Teacher Preparation Classroom

See a demo at
www.prenhall.com/teacherprep/demo

Your Class. Their Careers. Our Future. Will your students be prepared?

We invite you to explore our new, innovative and engaging website and all that it has to offer you, your course, and tomorrow's educators! Just click on "go" on the login page to begin your explanation.

Organized around the major courses pre-service teachers take, the Teacher Preparation site provides media, student/teacher artifacts, strategies, research articles, and other resources to equip your students with the quality tools needed to excel in their courses and prepare them for their first classroom.

This ultimate online education resource will provide you and your students access to:

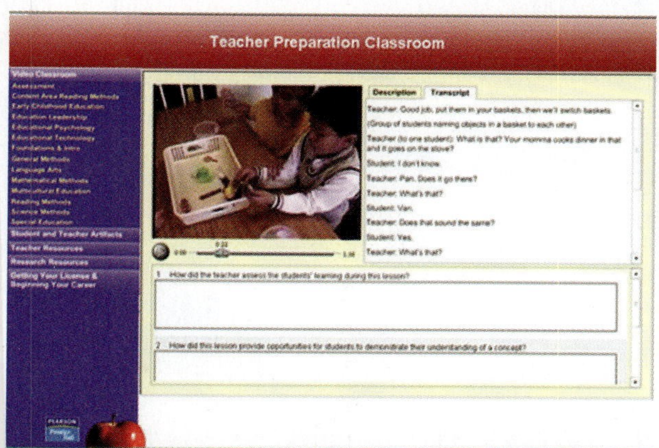

Online Video Library. More than 250 video clips—each tied to a course topic and framed by learning goals and Praxis-type questions—capture real teachers and students working in real classrooms.

Student and Teacher Artifacts. More than 200 student and teacher classroom artifacts—each tied to a course topic and framed by learning goals and application questions—provide a wealth of materials and experiences to help make your students observe children's developmental learning.

Lesson Plan Builder. Offers step-by-step guidelines and lesson plan examples to support students as they learn to build high-quality lesson plans.

Articles and Readings. Over 500 articles from ASCD's renowned journal *Educational Leadership* are available. The site also includes Research Navigator, a searchable database of additional educational journals.

Strategies and Lessons. Over 500 research-supported instructional strategies appropriate for a wide range of grade levels and content areas.

Licensure and Career Tools. Resources devoted to helping your students pass their licensure exam; learn standards, law, and public policies; plan a teaching portfolio; and succeed in their first year of teaching.

Access Code previously been used?
Students:
To purchase or renew an access code, go to **www.prenhall.com/teacherprep** and click on the "Register for Teacher Prep" button.
Instructors:
Email **Merrill.marketing@pearsoned.com** and provide the following informatio
- Name and Affiliation
- Author/Title/Edition of Merrill text

Upon ordering *Teacher Prep* for their students, instructors will be given a lifetime *T*

Exploring Your Role

An Introduction to Early Childhood Education

Third Edition

Mary Renck Jalongo
Indiana University of Pennsylvania

Joan Packer Isenberg
George Mason University

Upper Saddle River, New Jersey
Columbus, Ohio

Library of Congress Cataloging-in-Publication Data
Jalongo, Mary Renck.
Exploring your role: an introduction to early childhood education/Mary Renck Jalongo, Joan Packer Isenberg.—3rd ed.
p. cm.
Includes bibliographical references and index.
ISBN 978-0-13-172799-1 (alk. paper)
1. Early childhood education—United States. 2. Early childhood teachers—United States.
I. Isenberg, Joan P. II. Title.
LB1139.25.J35 2008
372.210973—dc22 2007007028

Vice President and Executive Publisher: Jeffery W. Johnston
Publisher: Kevin M. Davis
Acquisitions Editor: Julie Peters
Editorial Assistant: Tiffany Bitzel
Production Editor: Linda Hillis Bayma
Production Coordination: Norine Strang, Carlisle Editorial Services
Design Coordinator: Diane C. Lorenzo
Photo Coordinator: Sandy Schaefer
Cover Designer: Candace Rowley
Cover image: SuperStock
Production Manager: Laura Messerly
Director of Marketing: David Gesell
Marketing Manager: Amy Judd
Marketing Coordinator: Brian Mounts

This book was set in New Caledonia by Carlisle Publishing Services. It was printed and bound by Courier Kendallville, Inc. The cover was printed by Phoenix Color Corp.

Photo Credits for Chapter Openers: Superstock Royalty Free, p. 2; Anthony Magnacca/Merrill, p. 32; Dick Blume/Syracuse Newspapers/The Image Works, p. 70; Krista Greco/Merrill, pp. 108, 378; © Ellen B. Senisi/Ellen Senisi, p. 146; Michelle Pearlstein, p. 180; David Mager/Pearson Learning Photo Studio, pp. 218, 258, 310, 412; David Young-Wolff/PhotoEdit, Inc., p. 342.

Pearson Education Ltd.
Pearson Education Singapore Pte. Ltd.
Pearson Education Canada, Ltd.
Pearson Education–Japan
Pearson Education Australia Pty. Limited
Pearson Education North Asia Ltd.
Pearson Educación de Mexico, S.A. de C.V.
Pearson Education Malaysia Pte. Ltd.

10 9 8 7 6 5 4 3
ISBN-13: 978-0-13-172799-1
ISBN-10: 0-13-172799-0

To practitioners everywhere who devote their professional lives to the education and care of young children. It is through the concerted efforts of early childhood educators that people throughout the world learn to appreciate the importance of the early years and recognize the enduring benefits of high-quality programs that support the learning of all young children and create positive relationships with their families.

M.R.J.

I dedicate this book to my husband, George, with love and appreciation for all of his interest and support.

J.P.I.

Preface

Why do people decide to make the care and education of young children their life's work? When we ask undergraduate students this question, their answers vary. Some will simply say, "I love children." Others will be more specific and say things like the following:

I idolized my second-grade teacher, Ms. Cardill. When I was in second grade, I found out that I had a learning disability. Ms. Cardill helped me learn how to cope and inspired me to become a teacher in the process.

My mother and sisters are teachers; so is one of my uncles. I grew up with teaching and come from a teaching family. I guess you could say that I am carrying on the family tradition.

Because I am the oldest and my family lives nearby, my job when I was growing up was to babysit for my little brother, nieces, and nephews. There were always children around the house and I found that I really enjoyed their company.

By way of introduction, here is what we have to say about what precipitated our decisions to pursue a career in early childhood.

Mary: I've always wanted to be a teacher just like Ms. Klingensmith, my kindergarten teacher. Throughout early childhood, my favorite play theme was playing school—and when I did, I was always Miss K. When I was in high school, my little sister was in first grade. After 6 months with a mean teacher who was a former Marine sergeant, my sister was crying and throwing up every morning before school started. At age 7, she developed a stomach ulcer. Her teacher was fired at the end of that year, but when I saw the damage that one bad teacher could do, I made the commitment to go into teaching and become a good teacher.

Joan: As the oldest of four siblings, I spent much of my childhood and adolescence with young children. When I was a teenager, my best friend and I planned and organized children's birthday parties. In the summers, I worked at a camp and was a swimming instructor for young children who were learning to swim for the first time. These experiences helped me to see many different ways to teach things that children really wanted to learn. They also differed dramatically from the kind of in-school learning I remembered from my early childhood days, where I was expected to sit quietly, memorize information, and tolerate boredom. My work at camp and in my neighborhood allowed me to see children's delight in learning and led me to become an early childhood teacher.

Krista Greco/Merrill

Whether you are a beginner or a veteran in the field of early childhood, the underlying message is clear: We decide to teach children because we feel that early childhood is one of the most delightful periods in life, because we are intrigued and charmed by the young child's newcomer's perspective on the world, and because we feel well suited to fulfill the early childhood educator's multiple roles. In short, we seek careers in early childhood education because we believe that we can exert a powerful and positive influence on children's lives.

How does a college student move from dreams of teaching well to becoming an effective professional educator? One thing is certain: In that journey from imagining ourselves as effective teachers to actually becoming outstanding teachers, good intentions are not enough. It is almost inconceivable that anyone would enter into teaching with the thought, "I plan to be a terrible teacher and make children's lives miserable," yet there are many examples of teachers who have drifted from a firm commitment to fostering students' development and learning. Generally speaking, they are the teachers who have neglected their own learning, who became jaded by the futile search for one method that works equally well with all children, who waited to be told what to do, or who failed to put children at the center of their practice. In his book *To Become a Teacher: Making a Difference in Children's Lives,* William Ayers (1995) raises and answers a simple yet profound question:

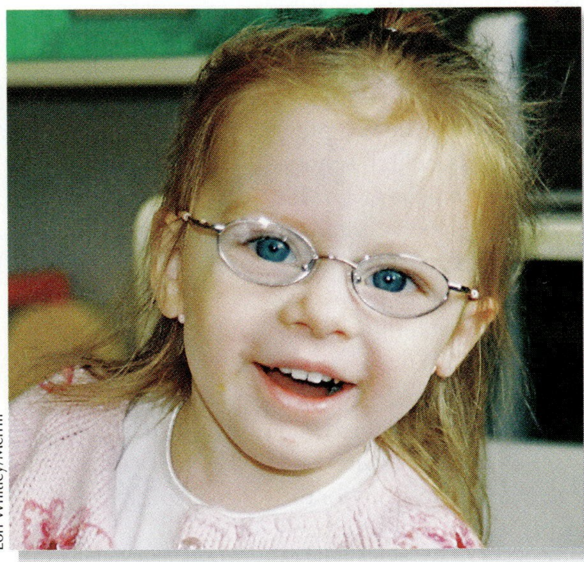
Lori Whitley/Merrill

> What makes a good teacher? When I ask college students this question, they typically come up with a wide and interesting assortment of qualities: compassion, love of children, sense of humor, kindness, and intelligence. My own list includes passion, commitment, curiosity, a willingness to be vulnerable, and authenticity. When I ask kindergartners the same question, they too have ready answers: a good teacher is fair, funny, smart, nice. . . . Teaching at its best requires knowledge of students, knowledge of hopes, dreams, aspirations, skills, challenges, interests, preferences, intelligence, and values they bring with them to the classroom. Teaching at its best is first an act of inquiry, investigation, and research into the lives of children. (pp. 5–6)

The third edition of *Exploring Your Role: An Introduction to Early Childhood Education* is designed to inaugurate your investigation into the lives of children, your research in the field of early childhood education, and your inquiry into the multiple roles that you will need to play as someone who cares deeply about the care and education of children, ages birth through 8.

Audience for This Book

David Mager/Pearson Learning Photo Studio

The third edition of *Exploring Your Role: An Introduction to Early Childhood Education* is written for college students who are relatively new to formal study of the field of early childhood education. Typically, these students are enrolled in specialized programs at 2- or 4-year colleges or universities that prepare them to work with children ages birth through 8. This comprehensive introduction to the field is most appropriate as the primary textbook for the initial course. It will meet the needs of instructors who teach in baccalaureate (4 or 5 year) programs as well as the needs of instructors who teach in 2-year associate degree programs at community colleges.

Body of the Chapter

As the Table of Contents details, the body of each chapter follows a clear organizational pattern. Every chapter defines the professional role, provides a rationale for its importance, and addresses the classroom practices that support that role. The body of the chapter then moves to the most influential paradigms that have resulted from theory and research. Finally, each chapter leads readers to practical applications of what was learned.

General Focus and Purpose

Traditionally, introductory textbooks in early childhood education have been organized by curriculum. The typical introductory text begins with a history of the field and a chapter on developmental theory followed by one chapter on each major subject area—language, mathematics, science, the arts, and so forth. *Exploring Your Role* takes a more integrated and innovative approach:

- This text is organized around the essential roles and responsibilities that effective early childhood educators must fill, according to **NAEYC standards**.
- Another fundamental difference between *Exploring Your Role* and traditional textbooks is that it is **interactive**: readers are encouraged to respond to what they are reading while they are reading it.
- This edition contains a new, unique chapter on **Diversity,** Chapter 3 by Beatrice Fennimore.
- **Videos** and other resources referenced in the text are available on the **Teacher Prep Website**. Practice and application opportunities are available via the **Companion Website**.
- This edition focuses on **program and academic standards** more than ever before.
- Finally, many features provide an **authentic classroom experience** by presenting and discussing real teaching situations.

The following pages will illustrate and describe these key characteristics, as well as some existing and new features of the book.

Organized Around NAEYC Standards

In *Guidelines for Preparation of Early Childhood Professionals,* the National Association for the Education of Young Children (NAEYC) characterizes early childhood education as "a diverse field encompassing a broad age-range of the life-span, birth through age eight, including children with special development and learning needs. Early childhood education occurs in diverse settings, including public and private schools, centers, and home-based programs, and encompasses many roles in addition to the traditional role of 'teacher'" (1995, p. 1). *Exploring Your Role's* 12 chapters are based on NAEYC's professional roles for early childhood educators. These roles that the NAEYC (1995) identifies and that we have adapted here include:

1. The *reflective practitioner* who carefully considers educational issues and is capable of ethical decision making (Chapter 1);
2. The *child advocate* who can engage in informed advocacy for children and the profession by understanding both traditional and contemporary perspectives on early childhood education (Chapter 2);
3. The *professional with a commitment to diversity, equity, and justice* for children and families (Chapter 3);
4. The *professional with knowledge of child development* who understands young children's characteristics and needs and uses this professional knowledge to address the needs of all children (Chapter 4);
5. The *facilitator of learning* who understands the multiple influences on young children's development and learning (Chapter 5);
6. The *creator of environments* who uses knowledge of child development to provide a safe, healthy, respectful, and challenging environment for learning (Chapter 6);
7. The *curriculum developer* who can design, implement, and assess learning across the content areas and provide meaningful programs that respect diversity and promote positive outcomes (Chapter 7);
8. The *educational planner* who understands different types and levels of collaborative planning/organization and can use a wide array of effective approaches, strategies, and tools that respond to children's needs and interests and yield positive learning outcomes (Chapter 8);
9. The *professional skilled in assessment and documentation* who works in partnership with families and other professionals to document children's learning using appropriate assessment strategies (Chapter 9);
10. The *professional who guides children's behavior* by building a sense of community in early childhood settings and teaching the skills of self-regulation (Chapter 10);
11. A *collaborator with families* who builds trust and respect between, among, and with families and the larger community (Chapter 11); and
12. The *emerging professional* who seeks and self-monitors professional growth through research-based practice and professional collaboration (Chapter 12).

Brief Contents

Chapter 1 Exploring Your Role as a Reflective Practitioner 2
Chapter 2 Exploring Your Role as a Child Advocate and Understanding History 32
Chapter 3 Exploring Your Role in Respecting Diversity and Promoting Equity and Fairness 70
Chapter 4 Exploring Your Role in Promoting Children's Development 108
Chapter 5 Exploring Your Role in Fostering Children's Learning 146
Chapter 6 Exploring Your Role in Creating High-Quality Early Childhood Environments 180
Chapter 7 Exploring Your Role as a Curriculum Developer 218
Chapter 8 Exploring Your Role in Planning for Children's Learning 258
Chapter 9 Exploring Your Role in Documenting and Assessing Children's Learning 310
Chapter 10 Exploring Your Role in Guiding Children's Behavior 342
Chapter 11 Exploring Your Role in Supporting Families and Communities 378
Chapter 12 Exploring Your Role as a Professional in the Field of Early Childhood Education 412
Appendix Compendium of Early Childhood Materials and Resources 437

In addition, early childhood professionals need to know how to locate and use resource materials from authoritative sources (see the Compendium of Early Childhood Materials and Resources at the end of the book).

From this list alone, it is clear that working effectively with young children is a challenging and demanding avocation. As Johnson (2006) points out,

> For all of its potential rewards, teaching is uncertain work. In some professions goals are clear and explicit, and success is easily measurable.
>
> The purposes of schooling extend well beyond the intellectual; schools are also charged with the social, emotional, and moral development of children. Given the various purposes of education, teaching's goals are hard to define, in turn making their attainment hard to measure.
>
> Teachers receive multiple, sometimes conflicting, messages about their roles. They are supposed to build skills while nurturing creativity and a love for learning, foster development of the "whole child" while closing their achievement gap, and respond to the individual needs of students while managing the group. The goals are overarching; one of the "givens" of being a teacher is knowing you will not be able to do all the society asks of you. (pp. 71–72)

Teaching young children is qualitatively different from the way it was 20, 10, or even 5 years ago. Our field has been profoundly affected by changes in families, advances in cognitive psychology, perspectives on the preparation of teachers, political influences on early childhood education, and a new era of sensitivity to cultural diversity and children with exceptionalities (Isenberg & Jalongo, 2003). As you enter early childhood education, you will be engaged in the rigorous work of figuring out who you are as a professional and flexibly adapting to a wide array of early childhood settings.

Interactive Approach

We rely upon case material and verbatim comments from students to make the content come alive and to encourage your participation in reading and thinking.

"Pause and Reflect About . . ."

In the margins of the book, **Pause and Reflect About** encourages you to relate what you have read to your own experiences and guide you to reflect more deeply on important topics.

> **PAUSE AND REFLECT**
> **About Early Leaders and Prevailing Views of Childhood**
>
> After reviewing the material in Figures 2.2 and 2.3, consider these questions:
>
> - What echoes of the past do you see in your teaching philosophy?
> - Which of these notable individuals whose commitment to the very young has made an indelible impression on your field made the greatest impression on you? Why?
> - Did you encounter any ideas that surprised you? Are any of the ideas consistent with your beliefs?

Meet the Teachers

Readers will first **Meet the Teachers** through case material that describes one infant/toddler caregiver, one preschool teacher, and one kindergarten or primary-grade teacher. In this way, we provide a balance of the three age groups every early childhood teacher needs to know—infants/ toddlers (0–2), preschoolers (3–5), and children in the primary grades (6–8). Unlike some introductory textbooks that focus almost exclusively on 3- to 5-year-olds, our emphasis is on the education and care of young children ages birth through 8.

> **Meet the Teachers**
>
> MARISSA has been a parent volunteer in a county-sponsored child-care program for the past 3 years while she has earned her Child Development Associate (CDA) credential. Today is the day of her interview for a position as a family child-care provider. As she scans the faces of the interviewers seated at the conference table, she worries that she will have difficulty putting her ideas into words. When she is asked about her approaches to working with toddlers, she replies, "I believe that learning is natural and that a warm, homelike setting is the ideal way to offer care and education to toddlers. Although learning in the early years is playful, this is also a time of life when the brain is developing and a firm foundation for real learning is built."
>
> ERIN has taught kindergarten for 4 years in a parochial school, and she is meeting with a college faculty member who coordinates the master's program. Erin knows that the professor will expect her to give some reasons why she is interested in the graduate early childhood program. When the discussion comes around to her philosophy, she says, "I want to become more knowledgeable about early literacy. It seems to me that some of the approaches to early reading instruction are part of a 'push-down' curriculum that is used with the upper elementary grades. My goal is to more fully understand how young learners become readers and to support them in their efforts."
>
> BRIAN is a private nursery-school teacher in Miami, Florida. When parents visit the school, Brian knows that he must make the program philosophy clear so that families can make informed decisions about whether or not his program is right for their children. In explaining his program to parents, Brian says, "Children need real-world experiences and meaningful learning activities, not mindless paper shuffling. The early childhood years are formative, so children need a balanced approach that includes experiences to support their development physically, socially, intellectually, emotionally, and artistically."

Each Meet the Teachers feature is followed by an invitation to *compare* the three teachers, *contrast* the three teachers, and *connect* the teachers' experiences with the reader's experience.

COMPARE	What are some commonalities among these three teachers' philosophical perspectives? What are some influences that might have shaped these teachers' ideas about early childhood education?
CONTRAST	In what ways are the teachers' philosophies distinctive?
CONNECT	Do you think that these ideas originated with these teachers? In what ways are their views similar to or different from your own? Surprisingly, the views of each of the contemporary teachers just described can be traced to ideas about children, learning, instruction, curricula, and evaluation that have been in existence for decades or even centuries.

New Chapter on Diversity and Equity

Although information on inclusion and diversity is interspersed throughout the text, the third edition devotes an entire chapter to this important topic. Beatrice S. Fennimore, author of numerous book chapters and articles on equity issues as well as two books, *Child Advocacy* and *Talk Matters*, graciously wrote this new chapter.

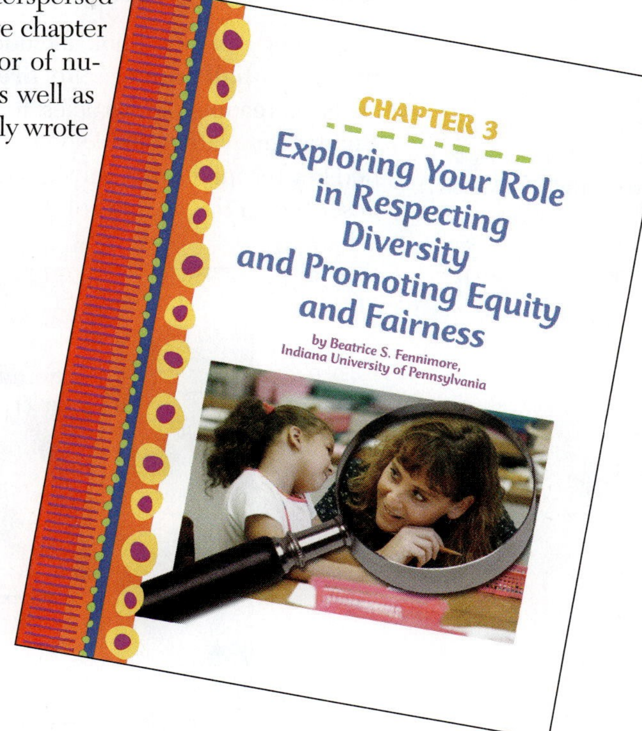

Diversity Icon

In order to make readers more aware of the chapter content *throughout the text* that focuses on diversity, we have used a special icon to highlight the sections that are particularly relevant to building readers' awareness of and appreciation for diverse learners.

Integrated Videos/Media

TEACHER PREP WEBSITE 3.3

Go to Video Classroom, select General Methods, choose Student Learning in Diverse Classrooms (Module 2), and select Incorporating the Home Experiences of Culturally Diverse Students (Video 1).

Teacher Prep Website Video Integration

Every copy of this book includes an access code to the Teacher Prep Website at **www.prenhall.com/teacherprep**. This site contains videos, children's and teachers' artifacts, readings and articles, teaching strategies, sample PRAXIS test items, a Lesson Builder template to help you create lesson plans, and more. Your authors have identified key resources that will enhance what you are reading about in this book. These are described in the margins of the book. See an example of this to the left.

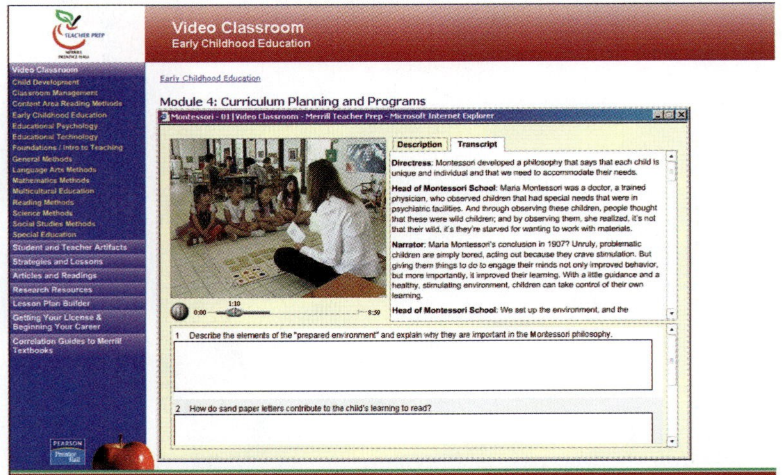

COMPANION WEBSITE 10.5 For more information about technology and early childhood, go to *Web Links* in Chapter 10 of the Companion Website at http://www.prenhall.com/jalongo.

Links to the Companion Website

Interspersed throughout the chapters are margin notes that make readers aware of the wealth of resources available on the Companion Website. These margin notes encourage readers to consider their professional roles, reflect on important topics, research the topic further, link with technology resources, collect artifacts for their professional portfolio, and complete a practice test. See a description of the Companion Website modules on page xviii.

Focus on Academic Standards and Program Accreditation

Early childhood education today is more standards-based than ever before (Hyson & Biggar, 2006). From its inception, *Exploring Your Role* was built around the National Association for the Education of Young Children Standards. In 2004, those standards were revised. The third edition addresses not only the 2004 NAEYC Initial Licensure Standards, but also the standards of the Association for Childhood Education International (ACEI) and the Interstate New Teacher Assessment and Support (INTASC). The first learning outcome of each chapter matches that chapter's content to the three sets of standards (NAEYC, ACEI, INTASC).

Learning Outcomes

Every chapter includes a list of outcomes for the student. This shift away from behavioral objectives to outcomes statements is consistent with current program accreditation requirements. Increasingly, teacher educators are being asked to provide more holistic and performance-based evidence that their early childhood programs make significant contributions to the students' growth as professionals.

Learning Outcomes

- ✔ Become familiar with standards for helping all children learn (NAEYC #1 and #4, INTASC #1 and #4, ACEI #3a and 3c)
- ✔ Understand the learning processes in early childhood education
- ✔ Examine the features of authentic learning
- ✔ Explore learner-centered teaching and learning and explain the cycle of learning
- ✔ Describe the major learning theories and their implications for young children
- ✔ Examine the effect of teachers' beliefs on children's learning
- ✔ Consider the central role of play in children's learning

Lesson Plans

With the increased focus on standards, learning how to plan lessons in teacher education programs has become more important than ever. This edition has more detailed coverage and examples of lesson plans, and the Teacher Prep Website has a Lesson Builder module that students can use to practice creating lessons that are developmentally appropriate and child-centered. In addition, the site provides links to content area, state, and association (NAEYC, CEC, etc.) standards Websites that students can link to and include in their lesson plans.

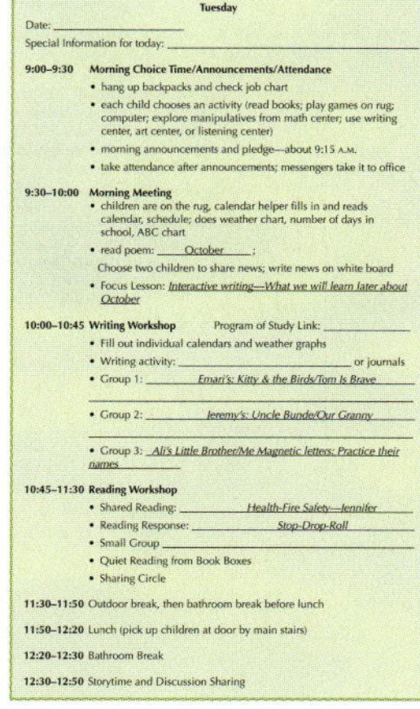

Tuesday

Date: ______

Special Information for today: ______

9:00–9:30 Morning Choice Time/Announcements/Attendance
- hang up backpacks and check job chart
- each child chooses an activity (read books; play games on rug; computer; explore manipulatives from math center; use writing center, art center, or listening center)
- morning announcements and pledge—about 9:15 A.M.
- take attendance after announcements; messengers take it to office

9:30–10:00 Morning Meeting
- children are on the rug, calendar helper fills in and reads calendar, schedule; does weather chart, number of days in school, ABC chart
- read poem: October;

Choose two children to share news; write news on white board
- Focus Lesson: *Interactive writing—What we will learn later about October*

10:00–10:45 Writing Workshop Program of Study Link: ______
- Fill out individual calendars and weather graphs
- Writing activity: ______ or journals
- Group 1: *Emari's: Kitty & the Birds/Tom Is Brave*
- Group 2: *Jeremy's: Uncle Bunde/Our Granny*
- Group 3: *Ali's Little Brother/Me Magnetic letters: Practice their names*

10:45–11:30 Reading Workshop
- Shared Reading: *Health-Fire Safety—Jennifer*
- Reading Response: *Stop-Drop-Roll*
- Small Group ______
- Quiet Reading from Book Boxes
- Sharing Circle

11:30–11:50 Outdoor break, then bathroom break before lunch

11:50–12:20 Lunch (pick up children at door by main stairs)

12:20–12:30 Bathroom Break

12:30–12:50 Storytime and Discussion Sharing

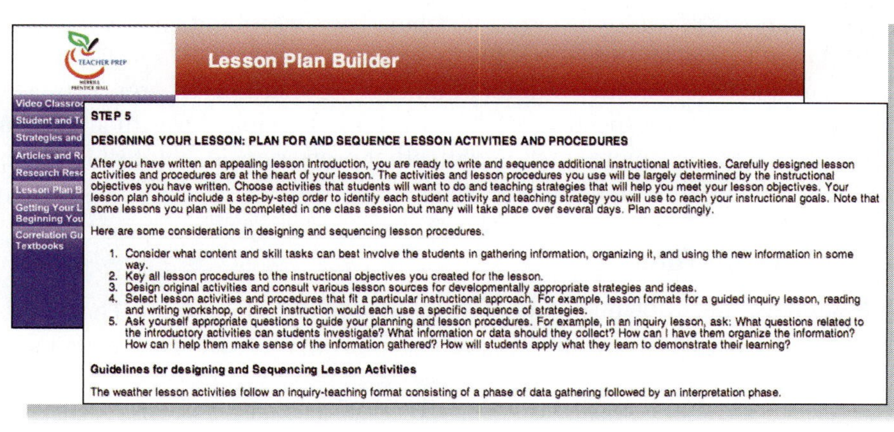

Provides an Authentic Classroom Experience

ASK THE EXPERT

Amy Driscoll on Exemplary Early Childhood Programs

Amy Driscoll

The first question often asked about my visits to programs is, **"What's the best program you've seen?"** It's impossible to respond to that question without one or two of my own. My response questions are, "Best program for whom? Or for what community? Or for what purpose?" What became clear in my visits to exemplary programs for *Cases in Early Childhood Education* was the importance of the fit between program and children, families, and community. Programs must reflect the cultural values of the children and families they serve, so they must look different from place to place. Consequently it is impossible to assess the quality of a program without looking at the context in which it serves children and families. While all good programs appear to be based on developmentally appropriate practices (DAP) and curriculum, there is huge variation in the way DAP is translated into the program. That variation is connected to the diversity of children and families—lifestyles and values, needs and strengths, and environment in which they live. For that reason I clearly avoid the idea of program models because model suggests a framework that can be transported and duplicated in other places. I don't think that models are appropriate when we talk about programs for young children. Their individuality and that of their families must be cherished and strengthened, and to do so, a program must be developed with that individuality as a foundation.

The other aspect of fit is one that connects educators with specific beliefs about children and learning with an environment and curriculum that supports those beliefs. In my visits, I encountered early childhood professionals who placed a high priority on finding programs in which they could teach in ways that matched their philosophy. A number of those professionals had searched for and tried out varied programs before finding a place where they could really be true to their beliefs. Once found, they were able to do their very best work for children.

The second question that I was asked after my visits to early childhood education (ECE) programs was, **"What did the programs have in common to make them unique and outstanding?"** I too was curious to answer that question as I began my visits. When I finished my travels and after much reflection, I have to say that it was people. In each case it was an individual or a group of individuals who were committed to an idea or an ideal. For example, Bebe Fearnside in Gainesville, Florida, decided to abandon traditional approaches to serving children and families in order to meet their needs in a comprehensive program. In her words, she "colored outside the lines"—interpreted policies and formed collaborations in ways that better served children. Like so many early educators she looked beyond what was happening and broadened her view of what was possible. The lesson we can gain from thinkers and professionals like her is that we have to push the boundaries of resources, of tradition, and even of policy and regulations to achieve the best programs for children.

When observing exemplary programs, the question is often raised about a focus, **"What should I look for?"** My answer is to go beyond what can be observed. You must begin, of course, with what you can see and hear, but after extensive observations, it is important to reflect and to inquire. The most outstanding programs I observed were those in which individuals reflected carefully about decisions and could articulate a clear rationale. In order to learn about those reflections, I had to raise questions. Most educators are willing to talk about their ideas, so it is not a difficult process. What I learned from the conversations about decisions were rationales consistently based on children's needs, or goals for children, or children's development. When Angela Pino, a teacher of 2-year-olds at City Country School in New York, was asked about why the staff went around cleaning up after children instead of leaving it all for the cleanup time or insisting that children clean before going to another activity, she could clearly describe the thinking behind their procedure:

> We feel that teaching children of this age to clean up after themselves during play interferes with spontaneous play and creative activity. After we

Ask the Expert

Each chapter includes the text feature we call **Ask the Expert**. These reflections from leading authorities in the field of early childhood education are matched to their areas of specialization as well as to each chapter's content. In order to highlight developmentally appropriate practice in Chapter 7, for example, we invited Sue Bredekamp, a leading expert on this issue, to contribute. In this way, *Exploring Your Role* provides the most up-to-date and authoritative information available on specialized topics by including the insights of prominent early childhood educators.

David, a Newly Immigrated Child

While there are many kinds of families, people have strong opinions about the ability of single parents to provide the appropriate environments in which to raise children. Much of the concern centers around whether or not single parents can appropriately raise a well-socialized child who will become a productive and contributing citizen. Increasingly, however, women who have never married are choosing to become parents and adopting children to create a family. The case of David is a good example.

David was adopted from a Russian orphanage at 26 months of age. His never-married adoptive mother, Marsha, had invested 18 months of working intensively with a social worker through extensive interviews, a personal history, financial statements, fingerprinting, evaluations by a psychologist and a psychiatrist, and a series of parenting classes. Next, Marsha worked with adoption agencies until a child was identified as a good match. She spent 2 weeks in Russia getting to know David and preparing to bring him home. Although Marsha knew very little about David's birth history, she did learn that he had been in the orphanage since he was 2 weeks old.

One Child, Three Perspectives

A text feature that makes our book exceptionally timely is what we call **One Child, Three Perspectives**. This component of the chapter highlights a child we have known and presents several different points of view on how best to meet that child's needs. Included among the perspectives are the views of parents, classroom teachers, social workers, school administrators, child guidance experts, health-care professionals, and others who are committed to helping the child. This approach is in keeping with the new NAEYC Standards that call for the preparation of early childhood professionals who have developed the skills of collaboration necessary to work with teams consisting of parents, families, colleagues, and professionals from many different fields who are committed to the education and care of young children.

One of the complaints of trained professionals in virtually every field is that nobody ever told them how challenging it would be to work in the "real world" of the profession for which they were prepared. In *Exploring Your Role* we attempt to rectify that error. Rather than restricting our accounts of young children to charming anecdotes, we present a wide array of more realistic situations that early childhood educators are likely to encounter. For instance, the case of a drug-exposed child and a case describing a newly immigrated child with limited English proficiency are included. "One Child, Three Perspectives" develops your ability to consider different points of view such as a parent's, psychologist's, or administrator's perspectives on how to support a child's growth and learning and will equip you to work more skillfully with other professionals. This text feature also emphasizes the theory/research/practice connection.

Collaborating with Families

Families figure prominently in any successful early childhood program. Therefore, we have not only devoted an entire chapter to this topic, but also include a recommended

strategy for working more successfully with families in all of the chapters. **Collaborating with Families** illustrates specific ways that skillful practitioners we know convey information on a variety of topics to the significant adults in each child's life. These text features were collaboratively designed with Ruth K. Steinbrunner for the second edition and updated by Denise Dragich for the third edition of the text.

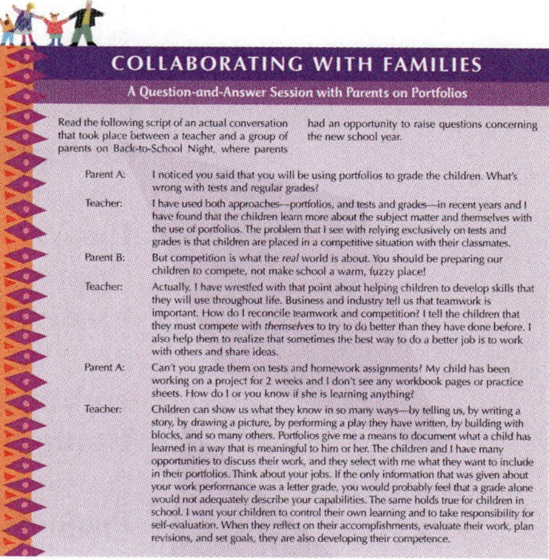

COLLABORATING WITH FAMILIES

A Question-and-Answer Session with Parents on Portfolios

Read the following script of an actual conversation that took place between a teacher and a group of parents on Back-to-School Night, where parents had an opportunity to raise questions concerning the new school year.

Parent A: I noticed you said that you will be using portfolios to grade the children. What's wrong with tests and regular grades?

Teacher: I have used both approaches—portfolios, and tests and grades—in recent years and I have found that the children learn more about the subject matter and themselves with the use of portfolios. The problem that I see with relying exclusively on tests and grades is that children are placed in a competitive situation with their classmates.

Parent B: But competition is what the *real* world is about. You should be preparing our children to compete, not make school a warm, fuzzy place!

Teacher: Actually, I have wrestled with that point about helping children to develop skills that they will use throughout life. Business and industry tell us that teamwork is important. How do I reconcile teamwork and competition? I tell the children that they must compete with *themselves* to try to do better than they have done before. I also help them to realize that sometimes the best way to do a better job is to work with others and share ideas.

Parent A: Can't you grade them on tests and homework assignments? My child has been working on a project for 2 weeks and I don't see any workbook pages or practice sheets. How do I or you know if she is learning anything?

Teacher: Children can show us what they know in so many ways—by telling us, by writing a story, by drawing a picture, by performing a play they have written, by building with blocks, and so many others. Portfolios give me a means to document what a child has learned in a way that is meaningful to him or her. The children and I have many opportunities to discuss their work, and they select with me what they want to include in their portfolios. Think about your jobs. If the only information that was given about your work performance was a letter grade, you would probably feel that a grade alone would not adequately describe your capabilities. The same holds true for children in school. I want your children to control their own learning and to take responsibility for self-evaluation. When they reflect on their accomplishments, evaluate their work, plan revisions, and set goals, they are also developing their competence.

In-Class Workshop

The 12 chapters conclude with a component that offers an additional opportunity to work with the information that you are learning in class. We call it an **In-Class Workshop**. These activities can be used with the total group or small groups to give you a chance to apply the basic principles you have acquired from reading the chapter. In Chapter 12 on professional development, for example, we lead you in beginning to develop a teaching portfolio. All of these In-Class Workshop activities have been extensively field-tested with students in our classes over the years and have been well received in presentations at professional conferences.

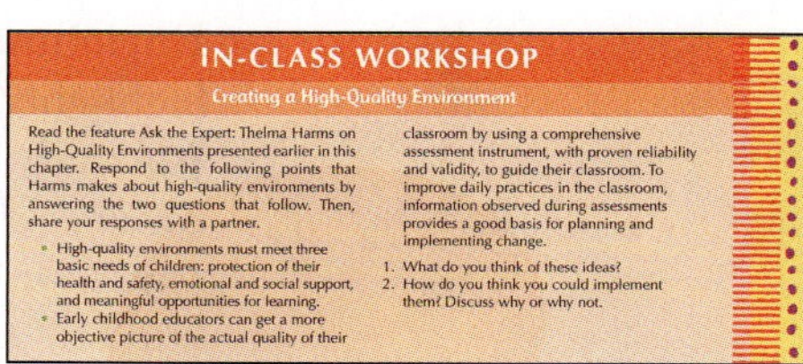

IN-CLASS WORKSHOP

Creating a High-Quality Environment

Read the feature Ask the Expert: Thelma Harms on High-Quality Environments presented earlier in this chapter. Respond to the following points that Harms makes about high-quality environments by answering the two questions that follow. Then, share your responses with a partner.

- High-quality environments must meet three basic needs of children: protection of their health and safety, emotional and social support, and meaningful opportunities for learning.
- Early childhood educators can get a more objective picture of the actual quality of their classroom by using a comprehensive assessment instrument, with proven reliability and validity, to guide their classroom. To improve daily practices in the classroom, information observed during assessments provides a good basis for planning and implementing change.

1. What do you think of these ideas?
2. How do you think you could implement them? Discuss why or why not.

Supplementary Materials

- The **Online Instructor's Resource Manual** is exceptionally comprehensive and is another way in which our textbook supports instructors and distinguishes itself from other texts on the market. All of the supplements for the third edition of the book were revised by DeAnna Laverick, D.Ed. The Instructor's Resource Manual for the first edition was developed by Ruth K. Steinbrunner, Ph.D., while she was a doctoral student at George Mason University, and was revised by Natalie K. Conrad, D.Ed., a professor at the University of Pittsburgh, Johnstown, for the second edition.
- **Online Test Bank.** The Test Bank includes various types of items, including multiple choice and true/false questions. Short-answer and constructed-response questions address chapter themes and prompt students to respond to authentic classroom scenarios.
- **TestGen.** Test management software is also available for instructors. Ask your Prentice Hall Sales representative how to obtain a copy.
- **WebCT and Blackboard.** Test items in WebCT and Blackboard format are available for download at **www.prenhall.com** in the Instructor's Resource Center.
- **PowerPoint Slides.** The first edition had transparencies in the Instructor's Manual but, with the third edition, all of these transparencies have been converted to PowerPoint slide shows that are not only available to instructors at **www.prenhall.com** at the Instructor's Resource Center, but also available to students in a note-taking format on the Companion Website (**www.prenhall.com/jalongo**).
- **Companion Website.** The Companion Website (CW), at **www.prenhall.com/jalongo**, is a resource for student practice.

The material that once was in a Student Study Guide has now been incorporated into the Companion Website. The various modules on the CW include the following:

- **Objectives**—Outline key concepts from the text.
- **Multiple Choice**—Complete with hints and automatic grading that provide immediate feedback for students.
- **Essay: Observations**—Hints and feedback connect classroom observations with chapter content.
- **Essay: Short Answer**—Complete with hints and feedback that challenge students to apply chapter concepts to their roles as educators.
- **Web Links**—Links to Internet sites that relate to chapter content.
- **Examples/Samples**—Checklists and other forms from the text are provided for download and printing.
- **Projects**—In-depth research activities encourage students to build on chapter concepts.
- **Enrichment Content**—PowerPoint lecture notes, key terms, research highlights, and additional readings are provided for each chapter.
- **Journal: Defining Your Role**—Web resources and reflective questions that connect chapter themes to student experience.
- **Journal: Constructing Your Professional Portfolio**—Prompts students to build their growing professional portfolios.
- **Journal: Pause and Reflect**—Activities and questions connect to each chapter's "Pause and Reflect" features.

To take advantage of the many available resources, please visit *Exploring Your Role: An Introduction to Early Childhood Education*, Third Edition, Companion Website at **www.prenhall.com/jalongo.**

A Final Word

In writing the third edition of *Exploring Your Role: An Introduction to Early Childhood Education,* we drew upon our many years of teaching toddlers, preschoolers, and children in the primary grades; supervising student teachers; as well as our work with practitioners in child care, nursery school, Head Start, and public school so that we could offer a useful, contemporary, and comprehensive perspective on the field.

Welcome, then, to an exploration of your role as an early childhood educator. You are joining the ranks of a profession with a long and distinguished history of dedication to the care and education of children. You are becoming a member of a field characterized by compassion, commitment, enthusiasm, and joy in the growth, development, and learning of young children.

Acknowledgments

More than 10 years ago, Joan and I were in Atlanta attending an NAEYC conference and standing in line, waiting to be seated for dinner. We saw Dave Faherty, then Merrill's Senior Editor, walk in with Joanne Hendrick, an early childhood educator and Merrill author whose books we both greatly admired. At the time, I dreamed aloud that

that might be us someday as we approached the end of our careers. I imagined us celebrating with our editor after the successful publication of our book with Merrill. Little did we know that we would be thinking about an introductory textbook going into its third edition with our current editor, Julie Peters. We thank the Merrill/Prentice Hall staff, including Ann Davis, our former editor, for their faith in us as thinkers, their support of us as authors, and their willingness to try a very different type of introductory textbook in early childhood education. We thank them also for their creativity and expert knowledge of the publishing field. Now that the book is published, we even thank them for the long conference calls on the telephone that crossed the line between nudging and pushing! Their support has enabled us to revise our introductory text more extensively and more frequently than we ever expected.

We also want to express our gratitude to the reviewers of this book, Velynda Cameron, Ozark Technical College; Ivy M. Cobbins, Olive Harvey College; Judy Hudson, San Juan College; Jennifer M. Johnson, Vance-Granville Community College; Marilyn K. Moore, Illinois State University; Peggy R. Owens, University of Houston–Clear Lake; Karen Paciorek, Eastern Michigan University; Kaarin Perkins, University of Houston–Clear Lake; and Elsa K. Weber, Purdue University–Calumet, for their thoughtful criticisms and many contributions that refined and polished our first draft of *Exploring Your Role.*

Finally, we want to thank our former graduate assistants, Natalie K. Conrad and Ruth Steinbrunner, who helped with the ancillary materials and suffered through the early drafts of the manuscript. Thanks also to Denise Dragich, who revised the Collaborating with Families feature that Ruth Steinbrunner developed originally. Dr. DeAnna Laverick merits recognition for completely revising the Companion Website for the third edition. Marjorie L. Stanek converted the "plain vanilla" transparencies into PowerPoint slide shows while Robin Quick updated the practice test items to be more like the Praxis exam in format.

We thank doctoral student Nadine Bolkhovitinov, who updated the "Did You Know" features in chapters 4 to 8 and updated the Compendium. Special thanks goes to Nancy Miller who worked tirelessly on the many details of this book, and, of course, we want to thank our families for tolerating our passion to try to make a contribution to the early childhood field through writing and for supporting us in many ways, ranging all the way from taking care of household duties to reading and critiquing drafts of chapters so that we could concentrate on writing.

About the Authors

Mary Renck Jalongo is a professor at Indiana University of Pennsylvania where she was named the university's outstanding faculty member in 1991–1992. She serves as coordinator of both the doctoral program in curriculum and instruction and the master's degree/initial teacher certification program in elementary education. Dr. Jalongo has written, co-authored, or edited over more than 20 books and has earned four national awards for excellence in scholarly writing. Since 1995 she has been the editor-in-chief of the international, bi-monthly publication *Early Childhood Education Journal*. Prior to teaching at the university, Dr. Jalongo taught in a cooperative for preschool children, many of whom were English language learners. She also gained classroom experience as a second and first grade public school teacher in low-income areas and did demonstration teaching of 2- to 5-year-olds for the University of Toledo laboratory school. Dr. Jalongo continues to work with young children on a regular basis through community service as a reading tutor in early childhood and special education classrooms.

Joan Packer Isenberg is an Associate Dean and Professor of Education at George Mason University in Fairfax, Virginia, where she has twice received the distinguished faculty award for teaching excellence. She received her bachelor's and master's degrees in early childhood education from Wheelock College and her doctorate in elementary education from Rutgers University. She has taught preschool, primary and elementary age children and held administrative positions in both public and private school settings. As a writer, Dr. Isenberg has also authored or co-authored 12 books and more than 50 journal articles. Among her most recent publications are two co-authored books, *Creative Thinking and Arts-Based Learning: Preschool Through Fourth Grade,* 4th ed. (Merrill/Prentice Hall) and *Exploring Your Role: An Introduction to Early Childhood Education,* 3rd ed. (Merrill/Prentice Hall) and a co-edited book, *Major Trends and Issues in Early Childhood Education,* 2nd ed. (Teachers College Press). She has been a Visiting Scholar for the National Board for Professional Teaching Standards (NBPTS), where she led higher education initiatives and the reform of advanced master's degrees for practicing teachers, and has served on the NCATE Board of Examiners, as President and in other elected offices of the National Association of Early Childhood Teachers Educators (NAECTE) and of the Metro Area Branch of the Association for Childhood Education International (ACEI). Her research interests are in teachers' professional development, arts integration, and early childhood curriculum. She was the 2006 NAECTE recipient of the Pearson/Allyn and Bacon Outstanding Early Childhood Teacher Educator Award.

Brief Contents

Chapter 1 Exploring Your Role as a Reflective Practitioner 2

Chapter 2 Exploring Your Role as a Child Advocate and Understanding History 32

Chapter 3 Exploring Your Role in Respecting Diversity and Promoting Equity and Fairness 70

Chapter 4 Exploring Your Role in Promoting Children's Development 108

Chapter 5 Exploring Your Role in Fostering Children's Learning 146

Chapter 6 Exploring Your Role in Creating High-Quality Early Childhood Environments 180

Chapter 7 Exploring Your Role as a Curriculum Developer 218

Chapter 8 Exploring Your Role in Planning for Children's Learning 258

Chapter 9 Exploring Your Role in Documenting and Assessing Children's Learning 310

Chapter 10 Exploring Your Role in Guiding Children's Behavior 342

Chapter 11 Exploring Your Role in Supporting Families and Communities 378

Chapter 12 Exploring Your Role as a Professional in the Field of Early Childhood Education 412

Appendix Compendium of Early Childhood Materials and Resources 437

References 473

Name Index 497

Subject Index 505

Contents

Chapter 1 Exploring Your Role as a Reflective Practitioner 2

Meet the Teachers 3
Learning Outcomes 4

Defining Teaching in Early Childhood 5

Did You Know . . . ? 6

Understanding Reflective Practice 8

Getting Started with Reflective Practice 11

Levels of Reflection 11

Developing the Characteristics of a Reflective Practitioner 14

The Disposition to Become a Reflective Practitioner 16

Make a Firm Commitment to the Care and Education of Young Children 16
Take Delight in, Be Curious About, and Learn to Understand Children's Development 18
Maintain a Fundamentally Positive Outlook on Children, Families, and Teaching 19
Be Willing to Take the Risks and Make the Mistakes That Are Part of the Learning Process 20
Adapt Flexibly to Continuous Change and Expect Perpetual Challenge 20
Master the Content and Pedagogy, Adjust Teaching, and Adapt the Curriculum to the Needs of Children 21
Build a Sense of Community; Seek Collaboration and Peer Support 22
Address Problems and Make Ethical Decisions 24
Pursue Professional Growth as an Educator of the Very Young 26

Conclusion 28

In-Class Workshop: Working with Teacher Reflection 30

Chapter 2 Exploring Your Role as a Child Advocate and Understanding History 32

Meet the Teachers 33
Learning Outcomes 34

Your Role as a Child Advocate 34

Did You Know . . . ? 35

Historical Influences on Contemporary Programs 37

Time-Honored Precepts of Early Childhood Education 46

Young Children Need Special Nurturing 46
Young Children Are the Future of Society 47

Young Children Are Worthy of Study 48
Young Children's Potential Should Be Optimized 49
How Programs Begin and Change 49
Societal Trends 49
Educational Theories 49
Knowledge of Child Development 52
Curriculum Standards 52
Community Expectations 53
Evaluation Criteria 53
Human Resources 55
Financial and Material Resources 55
Pedagogy 56
Early Childhood Programs, Past and Present 56
Articulated Philosophy and Goals 61
Appropriate Structure and Organization 61
Emphasis on Concept Development 61
Attention to All Five Domains 62
Increased Opportunity for Social Interaction 63
Respect for Individual Differences 63
Recognition and Inclusion of the Contributions of Many Ethnic Groups 63
Interdisciplinary Approaches to Subject-Matter Teaching 63
Conclusion 65
In-Class Workshop: Drafting Your Teaching Philosophy 68

Chapter 3 Exploring Your Role in Respecting Diversity and Promoting Equity and Fairness 70
Beatrice S. Fennimore
Meet the Teachers 71
Learning Outcomes 72
Did You Know . . . ? 73
Defining Diversity and Equity in a Multicultural Context 73
Diversity Means Everyone 74
Some Diversities Bring Challenges 75
Everyone Needs to Be Concerned 75
Attitudes and Dispositions Are Important 76
From Civil Rights to Multicultural Education 76
Culturally Deficient or Multicultural? 79
The Big Multicultural Picture 80
From Multicultural to Anti-Bias 82
Your Role in Building a Fair Chance for Children 83
Ecological Understanding of Difficult Childhood Realities 85
Thinking About the Concept of Social Justice 86

Ethics and Social Justice 87
Developing a Personal Position on Issues 88
Conflicts Between Needs of Children and Interests of Adults 90
Becoming an Advocate for Children 92
Advocacy in Action 92
Ways of Being an Advocate 93
Fairness and Equity in Your Classroom 99
Focus on Relationships 99
Focus on Safety and Responsibility to Others 100
Focus on Curriculum 100
Focus on Families and Community 101
Commitment to Diversity and Fairness in Public Spaces 102
Looking Toward the Future 102
Observe Carefully in the Field 102
Take Advantage of Opportunities to Develop Skills 103
Conclusion 104
In-Class Workshop: Becoming a Culturally Competent Teacher 106

Chapter 4 Exploring Your Role in Promoting Children's Development 108
Meet the Teachers 109
Learning Outcomes 110
A Definition of Development 110
Did You Know . . . ? 111
Characteristics of Young Children 111
Patterns of Development 111
Essential Needs 112
Developmental Milestones 114
What Are Infants Like? 114
What Are Toddlers Like? 116
What Are Preschoolers and Kindergartners Like? 119
What Are School-Age Children Like? 122
Your Role in Promoting Children's Development 123
Why Understanding Children's Development Is Important 126
The Brain and Children's Development 126
Learners with Exceptionalities 128
Children with Disabilities 129
Children with Special Gifts and Talents 133
Children from Diverse Backgrounds 133
Major Child Development Theories 134
Psychosocial Theory of Erik Erikson (1902–1994) 135
Cognitive-Developmental Theory of Jean Piaget (1896–1980) 138

Ecological Theory of Urie Bronfenbrenner (1917–2005) 141
Hierarchy of Needs Theory of Abraham Maslow (1908–1970) 142

Conclusion 143

In-Class Workshop: Understanding Inclusion 144

Chapter 5 Exploring Your Role in Fostering Children's Learning 146

Meet the Teachers 147
Learning Outcomes 148

A Definition of Learning 148

Did You Know . . . ? 149

Features of Authentic Learning Experiences 149

Your Role as a Facilitator of Learning 152

The Importance of Learner-Centered Experiences 153

Learner-Centered Experiences Meet the Needs of Diverse Learners 154
Learner-Centered Experiences Are Based on Brain Research 155
Learner-Centered Experiences Focus on Lifelong Learning 156
Learner-Centered Experiences Are Child-Initiated and Child-Directed 158

How Play Contributes to Children's Learning 158

A Definition of Play 158
The Importance of Play 160
Play and Children with Exceptionalities 160
Play and Children from Diverse Backgrounds 162
Stages and Types of Play 163

Fostering Learning Through Technology 163

Using Computers to Facilitate Learning 163

Major Learning Theories 165

What Is a Theory? 165
Maturation Theory of Learning 166
Behavioral Theory of Learning 167
Social Learning Theory of Learning 168
Constructivist Theory of Learning 169

Conclusion 177

In-Class Workshop: Learning Environments for Multiple Intelligences 178

Chapter 6 Exploring Your Role in Creating High-Quality Early Childhood Environments 180

Meet the Teachers 181
Learning Outcomes 182
Did You Know . . . ? 183

A Definition of Environment 183

Features of High-Quality Early Childhood Environments 184

Your Role in Creating High-Quality Environments 187

Arrange Space to Meet the Needs of All Learners 188
Use Time Flexibly 190

Select Appropriate Materials 190
Create a Climate That Affirms Diversity 190
Show Students That You Care About Them and Their Learning 190
Connect with the Children's Families 193

Why the Environment Is Important 193

Ambiance: Light, Color, Texture, and Noise 195
Privacy 195
Size 196
Density 196
Space 197

The Culturally Responsive Classroom 198

Creating High-Quality Early Childhood Environments 198

Preparing the Indoor Environment 198
Evaluating the Indoor Environment 207
Preparing the Outdoor Environment 207

The Inclusive Environment 211

Adapting Environments for Children with Limited Motor Abilities 213
Adapting Environments for Children with Sensory Impairments 214
Adapting Environments for Children with Diverse Academic Needs 214

Conclusion 214

In-Class Workshop: Creating a High-Quality Environment 217

Chapter 7 Exploring Your Role as a Curriculum Developer 218

Meet the Teachers 219
Learning Outcomes 220

A Definition of Curriculum 220

Did You Know . . . ? 221

Why the Curriculum Is So Important 221

Influences on the Curriculum 223
Developmentally Appropriate Practice and the Curriculum 224
What Does Research Say About Appropriate and Effective Early Childhood Curricula? 226

Your Role as a Curriculum Developer 228

Understanding the Written Curriculum 231

Standards-Based Curriculum 231
Content Standards 232
Performance Standards 232
Content Areas of the Early Childhood Curriculum 232
Organizing the Written Curriculum 236
Integrated Curriculum 239
Emergent Curriculum 242
Culturally Responsive Curriculum 242

Understanding the Taught Curriculum 243
Characteristics of Meaningful Curriculum 243
Building a Meaningful Curriculum 245
Unit Approach 245
Project Approach 247
Curriculum Theories 251
Conclusion 253
In-Class Workshop: Brainstorming with Curriculum Webs 255

Chapter 8 Exploring Your Role in Planning for Children's Learning 258
Meet the Teachers 259
Learning Outcomes 260
A Definition of Planning 260
Did You Know . . . ? 261
Types of Planning 262
Your Role as a Planner 273
Know the Children, Families, and Community for Whom You Are Planning 279
Be Knowledgeable About the Content and Concepts You Plan to Teach 279
Plan a Variety of Experiences to Meet the Needs of Diverse Learners 281
Plan Appropriate Methods of Assessing Children's Learning 281
Plan to Reflect on Your Teaching 282
Allow Plenty of Time to Plan Ahead 282
Why Is Planning So Crucial to Successful Teaching? 284
Planning for Accountability to Standards 284
Planning for Individual and Group Learning 285
Planning for Each Child's Success 286
Research on Teachers' Planning 286
Elements of Effective Planning 288
Long-Term Plans 290
Short-Term Plans 295
Planning for Diverse Learners 303
Conclusion 305
In-Class Workshop: Planning for Diverse Learners 307

Chapter 9 Exploring Your Role in Documenting and Assessing Children's Learning 310
Meet the Teachers 311
Learning Outcomes 312
Assessment Defined 312
Did You Know . . . ? 313

Your Role as an Evaluator 316

Recognizing Unethical, Illegal, and Otherwise Inappropriate Assessment Methods and Uses of Assessment Information 316

Choosing and Developing Appropriate Assessment Methods 317

Administering, Scoring, and Interpreting the Results of Various Assessment Methods 318

Using Comprehensive Assessment Data to Make Decisions About Individual Students, Instructional Planning, Curriculum Development, and Programmatic Improvement 318

Communicating Assessment Results to Students, Parents, Educators, and Other Audiences as Appropriate 318

Involving Children and Families in the Assessment Processes 319

Approaches to Assessment 320

Norm-Referenced (Standardized) Tests 320

Criterion-Referenced Tests 322

Principles of Performance Assessment 324

Evaluating Individual Children's Progress 326

Evaluating Program Effectiveness 332

General Indicators of a Balanced Assessment Program 334

Conclusion 337

In-Class Workshop: Designing Portfolios of Children's Work 339

Chapter 10 Exploring Your Role in Guiding Children's Behavior 342

Meet the Teachers 343

Learning Outcomes 344

Children's Needs and Rights 344

Did You Know . . . ? 345

Your Role in Child Guidance 349

Discipline and Child Guidance 351

Violence, Aggression, and Conflict 355

Positive Guidance Strategies 360

Conflict Resolution and Classroom Communities 362

Coping with Different Types of Conflict 364

Possession Disputes 364

Attention Getting 364

Power Struggles 365

Personality Clashes 366

Group-Entry Disputes 366

Aggressive Play 367

Teasing and Name Calling 367

Shifting Blame 367

Guiding Children to Appropriate Behavior 368

Conclusion 371

In-Class Workshop: Role-Playing Ways of Talking with Children 375

Chapter 11 **Exploring Your Role in Supporting Families and Communities 378**

Co-authored by Laurie Nicholson

Meet the Teachers 379

Learning Outcomes 380

Understanding Contemporary Families 380

Did You Know . . . ? 381

The Family as a Social System 382

The Family in the Larger Social Context 384

Respecting Diversity in Families 386

Teachers' Concerns About Working with Parents/Families 389

What Parents and Families Expect from Teachers 390

Promoting Parent/Family Engagement in Education 391

Toward More Effective Interactions with Parents/Families 393

Conferencing: Inviting Communication 402

Conclusion 407

In-Class Workshop: Creating an Informational Brochure on a Topic of General Interest to Parents 410

Chapter 12 **Exploring Your Role as a Professional in the Field of Early Childhood Education 412**

Meet the Teachers 413

Learning Outcomes 414

Did You Know . . . ? 415

A Definition of Professional Development 416

Your Role as an Early Childhood Professional 418

Ways of Supporting Professional Development 423

Stages in Teachers' Professional Development 424

Lifelong Learning and the Early Childhood Practitioner 428

The Concerns of Beginning Teachers 430

Conclusion 433

In-Class Workshop: Becoming a Valued Colleague 434

Appendix **Compendium of Early Childhood Materials and Resources 437**

References 473

Name Index 497

Subject Index 505

Note: Every effort has been made to provide accurate and current Internet information in this book. However, the Internet and information posted on it are constantly changing, so it is inevitable that some of the Internet addresses listed in this textbook will change.

Special Features

Ask the Expert

Elaine Surbeck on Keeping a Journal 10
Lilian Katz on Becoming an Early Childhood Educator 25
Amy Driscoll on Exemplary Early Childhood Programs 51
James L. Hoot on Early Childhood Programs Outside the United States 64
Linda M. Espinosa on Working with Children from Different Backgrounds 78
Stephanie Feeney on the NAEYC Code of Ethics 89
Rosalind Charlesworth on the Importance of Child Development and Early Childhood Education 127
Richard M. Gargiulo on Young Children with Exceptional Needs 132
Carol Brunson Day on Cultural Influences on Learning and Anti-Bias Education 155
Doris Pronin Fromberg on the Value of Play 161
Thelma Harms on Evaluating High-Quality Early Childhood Environments 209
Joe Frost on Outdoor Environments 212
Sue Bredekamp on Developmentally Appropriate Practice 227
Diane Trister Dodge on Early Childhood Curriculum 241
Marjorie Kostelnik on Teaching Young Children Using Thematic Units 298
Jeanette Allison on the Project Approach 304
Sue Wortham on Assessment 315
Deborah Leong on Assessment, Development, and Technology 331
Marjorie Fields on Effective Child Guidance 353
Edyth Wheeler on Conflict Resolution 369
Kevin Swick on Homeless Children and Families 387
Eugenia Berger on Family Involvement 395
Marilou Hyson on the Importance of Professional Preparation 422
Sharon Lynn Kagan on Public Policy and Teachers' Professional Growth 429

Collaborating with Families

A Checklist to Guide Parents in Selecting an Early Childhood Program 26
Writing a Program Philosophy Statement 62
Leslie's First Year as an Urban Public School Kindergarten Teacher 104
Is This Typical? Insights into Child Development 126
What Is a Good Learning Experience? 153
Why Use Learning Centers? 194
Building Connections with Families About the Curriculum 246
Communicating with Families About Meaningful Activities at Home 283
A Question-and-Answer Session with Parents on Portfolios 336
Common Conflict Scenarios 372
Coping with Conflict and Conducting Home Visits 406
Maintaining Positive Relationships with Families 432

One Child, Three Perspectives

An Instructional Support Team Designs an Educational Plan for Michael 29
Giselle's After-School Care 67
Brianna's Urban Public School Evening Art Class 105
Angelica's Baby Pictures 143
Alexander's Struggle to Learn to Read as an English Language Learner 177
Creating a Sensory-Rich Environment for Robert 215
Benjamin's School Play 254
Shayna Goes to Kindergarten 306
Damien, a Drug-Exposed Child 338
Earl's Disruptive Behavior 374
David, a Newly Immigrated Child 408
Rolando's Mother Gets Involved in Head Start 433

Exploring Your Role

CHAPTER 1

Exploring Your Role as a Reflective Practitioner

> **When educators reflect we look carefully at our own practice and think about how our actions could have more effectively supported student learning. It is as though we are looking through a lens to examine our behaviors and then thinking about ways to improve. . . . Revisiting their experiences and considering alternative actions allows educators to assess the benefits of specific teaching strategies. One of the most powerful is reflection itself.**
>
> **Ardith Z. Harle and Karen Trudeau, 2006, p. 101**

Meet the Teachers

DARLENE has been a toddler caregiver for 7 years. She arrives at a Saturday workshop wearing a sweatshirt that shows a cartoon face shouting the word, "Mine!" If you spent the day with Darlene's toddler group, you would see that she spends most of her time on the floor interacting with the six toddlers for whom she is responsible. Darlene explains her perspective this way: "Toddlers need, first and foremost, to learn social skills. At this age, disputes over toys are common, and a frustrated toddler tends to respond physically—hitting, crying, or biting—because the words aren't there yet. I see my primary roles as caring deeply about them, teaching them to get along with one another, and meeting their basic needs. I know that parents trust me to do what is right for their little ones, and I take that trust very seriously."

MS. THOMAS and her aide, Mrs. Grant, teach in a special public school prekindergarten program for children of low-income families. After children arrive, the day begins with a complete breakfast served in the school cafeteria. As they eat, the 4-year-olds engage in informal conversations with their teachers and peers. After cleanup, the children return to the classroom and gather on the carpet for a planning session. They review the day's events and choose the centers that they will visit. Each day, one child is responsible for drawing a picture depicting an important classroom event and dictating a sentence about the picture. The picture and caption become part of a journal that chronicles the school year. Following center time the children meet in small groups to review their accomplishments. Some of their comments are, "I made a farm with a fence out of blocks," "We put together a big dinosaur puzzle," and "Kerri and Lakisha and me played house."

MS. RITCHIE organized her classroom so that all of her first graders began completing the same worksheet the moment they arrived at school. After learning about the importance of providing time for children to make the transition from home to school each day, she changed her morning schedule and offered instead many choices of activities for children: writing, science, building, puzzles, or drama. Afterwards Ms. Ritchie began to see her first graders in a different way because she had more opportunity to talk with them, observe and assess their work, and help them to become independent learners. About this she said, "In all my years of teaching, this has been my easiest. Now I see the children beginning their long day happily. They are sharing and practicing different skills." For Ms. Ritchie, changing her schedule enabled her to work more closely with individual children (Isenberg, 1995, p. 121).

Each of these teachers is inviting children into the learning process as well as acting upon certain beliefs about early childhood education. Think about these teachers in

FIGURE 1.1 Characteristics of outstanding early childhood educators.

Good teachers . . .

- are open minded, flexible, culturally responsive, and committed to the principles of social justice
- regard themselves as learners and sustain an interest in learning throughout their careers
- exercise sound judgment and apply ethical principles in their decision making
- are dedicated to principles of inclusion and fairness in all of their dealings with children, families, and colleagues
- have a passion for teaching and pursue continuous improvement in their teaching effectiveness
- are capable of creating an orderly and productive learning environment
- believe that all children can learn and strive to maximize the potential of each and every one of their students
- understand how young children learn and are keen and thoughtful observers of the learning process
- analyze the results of student assessment and use it as the basis for curriculum planning
- can plan and teach in ways that support all young children's attainment of high academic standards
- can adjust their teaching and adapt the curriculum to children's special needs
- pose intriguing questions and design activities that motivate children to achieve at higher levels
- work collaboratively with administrators, colleagues, professionals in other fields, families, and communities
- learn to take constructive criticism and use it to improve as early childhood educators
- are willing to take an unpopular stand in order to advocate for the needs and rights of others (See Chapters 2 and 3).

relation to the characteristics of outstanding early childhood practitioners outlined in Figure 1.1. Then respond to the following questions.

COMPARE	*What are some commonalities that these three teachers share, even though they are working with children of various ages?*
CONTRAST	How do these teachers think about teaching? How would you characterize the outlook of each one?
CONNECT	*What aspect of these teachers' experiences made the greatest impression on you, and how will you incorporate this into your teaching?*

Now that you have reflected on the perspectives of three different teachers, here is a preview of the knowledge, skills, and dispositions you will need to acquire in order to fulfill your role as a reflective practitioner.

Learning Outcomes

- ✔ Become familiar with national standards and guidelines governing the early childhood educator's role as a reflective practitioner **(NAEYC #5, INTASC #9, and ACEI #5b)**
- ✔ Understand the characteristics and roles of effective practitioners in the field of early childhood education

FIGURE 1.2 Categories of early childhood programs.

FAMILY CHILD CARE

Setting: The family child-care provider's home
Examples: County child-care programs, American Nanny Program, Home-Based Intervention Programs
Children/Families Served (6 weeks–pre-K): Young children are cared for in a very home-like and family-like setting. Number of children served is smaller than in group care; multi-age groups are common. May be less formal arrangements or they may be licensed or accredited.
Typical Funding Source: Local, county, or state taxes; United Way; tuition on a sliding scale; or some combination thereof
Family Eligibility: Usually based on parent's proximity to home, ability to pay tuition, and eligibility criteria of specific programs
Teacher's Title and Credentials: Child caregiver or family child-care provider; at least a high school diploma and often state license or Child Development Associate (CDA) is required.

GROUP CHILD CARE

Setting: Classrooms designed for infants, toddlers, preschoolers, and school-age children that may be located a child-care facility, at the parent's/families' place of work, in churches or synagogues, and so on
Examples: Private child-care and preschool programs, Montessori schools, child-care franchises such as Kindercare, campus child-care centers, before- and after-school care for children in elementary school, corporate child care
Children/Families Served: Typically offer extended hours that would accommodate the needs of working parents/families; adult-to-child ratios and other program elements governed by state regulations
Typical Funding Source: Tuition paid by parents and/or donations
Family Eligibility: Generally based on parent's ability to pay tuition and fees
Teacher's Title and Credentials: Child-care provider; usually requires at least a high school diploma and a state license, CDA, or other teaching credentials.

PRESCHOOL OR NURSERY SCHOOL PROGRAMS

Settings: May be housed in many different locations: at community centers, in churches/synagogues, in buildings provided by commercial chains, in private homes or special facilities built near private residences, and so forth.
Examples: Child care at community centers such as YMCA, Kindercare, Montessori schools
Children/Families Served: Preschool is generally defined as the 3- to 5-year-old age group. Preschool programs may be half day, full day, alternating days (e.g., T/R or M/W/F), combined with other programs (e.g., child care before and after regular preschool program hours), or some combination of these options.
Typical Funding Source: Grant funded, privately funded, supported by tuition, or a combination thereof
Family Eligibility: Usually determined by the parent/family members' place of residence and/or ability to pay for the services
Teacher's Title and Credentials: Child-care provider; usually requires at least a high school diploma and a state license, CDA, or other teaching credentials

DROP-IN CHILD CARE

Setting: Located on-site to provide child care on an as-needed basis.
Examples: Child care at health-care facilities, the family member's employer, Ronald McDonald House, exercise studios, airports, shopping malls, or during religious services.
Children/Families Served: Provide temporary care for young children; children participate in the center on an as-needed basis. May offer 24-hour care if a parent needs to leave town for a family emergency, or just a few hours of care if a single parent needs to run errands and shop, for instance.
Typical Funding Source: Grant funded, privately funded, supported by tuition, or a combination thereof
Family Eligibility: Usually determined by the parent's participation in the business or services of an organization

(*Continued*)

FIGURE 1.2 Continued

Teacher's Title and Credentials: At least a high school diploma; may be a licensed babysitter or have a credential as a nanny; possibly an associate's degree

PUBLIC SCHOOL PREKINDERGARTEN, KINDERGARTEN, AND ELEMENTARY SCHOOL

Setting: Supported by tax dollars and typically housed in public school buildings or in a space rented by the public schools for that purpose. Most states have prekindergarten programs, particularly for children from low-income families.
Examples: Head Start classes for 3- and 4-year-olds located in the public schools, early intervention programs for young children with special needs, prekindergarten through third-grade classes
Children/Families Served: Kindergarten is generally for 5- and 6-year-olds and the primary grades in an elementary school are grades 1 through 3, serving children from approximately age 6 or 7 up to and including age 8 or 9.
Typical Funding Source: Federal, state, and local taxes
Family Eligibility: Some of these programs are reserved for low-income parents and children but others are open to any child who resides in the school district and meets the age requirements.
Teacher's Title and Credentials: A certificate or license awarded by the state is required—usually an early childhood or elementary endorsement. A 4-year baccalaureate degree from an accredited institution is mandatory.

Understanding Reflective Practice

Many experts believe that early childhood education students grow into effective teachers through the practice of reflection. What is teacher reflection? **Reflective practice** is defined as taking the scarce time to rethink, reconsider, reflect, and rework one's craft, all the while making informed and logical decisions on educational matters and assessing the consequences of those actions for all stakeholders in the process (Glickman & Alridge, 2001; Taggart & Wilson, 2005). Prominent educator John Dewey (1933) described reflective thinking as "the active, persistent, and careful consideration of any belief or supposed form of knowledge in light of the grounds that support it" (p. 9). "Rather than behaving purely according to impulse, tradition, and authority, teachers can be reflective—they can deliberate on their actions with open-mindedness, wholeheartedness, and intellectual responsibility" (Cruickshank, 1987, p. 8). To illustrate, imagine that you are going to read a picture book aloud to a small group of children. It is one of your first responsibilities in your practicum experience and your mentor teacher is observing you. You selected the book carefully with attention to the interests and cognitive levels of the children. The book is called *Bear Wants More* (Wilson & Chapman, 2003) and you have planned for it to be an interactive story reading in which you will ask children to chime in on the phrase that is repeated frequently throughout the book ("but bear wants more!"). Now you invite the students over to a carpeted area of the classroom to sit and listen. One child begins to race around the room, singing loudly. The process of reflection often goes something like this:

PAUSE AND REFLECT
About First Teachers

Think about your first teachers. How did they influence your ideas about your talents and capabilities? How did they affect your sense of belonging to the group? What were the most important lessons that you learned from them? Did any of these teachers from your early years in school inspire you to become a teacher and play school? How will you exert a powerful, positive influence on the lives of children and families?

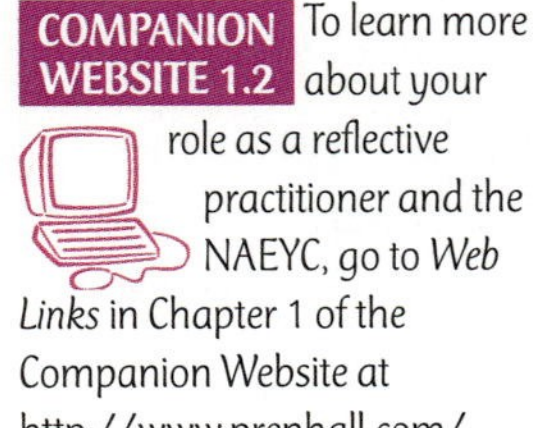
COMPANION WEBSITE 1.2 To learn more about your role as a reflective practitioner and the NAEYC, go to *Web Links* in Chapter 1 of the Companion Website at http://www.prenhall.com/jalongo.

- **Thinking about myself as a teacher—"What am I supposed to do?"** "I tried so hard to be well-prepared and it's not working. I even have a big bear puppet that I borrowed and a shopping bag 'cave' that I made to focus the children's attention. I'm being evaluated! He's ruining my lesson. I want him to sit down and be quiet. Should I just tell him to stop it? What if I do and he ignores me?" Note that at this stage in the process, the focus is on immediate impressions and impulses. It is often at this stage that we turn to traditions (what our teachers or parents might have done) or authoritarian approaches (trying to assert power over the child by yelling or punishing).

David Mager/Pearson Learning Photo Studio

Reflective practitioners think about teaching before, during, and after their interactions with children.

- **Seeing the child—"I notice that. . ."** "We didn't have outdoor recess today because it has been pouring down rain so he might be full of energy. It does not appear that he will grow tired of this quickly—if anything, he is running faster. I now notice that he is singing some of the words from the song 'The Bear Went Over the Mountain.'" At this stage in the process, the focus begins to shift to an examination of the context as you search for explanations.
- **Hypothesizing—"Maybe it's. . ."** "It might be the bear puppet that got him all excited. I think I'll go over to him, kneel down and speak quietly to him, and then lead him over to the circle with the group, but I'd better remind the rest of the students to stay on the carpet." At this stage, you begin to generate ideas about what might be causing or contributing to the behavior and formulate a strategy for how to address it effectively.
- **Questioning—"I wonder. . ."** "I could just say 'Justin! Sit down!' but knowing him, his feelings would be hurt. I wonder what he is thinking and I wonder if what I have planned will stop the behavior. Should I leave the rest of the group for a moment or will that spell disaster?" At this stage, you are deliberating about the outcomes of your actions.
- **Trying out—"I've decided to. . ."** "Here's what I've decided to say to the group: 'We are going to hear a funny story about a bear. Before we begin, I want you to close your eyes and try to think of all the things you know about bears. Think about where bears live and what they do in the winter time.' Then I'm going over and saying, 'Justin, I noticed that you are excited about the bear story and the puppet. You need to come with me and sit on the carpet so that you can see the puppet and the pictures in the story—they are funny!' Let's see how this works." At this stage, you are taking action and implementing your decision.
- **Reflecting afterward—"From this incident, I've learned. . ."** "Justin did come along to the circle. My professor had cautioned us about shouting out orders to children from across the room so I decided not to do that, although it would have been easier and it is what I recall most of my teachers doing. I did manage to get everyone settled down and ready to listen. My mentor teacher was impressed with the strategy that I used. Justin did cooperate and was not embarrassed because I spoke softly to him and did not make it into a battle of wills. My approach also did not label him as a troublemaker."

If you had stopped with your initial impressions—the "all about me" stage—you can see how limiting it would become. Inexperienced teachers often go in search of strategies

ASK THE EXPERT

Elaine Surbeck on Keeping a Journal

Elaine Surbeck

What is a teacher's journal? Who will read it?

I think it is natural that students are a bit uncertain about writing down their thinking, since often their notion of a *journal* is similar to that of a *diary*. It is important to make the distinction that although a journal does contain personal contemplation and rumination, the focus of the journal is on professional development and their thinking about the process of becoming a teacher. In the context of teacher preparation, it is not intended to be a vehicle for revealing intimate details of personal existence. Unless the journal is specified as interactive among agreed-upon readers and participants, the information and thinking students share in dialogue journals with the professor is confidential. Students should be encouraged to write those things that they are comfortable revealing about themselves as developing prospective teachers. In many cases, the entries that students make grow in length and depth as they begin to trust me, and to value their learning as they recognize the power of reflective thinking.

Why keep a teacher's journal?

While I have written rationales and voiced my beliefs, I think the best testimony comes directly from students themselves. With their permission, I am quoting two undergraduate students about what *they* found valuable in keeping a reflective dialogue journal.

> (Student One) "I found keeping a journal this semester to be a very useful and insightful experience. When I look back to my beginning entries it is so easy to see how far I have come in my thinking. Before this semester I don't think I could have expressed my philosophy about teaching as clearly as I feel I now can. Writing in my journal has helped me to bring my thoughts together. Drawing upon classroom experiences, lectures, notes, and readings to 'think' about in my entries helped me make my own meaning from what I was learning. As I wrote I felt I was constructing knowledge instead of just memorizing. . . . Journal writing is not an act of memorization; it is an act of thinking."

> (Student Two) "Journals . . . I am glad we were required to keep them—I wasn't at the time of course, but now I am very glad. I learned so much more in this class than any class I have ever taken. The journal helped me to grow. I had to think, reflect, and think again and that was good. I know more about who I am and what I want than ever before. What's more, I believe in what I am preparing to become. I know I will be the best teacher I can, and I know I will keep learning and learning and learning."

What is the process of reflection?

A common problem that is encountered in asking students to write in journals is how to help them to take their reflections further and to deepen their thinking about content. Through naturalistic research, my colleagues and I discovered that many students organized their journal entries using a particular sequence that started with *reactions* to something about teaching or class, then they might continue on to *elaborate* more about the topic, and finally, some students progressed to the level of *contemplation*. Not all students do so, so the question becomes one of whether it is possible to encourage reflective thinking in all students. As one way to investigate this possibility, I now ask students to use this same framework to assess their own entries, and challenge them to strive to reach the contemplative part of the sequence. [For more information about this framework, see Surbeck, Han, & Moyer, 1991]. Although additional research needs to be conducted to examine whether using the framework for self-assessment of journal entries increases students' ability to be reflective, we have some informal evidence that knowledge of the sequence and levels in the framework does encourage students to inquire further into their thinking. I believe that journal writing is one way to develop in our undergraduate students the disposition to be reflective and to assist them in creating their individual teaching theory, processes critical to becoming a child-sensitive teacher.

Elaine Surbeck is Dean of Teacher Education at Arizona State University in Tempe, Arizona.

and techniques that will make them more effective. In that quest they frequently overlook the fact that one of the most powerful tools for improving teaching is thinking about our own thinking, or reflection. As Nel Noddings (2006) notes, "Possibly no goal of education is more important—or more neglected—than self-understanding. . . . We need to ask not only what we believe but why we believe it. Similarly, we need to ask, What do I feel? Why? What am I doing? Why? And even, what am I saying and, again, why?" (p. 10). Watch the reading lesson in a K–3 classroom to reflect on what this teacher does to engage all of her students in learning in the "Shared Reading" video clip online at the Teacher Prep Website.

TEACHER PREP WEBSITE 1.2

Go to the Video Classroom, select Reading Methods, choose Fluency (Module 3), and select Shared Reading (Video 1).

Getting Started with Reflective Practice

From the earliest days of teaching, one of the defining characteristics of good teachers is reflective practice (Ayers, 2001; Nieto, 2005; Schon, 1983) because

> Teaching demands thoughtfulness. There is simply no way to become an outstanding teacher through adherence to routine, formula, habit, convention, or standardized ways of speaking and acting. Thoughtfulness requires wide-awakeness—a willingness to look at the conditions of our lives, to consider alternatives and different possibilities, to challenge received wisdom and the taken for granted, and to link our conduct with our consciousness . . . [it also] requires strength and courage—the strength to think in a time of thoughtlessness, the courage to care in a culture of carelessness. (Ayers, 1995, p. 60)

COMPANION WEBSITE 1.3 For more information about reflective practice, go to *Web Links* in Chapter 1 of the Companion Website at http://www.prenhall.com/jalongo.

Teachers who fail to reflect will discover that "chance and necessity are the sole rulers of those who are incapable of reflection" (Csikszentmihalyi, 1993, p. 17). Novice teachers often are eager to dispense with reflection, thinking it is a waste of time. But they are like the impatient gardener who neglects to prepare the soil and hastily scatters seeds upon the hard ground—they may proclaim "Finished!" sooner than the patient gardener who took the time to till the soil but, at harvest time, it will become apparent which person really invested time in planning and preparation and which one took the shortcuts.

One of the questions that we hear frequently from those novice teachers is "What am I supposed to reflect on?" A place to begin is with yourself, with your reasons for pursuing a teaching career.

> As teachers, we need to know a few things about ourselves as learners before we set out to plan for the learning of others. Maybe the primary question to ask here is, what led you to teaching in the first place? The reasons are familiar . . . I teach because I love teaching. I teach because I love kids. I've always wanted to be a teacher. Nothing is better than being a teacher. . . . Teaching is hard work. Choose teaching because you want to teach. Teach because you believe that the human spirit is capable of learning at any age and you strongly desire to be part of the dynamic interactions that characterize positive learning—total engagement of the mind, body, and spirit in an inquiry about those things that are known as well as those that seem distant and impossible (Carothers, 1995, p. 27).

Figure 1.3 is a list of questions to get you started with the process of reflection.

Levels of Reflection

TEACHER PREP WEBSITE 1.3

Go to the Video Classroom, select Social Studies, choose Connecting to Literature (Module 5), and select The Supply Chain (Video 1).

Research suggests that teachers' reflection often begins with a focus on themselves, then moves to a focus on the task of teaching, and finally progresses to a focus on the impact of their teaching on students (Fuller & Bown, 1975; Taggart & Wilson, 2005). So the sequence moves from *self* (level 1), to *task* (level 2), and to *impact* (level 3). Reflect on how children's literature can be a resource for effective teaching as you watch an

FIGURE 1.3 A self-questioning framework.

What led me to this career choice?

- Why do I want to work with young children?
- What do I believe about how young children learn?
- How do I think about concepts such as equality, freedom, individuality, and honesty as they relate to teaching and learning?
- What personal qualities and abilities do I possess that will make me successful in working with young children?
- What kind of early childhood teacher do I want to become?
- How will I demonstrate my commitment to young children and families through my work?

How are my personal characteristics matched to the job? Am I . . .

- Convinced that all children can learn?
- Committed to maximizing the potential of each and every one of my students?
- Dedicated to principles of inclusion and fairness in all of my dealings with children, families, and colleagues?
- Responsible in fulfilling my duties and capable of exercising sound judgment?
- Reliant on ethical principles in my decision making?
- Enthusiastic about and able to sustain a lifelong interest in learning?
- Willing to take constructive criticism and use it to improve?
- Passionate about becoming a teacher and determined to pursue continuous improvement in my effectiveness?
- Genuinely interested in young children, their development, ways to help them achieve high standards, and strategies for assessing their progress?
- Proud to be entering the field of early childhood education and eager to contribute to it?

elementary teacher developing the concept of a supply chain with students in "The Supply Chain" video clip on the Teacher Prep Website.

Level 1: Self as Teacher. Initially (and understandably), teachers tend to be preoccupied at first by their ability to fulfill the teaching role. They have a limited repertoire and therefore want quick, definitive answers to their questions about student behavior, teaching ideas, and solutions to various dilemmas. The typical novice who is confronted with the task of writing a lesson plan turns not to published resources written by professionals, but to memories of childhood and the activities they enjoyed back when they were young (Whitbeck, 2000). Novices tend to rely on firsthand experiences, follow their instincts, and have little interest in learning theory. Yet if a new teacher simply repeats what he or she experienced as a child, it is not good enough for at least four important reasons. First, it does not take into consideration the 15 or more years of educational research that was produced in between the time the novice teacher was a young child and matured into a prospective teacher—the teaching is old fashioned before it has even begun! Second, although children may participate in many different enjoyable activities, not all of them produce good learning outcomes. Third, relying on personal experiences does not take the new context into account and "each school, each community, each culture that a teacher faces call for different understandings and different responses" (Birmingham, 2003, p. 1). Fourth, chances are that the activities generated from memory are inadequate to sustain a teacher on a daily basis, are already overused with children, and are clouded by a personal childhood perspective rather than approached from a professional point of view. To see a teacher talking with a parent about sharing music, view "What Are Our Assumptions?" video clip online at the Teacher Prep Website.

TEACHER PREP WEBSITE 1.4

Go to the Video Classroom, select Foundations & Intro, choose Diversity (Module 4) and select What Are Our Assumptions? (Video 4).

Level 2: The Task of Teaching in Context. The second level of reflection focuses on the task. This occurs when teachers begin to look for relationships between pieces of their experiences, interpret the specific teaching situation, search for "why it was" a particular way, and try to arrive at principles to guide their actions (Lee, 2005). Part of becoming a reflective practitioner is to think about the assumptions that we bring to the classroom. A student teacher who typifies this stage said, "Some days I feel like such a good teacher and other days I am so disappointed in myself. My supervisor said that my teaching was 'uneven' and I don't disagree. The problem for me is, how do I get steadier, more consistent? Why is one activity so successful and another, a big disappointment?" With time and experience, this student started to see the connection between his level of planning, and the success of his lessons. True, he sometimes "got away" with a lesson that wasn't particularly well planned, but when lessons verged on disaster, it was nearly always attributable to failing to think through the procedures. Recognizing the need to plan more thoroughly, considering the particular characteristics of the learning situation, anticipating the difficulties that specific children might have, and talking through lessons with colleagues all supported this teacher's professional growth.

Scott Cunningham/Merrill

Children's first teachers often leave an indelible impression.

If you can step away from a preoccupation to "get through" the lesson and begin to make decisions in a more thoughtful way you are well on your way to the second level of teacher reflection (Ball, 2000; Birmingham, 2003; Carpenter-LaGattuta, 2002). At level 2 of reflection, the teacher considers alternative practices, makes choices based on knowledge and value commitment, selects content related to context and student needs, and seeks to analyze, clarify, and validate basic principles to guide teaching (Taggart & Wilson, 2005). In teaching, there are literally hundreds of daily decisions to be made. Anyone who aspires to become a good teacher will need to arrive at those decisions based on something more compelling than "This is what we did back when I was a child."

A strategy for moving beyond a focus on self to a focus on the task is to examine a critical incident—either one that you personally experienced or one that someone else has provided in the form of case studies (Quisenberry, McIntyre, & Duhon, 2002; Rand, 2000). For example, Kiera was teaching in a Head Start classroom when 4-year-old Ben fell on the playground and scraped his knee. Tina, one of his classmates, did what she had seen a teacher do—she moistened a paper towel and placed it on Ben's knee. The problem arose after the teacher praised Tina for helping Ben and Tina began to pursue him around the classroom, pressing more firmly, until he yelled, "Stop it, Tina! You're hurting me." This situation really challenged Kiera in several ways. She wondered if her positive reinforcement had backfired. And, although she was glad to see Ben "using his words" instead of lashing out physically, she sensed that Tina's feelings were hurt. In an instructional methods course back on campus, Kiera's professor suggested that the practicum students use the following series of questions as a tool for reflection (Korthagen & Vasalos, 2005, p. 50):

What was the context?
What did the children want?
What did you want?
What did the children do?
What did you do?
What were the children thinking?
What were you thinking?

How did the students feel?
How did you feel?

After describing the situation fully, Kiera and her fellow practicum students used the following questions to write a reflective essay:

What problems did you encounter or are you still encountering?
What was the ideal situation that you wanted to bring about?
What limiting behaviors in you—actions, feelings, images, beliefs—got in the way of achieving the ideal? What core qualities do you need in order to overcome the limitations and realize the ideal situation?
How can you mobilize these core qualities and begin to experiment with new behaviors? (adapted from Korthagen & Vasalos, 2005)

As Kiera wrote her essay, she realized that the main difficulty for her was that she wanted to promote compassion in her students and had not been successful in doing this. Ben wanted his classmate's overzealous mothering to stop. Tina evidently wanted the teacher's approval and had gotten a little carried away. Kiera had directed Tina to stop pursuing Ben but, on further reflection, she decided that such incidents would continue to happen unless Tina really understood how to read her classmate's responses and the difference between helping and hurting. Through reflection, Kiera decided to coach Tina in the skills of interacting more successfully with peers.

Level 3: Focus on Outcomes for Students. The third and highest level of reflection occurs as teachers become more student-centered and consider the outcomes that their teaching has for students. Mature professionals in the early childhood field are capable of striving for continuous improvement, of analyzing experiences from multiple perspectives, and of appreciating the influence that they exert over students' values/behavior/achievement. They are involved in the school and community (Buchanan, Baldwin, & Rudisill, 2002).

To summarize the impact of these levels of reflection, think for a moment about yourself at age 13. Remember how important it was to have certain clothes, musical tastes, hairstyles, or ways of speaking? During that time in our lives, most of us go along with the crowd to a greater extent than at other times. Most teenagers try to be like other teenagers to win peer acceptance. It is not until later that they recognize the value of or even understand the expression "Be yourself."

Becoming an early childhood professional frequently follows a similar course—we begin by trying to act like other teachers we have known and to simply fit in; there is a preoccupation with our own ability to fulfill the role of teacher. But then we begin to reflect on the consequences of our teaching decisions (Many, Howard, & Hoge, 2002). The In-Class Workshop at the end of this chapter will guide you through the stages in becoming a reflective practitioner.

Developing the Characteristics of a Reflective Practitioner

A **disposition** is a habit of mind, a characteristic way of approaching a situation. Suppose that you are writing a paper for a class about a leader in early childhood education and you encounter conflicting information about the person's birth date—what do you do? It depends on your disposition. Some students would just pick one of the dates to save time; others would consult additional, authoritative sources to make sure that the information is accurate. If you persist until the information is correct, you have the disposition to use

FIGURE 1.4 The basic dispositions for reflection.

Open-mindedness that includes:

- Interrogating beliefs and assumptions—our own and those of others
- Listening to others' points of view and interacting in productive ways
- Responding to surprises and unexpected outcomes in ways that improve the situation for learners
- Willingness to revise opinions based on data or admit that we may be wrong

Responsibility that includes:

- Accepting responsibility for our own intellectual beliefs and their consequences
- Having social awareness and regard for moral, political, and ethical issues
- Being responsible for oneself yet dedicated to the common good
- Testing out new thinking and seeking alternatives

Wholeheartedness that includes:

- Approaching teaching with enthusiasm, energy, and dedication
- Posing meaningful and searching questions that frame and reframe thinking
- Accepting that there are few easy answers in teaching and persisting at finding appropriate solutions
- Expecting teaching to be unpredictable and challenging

Ways to move toward "mindful, relationship-based practices":

- Attend to the individuals you are working with at any given time rather than dwelling on the past or future.
- Respect the individual knowledge, strengths, and needs of the children, families, and professionals with whom you work.
- Engage in the reflective cycle ("Think before doing, think while doing, think after doing"); carefully consider, plan, observe, and assess all of your actions and behaviors as a teacher.
- Develop an understanding of how your values and beliefs affect your practices, which in turn affect your students, their families, your colleagues, other professionals, and the community at large.
- Listen carefully, observe thoughtfully, and ask questions that can clarify and promote greater understanding.
- Foster positive relationships between and among all of the stakeholders in the child's education.

To reflect on samples of children's efforts to learn numbers, see the "Curriculum and Instruction–Numbers" artifact online at the Teacher Prep Website.

SOURCES: Adapted from Bolton, 2001; Chilvers, 2005; Dewey, 1909, 1933; McMullen & Dixon, 2006; Schon, 1987; Stronge, 2002.

resources effectively and seek the truth. Becoming a reflective practitioner also has a set of dispositions. There are three very basic ones—open-mindedness, responsibility, and wholeheartedness (Dewey, 1903; 1933). Figure 1.4 explains them further.

You will know that you are moving toward reflective practice when you display the following characteristics, based on Dewey's definition (Eby, Herrell, & Jordan, 2006):

- **Reflective practitioners are *active*,** meaning that they *search energetically for information and solutions to problems that arise in the classroom.* An example of taking action is learning more about the medical condition of a child through collaboration with colleagues and professionals from other fields.
- **Reflective practitioners are *persistent*,** meaning that they *think through difficult issues and persist even though it may be difficult or tiring.* For example helping preschoolers and kindergartners adjust to a new school year typically requires a long-term commitment.
- **Reflective practitioners are careful,** meaning that they have concern for self and others, respect students as human beings, and try to create a positive, nurturing classroom. An example of behavior that demonstrates care is the practice of involving children in establishing and monitoring school rules.

TEACHER PREP WEBSITE 1.5

Go to Student and Teacher Artifacts, select Foundations & Intro, choose Curriculum and Instruction (Module 10), and select Numbers (Artifact 1).

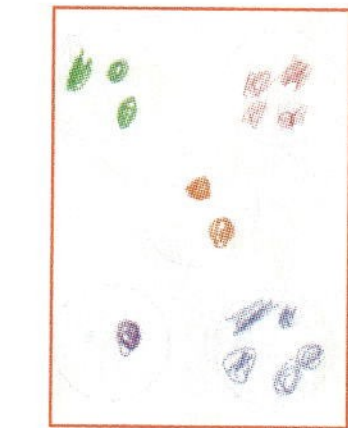

PAUSE AND REFLECT
About Caregivers of Young Children

Imagine that you had to trust someone else to help you care for and educate your sibling, your own child, or another child you love. What concerns would you have? What characteristics would you look for in the person responsible for your young child's care and education? Such questions are a good place to begin when thinking about the characteristics of effective early childhood educators. Now look at the Collaborating with Families feature at the end of the chapter to see a parents' checklist for evaluating early childhood programs. How did your ideas and concerns compare?

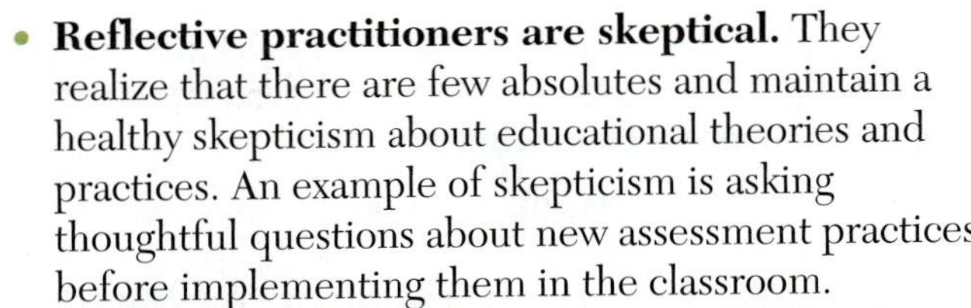

- **Reflective practitioners are skeptical.** They realize that there are few absolutes and maintain a healthy skepticism about educational theories and practices. An example of skepticism is asking thoughtful questions about new assessment practices before implementing them in the classroom.
- **Reflective practitioners are rational.** They demand evidence and apply criteria in formulating judgments rather than blindly following trends or acting on impulse. An excellent example of rational behavior as it applies to teaching is referring to professional journal articles to gather additional information on a topic before arriving at an opinion.
- **Reflective practitioners are proactive,** meaning that they are able to translate reflective thinking into positive action, such as explaining the rationale for new classroom practices to parents so that their questions and concerns are addressed before problems arise.

COMPANION WEBSITE 1.4 To learn more, go to the *Enrichment Content: Research Highlights* in Chapter 1 of the Companion Website at http://www.prenhall.com/jalongo.

To summarize, the goal is to become "reflective decision makers who can carefully observe, inquire, diagnose, design, and evaluate learning and teaching so that it is continually revised to become more effective" (Darling-Hammond, 2006, pp. 82–83).

The Disposition to Become a Reflective Practitioner

Now that you are familiar with the process of reflection, you will want to begin reflecting on the characteristics of effective early childhood educators and your suitability for the role. Figure 1.5 is a summary of the roles and behaviors associated with effective teaching. Some questions to ask yourself include:

What have you already done, what evidence do you have, to demonstrate that you will . . .

- Make a firm commitment to the care and education of young children?
- Take delight in, be curious about, and strive to understand children's development?
- Maintain a fundamentally positive outlook on children, families, and teaching?
- Accept the risks and make the mistakes that are part of the process of learning to teach?
- Adapt flexibly to continuous change and expect perpetual challenge?
- Master the content, adjust your teaching, and adapt the curriculum to the needs of individual students?
- Build a sense of community, seek collaboration, and offer peer support?
- Approach problems responsibly and make ethical decisions?
- Pursue professional growth and concentrate on becoming the best teacher I can be?

Make a Firm Commitment to the Care and Education of Young Children

As you begin your professional career in the care and education of the very young, it is helpful to remember that "early childhood education is not an exercise or a schedule or a

FIGURE 1.5 Roles and behaviors of effective teachers.

1. **Reflective Practitioner.** A teacher who thinks deeply about students, learning, pedagogical practices, and curriculum.

   Behaviors:
   - examines personal experiences as a learner and uses them to increase identification with children
   - expects uncertainty, tension, struggle, and intermittent crises and senses of failure
   - views frustration or discomfort as a necessary and predictable aspect of learning to teach
   - is open to professional advice and constructive criticism
   - engages in meaningful professional dialogue rather than merely complaining
   - resists the pull of tradition and tendency to teach as he or she was taught
   - demonstrates desire to accomplish the goal of becoming a new kind of teacher

2. **Teacher/Researcher.** A practitioner who collects and uses data from students to improve the teaching/learning process.

   Behaviors:
   - is capable of finding a focus for self-improvement and raises challenging questions about effective teaching
   - experiments with new teaching techniques
   - engages in professional dialogue with other teachers
   - expects to adapt or change teaching rather than viewing modifications as a sign of failure
   - modifies approaches to teaching and learning based on students' responses

3. **Professional and Collaborative Community Member.** A teacher who reads and synthesizes the literature in the field, carefully considers educational issues, and uses human resources to improve practice and reform education.

   Behaviors:
   - expects moral, political, and emotional uncertainty
   - compares/contrasts personal teaching philosophy with that of others
   - thinks about personal stance on an issue
   - provides clear rationales for choices to the public, to colleagues, and to supervisors
   - models enthusiasm for learning
   - seeks collegial input on important professional concerns
   - works collaboratively with professionals from other fields
   - gains an awareness of the politics of schooling and the ideologies of the institution

4. **As Evaluator of Child's Learning, Program, and Self**. A teacher who plans meaningful assessment tasks, gathers appropriate evidence, and monitors/supports students' progress in ways that enable every child to succeed and the program to flourish.

   Behaviors:
   - develops criteria for evaluating student learning
   - creates a system for tracking progress
   - reports in appropriate ways to the intended audiences for assessment data (e.g., feedback to students, progress reports to parents/families, and data to schoolwide, districtwide, statewide, or national groups)
   - engages in self-assessment by documenting professional growth and making it visible to others

SOURCES: Abdal-Haqq, 1998; Carroll, Conte, & Pan, 2000; Hargreaves, 1995; Wideen, Mayer-Smith, & Moon, 1998.

machine. It is young children exploring their world with sensory thoroughness, experimenting with people and places and materials, encouraged by a teacher who respects and uses their ideas and ways of learning to help them discover what has meaning for them in our society" (Law, Moffit, Moore, Overfield, & Starks, 1966, p. 12). Caring about children, enjoying their company, respecting them as individuals, and treating them equitably form the cornerstone of early childhood practice. In early childhood education, we speak of educating the "whole child"—the physical, social, emotional, cognitive, and aesthetic aspects (Hendrick & Weissman, 2007). As a group, early childhood educators do not consider covering material to be their primary responsibility in the way that some teachers at other levels do. Rather, they see children first. For example, if you ask a high school biology teacher what she teaches, she is likely to say, "biology," while an early childhood practitioner is more apt to respond with the particular age of children taught (e.g., infants; toddlers; preschoolers; first, second, or third graders; a mixed-age group).

What have you done to show your commitment to children?

Here is one preservice teacher's journal entry about commitment to children:

This may be a small thing but I think it shows that I am willing to stick up for kids. There is a trailer park not far from the dollar store I go to and they sell cheap candies there. The children gather up their money and the younger kids go with the older ones to buy the candy. I've noticed that the one cashier, in particular, will keep going to the next adult in line and will ignore the children until they either give up or no one else is left at the counter. This happened while I was waiting in line. When she turned to me, I said, "I think that these children were in line ahead of me so please go ahead and wait on them first." The children just beamed when I said that! At least this forced the cashier to think about her behavior, if only for a few seconds. I can tell by the look on her face that she considers these children without much money to be a nuisance. The manager has used his "No shirt, no shoes, no service" sign to keep them out and people in my town call them "trailer trash," thinking that it is so funny. I think it is cruel.

Think about the ways that you already have or might begin to intercede on behalf of children.

Take Delight in, Be Curious About, and Learn to Understand Children's Development

Knowing young children well is crucial to effective teaching. That is why one of the key concepts in early childhood education is developmentally effective practice (Copple & Bredekamp, 2006). Developmentally effective practice has two key components: age appropriateness, what children of that age are capable of doing, generally speaking, and individual appropriateness, what is suitable for that particular child at that time and in that situation, including the child's culture and ethnicity. The following is a journal entry from a student on the topic of developmentally effective practice:

During the summer I worked at a private child-care center inside a gated community where most of the homes are a million plus. The pressure on these kids is unbelievable and the center director has stated that parents won't pay unless they see results. We actually stayed after school to "fix up" the three-year-olds' projects—rearranging and repasting to make them appear more presentable. I think that the cut-and-paste activity was too hard for them and that doing this only tricked the families into believing that their children were more advanced but I wanted to keep my summer job and figured that the director knew more than me so I didn't say anything at the time.

What have you done that demonstrates your interest in understanding child development?

Here is an example of a preservice teacher's reflections on her efforts:

A group of children in my neighborhood were gathered for Scotty's third birthday party. The parents had made a videotape of the birthday boy at various ages. One of the things that he did when he was about 11 months old was to lie down on his stomach and slide quickly down five padded, carpeted stairs. One child begged to see the film run backwards, and the father obliged while the children laughed and squealed at the funny situations, such as a bite of birthday cake going backwards from a person's mouth and back onto the fork. When the film segment that showed Scotty shooting down the steps was run backwards, it looked like he was being propelled up the stairs. About half an hour later, a one-year-old who had watched the film was observed stretched out on the same stairs that were in the video. Suddenly I realized that he was trying to launch himself up the stairs, just as he had seen in the video run backwards! When I said this to my neighbors, they saw it too. This is an example of my being curious about why children do what they do. I was pleased that I was able to see more than the average person and make sense out of a child's behavior when no other adult at the party had seen it.

As this example illustrates, early childhood educators are intrigued by children's behavior and work harder than most to try to interpret it. Another opportunity to observe children occurs when teacher candidates are required to complete an in-depth study of a particular child, often in conjunction with a course in child development. Use this as an opportunity to practice higher-order thinking skills by analyzing, applying, synthesizing, and evaluating what you have learned in various classes and via your observations. Effective early childhood educators take the time to notice children's behavior and glean important information from those observations.

Maintain a Fundamentally Positive Outlook on Children, Families, and Teaching

No one goes into teaching with the thought, "I will become a mediocre, marginal, or destructive teacher who does just the minimum," yet it is clear that such teachers exist. One powerful indicator of whether a person will become one of these teachers is the individual's behavior right now. Students who will not expend much effort or do only what is directly rewarded are unlikely to become teachers who will do more than what is required. Look for evidence of your attitudes toward children, families, and teaching in your own behavior and that of your classmates. Do some people drag themselves in, collapse into a chair at the back of the room, and complain when the work is demanding? If so, chances are that if these people manage to get into teaching, they will quickly deteriorate into poor teachers. Are you and your classmates willing to do more than what is required? How many of you would go to hear a guest speaker even though there is no extra credit involved? As you work with faculty and supervisors, they are continuously evaluating these traits because they will be asked to write recommendations of your performance. Those recommendations will be based not only on your current level of performance, but also on your teachers' and supervisors' predictions about how you will fare in an early childhood setting. Anyone who is lukewarm at the very beginning of a career can hardly be expected to become enthusiastic in later years. Evidence of how you'll be in the classroom tomorrow is reflected in how you behave as a learner today.

What have you done to demonstrate a positive outlook on children and families?

Evidence of your belief in the importance of the early years may be found in your fulfillment of professional responsibilities. Are you on time for your practicum experiences and well prepared? Do you plan engaging and appropriate activities that do not waste children's precious time? Effective early childhood educators act upon their care, concern, and commitment to the very young; their behavior speaks louder than words ever could (Fennimore, 1989).

Be Willing to Take the Risks and Make the Mistakes That Are Part of the Learning Process

Psychologists usually define learning as a change in behavior. If your behavior remains the same, then you have not learned. The difficulty with changing behavior is that we feel unsure of ourselves, uncertain about whether we are acting appropriately. A good example is writing a lesson plan for the first time. Students typically say such things as, "I never wrote a lesson plan before," "I'm so confused," or "I have no idea what to do." In other words, these students are being asked to change their behavior and they are afraid of taking a risk. Yet real learning is, by definition, risky—no risk of mistake, no learning. When you are confronted with new challenges and unfamiliar tasks such as lesson planning, it is helpful to take stock of what you *do* know, based upon your experiences as a student. You probably know quite a few things about planning activities that are simply common sense, such as the need to teach something significant (a concept), the need to specify your goals (the objective), the need to capture children's attention at the beginning of the lesson (an introduction or motivation), the need to identify what materials are necessary to teach the lesson (materials), the need to think through your lesson in a logical sequence (the procedure), and the need to make certain that your information is current and accurate (resources or references).

What have you done that demonstrates taking appropriate risks and learning from mistakes?

TEACHER PREP WEBSITE 1.6

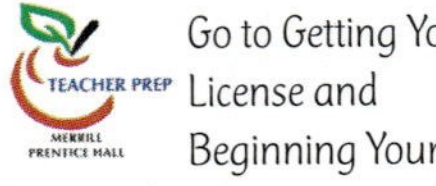

Go to Getting Your License and Beginning Your Career, select Preparing a Portfolio, and choose Reflection as an Essential Component of the Teaching Portfolio.

Incidents that prompted you to take a stand or to change your behavior in some significant way are another type of insight that can be recorded in your journal entries. A framework for analyzing such experiences might be:

The mistake I made (and why):
How I handled the mistake (and why):
What I learned from the mistake:

To learn more about the process of teacher reflection go to "Getting Your License and Beginning Your Career" section of the Teacher Prep Website.

Adapt Flexibly to Continuous Change and Expect Perpetual Challenge

"Teaching is a complex, situation-specific, and dilemma-ridden behavior" (Sparks-Langer & Colton, 1991, p. 37). If you want a large measure of control, predictability, and guaranteed results, it is preferable to work with objects rather than human beings.

As everyone knows, we human beings are highly individual. What encourages one person undermines the confidence of another. For example, "Doctors do not walk into surgery with an instructional manual. Attorneys do not defend clients using prescribed dialogues that are guaranteed for all cases. These professionals interpret cases individually, and then apply the most appropriate interventions. Each patient is unique, each client an individual" (Glasgow, 1994, p. 132). The uniqueness of human beings requires you to constantly adapt and adjust your instructional strategies, the examples that you give, and the ways that you interact with students. In most cases, the work of the early childhood professional is accomplished in group rather than individual settings. Responding to these complex, multiple demands requires a large measure of flexibility.

What have you done that demonstrates your flexibility in thinking and ability to adapt?

Try audiotaping one of your lessons. Type your actual words in the right-hand column, then go back and try to fill in the thoughts that were going through your head at the same time.

Teacher's Thoughts	**Teacher's Words**
Using real objects to introduce this lesson on plants has captured their attention. . . . Elisa seems very quiet today. *Wow, it's hot in here with these warm fall days and all of these windows.*	"Let's look at these plants I brought today. What are some of the parts of plants that you know about? Tell me and I'll make a list. Cara says that she sees leaves. Cara, can you come up and point to some of the different kinds of leaves you see?. . . "
Taylor and Jason are lying down. Should I say something or ignore it? I have to remember that Jaime's mom is picking him up for a doctor's appointment.	"I want to see everyone sitting up. That way you can all see all of the plants. How about another part that is below the ground and that you can't see unless you pull the plant out of the soil? Ritchie? Yes, roots. I'll put that word up here on our list."
Maria really seems to be into the lesson today. . . .When we have our student teaching seminar, I want to be sure to share the flannel board cutouts I got from a book to show the parts of a plant and how flowers grow.	

Master the Content and Pedagogy, Adjust Teaching, and Adapt the Curriculum to the Needs of Children

Think about something that you do exceptionally well. What were your first attempts like? How about all of the stages in between? It is unrealistic to expect that any less effort would be expended in becoming a teacher than in learning to swim or cook or play a musical instrument, for instance. Yet over and over again, beginning teachers secure their first jobs and lament that they were not adequately prepared for the realities of teaching (Ryan, 1986), as if they expected to be a finished product churned out on an assembly line.

The truth is that most colleges and universities are all about possibilities—about what education could and should be rather than about what it is or the status quo. In other words, there is a discrepancy between centers and schools as they routinely exist and centers and schools at their very best. If your college and university instructors are doing their jobs, they are preparing you to be the best possible early childhood educator, not a mediocre one. They are hoping that you will be strong enough to resist routine and expedience. They are trusting you to become a change agent, a person who will continually strive to improve centers, schools, and other educational contexts by making them more responsive to young learners.

Are you genuinely interested in education and do you sustain concentration throughout your program, even when the content of a particular course or the style of an instructor is not what you prefer? You will know that you are concentrating fully on your goal when you become so involved in learning activities that you lose track of time, instead of watching the clock. Another indicator of this concentration on your goal is the tendency to seek feedback from others rather than fearing recommendations for improvement or resenting the extra effort it takes to become an even better teacher. Yet you could probably stand outside the classroom door of a typical education course on the day when major projects are returned to the students and overhear some students complaining bitterly because they were asked to revise their work. Although they are, in effect, saying, "How dare the instructor ask more of me!" the truth is that asking more of teachers is commonplace. The worst in our field are satisfied to be uninformed, less skilled, and disaffected. The best in our field are constantly striving to learn more, teach better, and demonstrate their care and concern for young children.

What have you done that demonstrates your determination to master the content and pedagogy?

Gordon and Browne (2006) suggest that teachers ask themselves, Do I see myself as a learner? Where does my learning take place? How? What happens to me when something is hard or when I make a mistake? Do I learn from other teachers? Do I learn from children?

A good reflective exercise is to interview an early childhood educator who has a wonderful reputation. You will undoubtedly be amazed by all of the duties, both required and volunteer, that this person has undertaken and the clear focus with which those duties are approached. If you immediately establish a sense of purpose, you will make the most of your education.

Build a Sense of Community; Seek Collaboration and Peer Support

Have you ever felt a strong sense of affiliation with a group other than your family? If so, you were part of a community. Communities provide opportunities to reveal ourselves fully, know others well, and reach out, connect, and help (Sapon-Shevin, 1995). A school community is characterized by a clear and vital mission and a shared sense of purpose (Boyer, 1995). This means that all stakeholders—children, parents, family members, teachers, administrators, support staff, and the community at large—understand what is happening in school and why. Another important dimension of a learning community is classroom climate, the feeling or tone of a classroom. A classroom community that supports learning is

- *communicative,* meaning that all members strive to make themselves understood as well as understand others
- *just,* meaning that everyone expects and receives fair treatment
- *disciplined,* meaning that expectations for and limits on behavior are made clear
- *caring,* meaning that every person in the room is treated with love and respect
- *celebratory,* meaning that achievements and milestones are honored and savored (Boyer, 1995)

Whenever a sense of community is built, we feel that we belong and feel responsible for ourselves yet committed to one another.

What have you done to document your efforts to build community in interactions with classmates, families, and professionals?

One way to build a sense of community is to discuss lesson plans thoughtfully with others, using the professional terminology that you are acquiring in your classes. The following is a dialogue about using academic standards between a sophomore, Miranda, who has just taught her first lesson in preschool, and two junior-level students in the same program.

Rachael: This is the first time you've used the academic standards, right? What did you think about that?

Miranda: Actually, as I was searching through the packet to determine which standards I felt were appropriate, I really enjoyed it and read through—even the ones that didn't apply. I think they're the basis for a lot of things in education. It was interesting to see, on that level—a preschool level—what would be expected.

Kaylee: Did the standards help to guide the lesson?

Miranda: Yes, they did. . . . I found that one lesson could cover so many standards. I probably could've listed more.

Kaylee: Our professors want us to list all of them too.

Rachael: You get used to reading through page upon page [of standards]! For closure to the story, you might complete an activity like using the song again with finger puppets and having them do the motions with you.

Miranda: Right.

Kaylee: I know you said in your reflection paper some children were doing the motions. You could teach the motions first and make sure each student is doing them.

Miranda: I sort of struggled with that. It's something you sort of go with while you're there. . . .toward the end I just wasn't sure how to close it. That would be a good idea.

Kaylee: Even when I write lessons and someone else reads over them, they think of tons of ideas. And it's not that any of your ideas are wrong. You could bring in. . . something that they can touch, that could be a manipulative.

PAUSE AND REFLECT
About Building Community

Think back to your very first college class. How did you respond to a new environment with unfamiliar people? How might those feelings help you to understand the child who cries on the first day of school? What is it that causes you to feel enthusiastic about a college course? What is it that causes you to dread attending a class? How might these feelings enable you to better understand the young child's perspective on a high-quality early childhood setting?

Rachael: Every time you write a lesson you need to think, "What will the children be doing?" Every activity we do, "What will their behavior be like?" And think, "If I were a 3-year-old, what would I be doing while waiting?" It's definitely something good to remember as you write more lessons. Always have something for them to do (Jalongo, Rieg, & Helterbran, 2007).

Address Problems and Make Ethical Decisions

William Ayers (1995) explains why this ethical dimension is so critical to becoming a successful teacher:

> Teaching is intellectual and ethical work. It requires the full attention—wide awake, inquiring, critical—of thoughtful and caring people if it is to be done well. Although there is always more to learn and more to know as a teacher, the heart of teaching is a passionate regard for students. With it, mistakes and obstacles will be met and overcome; without it, no amount of technical skill will ever fully compensate. The work of teaching involves struggling to see each student in as full and dynamic a way as possible, to create environments that nurture and challenge the wide range of students who are actually there in classrooms, and to construct bridges with each learner from the known to the not yet known (p. 60).

COMPANION WEBSITE 1.5 For more information about technology and early childhood, go to the *Web Links* in Chapter 1 of the Companion Website at http://www.prenhall.com/jalongo.

Ethical teachers use moral principles to guide behavior (e.g., equity, freedom, respect), and identify and empathize with the welfare of others beyond duty or common decency (Tennyson & Strom, 1988). Suppose that a child in your class is being seriously neglected, arriving at school tired, hungry, unwashed, and dressed in clothes that will not protect her against the weather. Some teachers would complain bitterly about the family. Many would contact local social services agencies for support. Some would try to arrange a meeting at school with the family. Others would make a visit to the home. Still others would intervene directly and see to it that the child was fed, clothed, and bathed. At one time or another, most teachers have tried several of these strategies. Unlike situations in some other occupations, no one told the teacher precisely what to do or when to act. Rather, these teachers relied upon their general care and concern for children and families, the input of colleagues and other professionals, and their familiarity with the particular child's situation. When a teacher is solving a complex (yet common) problem such as helping a neglected child, breaking it down into smaller steps and proceeding confidently toward a solution seldom occurs. More often than not, teachers have to feel their way through many possible courses of action and proceed cautiously, guided by their "ethic of caring" (Noddings, 1984).

What have you done to document your problem solving and ethical reasoning?

Select a teaching dilemma and analyze it using the following questions.

- What are all the possible responses to this situation?
- Which decisions are reasonable and ethical? Why?
- Who benefits from the decision?
- Whose interests are being served? With what effects?
- What is the significance of these effects on children's lives?
- To what extent do teacher decisions have a limiting or distorting effect on the opportunities open to children? (Tennyson & Strom, 1988)

Reflection on ethical dilemmas is enhanced by interaction (Harle & Trudeau, 2006).

ASK THE EXPERT

Lilian Katz on Becoming an Early Childhood Educator

Lilian Katz

Throughout this chapter we have emphasized that individuals develop into early childhood practitioners. The following describes the experiences that led one prominent early childhood educator into the field.

What was your path to becoming an early childhood educator?

My interest in child development and the field of early childhood education grew out of 5 years of experience as a participating mother in parent cooperative preschools in the San Francisco Bay area with my children. Over a period of 5 years I watched several teachers interact with my own three and with whole classes of other people's children and became impressed and intrigued by their skills and insights. In those days each mother had to participate as an assistant teacher one day per week and to attend evening classes on parenting and related content one evening a week. These teachers encouraged me to read the literature on early development and education that was new to me.

After my youngest child moved on to kindergarten, I enrolled in a class in child development for preschool teachers at the local community college. Dr. Mary Lane of San Francisco State University was the instructor of that interesting and inspiring class, and she strongly encouraged me to complete my bachelor's degree, which I did in 1964. Dr. Lane also urged me to accept a position as a preschool teacher in a nearby parent cooperative nursery school. After teaching 3-year-olds for 2 years, I was offered a fellowship to study child development at Stanford University with Professor Pauline Sears. Because Stanford had no master's program at that time, I had to register for a Ph.D.—a completely unanticipated change in the direction of my life as the mother of three young children!

As I was completing my doctoral work, I was offered the position I had at the University of Illinois, Urbana–Champaign for 31 years. The University then housed the National Laboratory of Early Childhood Education and the ERIC Clearinghouse on Early Childhood Education, a part of the national information dissemination network. In 1970, I was appointed director of the ERIC Clearinghouse and continued in that role until it was closed down in 2003.

During the nearly 40 years since the beginning of my career, I have engaged in a rich mix of teaching, lecturing, writing, consulting, and service to various groups, including the first president of the Illinois AEYC, 8 years on NAEYC's board, 4 as vice president and 2 as president (1992–1994), and have lectured in 57 countries.

What is a key issue in teacher development?

One of my earliest papers focused on the developmental stages of teachers, in which I suggested that no one can begin any professional role as a veteran or expert, and that there are probably stages or sequences in which knowledge, skills, and dispositions related to the work are learned (Katz, 1972). Interest in this paper has continued for more than 30 years, and I have recently updated it to reflect some more recent characteristics of our field. In several papers over the years, I have also discussed the "feed-forward" problem associated with teacher development. This refers to the idea that preservice professional training experiences (in all professions) frequently give students answers to questions they have not yet asked and solutions to problems they have not yet encountered. While the nature of those training experiences remains constant, the meanings attributed to them change in retrospect, in the light of subsequent experience. So that, for example, a student might say of an undergraduate course "at the time I was enrolled in that course it was not interesting, not practical enough, or too much work"; but 5 years later, as a practicing teacher, the former student might say, *in retrospect*, "I hated it then, but now I'm so glad I had it." Or, vice versa, a student might say of a current experience, "This is fun," but 5 years later, in retrospect, might describe it as a waste of time in the light of current experience and needs.

If this formulation of the feed-forward problem is accurate, then teacher education cannot be designed on the basis of how students experience it at the time of enrollment in it. Rather, it must be designed on the basis of our very best understanding of the long-term developmental processes through which the professional must pass in the journey from novice undergraduate to inservice practitioner.

Lilian G. Katz is Professor Emerita of Early Childhood Education at the University of Illinois, Urbana–Champaign and Co-Director of the Clearinghouse on Early Education and Parenting.

Pursue Professional Growth as an Educator of the Very Young

Many psychologists contend that human beings naturally are growth seeking. Harvard psychologist Mihalyi Csikszentmihalyi (1993) explains it this way: "Boredom directs us to seek new challenges, while anxiety urges us to develop new skills; the net result is that, in order to avoid negative feelings, a person is forced to grow in complexity" (p. 191). This, of course, is what outstanding teachers do as they mature professionally—they become more complex and seek professional growth throughout their careers.

What evidence do you have that you seek professional growth?

Novices acquire expertise more quickly when they capitalize on professional development opportunities. Try talking over and thinking through surprising situations, persistent doubts, or nagging problems with more experienced teachers. Select a topic that you find intriguing, read the latest professional literature about it, and then join in an online discussion group. Attend a professional conference session that is interactive and participate in the discussion, even if it is to ask a question rather than provide an answer. Ask yourself: Am I an active member of a professional organization? If there is a professional conference nearby and I can attend, do I? If my instructors recommend a useful resource, in print or online, do I follow through? Do I maintain a log of my professional development activities with the date, purpose, time allocated, and outcomes recorded for inclusion in my professional portfolio? (For more about portfolios, see the Companion Website and Jones and Shelton, 2005).

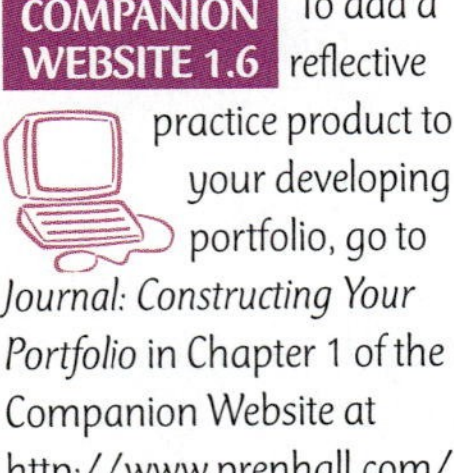

COMPANION WEBSITE 1.6 To add a reflective practice product to your developing portfolio, go to *Journal: Constructing Your Portfolio* in Chapter 1 of the Companion Website at http://www.prenhall.com/jalongo.

COLLABORATING WITH FAMILIES

A Checklist to Guide Parents in Selecting an Early Childhood Program

Parents choose a program for their children for a variety of reasons. According to the research (Fuller, Holloway, & Bozzi, 1997), the major considerations are as follows:

- convenience and affordability (Evans, 2006)
- supportive relationships with teachers and providers
- caregivers and teachers with positive affect (e.g., warm, sensitive, caring)
- cognitive stimulation that will lead to children's success in school

The following checklist describes features of high-quality early childhood settings that parents should consider when they are seeking an early childhood program for their children.

The Teacher

__ is warm, friendly, and supportive
__ treats each child as a special person
__ has training and experience working with children
__ respects and accepts different races, cultures, religions, and ethnic groups
__ listens to children intently
__ interacts with children in positive ways, nonverbally and verbally
__ clearly states a personal philosophy of education

The School, Center, or Family Child-Care Setting

__ is pleasant, comfortable, and clean
__ has disease-prevention policies and first-aid procedures in place
__ has space for both active and quiet play
__ has appropriate light, heat, and ventilation
__ is regulated and approved by a state and/or federal agency
__ provides a safe outdoor play area
__ is supplied with appropriate learning materials and equipment, indoors and out
__ informs families about policy for release of students and emergency procedures

The Family Support System

__ encourages family participation in the program
__ provides information to families about the program and the child's progress on a regular basis
__ offers scheduled opportunities for conferencing as well as informal opportunities for parents, families, and teachers to interact
__ uses community resources to support families and children

The Program

__ gives every child a sense of belonging
__ guides children in dealing with powerful emotions
__ encourages self-help skills and builds independence
__ prevents behavior problems and resolves conflicts in ways that respect children

Time Is Planned for

__ active and quiet play
__ indoor and outdoor activities
__ trips, excursions, and special events
__ artistic and musical expression
__ creative expression and the arts
__ language and literacy development activities
__ concrete early math and problem-solving activities

Opportunities Are Provided to

__ learn to get along, to share, and to respect differences
__ learn about own and others' cultural and ethnic backgrounds
__ speak English as well as to speak each family's native language
__ develop each child's unique talents
__ establish healthy self-esteem
__ develop good health habits

Toys and Equipment You Should See Include

For Infants:

__ cribs, mobiles, soft toys, and blankets
__ rocking chairs, lullaby tapes, and soft lighting
__ safe places to crawl and explore

For 1- and 2-Year-Olds:

__ cloth, cardboard, and plastic books
__ items to sort by shape and color, and large hollow blocks
__ baby dolls, beds, bottles, and other related materials
__ toys with which to practice filling and emptying, and pushing and pulling
__ low climbing equipment with padding underneath
__ simple equipment for practicing motor skills (e.g., rocking boat, large wooden toys with wheels)

For Preschoolers:

__ clay, paint, books, puzzles, games, and blocks
__ tapes or CDs and simple musical instruments
__ computers and software
__ dress-up clothes, small toys (e.g., miniature farm or house setup), house area (with toy refrigerator, stove, etc.)
__ tricycles, wagons, and climbing equipment
__ sensory materials such as water and sand
__ variety of paper and writing utensils for drawing, writing, and bookmaking
__ labeled objects and areas to help children develop independence

To test your knowledge of this chapter's content, go to the *Multiple Choice* and *Essay* modules in Chapter 1 of the Companion Website at http://www.prenhall.com/jalongo. These items are written in the same format that you will encounter on the Praxis test to better prepare you for your licensure exam.

Conclusion

Perhaps the best way to conclude this chapter is to return to what has surely brought you to teaching in the first place: the children. Reflect for a moment on your personality and characteristics. If you were asked to identify what you like best about yourself, what would it be? If you had to identify five personal characteristics and qualities that will enable you to succeed as an early childhood educator, which ones would you choose? Why? This is how you can begin to explore your role as a practitioner. If you invest your heart and mind in becoming an effective early childhood practitioner, you will discover new ways to deepen insight about yourself as a professional, think systematically about your teaching practice, expand your repertoire of skills and techniques, and work with other professionals to improve your school or center (Kochendorfer, 1994).

> Inside each person there is a wonderful capacity to reflect on the information that the various sense organs register, and to direct and control these experiences. We take this ability so much for granted that we seldom wonder about what it is. . . . If we ever think about it, we give it such names as awareness, consciousness, self, or soul. Without it, we could only obey instructions programmed in the nervous system by our genes. But having a self-reflective consciousness allows us to write our own programs for action, and make decisions for which no genetic instructions existed before. . . . Like air, it is always there; like the body, it has its limits. It is something that can get hurt, but it can also soar; it grows, and its powers slowly expand. Although every human brain is able to generate self-reflective consciousness, not everyone seems to use it equally. (Csikszentmihalyi, 1993, pp. 22–23)

You are embarking on a lifelong project—becoming a caring and competent teacher of the very young. Many students have the mistaken impression that if they put their 2 or 4 years into a program, they are finished with the project of becoming a teacher. Nothing could be further from the truth. Initial teacher preparation is just that, a beginning in the transition from novice to expert.

ONE CHILD, THREE PERSPECTIVES

An Instructional Support Team Designs an Educational Plan for Michael

The instructional support program was designed to reduce the number of students being placed in special education. It consists of a team approach to intervening when a child is experiencing serious difficulty in the classroom and has been identified as a possible candidate for special education. Members of the instructional support team (IST) include the principal, the guidance counselor, the instructional support teacher, the classroom teacher of the child, and the parent or parents. A teacher accesses these services by requesting assistance from the team. The process continues with the instructional support teacher collecting information, including observations of the child in class; an interview with the child, teacher, and parent(s); and other information as necessary. Then the IST meets to share information, set a reasonable goal, brainstorm about interventions to attain the goal, delegate responsibility for implementing the suggestions, and establish a timetable. The plan is put into action for 30 days, then the team meets to review the case. Several decisions are possible: (1) the child is making progress or has met the goal, (2) the interventions should continue and be monitored for another 30 days, or (3) the child should be referred for further evaluation and possible special education placement.

Ms. Mong has been the IST teacher for 2 years. In October, a second-grade teacher submitted a referral for five students in her second-grade class. Ms. Mong began with classroom observations. Michael was paired with a partner who had a higher reading level. When Ms. Mong interviewed Michael and asked him to read a passage from the new reading series, he said, "I can't read this book. Someone always reads it to me." Ms. Mong decided to check on Michael's progress during first grade. His teachers reported that his progress was slow but satisfactory. The first-grade teachers used a variety of children's books in addition to the reading series. They did not emphasize worksheets. They also mentioned that Michael's second-grade teacher, Ms. Orr, had been to see them to complain that "This kid can't read."

When she went to confer with Ms. Orr, the IST teacher suggested that it might be helpful to give Michael some reading choices. Ms. Orr refused, saying that this would single Michael out from his peers and be too confusing. She further pointed out that she was using a second-grade-level reading series, and said that therefore, a child assigned to her class ought to be able to read second-grade material. When the IST teacher invited her to bring some ideas to the team meeting, Ms. Orr said, "Why do I have to go through instructional support anyway? I just want him in remedial reading." When the IST meeting convened, Michael's father said angrily, "We never heard about any of these problems before. Why is this happening now? It's not *my* job to teach him to read, it's yours." Ms. Orr replied, "And that's exactly what I'm trying to do, but how can I give him the individual help he needs when there are 28 other children in the class? Now you see why I am advocating for special placement." The IST teacher said, "Remember that our goal is to give Michael support and enable him to stay with his peers." "What should we do, then?" Michael's mother asked. "We only want what is best for Michael."

REACT	*With whom do you identify most strongly in this case, and why?*
RESEARCH	*What particular professional and ethical issues are represented by Michael's situation?*
REFLECT	*What are the underlying issues?*

IN-CLASS WORKSHOP

Working with Teacher Reflection

Most teacher preparation programs gradually increase your responsibility for teaching through a carefully sequenced series of experiences. You might begin with some observation, then have responsibility for working with one child or a small group, then work with the total group of students with close supervision during selected portions of the school day, and then, finally, take major responsibility for teaching and managing the classroom throughout the day. Use the stages and the questions that follow to chart your progress toward becoming a more reflective practitioner. Discuss each of the questions within your group and compare/contrast your experiences with those of your classmates.

The exploring practitioner: Self-directed experiences with students

What experiences have you had that might fall into this category? Have you been responsible for the care of younger siblings? Have you been a babysitter for family, friends, and neighbors? Are you a parent? Have you volunteered to work with children in a less formal setting, such as in a recreational program, at a camp, or at a church or synagogue? How did these experiences influence your decision to become a teacher?

The inquiring practitioner: Understanding teaching and schools in modern society

What experiences have you had/will you have that might be categorized as initial inquiries into what school life is like? Does/did your teacher preparation program provide you with some early field experiences in which you are an observer/participant in schools? What understandings did you acquire or do you expect to amass through such experiences?

The problem-solving practitioner: Developing skills to meet the needs of society and students

What experiences have you had in developing your skill to teach a concept and plan the related activities? Have you learned to identify appropriate learning outcomes for children? Where and how did you learn this? Have you learned how to write a lesson plan? Where and how did you learn this? In what areas of the curriculum do you feel most confident? Why? Have you worked with one child or a small group of children? Have you conducted in-depth observations of a particular child, as in a case study? What did you learn from that experience?

The decision-making practitioner: Developing and demonstrating effective teaching and learning processes

What experiences do you expect to have or have you had in which you were given major responsibility for teaching children in an early childhood setting?

Briefly review your teacher preparation program. What courses and experiences seem to match each of these processes just described?

SOURCE: The four categories are adapted from Peters, 2000.

CHAPTER 2

Exploring Your Role as a Child Advocate and Understanding History

> Many early childhood educators feel that they must implement programs that conflict with their understanding of best practice . . . .we may have to act beyond our schools to support authentic learning in our classrooms and preserve the integrity of our profession. . . Studying the past could provide examples for us as we advocate for good teaching practices.
>
> Richard J. Meyer, 2005, p. 28

Meet the Teachers

MARISSA has been a parent volunteer in a county-sponsored child-care program for the past 3 years while she has earned her Child Development Associate (CDA) credential. Today is the day of her interview for a position as a family child-care provider. As she scans the faces of the interviewers seated at the conference table, she worries that she will have difficulty putting her ideas into words. When she is asked about her approaches to working with toddlers, she replies, "I believe that learning is natural and that a warm, homelike setting is the ideal way to offer care and education to toddlers. Although learning in the early years is playful, this is also a time of life when the brain is developing and a firm foundation for real learning is built."

ERIN has taught kindergarten for 4 years in a parochial school, and she is meeting with a college faculty member who coordinates the master's program. Erin knows that the professor will expect her to give some reasons why she is interested in the graduate early childhood program. When the discussion comes around to her philosophy, she says, "I want to become more knowledgeable about early literacy. It seems to me that some of the approaches to early reading instruction are part of a 'push-down' curriculum that is used with the upper elementary grades. My goal is to more fully understand how young learners become readers and to support them in their efforts."

BRIAN is a private nursery-school teacher in Miami, Florida. When parents visit the school, Brian knows that he must make the program philosophy clear so that families can make informed decisions about whether or not his program is right for their children. In explaining his program to parents, Brian says, "Children need real-world experiences and meaningful learning activities, not mindless paper shuffling. The early childhood years are formative, so children need a balanced approach that includes experiences to support their development physically, socially, intellectually, emotionally, and artistically."

COMPARE	What are some commonalities among these three teachers' philosophical perspectives? What are some influences that might have shaped these teachers' ideas about early childhood education?
CONTRAST	In what ways are the teachers' philosophies distinctive?
CONNECT	Do you think that these ideas originated with these teachers? In what ways are their views similar to or different from your own? Surprisingly, the views of each of the contemporary teachers just described can be traced to ideas about children, learning, instruction, curricula, and evaluation that have been in existence for decades or even centuries.

Now that you have reflected on the perspectives of three different teachers, here is a preview of the knowledge, skills, and dispositions you will need to acquire in order to fulfill your role in learning about the traditions of early childhood education and becoming an advocate for children.

Learning Outcomes

- ✔ Become familiar with national standards and guidelines governing teachers' knowledge of the history of early childhood education and their role as child advocates **(NAEYC #5, INTASC #9, and ACEI #3b)**
- ✔ Gain a historical perspective on the field of early childhood education
- ✔ Identify the ways that teachers can function as child advocates
- ✔ Explore traditional and contemporary roles and responsibilities of early childhood educators in providing quality programs
- ✔ Describe the major curriculum models for programs serving young children, ages birth through 8 years
- ✔ Articulate a philosophy of teaching that reflects an understanding of the history of the field of early childhood education

COMPANION WEBSITE 2.1 To learn more about child advocacy and the history of early childhood, go to *Journal: Defining Your Role as a Child Advocate* in Chapter 2 of the Companion Website at http://www.prenhall.com/jalongo.

Your Role as a Child Advocate

Throughout history, individuals have used their intelligence, influence, powers of persuasion, and monetary resources in the service of children and families. Child advocacy is the willingness to take a stand on behalf of children and families that goes beyond common decency or expectations (Robinson & Stark, 2002). In 1997, the world mourned the loss of two prominent child advocates, Mother Teresa and Princess Diana. Mother Teresa used her unselfish commitment to humanitarian goals and the Catholic nuns who joined her order to help children around the world. In a very different way, England's Princess Diana used her access to power, wealth, and influence to raise money for various charities, particularly her goal of disarming land mines and bombs so that horrible injuries to children worldwide could be averted. To consider the contributions of well-known people such as Mother Teresa and Princess Diana can be rather daunting to a person who is just entering the early childhood field. You may ask yourself, "But what can *I*, as just one person, ever do that would qualify as being an advocate for young children?" There are many different types of child advocacy activities. The three main approaches are

1. Early childhood professionals addressing the needs of children and families—for example, locating community support for housing, medical services, government assistance, extended child care, tutoring, counseling, and other intervention services.
2. Accessing services for children with exceptionalities—for example, assisting parents in negotiating the multiple agencies servicing their child.
3. Professional advocacy on behalf of teachers, administrators, and caregivers—for example, developing the self-confidence and skills to become an advocate

DID YOU KNOW...?

- The history of the early childhood field reflects society's struggle to become more humane, decent, and nurturing (Osborn, 1980; Swick & Brown, 1999).
- Many children of families at all income levels seeking child care in the United States are on a waiting list for 12 months or more (www.daycareuniverse.com).
- In 2002, 11.9 million children younger than age 5 were enrolled in early childhood settings (*Education Week,* 2002). In 2007, there were 11,000 accredited early childhood programs (NAEYC, 2007).
- Low-income families often are earning salaries rather than unemployed. Among low-income families with children, 6 in 10 have at least one parent who worked full-time all year, and another 1 in 10 have a parent who worked at least half-time all year. (For more facts on families, see http://newfederalism.urban.org.)
- In what settings are American children cared for and educated? The distribution is as follows: 40% in a self-contained center; 28% in a place of worship; 12% in public school; 7% in a home; 6% in a private school; 4% in a community center; 2% someplace else; 1% college/university (*Education Week,* 2002).
- Who is responsible for the care of young children in the United States? The breakdown is as follows: 13% of caregivers are paid nonrelatives, 24% are center staff, 28% are family child-care providers, and 35% are relatives who are paid (Center for the Child Care Workforce and Human Services Policy Center, 2002).
- During 2002 and 2003, 23.9% of 3- and 4-year-olds in the United States were enrolled in state prekindergarten, Head Start, or IDEA Preschool Grant Programs (Barnett, Hustedt, Robin, & Schulman, 2004). During school year 2002–2003, these programs served nearly 740,000 children, or 10% of the nation's population of 3- and 4-year-old children (Barnett et al., 2004).
- At least 40 states are working on or offer prekindergarten programs (Barnett, Lanny, & Jung, 2005). Most are located in schools where 75% or more of the student population comes from low-income families determined by the students' eligibility to receive free or reduced-priced lunch (Zaslow & Martinez-Beck, 2006).
- Barnett et al. (2005) found that when children attended state-funded pre-K programs in Michigan, New Jersey, Oklahoma, South Carolina, and West Virginia, gains in math skills were 44% higher than for children outside the program.
- Based on 10 critical areas—curriculum, teacher degree requirements, specialized training, assistant teacher degree requirements, teacher inservice work, maximum class size, staff–child ratio, screening and referral requirements, support services, and meal requirements—just 16 states have established comprehensive quality standards for preschool programs (Barnett et al., 2004).

yourself, to assess needs and issues for advocacy, to develop persuasive communication skills, and to participate in providing professional growth opportunities for other professionals (adapted from Liebovich & Adler, 2007, in press).

Child advocacy includes a wide range of behaviors and activities, all unified by care and concern for children, families, colleagues, and other professionals. "Early childhood

Richard Hutchings/Silver Burdett Ginn

The role of child advocate sometimes requires discovering and marshalling community resources.

teaching is simply and completely about children and their well-being" (Glasgow, 1994, pp. 131–132). It might be something straightforward such as speaking up when a child is being treated unfairly in the school system. It might involve putting a child and family in contact with needed services, such as getting glasses through the local Lions Club for a visually impaired child from a low-income family. It might involve taking political action, such as participating in NAEYC's Week of the Young Child activities at the local, state, or national level. At other times, legal action, such as reporting a suspected case of child abuse, might be the most appropriate way to defend a young child.

As a first step in any child advocacy activity, you must *believe that just one person truly can make a difference.* After college student Jamie Barron Jones studied child advocacy, she found herself at a flea market where a vendor was selling a game that had been pulled off the market by the Product Safety Commission—large darts with weighted metal tips that were to be pitched like horseshoes outside in a yard. The darts had been responsible for the deaths or serious injuries of several children. Rather than remaining silent, Jamie deliberately made a scene and challenged the man at the booth about his unscrupulous business practices. She announced to all of the people there that these toys were dangerous. When the seller dismissed her concerns by saying that people were allowed to buy whatever they liked, she reported him to the police. Her reasoning was that even if she only prevented the man from selling a few sets of these banned toys, she might have protected a child from serious harm.

As Jamie's situation illustrates, another critical feature of child advocacy is *taking a stand and knowing to whom to turn for support.* Sources of support might be close to home, as in asking one of your family members to volunteer time to read to the children in your class. You might reach out to the community, inviting people, such as a florist, to speak about their jobs, to teach children a skill such as making tortillas, or to provide free services such as dental care to needy children. At other times, the special services, political influence, or financial resources represented by individuals or groups may be the resource that you need. Collaboration with the local librarian, a letter to your senator, or a donation from a local business can supply needed human and material resources. Mrs. Morrison, an infant-and-toddler caregiver, used local resources to create a playground for the young children in her center. She managed to get money for materials from local businesses, to convince parents to help assemble the play equipment at a Saturday picnic, and to publicize the event through the local media. Likewise, Mr. Shaughnessy helped to organize a community-wide effort to help families whose trailer homes had been destroyed in a tornado. By working with United Way, churches, the fire department, school personnel, and school students, he was able to collect many useful household items that enabled these families to rebuild their lives.

The third key element in child advocacy is *putting the child's agenda first.* When children are in desperate circumstances as a result of neglect, it is sometimes tempting to blame the victims rather than taking action. Ms. Ditka, an intern teacher, was surprised to learn from the school nurse that Autumn, an 8-year-old in her class, had head lice and fleas. Although it is common for head lice to appear at school and possible for anyone to get them, Autumn's situation was extreme. When an outbreak of head lice occurred in her classroom, many of the parents were angry with the teachers for not noticing it sooner, and some blamed the school for unsanitary conditions. Soon, everyone was blaming Autumn and her family and treating them like outcasts. Ms. Ditka had to overcome her own fears about getting lice and fleas. She did this by getting accurate medical information about how to halt the transmission of these insects from one child to another and by working with the custodians to kill the insects that had infested her classroom. When Health Department officials first went to Autumn's house to fumigate, they were met on the porch by her grandfather, his shotgun, and his hunting dogs; the next time, the sheriff accompanied them and the house was fumigated. Throughout this time, Autumn was kept out of school for over a week. When she returned, Ms. Ditka had to confront her uneasiness about physical contact with Autumn. She also found it necessary to intercede on Autumn's behalf with the class because so many of the children had been cautioned to "stay away from that dirty girl." Ms. Ditka knew that her response when Autumn walked into the room would speak volumes, so when Autumn stood hesitantly in the doorway, she welcomed her warmly and gave her a hug. What prevented Ms. Ditka from resenting Autumn, as many of her coworkers did, was simply her remembering that Autumn had no choices in or control over her physical environment. Without Ms. Ditka's advocacy, Autumn's second-grade year would have been a story of alienation from peers and damaged self-esteem. But because a caring teacher stood up for Autumn, calmed others, and controlled her own fears, Autumn was able to succeed academically and socially. She succeeded because her teacher approached the situation from the perspective of a child advocate rather than rushing to judge Autumn and her family. Figure 2.1 summarizes ways to prepare for and take action in a child advocacy role.

Library of Congress

What does *childhood* mean to you?

Historical Influences on Contemporary Programs

COMPANION WEBSITE 2.2 To learn more about your role as a child advocate and the NAEYC, go to the *Web Links* in Chapter 2 of the Companion Website at http://www.prenhall.com/jalongo.

The field of early childhood owes much to the early leaders—philosophers, scholars, educators, theorists, religious leaders, physicians, and scientists—who have made significant contributions to contemporary thinking about young children. As you read their profiles in Figure 2.2, consider how the philosophy statements of the three early

FIGURE 2.1 Child advocacy strategies.

PREPARING FOR ADVOCACY

1. **Arrive at a Definition of Advocacy**. Learn from history. Think about what you can do, both subtle and bold, that would put children and families first.
2. **Observe Advocacy in Action**. Look for evidence of a professional commitment in practicing teachers. Watch for ways that they strive to meet the needs of children and families and to promote respect for the profession of early childhood education. Reflect on models of advocacy from your past experiences in and out of the classroom. Participate in activities such as letter writing campaigns, public political marches or rallies, or public policy meetings.
3. **Reflect and Share**. Get involved in keeping a journal, and participating in group discussions. Get involved with advocacy groups, such as NAEYC's annual Stand for Children. Partner with teacher educators. Explore organizations such as the World Schooling Consortium, FairTest, and the Rouge Forum.
4. **Develop Leadership Qualities and Take Reasonable Risks**. Advocacy is a political act. Start small and gradually increase the challenge to build your confidence with advocacy activities. Match your style with the population served and the gatekeepers of resources and power. Work with community agencies. Vote.
5. **Understand the Context of the School Community**. Take the student population, the socioeconomic status of the school population, and the funding available to the school into consideration.
6. **Develop an Action Plan**. This process typically involves a needs assessment, mobilizing support for pursuing change, prioritizing advocacy issues and concerns, making a plan, implementing the plan, assessing the outcomes of the plan, and revising the plan as necessary.

TAKING ACTION

Speak Out on Issues of Concern to Children and Families

Lend your voice to public discussions of positive action on behalf of children. Write a letter to a legislator, create your own Web page on an issue of concern, wear a message on a T-shirt or badge, write a letter to the newspaper editor, research a topic and share the information with others, work with professionals and parents to make a presentation at a conference, choose an assignment for a college course that will develop child advocacy skills, attend a meeting to find out more about what you can do, volunteer time to community service projects, offer to be a guest speaker for high school students who are considering the early childhood field, participate in a political protest against an injustice, advocate QCA (quality, compensation, affordability) in a national system of child care.

Share Knowledge and Share Experience

Draw upon and expand your knowledge base and experience so that you can become an information resource for others. Speak with families on issues of concern, create an information board for parents, plan cooperatively with fellow teachers, educate administrators about early childhood, join a special interest group of NAEYC and read Voices of Practitioners (found on the Beyond the Journal page: www.journal.naeyc.org/btj), collect and disseminate information (newspaper articles, magazines written for parents, brochures from various organizations, items from the Internet from highly respected organizations, brochures on various topics published by professional groups), speak with your neighbors and community members about the challenges that today's children and families confront.

Empower Parents and Families

Collaborate with colleagues, professionals from other fields, and families to find sources of support and to coordinate services. Develop good working relationships with child advocates from other fields so that you can make referrals; defend families' rights to services and show them how to cut through "red tape"; communicate in many ways (e.g., home visits, e-mail correspondence, notes home, telephone calls, informal conferences); share children's work in a variety of ways—on videotape, in photographs, in a class journal, in books that children author, illustrate, and take home; extend personal invitations to engage parents in school governance activities and shared decision making; donate time, materials, clothing, and household goods to charities.

FIGURE 2.1 Continued

Stand Up for Ourselves
Educate others about the challenges the early childhood profession faces and affiliate with professional organizations that represent our needs and concerns. Get involved in a worthy wage campaign for child care, conduct a survey and publish the results in a newsletter, join a professional association and bring along a friend, work toward accreditation and licensure for yourself and/or your program, participate in political lobbies designed to improve the working conditions for early childhood educators, read all about a topic of concern and gather authoritative evidence to support your arguments.

Engage in Teacher Research
Inquire into the effectiveness of our own classroom practices. Analyze sets of student work and use the insights gained to fine tune teaching. Investigate the process of Japanese Lesson Study, in which teams of teachers analyze student responses to lessons as a way to improve their teaching.

SOURCES: Adapted from Goffin & Lombardi, 1988; and Meyer, 2007.

childhood practitioners from Meet the Teachers reflect these long traditions in early childhood education.

There are many compelling reasons for studying the historical foundations of early childhood education (Feeney, Christensen, & Moravcik, 2006). The study of history and an overview of the leaders in early childhood education will enable you to gain insight into the following questions: How have current policies and educational innovations evolved from past thought and practice? What are some of the enduring achievements and continuing controversies in the field of early childhood education? What were the origins of many of the teaching methods and instructional materials in common use today? Figure 2.3 illustrates some of the teaching materials invented by leaders in the field of early childhood education that are standard equipment in most classrooms. To see a Montessori program in action, view the "Montessori" video clip online at the Teacher Prep Website.

TEACHER PREP WEBSITE 2.1

Go to the Video Classroom, select Early Childhood Education, choose Curriculum Planning and Programs (Module 4), and select Montessori (Video 2).

When we hear accounts of neglect or abuse of young children on the news, we cannot help wondering what this world is coming to. But before a culture can determine whether it has made progress, it must first review where it has been. In other words, you need a historical perspective on attitudes toward and treatment of children.

Actually, exploitation and abuse of young children has been in existence throughout history; at times, the maltreatment of children was commonplace and generally accepted as a prerogative of adults. Although contemporaries may argue that the treatment of children today is worse than ever before, the truth is that the further one goes back in history, the greater the likelihood that young children—particularly young children living in poverty—were mistreated and exploited by adults (DeMause, 1974). By today's standards of treatment, the majority of children in previous eras would have been categorized as abused. This is not to say that adults who cared about children did not exist previously, only that prevailing views of children were far from positive in previous eras. An overview of the dominant perspectives on children in different historical eras of Western culture follows:

- **Antiquity:** Little evidence of parental attachment; occasional infanticide was socially acceptable
- **Middle Ages:** Poverty and high mortality rates contributed to indifference and abandonment

FIGURE 2.2 Early leaders of early childhood education.

Plato (427–347 B.C.) and Aristotle (394–322 B.C.)
Country: Ancient Greece
Occupation: Philosophers
Both believed that a child's education should begin well before age 6, and both discussed individual differences in children's learning and personalities.

Martin Luther (1483–1546)
Country: Germany
Occupation: Religious Leader
First to advocate universal education and teaching all children to read so that they could read the Scriptures in their native language (rather than Latin). Believed that the family was the most important educational institution. Is considered the father of religion-affiliated education.

John Comenius (1592–1671)
Country: Now the Czech Republic
Occupation: Educator and Bishop
Wrote the first known picture book, *Orbis Pictus (World of Pictures)*, in 1658. Advocated that the child learn at the mother's knee until age 6. Believed that firsthand experiences were important to children's learning and that play was the natural learning medium of young children. Argued that the very young were more flexible in their thinking and that the early years were a crucial time for shaping character.

John Locke (1632–1714)
Country: England
Occupation: Medical Doctor, Philosopher, and Political Theorist
In his influential book *Some Thoughts Concerning Education*, he took issue with the prevailing views of his contemporaries, who believed that heredity was the major influence on children's futures and that harsh discipline was necessary to keep children under control. He argued, rather, that the child's mind was comparable to a *tabula raso*, or blank slate, upon which experience would draw the mind's contents. His belief that the child was impressionable and malleable had a profound influence on the role of education in improving children's lives.

Jean-Jacques Rousseau (1712–1788)
Country: France
Occupation: Philosopher and Writer
Considered to be the originator of our modern concept of childhood development. Wrote a novel about a fictitious child named *Emile* in 1760. This book captured the imagination of many adults by enabling them to look at things from a child's point of view; this was a revolutionary way of thinking at the time. Believed that children are naturally good and innocent but that they are corrupted by society. Argued for greater freedom for children and believed that their education should be based upon their interests and adjusted to their innate timetables for learning, which he called unfolding. Also wrote *How Gertrude Teaches Her Children*, a book intended to model a natural style of educating the very young.

Johann Heinrich Pestalozzi (1746–1827)
Country: Italy
Occupation: Educator
Advocated teaching children with love, respect, patience, and understanding. Believed that the senses could be sharpened or cultivated by practice. Emphasized the importance of play and sensory experiences. Further developed Froebel's concept of the "object lesson," in which the child moves from concrete objects to ideas to words via careful observation and teacher-guided discussion, which often takes place outdoors. Designed schools based on Rousseau's idea of naturalism and argued for attention to three elements of the individual: the head, the heart, and the hand.

FIGURE 2.2 Continued

Robert Owen (1771–1858)
Country: Scotland
Occupation: Religious Leader, Educator
Fought against child labor and created the first factory day-nursery for children 18 months to 10 years to care for children while their parents worked in his mill. The program emphasized dance, song, and outdoor play. Disagreed with harsh punishment and fear as ways to train children.

Friedrich Froebel (1787–1852)
Country: Germany
Occupation: Educator
Considered to be the father of kindergarten (literally, "a garden of children"). Concluded that the early years were the most critical. Designed carefully sequenced materials and detailed instructions for their use. The program included gifts—toys such as balls, blocks, and cubes—and occupations—tasks that taught skills useful in later life such as weaving, folding paper, stringing beads, perforating paper, and modeling with clay. Believed that children were brought closer through song, dance, plays, and games.

Horace Mann (1796–1859)
Country: United States
Occupation: Teacher, Lawyer, Senator,
Secretary of Massachusetts Board of Education
Initiated the Common School movement, the basis for public education. Argued that free education should be universal regardless of economic status, that religious training and schools should be distinct (separation of church and state), and that classrooms should be staffed by well-trained male and female teachers. Advocated the preparation of female teachers for work with younger children, an idea unheard of in his day. Started the first teacher-training school, an institution that prepared teachers by focusing on educational theories and giving them experiences with children that were closely supervised. Opposed the harsh punishment characteristic of the era and advocated a bond of mutual trust, respect, and rapport between teachers and children.

Maria Montessori (1870–1952)
Country: Italy
Occupation: Medical Doctor, Program Developer
A medical doctor who was not permitted to practice due to social sanctions against a woman studying male anatomy. Was given a post working with slum children in Rome to try to resolve the problem of unsupervised, neglected children. Believed that children enjoy order and structure and should be taught practical, sensory, and formal skills, such as reading, writing, mathematics, and motor coordination. Her school, the Casi dei Bambini (Children's House) opened in 1908 and attracted attention because it taught academic skills, manners, and cleanliness to children younger than age 5. Promoted the idea of a prepared environment in which the teacher was a directress, and designed highly detailed instructions on how to teach. Believed that the major outcome of a quality education was the ability to focus and concentrate. Invented self-correcting materials, child-sized furniture, and a self-help skills curriculum. The focus of the program was unique in that in was child centered rather than group centered and children were encouraged to expand their interests.

John Dewey (1859–1952)
Country: United States
Occupation: Teacher, Scholar
Established the Dewey Laboratory School at the University of Chicago as a way of studying curricula (Tanner, 1997). Considered to be the father of progressive education. Dewey's primary concern was the preparation of citizens for a democratic society, as described in his major work, *Democracy and Education* (1916). Believed that curricula should be child centered and include topics of study that would enable children to understand social purposes and community life. Topics of study began with the family and led out to the community. His emphasis was on active learning in which children used open-ended materials to understand problems, questions, relationships, and connections.

FIGURE 2.3 Where did it come from? A historical view of the origins of early childhood materials.

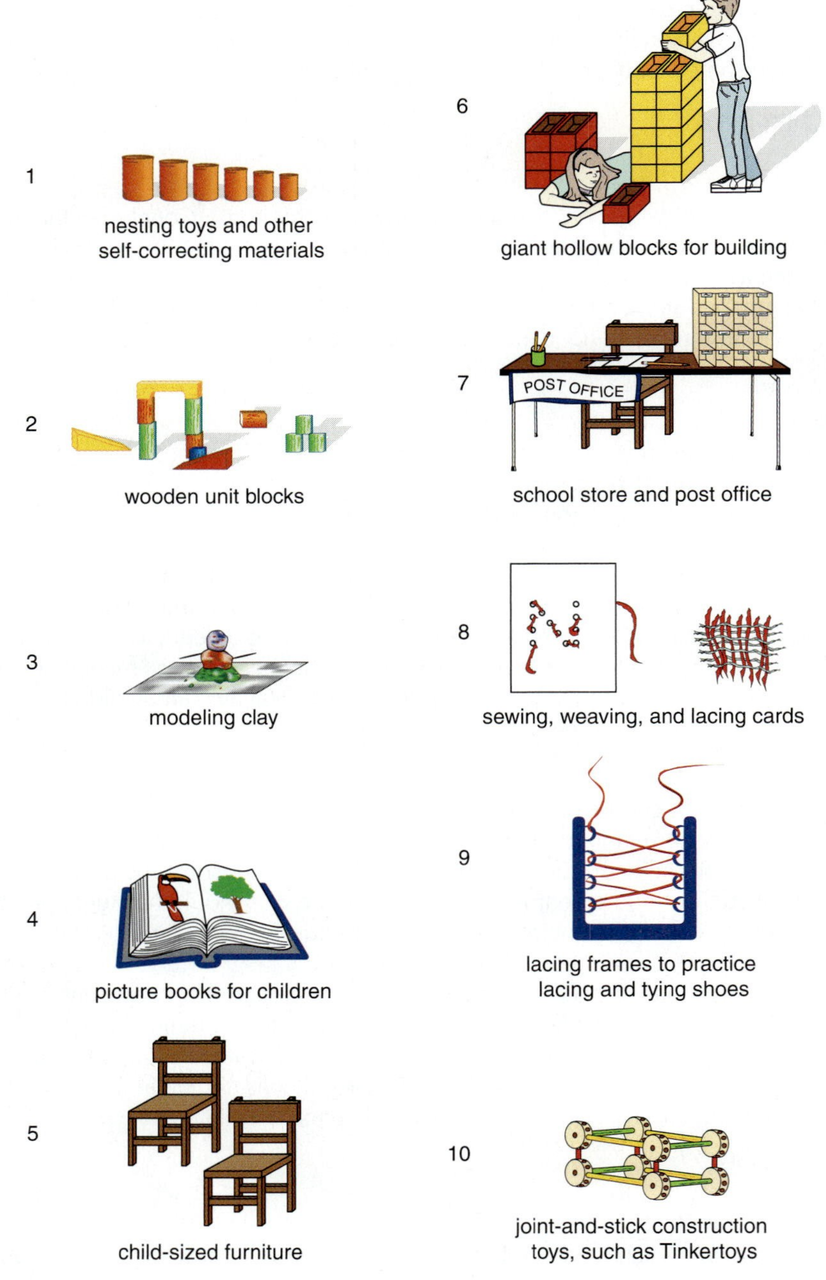

Answers: 1. Maria Montessori; 2. Carolyn Pratt; 3. Friedrich Froebel; 4. John Amos Comenius; 5. Maria Montessori; 6. Patty Smith Hill; 7. Carolyn Pratt; 8. Frederick Froebel; 9. Maria Montessori; 10. Frederick Froebel (who used toothpicks and peas).

- **Renaissance:** Ambivalent attitude toward children
- **18th Century:** Children were valued for their potential as laborers; industrialization led to use of children as workers in factories, farms, mills, and mines
- **19th Century:** Child labor and exploitation continued; significant medical and educational advances enabled a much higher percentage of children to survive to adulthood
- **20th Century:** Concern with the rights and plights of children; however, instances of abuse, neglect, starvation, exploitation, and unnecessary mortality continue (G. LeFrancois, 2000).

Why were so many children treated with indifference or hostility in the past? Historians believe that there were several reasons, including (a) an infant mortality rate so high that few children lived to age 5 due to disease and poor living conditions; (b) the view of pregnancy as an often undesirable state and the absence of reliable methods of birth control; (c) the abject poverty in which large numbers of families existed as a result of the virtual absence of a middle class; and (d) perhaps most important, the fact that many adults lacked the ability to identify and empathize with children or to regard the early years of life as a qualitatively different and valuable time period in human beings' lives (Postman, 1982; Tuchman, 1978).

PAUSE AND REFLECT

About Early Leaders and Prevailing Views of Childhood

After reviewing the material in Figures 2.2 and 2.3, consider these questions:

- What echoes of the past do you see in your teaching philosophy?
- Which of these notable individuals whose commitment to the very young has made an indelible impression on your field made the greatest impression on you? Why?
- Did you encounter any ideas that surprised you? Are any of the ideas consistent with your beliefs?

Of course, it can be demonstrated that deplorable examples of the treatment of young children continue to exist. Consider the following four true incidents involving children that have recently been reported in the newspaper:

1. Two young children are left to fend for themselves while their parents go on a vacation.
2. Preschool girls with teased hair and heavy makeup compete in a beauty contest and perform in a sexually suggestive way during the talent portion of the show.
3. A mother is recorded on videotape attempting to sell her preschool daughter to the child's babysitter.
4. A nanny is convicted of shaking a crying infant and causing its death.

Each of these contemporary situations will be discussed in light of historical practices (Aries, 1962; Bloch & Price, 1994; Cleverley & Phillips, 1986; Osborn, 1980).

As to the first case, in which children were left home alone, child abandonment and neglect has been a recurrent practice throughout history. In different cultures and at various times, children were seen as a drain on limited resources. In ancient times, infants were left to die from exposure to the elements as a way of controlling family size and overpopulation. Nearly all children with physical defects were left outside to die of exposure in the Greek city-states. Grain allocations were limited to one female child per family (boys were more valued for their potential as warriors), so firstborn girls were often the only ones saved. In Rome, "potting" children was common: Babies were abandoned by the roadside in clay pots or in the river in baskets and adorned with ornaments to invite others to take the children in if they wished. In other words, the Bible story of Moses as an infant floating down the Nile in a basket typified practices of the era. Even in the 20th century, children with disabilities were viewed by many people around the world as embarrassments or liabilities, and parents were pressured to institutionalize them. An excellent film that accurately portrays this attitude is *My Left Foot.*

In 318 A.D., during Roman Emperor Constantine's reign, killing a child became a crime. Emperor Augustus offered stipends to families who would raise foundlings. It was not until 400 A.D. that the first orphanages were established. Although laws against infanticide existed at that time, the practice of killing infants remained common. During the Dark Ages, most people were peasants who spent their short lives (life expectancy was about 30 years) working for landowners and the aristocracy. Disease, near starvation, and generally poor living conditions resulted in a high infant mortality rate. Children were frequently viewed as just another mouth to feed rather than a privilege or a treasure. During the Middle Ages, a distinction was made between willful disposal of children and other causes of death. One way of disposing of children was to smother them and claim that it was an accident. Even if a parent was convicted of willfully disposing of a child, the punishment for infanticide was only a year of penance. By the 1700s, opiates, starvation, dunking babies in cold water, and leaving them on doorsteps or at the hospital were ways to get rid of unwanted children. In 19th-century France, hospitals actually were equipped with turntables so that mothers could abandon their infants without being identified. This was more apt to occur when the child was disfigured in some way, and, with the high incidence of venereal disease, infants were frequently born blind until medical advances were made in the late 1800s. The novel *The Hunchback of Notre Dame* is representative of the way that children with disabilities were treated. Even during the Industrial Revolution, there were "nurses" who would take infants for the purpose of disposing of them and adults who bought children and turned them into slaves or criminals, as depicted in the Charles Dickens novel *Oliver Twist.*

As to the second news story, about a children's beauty pageant in which preschoolers are treated like Barbie dolls, the view of children as miniature adults has long been with us. If you examine pre-18th-century Western artwork, you will notice three things. First, children are seldom depicted (other than in a few pieces of sculpture), presumably because they were not considered worthwhile subjects. Second, any child portrayed in art probably was from a wealthy, titled family and was dressed exactly like the adult he or she was expected to become someday. Finally, you will notice that typical childish facial features (e.g., turned-up nose), body configuration (e.g., large head in proportion to the body), and interests (e.g., play) are rarely represented. Mainly, children were valued for their potential as adults. Throughout history, the point at which children were expected to think more logically was age 6 or 7—the "age of reason." It was assumed that this ability to reason equipped them to take on adult roles, such as caring for other children, hunting, gardening, tending animals, performing household chores, and, in industrial societies, working in factory settings (Sameroff & McDonough, 1994). Anthropological studies of 50 cultures suggest that even now, most cultures begin assigning more responsibilities to children and initiate formal education for children between ages 5 and 7 (Rogoff, 1993). Two films, *The Last Emperor* and *Little Man Tate,* offer a valuable perspective on children being treated as adults, in the first case, a Chinese child of royal birth, and in the second, a child genius in mid-20th-century America.

As to the recent news account of the child being offered for sale, the treatment of children as property or as a commodity has long been in existence. Throughout history, children have been exploited for their potential as workers in factories and on farms. In 1535, during English King Henry VIII's reign, a law was enacted to apprentice children so that they could begin working as early as possible. Beginning in 1618 and for many years thereafter, children as young as 10 years of age were shipped from London to work as indentured servants in colonial America. In 1619, the first African children landed in America and became slaves. In many states, African children were not viewed as human beings but as the property of slave owners, as depicted in the *Roots* television series. Because slaves were valuable property, some consideration was given to the care of the very young. But by age 5 or 6, most slave children were working, and by age 12, they were expected to perform one-fourth of an adult's workload on a daily basis. The first factory to employ children opened in England in 1719, and it was not until the Factory Act was passed in 1833 that children under age 9 were prohibited from working in mines. Children without parents often were "trained for service," meaning that they were taught to become servants. After the American West was settled, "orphan trains" brought city children without families to work on farms. It was not until 1842 that the working day for children under age 12 was limited to 10 hours in Connecticut. Laws controlling the use of children as workers first were proposed in 1906, but 32 years passed before the first enforceable work law for the protection of minor children was passed in 1938. To this day, the notion that young children ought to be pushed to work very hard continues, although the definition of work differs. Most often, extreme pressure comes in the form of pushing children to achieve in sports, in the performing arts, in academic pursuits, or, in some cases, to achieve fame and fortune as a star in the media.

As to the case of the nanny who was convicted of murdering an infant, the view of the child as innately bad or needing harsh discipline has also been revisited throughout history. In the 1600s, children in America were expected to obey their parents without question and to address them as "honored sir" or "esteemed parent." Children were expected to be seen and not heard, and the prevailing opinion about child rearing was "Spare the rod and spoil the child." One of the first illustrated textbooks, *The New England Primer,* included the following verse to teach the letter *F:* "The Idle **F**ool is whipt at school." In colonial America, parents were advised to dress up as ghosts and enter a disobedient child's room at night to frighten the child into obedience. Children's natural playfulness and toddlers' willfulness were seen as the work of the devil, which had to be beaten out of them. Long after harsh discipline was generally frowned upon for most children in America, children who were from different cultures—such as Native Americans kidnapped from their families and forced by government law to attend boarding schools—were likely to be subjected to extreme methods of punishment in order to force them to fit into mainstream society. The film *The Dollmaker,* about an Appalachian woman and her family who moved to Detroit in the late 1940s, exposes the indifference and cruelty visited upon American children who were not part of the mainstream culture.

As the preceding historical overview suggests, conditions for children have improved, but there is still much work to be done. Fortunately, enlightened views on children's early years have existed alongside the more repressive views throughout history, and these ideas

FIGURE 2.4 Contemporary leaders in early childhood education.

Scholars/ Researchers	Prominent Authors	Child Advocates	Practitioners	Experts from Other Fields
Urie Bronfenbrenner	Bettye Caldwell	James Hymes	Vivian Paley	T. Berry Brazleton
Constance Kamii	Alice Sterling Honig	Marian Wright Edelman	Docia Zavikovsky	Howard Gardner
Bernard Spodek	Sue Bredekamp	Bertha Campbell	Loris Malaguzzi	Daniel Goleman
David Weikart	Barbara Bowman	Edward Zigler		Stanley Greenspan
Larry Schweinhart	Lilian Katz			

SOURCE: Reprinted with permission from Child Care Information Exchange, P.O. Box 3249, Redmond, WA 98073, (800) 221-2864, www.childcareexchange.com.

COMPANION WEBSITE 2.3 For more information about child advocacy, go to the *Web Links* in Chapter 2 of the Companion Website at http:// www.prenhall.com/jalongo.

form the foundation for your role as a contemporary early childhood advocate. Figure 2.4, based on survey data, lists some of the most prominent contemporary early childhood advocates (Neugebauer, 1995). These individuals, combined with the early childhood experts whom we interviewed for the Ask the Expert features that occur throughout this book, form a veritable "who's who" of those who have exerted a profound influence on the early childhood education field.

Time-Honored Precepts of Early Childhood Education

Throughout history, various facets of the child have been emphasized, such as physical development, religious training and character development, social and emotional growth, and intellectual growth (Osborn, 1980). Although different cultures and individuals have always differed in their responses to young children, some points of view have prevailed in Western thought. The field of early childhood education is part of a rich tradition of care, concern, and education for the very young. Teachers, researchers, and theorists in the field and in related fields have paved the way for your career by advocating for young children's needs, developing programs, and inventing the materials that are still in wide use. Some of the guiding principles of early childhood programs and their origins are discussed in the remainder of this section.

Young Children Need Special Nurturing

A recurring stance toward early childhood is the view that young children require special forms of care, protection, education, and sympathetic understanding from adults. Smith (1996) typifies this view: "If we are to make the best use of every country's most precious resource, its children, we must better define what we mean by quality and, through whatever means possible, deliver the resources necessary to foster and nurture children's development" (p. 330). How did kindergartens, nursery schools, and parent involvement in early childhood get their starts in the United States? Interestingly, the early efforts to provide care and education for the young were led by "dauntless women" who went against the general thinking of their day (Snyder, 1972; Wortham, 1992; Wyman, 1995).

The history of the kindergarten movement in the United States, prompted by Froebel's work in Germany, documents the growth of the commitment to the care and education of the very young. In 1855, inspired by the German kindergarten movement, Mrs. Carl Schurz opened the first kindergarten in Wisconsin for German immigrant children, Elizabeth Peabody established the first kindergarten for English-speaking children in 1860, and Susan Blow of St. Louis opened the first publicly supported kindergarten in 1873.

Nursery schools in the United States have a similar history. Carolyn Pratt founded the City and Country School in New York (now the Bank Street School). Her curriculum included field trips and child-run enterprises, such as a school store and post office. In 1922, Abigail Adams Eliot founded the Ruggles Street Nursery School in Boston, whose program was based on the work of the McMillan sisters in England. An early effort to involve parents meaningfully in programs for young children was the Parent Cooperative Nursery (a program in which parents volunteered to work in the classroom), which was established by wives of faculty members at the University of Chicago in 1915.

Professional organizations have long been a significant support system for educators acting upon their commitment to nurture the young. Patty Smith Hill (1868–1946), a professor at Teachers College, Columbia University, was the founder of two major professional organizations that play a vital role in professional development today. She worked with the International Kindergarten Union, now the Association for Childhood Education International (ACEI), and in 1929, she called a meeting of the National Association for Nursery Education, which changed its name to the National Association for the Education of Young Children in 1964 and includes over 100,000 members today. For more on the history of early childhood education, see Lascarides and Hinitz (2000).

Young Children Are the Future of Society

"I touch the future, I teach." Perhaps you have heard these words of the first American teacher to become an astronaut, Christa McAuliffe. Actually, this view of children as the future of society has an extensive history. Beginning in ancient times, philosophers noted the influence of early experience on later experience. Socrates (470–399 B.C.) spoke of the education of children under age 6, and Aristotle believed in educating the young and recognized individual differences. Much later, German religious leader Martin Luther (1483–1546) argued that girls as well as boys should be taught and advocated a wide range of courses in school, including music. In Czechoslovakia (now the Czech Republic), educator John Comenius (1592–1670) designed the first illustrated children's textbook, *Orbis Pictus (World of Pictures)* (1658), and one of the first books for parents, *School of Infancy* (1628), in which he advocated the "school of the mother's knee," whereby mothers would informally teach their children the basic foundations of all knowledge by age 6.

PAUSE AND REFLECT

About Your Personal History

Interview a partner using the questions provided. After the interview, be prepared to introduce your partner to the class. As the interviewer reports to the class, you will do the following:

1. **Introduce your partner.** On the chalkboard, write your partner's first and last name large enough so that everyone can read it.
2. **Briefly summarize the interview responses your partner gave to each of the questions.** Choose the most interesting things that your partner said during the interview.
3. **Make a concluding statement.** While you are listening to your partner, try to "listen between the lines" and infer the values, beliefs, talents, strengths, and attitudes that your partner might bring to teaching. Try to capture that in a sentence or two that characterizes your partner in a positive, memorable way for the class. When you are finished, switch roles.

Interview Questions

1. What is your first and last name?
2. When did you first say, "I want to work with young children"?
3. How did you get interested in becoming an early childhood educator? What influenced you the most?
4. If you were forced to choose a career other than teaching, what would it be? Why?

Young Children Are Worthy of Study

Recently published child development textbooks offer several reasons for studying children, including the following: studying children enables us to investigate development from its very beginnings and thus explain behavior; studying children offers practical guidance in child rearing, programs, and so forth; and studying children offers a means of predicting adult behavior. Again, there are long-standing traditions that emphasize the importance of child study, but they occurred much later than most people imagine. A survey of major research journals found only 35 empirical studies of children in the 9-year period from 1890 to 1899, and even in the time period from 1950 to 1958, only 362 studies of children were published (Cleverley & Phillips, 1986). One of the first published attempts at child study was written by physiologist William Preyer in 1881. His book *The Mind of the Child* was a 3-year diary about his son's behavior, which he studied from the normative perspective of when and in what order the child would display certain adult characteristics (Cleverley & Phillips, 1986). Evolutionist Charles Darwin and novelist Louisa May Alcott, among other famous people, published baby biographies consisting of detailed observations of their infant children. In 1911, Arnold Gesell established the Child Development Clinic at Yale University, where he studied infants and identified general and predictable markers of development. Based on these studies, Gesell concluded that development must be controlled by an inner timetable of growth, or maturation. In 1926, Jean Piaget, who had completed advanced study in biology and was engaged in a study of epistemology (the study of knowledge), worked as a graduate student administering intelligence tests to young children. He became fascinated by the reasoning behind children's answers that he had to score as incorrect on the test. Piaget studied his own children's intellectual development intensively and published *Language and Thought of the Child,* in which he set forth a proposal that was surprising for his day. Unlike his contemporaries, he did not argue that nature (heredity) was the most important influence on children's development, nor did he argue that nurture (environment) was the most important influence. Rather, he described a dynamic interaction between the child's heredity and environment and proposed a theory of cognitive (knowledge) development and stages of reasoning through which children progress. Piaget also emphasized a concept called constructivism, or the belief that children actively build their own understandings about the world rather than merely soaking up information and experiences. This too was a departure from the thinking of the day.

Young Children's Potential Should Be Optimized

Another idea that is fundamental to early childhood education is the concept that every child is a unique individual who deserves to have her or his potential optimized. Some popular contemporary slogans include "Put children first," "Leave no child behind," and "Level the playing field" so that children can excel. Thoughtful discussions of young children's individuality first appeared in ancient times, when Aristotle wrote about differences in children and the importance of developing their talents.

There have been adults throughout history, then, who have advocated for children's basic needs and recommended educational programs for them, even when these adults were at odds with their contemporaries. Your role in providing quality care and education for the very young is consistent with the finest contributions of these leaders. Figure 2.5 summarizes the principles underlying and characteristics of high-quality programs.

TEACHER PREP WEBSITE 2.2

Go to the Video Classroom, select Early Childhood Education, choose Curriculum Planning and Programs (Module 4), and select Reggio Emilia (Video 3).

How Programs Begin and Change

There are several sources for and influences on early childhood programs. Each influence is described in its historical as well as contemporary context in the following paragraphs. To see what the Reggio Emilia program looks like, watch the video "Reggio Emilia" online at the Teacher Prep Website.

Societal Trends

Societal trends, such as economic conditions, national and world events, political policies, and technological advances, influence early childhood programs. Despite the fact that the United States currently is one of the few developed countries without federally funded child care and nursery schools for all young children, such programs have existed in the past in the United States. After the Great Depression of the 1930s, the Works Progress Administration (WPA) established nursery schools to help address the social issues of unemployment and poverty. Later, during World War II, child-care centers were funded because men were at war and women were needed to work in munitions factories to support the war effort. The Lanham Act of 1942 authorized federal support for child-care centers, which were often located near women's places of employment. Today the United States remains without a national system of child care for infants, toddlers, or preschoolers, or before- and after-school care for children in the primary grades.

Educational Theories

Educational theories, research, and philosophies are another influence on programs. Throughout the first half of the 20th century, many parents were encouraged to institutionalize children with exceptionalities or to keep them at home. When children with disabilities were sent to school, it was often to sit in the back of the room or to perform some menial task in the building. Even after special education became widely available in public schools, these students were removed from the company of their peers and relegated to a remote area of the school, such as the furnace room or a storage area. When

FIGURE 2.5 Programmatic precepts and features.

ESSENTIALS

Five Essentials for Excellence in Early Childhood Programs:

1. Interdisciplinary preparation for diverse early childhood settings
2. A system that balances specialized preparation with realism and accessibility
3. Faculty with resources needed to prepare tomorrow's professionals
4. Structures and processes that will support and sustain innovation
5. Tools to define, recognize, and assess high-quality early childhood teacher preparation

PROGRAMMATIC PRECEPTS

1. **Learning Is Fundamentally Social.** Children's development and learning begins with social interaction. Close human relationships and mutual understandings facilitate learning. Therefore, adult/child intersubjectivity is important to the learning process and teachers must get to know every child.
2. **Cultural Contexts and Environmental Influences Are Powerful Determinants of Learning.** Warm, secure, and responsive environments promote learning and development while cold, restrictive, and unsafe environments retard learning because they do not nurture children's physical and emotional well-being. Therefore, an early childhood perspective acknowledges the importance of providing children with opportunities to interact, understand, and cooperate in groups.
3. **Learning Drives Development Rather Than Being Driven by it.** Early childhood teachers should set goals, implement them, and guide children's development rather than stand by and wait for development to occur spontaneously. Optimizing children's learning and development is the prime directive of early childhood education, irrespective of the setting.
4. **Children Are Not Passive Recipients of Information; Rather, They Play an Active Role in the Construction of Their Own Understandings within the Cultural Context.** Therefore, every society needs to carefully consider what is worthwhile for children to learn, the skills that they need to develop, and the dispositions they should have.
5. **Although Patterns of Development Can Be Identified, Each Child Is an Individual with Unique Characteristics That Have to Be Respected.** Therefore, early childhood professionals are expected to plan flexible programs that accommodate individual growth.

STRENGTHS AND WEAKNESSES OF CHILD-CARE PROGRAMS

An evaluation of 390 child-care preschool classrooms using the 37-item *Early Childhood Environment Rating Scale* (Harms & Clifford, 1997) indicated the following strengths and weaknesses in the programs:

Strengths

- scheduled time for gross motor activity
- furnishings for routine care
- supervision of creative activities
- time for fine motor activities
- music experiences
- space for gross motor activities
- scheduled creative activities
- provisions for parents
- supervision of gross motor activity
- overall tone of the classroom

Weaknesses

- cultural awareness
- space for child to be alone
- dramatic play
- art
- opportunities for professional growth
- furnishings for relaxation
- displays of children's work
- personal grooming
- meals/snacks
- personal area for adults

SOURCES: Adapted from *New Teachers for a New Century: The Future of Early Childhood Education*, by U.S. Department of Education, 2000; Glasgow and Smith, 1996; and *Quality Details: A Close-up Look at Child Care Program Strengths and Weaknesses, Young Children, 52*(2), (pp. 51–61).

ASK THE EXPERT

Amy Driscoll on Exemplary Early Childhood Programs

Amy Driscoll

The first question often asked about my visits to programs is, **"What's the best program you've seen?"** It's impossible to respond to that question without one or two of my own. My response questions are, "Best program for whom? Or for what community? Or for what purpose?" What became clear in my visits to exemplary programs for *Cases in Early Childhood Education* was the importance of the fit between program and children, families, and community. Programs must reflect the cultural values of the children and families they serve, so they must look different from place to place. Consequently it is impossible to assess the quality of a program without looking at the context in which it serves children and families. While all good programs appear to be based on developmentally appropriate practices (DAP) and curriculum, there is huge variation in the way DAP is translated into the program. That variation is connected to the diversity of children and families—lifestyles and values, needs and strengths, and environment in which they live. For that reason I clearly avoid the idea of program models because model suggests a framework that can be transported and duplicated in other places. I don't think that models are appropriate when we talk about programs for young children. Their individuality and that of their families must be cherished and strengthened, and to do so, a program must be developed with that individuality as a foundation.

The other aspect of fit is one that connects educators with specific beliefs about children and learning with an environment and curriculum that supports those beliefs. In my visits, I encountered early childhood professionals who placed a high priority on finding programs in which they could teach in ways that matched their philosophy. A number of those professionals had searched for and tried out varied programs before finding a place where they could really be true to their beliefs. Once found, they were able to do their very best work for children.

The second question that I was asked after my visits to early childhood education (ECE) programs was, **"What did the programs have in common to make them unique and outstanding?"** I too was curious to answer that question as I began my visits. When I finished my travels and after much reflection, I have to say that it was people. In each case it was an individual or a group of individuals who were committed to an idea or an ideal. For example, Bebe Fearnside in Gainesville, Florida, decided to abandon traditional approaches to serving children and families in order to meet their needs in a comprehensive program. In her words, she "colored outside the lines"—interpreted policies and formed collaborations in ways that better served children. Like so many early educators she looked beyond what was happening and broadened her view of what was possible. The lesson we can gain from thinkers and professionals like her is that we have to push the boundaries of resources, of tradition, and even of policy and regulations to achieve the best programs for children.

When observing exemplary programs, the question is often raised about a focus, **"What should I look for?"** My answer is to go beyond what can be observed. You must begin, of course, with what you can see and hear, but after extensive observations, it is important to reflect and to inquire. The most outstanding programs I observed were those in which individuals reflected carefully about decisions and could articulate a clear rationale. In order to learn about those reflections, I had to raise questions. Most educators are willing to talk about their ideas, so it is not a difficult process. What I learned from the conversations about decisions were rationales consistently based on children's needs, or goals for children, or children's development. When Angela Pino, a teacher of 2-year-olds at City Country School in New York, was asked about why the staff went around cleaning up after children instead of leaving it all for the cleanup time or insisting that children clean before going to another activity, she could clearly describe the thinking behind their procedure:

> We feel that teaching children of this age to clean up after themselves during play interferes with spontaneous play and creative activity. After we

finish play, we all stop to pick up and ready the area for tomorrow. Then we're fostering the idea of group responsibility.

Or when asked about the procedure of opening children's lunch boxes, and unscrewing tops from thermos bottles and other containers, Angela explained:

Children stay here for lunch for social reasons. With twos and threes it could take the whole lunch period for them to get everything opened or arranged. Our goal during this period is not independence or fine motor skills. It's social development. The other aspect is that it's done for management reasons. It frees up the teachers to stay sitting at the tables to interact socially with the children.

Whether we agree with her rationales or not, the important quality of her program is the reflection that goes into her decision making. She doesn't rely on tradition—the way it's always done—she thinks through many of the daily management details with attention to what children need, and to goals for children. Such reflection and decision making truly characterizes the professional educator and quality programs.

Amy Driscoll is an Associate Senior Scholar at the Carnegie Foundation for the Advancement of Teaching.

Public Law 94-142 was funded in 1977 with 1.1 billion dollars to support educational programs for children with disabilities, it called for mainstreaming, meaning that these children were to be taught in the least restrictive environment, in other words, in the company of their peers. Today, strategies for supporting the development of children with exceptionalities have been clinically researched and carefully articulated (Greenspan & Wieder, 1998); young children with exceptionalities are included in most early childhood settings, and most teachers study various handicaps and medical conditions as part of their preparation programs. **Inclusion,** the practice of adapting early childhood environments and curricula so that children with disabilities can be educated with their peers and experience success, is a major achievement of contemporary early childhood education.

Knowledge of Child Development

Knowledge of learners and child development, such as developmentally appropriate practice, observational research on young children, and educators' practical experiences, also influences programs. It has taken time for infants and children to be considered worthy of careful study. It was not until the early 20th century that child development emerged as a field of study. As recently as the 1970s, many people who had not studied child development continued to believe that babies were totally lacking in intellectual abilities. Some people actually thought that babies' senses, such as vision and hearing, were not operative during the early months! Today, brain research has persuaded educators and the general public that infants are much more competent than was previously imagined and that early experience exerts a profound influence on the mature human brain's capabilities (Grunwald, 1996/1997; Jensen, 1998, 2006; Sylwester, 1995). As a field, early childhood education owes much to research on children's growth and development.

Curriculum Standards

Curriculum standards, such as the national curriculum, local policies, and school traditions, also affect early childhood programs (Grudlund, 2006). Prior to the mid-20th century, many early childhood programs focused on socialization; however, during the 1950s and 1960s, there was a national effort to improve the academic performance and social skills of "disadvantaged" children (Bronson, 2006, p. 47). Referred to as compensatory education, the goal was to support low-income children in attaining the academic and social skills that were more typical of their middle-class peers. "Over the last decade, an increasing emphasis on standards and accountability has led to a greater tendency in kindergarten to teach academic subject matter such as literacy and mathematics, to assess children's progress, and to focus on the types of social and emotional skills that allow young children to benefit from instruction, such as self-control, curiosity, self-direction, and persistence (Bronson, 2006, p. 47). The standards movement has swept the nation, and as a result teachers "are encountering unprecedented demands. . . . The public now expects schools to teach all students so that they achieve high standards—rich and poor, immigrant and native-born, white and minority, special needs and mainstream—and to take on new functions beyond the traditional scope of schools' responsibility" (Johnson, 2006, p. 7).

> Responding both to the public's demand for accountability and to the requirements of *No Child Left Behind,* all states now have instituted standardized tests to monitor students' academic progress. Some of these assessments carry "high stakes" because they determine which students will be promoted to the next grade or graduate from high school. Schools that fall below the established performance standards can be taken over by state officials or closed down altogether, and parents have the right to remove their children from low-performing schools. Faced with exams that carry such far-reaching consequences, teachers experience increased pressure to deliver high test scores for the sake of their students, their schools, and themselves. (Johnson, 2006, p. 73)

It is teachers who bear the burden of society's newer, higher expectations for schools (Hargreaves, 2003). Figure 2.6 highlights the consequences of and appropriate responses to the standards movement in early childhood education. To learn more about early learning standards, see http://www.naeyc.org/resources/position_statements/positions_2003.asp

Community Expectations

Community expectations, such as national public opinion, regional issues, and local controversies, are another influence on programs. During the 1960s, *Life* magazine published pictures of FBI agents chasing Amish children through the fields to force them to attend the public school in accordance with the compulsory attendance laws. Today, it is considered perfectly acceptable for a wide array of schools and schooling methods with differing philosophies to exist, including home schooling, private programs, church-affiliated programs, programs that teach cultural perspectives different from the mainstream, university-affiliated preschools, and so forth (Driscoll, 1995). The history of education includes numerous examples of community pressures that shaped educational practices. For example, after *Sputnik* was launched in 1957 and the United States feared that it would lose the space race to the Russians, there was tremendous pressure on public schools to increase students' achievement in science and mathematics. To view the High/Scope curriculum in action, watch the "High/Scope" video clip online at the Teacher Prep Website.

TEACHER PREP WEBSITE 2.3

Go to the Video Classroom, select Early Childhood Education, choose Curriculum Planning and Programs (Module 4) and select High/Scope (Video 4).

Evaluation Criteria

Evaluation criteria, such as accreditation standards, large-scale testing programs, and the individual progress of children in the curriculum, affect early childhood programs. Head Start, a federally funded program for low-income families and their children, has

FIGURE 2.6 Standards for early childhood education: positives and negatives.

Standards can be a positive influence when they . . .

- enhance educators' conversations about children's growth and learning as well as set higher expectations for children
- foster communication across the grades and among various stakeholders—with families, colleagues, and the general public
- support what teachers are already doing and serve to further professionalize the field
- provide continuity as preschool standards are linked to primary standards
- help to identify appropriate next steps in curriculum
- make the connection between curriculum and assessment more explicit, thereby supporting accountability

Standards can be detrimental if they . . .

- lead to teaching to the standards only and an inflexible curriculum
- result in undue pressure of accountability on educators
- push the type of curriculum suitable for more mature learners with less mature students
- lead to a mistrust of self-directed, exploratory ways of learning and treat direct instruction as the only way to guarantee that standards are addressed
- cause a rift between teachers/families and early childhood/elementary teachers in which each ascribes blame to the other for low performance
- reduce the amount of time for teachers to reflect, interact, and figure out best practices
- result in the inappropriate use of testing and other assessment
- neglect the need for teachers to have specific training and support in implementing standards

TACTICS THAT CANNOT ACHIEVE HIGH STANDARDS: FAILED SOLUTIONS

1. **Raise the Kindergarten Entrance Age.** The idea of postponing education is proposed perennially yet the idea makes little sense. Some educators may argue that a child needs "a year to grow," while at the same time suggesting that the home environment is not sufficiently enriching from an educational standpoint. If the child is kept out of school for another year, who benefits from such a decision? (Kluth & Straut, 2001). *It does not help to postpone education.*
2. **More Screening and Testing.** Tests are like taking a patient's temperature repeatedly—they are an indicator but do not suggest an underlying cause. *It does not help children achieve high learning standards to employ screening and/or readiness testing in connection with kindergarten entrance.*
3. **Add a Year.** Some advocate providing a year of school between kindergarten and first grade (i.e., "junior" first grade) or retaining children at the same grade level for another year. The research on holding children back or "flunking" them is very clear: it lowers expectations from parents/families and damages children's self-esteem (Black, 2007; Estok, 2007). *It does not help children achieve high standards to reinstate extra-year programs or to increase grade retention at the primary level.*

WHAT *CAN* ACCOMPLISH HIGH STANDARDS?

- **Direct Interaction with Materials**
  Young children's learning is enhanced through direct interaction with materials, adults, and other children (Helm & Beneke, 2003).
- **Rich Verbal Interaction**
  Children show growth when classrooms are rich in verbal interaction with one another and with adults about what they are doing, experiences with quality literature, and planned opportunities to write about their experiences.
- **Choice Among Learning Activities**
  Effective classrooms are arranged so that for much of the day children are able to make choices about what materials they will use and with whom they will work.
- **Open-Ended Learning Materials**
  Broad curriculum goals are implemented through careful preparation of the physical environment (Cassidy, Mims, Rucker, & Boone, 2003).
- **Heterogeneous Groups**
  Children are assigned to heterogeneous groups, preferably multiage groups that have the same teacher for multiple years.
- **Varied Instructional Approaches**
  Teachers regularly employ a variety of instructional approaches to assure that children learn both the skills they need and challenging, worthwhile content.

SOURCES: Adapted from *Make Early Learning Standards Come Alive: Connecting Your Practice and Curriculum to State Guidelines,* by G. Gronlund, 2006, St. Paul, MN: Wadsworth; and *Dimensions of Early Childhood, 32*(1), pp. 3–9.

provided education, health care, nutrition, parent involvement and education, and career opportunities for adults since the mid-1960s. Yet when it was evaluated in the 1970s based on increases in children's intelligence test scores alone, and these other important contributions were not considered, its funding declined. More recently, nationally recognized statistician Harold Howe calculated that every dollar invested in Head Start had saved approximately $7 in later support services, and the program's funding was increased.

Human Resources

Human resources, such as competent teachers and administrative support, as well as characteristics of the school as a learning organization, also affect programs. Recurring criticism of child care has been directed at its inadequate training for teachers and high turnover rates in centers. The difficulty with child care in the United States, of course, is that the salaries are low, the benefits are often nonexistent, the hours are long, and the expectations for professionalism from parents and the community are high. One major initiative that has attempted to address the professional status of child-care workers is the establishment in 1972 of the Child Development Associate (CDA) credential, which is based not only on coursework, but also on practical experience. In addition, the 2-year community college programs are assuming major responsibility for preparing America's child-care professionals. Through organizations such as the National Association for the Education of Young Children, the Day Care Workers of America, and the National Association of Early Childhood Teacher Educators, these community college programs are working to elevate the status of the profession and to improve working conditions for staff members.

Financial and Material Resources

Financial and material resources, such as funding, special grants, equipment, and curriculum materials, also have an influence on programs. During the 1800s and early 1900s, the majority of teachers were women without means; their families could not support them financially or find them suitable husbands. These women volunteered to teach in less-populated areas in order to survive (at that time, states such as Michigan and Ohio were considered to be "out West"). Few towns had school buildings, much less equipment and materials, and it was common practice for teachers to move from home to home and rely upon the hospitality of families. Each year, the town decided whether it could afford the teacher's services, a site for the school, and so forth based on the success of farming and industry and on charitable contributions. Accounts of the "dame schools" for young children in the 1800s and historical accounts of teachers' lives based on their letters and diaries (Wyman, 1995) make interesting reading on this phenomenon in the field of early childhood. Eventually, property taxes were used to establish a funding base for schools and to provide free public education. This system is now under scrutiny as a result of Jonathan Kozol's (1991) exposé of inequities in school funding formulas; his book is appropriately titled *Savage Inequalities.* When Kozol's book became a bestseller, it created a public outcry because it demonstrated how a system of school support based on property values consistently favors those residing in wealthy areas and puts those residing in low-income areas at a disadvantage.

James L. Shaffer

What does the similarity of these children's responses tell you about the value of the assignment?

Pedagogy

Pedagogy, or the agreed-upon set of standards for effective instructional practice, also has an impact on early childhood programs. It includes such things as integrated curricula, cooperative learning, and ways of presenting material to children. When the British infant schools that emphasized children's play and child-initiated activities were heralded as a major step forward during the 1970s, many American public schools attempted to transplant the ideas, most with limited success. Evidently, American educators found it difficult to abandon the assembly-line approach to education that dominated at the time.

Early Childhood Programs, Past and Present

Throughout history, early childhood educators have been striving to develop high-quality programs for young children. Some of these programs have existed for centuries, such as the kindergarten concept that was begun by Friedrich Froebel in the 1800s. There are at least five major philosophies/curricula/approaches to early childhood that have been in existence for many years and are widely recognized in the field of early childhood education (Walsh, 2007, in press). Montessori has over 100 years of history, and Reggio Emilia began in the 1940s. Three gained recognition during the 1960s in the United States: Bank Street (also known as the Developmental Interaction Approach), High/Scope, and Head Start (Roopnarine & Johnson, 2005). Figure 2.7 provides a brief history of each approach, its current status, an overview of the teacher's role, a synopsis of its teaching strategies, and a website that supplies further information about the approach.

COMPANION WEBSITE 2.4 To learn more about linguistic and cultural diversity, go to *Enrichment Content: Research Highlights* in Chapter 2 of the Companion Website at http://www.prenhall.com/jalongo.

We have adapted the following list of questions from Kamerman and Kahn (1994) to stimulate reflection about the distinguishing features of the wide array of programs offered for the very young. As you read them, think about a particular early childhood program with which you are familiar.

Need for a Program. What is the apparent demand for early childhood education? For example, what percentage of mothers with young children at various ages are employed out of the home in this nation?

Types of Programs. What different kinds of programs for young children are offered? A system of family child care? Center-based care? Public school? On what hours, schedules, and calendars do these programs typically operate? How well do these programs meet the needs of families?

Children Served by a Program. Who is served by the program? All children? Children who are economically privileged? Children at risk? Children who have been identified as gifted and talented? What is the program's basic view of the child?

FIGURE 2.7 Historical overview of early childhood programs and initiatives.

GENERAL INFORMATION: EDUCATIONAL THEORY HOME PAGE
www.ed.uiuc.edu/coe/eps/Educational-Theory/Et-welcome.html

MONTESSORI

History and Current Status
Now more than 100 years old, the Montessori method is named after its founder, Maria Montessori (1870–1952). She was the first female medical doctor to graduate from the University of Rome. She began her work in a psychiatric clinic. In 1907, she accepted a position as a child-care-center director for a housing project. Sixty children between the ages of 3 and 7 enrolled in the project. Equipment and materials were absent so Montessori invented her own, based on the multisensory approaches she used previously with children who had intellectual handicaps. After many of her students passed the standardized tests necessary to be admitted to the Italian public schools, her program attracted national and international acclaim. Montessori began to educate teachers and visited the United States in 1913. She was regarded as an innovator in the education of young children, and by 1914 there were 100 Montessori schools in the United States. In 1922, Montessori was appointed government inspector of schools, but because of her opposition to Mussolini's fascism, she was forced to leave Italy in 1934 and opened the Montessori Training Centre in the Netherlands. Montessori wrote 25 books on the various aspects of her theory and practice. Following her death in 1952, Montessori's methods were embraced in America as parents sought new learning options for their children. In 1960, Nancy McCormick Rambusch founded the American Montessori Society (AMS). Today there are about 4,000 Montessori schools in the United States and about 7,000 worldwide. (See www.montessori.org.nz/drmariamontessori.shtml for more information.)

Goals
The goal of a Montessori education is for all children to become self-motivated, independent, and life-long learners. A carefully prepared learning environment promotes experiences with academic concepts, practical life skills, development of the senses, and character (Epstein, Schweinhart, & McAdoo, 1996; Roopnarine & Johnson, 2005).

Role of the Teacher
The teacher's primary role is to prepare the environment so that children can learn from and through it. Teachers recognize that materials in the Montessori environment, such as sand trays, chalkboards, and language cards, encourage children's self-directed learning and overall development. Materials in a Montessori classroom are presented to children in a natural and orderly manner (Lillard, 1996) and children freely choose the Montessori materials they like to use (Epstein et al., 1996).

Strategies
The Montessori method is characterized by concrete learning materials, multiage classes, involvement of the children in establishing their own learning goals, teaching to meet individual needs and strengths, process-focused assessment, development of an integrated curriculum across subject areas, and an appreciation for children's imaginative interpretation. Children learn to respect the work of others. They engage in communication and language by talking to each other, writing, drawing pictures, and listening to books that teachers read aloud or that they can read by themselves (Lillard, 1996).

Websites
www.montessori.org
www.stkate.edu/~mdorer/
www.montessori.co.uk/index.htm

BANK STREET/DEVELOPMENTAL INTERACTION APPROACH

History and Current Status
In 1918, an innovative nursery school was opened in New York City; by 1930, it had expanded and moved to a large factory building on Bank Street. The school's innovative methods gained recognition and in 1943, the New York City Board of Education requested workshops for its teachers on Bank Street's child-centered methods. Bank Street College of Education is a leader in child-centered education. Some of the college's accomplishments

(*Continued*)

FIGURE 2.7 Continued

include working with the federal government to design the Head Start and Follow Through programs; publishing the first multiracial, urban-oriented readers for young children (*Bank Street Readers*); and creating a widely used word processing program for children (*Bank Street Writer*).

Goals

The mission of Bank Street College has been and continues to be maximizing human potential, improving the education of children and their teachers, and connecting teaching and learning meaningfully to the outside world. Bank Street College aims to build a better society by working with diverse groups of children, families, and their communities. The overarching goal of this approach is to develop the child's social competence and assist children in becoming responsible members of the classroom community.

Role of the Teacher

Teachers are responsible for modeling enthusiasm for learning, adapting appropriately to new circumstances, promoting gentleness and sensitivity, and demonstrating a commitment to live democratically and strive to improve society.

Strategies

The Bank Street model provides a structured environment with clear expectations (Epstein et al., 1996). Children are free to choose group or individual work or to select unstructured materials (water, paint, sand, etc.) and structured materials (puzzles, Cuisenaire rods, books, etc.) or to select dramatic play and block building (Roopnarine & Johnson, 2005). Because the program seeks to advance democratic ideals inside and outside schools, children frequently engage in social studies activities as part of the curriculum (Roopnarine & Johnson, 2005).

Websites

www.bnkst.edu/
www.edc.org/CCT/mlf/bankst.html
www.cc.Columia.edu/cu/cerc/wildOnes/bnkst.html

HEAD START

History and Current Status

In 1964, the federal government asked a panel of child development experts to draw up a program to help communities meet the needs of disadvantaged preschool children. The panel report became the blueprint for Project Head Start. This federally funded program was established to provide an array of support services that would enable low-income children to achieve in ways more characteristic of their middle-class peers. Its purpose is to break the cycle of poverty during the preschool years through a comprehensive program to meet the child's emotional, social, health, nutritional, and psychological needs (Zigler & Styfco, 2004). Recruiting children age 3 to school-entry age, Head Start has been enthusiastically received by education personnel, child development specialists, community leaders, and parents across the nation. Head Start serves children and their families each year in urban and rural areas in all 50 states, the District of Columbia, Puerto Rico, and the U.S. territories.

Goals

Head Start is one of the largest and most popular approaches to early childhood education (Spodek & Saracho, 2003). Head Start and Early Head Start are comprehensive child development programs that serve children from birth to 5 years and pregnant women and their families. Children from low-income families are eligible for Head Start if their families' incomes are below the federal poverty level or if their families are eligible for public assistance. Educational as well as nutritional, dental, and social services are provided (Spodek & Saracho, 2003). In 2003, Head Start was appropriated more than $6.7 billion dollars for programs, technical assistance, research, and other activities (Zaslow & Martinez-Beck, 2006, p. 7).

Role of the Teacher

Teachers nourish learning through social interaction and play, balanced with direct teaching (Roopnarine & Johnson, 2005). Parent involvement is an important aspect of the Head Start philosophy and the program provides career opportunities for parents to become aides and teachers (Bronfenbrenner, 1974; Duch, 2005).

FIGURE 2.7 Continued

Strategies

Strategies include: a range of individualized services in the areas of education and early childhood development; medical, dental, and mental health services; nutrition; and parent involvement (Zaslow & Martinez-Beck, 2006, p. 7). Head Start and Early Head Start programs served more than 900,000 children in approximately 50,000 classrooms in 19,000 centers in 2002 (Zaslow & Martinez-Beck, 2006, p. 7).

Websites

www.teacherquicksource.com
www.acf.hhs.gov/programs/hsb/
www.ci.chi.il.usworksMart/HumanServices/ChildrenServices/HeadStart.html
www.cardmall.com/NBHS
www.infomagic.com~nacog/na01006.htm

HIGH/SCOPE

History and Current Status

The High/Scope curriculum began with the Perry Preschool Project in Ypsilanti, Michigan, during the late 1960s. It was an experimental program based on the cognitive-developmental theories of Jean Piaget. Children enrolled in the program were from low-income families. The program's founder, David Weikart, conducted a longitudinal study of children who participated in the preschool and a comparison group that did not have a preschool experience. The evidence suggested that the High/Scope Perry Preschool program contributed strongly to the successful life adjustment of children who participated in it.

Goals

Based on the cognitive-developmental theories of Piaget, the High/Scope program emphasizes child-initiated (tasks chosen by the child) and child-directed (work monitored by the child) activities. Children learn to work effectively—individually, with other children, and with adults—thereby developing skills and traits that enable them to become successful students in later educational experiences.

Role of the Teacher

Teachers' and children's work go hand in hand as High/Scope emphasizes the plan-do-review method (Epstein et al., 1996). Children plan what is to be done, engage in activities, and review their progress (Schweinhart & Hohmann, 1992). This type of learning is promoted by teachers' use of a questioning style as well as their overall emphasis on conversations with children (Roopnarine & Johnson, 2005).

Strategies

The High/Scope classroom is divided into interest areas (Epstein et al.,1996) and a consistent routine is practiced, with children receiving advanced notice of schedule variation (Roopnarine & Johnson, 2005). The approach requires no special equipment, materials, or environment other than those found in typical early childhood settings.

Websites

www.highscope.org/
www.ed.gov/pubs/EPTW/eptwll/eptwlld.html
www.sccoe.K12.ca.us/child/highscop.htp

REGGIO EMILIA

History and Current Status

Reggio Emilia is the name of a municipality in Italy. In 1946, after World War II, the members of this community sold the tanks and other equipment that had been abandoned in their town and used the funds to establish a preschool. Members of the community salvaged materials, contributed money, donated their time, and became fully engaged in operating the school. Teacher Loris Malaguzzi became a leader in this effort (Edwards, Gandini, & Forman, 1998). The curriculum was based not on a curriculum guide, but on following children's interests. It

(*Continued*)

FIGURE 2.7 Continued

had a particularly strong art component, and eventually became a model of preschool education worldwide. Traveling exhibitions throughout Europe and the United States shared the Reggio Emilia approach—especially children's art work—with educators, parents, and policymakers (New, 1992).

Goals

The heart of the Reggio Emilia approach is that the child has needs and rights. Important to this approach is the teacher's documentation of children's development (Vakil, Freeman, & Swim, 2003). For instance, displays of photographs and examples of children's work, as well as teacher's recordings and note-taking of conversations, provide records of children's development (New, 1992). It is also characteristic of this approach to keep teachers and children in the same group for 3 years (New, 1992).

Role of the Teacher

The interests of children, as evidenced by their questions and curiosities, help to guide learning (Roopnarine & Johnson, 2005). Additionally, individual and group work is supported. Multiple forms of knowing are embraced (Hewett, 2001). Keeping within this framework, projects that support children's expressions in an aesthetic environment are emphasized in the curriculum. Rather than working in isolation, the teacher's role is expanded to that of a collaborator with other teachers, parents, an art specialist, and experts from the community (New, 2000).

Strategies

Three key concepts in Reggio Emilia are emergent curriculum, project work, and documentation. An emergent curriculum is one that builds upon the interests of children. Topics for study are captured from the talk of children, through community or family events, and from the known interests of children. Projects are in-depth studies of concepts, ideas, and interests that arise within the group. Considered as an adventure, projects may last one week or could continue throughout the school year. Throughout a project, teachers help children make decisions about the direction of study, the ways in which the group will research the topic, the representational medium that will demonstrate and showcase the topic, and the selection of materials needed to represent the work. Similar to the portfolio approach, documentation of children's work in progress is viewed as an important tool in the learning process for children, teachers, and parents. Pictures of children engaged in experiences; their words as they discuss what they are doing, feeling, and thinking; and the children's interpretation of experience through the visual media are displayed as a graphic presentation of the dynamics of learning.

Teacher Role

The teacher's role within the Reggio Emilia approach is complex. Working as co-teachers, the role of the teacher is first and foremost to be that of a learner alongside the children. The teacher is a teacher-researcher, a resource and guide as she or he lends expertise to children (Edwards et al., 1998). Within such a teacher-researcher role, educators carefully listen, observe, and document children's work and the growth of community in their classroom and are to provoke, co-construct, and stimulate thinking, as well as support children's collaboration with peers. Teachers are committed to reflection about their own teaching and learning.

Websites

www.ericdigests.org/2001-3/reggio.htm
www.latelier.org/usefullinks/
www.ericps.ed.uiuc.edu/eece/reggio.html
www.naeyc.org/naeyc/resource/affjul.htm

Funding for a Program. How is the program funded? With federal funds? Through other public sources? By parents? Through some combination of these?

Families in a Program. What forms of family support are available? Family leaves? After-school care? Health care? Social services? How are the roles of parents and families defined in the program?

Professionals in a Program. How are the staff members trained? What qualifications are necessary to work in the program? What is the status and income level of the profession? What benefits are offered? What is the turnover rate?

Goals of a Program. What is the program's primary focus? What purposes does it serve? What type of curriculum does it have, custodial or educational? How is the program's quality monitored?

Cultural Context of a Program. What uniquenesses does this early childhood program have? How has the culture and the society in which the program operates influenced standard practices?

Despite differences in specific characteristics, excellent early childhood programs share several important attributes (Carbo, 1995; Erwin, 1996); these are described in the following paragraphs.

Articulated Philosophy and Goals

In any excellent program, everyone clearly knows about the goals of the program, their specific roles, and the early childhood principles and practices that will support the program's purpose. A curricular philosophy is not a written statement of lofty ideals without much connection to classroom practices. Rather, the program's philosophy should be apparent in the daily experiences of children, families, and educators. A clearly articulated curricular philosophy is translated into goals and is evident to those who observe the program in action. Above all, the emphasis of a good early childhood program is on being of service to children and families. Respect for different family structures, cultural backgrounds, and community affiliations is essential in order to reach and teach every child (see Collaborating with Families feature on the next page).

Appropriate Structure and Organization

A good program is well organized so that it can make the most of team members' strengths and available resources. The program has leadership, yet it is characterized by a cooperative and democratic spirit. It has structure yet sufficient flexibility to adapt to individual needs, choices, and preferences of children, families, and educators. Evaluation is a major part of appropriate structure and organization. To monitor the program's progress, a high-quality curriculum includes an ongoing system of evaluation that guides improvement, acknowledges effort, and celebrates successes.

Emphasis on Concept Development

High-quality curricula emphasize concept development, depth of learning, and interpretation of meaning rather than the memorization of isolated bits of information. Good teaching involves more than telling children information. Perhaps the best indicator that meaningful concepts are being developed is the quality of children's work. If children's responses all look alike, there is little chance that real thinking is taking place, because the lesson was simply an exercise in following directions. Every early childhood curriculum

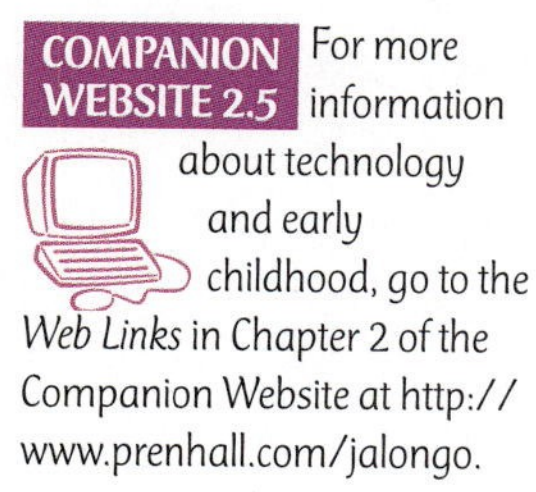

For more information about technology and early childhood, go to the *Web Links* in Chapter 2 of the Companion Website at http://www.prenhall.com/jalongo.

COLLABORATING WITH FAMILIES

Writing a Program Philosophy Statement

In addition to preparing a teaching philosophy statement, you may also be asked to write or revise a program philosophy statement. A program philosophy statement clarifies what is emphasized in the program, prioritizes long-range goals for students, and puts the entire program into perspective. **Work as a child advocate with the children in your classroom by building open communication with families:** Ask parents to share with you their beliefs about education and their hopes for their child.

At a parent meeting early in the year, begin to build community with the families in your classroom. Model a class Morning Meeting with the use of an interactive message. Read the article "Morning Meeting begins at 7:15 PM!" at www.responsiveclassroom.org/newsletter/15_3NL_2.asp. As they enter your room, ask families to write one hope they have for their child for this school year. Discuss the hopes and relate them to your program's philosophy.

The following is an excerpt from the Five Oaks School's program brochure and parent handbook that explains the program philosophy. Read it as you would if you were in the process of choosing a program for your sibling or child. How does this statement orient you to the goals and philosophy of the program? How does it communicate respect for your role? What questions do you still have about the program after reading it?

> Five Oaks is a nondenominational early childhood program that is licensed by the state Board of Education and Department of Social Services to serve children from age 3 to 8 years. We have preschool groups and a primary school for grade kindergarten through third that conform to all state requirements.
>
> Your child has learned a great deal during the first three years of life. When you compare the helpless infant you nurtured with the behavior of your talking, playful, active, competent three-year-old, what your child has learned in skills and knowledge is readily apparent. The early years from birth through eight lay the foundation for the learning that will continue throughout your child's entire life. Probably even more important than the knowledge and skills your child acquires are attitudes about school, learning, personal abilities, and work with others. The goal of Five Oaks is to promote learning, a venture that begins at home and continues through school. At Five Oaks, your child will learn to feel confident, capable, and accepted by the group.
>
> Young children are naturally curious about their world and are motivated by that curiosity to make sense of their environments. Children learn from active interaction with their surroundings, with each other, and with caring adults. At Five Oaks, we nurture that curiosity and the development of skill and mastery of the whole child. The setting and the program are designed to be challenging, rewarding, and stimulating in all areas of the child's development—physical, social, emotional, and intellectual. We use a project approach to instruction and children often work in multi-age groups. Normally, one teacher will stay with a group of children throughout the preschool years and then will assist with the transition to the primary school. Each child will have the same lead teacher while attending the primary school.
>
> You, as your child's first teacher, are an important member of the school community. Five Oaks looks to you for support and partnership that will further your child's development and learning.

should challenge young children's intellects by raising questions that intrigue young minds and encouraging the very young to explore answers in their own ways.

Attention to All Five Domains

Leaders in the field of early childhood education often speak of the whole child, which refers to supporting the young child's development and learning in five interrelated domains. In a high-quality curriculum, there are many activities that support every child's cognitive growth (the intellectual strategies used in learning), literacy learning (the ability to communicate through words), affective development (the emotional and social dimensions of development), psychomotor abilities (the mastery of physical motor skills), and aesthetic development (the ability to appreciate and respond via the arts).

Increased Opportunity for Social Interaction

An excellent early childhood program develops the group process skills of young children. Rather than working in solitude and silence on routine tasks, small groups of children are given interesting challenges and are invited to use their problem-solving skills and seek guidance from the teacher as necessary. A good example might be a group of children who are asked to create a simple map of their indoor or outdoor play area.

James L. Shaffer

Young children with special needs are included in most early childhood settings.

Respect for Individual Differences

In an excellent early childhood program, children's interests, backgrounds, and learning styles are acknowledged, respected, and used as the basis for adapting the curriculum to meet their learning needs. Because the fundamental goal in an open society is for all children to experience success in school rather than to label and sort children, effective instructional practice means that teachers use diversified teaching strategies to optimize each child's potential. Too many early childhood curricula borrow their teaching strategies from the ones used with limited success with older children, yet it is obvious that early childhood is a unique phase of development that requires a different approach to instruction.

Recognition and Inclusion of the Contributions of Many Ethnic Groups

Yet another indicator of a high-quality curriculum is a multicultural perspective that appreciates the different people from every nation in our increasingly global society. Where cultures are concerned, the whole is truly more than the sum of its parts, because the contributions of each group interact with one another and are recombined to create something new. A high-quality early childhood curriculum does not emphasize the majority culture and disregard or ignore other groups that constitute the community at large.

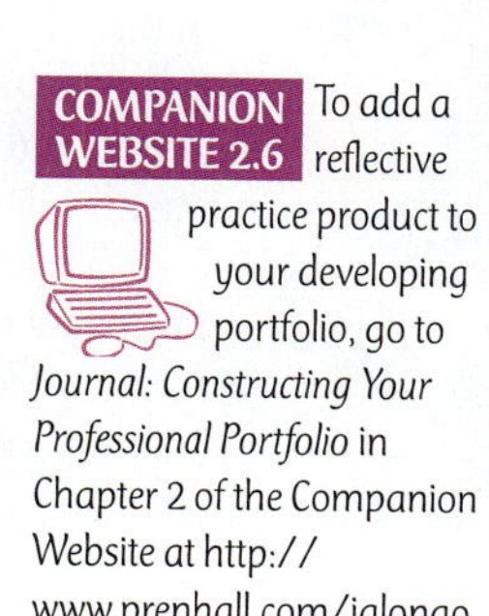

COMPANION WEBSITE 2.6 To add a reflective practice product to your developing portfolio, go to *Journal: Constructing Your Professional Portfolio* in Chapter 2 of the Companion Website at http://www.prenhall.com/jalongo.

Interdisciplinary Approaches to Subject-Matter Teaching

In a high-quality curriculum, teachers help children to see the interrelationships between and among concepts and experiences. When early childhood programs have rigid schedules that provide a few minutes for each subject, children do not have sufficient time and opportunity to pursue ideas in depth, and the content becomes fragmented. Therefore, it is important to use the curriculum to demonstrate to children that ideas

ASK THE EXPERT

James L. Hoot on Early Childhood Programs Outside the United States

James L. Hoot

Why should prospective teachers in the United States be interested in early education in other countries?

During my first 8 years of schooling, I attended a parochial school. Students at this school had many things in common. They were all residents of a suburban midwestern community. They were all of Anglo-Saxon ancestry. They all spoke the same language, shared many of the same values, and were all American. As we begin the 21st century, America's classrooms are changing dramatically.

Demographic projections consistently support the view that within the next decade, those of Anglo-Saxon ancestry will be minorities in many of our nation's schools. Further, while minorities of earlier decades were composed primarily of blacks and Hispanics, today's growing minorities include children of Vietnamese, Hmong, Cantonese, Cambodian, Korean, Arabic, Eastern European, and other ancestries. Along with this diversity of students is a concomitant diversity of languages and values.

Why should we study what early childhood educators in other countries are doing?

Compared to other countries, America has truly been blessed. Our abundance in terms of wealth, however, often creates misleading notions that we are the best in everything we do. One has only to look at the Olympics and other international competitions to see the fallacy of this viewpoint. As it relates to children, this fallacy was recently well expressed by an American teacher attending a conference presentation on the topic "Excellence in Teaching Young Children—A World Perspective." After teachers from Australia, Finland, and Hungary made short presentations regarding child care in their respective countries, I overheard a stunned American teacher sheepishly whisper to her colleague, "My God! We're a third-world country when it comes to child care."

Clearly, the foundations of our field were laid by thinkers from abroad such as Pestalozzi, Froebel, Piaget, Vygotsky, and Montessori. Likewise, programs of today are enriched by the work of other international colleagues (e.g., Malaguzzi's work with Reggio Emilia). Considering international ideas provides us with an opportunity to assess what we have done and what we might do in the future to improve our own programs. While it would be a mistake to flit from one new international (or national) model to another for the sake of change, thoughtful consideration of the world of ideas for improving the lives of children can move us toward a better educational system for all children.

Learning about other approaches to early education can also provide dividends in advocating for all children of the world. Recently, a state politician was speaking to a group about what his administration was doing to improve child care. In a question-and-answer period following the session, this politician's self-accolades were quickly humbled by an educator who had just returned from Finland. The lady asked why people with as little as 12 hours of training and no formal postsecondary education were allowed to be preschool teachers. "Teachers in Finland," she continued, "must have 3 years of postsecondary education in early education to qualify." Both the politician and many other participants were quite surprised by such an inequity. Another teacher, who had just returned from a visit to Hungary, expressed amazement that preschoolers there nap in separate rooms on youth-sized beds complete with full bedding, in contrast to the cots and floors where children in the United States commonly take their naps. The remaining questions centered upon other inequities and what can only be interpreted as our national lack of commitment to very young children.

While some of the best early childhood programs I have seen are not in the United States, we have, nevertheless, made major contributions to the field. The relatively recent construct of developmentally appropriate practice by the National Association for the Education of Young Children and the resulting publication of its operational definition, for example, has advanced increased international discourse regarding acceptable practices for educating children. Use of this document by colleagues in other countries might assist their lawmakers in moving toward higher-quality programming for their children.

How can we learn more about what is going on in other countries?

There are a number of ways in which beginning professionals can learn about early education in other countries. One of the best ways is to travel. In Europe, preservice teachers frequently study in other countries as part of their teacher education programs through such programs as Erasmus, which is funded by the European Community. Over the past couple of years, many American universities have joined this early childhood teacher exchange network. In addition, increasing numbers of universities now have independent, yearlong international student exchange programs for preschool teachers. If such travel or time commitment is not possible, preservice professionals can also join international early childhood education professional organizations, such as the World Organization of Early Childhood Education (OMEP) and the Association for Childhood Education International (ACEI). In addition to hosting a major professional conference outside of the United States every third year and producing numerous publications relating to international issues, the ACEI also has a home page on the Internet (www.acei.org). This home page includes information about the organization, a system for setting up an international pen-pal program for your classroom, and a way of contacting international teaching colleagues.

Nations of the world are becoming increasingly interdependent. By working together with international colleagues, we are more likely to improve the quality of education for our world's children.

James Hoot is Director of the Early Childhood Research Center, State University of New York, Buffalo.

are connected and that what is learned in one context can be applied to similar situations or modified to fit a different situation. As noted in Figure 2.6, an evaluation of 390 child-care preschool classrooms using the 37-item *Early Childhood Environment Rating Scale* (Harms & Clifford, 1997) indicated that the features of early childhood programs that are ranked highest include scheduled time for gross motor activities, furnishings for routine care, supervision of creative activities, and time for fine motor activities; those ranked lowest included a personal area for adults, meals and snacks, personal grooming, and displays of children's work (Cryer & Phillipsen, 1997).

PAUSE AND REFLECT
About Exemplary Programs

Work in small groups to identify the characteristics of your "dream program" in early childhood. Consider how teachers would behave, what the physical facility would look like, how the children would be taught, what equipment and materials would be provided, and how families would be supported. What ideas did you have in common? After brainstorming your list, compare and contrast it with the checklist in the Collaborating with Families section of Chapter 1.

Conclusion

As Judith Schickendanz (1995) notes,

> History has given early childhood programs a complicated and distinctive character, one filled with various strains and tensions. Some of these derive from questions about the relationship or balance to be achieved between families and society, and parents and teachers. Other tensions and strains derive from such things as the competing demands that are made on teachers of the very young because they must provide both education and physical care, while still others arise

> from contradictory conceptions of development that pit nature versus nurture. Early education has also been tugged and pulled by differing theories and beliefs about the origins of poverty and how people escape it; by differing conceptions of play and the proper balance to be struck between play and work; and by clashing beliefs about the benefits of didactic and holistic methods of instruction. (p. 7)

Based not only upon the historical foundations of the early childhood field, but also upon current best practices, we know that high-quality programs for young children have enduring consequences. Early childhood programs, according to Schweinhart (1994), contribute to children's development when they *empower young children* by encouraging them to initiate their own learning activities, *empower parents* by involving them as partners with teachers in supporting their children's development, and *empower teachers* by providing them with training and supervision that offer hands-on workshops, observation and feedback, and follow-up sessions.

COMPANION WEBSITE 2.7 To test your knowledge of this chapter's content, go to the *Multiple-Choice* and *Essay* modules in Chapter 2 of the Companion Website at http://www.prenhall.com/Jalongo. These items are written in the same format that you will encounter on the Praxis test to better prepare you for your licensure exam.

You can best fulfill your role as a child advocate when you work to provide early childhood programs that are "comprehensive, individualized, community based, generalizable, and age appropriate" (Erwin, 1996, p. 213). As Santrock (2004) reminds us, the well-being of children is a primary concern, for when children fail to reach their full potential, they make fewer contributions to society than society needs and the future of everyone is diminished. Viewing children as the "living messages" that we send to a time we will not see, Postman (1982) underscores the importance of understanding the traditions in the field and striving to become a child advocate.

ONE CHILD, THREE PERSPECTIVES

Giselle's After-School Care

Giselle is an 8-year-old who lives in an upper-middle-class suburban neighborhood with her father, mother, and 4-year-old brother. Every day after school, she goes out into the yard with her brother and calls out to the retired woman who lives next door, "Anna, is it okay if we jump the fence?" Then the two young children climb over the fence that separates the two yards and spend the next hour or two on the patio with their neighbors. About this, Giselle says matter-of-factly, "My mom said that after-school care costs too much and that we can just play or watch TV until she gets home from work. This house cost a *lot* of money." The neighbor who unofficially watches Giselle and her brother says, "They are a nice family but I worry about those young children being by themselves. Giselle is really mature for her age, but she wouldn't know what to do in an emergency. My husband and I just try to arrange to be home every weekday afternoon. It's only for about an hour, and then their mom is home from her shift at the hospital."

When Anna's daughter, who is a college student in education, visits her parents, she says, "I know you and Dad like children and all, but have you considered the legal implications? You don't really have any agreement with this neighbor about responsibility for care. If something happens to those children, they could sue you for trying to do them a favor."

Giselle's mother says, "I don't know what I would do if we couldn't rely on Anna. It doesn't help me much to have my children in after-school care because I have to leave work on my break to take them there, take a chance on being late getting back to work, and then go through rush-hour traffic to pick them up after my shift. I think that after-school programs should be right in the school building and supported by the community like they were when we lived in Los Angeles. We were totally unprepared for the lack of services here."

REACT	What is your initial response to Giselle's situation? What would you like to say to each of the adults in this scenario?
RESEARCH	Go to the library and read a recent article about after-school programs, policies, curricula, or philosophies. Is your reading consistent with your reaction or not?
REFLECT	Discuss what you and your classmates found in your readings. How has this information altered or enriched your initial reaction to the situation?

IN-CLASS WORKSHOP

Drafting Your Teaching Philosophy

What do you believe about how children learn? What do you believe about the teacher's role? Generally speaking, beliefs are mental constructions of experience held to be true that guide behavior (Birmingham, 2003; Sigel, 1985). A large portion of what individuals believe evolves from personal experiences or from cultural indoctrination (Abelson, 1979). Beliefs are based on what you value and emanate from evaluation and judgment (Pajares, 1992).

What do we know, based on research, about teachers' belief systems and how they shape teaching behavior?

1. **The Belief/Philosophy Connection.** A teaching philosophy is a subset of beliefs about how children learn and develop (Many, Howard, & Hoge, 2002), which is drawn from general knowledge, experiences, and reflection (Fang, 1996).
2. **The Influence of Autobiography.** A teacher's belief system is constructed, first and foremost, out of autobiography—from personally significant experiences and intense emotional responses that make experiences memorable (Bullough & Gitlin, 2001). Novice teachers are apt to rely on childhood experiences to direct their behavior in classrooms rather than what they have learned during teacher preparation (Whitbeck, 2000). Consequently, the belief systems of many entry-level early childhood students conflict with theories of the teacher education program (Pajares, 1992).
3. **The Effects of Reflective Practice.** As teachers gain experience and reflect upon it, they develop rich case material, consisting of particular children in particular settings, that they can use to guide their responses (Jalongo & Isenberg, 1995). A teacher's actions and beliefs emanate from experiences, education, and the specific setting in which she or he is teaching (Mueller, 2003).
4. **The Philosophy/Reality Conflict.** Discrepancies often exist between teachers' stated theories of practice and their actions in the classroom (Anderson, 1997; Buchanan, Burts, Bidner, White, & Charlesworth, 1998; Cassidy & Lawrence, 2000; Hatch & Freeman, 1988; Vartulli, 1999). Some reasons why teachers do not act upon their stated beliefs include: pressure from administrators and parents (Kowalski, Pretti-Frontczak, & Johnson, 2001), concern about students' performance on tests (Charlesworth, Hart, Burts, Mosley, & Fleegle, 1993), class size, and time limitations (Brown & Rose, 1995).

Individual Response

In an entry from her student teaching journal, Jane Mize describes how she overcame her initial disillusionment and made major changes in her teaching. As you read the excerpt, what can you infer about her beliefs? What kind of professional is she striving to become?

> I had a lot of information I needed to "teach" to the children. I envisioned them, eyes glued, listening to me intently. In reality, I kept having to stop during the lesson to refocus the children or attend to behavioral problems, sometimes losing my calm demeanor. After one particular lesson that had not gone well, I just stopped and sent the children back to their seats early. I realized that I was getting more and more frustrated. At first, I thought it was the children. The more I thought about it and analyzed my teaching methods, the more I realized that I had to make some changes in my approach.
>
> Within the next several days I had my "pet invention lesson" (where the children were to create imaginary pets out of cloth and other materials). I kept my focus on the children's literature that I selected to go along with the lesson and tried to concentrate on giving clear instructions to the children about the accompanying activities. Then off the children went, and for the rest of the morning I helped with the materials, observed children eagerly learning, and listened to them tell me excitedly about what they had made. This lesson was the beginning of the change in my approach to teaching. I realized that I had been keeping the children in their seats too long and doing most of the talking instead of engaging them in good dialogue, not only with me, but also with each other. Also, I realized that in my old approach I was getting responses from the same children while

others were sitting there squirming or tuning me out. I was not using the time I had with the children to the best advantage.

I decided to try to revise my approach. We still came together as a group, but not as often and not as long. I tried doing more in small groups or pairs, having the children share information with each other. I hoped that this would encourage some of the more reticent children to become involved and gain confidence with their ideas. When we did come together as a group, I read good literature. I also attempted to improve my divergent questions and tried to encourage more children to participate (Jalongo & Isenberg, 1995, pp. 192–193).

Discussion Questions

Now that you have collected your impressions of Jane Mize's experience, work in small groups and discuss the following questions.

What can you infer about Jane Mize's beliefs about teaching and learning? How would you characterize her philosophy?

What role did observation play in helping her to decide upon a course of action?

What processes did she use to improve her teaching?

What seemed to be getting in the way of teaching effectively?

Writing a Teaching Vignette

A vignette is a short description of an incident or episode about teaching and learning. A good teaching vignette includes the following elements:

Setting: Describe the who, what, when, and where involved in the situation. Include only those things that are essential to understanding the story.

Beginning: Start with something that will get the reader into your teaching vignette immediately. A good vignette does not necessarily arrange things chronologically. It starts with the most interesting part.

Reaction: A good teaching vignette is not like a book report; it does more than summarize. It also honestly and clearly describes your thoughts, feelings, and reflections as a teacher or as a learner.

Attempt: A vignette helps the reader to understand how you, as a teacher or learner, responded to the situation and why you responded as you did.

Outcome: A vignette makes the results of the actions for the teacher and the learner clear.

Ending: Every story needs to build to a satisfying conclusion. A vignette should give the reader a sense of completion, a sense that the incident has been "wrapped up."

You should choose a situation to write about that has powerful emotions associated with it, because these are the kinds of experiences that exert the greatest influence on behavior. Following are some ideas to get you started.

- **Role Models and Mentors:** Write a vignette about an educator who had a positive influence on your decision to become a teacher. What, exactly, did that person do for you? Why did it matter so much?
- **Echoes of Childhood:** Write about a particular incident from your childhood that has enabled you to develop greater empathy for students. How will you use that experience, good or bad, to be a more caring teacher?
- **Best and Worst Learning Experiences:** Write about a particular situation in which you felt very successful or unsuccessful as a learner. Why did this occur? What did you do about it?

CHAPTER 3

Exploring Your Role in Respecting Diversity and Promoting Equity and Fairness

by Beatrice S. Fennimore,
Indiana University of Pennsylvania

> **If you look around, about every single major American issue that needs to be addressed is around the way we treat our children. . . . What are we going to leave our children? It's a major issue. It is the great purpose that we need to revive. We don't have a lot of public purposes in America. We need this kind of movement around children's issues to determine whether we can protect people who don't have the power of the vote.**
>
> **Marian Wright Edelman, 2004, p. xv**

Meet the Teachers

MS. LI is an early childhood educator in a school that serves many children who experience challenges in their families and communities. Some of the children have parents struggling with substance abuse, and others have parents who are serving prison sentences. A number of teachers in the school are seeking transfers to "better schools," and ask Ms. Li why she wants to stay. She replies, "It is important to me to make a difference with children who are not experiencing privilege in our society. While some think of the children here as deficient because of difficulties experienced by their parents, I try always to see their strengths and their resiliency. They have the right to be respected for who they are. I want to stand up for them and be part of their fair chance for a positive future."

MR. LUKAS works with children in a preschool program that has started to prepare children for state-mandated standardized tests. He thinks that these tests contain information that is culturally unfamiliar to some of the children, and is also aware of the ways in which some teachers feel compelled to drill small children on test items without helping them to construct meaning from what they are being taught. Mr. Lukas recognizes that he must cooperate with the state mandate to keep his job, but is determined to take what he perceives as an ethical stance regarding the tests. With his administrator's permission, he has started a study group within the program for teachers who want to discuss fairness in assessment as well as developmentally appropriate approaches to preparing young children for assessment. Several other teachers have criticized him for taking on this extra responsibility without pay.

MRS. HERNANDEZ is a kindergarten teacher in a large urban public school. She is concerned when she hears other teachers refer to "at risk children" and "parents who don't care." Seeking to contribute to a positive climate of ethical language about children in her school, she tries to model language that recognizes challenges while respecting children. After overhearing a teacher call a child named Helen a "little troublemaker," she casually dropped in on that same teacher after school. Gently, she mentioned that Helen was helpful to other children in her class and persistent in correcting errors on papers. "I know she has problems, but I want to be compassionate and kind in my treatment of her." Mrs. Hernandez was prepared for the possibility that her words might not be well received, but felt that they were very important to say for the sake of the child. The teacher was polite but slightly unfriendly in her response: "Well, we all have our own opinions." Mrs. Hernandez gently replied "Yes, but of course we are all here for the children." She remained positive and professional, and committed to always being an advocate for children.

Now that you have reflected on the perspectives of three different teachers, here is a preview of the knowledge, skills, and dispositions you will need to acquire in order to fulfill your role in understanding diversity and promoting equity and fairness in your classroom.

COMPARE	What behaviors can you point to in each of these instances that demonstrate the teacher's respect for diversity and compassionate commitment to fairness?
CONTRAST	Why might each of the teachers be seen as controversial by others in their schools or programs? Should teachers speak out about their commitments to children where they work?
CONNECT	Review the problems and challenges of children and families in Figure 3.1 and think about the ways in which you will design approaches to children who encounter these situations. How will you make certain that the children, their families, and your professional colleagues know you are committed to fairness or equal treatment of others? Name something you will try always to do and something you will try never to do in your own classroom.

Learning Outcomes

- ✔ Become familiar with national standards and guidelines governing teachers' knowledge of the history of early childhood education and their role as child advocates **(NAEYC #1, INTASC #3, and ACEI #3b)**
- ✔ Connect the emergent history of civil rights to current concerns about diversity and equity in American education
- ✔ Analyze the way in which multicultural and anti-bias approaches to early childhood education link the issues of diversity and equity
- ✔ Understand your role in working toward a fair chance for all children in America
- ✔ Analyze ways in which a commitment to diversity, equity, fairness, and advocacy can create conflicts between the needs and interests of children and those of adults

FIGURE 3.1 What do these words mean to you?

The *Brown* decision of 1954 gave American children the constitutional right to an equal educational opportunity. In writing the decision of the Supreme Court, Chief Justice Earl Warren made it clear that a fair chance to get a good education was important for every child:

> In these days, it is doubtful that any child may reasonably be expected to succeed in life if he is denied the opportunity of an education. Such an opportunity, where the state has undertaken to provide it, is a right which must be made available to all on equal terms.

Think about these words. How do they make you feel and think about your future role as an early childhood professional and advocate for children?

SOURCES: Brown et al. v. Board of Education of Topeka, Shawnee County et al., and Companion Cases, 74 Sup.Ct.686 (1954).

DID YOU KNOW...?

- Our country today is a far different place than it was even half a century ago. As of the year 2000, people of color made up 25% of our total population, a 5% increase from just a decade earlier (Nieto, 2005, p. 5).
- In 2000, the number of foreign-born or first-generation U.S. residents reached the highest level in U.S. history—56 million, or triple the number in 1970. And unlike previous immigrants who were primarily from Europe, only 15% are now from Europe, with over half from Latin America and a quarter from Asia (U.S. Bureau of the Census, 2002).
- Whites still make up more than half of all students, but it is a dwindling majority at just 61.2%. Blacks now make up 17.2%, Hispanics 16.3%, Asian/Pacific Islanders 4.1%, and American Indians/Alaska Natives 1.2% of students in public schools (National Center for Education Statistics, 2002).
- The strongest statistical correlation with school success is income, and minority families are statistically more represented in the low-income category. Schools in low-income areas tend to have fewer resources, less experienced teachers, and more discipline problems (Hout, 2002).
- In 2003, nearly 40% of U.S. public school students were members of minority groups, compared to less than 10% of teachers. While the nation's student population becomes more and more racially diverse, the teaching force is moving in the opposite direction, becoming more racially homogeneous (Johnson, 2006; Snyder & Hoffman, 2003).
- About one in four workers in the United States earned poverty-level hourly wages in 2004. Nearly 39 million Americans, including 20 million children, are members of low-income working families—with barely enough money to cover basic needs like housing, groceries, and child care (Children's Defense Fund, 2005).
- One source of diversity in U.S. classrooms is the growing population of children from other nations. Nearly 90% of the children placed into international adoption are under the age of 8. These children almost always come from environments that do not meet their basic needs due to poverty, war, famine, overpopulation, or natural disasters (Meacham, 2006).

✔ Apply principles of ethics and fairness to the ways in which early childhood professionals talk about and describe children and families

✔ Identify ways in which a commitment to diversity and equity can be reflected in curriculum, relationships with children/families, and in your contributions to the profession and society

Defining Diversity and Equity in a Multicultural Context

Opportunities to explore the issues of diversity, fairness, and equity play a very important role in the preparation of early childhood professionals. Since the *Brown* decision of 1954 and the civil rights movement of the 1960s, American educators have been developing progressive approaches to understanding and accepting the diversities of childhood while also seeking ways to create more equal opportunities for children in school and society (Banks, 2001).

COMPANION WEBSITE 3.1 To learn more about diverse learners, equity, and fairness, go to *Journal: Defining Your Role* in Chapter 3 of the Companion Website at http://www.prenhall.com/jalongo.

How should early childhood professionals define diversity and equity in a democratic society? *Equity* is a simple sense of fairness in the distribution of primary goods and services that define the social order (Edmonds, 1979). *Diversity* is the presence of

human beings with perceived or actual differences based on a variety of human characteristics (Koppelman & Goodhart, 2005). Caring about equity and fairness for children involves wondering how society can better protect and ensure their rights to the basic essentials necessary for full, healthy development. These essentials include nutrition, health care, safety, and adequate educational resources (Brazelton & Greenspan, 2000). Caring about diversity involves respecting the rights of children to be valued for themselves while recognizing the fact that diversity can bring undeserved discrimination to some and unearned privilege to others. It is often the presence of discrimination or the sense of privilege that ultimately leads to greater inequities in society.

Laura Bolesta/Merrill

Teachers must demonstrate a commitment to equity and fairness.

The challenges of human diversity and equity are thus linked, and have long been a part of the American experience. Today, however, there is a growing awareness of the ways in which changing demographics make it necessary for all educators to enter their relative fields knowledgeable about issues in equity and prepared to work with a highly diverse child population. It has been estimated that by 2020, almost half of the American elementary and secondary students will be children of color. Children who are White make up less than one-fourth of the student population in the nation's largest cities, and in some states students who are Latino, Asian American, American Indian, and African American comprise more than half of the student population (Gollnick & Chinn, 2005). If you seek to be an excellent and ethical early childhood educator, you will need to enter your field prepared for its challenges and determined to respect, support, and work successfully with all children and families.

PAUSE AND REFLECT
About Changing Demographics

How do you feel about the fact that our nation is becoming more diverse? Does this give you a sense of excitement as a future teacher? Or do you feel uncertain about how you will be able to work with children very different from yourself? How do you think you might learn more about new immigrants to America? Can you make a greater effort to socialize with peers who are different from you in terms of race, culture, or language? Are there people from other parts of the nation or the world in your immediate setting whom you might try to get to know better? Plan to be more outgoing in terms of diversity while you are studying to be a teacher.

Diversity Means Everyone

The term *diversity* applies to everyone in every early childhood setting! Each individual belongs to familiar social groups and has an ethnic and cultural identity, and each individual is also different from many other people on a local, national, and global level. Thus, each of us needs to learn not only how to function and communicate within our own culturally familiar groups, but also how to be respectful of and open to different forms of function and communication with groups or individuals who are different from ourselves. Rather than thinking of diversity in terms of people who are *different from you,* it is important to *place yourself* and your cultural experiences in the context of a vast world of many human differences.

Along with your colleagues and students, you will constantly be striving to understand and articulate your own cultural experiences as you also seek to understand, respect, and work well with those whose cultural experiences are different from your own throughout your career. Whether you are teaching diverse groups of children or teaching in more homogeneous settings, it will be very important to help the children understand differences and prepare them to become people respectful of diversity and capable of thriving in our increasingly global society (Derman-Sparks & Ramsey, 2006). To see a child's drawing of an extended family, see "Multicultural Education–Age" student and teacher artifacts online at the Teacher Prep Website.

TEACHER PREP WEBSITE 3.1

Go to Student and Teacher Artifacts, select Multicultural Education, choose Age (Module 8), and select My Family (Artifact 1).

Some Diversities Bring Challenges

Diversity is a very valuable dimension of human life. Differences in human culture, religion, gender, ability, language, and lifestyle enrich our lives and make the world a far more interesting place in which to live (Noddings, 2005). However, it is important to understand that some forms of diversity also pose a threat to the well-being of children. Poverty, for example, is an economic diversity that takes a tremendous toll on children (Duncan & Brooks-Gunn, 1997). Other diversities such as race, language, gender, ability, and social class can elicit discriminatory beliefs and actions in many social settings (Derman-Sparks, 1989; Goodwin, 1997). Thus, though early childhood educators should not approach diversity as a *problem* in and of itself, they must be aware of the problems that many forms of diversity can create for children and their families.

Everyone Needs to Be Concerned

It is not only those early childhood educators who plan to teach in urban or high-poverty communities who must be concerned about the more negative ramifications of diversity and equity. Every teacher in every setting will almost inevitably encounter some ways in which differences are creating potential problems for children and some ways in which some children may be at risk for being treated unfairly.

For example, Nicholas Jones is a second-grade teacher in an affluent suburban school district who has recently encountered several diversity and equity issues. The two children with special needs in his classroom are often excluded from games or groups by many other classmates. Nicholas constantly intervenes to work toward creating a friendly and inclusive classroom community. He is also aware of the fact that the district recently changed the way in which children were assigned to one of three elementary schools. More affluent parents had been pressuring the district

Elena Rooraid/PhotoEdit Inc.

Children need to be taught to be respectful of others.

to send their children to a school different from the one that served some children from lower-income housing, and the teachers believe that this was the reason for the change. It is Nicholas's commitment to acceptance of diversity and fairness for all children that motivates him to strive for inclusiveness in his classroom and also inspires him to think carefully about the ways in which political decisions can affect equal treatment of children in his district.

TEACHER PREP WEBSITE 3.2

Go to Student and Teacher Artifacts, select Multicultural Education, choose Ethnicity and Race (Module 3), and select Girl with Friends (Artifact 3).

Attitudes and Dispositions Are Important

In addition to all the pedagogical skills you will need as an early childhood educator, you will also need the attitudes and dispositions that will help you to embrace diversity and strive constantly to create equal opportunities for children. You will need to become a *culturally competent educator* (Irvine, 2003)—aware of your own cultural limitations, respectfully open to cultural differences, and able to use cultural resources and acknowledge the integrity and value of all cultures (Ramsey & Williams, 2003). If you have grown up in a homogenous background and gone to schools that did not emphasize cultural awareness, you may be feeling nervous about some of the diversities that await you. Be assured that there is no need to feel fearful or intimidated. It is entirely possible for you to develop enthusiastic confidence in yourself as a person who can function well in cross-cultural settings (Gay, 2003). You can view an example of a child's drawing that illustrates the experience of being a racial minority in her classroom in the "Multicultural Education–Ethnicity and Race" student and teacher artifacts online at the Teacher Prep Website.

Early childhood professionals need a broad perspective on the issues of equity, fairness, and diversity. It is not enough to think on a surface level about important social problems or to collect some good classroom ideas for teaching children about diversity. Rather, once you have developed strong dispositions toward fair treatment of diverse children, you will constantly seek curriculum and activities that help your students to learn about and respect themselves and others. The In-Class Workshop at the end of this chapter will help you develop greater self-awareness as you begin planning to be a culturally competent teacher in your future classroom.

Keep in mind that all the important ideas and guidelines in every chapter of this book *will need to be implemented with a diverse population of children*—many of whom will not yet be getting a fair chance to develop their full developmental potential for a variety of reasons. However, if you are prepared to understand and respect diversity in all of its forms, and to advocate for fair treatment of children in any circumstance, you can face any future challenges with optimism and dedication. A very important intended outcome of this chapter is an understanding of the resilience and determination that you will need as you encounter the reality of being a lifelong advocate for children in school and society. Continue to think about the importance of advocacy for diversity and fairness as you read future chapters and the case in Collaborating with Families on page 104.

COMPANION WEBSITE 3.2 To learn more about your role in promoting equity and fairness with diverse learners, go to the *Web Links* in Chapter 3 of the Companion Website at http://www.prenhall.com/jalongo.

From Civil Rights to Multicultural Education

A discussion of diversity and equity for young children necessarily leads one back to the American civil rights movement of the 1960s. If you are new to the field of early childhood education today, chances are that your "experience" with the civil rights movement may have been a few pages in a social studies textbook. On the other hand, many of the more mature and experienced early childhood educators in our field today were "baby boomers" born during a time of rapid population growth after World War II. Those who were high school or college students during the civil rights movement often have a vivid memory of the tension and excitement of a historical period when many Americans stood up for their rights and opposed unjust laws that supported racially segregated schools and other forms of discrimination. Whether you personally experienced that time in history or not, you will undoubtedly encounter many of its ramifications throughout your career. And, hopefully, you will be able to envision the many ways in which civic action and civil responsibility in any generation can create a vision for social change.

Thinking about the civil rights movement of the past helps educators today to realize that it was possible and continues to be possible for American citizens to care deeply and publicly about fairness and social justice. Many Americans continue to actively promote equal rights and fair treatment of all people (Children's Defense Fund, 2005). As you think about the fact that injustice and discrimination continue to harm children today, your growing sense of the importance of child advocacy can help you to develop your own sense of passion about standing up for what you believe is right and working with others to create a fair world for children.

During the civil rights movement, many American citizens actively resisted school integration and other efforts to create fairness and equal treatment in society (Spring, 1994). The issues of justice and fairness were controversial then, and they continue to be controversial today. This means that you can not naively believe that everyone in our nation is in agreement about equal human rights. Unfortunately, discrimination based on race, culture, socioeconomic status, and language continues to exist and continues to have a negative impact on the lives of many individuals (Edelman, Holzer, & Offner, 2006). Also, as people who were historically oppressed have gained more access to their rights and grown more assertive in confronting discrimination, new tensions have arisen. For example, you may know some people who resent compensatory programs or economic social supports given to those who endured historic discrimination. Or, perhaps you have encountered people who seem to feel uncomfortable when encountering assertiveness and a stronger sense of identity in those who were once intimidated by the prejudice of others.

Finally, those who have been *privileged* in society (those whose economic circumstances are comfortable and whose physical or cultural characteristics do not encounter prejudice and discrimination) may believe that they are superior to others. Often, they fail to see the ways in which their success in life, even though they may have worked very hard to achieve it, may also have been supported with circumstances they did not earn, such as affluent families, communities offering first-rate public education, or light skin color.

The social issues of diversity and equity are clearly complex, but the *responsibility of the educator to the well-being of all children* is clear. If you reflect on your own life, you can probably recall times that you were treated unfairly and felt hurt and upset. Looking to the future, you will have the exciting opportunity to try to protect other children from discrimination and hurt. You will need to become a skilled thinker and a thoughtful speaker as you balance many social beliefs and disagreements with your deep commitment to equity and fairness for children. This may be complicated at times, but as a child advocate you can persist with career-long success in your efforts to try to accept all children and protect them from harmful forms of discrimination. To watch diverse young learners in the classroom, view the "Incorporating the Home Experiences of Culturally Diverse Students" video clip online at the Teacher Prep Website.

TEACHER PREP WEBSITE 3.3

Go to Video Classroom, select General Methods, choose Student Learning in Diverse Classrooms (Module 2), and select Incorporating the Home Experiences of Culturally Diverse Students (Video 1).

ASK THE EXPERT

Linda M. Espinosa on Working with Children from Different Backgrounds

Linda M. Espinosa

Children who enter group early care and educational programs from families with low incomes, speak a language other than English, represent an ethnic group that is non-White such as Latino/Hispanic, African American, or American Indian, or are recent immigrants to the United States are at a higher risk for school failure. Those children from non-White cultures and low-income households who enter school programs speaking little or no English are highly vulnerable to chronic academic underachievement and eventual school failure. There are dramatic differences in young children's achievement in mathematics and literacy by race, ethnicity, and socioeconomic status (SES) at school entry that persist throughout the schooling process.

Do these children struggle in school because they come from poor families, because they don't speak English, or because they are unfamiliar with school expectations?

Children from nonmainstream backgrounds often experience "double jeopardy." They frequently live in households that have few economic, educational, and social resources and they are more likely to attend schools that have fewer resources, which magnifies any existing educational inequalities. Children who enter school not speaking English must also face the increased demand of learning a new language while also learning academic subject matter. Children whose home culture is substantially different from that of the school culture also face sociocultural discontinuity; this disharmony can create school adjustment difficulties. The family economic, social, cultural, health, and educational conditions interact with the school characteristics and result in early inequities that often persist throughout a child's schooling.

How can early childhood professionals improve the educational success of children from diverse backgrounds?

Early childhood educators can improve the educational outcomes for children from diverse backgrounds by:

- providing a culturally responsive curriculum that integrates features of the child's family practices into the classroom.
- providing continuous support for home language development as the child is acquiring English.
- hiring qualified bilingual and bicultural teachers and staff.
- individualizing curriculum, interactions, learning opportunities, and assessment approaches.
- conducting continuous assessment to identify children's individual preferences, interests, and abilities in their home language and English.
- engaging families as true partners.
- recognizing and embracing the belief that diversity is a strength and bilingualism is an asset.
- recognizing that children from diverse backgrounds and non-English-speaking homes can become fully bilingual and biliterate and achieve to high standards when provided with high-quality early education combined with effective family partnership programs.

Linda Espinosa is a Professor of Early Childhood Education in the College of Education at the University of Missouri–Columbia.

John Coby is a kindergarten teacher in a large urban school. He has a very diverse group of children in his class, including a few with special needs who have individualized education programs (IEPs.) The professional development offered by John's school district this year has included a focus on greater awareness of equity in the ways in which he treats boys and girls, bilingual approaches to education, and the need to focus on the understanding of racially based conflicts and cultural differences. John knows from his undergraduate studies that the roots of a special education and equitable treatment of children stem from the civil rights movement. Moreover, he believes that he has a personal continuing role in promoting civil rights and equal treatment of children.

Many of John's college classmates have questioned his continuing work with "children from that kind of neighborhood," which helps him to realize the ways in which stereotyping of children who live in certain environments continues to exist in society. The parents of children in John's class sometimes tell him about the difficulty they experience in finding doctors or dentists who will accept the publicly funded health insurance covering their children, which has made him aware of some of the social difficulties still faced by children with less-privileged economic backgrounds.

Culturally Deficient or Multicultural?

Early childhood education has played an important role in the transition from the civil rights movement to the emergence in the 1970s of the comprehensive field of multicultural education. During the "war on poverty" that followed the civil rights movement, and the evolution of the Head Start program starting in 1965, there was a renewed interest in early educational experiences of American children (Roopnarine & Johnson, 2005). Subsequent research and literature focused on the needs of children who were poor unfortunately led to some troubling stereotypes. New terms such as *cultural deprivation, culturally deprived child,* and *disadvantaged child* carried assumptions about inherent deficits in the children and their families. The impression was made not only that children who experienced poverty were very different from those in the middle-class culture, but also that they *did not have a valuable culture of their own.* The economically impoverished children who were labeled as culturally deprived were presumed to be less intelligent, less motivated to learn, less able to control their impulses, and less capable of using effective spoken language. The families of these children who were poor were described as lacking in moral values and failing to recognize the importance of education in the lives of their children. These negative and deficit-based descriptions of children who were poor found their way into education textbooks and teacher education classrooms where courses on the culturally deprived child might be taught. Thus, while compensatory early childhood programs were being developed with the purpose of helping the children to catch up to their more advantaged peers, the ways in which the children were commonly described as deficient could simultaneously serve to lower expectations for their success.

Ultimately, a dedicated group of educators countered what they considered the discriminatory idea that compensatory programs (such as Head Start) for "culturally deprived children" might be unsuccessful because of inherent genetic weaknesses or inferiorities in the children themselves (Jensen, 1969). These educators created and promoted the field of *multicultural education.* Through their dedicated work, more and more educators became convinced that children had the right to be accepted and valued within the context of their race, culture, language, family, and community (Fennimore, 2000). Nieto (2005) offers an explanation of the circumstances that affect teachers' views of diverse student populations:

> As a result of the continuing inequality in schooling, children in our nation attend vastly different schools based largely on where they live, and where they live is based largely on their social class and race. Given the situation of immense inequality in our public schools, we no longer can naively state that equality is a driving force of our educational system. It is for this reason that, probably more than at any time in our recent past, the question of why people enter teaching has become so vital. Nothing less than the future of public education is at stake.
>
> At the same time, we must remember that many teachers have not had sustained contact with people of diverse backgrounds, nor have they learned about people different from themselves in other ways. As a result, it is no surprise that some teachers have negative perceptions, biases, and racist attitudes about students they teach, and about the students' families, cultures, and communities. These things also must be challenged. Nevertheless, it will do no good to either moralize or blame teachers for their negative attitudes and biased behaviors. Teachers are not superhuman; they pick up the same messages and misconceptions that we all do, it is only by confronting the ones that get in the way of student learning that change will occur. This means encouraging prospective and practicing teachers to reflect deeply on their beliefs and attitudes so that a shift can take place. (p. 217)

Today, multicultural education continues to serve as a pathway to respecting, understanding, valuing, and including the many different cultures and experiences of children in America. Also, it continues to inspire educators to help children, families, educators, and all citizens to move forward in their acceptance of diversity and commitment to equal and fair treatment of all people.

Krista Greco/Merrill

Multicultural education is a pathway to acceptance of diversity.

The Big Multicultural Picture

While there are many ideas for classroom materials and activities that support multicultural education, it is essential that educators first develop the bigger picture of how an understanding of the goals of multicultural education can inspire a lifelong commitment to equal opportunities for diverse children. Multicultural education is much more than a curriculum or a designated way of teaching! Rather, multicultural education should be viewed as a dynamic field of study and a *process* that continually confronts prejudice and discrimination as it builds understanding and respect between diverse people (Banks, 2001).

One important central assumption of multicultural education is that many schools are currently structured in a way that gives some students with certain characteristics a greater chance to be successful than other students who have different cultural characteristics (Banks, 2001).

Perhaps you can recall, from your own education, ways in which different students were labeled, tracked, or treated within your school.

Elizabeth Kelly, who teaches first grade in a rural school serving children from homes ranging from affluent to impoverished, vividly recalls her own elementary school years. Her mother had died and she lived with her struggling single father on disability because of a work-related injury. Elizabeth attended a school that placed children in classrooms according to perceived ability at an early age. She was an eager and able student who recalls feeling confused when her teachers acted as though she was not capable of some very easy class activities. Most of the children in her elementary school classrooms were from her housing project, and she never made friends with children from different neighborhoods.

When Elizabeth got to middle school, she was given an intellectual ability test on which she achieved a very high score. A few weeks into the first year of middle school, she was moved into a classroom in which many of the students came from wealthier neighborhoods. Elizabeth never felt as though she really fit in with the other students, but she got excellent grades throughout high school in a gifted academic track. It was only after she graduated from college, where she had taken a course in multicultural education, that Elizabeth realized that her economic and family situation resulted in a significant impact on assumptions about her ability in elementary school. Today, in her own classroom, she is very careful to demonstrate respect and high expectations for all her students. Elizabeth, through her own experiences, has come to understand first-hand the ways in which prejudice can harm children and then to embrace the ways in which multicultural approaches to education can counteract bias and support equity for children. As she and many other committed early educators now realize, the concept of multicultural education is very complex because its ultimate task is so great. It incorporates the idea that all students—regardless of social class, gender, and racial, ethnic, or cultural characteristics—should have an equal opportunity to learn in school. To watch a discussion between a Native American parent and a teacher, view "Multicultural Perspectives in Curriculum" video clip online at the Teacher Prep Website.

TEACHER PREP WEBSITE 3.4

Go to Video Classroom, select Foundations and Intro, choose Diversity (Module 4), and select Multicultural Perspectives in Curriculum (Video 5).

James Banks (2001) describes multicultural education as serving at least three purposes: It serves as an important idea, an evolving process of strengthening respectful and equitable human relationships, and a valuable method of reform in school and society. As an *idea,* multicultural education is an educational strategy used to support and extend the concepts of culture, diversity, equality, democracy, and social justice in the school setting (Gollnick & Chinn, 2005). As a *process,* multicultural education is a powerful way to continue to work through the conflicts, tensions, and ultimate positive outcomes for children that emerge when people honestly address differences and talk about privilege and discrimination in school and society (Gonzalez-Mena, 2007). Finally, as a *reform,* multicultural education enables educators to express their beliefs in equity for children and to work with others for social change (Cochran-Smith, 1995).

For example, Jamaal has been a teacher of 4-year-old children in a child-care center serving a highly diverse child population for many years. He has used the *idea* of multicultural education to support the design of his curriculum and activities with the children. With the support of his director, he has purchased books that help children to think in a positive way about their own cultures and experiences as well as those of others. During periods of traditional holidays such as Christmas, Jamaal is very aware of the fact that many of his families cannot afford to purchase expensive gifts for the children. It makes him sad to hear some of the children pretend that they are going to get the toys they see advertised on TV. So, with the help of a large box turned into a "TV,"

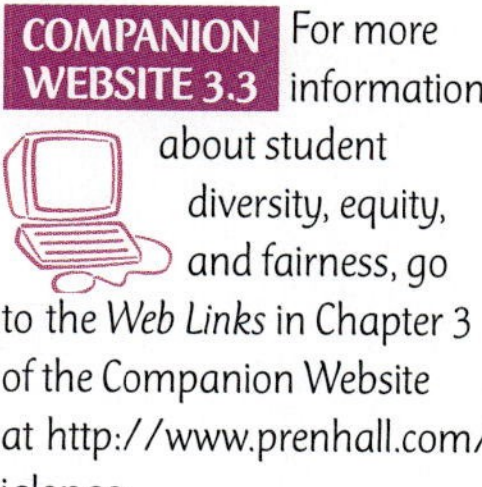

COMPANION WEBSITE 3.3 For more information about student diversity, equity, and fairness, go to the *Web Links* in Chapter 3 of the Companion Website at http://www.prenhall.com/jalongo.

he advertises the special winter holiday that he and the children will celebrate. This holiday includes kind words, helping deeds, and creation of small "winter time" gifts for family members. Jamaal also talks to the children about the principle of *unity* imbedded in the holiday of Kwanzaa.

As a *process,* Jamaal has used his understanding of multicultural education to continually help to resolve conflicts with staff. As an African American educator, Jamaal has confronted colleagues in a strong but positive way when they have expressed ideas with which he disagreed. For example, when a colleague at a faculty meeting expressed the opinion that the discussion of racial and cultural differences led to unnecessary tensions and disagreements, Jamaal reminded him that those who were more likely to suffer from discrimination and prejudice really did benefit from discussions of multicultural issues, as did those who needed to grow in their own awareness of their beliefs and actions through constructive discussion. His colleague ultimately responded in a positive way to the idea that tensions caused by talking about differences could yield very positive results.

COMPANION WEBSITE 3.4 To learn more about student diversity, equity, and fairness, go to *Enrichment Content: Research Highlights* in Chapter 3 of the Companion Website at http://www.prenhall.com/jalongo.

As a *reform,* Jamaal demonstrates his commitment to multicultural education by serving as program representative on a committee of teachers from his program, people from the community, and early childhood teachers in the public school his children will ultimately attend. He is aware of the fact that many of the public school teachers have a negative view of parents and children in his community. He works hard to counteract negative statements about the children, and to build positive attitudes toward them in the public school.

From Multicultural to Anti-Bias

There are many ways to interpret and implement the "big ideas" of multicultural education. Concern has grown that multicultural education for young children may become trivialized into forms that do not really address the prejudice and bias that create the greatest social and educational problems for diverse children (Derman-Sparks, 1989; Derman-Sparks & Ramsey, 2006). For example, teachers may focus only on different foods or on activities such as creation of crafts or costumes that reflect other cultures. This is known as a "tourist curriculum" and, though part of multicultural education, does not address real-life daily experiences and problems encountered by people who are different in any setting.

Other concerns include the fact that some educators in all-White classrooms may not see the importance of teaching about diversity, that some standardized multicultural curricula do not take the actual experiences of the children in the classroom into account, and that a pure focus on international education does not allow the children to explore the uniquely American contributions of and conflicts relating to diversity (Ramsey, 2004).

In response to these concerns, the idea of *anti-bias education* has been developed. This is an active approach to challenging prejudice, stereotyping, and bias. Of particular concern are "isms," or the tendency to make generalized assumptions about some people based on certain characteristics. Gender, race, ethnic and cultural attributes, age, ability or disability, and social class are all potential "isms." Anti-bias approaches assume that it is not enough to just speak in a positive way about differences or try to help everyone appear to get along with one another all the time. Rather, it is necessary for committed individuals to actively intervene and challenge the personal and institutional behaviors that oppress others (Derman-Sparks, 1989).

Sharon considers herself to be an anti-bias teacher. When children make comments indicating bias, she works hard to try to open up their thinking without making them feel they have said something wrong. For example, one day she asked the children what doctors do. One little girl said, "A doctor is a man who helps people." Sharon said, "Yes, a doctor can be a man. But a woman can be a doctor too! You could be a doctor one day." Then a little boy in the class said, "No, she can't be a doctor. She's not big enough. Doctors have to be very tall." Sharon replied, "I think maybe *your* doctors are very tall. Remember that you will all grow up to be bigger, and that there are grown up men and women doctors of all sizes. Also, you learn how to be a doctor with your mind, no matter what size body you have." Later that week, Sharon made a doctor learning center with a display of photographs of diverse male and female doctors. Children could draw themselves in doctor outfits and hang their creations near the photographs.

In conclusion, this section on multicultural education has focused on ways in which your career as an early childhood educator can be empowered and invigorated by knowledge of the past and awareness of a present in which we still need to focus on the issues of diversity and equity. To work with many others in your profession to strive for a better world for children, you will need to apply your multicultural skills to an understanding of the dynamics of child advocacy in school and society.

It is clear that diversity and equal treatment of children are issues that are linked in important ways. While multicultural approaches do help us to think about ways in which human harmony can be created, they also help us to create the tensions necessary to address injustices that are harmful to children. Thus, while early childhood educators can certainly think of themselves as nurturers who want to promote positive relationships among diverse people, they also can think of themselves as politically astute and courageous advocates who take a stand for children (Fennimore, 1989).

It can be difficult to think about the political and thus controversial aspects of child advocacy when a great deal of your preparation as an early childhood educator is focused on helping and teaching children and families in peaceful environments. Yet, to be an educator whose determination leads you to try to support diversity and equity, you will also need to be prepared to think and talk about very complex social and political problems. The following sections will help you to envision positive and productive participation in protecting and enhancing the rights of children to a fair start in life. To see a Native American parent discussing how disregard for his culture in the curriculum is damaging to the child, view the "Teacher Rigidity" video clip online at the Teacher Prep Website.

TEACHER PREP WEBSITE 3.5

Go to Video Classroom, select Multicultural Education, choose Language (Module 7) and select Teacher Rigidity (Video 1).

Your Role in Building a Fair Chance for Children

The goals and methods of multicultural education can be of great assistance to early childhood educators as they try to meet the needs of the diverse children in their classrooms. Yet, these educators will continue to encounter some of the most challenging questions faced by professionals committed to equity in early childhood education. Why are some children economically poor? Why don't their families have adequate incomes or homes or health care coverage? Why are their parents struggling with problems such as abuse or addiction? The answers to these questions are complex and change from family to family. While some in our society believe that we need stronger social policies

Pearson Learning Photo Studio

Anti-bias education challenges stereotypes, prejudice, and injustice.

to protect children from poverty and other serious social problems (Children's Defense Fund, 2005), others believe that individual families need to take personal responsibility for correcting faults or inadequacies that lead to economic problems.

Americans have a traditional belief in the concept of *meritocracy*, which is the idea that all people have the same chance to succeed, and that people who are poor simply do not take advantage of opportunity or work hard enough (Stevens, Wood, & Sheenan, 2002). Maria Carmelino, for example, has a grandfather who continually reminds the family of what it was like to come to America as an immigrant from Italy in the 1920s. Grandpa Carmelino recalls how hard he worked 7 days a week in a small grocery store that he eventually bought and made into a family business. Based on his experience, he blames people on public assistance for not working hard enough and not helping out their families. It is hard for him to understand, because he had to endure discrimination and work very hard, how the forces of racism, classism, and inadequate opportunities for employment with a living wage present different challenges to diverse members of the American population. For example, Grandpa Carmelino might not be fully aware of the powerful and enduring negative effect of skin color discrimination on the lives of many Americans in the past and today. Also, he may not be aware of the ways in which different challenges, such as the globalization of the American market, are deeply affecting the economic experiences of many American people today.

Maria Carmelino is a kindergarten teacher who understands her grandfather's point of view but was helped—through an undergraduate program with a strong emphasis on awareness of issues in equity and diversity—to recognize that there are many cultural, economic, and political forces in our nation that enhance the opportunities of some people while potentially harming and limiting the opportunities of others. Maria knows that every family is different, and should be understood in its own individual circumstances. Although Maria feels strongly that we should expect families to be responsible for self-support and protection of their children, she also tries very hard to recognize the many ways in which the struggle for some families to do this is much too difficult. Also important, Maria realizes that her fundamental commitment to excellent educational services for children must remain strong in spite of the fact that they or their families are experiencing difficult problems or even severe distress.

Some children and adults in America, in spite of a tremendous effort on their part, still do not have access to what is most valued in our society. One reason for this is that many families in which parents are working for minimum wage are still falling below the poverty line (Children's Defense Fund, 2005). Another reason is that families may be experiencing poverty and disadvantage that has accumulated and worsened in their communities over several previous generations. For example, does a little girl who is born to a single mother who lives in extreme poverty in a community experiencing violent crime and drug abuse, and who attends schools characterized by inadequate resources and low expectations, have a fair chance to compete with affluent children in communities privileged by many resources including well-funded schools? Even if this child works very hard and makes an outstanding effort in her poorly funded and disintegrating school, in which some of her teachers may be devoted to her while others have very low expectations, how reasonable is the expectation that *through her own effort alone* she can overcome the long-term effects of generational poverty experienced by her family, community, and school? How will she fare with the prejudice often experienced by children who are poor because of their race and designated social class? And, in retrospect, what were the experiences and opportunities of her single mother during her own childhood in the same community? Was her mother affected by poverty, community violence, and impoverished schools? Was she affected by gender bias that limited her expectations and aspirations? Did she seek to enter a responsible relationship but was later abandoned by someone she trusted and loved who did not honor his commitment to his family? Did her partner abandon her because he could not find an opportunity to make enough income to support a family? Was it possible that he could not take the minimum-wage jobs available to him because his mandated child support payment (which could be taken out of his paycheck) would be higher than a monthly salary he could earn (Edelman et al., 2006)? Did he experience a lack of opportunity based on his race or primary language? Was he excluded from employment opportunities because of one unfortunate bad decision and brief imprisonment? These are the kinds of questions that early childhood educators interested in fairness to children might ask when they meet families that are struggling to survive.

Think about the child just described as *your* child. You would have a great compassion for her problems and a strong desire to protect her and enhance her ability to survive and do well. It is all too easy to apply negative judgment to other people who do not seem to be functioning well in society, and to blame them for what appears to be their lack of success. However, the habitual blaming of those who are struggling in our society can stand in the way of the ethical obligation of educators to do their very best for all children. While it is important to honestly recognize the ways in which some families can and should seek to become stronger and more responsible, it is also important to remember that the time is *now* for children in our care, no matter how difficult their lives, to get a fair chance at the education that we *can* provide.

As a teacher committed to accepting and helping all children, you will need to rise above negative responses to family and community realities and reflect real respect for the diverse experiences and circumstances of all the children in your classroom. This will help you to do your very best to give the children a fair chance at developing their full potential.

Ecological Understanding of Difficult Childhood Realities

Many teachers have the tendency to believe that problems experienced by children are caused only by their direct home environments. Though it is true that many serious problems can be created and experienced within the home itself, the ecological developmental theory of Urie Bronfenbrenner (discussed in Chapter 4) helps us to understand how other circles of social systems and events also affect the lives and development of children. In addition to the immediate family environment, children gain important developmental experiences through contact with many others such as child caregivers, people serving their church, medical personnel, and friends. Some influences are beyond the direct experience of the child but still very influential in his or her development. For example, the kind of employment held by the parent, and the ways in which the employer does or does not provide benefits such as health insurance and sick days that can be taken for sick children, has an important influence on the child.

On a larger scale, the ways in which the government does or does not provide funding or create protective policies for children and families is important, as are the attitudes of the general public toward social and civic responsibility for equal opportunities for children (Barbour, Barbour, & Scully, 2005). For example, if our nation made the economic commitment to excellent preschool education for all children, the lives of children would change very dramatically. Bronfenbrenner's theory helps us to look at communities and the larger society for responsibility to children, and also helps us to think about fairness in the ways that public resources are made available for the protection and well-being of all the children in our nation.

Shannon, for example, is a 6-year-old child. Her teenage mother has tried very hard to create a nice home environment for her, but their apartment is very small and in poor condition. Although there is a law that the landlord has to remove all the lead-based paint on the property, he has ignored several requests to do so.

Shannon's mother has been at home with her while receiving public assistance and attending class a few days a week to become a practical nurse. However, because of new government policies, she must now work 40 hours a week to retain her food stamps and medical insurance. Thus, Shannon's mother had to leave school without finishing. Because she does not own a car, she takes several public buses to work in a fast food restaurant that pays minimum wage. Shannon's mother cannot afford a good local after-school program for her, so she pays an older woman in poor health a small amount to provide care. The woman frequently sleeps while Shannon watches TV all afternoon. Because of a cut in state funds, Shannon's local library has had to close. This means that she and her mother can no longer spend Saturday mornings reading and looking at books.

Do you see how many of Shannon's challenges in life extend beyond her mother to many other institutions and social policies and trends? An advocate for Shannon might lobby for reopening the library, or for public assistance policies that help mothers work while also helping them to spend enough time with their children and go to school to earn qualifications for better-paying jobs.

Thinking About the Concept of Social Justice

Early childhood educators who utilize the ecological model of human development understand the impact of government as well as many public and private social institutions on the lives of children. When they are aware of the ways in which some of these institutions seem to be uncaring or to be shortchanging children, it is natural for them to develop an interest in public action and advocacy (Goffin & Lombardi, 1988). Many early childhood educators write and speak about the importance of *social justice,* which is an equal right to basic liberties and opportunities in a fair social system characterized by cooperative relationships between citizens over time (Rawls, 2001). A concern about social justice tends to focus on those who have far fewer advantages than others, considering the ways in which many others in the same society are faring (Kumashiro, 2004).

As a student in education, you may be interested to know that the concept of social justice in teacher preparation has become controversial. While many have considered it essential for new teachers to develop a belief in fairness and equity related to social justice during their preparation, a concern has now arisen about whether this concept should be included in teacher education language and standards. The reason for the concern is that the concept of social justice is hard to define and, if inappropriately used, might subject students to coercion (Wasley, 2006). For example, there is a concern that you might hesitate to say in a class discussion that you were in support of a certain political candidate for president because the professor had earlier indicated that anyone committed to social justice should vote for the other candidate. If this happened, your desire to become a teacher might mean that your personal right to express opinions and make political choices might be curtailed.

This controversy over the term *social justice* is an excellent example of the kind of tension that early childhood educators, who are advocates for diversity and equity, often encounter. On one hand, of course, it would seem that students in education should not be coerced into stating that they have political beliefs other than the ones they actually hold in order to gain teacher certification. On the other hand, however, a determined concern about the welfare of children in our society does seem central to the development of dispositions leading to compassion and commitment in teaching practice.

PAUSE AND REFLECT

About Social Justice

Have you had the opportunity to think about the concept of social justice as a high school or college student? How do you feel about the fact that some children are extremely poor and living without homes or basic necessities? As a future teacher, how do you think you will respond to children who are experiencing tremendous hardship? To what provision of basic services do you think all American children should be entitled? Can you envision a role for yourself in contributing to a society in which respect and concern for the needs of all children and families is more evident? Can you see yourself, in family or social settings, trying to help others understand the plight of children and the need for better social policies to protect them?

Ethics and Social Justice

The NAEYC Code of Ethical Conduct, as indicated on page 447 of this text, upholds the ethical responsibility of early childhood educators to speak out for the welfare of children. It states that, "Because the larger society has a measure of responsibility for the welfare and protection of children, and because of our specialized expertise in child development, we acknowledge an obligation to serve as a voice for children everywhere." Certainly, if we are a voice for children, we are logically a voice for their economic well-being, nutrition, safety, medical and dental care, and protection from violence and abuse, among many other things. If children need this voice, it is because they are currently living without basic needs being met (Brazleton & Greenspan, 2000). Caring about these unmet needs and feeling a sense of determination to contribute to a public sense of the importance of respect for diversity and fairness means that we almost inevitably must work within a framework of commitment to social justice.

Krista Greco/Merrill

Speaking out for the welfare of children is an important professional responsibility.

FIGURE 3.2 Demonstrating commitment to children: Hurricane Katrina.

In 2005, Sue was a teacher in a child-care center in New Orleans. Children whose parents were very poor were enrolled at her center when Hurricane Katrina made landfall. Fortunately, she and her husband, children, and pets were able to drive to Texas and stay with relatives before the storm hit. To her sorrow, she later learned that the grandfather of one of her students had died in front of the child while helping her to cross a bridge on foot after the storm. Apparently he had run out of medication for a serious heart condition. The child sat alone crying for hours before being aided by a rescue worker. Many of Sue's other students lost their homes and were economically devastated.

Today, Sue is deeply concerned that so many of her students continue to be homeless or lacking in basic necessities. The children are sad and upset, and most do not have access to the emotional support they need through mental health care. Sue feels angry that more public resources have not been given to the children and has written many letters to government officials about their condition. She has also volunteered many hours with a local social service agency to bring food to families and urge community donations to a local food bank. Her actions are based not in political beliefs or membership in a political party but in her passion for fair and humane treatment for the children.

As you read each of the following statements, think about more skillful ways of talking about controversial issues that are modeled throughout this chapter (see, for example, Figure 3.3). Make a deliberate effort to formulate a response that is *different* from what you might have said prior to studying this material. Review the NAEYC Code of Ethical Conduct in the Compendium on p. 447 before you begin.

- A former resident of New Orleans now living in the same Texas community as Sue tells her, "You're wasting your time trying to help. No one cares about the poor. They would rather keep them out of the 9th Ward so that big business can take over their land."
- At Thanksgiving, Sue's uncle says what her other family members have been thinking, "Aren't you getting a little overinvolved? After all, you don't teach there anymore and you weren't making much money when you did. By now, these people should have gotten their lives back on track."
- Sue has decided to return to school to earn her undergraduate degree in early childhood education and, after she shares this story during class, the professor says, "Your actions are entirely consistent with the NAEYC Professional Code of Ethics. Working with parents and communities is not limited to in-school activities." Afterward, two of her classmates speak with Sue. One says, "My family came here from Poland and they managed to be successful without anyone's help. How is this different?" Another one says, "Yes, my family came here as refugees after the Vietnam War with nothing and now we're doing fine. Why aren't they doing better now that so much time has passed?"

It is not really necessary to think about fairness and social justice as terms connected to a political party or to being "liberal" or "conservative." Most of us have some strong political commitments as well as a more flexible mix of political and personal ideas that change over time. Whatever our political persuasions, we can retain an open mind and a strong sense of compassion for the children who have so little in our society. When we encounter children who experience deprivation and suffering, we may very well be reinforced in our beliefs that society should provide a greater level of justice or fair treatment for all children. Figure 3.2 illustrates a contemporary situation in which a teacher's commitment to children goes beyond her political affiliations.

Developing a Personal Position on Issues

You are no doubt realizing that the concepts of diversity, equity, and social justice can actually be quite controversial. Considering the level of controversy, why should early childhood educators need to develop a full professional and philosophical stance in issues of

ASK THE EXPERT

Stephanie Feeney on the NAEYC Code of Ethics

Stephanie Feeney

Why do early childhood educators need to be concerned about ethics?

Morality is based on values and refers to deeply held beliefs about right and wrong that guide people's behavior. Ethics involves making choices between values and thinking about duties and obligations to others. Professional ethics involves reflection on values and morality relating to the work that is done by the members of a profession. Early childhood educators need to be concerned with professional ethics because we work with children at a time in their lives when they are very young and therefore vulnerable. Because young children are so defenseless, it is important that those who work with them be aware of the tremendous power that they have over their lives. They need to be aware of their obligation to do what is right and to be certain that nothing they do is harmful to children.

Another reason that professional ethics is important is that early childhood educators often find themselves in situations where they have conflicting responsibilities. They have obligations to children, families, the agencies they work for, and their communities. Each of these has needs and makes demands. Knowing about professional ethics helps educators to weigh and balance the demands of each of these groups in ways that help them put the best interests of children first.

What is a code of ethics, and why is it an important part of a profession?

The goal of a profession is to contribute to society and to meet the needs of the people it serves. A code of ethics reflects the wisdom and commitments of a profession and describes its responsibilities. A code assures the society that the people who do an important job will have high standards and conduct themselves in a moral way. One way to determine if an occupation is a profession is to ask if it has a code of ethics.

A code of ethics is based on the moral reflection of the profession and addresses the obligations that each practitioner shares in meeting its responsibilities. It is not a legal or regulatory document. A code supports professionals in choosing to do what is right, not what is easiest, most comfortable, or will make them most popular. It gives professionals guidance as they seek to understand and resolve moral dilemmas they encounter in their work.

How can knowing about the NAEYC code of ethics help teachers of young children?

A commitment to ethical behavior is an essential part of every profession. Because early childhood educators make a significant contribution to young children in our society, it is important that they commit themselves to behaving ethically. For this reason the National Association for the Education of Young Children (NAEYC) has developed a Code of Ethical Conduct. The NAEYC Code was first published in 1989 and was updated in 1992, 1997, and 2005. This Code is part of the identity of the field of early care and education. It identifies the issues the profession cares about and wants new members to care about, communicates with those outside the profession about what they can expect from its members, and provides guidelines for ethical conduct. It identifies the field's core values, identifies relationships that are fundamental to members' work (children, families, colleagues, and community and society), spells out ethical responsibilities, and guides in the resolution of ethical dilemmas.

The Code is based on core values that reflect members' central beliefs, history, commitment to society, and common purpose embraced by the early childhood field. These core values are the foundation that makes it possible for early childhood educators to move from personal values and beliefs to a shared understanding of the professional values held by everyone in the field.

Stephanie Feeney is Professor Emerita in the Department of Curriculum Studies at the University of Hawaii.

fair treatment of children? Isn't it better just to create a pleasant environment in your own classroom, and leave the other problems to other institutions and government officials? The answer is no. You will *need to develop a personal point of view and get involved.*

Why is a personal point of view about the problems of children and families so important? First of all, many of you will encounter the troubling ramifications of unequal access to income, jobs, and services in your own students. When children lack adequate food, clothing, and medical or dental services, you could possibly become demoralized by visible signs of the powerful impact of poverty on their everyday lives. If you have not developed a personal sense of commitment to fair treatment of children, you might fall into the habit of blaming families and excusing yourself from providing an excellent and enthusiastic educational opportunity to the children (Edmonds, 1979; Fennimore, 2000; Irvine, 2003).

Also, as you enter your career you will become more aware of the continuing damage done to children by racism, classism, and other forms of bias. For example, you may hear some educators in your school say things like, "We can't help that kind of child" or "Only a few of these kids will be able to make it." Knowing that they are talking about children whose diversities have unfortunately created discriminatory reactions, you will need a sense of personal determination to have a continually positive approach in a potentially negative professional environment. Your understanding of multicultural education and commitment to fairness for children can be an inoculation against the kinds of teacher "burn out" that can pose a genuine threat to the well-being of children in schools. Throughout their careers, all early childhood educators who do not accept child poverty or discrimination against children as inevitable can speak out for social change. As an early childhood professional, it is possible that your career will lead you to many ways in which you might contribute to better attitudes and increased public willingness to protect the needs of children in greater society.

Conflicts Between Needs of Children and Interests of Adults

If we ask any assembled group of American adults if they care about children, they are likely to say that they do. Likewise, if we ask if they think that it is acceptable for American children to go hungry, or be without basic health care, or be homeless, they are likely to indicate that it is not acceptable. In the broad sense, most people feel that children should have good lives and be protected from harm (Kozol, 1995). So, early childhood educators might wonder why a nation in which so many express the belief that the basic needs of all children should be met has so many deeply disadvantaged children living within its borders. Leah Jordan, who spent 2 years after college volunteering at a community health and education center in a poor rural area, believes that she has some answers. "Every time we tried to do something for a group of impoverished people, someone else objected! We tried to get health services for pregnant teen mothers, but a group of people from a religious faith objected to the sexuality education component of the services. We tried to start a free breakfast program for the children in the schools, but people from a social service agency were afraid that it would interfere with the funding for their own breakfast program. We tried to start a free kindergarten tutoring program in the community center, but the school district was concerned that the tutors would not understand the standards and assessments important for testing outcomes. We even had a group of citizens who were concerned that the proximity of our center to their homes might affect real estate values. They felt that too many people who were poor were walking through their neighborhood!"

Leah's experience points to the dilemma of public service to children in a national democracy of many competing private and public interests. Efforts to help or support one group of people can often be opposed by another group. Just beneath the surface of many efforts to help or protect children lie conflicts of public and private interests, beliefs, and values. For example, one group of citizens may be advocating for public funds for child-care centers that are demonstrably needed by a large group of children in the community. However, another group of citizens in the same community who are making economic sacrifices so one parent can stay home with their own children may well oppose use of their tax dollars to pay for the care of others.

Arguments about financial matters are often central to conflicts over what should be done to help children experiencing significant dilemmas in society. Senator Walter Mondale, who was a strong advocate for children and families, would speak of this problem frequently. He said that groups would come before legislators to advocate for a need of children but then abandon the legislators in their efforts if they discovered that the money for services would not be going to their particular service or profession (Senn, 1977).

There are also many different personal and religious beliefs and ideologies in our nation. One group might indicate that it was concerned about the hunger and educational failure of children who are immigrants, but then object to bilingual education because it believes that all children in America should only speak English. Another group might indicate concern about child abuse in families where parents are addicted to methamphetamines, but then argue vigorously about the legalities of terminating parental rights and placing the children with adoptive parents.

Barbara Shell, who teaches in a preschool intervention program for children whose parents are addicted, understands how complicated these issues can be. "We have teen mothers with short-term addiction and supportive families who might quickly respond to outpatient rehabilitation and parenting classes, but we also have teen mothers who have grown up in foster care, been addicted for several years, and are living with men who are addicted and abusive. Some of our children have been treated fairly well or even very well by their parents, while others have experienced abject neglect and severe physical abuse. It is hard to know what is best to do! But the people who argue that we should *always* place the children for adoption, and the people who argue that we should *never* place the children for adoption, just don't understand that every family is different."

It has been common for Americans to embrace the African proverb "It takes a village to raise a child." However, unlike other nations in which there is a strong focus on social and community responsibility for the well-being of children, America has focused historically on the privacy of the individual family. The commonly held assumption has been that each family should be self-supporting, with government intervention necessary only when a family fails to meet its own basic needs (Fennimore, 1989).

This assumption often stands in the way of a wider feeling of social responsibility. For example, Elisha Williams, who teaches in a preschool program for teenage mothers and their children, grew up with a single mother who held several jobs. Her mother was able to help Elisha and her sister do well in school and finish college successfully, without receiving public assistance when they were growing up. "I saw my mother do it, and I know other mothers can do it," says Elisha, "so it is hard for me to see some of these mothers on public assistance who don't seem to make much of an effort. In my heart, I'd like to think anyone can support his or her family if enough effort is made."

Yet, Elisha's colleague Wanda reminds her, "Don't forget your mother had a strong mother of her own who often helped her. Many of these young single mothers have no one at all in their lives. And remember that your mother, who was a wonderful and courageous woman, did get a scholarship to a community college. Some of our mothers dropped out of high school. Even if they want to work—what kinds of opportunities are really available to them?"

After thinking through all these complicated issues, early childhood educators can feel overwhelmed. How much difference can one person make in such a complex world of problems and competing ideas? It is important to realize that, as an educator, you are *preparing to take your part in some very problematic social dilemmas.* Do not let this discourage you! Remember that you did not create these problems, but as an early childhood educator you are choosing to enter a field where you can contribute to their solutions. Later in this chapter, we will discuss some specific strategies that can help early childhood educators to remain optimistic and resilient even while dealing with a variety of different problems. The children of our nation need teachers with a vision—teachers who won't give up on them or their future.

Becoming an Advocate for Children

As a student in the field of early childhood education, your main focus is on meeting all the professional expectations of that role. In addition to preparing for classroom teaching you also need to develop a *philosophy* or a set of personal beliefs that that serves as a bridge between your college studies and your actual work with children. Your philosophy, as you develop it, will probably include your sincere intention to be nice to every child and to give every child a fair chance.

Most educators begin their careers with a large measure of idealism that will be affected by the challenges that they experience. How do early childhood professionals stay resilient and dedicated to all the children after a few years of the realities of teaching? What if your students are experiencing extreme poverty or troubling family problems? What if some of the other teachers in your school are very negative about the children? You can remain a strong and positive teacher, but to do this you will need to be sure to fit the concept of *child advocacy* into your emerging philosophy of teaching.

> **PAUSE AND REFLECT**
> **About Expressing Disagreement**
>
> Have you ever thought about positive and productive ways in which you might disagree with the ideas of others? How do you tend to react when someone makes a prejudiced comment? Are you silent, or do you say something? If you were encouraged as a child to always be pleasant so you would be well liked, how will you feel about taking a stand in controversies regarding children? Will you be able to be kind and respectful but also clear and determined when you counter negative comments about children and families with your own positive point of view? Can you practice this skill now by making contributions to class discussions about important issues in early childhood education?

Advocacy in Action

As discussed in Chapter 2, child advocacy is the commitment to equitable opportunities for all children to reach their highest potential for human development that transcends paid employment and assumes a lifetime of social and political action on their behalf. Teachers who are

David Mager/Pearson Learning Photo Studio

Community fundraising is one way to act upon care and concern for others.

advocates support basic democratic rights for children and seek to actively represent those rights in school and society. They look for responsible and meaningful ways to speak and act on behalf of children (Fennimore, 1989).

When teachers who are advocates encounter situations in which children are not being treated nicely or fairly, they are concerned. While they need to be courteous and professional in all their encounters, they can also be known as teachers who pleasantly counter negative comments about children with positive comments. Further, part of their professional reputation can be that they act with compassion toward children and raise questions about their well-being when they are suffering or in difficult situations. If you look back at the "Meet the Teachers" feature at the beginning of this chapter, you will read stories of teachers who have put their advocacy into action.

You may hear the advice that you should not raise questions or express criticism in your school or program until you have tenure. It is true that you will need not only to be an excellent teacher, but also that you will need to have positive relationships with your colleagues and administrators. This is especially important at the beginning of a teaching career, when you will still have a great deal to learn. You can achieve these goals while also being determined every day to stand up for children and to represent respect for diversity and commitment to equal treatment whenever you can. You can be sensible and careful about what you do or say while making sure everyone knows how dedicated you are to all the children. And, as your career develops and your success with tenure is achieved, you can consistently grow stronger in your advocacy for children in the context of school and community.

Ways of Being an Advocate

There are countless ways to be an advocate for children. No one can predict the exact situations you will encounter or the conflicts or tensions that you will face during your career. Rather than learning specific advocacy skills, you will be well served by your understanding of the broader ways in which your advocacy for children will be evidenced by your caring, ethical decisions, use of language about children, and involvement in political contexts.

Advocacy as Caring

First of all, advocacy is a state of mind. It makes you determined to *care* about children. The answer to the question "What can you really do when children and families have such terrible problems?" is always the same—you can care. The fact that you care will always assist you in doing two things. First, you will try to alleviate a difficult childhood situation by being the best teacher you can possibly be and by doing anything else within the scope of your role that might be helpful. Second, because our caring and efforts so often do fall short of solving the entire problem, you can *continue to wonder* what might be done in the future, not only for the particular child and family but in society as a whole, that could keep such problems from happening in the first place (Noddings, 1995).

Keith, for example, is a student teacher in a prekindergarten class in a large urban school district. He is not comfortable with some of the ways in which his cooperating teacher treats one of the students. The little boy comes to school without bathing and in clothes that have not been washed. Every morning he forgets to bring the small homework paper the children were given the day before. After he is scolded about this, he sits at his desk and cries. Keith has learned that the little boy's mother died of a drug overdose, and that his father also uses drugs. Because he cares very much about the situation this child is facing, he decides to decorate an old folder he has at home, write the child's name in the center, and bring the folder to school.

Keith says, "I put your name on this! It's special for you! Maybe you could remember better to do your homework paper and bring it back now. Let's give it a try." Keith knows his power to affect this sad situation is very limited, but he takes some action to help and also makes a decision about the future. He is going to try to establish a program in the school in which he is employed that invites older people who are retired to team up with children who need more parental support than they can possibly get in their current situations.

You will need a very strong cultural eye to respect and support the children whose nightmares come both night and day (Irvine, 2003). Every single person who "chips away" at major childhood problems makes an important contribution in some way (Shorr, 1988). Because the contribution may not be visible and the outcome of the contribution may take place far into the future, teachers can get discouraged. They do not get immediate feedback that reinforces their sense of what is accomplished by their advocacy. If you are an advocate for children, however, you can counteract discouragement by focusing on the fact that any positive act on your part will undoubtedly contribute to the *resilience* of the child. Studies of childhood resiliency indicate that every form of support that is provided to children with serious troubles makes it more possible for them to make some developmental progress (Jenson & Fraser, 2006).

Think back to your own early childhood and elementary teachers. Don't you still remember some of their words and actions? Weren't there some kindnesses (or lack of kindness) that have always stayed with you? The memory of your compassion and understanding will undoubtedly stay with your students as well. It is best to focus not on proof that your advocacy is yielding good results but rather on the faith that any advocacy characterized by caring should have a positive future result.

Advocacy as Ethical Decision Making

The ethical responsibilities of early childhood professionals dictate that we not only care and support resilience but that we uphold human dignity at all times. In every interaction with people as educators, we have a serious responsibility to avoid doing harm and to seek doing good (Feeney & Freeman, 1999). Thus, advocacy and ethics go hand in hand. Just as caring advocates must often *wonder* what might be done in the future to alleviate a problem faced by children or families, ethical advocates must continually wonder about *what is the right thing to do.* It is often easier to agree with a general statement of ethics than it is to know what to do in a specific situation. Ethical actions require careful thought and analysis of possible alternatives and outcomes. It is usually a good idea to first take time to *define* the actual ethical dilemma in some clear way. Then, it helps to think of the ideal response. Once you have done this, you can start to analyze different possible outcomes, including possible negative outcomes, of the idea. You may need to implement important concepts from ethical codes in the best possible way, considering the complexities of the specific situation. Your ethical decision about how to ultimately act may in some circumstances be less than what you perceive as the ideal action.

Mary Lyn, for example, is student teaching in a small rural first-grade classroom. She has talked several times with her cooperating teacher about bruises on one little girl in the class. The child has told her several times, "My Daddy hits me." Mary Lyn has been surprised by what she has perceived as her cooperating teacher's somewhat passive acceptance of this situation. The teacher has indicated that the family has had problems with alcohol addiction, unemployment, and commitment of occasional petty crimes for years. Mary Lyn thinks she has encountered the ethical dilemma of her need to act responsibly toward a child who may be abused. As she thinks about what she would identify as the ideal response, she recalls her school law class and feels that she should call the local child protection agency as a mandated child abuse reporter. Her cooperating teacher cautions her to talk with the principal about such an action.

The principal does speak with Mary Lyn, and asks her to review the district child abuse reporting policy. The written policy explains that she has met her duty as a mandated reporter by bringing the situation to the attention of the principal, and that the decision to make an actual report will be decided later by the district guidance counselor. The principal indicates that Mary Lyn should understand that the situation faced by the family in question is highly complex and that she will have no further involvement in the decision to report. In her heart, she still feels that she would like to do the ideal (call protective services as a mandated reporter). However, after speaking with her university supervisor, she also understands that she has done what could be done within her power and that any violation of the district policy could have very negative professional outcomes.

Mary Lyn decides to focus on what she realistically can do, which is first to try to be very kind and supportive of the child. She also decides to add two excellent articles on ethical dilemmas in child abuse reporting to the library in the faculty room. Mary Lyn also plans to continue to think about ways to help children experiencing abuse or neglect, even when it is considered too mild for schools to report.

Early childhood professionals often have the challenge of implementing idealistic ideas in professional settings that are less than perfect. They will need to accept discouragement and setbacks at times, while continuing to find positive ways to be ethical child advocates. What is most important is that early childhood teachers never stop caring and never stop seeking the most ethical possible solutions to complicated dilemmas.

Advocacy as Talk About Children

There is one effective method of child advocacy that has no cost, is readily available, and can be easily used by all early childhood educators: the area of descriptive language about children. Think back to the discussion of the emergence of the conceptualization of *cultural deprivation* and *compensatory education* earlier in this chapter. Programs that were designed to help children were often based on deficit-based descriptions with the potential to also hurt the children. This is because the deficit-based labels applied to the children who met the criteria for compensatory programs implied that they were very different from their more advantaged peers and likely to retain deficiencies in spite of help. The lowered expectations caused by these labels could actually counteract the positive effects of the compensatory interventions.

When you enter schools and programs for field experiences, you may hear some educators say things like this:

"These are the slower children."
"Some of these kids are crack babies."
"Our students are poor so we expect low scores."
"This is our emotionally disturbed student."

What's wrong with statements like this? First, consider how you would feel if such statements were made about your own child. Wouldn't you feel hurt and concerned about how your child might be treated when such assumptions existed in the school? Then, consider how such statements could harm any child by creating a negative school climate and lowered expectations. Teachers who say such things are not demonstrating respect for their students.

Effective early childhood educators understand that part of their ethical responsibility to children is speaking about them in compassionate ways that honor their cultures, personal characteristics, and human potential. Whatever the very real problems of poverty, abuse, or other debilitating circumstances, children should never be personally diminished by the ways in which their teachers describe and discuss them. Teachers can be honest ("many students in our program are poor") and discuss real problems ("and we are also concerned that many of them are not meeting state standards at this time") even as they express their professional commitment ("we are determined to do our best for them") and respect for the children ("and they deserve nothing less!"). All teachers must be aware of the three main areas of "teacher talk" that early childhood professionals should consider carefully in terms of advocacy and ethics: confidentiality, deficit terminology, and information about test scores and other forms of assessment (Fennimore, 2000). Figure 3.3 provides examples of appropriate teacher talk.

In terms of *confidentiality*, we need to be aware of the fact that we are trusted as professionals with a great deal of very personal information about children. They may have an imprisoned parent, a parent undergoing drug rehabilitation, or a sibling who has encountered a serious problem in the school or community. A child may have experienced sexual abuse, been in several foster placements, or had a serious illness. Personal information about children and families should be shared only when necessary *to help the child* and should be shared only with those who need to know it *to also help the child.* Careless gossip about sensitive information is wrong because it creates further danger for a child who is already encountering some kind of serious dilemma. The danger is that the information will foster a discriminatory school environment in which some or many professionals change the way they act toward the child because of their unnecessary awareness of confidential personal information. Likewise, parents and community volunteers may overhear inappropriate gossip by educators and spread sensitive information about children and families in the community.

In terms of *deficit terminology*, early childhood professionals should be careful to avoid using terms or labels that imply some kind of automatic deficiency. For example, children are not "at risk" just because they live in some kind of neighborhood or belong to a specific

FIGURE 3.3 How would you respond?

You are an early childhood professional who is committed to ethical descriptive language about children. Think about what you would actually say in the following situations:

- The father of a little girl in your class has been arrested. Her mother has shared this with you but asked that you not repeat it unless absolutely necessary. Another teacher comes into your room and says, "I heard that a father of someone in your class was arrested. Did you hear anything about it?"

Possibly you would say, "I hope you understand, but I have been asked not to repeat confidential information about this. If you do hear more from others, I hope you will protect the confidentiality of the situation with me. I appreciate your understanding."

- Three children in your class have been recommended for diagnostic testing to determine possible learning disabilities. All three receive low scores on an IQ test. The school psychologist shares the information with you, but indicates that the children will remain in your class with learning support. She says, "You are going to have it rough with these low-IQ kids in your room."

Perhaps you might say, "I have enjoyed having these children in my class this year, and I am sure I will continue to enjoy it. All three of them have some very nice characteristics and good abilities. If you might be able to share some specific strategies that could make me more successful in supporting them, I would really appreciate your help."

- You are on vacation, and find yourself sitting on a beach next to a teacher from a different part of your state. He is telling you about all the resources and opportunities the children get in his affluent suburban school district. When you indicate that you teach in a high-poverty urban area, he says, "You are kidding! Can't you get out of there into a better district?"

Perhaps you might say "I know that many people have a very negative image of children in the neighborhood where I teach. It's true than many of them are extremely poor, and that some of them bring significant problems to school. But I am dedicated to my students. They need excellent teachers, and I am so proud of my efforts to try to be one. You'd be surprised at all the great skills and characteristics my students have!"

cultural, ethnic, or linguistic group of people. Originally created to avoid the use of labeling, the term "at risk" has unfortunately evolved into what can be a discriminatory label that unfairly implies a deficiency that is anticipated just because of a personal circumstance or characteristic. If children are facing significant challenges such as extreme poverty or loss of parents to HIV/AIDS, they are *placed at risk* by circumstances beyond their control. Such problems deserve recognition and compassionate concern, but should not be made even more difficult by the automatic application of insensitive and derogatory labels.

The area of special education creates many potential problems in terms of labeling children. When a specific problem has been diagnosed and an individualized education program (IEP) created, children will also have labels such as ADD (attention deficit disorder) or LD (learning disability). Be sure to remember the "people first" rule—always put the *person* in front of the *label* when describing the child. Compare these two statements:

"I have three ADD children in my class."
"I have three children diagnosed with ADD in my class."

What is different about the second statement? It follows the "people first" rule because the disability (ADD) is mentioned after the personhood (children) is established. In the second statement the ADD becomes a diagnosis, not the central identity of the child (Fennimore, 2000).

If you become aware of a label or special education term applied to a child, ask yourself if use of that label in any setting is really necessary to understand and help the child. For example, if you are making arrangements to take your class on a trip to the zoo, it is fine to call ahead and tell the zoo education coordinator that one of your children is in a wheelchair and another is deaf. The zoo may offer some special arrangements for those children. On the other hand, complaining to another teacher about having "these special ed kids" in your classroom would be unethical and uncaring.

Finally, as an early childhood professional you will have access to the scores children achieve on developmental screening tests, intelligence tests, readiness tests, and standardized achievement tests. Remember that a *score on a test* is never a central personal characteristic. For example, a child does not "have an IQ of 90." Rather, a child has received a *score* of 90 on an assessment called an Intelligence Quotient test taken on one day of his young life. While this score may help you and other educators to plan appropriately for his educational program, it should not be used casually to describe him in a negative way on a daily basis.

All scores on tests and assessments, particularly those that are very low, have tremendous power to prejudice the minds of teachers. It is actually very difficult to retain a neutral enthusiasm for the potential of a child to be successful once knowledge has been gained of low test scores. Thus, teachers who are advocates have two important responsibilities in this regard. The first is to use scores on tests to make appropriate decisions in terms of curriculum and teaching strategies. The second is to make a sincere effort to continue to think and speak of the child as a person who will continue to grow and develop in positive and possibly surprising ways (Fennimore, 2000).

Advocacy as Activism

Early childhood educators, no matter how talented and dedicated, know that schools and programs for children cannot solve social problems all by themselves. Thus, their internal focus on their schools must also turn outward into larger society. Opportunities will undoubtedly arise that will enable them to participate in *personal advocacy, public policy advocacy,* and *private sector advocacy* (Robinson & Stark, 2005).

Personal advocacy is the means by which you can share your personal views and philosophies with other groups or individuals. It is often spontaneous and informal. For example, at a professional development session for all the early childhood educators in your geographical area, you might organize a group to meet and communicate about the need for better nutrition and more physical education in your programs. *Public policy advocacy* is action that you can take to influence public policies and practices implemented by school boards as well as local, state, and federal policymakers. For example, you might organize a group of educators to write to legislators about concerns related to fat content in school lunches and lack of funding for school playgrounds. *Private-sector advocacy* focuses on the need for business to better respond to the needs of children and families. In this area, you and other advocates might have a campaign of letters and phone calls to encourage a local fast food chain to offer more fruits and vegetables on their menus (Robinson & Stark, 2005).

Fairness and Equity in Your Classroom

All your beliefs about fairness and diversity must come alive in your own classroom. Teachers make many decisions every day, and hopefully your decisions will be firmly grounded in your respect for diversity and your commitment to fair treatment of children. Remember that there is clear evidence that children do notice differences from a very early age and that these differences become part of their earliest constructions of their social world (Ramsey, 1998). You see the differences too! The way you help the children to process their understanding and acceptance of difference, and the way in which you model your own approach to difference is extremely important.

Focus on Relationships

The standards of the National Association for the Education of Young Children for accreditation of early childhood programs focus first on the importance of *relationships* (Wien, 2004). Your respect for diversity and fairness will be reflected most in the ways in which you speak to children, describe children to others, encourage children to interact with each other, and foster a sense of community and fairness in your classroom. A genuine respect for children from all backgrounds combined with empathy and encouragement is the foundation of outstanding multicultural teaching in your own classroom. You are likely the most important daily role model for the children in terms of social interactions, and they will be observing you carefully. Treat them the way that you want them to treat each other, and design classroom experiences to build and nurture positive relationships. It is your job to lead the children from a world of *me* to a world of *us* (Stone, 2001).

Think about Mrs. Hernandez, whom we met at the beginning of this chapter. She is a teacher with great compassion for children, who tries also to foster empathy and care in other teachers. In her own classroom, Mrs. Hernandez is dedicated to helping the children to form an accepting community of friends. Many of the children in her classroom are very aware of violence in their communities. Some of them are exposed to inappropriate violent media by older siblings, and all of them have seen some real-life and fictional violence on television. Mrs. Hernandez talks constantly to the children about ways in which they can be peaceful with one another. No matter how frustrated she may feel with the children at times, Mrs. Hernandez is determined to respect them with her words and actions. She knows that if they seem themselves mirrored in her eyes as worthy of interest and respect, they will be better able to act respectfully toward others (Stone, 2001). Also, she knows that angry words that blame and scold can reinforce the feelings of rejection, fear, and helplessness that can make violence seem more attractive to children.

Mrs. Hernandez always looks for opportunities to help the children understand their similarities and differences more clearly. She makes a particular effort to include and welcome her two students with disabilities, and to help the other children feel comfortable through understanding of those disabilities. Whenever a child who speaks a primary language other than English enters her classroom, she makes a chart of several words in that language and hangs them on the wall so all the children can learn and use them each day.

Focus on Safety and Responsibility to Others

Your commitment to honor the dignity of the children you teach must include a desire to protect them and help them to feel safe in your classroom (Nieto, 1999). If there are potentially confusing differences between the culture of the home and that of the school, you will need to build a bridge for the children between these discontinuities (Ritchie & Howes, 2002). Charlie, for example, is a child who lives in a small apartment with a large number of adults and children. He shouts very loudly at school, as he often must at home in order to be heard. His teacher explains nicely that school is a different kind of place where people speak in softer voices. She says, "Practice a quieter voice, Charlie, because you'll find out that I can hear you. At school, children are asked not to shout. It is OK to act a little differently at school."

Part of safety and responsibility to others in school is the practice of fairness and helpfulness in a friendly classroom community. Children should see daily evidence that equal participation is encouraged and that exclusionary social behaviors are discouraged. Teachers can ask, "Is this fair?" and work with children to design a learning environment characterized by fairness (Paley, 1992). This also supports development of sociopolitical consciousness in children through modeling equitable treatment and expressing disapproval of unfair behaviors (Ladson-Billings, 2006). Ultimately, children in fair and safe classrooms may become adults who take action against discrimination and injustice (Banks, 2004).

Focus on Curriculum

Depending on your school or program, you may have relatively little latitude in the development of the curriculum that you are expected to implement. With the increasing national focus on testing and standards, there is a good chance that part of your curriculum will be to foster early academic learning, particularly in literacy and mathematics. You will always need to balance your understanding of the required curriculum with your understanding of the most respectful way to honor the current developmental needs and cultural experiences of the students. Hopefully, you will also have access to the kinds of children's literature that reflect respect for many forms of diversity and will be able to introduce cross-cultural materials and artifacts into your classroom life. Every early childhood professional, in every setting, should actively look for daily ways to interject activities, stories, and materials that foster learning about and respect for diversity in the children.

Your goal as you implement your curriculum is to be a culturally competent early educator who can promote academic achievement, support awareness and acceptance of human differences in the children, and help the children to understand the harm done by bias (Ladson-Billings, 2006). Another goal is to foster a sense of citizenship that helps children acquire the knowledge, attitudes, and skills necessary to make reflective decisions and take action on behalf of themselves and others (Banks, 2004). You can use the community of your classroom to help promote a sense of activism, leading to greater fairness in young children (Pelo & Davidson, 2000).

It is possible for determined educators to integrate multicultural knowledge and skills in any early childhood setting by widening the cultural diversity in the materials used for activities, play, art, and room decorations. Traditional holidays such as Christmas and Thanksgiving that are not inclusive of all beliefs or are not equally celebrated or valued by all people can be transformed into more universal themes focused on the season of the year and dimensions of celebration of human spirit and accomplishment (Ramsey, 1998). Don't forget that the *teacher* is an important part of the curriculum! Your attitudes, beliefs, knowledge, and dispositions will be an important component of education for fairness and diversity in your classroom. Think back to Mr. Lukas, another teacher introduced at the beginning of this chapter. In addition to his concern about the ways in which young children are being drilled to prepare for tests as part of the curriculum, he also worries that the curriculum is too narrow in terms of cultural diversity and citizenship education. He constantly shapes his teaching of the curriculum in a way that models respect for and interest in differences. Mr. Lukas makes sure that his class library includes books reflecting many important topics in diversity, and he regularly displays photographs and pictures in his classroom that help children talk about gender, race, language, age, and culture. Several children in his class may not participate in parties, including birthday parties, for religious reasons. Sensitive to this cultural difference, Mr. Lukas has talked to the parents of these children and discovered that his idea of a "community day" once a month, in which children share snacks and review all that they have accomplished that month, is acceptable to them. Thus, he helps the children to appreciate their accomplishments and enjoy relaxing time together without encountering the dilemmas raised by traditional holidays and celebrations. Mr. Lukas is acting as a sensitive cultural guide who is helping his students to process their cultural realities and those of others through an intentional developmental approach (Nieto, 1999).

COMPANION WEBSITE 3.5 For more information about technology and early childhood, go to the *Web Links* in Chapter 3 of the Companion Website at http://www.prenhall.com/jalongo.

Focus on Families and Community

All the important ideas about parents and families in other chapters of this book are applicable to diverse settings. It will be important for you to be aware of bias that you may have toward some parents that might keep you from implementing best practice. Respect for the children and desire for their positive outcomes dictates that educators must do their best to build positive communication with their parents and families. You will encounter educators who talk about "parents who care" and "parents who don't care." Often, the "don't care" designation is given to parents whose race, class, culture, or language differs from that of the teacher. While you may possibly encounter parents who do seem to be failing to meet the needs of their children and neglecting to support the goals of the school at home, there are also many deeply caring parents who are in a desperate struggle with poverty or the demands of their work or personal situation. The best goal is to create a plan of communication and positive interaction with all parents throughout the year (Wright, Stegelin, & Hartle, 2007). If differences in language or cultural understandings seem to create difficulties, continue to do your best to display respect and a desire for open communication for the sake of the child. As you get to know your diverse parents, you will undoubtedly learn that they have many strengths and positive characteristics. Remember that parents need support not only in helping their children to do well in school but in understanding the ways in which participating in school committees and school board initiatives can also help to ensure that their children get a fair share of school resources (Edmonds, 1979). Together, you can work to create a world of growth and acceptance for the child.

Commitment to Diversity and Fairness in Public Spaces

Hopefully you are looking forward to a long and successful career as an early childhood professional. Your role as an advocate can protect you from developing some of the negative attitudes and discouraged feelings that cause a sense of "burnout" in teachers. As you grow more confident and more determined to speak out for children, you can join initiatives in your program or district and within your profession to extend your advocacy for children. It will be important to participate in program or district committees, and to represent the needs of the children in a positive way as you work with others. Equally important will be joining professional groups that focus on advocacy and working with others to bring the voices of children and the teachers who care about them to the public. Remember that public participation in controversial issues, while very important, is never easy. As a competent professional, you will need to have the courage to promote fairness and justice through direct confrontation of social inequities reflected both in school practice and in larger society (Irvine, 2003).

COMPANION WEBSITE 3.6 To add a reflective practice product to your developing portfolio, go to *Journal: Constructing Your Professional Portfolio* in Chapter 3 of the Companion Website at http://www.prenhall.com/jalongo.

Looking Toward the Future

While it is exciting to speak out for the needs of children and families in society, it is rarely easy. As this chapter has established, adult controversies lie beneath the surface of just about every issue that affects children. Children do not have money of their own to give to political campaigns, and they cannot vote. Those who acknowledge their powerlessness but promote their causes must be very persistent and determined.

Observe Carefully in the Field

As your preparation to become an early childhood professional brings you to field experiences, pay careful attention to issues of diversity. Work to become a competent observer of language used to talk about and describe children as well as the kinds of relational interactions that take place between teachers and children. How do your role models appear to respond to issues of fairness and diversity? How are you responding, now that you are actually in classrooms with children? Are you wondering if your role models have adopted deficit approaches to forms of diversity? Are they warm and compassionate when children experience poverty or other forms of suffering? Do you find yourself reflecting on the possible prejudice to which you may have been exposed in your own home and community?

As you consider these and other important questions, why not "tell your story" as a beginning teacher by starting a personal reflective log with a specific focus on diversity and fairness (Gay, 2003). At the very start of your career, you may wisely refrain at times from openly challenging the actions and stated beliefs of your mentors in the same way as you might as a more experienced teacher. However, when you observe or hear things that do not seem to reflect a commitment to fairness and diversity, you can take note of them and think about them carefully. How might you have done things differently, and how do you plan to do them differently in your own classroom? All educators committed to fairness and respect for diversity will need to *work hard* throughout their careers to avoid falling into negative words and actions when confronted with some of the more difficult aspects of diversity. Your reflective journal will help you process the discrepancies you see and move forward into a frame of mind that will help you to support fairness and respect diversity during your own career.

Take Advantage of Opportunities to Develop Skills

Your years in college are a good time to start developing your personal voice and position in public spaces. Read the student newspaper, attend meetings of student leadership groups, and find out about the issues and controversies in which you might participate. Perhaps there is a group on campus that helps students to come together to talk about racial or religious differences. You will benefit from joining such a group to become more culturally aware and to become both a good listener and a clear speaker.

Advocates cannot be afraid to take a stand and express their beliefs in public or professional gatherings in which others may disagree. Responsible civic participation in a democracy often brings disagreement and tension (Swadener, 2003). If there is a student council or senate on your campus, consider running for office or joining a committee tackling a sensitive campus problem (perhaps gender violence or race relations). This will help you develop skills in the negotiation and resolution of important human problems. If you take advantage now of the opportunity to become involved in public issues and conversations, you will start to develop the skills and confidence necessary to be a persistent and courageous voice for children during your career.

Remember Ms. Li, one of the teachers we met at the beginning of this chapter. She is committed to staying at a school in which the children and community experience many challenges. During the years, she has joined several different district committees that focused on issues of diversity and equity. Some of the other educators on the committees openly disagreed with some of her positions and ideas. Although this upset her at first, she has become more skilled in remaining positive and confident as she advocates for children. For example, last year she was on a committee that talked about equity in the district's gifted program. A community group had complained that the vast majority of the children in the program were White and lived in the wealthiest section of the district. The committee was charged with discussing ways to include more children in gifted programming. Several teachers on the committee were opposed to any changes. One of them said, "The other kids aren't in the program because they don't qualify. Period!" Ms Li calmly replied, "I understand what you are saying, and I agree that entrance criteria are important. I am just wondering if the criteria are fair. So many of my children are so bright and capable, but their life circumstances have been hard. Some of them would really thrive in a gifted curriculum, and I'd love to see them have that chance." Although the other teacher did continue to disagree with her, the ultimate outcome of the committee work did include changes in the criteria that gave more children who were less affluent a chance to benefit from gifted resources.

COMPANION WEBSITE 3.7 To test your knowledge of this chapter's content, go to the *Multiple-Choice* and Essay modules in Chapter 3 of the Companion Website at http://www.prenhall.com/Jalongo. These items are written in the same format that you will encounter on the Praxis test to better prepare you for your licensure exam.

COLLABORATING WITH FAMILIES

Leslie's First Year as an Urban Public School Kindergarten Teacher

Leslie is very excited about her first year of teaching. Her principal has told her that her classroom will be very diverse. "Some of the parents are professionals and very involved," she said, "while other parents have several jobs or other challenges in their lives that can keep them from being involved." Leslie is determined to make a real effort to have good communication with all parents. With the information on the children's records, and help from the school social worker, she identifies five different categories of parents of children in her classroom:

- Parents whose employment situation makes them available during the day for phone calls or volunteering
- Parents whose employment situation makes it difficult or impossible for them to volunteer or take phone calls during the day
- Parents whose situations are special because they are foster parents, or family guardians such as grandparents caring for children (may overlap)
- Parents whose primary language is not English (may overlap)
- Parents who have been difficult to contact and seemingly unwilling to come to the school or communicate with teachers in the past—some of these parents may not have telephones (may overlap)

With this information in mind, Leslie makes a plan. She is going to try to identify people who can help her communicate with parents whose language she does not speak, and also try to identify older siblings of children with parents who are difficult to contact. The siblings can help to bring information to the parents. Leslie also plans a class newsletter and other communications that will let all the parents know how to contact her during the school day or through the school's "parent hotline" answering machine.

Conclusion

Everything you do as an early childhood professional will be affected by your dispositions toward diversity, equity, and fairness. If you are determined to be a lifelong multicultural learner and a committed educator, you will find ways throughout your career to honor and respect children and their families. It is exciting to think of how many contributions you will make to your profession, and how many people will benefit from those contributions, through your persistent efforts to be a culturally competent educator who seeks to provide and advocate for excellent and equitable opportunities for all children.

ONE CHILD, THREE PERSPECTIVES

Brianna's Urban Public School Evening Art Class

Brianna is a 7-year-old girl who lives with her father and three older siblings. Two years ago, her mother deserted the family and moved to a different state. Brianna's father is doing his best with his family, but is struggling with making child-care arrangements when he has the evening shift as a security guard at a local bank. Brianna, who is left to take care of herself in the evening, gets very lonely. Her teacher in her local public school had recently told the whole class that there would be an art program available to the children on Tuesday evenings, and gave the children a flyer. Brianna could not read the flyer, but walked to the school by herself on the next Tuesday evening. The art teacher told her she was not allowed to come into the room because she had not paid 5 dollars and did not have parent permission. When a parent volunteer found Brianna crying outside the door of the classroom, she asked the teacher if she could pay the 5 dollars for Brianna. The teacher said she would allow Brianna to enter only that evening, but without parent permission she could not come again. The teacher indicated that she had to follow the rules because of insurance liability, but the parent volunteer felt that she had been very unkind to Brianna. When the teacher talked to the principal the next day, the principal indicated that perhaps the evening classes could no longer be offered if children such as Brianna came on their own without payment or parent permission.

REACT	What is your initial response to Brianna's situation? What would you like to say to each of the adults in this scenario?
RESEARCH	Go to the library and read a recent article about children who are left on their own after school or in the evenings. How might schools respond to this situation?
REFLECT	Talk about this situation and the readings you have done in class. How might schools and teachers be sensitive to children who are alone a great deal of time outside of school?

IN-CLASS WORKSHOP

Becoming a Culturally Competent Teacher

Learning how to be a culturally competent educator is a lifelong process. It starts with determination to respect diversity and promote fairness for children, and continues as teachers reflect on their past experiences and future goals. No matter what your personal background may be, you have a culture of your own. This culture helps you to fit in well with some groups but may cause you to feel somewhat strange or less comfortable with other groups. Your developing cultural competency will help you to widen your abilities to communicate and work well with people most like you as well as people whose lives are very different from your own.

How would you describe your own cultural identity? This includes your family structure, socioeconomic status, language, religion, housing, aspirations, traditions, and a variety of other personal and family experiences.

How would you describe your opportunity to meet and learn about people who were different from you when you were growing up? Did you live in a community and attend a school characterized by diversity? Were neighborhoods stratified according to income and nature of housing? Did everyone in your school seem to be very much like you? Did you travel to other places or learn other languages as a child?

Can you identify times that you believe you experienced discrimination or unfair treatment during your childhood and adolescence? Did your family have problems or difficulties that seemed to set you apart from others? Were you aware of ways in which you were not well received in your school? Did you experience illness or disability that seemed to set you apart? Did another group of children exclude you from their activities?

Identify ways in which you may have been exposed to discriminatory or prejudiced attitudes during your childhood and adolescence. Do you recall hearing family members or friends talk about other people in discriminatory ways? Do you think now that you were encouraged to look down on or stay away from people different from yourself? Were you aware of your school or teachers treating different children or groups of children differently from the way you were treated?

Describe what you believe your major challenges will be as you seek to be a culturally competent educator and an advocate for children. Everyone has grown up with some form of bias or prejudice. It is fine to acknowledge this, and also to acknowledge that you do see differences such as skin color, disability, or economic attributes (such as quality of clothing). If you develop insight into some of the bias that you may have incorporated into your thinking as you were growing up, you can make a determined commitment to widening your thinking and becoming more respectful and accepting of diversity. Rather than feeling defensive about possible bias, be open to understanding and changing some of the ways you may think about difference.

Now create a plan for your future classroom. How will you include diversity and fairness in your curriculum? How will you plan to communicate regularly with diverse families? How will you try to interest your colleagues in developing greater cultural competency?

CHAPTER 4

Exploring Your Role in Promoting Children's Development

> **The study of child development is provocative, is intriguing, and is filled with information about who we are and how we grew to be this way. The more you learn about children, the better you can guide them.**
>
> **John Santrock, 2007, p. 6**

Meet the Teachers

MS. MITCHELL has been caring for infants and toddlers in her home for more than 15 years. She knows that infants and toddlers need varied sensory stimulation to help their brains grow, and she shares this information with the children's families. She also knows that very young children who do not have a stimulating environment develop smaller brains. So, in her home, you might see children's physical needs being met by being rocked or cuddled, playing pat-a-cake with an adult, or pushing and pulling toys by themselves. You would also notice bright objects or mirrors on the wall, colorful toys, and large pictures in books that are used to stimulate the infants' visual development. While feeding, diapering, or toileting these very young children, Ms. Mitchell talks to them in a soft, sing-song way to "bathe the children in language from the earliest days and to encourage them to explore and experiment with sounds."

MS. WU teaches in a public preschool program for children who are hearing impaired. The main goal of her program is to help the children learn to communicate. Ms. Wu makes weekly home visits to interact individually with each child and model appropriate ways for parents to support their children who are hearing impaired. If you visit Ms. Wu's class, you will notice 3-year-old Morgan, a child with Down syndrome who is hearing impaired and does not yet walk or talk. During her weekly visits to Morgan's home, Ms. Wu uses pictures, picture books, props, gestures, and firsthand experiences to help Morgan communicate with others about her world. During Ms. Wu's visits, Morgan's mother discusses her own needs as well as Morgan's. Ms. Wu listens to Morgan's mother and offers suggestions about ways to improve Morgan's language development and senses other than hearing, but she keeps the conversation focused on the best ways to meet Morgan's developmental needs. Ms. Wu says, "I am here to help Morgan grow and develop, but I also realize I must consider her mother's needs and education as well. This presents a real challenge for me."

MR. GUTHRIE teaches third grade in a school where children speak 17 languages and uses class meetings as a way to meet both individual and group needs. He notes that getting children to learn how to use a class meeting effectively takes a lot of time and understanding at first. So, he usually spends the whole month of September teaching children how to give and receive compliments. He then uses the entire month of October to help children identify and solve real classroom problems. This year, for example, during reading workshop time, children often argued about who could use the couch in Mr. Guthrie's classroom. Once the children identified the problem and placed it in the problem box for discussion, Mr. Guthrie put it on the agenda for the next class meeting. After suggesting several possible solutions, the third graders finally decided to add a different-colored set of cards to the book check-out pocket chart and rotate them daily to give everybody a turn using the couch. Mr. Guthrie says, "If you let yourself listen to children, they come up with great suggestions for solving their own problems."

These three teachers know what children are like. Now that you have met them, use the following questions to consider how they use their knowledge of child development, and compare, contrast, and connect them to your own thinking at this time.

COMPARE	What are some similarities in the ways these three teachers support children's development?
CONTRAST	What differences do you notice about the ways these teachers facilitate children's development?
CONNECT	What impressed you most about how these teachers meet children's developmental needs? How could you incorporate some of their ideas in your own teaching?

Now that you have reflected on the perspectives of three different teachers, here is a preview of the knowledge, skills, and dispositions you need to acquire in order to fulfill your role in promoting children's development.

Learning Outcomes

- ✔ Become familiar with your child in supporting children's development **(NAEYC #1, INTASC # 2, and ACEI #1)**
- ✔ Understand the developmental characteristics of children from birth through age 8
- ✔ Apply knowledge of child development in early childhood classrooms
- ✔ Describe the leading theorists influencing early childhood education
- ✔ Appreciate the importance of meeting the diverse needs, interests, and abilities of all young children

A Definition of Development

Consider the remarkable changes that have occurred in your body in your developmental journey from a newborn infant to a mature adult. Your growth and development depended on important biological and environmental factors. As you come to understand the process of typical development, it is easier for you to see how virtually any condition, biological or environmental, can contribute to or impair healthy growth and development.

COMPANION WEBSITE 4.1 To learn more about defining your role in promoting children's development, go to *Journal: Defining Your Role* in Chapter 4 of the Companion Website at http://www.prenhall.com/jalongo.

When we refer to *growth*, we mean the increases in children's overall physical size, or a specific aspect of size such as height, weight, or strength. In contrast, *development* refers to the complex and dynamic cognitive, language, physical, motor, social, emotional, and moral changes that occur over time. Development occurs throughout one's life (Berk, 2005). Consider, for example, physical/motor development. You began your life by not even being able to hold your head up. As your muscle development matured,

DID YOU KNOW...?

Key Facts About Children's Development

- 13.5 million children live in poverty in the United States.
- 9.3 million children lack health care and 22% of children have not completed their needed vaccinations.
- 20% of children ages 3 to 17 have one or more developmental, learning, or behavioral exceptionalities.
- About 12 million preschoolers—including 6 million infants and toddlers—are in child care.
- Quality child care has a lasting impact on both children's well-being and ability to learn.
- Each year, an estimated 3 million children are reported as suspected victims of child abuse and neglect and referred for investigation.

SOURCES: Children's Defense Fund, 2005; Federal Interagency Forum on Child and Family Statistics, 2005; KidsCount Data Book, 2005; National Center for Health Statistics, 2004.

you were able to eventually roll over, sit, crawl, stand, walk, run, and perhaps engage in even more complex physical skills. These changes over time are what make each person unique.

Characteristics of Young Children

All children develop in similar ways. They follow a predictable pattern of development, which is related to their age, and influenced by their family and cultural backgrounds, individual temperament, and biological makeup. Although children of certain ages behave in similar ways and have particular characteristics and needs, variations in development are always evident. Knowing what young children are like is the first step toward making good child development decisions. Essentially, there are three primary characteristics of what young children are like: (a) predictable patterns of development, (b) essential needs, and (c) developmental milestones.

PAUSE AND REFLECT

About Children's Development

Make a list of the biological and environmental factors (e.g., good nutrition, physical health) that you needed to develop into a healthy adult. Now think about what your own development would have been like if one or more of these factors had been lacking. What observations can you make about the necessary resources and supports that promote healthy development? Identify some current conditions that affect children's development.

Patterns of Development

Children all over the world develop in the same way, yet each child has a unique pattern of development. The following five principles of development will help you better understand these patterns and provide guidelines for your work with children in all early childhood settings (Berk, 2005; Bredekamp & Copple, 1997; Erikson, 1993; Piaget, 1992; Santrock, 2007; Vygotsky, 1978).

1. *Development in each domain—physical, motor, social, emotional, and cognitive—influences and is influenced by development in other domains.* When children master any physical skill, such as climbing on a jungle gym, riding a bicycle, or kicking a soccer ball, their self-confidence usually increases. However, if children are unable to reach, grasp, crawl, or walk, they are limited in how they explore their world, which influences their cognitive development. The interrelatedness of each domain is an important principle of development.

2. *Development occurs in an orderly and predictable sequence.* Development occurs from the top of the body to the bottom (cephalocaudal) and from the center of the body outwards (proximodistal). Cephalocaudal development works its way down from the head to the neck, trunk, and so forth. That is why an infant's head is proportionately so much larger than the rest of its body; the greatest growth in size, weight, and other features first occurs at the top of the body. Proximodistal development begins with the large trunk and arm muscles and works its way out to the smaller muscles in children's hands and fingers. That is why preschool children need lots of opportunities for large-muscle activities such as jumping, climbing, and running before they are expected to do activities that require control of the small muscles in their hands and fingers, such as writing and coloring in small spaces.

3. *Development proceeds at different rates within each individual and within each developmental area.* There is a wide range of individual variation in the timing of developmental changes that are influenced by biological and other sociocultural factors such as environment, family, temperament, learning style, and experience. Children first sit up, roll over, take a first step, lose a tooth, or learn to read at different rates. Only when children deviate considerably from the average ages for these developmental milestones is there cause to consider their development exceptional, either delayed or advanced.

4. *Development is greatly affected by the kinds of experiences children have.* Experiences are cumulative; therefore, they can either positively or negatively affect children's developing knowledge, skills, and attitudes. Experiences that occur regularly have more powerful, lasting effects than those that occur rarely. For example, children who hear a great deal of spoken language in the home and use books early and consistently are more likely to develop an understanding of the different functions of language, which is a clear advantage for later reading and writing. Conversely, young children who do not hear spoken language or have no experiences with books are often at a disadvantage for later literacy development.

5. *Development results from the interaction of each child's biological, environmental, and cultural influences.* No single theory adequately describes and explains the complex course of children's development. Today, it is widely accepted that three major factors—biological, environmental, and cultural—are so intertwined that their combination makes each person unique. *Biological influences* originate in the genes, which determine such characteristics as height, weight, metabolism, and brain development; *environmental influences* include such environmental experiences as language, nutrition, and health care; and *cultural influences* come from family, peers, community, and the media. If, for example, your genetic makeup predisposes you to healthy development but you have inadequate nutrition and medical care in your early years, your development will be adversely affected.

Essential Needs

Just as there are universal principles of development, there are universal basic needs that affect children's well-being. Even though each child has a unique personality, family situation,

Anthony Magnacca/Merrill

These children are the same chronological age; they show variation in the normal range of development.

and cultural background, *all children* have the same basic physical, social, emotional, and cognitive needs that contribute to their long-term healthy well-being and ability to thrive (Brazleton & Greenspan, 2001; Maslow, 1987; Santrock, 2007).

Minimal *physical needs* include food, clothing, shelter, and medical care. Basic *social and emotional needs* include a consistent and predictable relationship with an attentive, caring adult, strong peer acceptance, and freedom from abuse and discrimination (Maslow, 1987). Minimal *cognitive needs* include the "ability to communicate thoughts and feelings, to process information in a meaningful way, to engage in constructive problem-solving, and to experience success both at school and in the community" (White & Isenberg, 2003). How well early childhood professionals meet the following essential needs of children strongly influences what children will be like.

Need for Security and Safety

Children need to feel safe and valued. Their world must be predictable and include at least one adult upon whom they can depend. Feelings of security influence children's ability to take risks, explore, and establish a positive sense of self (Maslow, 1987). They also need to live in an environment that protects them from physical and psychological harm and exposure to violence.

Need for Love, Understanding, and Acceptance

Children of all ages need love and affection from the significant adults in their lives in order to thrive and feel supported. They also need adults in their lives who understand and accept them unconditionally as unique individuals throughout life. Young children need these nurturing relationships for most of their waking hours.

Need for Competency, Responsibility, and Independence

From the earliest years, children gradually need to learn to become competent and responsible for themselves and their own actions. Infants have a need to feed themselves, toddlers have a need to dress themselves, and school-age children have a need to use the tools of reading and writing that will help them be competent students. All children need realistic expectations and reasonable limits.

Need for Success, Guidance, and Respect

Closely related to children's need for competency is their need for success. Being successful in much of what they undertake helps children develop self-esteem, confidence, and motivation to learn. All children need reasonable limits, suitable to their level of understanding and development, that allow them to maintain their dignity and self-respect. And, in order for children to show respect for others, the adults who care for them must treat them with respect.

Developmental Milestones

All children develop in a universal sequence whose steps are often referred to as periods of development. Approximate age ranges that depict typical behaviors and abilities of children characterize each of these periods. As children develop, they face new and different demands and challenges. Knowing what children are like at these times will help you better use the most suitable methods to help them learn and grow. The following sections describe the developmental milestones of infants, toddlers, preschoolers and kindergartners, and school-age children.

What Are Infants Like?

Infancy, the first 12 months of life, is a time of total dependency on adults; it also is a time of the most rapid changes in development. By their first birthdays, infants, who were fully dependent upon adults to meet all of their needs as newborns, can often walk and feed themselves. Their well-being very much depends upon the nature of their early care and experiences. Infants vary in the rates at which they develop.

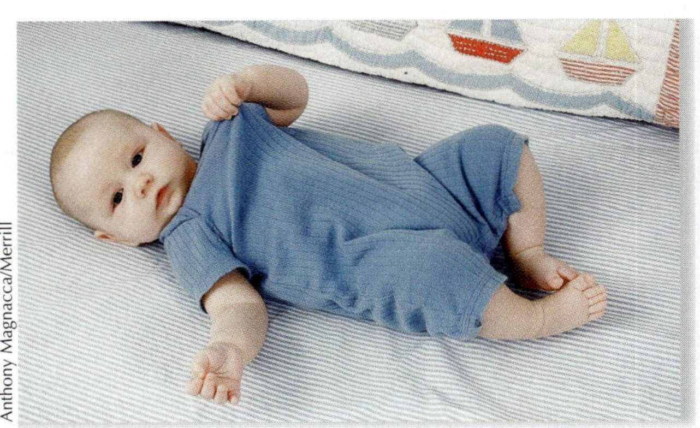
Anthony Magnacca/Merrill

Nancy Ritz/Merrill

Physical development is dramatic and rapid during the first year of life.

Physical/Motor Development

Physical development in infants is rapid and dramatic. Some of the more important milestones in infants' physical development are (a) increases in height and weight; (b) growth of the brain, bones, and muscles; and (c) a maturing central nervous system. During the first year, infants learn to sit up and move from place to place, hold and use objects, and increase their coordination. By 4 to 5 months of age, for example, an infant's birth weight will have doubled, and by 12 months, it will have tripled.

Social/Emotional Development

Healthy social and emotional development begins at birth. During infancy, children need to learn that they can trust and depend on those who care for them. Trust develops from consistency in the love, physical care, daily routines, and other experiences adults provide. Infants also must develop good feelings about themselves. They accomplish this by forming close attachments to loving, understanding adults who care for them and consistently meet their needs. By 6 months of age, infants need to have established one or more emotional ties to another human being—a process referred to as attachment. Developing trust and forming early attachments are both essential for children's mental health. These early attachments have an enduring effect on later social and emotional development and behavior.

Cognitive Development

Infants' cognitive development begins with reflexes (e.g., eye blinking, grasping), moves to simple motor movements centered around their own bodies and then to repeated actions, and eventually shows the beginnings of goal-directed behavior that makes things happen (Piaget, 1992). In just a few short months, infants' rapid cognitive development helps them to move from making things happen accidentally (e.g., making sounds by dropping a rattle) to deliberately making things happen by thinking about their actions (e.g., purposefully dropping a rattle to hear the sounds it makes). You can see an infant's deliberate actions in the "Cognitive Development–Infancy" video clip online at the Teacher Prep Website.

Go to Video Classroom, select Child Development, choose Physical Development (Module 2), and select Cognitive Development–Infancy (Video 5).

Language Development

Learning to speak and to understand what others say begins in the earliest days of infancy, when infants' parents or adult caretakers talk and respond to them. Babies listen to the words of the adults who care for them, begin to experiment with sounds, and try to repeat words they hear by cooing and babbling. Between 6 and 9 months of age, infants begin to name objects and imitate what they hear. Table 4.1 summarizes the major developmental milestones of infants.

Implications for Early Childhood Practitioners

As a caregiver for infants, you can provide regular and responsive care so that infants develop trusting relationships. You can nurture infants' development by preparing a rich, sensory, and safe environment in which infants are comfortable exploring new things. Caregivers must also engage in close personal contact, such as cuddling and the use of positive, soft voice tones during feeding and a quick response to their cries of distress.

TABLE 4.1 Developmental Milestones of Infants

Age	Physical/Motor	Social/Emotional	Cognitive	Language
1–3 months	• hold head up • hold rattle briefly • glance from one object to another • reach toward object	• begin to smile • use smiles and gurgles to get responses • prefer people to objects	• look at colorful objects and faces • practice sucking, looking, grasping, and crying • accidentally discover what their bodies can do (e.g., sucking thumb)	• are calmed by familiar voices • cry when uncomfortable • listen to voices and sounds • coo and babble • show startle response to sharp noises
3–6 months	• sit with support • double birth weight • visually follow ball • put objects in mouth • turn from stomach to back and then back to stomach • transfer object from hand to hand • grasp objects with thumb and four fingers	• begin to laugh • coo and smile at objects as well as people • cry in response to unpleasantness • anticipate and show interest in being picked up • show emotions: anger, surprise, sadness, fear	• try to make interesting sights and sounds last by repeating them (e.g., kicking to make a mobile move) • grasp reachable objects • recognize differences between self and objects • respond to their name • imitate interesting behavior	• have different cries for hunger, pain, and attention • babble with two syllables (e.g., ga-ga, goo-goo) • laugh • show interest in sounds • distinguish between friendly and angry sounds • imitate sounds • repeat vowels
6–9 months	• sit alone • crawl • pull string to obtain object • use pincer grasp • stand with help • need help to sit down again • show hand preference	• play social games (e.g., peek-a-boo and pat-a-cake) • sometimes react to strangers by screaming or crying • approach new situations and people with caution • consistently show emotions • shout to get attention • display shame and shyness	• intentionally try to make things happen (e.g., banging to make noise) • begin to recognize that objects can be used to cause things to happen (e.g., banging pot lids together to make noise)	• begin to understand first words • begin to say *mama* or *dada* and one or two other words • look at familiar objects when named • listen to own voice • respond to requests such as "Give me your rattle"
9–12 months	• push car along • pull up to stand beside furniture • take some steps • hold object with thumb and two fingers • triple birth weight	• may show possessiveness of adult by clinging or pushing others away • clearly communicate feelings and emotions • act socially toward other children by offering or taking away a toy • show affection by hugs • obey simple commands	• anticipate events (e.g., when mother gets the car keys, she is leaving) • look at object, reach for it, grasp it, and put it in mouth • search for hidden objects (e.g., look for a toy when they see it being hidden)	• babble to people • understand commonly used words and look at person saying them • understand 12 words (receptive vocabulary) • understand instructions (e.g., "Wave bye-bye") • speak first word between 10 and 15 months

What Are Toddlers Like?

The period of development from ages 1 to 3 can be somewhat challenging for toddlers and the adults caring for them. Toddlers are highly inquisitive and very active. They are determined to be independent and to make things happen. In addition, they tend to have frequent changes in mood. Because toddlers are into everything, they need constant supervision for their own safety. Toddlerhood is a time when children begin to become more competent and independent.

Physical/Motor Development

The average toddler is 32 to 36 inches tall and weighs 23 to 30 pounds. Even though physical growth slows during this period, toddlers' large muscles develop rapidly. Improved motor control, coordination, and balance keep toddlers constantly on the move, running, climbing, and jumping. As toddlers' small muscles develop, they become more skillful in using their hands; they can hold a cup with one hand, string beads, and stack objects. Although they are not skilled at dressing, they are quite skilled at undressing, particularly at undoing their shoes and taking off their socks. Toddlers use the new control they have over their bodies to express their feelings. They jump and chuckle when they are happy, and kick and scream when they are unhappy. Because their rate of growth has slowed, they need less food. Thus, many toddlers become fussy eaters and prefer to play with their food rather than eat it. They also begin to use the toilet alone, and they continue to need periods of rest and quiet during the day.

Social/Emotional Development

Toddlers seek independence from adults and show interest in children their own ages. They demand to do things for themselves and typically respond to requests with a resounding "No" or "Me do it!" These responses make them seem stubborn, willful, and defiant. In reality, however, they are simply trying to figure out who they are and to accomplish the important task of becoming more competent and independent. Toddlers also are meeting new expectations from parents and caregivers. When they were infants, the adults in their lives promptly and patiently responded to their needs and adjusted their own schedules to accommodate them. Now, these same adults often ask toddlers to wait and say "no" to them. Suddenly, toddlers' needs are not being met as promptly as they were during infancy, and conflicts arise. They often respond by crying or having temper tantrums.

Cognitive Development

Toddlers can recall and anticipate certain events they have experienced. For example, they not only ask for juice but also can remember where the juice is kept. This skill marks the beginning of memory. Toddlers also engage in imaginative play during which they act out their own ideas about objects and events without much regard for reality. What they think about their world depends upon the experiences they have. These early concepts about their world are the basis upon which later concepts are formed.

Language Development

Most toddlers understand about 300 words. From ages 2 to 3, they learn new words and grammatical forms at an astounding rate. They enjoy language for its rhythm and like to hear the same stories over and over again, more for the rhythm than the content. They also enjoy looking at books and magazines and naming familiar objects they see in pictures. Toddlers' first words name familiar people (e.g., *dada, mama*), animals (e.g., *kitty, doggie*), objects they see in pictures (e.g., *car, ball*); they also include social interaction terms (e.g., *bye bye, up*). Toddlers' speaking vocabulary includes single words that stand for a whole thought and averages 200 to 275 word by age 2 (Santrock, 2007). Table 4.2 lists some developmental milestones for toddlers.

TABLE 4.2 Developmental Milestones of Toddlers

Age	Physical/Motor	Social/Emotional	Cognitive	Language
12–18 months	**Gross motor** • stand alone • walk without support • climb onto chair • push and pull toys • roll ball using both hands • squat to pick up objects • move in place to music **Fine motor** • scribble on paper • pick up small objects with thumb and forefinger • feed self with fingers or spoon • pour, stack, and build • take off shoes and socks	• are deeply attached to adult who provides regular care • explore surroundings • can give and receive toys • enjoy chasing, hiding, and other games • play beside, but not with, other children • take turn rolling a ball	• try new ways to do things • imitate behavior of others • use trial-and-error method to learn • look at picture books	• say 2 words at 12 months, 4–5 words at 15 months, and 15–20 words by 18 months • use gestures, tone, and context • understand simple directions • repeat syllables • wave bye-bye • use words to make needs known
18–24 months	**Gross motor** • walk, run, and slide • throw and catch • balance self • bend to pick up objects • walk backward • imitate familiar adult behavior • move to music **Fine motor** • use cup and spoon awkwardly • turn 2–3 pages of book • place large pegs in pegboard • hold crayon in fist • squeeze toys	• anticipate expressions of love and return them • recognize self in mirror • show intense likes and dislikes • are easily distracted and entertained by others • alternate between dependence and independence from adults • understand ownership of own possessions • show disgust and guilt	• picture ideas, objects, and events in mind • think about and solve simple problems • imitate behavior seen days or even weeks earlier • are beginning to understand consequences of behavior	• understand simple questions • point to parts of body • have 20-word vocabulary at 18 months and a 272-word vocabulary by 24 months • use simple sentences and phrases by 24 months • begin to take turns in conversation • name familiar objects • "read" to doll or stuffed animal • fill in words in familiar stories
24–36 months	**Gross motor** • walk on toes • kick large ball • imitate animal movements • walk up and down stairs one at a time with alternating feet • ride tricycle • hang by hands from a support (e.g., jungle gym bar) • jump in place **Fine motor** • build towers • string 3–4 beads • manage spoon and fork • snip with scissors • hold crayon with thumb and forefinger • use one hand consistently • control grasp and release • find favorite pictures in books	• watch other children • make a choice between two alternatives • play house using simple role play • participate in small-group activities or 5–10 minutes • know gender identity • insist on doing things independently • take turns with one reminder • play alone for 15 minutes • express a range of emotions through actions, words, or facial expressions	• repond to simple directions • select and look at picture books, and identify several objects within one picture • touch and count 1–3 objects • match 4 colors • attempt to play with unfamiliar toys	• understand prepositions and pronouns • say "no" • use words to ask for things • make sounds for *p, m, n, w,* and *h* at the beginning of words • use question words (e.g., why, when) • use past tense and plurals • speak in 2- to 5-word sentences • understand negatives • enjoy simple storybooks for 10–15 minutes • read familiar book to self

Implications for Early Childhood Practitioners

Practitioners need to be protective, reassuring, and confident as toddlers assume self-care responsibilities of feeding, toileting, and dressing. They also need to provide toddlers with a variety of opportunities to develop initiative, autonomy, and self-reliance through the routines, schedules, simple choices, and clear limits that they need.

To enhance toddlers' language development, caregivers can teach toddlers the names of familiar objects and people such as chair, cup, and baby and support their efforts at saying new words. Looking at toddlers while talking with them, talking about what you are doing, and describing what they are doing is also important for practitioners.

What Are Preschoolers and Kindergartners Like?

The preschool-kindergarten period of development extends from 3 to 6 years. During this time, children show improved motor skills and make great strides in language development. Preschool and kindergarten children also become more self-sufficient in caring for themselves and begin to show less attachment to their parents. They engage in more complex play activities, are very curious, and want to explore their world outside their familiar surroundings. While older preschoolers and kindergartners show significant variation in aspects of their development, they typically have increased their ability to work cooperatively with others, to reason differently, to control their emotions, and to use verbal and written communication more skillfully.

Physical/Motor Development

Physical development during the preschool years is steady. During this time, children's height increases each year by about 2 to 3 inches and their weight by about 4 to 6 pounds. Their body proportions change from chunky and chubby to lean and tall, and their muscles, bones, and brains continue to develop (Puckett & Black, 2005). By age 5, children's brains have reached about 90% of their adult weight, and myelination, the process that facilitates the transfer of messages, makes children's increased motor abilities possible. Preschoolers and kindergartners are usually very active and have lots of energy. **Gross motor** (i.e., large muscle) skills are rapidly expanding, and children show increased facility with their arms, hands, and legs. They enjoy practicing their newly learned hopping, throwing, catching, and jumping skills. **Fine motor** (i.e., small muscle) skills become more refined, thus enabling children to perform such self-help skills as buckling, snapping, buttoning, and zipping. Mastering these skills involves a great deal of work and practice, but children enjoy the challenge. Older preschoolers and kindergarten children become even more agile; they show interest in sports, noncompetitive games, and physical fitness (Berk, 2005; Puckett & Black, 2005). Because of their increased fine motor skills, they communicate more in writing and can print recognizable letters and numbers. They do, however, often make letter reversals and write mirror images of letters.

Social/Emotional Development

Preschool and kindergarten children begin to spend more time with people outside their own families. They have a strong need to be with and accepted by other children of similar ages, and often become very attached to their playmates. They are generally happy, curious, compliant, imaginative, and pleased with their own ability to plan and complete projects, which are primarily carried out in imaginative play activities. New experiences interest them and they want to know more about other people, what other people do, and what they themselves are capable of doing. They spend much time experimenting with adult roles they have observed. Preschoolers show increased autonomy, yet they still move back and forth between their need to be independent and their need to be dependent. Although the ability to delay gratification of their needs and wants has increased, they still become easily frustrated, cannot tolerate waiting, and frequently cry when things do not go their way. Many children also experience an expanding range of emotions and learn how to express these emotions in socially acceptable ways. Fear and anxiety are common emotions during these years. Many preschoolers typically fear the dark, unfamiliar animals, and potentially dangerous situations such as fire or deep water. By the end of this period of development, most children outgrow these fears.

Cognitive Development

From the ages of 3 to 6, children's thinking is a combination of fantasy and reality, and their understanding is based upon their own limited experiences. Young preschoolers focus primarily on what they see in their immediate surroundings and upon present events. They have difficulty with concepts related to the past and the future, and they are able to think aloud about only one idea at a time. As they become more mature and have more experiences, preschoolers' thinking becomes more objective and realistic. Older preschoolers and kindergartners, for example, can sort objects by more than one attribute (e.g., color, size, shape), but their thinking is not systematic and they stop in the middle of what they are doing and go on to something else. Children between the ages of 3 and 6 ask many "why" questions. Although they sometimes do this to get attention, generally their questions stem from their strong need to find out about their world. This process of asking questions and finding out about things helps them learn. You can see an older preschool child grouping seashells by more than one attribute in the "Intelligence–Early Childhood" video clip online at the Teacher Prep Website.

TEACHER PREP WEBSITE 4.2

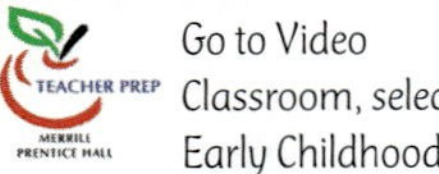

Go to Video Classroom, select Early Childhood Education, choose Child Development (Module 1), and select Intelligence–Early Childhood (Video 4).

Language Development

Children's vocabularies increase rapidly during this period. Usually, 3-year-olds have vocabularies of 200 to 250 words, 5-year-olds have vocabularies of about 2,500 words, and the vocabularies of 6-year-olds consist of about 20,000 words. Preschoolers usually understand more words than they actually speak. Most preschoolers love to talk and are curious about words. Sometimes, however, they use words that they do not understand merely for the practice and pleasure that new words bring. In doing this, they give the impression that they understand what they are saying. Adults, therefore, must be careful not to assume that young children understand all of the words they use. Table 4.3 describes the major developmental milestones of preschool and kindergarten children.

Implications for Early Childhood Practitioners

Adults who work with preschoolers and kindergarteners should provide a wide variety of interesting materials that encourage children to make and act on their choices of activities and offer opportunities for children to experience success. They are tolerant of children's learning mistakes, encourage children's independence, set reasonable expectations for each child's skill and ability levels, and make available a variety of authentic, real-life experiences.

TABLE 4.3 Developmental Milestones of Preschoolers/Kindergartners

Age	Physical/Motor	Social/Emotional	Cognitive	Language
3 years	**Gross motor** • stand on one foot briefly • kick and throw ball • ride tricycles • use swings, slides, and climbers; walk on tiptoes • do forward somersault **Fine motor** • make simple drawings • dress and undress self but will still ask for help • copy figures (e.g., 1) • cut paper • paste with forefinger • build eight-block towers	• like to please adults • have occasional, short temper tantrums • look to adults for security, recognition, and encouragement • take turns, share, and use language to settle disputes • try to follow directions • show interest in family activities • may act like a baby • accept suggestions • test limits	• stack objects by size • understand simple questions,statements, and directions • ask many questions and understand more words than they use • count by rote and recognize some letter names • like rhythm, repetition, and humor • put simple geometric shapes into correct slots	• use familiar words and longer sentences with plurals and past tense • talk to self • play with language for fun and practice • name objects, people and events in a picture • recite nursery rhymes and poems
4 years	**Gross motor** • balance self • run, jump, climb, and hop in place skillfully • bounce and catch ball • build bridges with blocks • walk backward **Fine motor** • copy *O* and *X* • use fork and safe knife • follow lines when cutting paper • use zippers and buttons • print letters • draw simple recognizable figures	• are proud of what they can do • prefer playmates of their own age • seek attention by showing off, making up stories, and being silly • express displeasure loudly and through aggression • tolerate some frustration • are developing a sense of humor • like nonsense words • show a balance between dependence and independence	• know own sex, age, and last name • point to six basic colors when asked • give long answers to questions • draw what they know • have limitless imagination • see differences among some shapes and colors • show interest in books and printed words • count objects when touching them	• answer out loud to "Hi" and "How are you?" • speak clearly in sentences • make up words • ask many "how" and "why" questions • speak of imaginary conditions • tell tall tales • use adverbs and 5 word sentences • like repetition of sounds and words
5 years	**Gross motor** • run on tiptoe • skip, jump rope, and walk a straight line • roll ball to hit objects • ride two-wheeled bicycle with training wheels • dribble and bounce ball **Fine motor** • copy designs, letters, and numbers • cut, paste, and fold paper • grip pencil correctly • show handedness • copy the numerals 1–10 and a triangle	• play together with others • enjoy visiting friends alone • cooperate with adults and peers • recognize the rights of others • try to conform to rules • generally feel good about themselves and their world	• understand yesterday, today, and tomorrow • know difference between reality and fantasy • can remember more than two ideas for a short time • have keen interest in numbers and counting • remember own address • identify pennies, nickels, and dimes • ask for information and facts • hear differences and similarities in letter sounds • remember number, letter, and counting sequences	• use sentences with correct grammar • talk to others with poise • ask direct questions and want real answers • use longer sentences with connectors (e.g., *but, because*) • are interested in word meanings • try out new words and can define some simple words • like stories • understand nouns and verbs

What Are School-Age Children Like?

School-age children, ages 6 to 8, also show dramatic changes in development. They are losing temporary teeth and gaining permanent teeth, their motor coordination continues to be refined, and they work hard at mastering the basic skills of reading, writing, and mathematics. School-age children's thinking also changes during this period as it becomes more orderly and logical. Friends assume an important role in their lives, and school-age children become increasingly aware of how they look to others (Berk, 2005; Santrock, 2007; Wood, 1997). Older school-age children prefer to work with peers of the same sex. Most school-age children delight in group projects and activities, have a delightful sense of humor, and respond to adults with beaming smiles when praised and sad looks when they are criticized.

Physical/Motor Development

The average school-age child is 45 to 51 inches in height and weighs from 45.5 pounds at age 6 to 60 pounds at age 8 for boys and somewhat less for girls. As children grow taller, their body proportions shift. During this period, their vision becomes sharper, they still have frequent illnesses, and they tire easily. Gross motor skills include such fundamental movements as running, kicking, and reaching, which prepare children for the more complex coordination needed to play organized sports. Playground games such as tag and hopscotch are very popular and important for school-age children. Fine motor development is evident in greater dexterity and control over drawing and writing, which makes copying from the chalkboard easier (Puckett & Black, 2005; Wood, 1997). Older school-age children produce smaller and more detailed pieces of art.

Social/Emotional Development

School-age children are now more responsible and independent, are more prosocial in their peer interactions, work harder at making friends, and are more self-critical. Younger school-age children still seek adult approval and tend to tattle, whereas older school-age children are more interested in forming clubs and selected groups. Older children also have fears and worries that they carefully mask; these take the form of nail biting, inattention, or changed eating and sleeping patterns.

Todd Yarrington/Merrill

The school-age child is learning to use symbols and understand detailed information.

Cognitive Development

School-age children are eager, curious, and delightful learners who thrive on opportunities to discover and invent. They rely on learning through such forms of play as puppet shows, story retellings, games, and secret codes. Younger school-age children's thinking is intuitive and based on concrete, active experiences. Older school-age children's thinking changes from an intuitive, concrete understanding to a more logical understanding. They can now think, plan, and reflect on what they are learning but their thinking, while growing more abstract, still needs to be related to familiar experiences. Older school-age children have a more focused attention span that enables them to assess their accomplishments; they also have more permanently stored information in their brain's memory that allows them to access information to facilitate learning. These abilities enable them to begin to understand differences, cause and effect, and multiple perspectives (Springer, 1999).

Language Development

School-age children have a good understanding of both oral and written language. Their oral language is quite adultlike, and they tend to dominate conversations. Their talk gleefully includes metaphors, jokes, puns, and riddles, because they now understand multiple meanings. They also use language to communicate their feelings and understand and use more appropriate grammatical structures such as plurals, possessives, and past tense in their oral and written language. Their vocabularies continue to expand, and they show a new interest in the meanings of words. The written language of school-age children typically includes invented spellings, which are evidence of their understanding of the connection between letters and sounds. Table 4.4 describes the major developmental milestones of school-age children.

Implications for Early Childhood Practitioners

Adults who work with school-age children need to provide developmentally appropriate materials and resources, such as projects, hands-on and other concrete, investigative activities, that offer opportunities for school-age children to set and achieve realistic goals. Teachers also need to communicate to all children that they can master the basic knowledge and skills in academic subjects by focusing children's attention on the progress they are making rather than stressing the deficits in their learning. In addition, teachers of school-age children need to ensure flexibility in the curriculum, respond to individual differences, and take advantage of these children's emerging ability to teach each other.

The miniportraits provided in Tables 4.1 through 4.4 of widely held developmental milestones of children from birth through age 8 can be a powerful tool for you. They can help you know what to expect and what challenges children may face at different periods of development. They also can give you a framework for understanding how to meet the needs of all children.

> **PAUSE AND REFLECT**
>
> **About Characteristics of Young Children**
>
> Think about a child you know very well. Make a list of the three most important age-related characteristics of that child—characteristics that you think a teacher ought to know to optimize the child's development. Use at least two of the developmental domains just discussed (i.e., physical/motor, social/emotional, cognitive, and language). Now that you have this information, what do you think this child needs to develop optimally?

Your Role in Promoting Children's Development

Child development is the study of the changes that occur in children from conception through middle childhood. As a teacher, you will be making hundreds of daily decisions about children that are based, in part, on their development. A good example of decision making based on child development comes from Ms. Cochran, a first-grade teacher.

> One of Ms. Cochran's first graders, Vu, is a 6-year-old bilingual child who reads fluently. During free choice time, children select from a variety of hands-on materials and

TABLE 4.4 Developmental Milestones of School-Age Children

Age	Physical/Motor	Social/Emotional	Cognitive	Language
6 years	**Gross motor** • enjoy challenging acrobatics and outdoor activities • ride two-wheel bike • can do standing long jumps • begin to use a bat **Fine motor** • have good visual tracking • make simple figures with clay • sew simple stitches • use table knife for spreading food	• are competitive and enthusiastic • test boundaries • can be bossy, teasing, and critical of others • get upset easily when hurt • believe in rules for others but not self • have pride in work • like surprises • enjoy routines and have difficulty with transitions	• use symbols • work in spurts • begin to use logic • can put stories and events in sequence • sort and classify information, groups, and objects	• explain things in detail • use enthusiastic language • have some speech irregularities
7 years	**Gross motor** • balance on one foot • walk on balance beam • hop and jump in small spaces • can do jumping jacks **Fine motor** • brush and comb hair • use table knife for cutting	• are sometimes moody and shy • rely on adults for help • are afraid to make mistakes • are sensitive to others' feelings • have strong likes and dislikes • draw and write about same theme repeatedly • are eager for adult acceptance	• engage in abstract thinking • like maps and detailed information	• talk with precision • converse easily with others • are curious about word meaning • send notes and use secret codes
8 years	**Gross motor** • are highly energetic and agile • alternate hopping to a beat • enjoy rough-and-tumble play • have coordinated skills for sports **Fine motor** • use common household tools (i.e., hammer, screwdriver)	• have keen awareness of adult and child worlds • show disappointment when things do not go their way • crave acceptance from peers and adults	• classify and sort spontaneously • discover, invent, and take things apart to investigate how they work • want perfection and erase constantly • work slowly	• explain things in detail • use enthusiastic language • have some speech irregularities

usually interact in small groups or pairs. Vu chooses to work alone and seldom speaks with his classmates. During these times, Ms. Cochran talks with Vu about what he is doing. While he does answer her, the conversation is very one-sided—initiated by Ms. Cochran and finished when she no longer asks questions or makes comments. Ms. Cochran has observed that Vu also needs help taking turns, sharing, cleaning up, using words to ask for something or to respond to a question or request, and during transitions. Based on her observations of Vu and what she knows about 6-year-olds, Ms. Cochran spoke with other specialists and Vu's parents to see how to best meet Vu's developmental needs.

Ms. Cochran is demonstrating her role in promoting children's development. Even though child development knowledge is essential for all early childhood professionals, it alone is not sufficient. Your role in using child development knowledge can be guided in the following ways.

1. ***Possess a thorough knowledge of child development.*** Early childhood practitioners rank knowledge of child development as the number one competency needed by teachers. Ms. Cochran knows that 6-year-olds typically talk to other children and the teacher in one-to-one, small-group, and large-group interactions. Vu was not using oral language in these ways. Using this knowledge, Ms. Cochran developed strategies to help Vu acquire the social skills he needs to become a more integral part of the group. She spoke with Vu's parents and encouraged them to establish a playtime for Vu each week, to have him play with children his own age, and to spend time talking with him at home.
2. ***Be a keen observer of children.*** Observation is essential for understanding and responding to children. It is your basic tool—your eyes and ears—and gives you important information about children's needs, interests, and strengths. Knowing what typical behavior is at certain ages enables you to observe and compare against expected behavior. When children's development is not typical, your documented observations provide the evidence needed to identify a child who may require additional services from other professionals such as a pediatrician, counselor, speech and language specialist, or social worker. In the preceding scenario, Ms. Cochran was aware that Vu's social development and oral language development were not typical of 6-year-olds and sought early support for him.
3. ***Create safe, caring, and appropriate environments for all children.*** All children need supportive environments for their optimal development. They also need adults who view them as unique, who know as much as they can about them, and who will adjust their goals based on each child's strengths, culture, interests, and abilities. Through her commitment to creating a supportive environment, Ms. Cochran enlisted lots of support for Vu. She knew that Vu needed to develop social skills, so she began asking him questions that could not be answered with a simple "yes" or "no." She also knew that children from Vu's culture often speak only when spoken to. Thus, Ms. Cochran arranged for other student helpers that Vu could contact if he needed something, and she chose children to be helpers who already had a trusting relationship established with Vu. These practices illustrate the importance of using child development knowledge to help children develop the necessary knowledge, skills, and abilities they need to be successful learners (Berk, 2005; Santrock, 2007).
4. ***Develop children's social and emotional competence.*** We know that teachers who establish firm boundaries, foster warm personal relationships in the classroom, and encourage students to have a say about their learning strengthen students' attachments to school, their interest in learning, their ability to refrain from self-destructive behaviors, and their positive behaviors (Goleman, 1998). Ms. Cochran's concern for Vu's well-being, feelings, and social competence clearly will help Vu to become part of the classroom community where his emotional and social competence is valued and cultivated.

To learn more about fulfilling your role in promoting children's development and the NAEYC, go to *Web Links* in Chapter 4 of the Companion Website at http://www.prenhall.com/jalongo.

The Collaborating with Families feature on the next page provides two strategies for helping families gain insight into the role of children's development in schools and learning.

COLLABORATING WITH FAMILIES

Is This Typical? Insights into Child Development

Many parents want to know if their child's behavior is typical of other children that age. They usually follow that question with, "What should I do?" Here are two suggestions that address parents' concerns about their child's development.

1. Conduct a family informational meeting on typical child development and show how your curriculum relates to the developmental levels of the children in your class. Ask family members to bring in a picture of them when they were the age of the children in your class. Have them share a memory of something they liked to do at that age. Compare their memories to the developmental levels and discuss what they remember as being easy or difficult at that particular age.
2. A teacher whose own children are grown and independent keeps pictures of them when they were her students' age on her desk. She tells families that the pictures help her to remember the needs and interests of children at that age as well as her hopes for how her own children would be taught and cared for by their teachers. Teachers who have no children could do the same with their own or another family member's picture.

These suggestions are a beginning for using your growing child development knowledge to help families make thoughtful decisions about what their children need and how best to support them.

Why Understanding Children's Development Is Important

Children develop faster during the first 5 years than at any other stage of their lives. In these critical early years, they are not only establishing the basic foundations for physical, cognitive, and social/emotional development, but also are forming beliefs, attitudes, and behavior patterns that influence how they view themselves and the world in which they live. As a teacher, the more you know about children's development, the more appropriate your teaching will be. Making good professional decisions considers children's brain development, exceptional learning needs, and cultural and social backgrounds. We will discuss each of these important aspects of child development separately.

The Brain and Children's Development

The human brain, the mind's organ, is deeply affected and shaped by its experiences. In fact, the same stimulus processes that shape the developing brain are also responsible for storing information and developing new skills throughout one's life. Thus, we can say that the brain mediates everything we were, are, and will be. Brain development is best understood when considered in relation to other areas of development because those developmental areas help us understand what is happening with the brain. Children's capabilities in each area of development mirror their brain development at any given time. For example, we know what is happening with children's brains as we see evidence of their developing visual skills, language capacity, or motor abilities.

COMPANION WEBSITE 4.3 For more information about child development, go to *Web Links* in Chapter 4 of the Companion Website at http://www.prenhall.com/jalongo.

ASK THE EXPERT

Rosalind Charlesworth on the Importance of Child Development and Early Childhood Education

How do theories of child development apply to all of our diverse populations?

Theories of child development can serve as guides for assessing children's developmental levels. They can help us know what children's competencies are and where we should begin instruction. Theories of development can also guide planning instruction for individuals and for groups. The constructivist theories of Piaget and Vygotsky are especially helpful in leading us to developmentally appropriate instruction. Concepts such as that of children constructing knowledge through their exploration of the world while adults determine their zone of proximal development and scaffold their learning experiences within the zone are invaluable. These concepts, along with Erikson's psychosocial theory, support the importance of play as the major vehicle for learning during early childhood. Interpretations of these theories may differ across cultures but provide a foundation for early childhood planning and practice.

If I consider development as the foundation of early childhood education, as in the concept of developmentally appropriate practice, will my classroom be unstructured?

Frequently I hear the comment that there are "structured programs" and "developmentally appropriate programs," which carries the implication that developmentally appropriate programs lack structure. Structure is necessary for any program in several areas: classroom space, guidance techniques, instructional methods, materials, curriculum, and assessment. Structure based on the development of young children includes some of the following factors:

- Classroom space is clearly divided into a variety of learning areas. The space includes table areas, a soft carpeted area, floor areas used as instructional space, and centers with open shelves where children can select materials.
- Guidance techniques should be clear, consistent, positive, and inductive; time blocks are broad and flexible but follow a consistent routine; children have choices of activities that fit their competencies, interests, and learning styles; children are involved in rule-making.
- Instructional methods include whole-class, small-group, and individual activities as appropriate; children are encouraged to construct their own knowledge; focus is on creative thinking and problem solving; peer interaction is encouraged; and play is the major vehicle for learning.
- Materials are carefully organized, are concrete and open-ended and promote creativity. Firsthand experiences are provided.
- Curriculum is guided by standards and scope and sequence but adapted for individual children's development; content is integrated; and there is equal emphasis on cognitive, affective, and psychomotor areas of development.
- Assessment is an organized process conducted mainly through observations and individual interviews as children work with appropriate materials. Daily observations provide information used for planning and relate to children's current competencies and interests. Planning can then focus on age, individual, and culturally appropriate teaching strategies.

With the increasing emphasis on standards and assessment, it seems that only cognitive development is important. What will happen to an emphasis on affective and psychomotor development?

All three areas of development are closely intertwined. The elements of self-concept in all three developmental areas combine to build children's self-esteem during their everyday experiences. Doing away with recess, physical education, the arts, and peer interaction in favor of more time on drill-and-practice academics does not necessarily increase achievement but *does* increase opportunities for failure. Children are more likely to learn the skills and knowledge required by standards through an integrated curriculum that focuses on practices that support all children's learning styles and provides learning opportunities based on the developmental strengths of young children. Instructional strategies focus on children being physically active, social, and creative.

Rosalind Charlesworth is Professor Emerita at Weber State University, Ogden, Utah.

Brain development continues throughout the lifespan and is consistent with the lifelong capacities for thinking, feeling, and adapting. Young children's brains are more plastic (impressionable) than those of older children and adults. On one hand, this means that young children's brains are more likely to develop typically and be open to learning from the enriching influences in their lives; on the other hand, this means that young children are also more vulnerable to atypical development should the learning and environmental influences in their lives be impoverished. Recent research on brain development provides educators with knowledge of the positive and negative influences on healthy brain development (Gallagher, 2005; Shonkoff & Phillips, 2001). Figure 4.1 identifies the key facts on brain development as well as the positive and negative influences.

Learners with Exceptionalities

By now you are probably aware that there will be all kinds of learners in the settings in which you will teach. Some may have physical or learning disabilities; others may have special gifts or talents. A *disability* is defined as "an inability to do something or a diminished capacity to perform in a specific way" (Hallahan & Kauffman, 2006, p. 7). Though exceptional learners need individualized supports and services to help them develop, learn, and be successful in school, they also need to have their *abilities* recognized and nurtured. The term *exceptional learner* refers either to children with disabilities or children with gifts and talents.

Although you are not expected to have in-depth knowledge of every disability, gift, or talent, you do need to learn about specific needs of the children in your setting. As an early childhood educator, you will interact with these learners in the same positive manner as you would with every other child, because children with exceptionalities are more similar to than they are different from other children. They have the same basic needs to be cared for adequately, be treated fairly, and be successful. It is beyond the scope of this book to discuss each category of special needs. However, we do want to introduce you to important legislation and services, categories of disabilities, and the notion of inclusion for children with disabilities as well as some characteristics of children with gifts and talents that are important aspects of their development.

FIGURE 4.1 Facts about brain development.

Brain development in the prenatal period of development:

- Brain growth begins shortly after conception and develops rapidly during the prenatal period. The brain develops more quickly than other organs or limbs.
- By the 6th prenatal month, the brain contains nearly all of the billions of neurons of a mature brain. The brain creates about 250,000 new neurons every minute. New neurons migrate to the areas of the brain where they will function.

Brain development after birth:

- Infants' brains are not fully formed at birth. Brain growth reaches 70% of its adult weight by age 2, 90% by age 6, and full weight by puberty.
- Neurons have specialized functions and form connections (*synapses*) with other neurons that enable them to store information.
- The brains of young children generate more synapses than the mature brain needs to function efficiently. Thus, the brain *prunes* unused synapses to make it operate more efficiently and *retains* synapses that are used often.
- Individual experiences foster new brain growth and refine existing brain structures that make each individual brain unique.

IMPLICATIONS FOR HEALTHY BRAIN DEVELOPMENT

Healthy brain development requires stimulation in all domains. The following effective early childhood practices contribute to healthy brain development:

- Talking, singing, reading, and playing with children.
- Protection from environmental hazards, such as alcohol and household chemicals.
- Proper prenatal and postnatal care, such as immunizations and nutrients for mother and baby.
- Environments that provide rich and varied experiences with age-appropriate expectations.

BARRIERS TO HEALTHY BRAIN DEVELOPMENT

Inadequate stimulation limits the number of synapses the brain generates. If not used, the synapses do not develop, leading to a child's difficulty in learning and in developing healthy social and emotional relationships. The following experiences lead to unhealthy brain development:

- Exposure to hazardous drugs (e.g., alcohol, heroin), viruses (e.g., HIV), and environmental toxins (e.g., lead and mercury)
- Diet lacking iron and folic acid
- Chronic maternal stress
- Head injuries from child abuse and neglect
- Environments that lack rich and varied experiences and have unrealistic expectations

SOURCES: Data based on Berk, 2005; Gallagher, 2005; and Thompson, 2001.

Children with Disabilities

Legislation

Since the mid-1970s, a variety of federal laws have been enacted to ensure that educational needs are met for children with exceptionalities and that the abilities of children with disabilities are recognized. These laws provide funding and guidelines for federal, state, and local schools and agencies to educate eligible children with disabilities from birth through age 21 in the most effective settings. In addition, the laws require that classroom aides or resources, specialized training for classroom teachers, therapy services, family training and counseling, and home visits be made available when needed. Table 4.5 lists the major federal laws and describes the eligibility guidelines for service.

TABLE 4.5 Legislation for Children with Exceptionalities

Law	Year	Major Highlights
Public Law 94-142, Education for All Handicapped Children (EHA)	1975	• identifies and provides all children between the ages of 3 and 5 with developmental disabilities with a free, appropriate public education • describes processes and procedures for determining eligibility for free intervention services • mandates provision of other services including transportation, testing, diagnosis, and parental rights to due-process hearings if parents disagree with an eligibility decision
Public Law 99-457, Education of the Handicapped Act Amendments	1986	• mandates intervention services for children with developmental delays or who are at risk for developmental delays from birth through age 2 • requires that intervention services for very young children be provided in settings in which other infants and toddlers are being educated, such as child-care settings, preschools, and family-care settings • requires family involvement in decision making and in plans for the transition to preschool special education programs • mandates an individualized family service plan (IFSP) for infants and toddlers that includes goals, needed services, and plans for implementation
Public Law 101-476, Individuals with Disabilities Education Act (IDEA) (Amended with same name 1997) (Reauthorized in 2004)	1990	• reauthorizes and extends PL 94-142 • changes language from "handicapped children" to "children with disabilities" and adds autism and traumatic brain injury to eligible categories for services • mandates that each state and local government must pay most of the costs of special education programs and must determine its own criteria and evaluation process for determining eligibility for services • critical mandates include the following: — identifying and screening all children with disabilities — free, appropriate public education — least restrictive environment (i.e., where possible, children are placed in regular education settings) — individualized education program (IEP) (i.e., written program for each child with a disability) — due process (i.e., schools and parents may protest an eligibility decision) — parental or guardian participation (i.e., they are to be included in all decision making)
Americans with Disabilities Act (ADA)	1990	• civil rights legislation that ensures that individuals with disabilities are protected from discrimination in the workplace and in all public facilities

Categories of Disabilities

The Individuals with Disabilities Education Act (IDEA) of 1990 lists 13 different disabilities that qualify children for special education services. Identifying these disabilities, their basic characteristics, and the services available for such children is essential to fulfilling your role in promoting the development of exceptional learners in a regular education setting. These 13 categories are:

1. ***Autism:*** a developmental disability that affects verbal and nonverbal communication and social interactions. Children who are autistic either do not speak or have immature speech patterns and limited understanding of ideas.

2. ***Deafness:*** a hearing impairment that ranges from mild to severe. Children classified as deaf cannot process language without an amplification device.
3. ***Deaf-blindness:*** a combined hearing and visual impairment that causes severe communication and related educational problems. These children must be educated in programs that attend to both disabilities.
4. ***Hearing impairment:*** a sensory, physical disability that can be temporary or permanent and adversely affects children's speaking abilities.
5. ***Mental retardation:*** a cognitive delay in which children consistently function below the level of the average population.
6. ***Multiple disabilities:*** two or more disabilities that result in motor and sensory deficiencies, delay development, and affect learning.
7. ***Orthopedic impairment:*** a motor skill impairment that impedes self-help, motor skills, and other areas of development. It includes such impairments as clubfoot and impairments caused by other diseases such as cerebral palsy.
8. ***Other health impairment:*** ongoing medical attention for such health problems as heart conditions, sensory integration issues, asthma, epilepsy, and diabetes. Although these health problems do not directly affect children's ability to learn, they often affect development in a negative way because these children have limited physical and mental energy.
9. ***Serious emotional disorders:*** social/emotional disabilities include abnormal social relations, bizarre mannerisms, inappropriate social behavior, and unusual language that interfere with a child's daily adaptation.
10. ***Specific learning disability:*** a processing disorder in children with normal intelligence that may occur in the areas of memory, visual and auditory discrimination and association, perceptual motor skills, attending, or verbal expression, all of which lead to an inability to remember, express ideas, focus on tasks, or discriminate between likeness and difference.
11. ***Speech or language impairment:*** a communication disorder that includes stuttering, impaired articulation, or an inability to gain meaning from language that is basic to many of the other disabilities listed here, especially hearing impairment, mental retardation, and specific learning disability. You can find instructional strategies to facilitate language development of 5 years-old Karen and identify advantages and disadvantages to encouraging her language usage through leadership roles in the "Special Education–Communication Disorders" student and teacher artifacts online at the Teacher Prep Website.
12. ***Traumatic brain injury:*** a neurological impairment caused by an outside influence that results in brain injury, either temporary or permanent, that may affect one or more areas of developmental functioning. This is a new category of disability under IDEA (1990) that provides services for children with brain injury.
13. ***Visual impairment:*** a disability that affects normal development, even with correction, including those with low vision, partial sightedness, or legal blindness.

Being knowledgeable about the different categories of needs that qualify for services is an important first step for all adults in regular early childhood settings. It will help your interactions with children who exhibit any of these special needs and perhaps help you to provide resources to them early, which will positively affect their development.

TEACHER PREP WEBSITE 4.3

Go to Student and Teacher Artifacts, select Special Education, choose Communication Disorders (Module 11), and select Leadership Roles Encourage Language in the Classroom (Artifact 1).

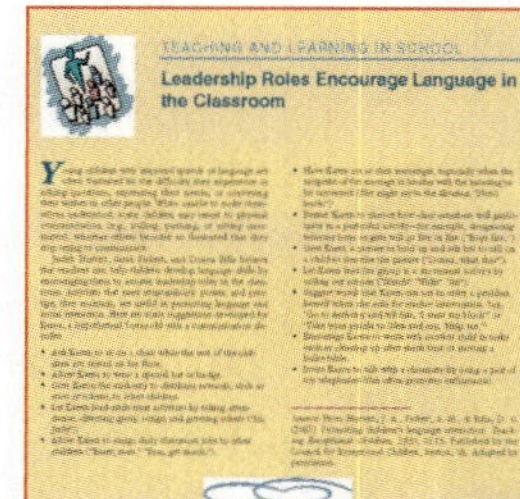
TEACHING AND LEARNING IN SCHOOL

Leadership Roles Encourage Language in the Classroom

ASK THE EXPERT

Richard M. Gargiulo on Young Children with Exceptional Needs

Richard M. Gargiulo

Why are so many early childhood teachers afraid or reluctant to teach young children with exceptional needs?

This perception is unfounded. Young children with disabilities are more like their typically developing classmates than they are different. I strongly encourage teachers to remember that a child with exceptionalities is first and foremost a child. Just because a child has exceptional needs should never prohibit professionals from realizing just how typical he or she is in many other ways. Good teachers look for similarities between all children and their peers, not differences. It is vitally important that early childhood teachers focus on the child, not the impairment; separate the abilities from the disability; and see the child's strengths, not the weaknesses.

In what kind of environment should I teach young children with exceptional needs?

Contemporary thinking suggests that *all* young children with exceptional needs should receive intervention and educational services in settings designed for children without those needs, that is, in typical environments such as child-care centers, Head Start programs, or regular classrooms. Known as *full inclusion,* this concept has evolved into one of the most controversial and complex practices in the field of early childhood education. Some early childhood educators mistakenly believe that federal laws require us to educate children with exceptional needs only in general education classrooms. This simply is not true. Where appropriate, we need to educate young children with exceptional needs in the least restrictive environment, that is, with their typically developing peers. This, of course, implies the need for a continuum of placement options. To illustrate, some children with exceptionalities need a more restrictive setting, such as a preschool program for children with disabilities or for children with multiple impairments, which is a more appropriate environment than a private preschool or a public school kindergarten.

If children with disabilities are so much like their typical counterparts and there is a push for full inclusion, why are early childhood teachers in the field of special education prepared differently from their classmates?

This is a perfectly valid question. I wonder the same thing. In fact, I believe the time is right for a collaborative or integrative personnel preparation program. Support for this proposal is growing both in early childhood circles and in the field of special education. I believe we need to develop a seamless or inclusive model for preparing teachers of young children so that all are prepared to teach all children regardless of the type of setting they work in. We teach children, not disability labels. A unified model of preparation makes good sense. Preservice teachers could draw upon effective practices from both fields and thus provide services that are age and developmentally appropriate while also being responsive to the individual needs of each learner. I am convinced that young children need teachers with multiple competencies capable of providing effective instruction in a variety of settings. Such professionals will be well suited to meet the challenges of today's workplace.

Richard M. Gargiulo is a Professor of Education at the University of Alabama at Birmingham.

Inclusion

Inclusion is a way of educating all children with exceptionalities in the most natural settings within their community, particularly in the early years (Division for Early Childhood of the

Council for Exceptional Children, 1993; Guralnick, 2001; Hallahan & Kauffman, 2006). As a teacher of young children, it is important that you create an environment that maximizes the learning potential for *all* children and adapt instruction to meet individual needs, be able to assess children's performance adequately, know when and if to refer a child, and be ready to participate in eligibility and IEP conferences. Advocates of *full inclusion* believe that all children, no matter what their disability, should be educated in the regular education classroom, with both special and regular educators sharing joint responsibility in a team-teaching model (Bergen, 2003). These educators do not believe that separating children with disabilities into isolated classrooms allows them to develop to their fullest potential. However, others support *partial inclusion,* a model that provides assistance when and where needed as well as the full-inclusion option (Bergen, 2003). They argue that full inclusion may not meet the unique needs of all children either academically or socially because these children need more intensive, individualized instruction, and separate, specialized settings that ensure an appropriate education.

Children with Special Gifts and Talents

Gifted children are characterized by high academic ability; talented children show excellence in such areas as art, music, drama, or sports. A gift or talent can occur in one or more areas of development. In a regular early childhood setting, children with special gifts and talents need to be challenged and stimulated just as every other child. Intellectually gifted children progress faster than their peers academically and often have a deep interest in books and reading, large vocabularies, a wide range of interests, and a desire to learn. To maintain their motivation they need a nurturing classroom social climate; learning activities that are challenging, relevant to their personal interests, and sometimes individualized; and teaching methods that match their learning styles (Hallahan & Kauffman, 2006).

Children with exceptional needs often experience greater academic and social challenges in school. Having knowledge of these needs will increase your awareness and sensitivity to all children. It will also help you to explore new ways of viewing and educating children with disabilities and children with gifts and talents. All early childhood professionals must accommodate individual differences and develop the skills necessary to work with the entire professional support team to maximize the potential of every child. This process necessitates a more inclusive interpretation of developmentally effective practices (National Association for the Education of Young Children, 2001; Puckett & Black, 2005).

PAUSE AND REFLECT

About Children with Exceptionalities

Think about a child you know or may have seen who has a disability, special gift, or talent. Describe the characteristics of the child and what you think the child's teacher did or did not do to support his or her development. What are your concerns about teaching children with exceptionalities?

Children from Diverse Backgrounds

Although children all over the world have universal developmental characteristics, the social and cultural settings in which children live significantly shape their development and contribute to each child's uniqueness. By *social setting* we mean the significant people in children's lives who influence their development; by *cultural*

TEACHER PREP WEBSITE 4.4

Go to Student and Teacher Artifacts, select Multicultural Education, choose Education That Is Multicultural (Module 9), and select Snow Scene, Art K–2, (Artifact 1).

setting we mean the values, behaviors, languages, dialects, and feelings about being part of a particular group that all children possess. Knowledge about these is critical "to ensure that learning experiences are meaningful, relevant, and respectful for the participating children and their families" (Bredekamp & Copple, 1997, p. 9). You can see a primary child's detailed snow drawing that illustrates a learning experience that is meaningful, relevant, and respectful in the "Multicultural Education–Education That Is Multicultural" student and teacher artifacts online at the Teacher Prep Website.

Since the civil rights movement of the 1960s, educators have become increasingly informed and sensitized to how deeply children's development is influenced by their social and cultural worlds. Just as you and I want to be accepted for who we are, so too do children from diverse backgrounds want the same full acceptance. Being aware of different cultures will help you be more open and accepting of children from cultures with which you may not be familiar and help all children learn to respect and care for one another and their world.

America has always been characterized by the blending of many cultures, which has shaped this country into what it is today. Yet, its basic values still reflect a Western European tradition. European-American characteristics, such as individual responsibility for one's own actions, a strong work ethic, and a focus on the individual rather than the group, dominate American culture (Banks, 2006; Berns, 2007).

The National Association for the Education of Young Children (NAEYC, 1996) has taken the following position regarding the affirmation of diversity:

> For optimal development and learning of all children, educators must *accept* the legitimacy of children's home language, *respect* (hold in high regard) and *value* (esteem, appreciate) the home culture, and promote and encourage the active involvement and support of all families, including extended and nontraditional family units. (p. 5)

It is beyond the scope of this book to provide selected characteristics from each cultural group that you might encounter as an early childhood educator. The very best way for you to learn about the diversity of the children in your classroom is from the families of your children. They will help you better understand the values, behaviors, language, and traditions of the individuals you will be teaching. Because each of these children will bring many different needs, you will be learning ways to affirm each child's diversity so that each one can develop the necessary feelings of self-worth so vital for healthy development. Knowing that children's development is shaped within their social and cultural worlds makes it imperative that you become sensitive to children's rich, diverse backgrounds in making the best educational decisions for them. As you grow in becoming a teacher of young children, you will enjoy and appreciate the richness of the diversity of the children you teach.

COMPANION WEBSITE 4.4 To learn more about linguistic and cultural diversity, go to *Enrichment Content: Research Highlights* in Chapter 4 of the Companion Website at http://www.prenhall.com/jalongo.

Major Child Development Theories

The best early childhood professionals use their knowledge of child development to guide their practice. The theories that follow are regularly used to explain what children are like. We discuss four theories from the fields of psychology and anthropology to portray different influences on children's development. We describe the key ideas of each theorist and then apply them to early childhood practice.

Psychosocial Theory of Erik Erikson (1902–1994)

Erikson's (1993) psychosocial theory emphasizes that development occurs throughout the lifespan in a series of stages, with each stage contributing to and being influenced by the one preceding and following it. He proposed eight psychosocial stages that are each characterized by a conflict or crisis that influences one's social development and reflects the particular culture unique to each individual (Berk, 2005). According to Erikson, healthy, lifelong social interactions come from the successful resolution of the unique developmental tasks that an individual faces. How individuals resolve the social conflicts at each stage influences their attitudes and skills. Erikson reinterpreted Freud's psychosexual stages and gave more emphasis to the interactive nature of development and less emphasis to biological factors. Consequently, Erikson believed that children play an active role in shaping their development through the kinds of experiences they have. He emphasized the role of developmental needs as a way to understand what age-appropriate social and emotional behavior should be. Erikson's theory is the most widely read and influential of the psychoanalytic theorists. Erikson was a German psychoanalyst who was strongly influenced by his studies with Sigmund Freud, the father of psychoanalysis. Table 4.6 describes each of Erikson's eight psychosocial stages and suggests applications for you to use in your role in promoting all children's development.

Applying Erikson's Psychosocial Theory in Early Childhood Practice

FOSTERING TRUST AND AUTONOMY IN INFANTS AND TODDLERS. Infants and toddlers need warm, loving, caring adults who understand their social needs during each period of development. Adults are their social and emotional models and have an extremely important role in helping infants and toddlers develop trust and autonomy.

Suggestions:

- Ensure that infants have adults who consistently meet their needs, who talk with them calmly, and who nurture their feelings of trust. In this way, infants develop "a sense of a safe, interesting, and orderly world where they are understood and their actions bring pleasure to themselves and others" (Bredekamp & Copple, 1997, p. 58).
- Provide opportunities for toddlers to engage in self-care routines such as feeding, dressing, and toileting. It is important to maintain a reassuring, confident attitude to support toddlers' basic attempts at mastering motor and cognitive skills.
- Select literature that fosters trust and autonomy, such as the lift-the-flap book *Baby Danced the Polka* (Beaumont, 2004) and *Llama, Llama Red Pajama* (Dewdney, 2005), which addresses bedtime and separation anxiety.

FOSTERING INITIATIVE IN PRESCHOOL CHILDREN. Preschoolers are interested in trying new tasks, assuming responsibility for themselves and materials, playing with others, and discovering what they can do with the help of adults. They also use pretend play as one way to make choices and decisions that increase their sense of autonomy and competence, and to master the social and cultural world in which they live (Erikson, 1993).

TABLE 4.6 Erikson's Eight Psychosocial Stages

Psychosocial Conflict	Developmental Ages	Key Characteristics	Major Outcomes	Significant Persons
Trust versus mistrust	Infancy (0–12 months)	• Infants' conflict centers on care and nurturance. • Their needs must be satisfied.	• If needs are met consistently, infants develop trust in others and a hopeful, confident outlook. • If needs are met inconsistently, infants do not develop the hope that they will receive the care they need.	• Responsive, sensitive, and consistent caregiver
Autonomy versus shame and doubt	Toddlerhood (1–3 years)	• Toddlers' conflict centers on their ability to exert ownership over their bodies and actions after they develop trust and good feelings about themselves and their environment.	• If toddlers have the opportunity to manage themselves and their environments appropriately, they develop autonomy, a sense of an emerging separate self, and will. • If the environment is so rigid that children feel overcontrolled by others, they resist such control and may become filled with doubt about their ability to control themselves successfully.	• Significant, consistent adult
Initiative versus guilt	Preschool years (3–5 years)	• Preschoolers struggle between their ability to undertake and complete tasks and their fear of failing at those tasks and feeling guilty. They go back and forth between the wish to be big and independent and also to be helpless like a baby. • They generally will take responsibility for self-care, want to belong to a group, and begin to play together cooperatively.	• Preschoolers who show initiative have a sense of direction and purpose to their work and play. • Preschoolers who cannot test their independence and are punished too quickly may feel unnecessarily guilty. • School-age children who show a sense of industry demonstrate feelings of competence by a "can do" attitude toward school tasks.	• Basic family
Industry versus inferiority	School-age years (6–12 years)	• Elementary children become increasingly focused on doing and making things. • They want to master intellectual and social tasks, do things well, and be competent.	• Elementary children who do not feel industrious feel incompetent, and often demonstrate a "can't do" attitude toward school tasks.	• Neighborhood, peers, and those at school
Identity versus role confusion	Adolescence (10 to 20 years)	• Adolescents try to find out who they are, what they are about, and where they are going in life.	• Adolescents who explore different roles and paths in a healthy manner are more likely to achieve a positive identity. • Adolescents who do not adequately explore many roles or are pushed into a particular adult role often experience identity confusion.	• Peers and adult role models

TABLE 4.6 Continued

Psychosocial Conflict	Developmental Ages	Key Characteristics	Major Outcomes	Significant Persons
Intimacy versus isolation	Early adulthood (20s and 30s)	• Adults at this stage are ready to form deep relations.	• If young adults have resolved their sense of identity, they develop a sense of love and loyalty. • A weak sense of self hinders the formation of intimate relationships and leads to a sense of isolation.	• Partners in sex, friendship, and cooperative ventures
Generativity versus stagnation	Middle adulthood (40s and 50s)	• Focus is on the future and preparing the next generation of citizens through productivity and care.	• Those who have positively resolved previous crises nurture younger generations for the future and have the virtue of caring. • An unhealthy resolution leads to questions about usefulness and a sense of purpose in life.	• Shared lives and mentoring relationships
Ego integrity versus despair	Late adulthood	• Focus is on reviewing life's accomplishments.	• Positive resolution leads to feelings of integrity, full growth, and wisdom about contributing to society. • Negative resolution leads to feelings of despair and hopelessness in being able to contribute to society.	• Society at large, and personal sphere of significant others

Suggestions:

- Provide children with many opportunities for choice, such as selecting and using materials in a variety of ways and allowing children long, uninterrupted periods for play.
- Encourage children to engage in all forms of play. Children practice appropriate social skills and develop feelings of competence through play.
- Use unbreakable cups and pitchers that are easy to pour and hard to spill.
- Show children how to clean up or revise a product that is not quite right.
- Acknowledge children's attempts at independence and make sure that each child has a chance to experience successes rather than failures by providing developmentally appropriate tasks.
- Select literature that fosters initiative and adventure, such as *Where the Wild Things Are* (Sendak, 1964), *Moss Gown* (Hooks, 1987), or *Min-Yo and the Moon Dragon* (Hillman, 1992).

FOSTERING INDUSTRY IN ELEMENTARY CHILDREN. A healthy sense of industry includes a positive but realistic self-concept, pride in accomplishment, moral responsibility, and cooperative participation with age-mates. During the elementary years, children continue to refine their sense of self.

Suggestions:

- Select literature that can help children with the struggles they face. For example, a sense of industry or task orientation can be understood through *Island of the Blue Dolphins* (O'Dell, 1960) for older children or *Daniel's Story* (Matas, 1993) for younger children.
- Make sure that students have opportunities to set and achieve realistic school and personal goals—for example, through assignments that are challenging but not overwhelming and engage their curiosity and motivation to master tasks.
- Provide students with opportunities to demonstrate responsibility such as caring for pets and plants, being accountable for their own belongings and homework, and using technology appropriately.
- Support students who feel discouraged through individual contracts that show student progress or portfolios that show work samples over time.

COMPANION WEBSITE 4.5 For more information about technology and early childhood, go to the *Web Links* in Chapter 4 of the Companion Website at http://www.prenhall.com/jalongo.

Cognitive-Developmental Theory of Jean Piaget (1896–1980)

Piaget's theory of the stages of children's intellectual development focuses on how children's thinking, reasoning, and perception differ from those of adults. Piaget's cognitive-developmental theory is based upon the in-depth, observational studies of his own children. These studies were used to figure out how children think about their world. Piaget's background as a biologist, with its emphasis on adaptation, strongly influenced his theory of cognitive development. The theory is based upon the following four assumptions about cognitive development (Woolfolk, 2007):

1. Biological and environmental influences interact continuously to develop an individual's thinking, reasoning, and perceptual ability.
2. Cognitive development is initially the result of direct experience in an environment; eventually children become capable of transforming their experience mentally through internal reflection.
3. The pace of an individual's development is influenced by the social context.
4. Cognitive development involves major qualitative changes in one's thinking.

Piaget hypothesized that the thinking ability of all children, including those with exceptional needs and from diverse backgrounds, moves through a series of four cognitive stages. The rate of progress through these stages varies from individual to individual, but each stage has unique characteristics. The first three stages occur during the early childhood years; these include (a) the sensorimotor stage (0–2 years), during which infants and toddlers use their senses and reflexes to respond to their immediate world but do not think conceptually; (b) the preoperational stage (2–7 years), during which children have an increased ability to think symbolically and conceptually about objects and people outside of their immediate environment, which is evident through children's increasing use of language and imaginative play; and (c) the concrete operational stage (7–12 years), which is characterized by the ability to use logical thought to solve concrete problems related to concepts of space, time, causality, and number. The fourth stage, formal operations (ages 12 and on), marks the beginning of logical and scientific thinking and is characterized by the ability to make predictions, think hypothetically, and think about

TABLE 4.7 Piaget's Stages of Cognitive Development

Cognitive Stage	Approximate Age Range	Key Behavioral Characteristics	Practical Applications
Sensorimotor	Birth–2 years	• react to stimuli with simple reflexes, such as rooting and sucking • develop first habits, such as sucking when shown a bottle • accidentally reproduce interesting events, such as kicking a mobile and hearing music (primary circular reaction) • focus on the world outside of self, such as imitating sounds of others (secondary circular reaction) • are curious about what objects can do, and what they can do with objects, such as rolling a ball to knock an object (tertiary circular reaction) • develop the concept of object permanence: the understanding that objects exist even when they cannot be seen	• provide stimulating, colorful, safe objects for infants and toddlers to reach for, grasp, and explore • encourage sounds and responses to stimuli such as clapping, singing, and cooing
Preoperational thinking	2–7 years	• have the ability to mentally represent an object that is not present, as in pretending to drive a car while playing (symbolic function) • are egocentric, able to focus only on own perspective, not on those of others • project animism, giving life to inanimate objects, as in thinking that clouds cry • show *centration* in thinking, focusing attention on one characteristic of an object or event, such as color, shape, or size, to the exclusion of others • display a rapid increase in language • use fantasy and imaginative play as natural modes of thinking	• provide props to represent images in children's environment • talk about how certain behaviors (e.g., pushing, grabbing) make others feel to reduce egocentrism • encourage classification of objects by shape, size, weight, or color • provide rhymes, songs, and poems that play with the English language and not similar sounds • provide opportunities to work in groups of two or three • encourage new gross motor activities that stretch children's comfort zones • provide open-ended activities (e.g., blocks, art, writing, pretend play) • provide sensory experiences
Concrete operations	7–11 years	• can coordinate attributes at one time (reversibility) • classify and divide sets and subsets and consider their relationships (e.g., understanding that one's mother can also be somebody else's sister and daughter at the same time) • become more analytical and logical in their approach to words and grammar	• use concrete, manipulative objects and materials to help children draw conclusions • provide concrete materials as a bridge to representational thought • provide opportunities to work decisions and exchange points of view

SOURCES: Data based on Piaget, 1992; Santrock, 2007; and Woolfolk, 2007.

thinking. Table 4.7 summarizes Piaget's first three stages of cognitive development and lists the major characteristics of each. (Piaget's cognitive development theory is discussed in greater detail in Chapter 5.)

Applying Piaget's Cognitive-Developmental Theory in Early Childhood Practice

Although Piaget never claimed to be an educator, his theory has greatly influenced our thinking about how early childhood teachers should promote children's intellectual development. His ideas have implications for how we prepare early childhood settings and how adults interact with the children they teach. In fact, several different early childhood programs and practices have been designed explicitly using Piagetian principles, particularly concerning the interaction patterns between the adult and the child. One such program is "Educating the Young Thinker," an inquiry approach aimed at promoting the development of representational competence by using language to provoke cognitive disequilibrium (Copple, Sigel, & Saunders, 1984). A second approach uses group games to promote the development of children's logic and social and moral values (Kamii & DeVries, 1980). You can see Maddie showing centration in her thinking as she focuses on the characteristic of the length of the rows of fish to the exclusion of others in the "Cognitive Development–Early Childhood" video clip online at the Teacher Prep Website.

TEACHER PREP WEBSITE 4.5

Go to Video Classroom, select Early Childhood, choose Child Development (Module 1), and select Cognitive Development–Early Childhood (Video 1).

Suggestions:

- Prepare early childhood settings that encourage exploration and discovery. Include a wide variety of interesting materials and experiences for all children. Because young children's thinking is based on motor experiences, the optimum learning environment has interesting materials available to children at different levels of development. Such materials might include colorful stacking toys for infants, ample puzzles and construction materials for preschoolers and kindergartners, and board games and manipulative materials for school-age children. These materials must be worthy of children's attention to develop their thinking through exploration, experimentation, hypothesis testing, and reflection (Bredekamp & Copple, 1997).
- Provide a variety of opportunities for play to enhance children's practice with symbols. During play, you will notice that children practice what they know and use important thinking abilities, such as problem solving, negotiation, and decision making. Practicing new skills in a safe context is inherently satisfying to children. Such repetition may be as simple as infants grasping and dropping an object or preschoolers repeatedly working the same puzzle, in and out of the frame, until all variations have been mastered. From Piaget we learn that as children develop, they practice different and more varied skills, and thus become more effective in their interactions.
- Understand that *preoperational children* think concretely. Guiding preoperational thinking should include using concrete materials, such as chips or cubes, whenever possible; keeping instructions as brief as possible and using actions as well as words; and providing a wide range of

Jo Hall/Merrill

Opportunities for children to practice new skills help them gain confidence.

experiences, such as field trips, cooking, and learning about community workers, in order to build a foundation for concept learning and language.

- Understand that the *concrete operational* child thinks concretely. Guiding concrete operational thinking should include the continual use of concrete materials and visual aids such as graphic organizers, diagrams, and timelines; keeping demonstrations and readings short and focused; and using familiar examples to explain difficult concepts such as measuring two different rooms to understand the concept of area.
- Select literature that capitalizes on preoperational children's growing intellectual capacity to enjoy fantasy and humor through books such as *Kitten's First Full Moon* (Henkes, 2004) and concrete operational children's growing intellectual capacity to use problem solving and perspective taking through books such as *The Cats in Krasinki Square* (Hesse, 2004) and *Hot Dog with Abbot Avenue* (English, 2004).

Ecological Theory of Urie Bronfenbrenner (1917–2005)

Bronfenbrenner (1981), an American developmental psychologist and a major proponent of the development of the Head Start program, is credited with the development of the interdisciplinary field of human ecology that emphasizes social and cultural influences on development (Santrock, 2007). These contexts—the family, educational setting, community, and broader society—are interrelated, and all have an impact on the developing child. For example, even though a child with a disability lives in a nurturing, accepting family, and has support from peers and neighbors, the child may be affected by stereotypes and biases held by the community at large that could affect his or her development. Bronfenbrenner's model includes the following four different societal systems, each of which influences the other and a child's development:

1. ***The microsystem*** is where the child lives and experiences most of his or her interactions, such as the home, school, and neighborhood.
2. ***The mesosystem*** involves the relations between the microsystem and the larger environment, such as the connections between the family and school and the relationship between the family and neighborhood.
3. ***The exosystem*** includes the social settings that affect, but do not include, the child—for example, the parents' work environment and government services such as parks and libraries. If, for example, a parent is highly stressed in the work environment, that parent's stress will often influence how the parent interacts with the child after work.
4. ***The macrosystem*** includes the values, beliefs, laws, and customs of a child's culture that are transmitted from generation to generation and affect the interactions among the family, school, and community in the child's immediate world.

Applying Bronfenbrenner's Ecological Theory in Early Childhood Practice

Bronfenbrenner's theory has a significant impact on how early childhood educators interact with children and their families. The most important applications occur at the microsystem level, where early childhood teachers can provide consistent support for children and their families.

Suggestions:

- Know children in more than one setting. Observing children in different social settings (e.g., the school, home) and inviting families to provide their perspective and knowledge is essential for obtaining the most complete picture of individual development.
- Study children in a variety of settings over a period of time. This look at the child helps early childhood educators see common as well as individual characteristics of children.
- Create and maintain good communication between home and school. Involve families in learning activities at home, welcome parents in your classroom in a variety of roles, and learn about the child's community and culture.

Hierarchy of Needs Theory of Abraham Maslow (1908–1970)

Humanistic psychologist Abraham Maslow (1987) formulated a theory of human motivation based upon a hierarchy of universal basic and growth needs. Maslow suggests that these needs motivate individual behavior and lead to healthy growth and development, when satisfied. He also believed that individuals must satisfy their basic needs before their higher-level growth needs can be met. *Basic needs* include physiological needs (e.g., food and drink) and safety and survival needs (e.g., physical and psychological security). *Growth needs* emerge as children's basic needs are being met. Growth needs include the need for *love and belonging* (e.g., being accepted and belonging to a group both in the family and in the school). They also include the need for *esteem* that comes from recognition, approval, and achievement from both peers and adults and leads to a sense of competence and can-do feelings. Such feelings of self-worth are derived from authentic, not trivialized, accomplishments. As needs are met, individuals naturally tend to seek higher needs, the highest of which is self-actualization, the desire to use one's abilities and talents to the fullest. Motivation to satisfy growth needs increases when they are being met and decreases when they are not being met. For Maslow, children whose basic safety needs are clearly being met will naturally seek stronger needs for love, belonging, and so forth, up the pyramid of needs.

Applying Maslow's Theory in Early Childhood Practice

Teachers of young children must know which of their basic and growth needs are or are not being met if they are to help them grow and develop in healthy ways. If children's needs for food, shelter, and safety are not being met, they will require additional support to be successful in school.

Suggestions:

- Provide predictable routines in the daily schedule to help children feel secure in their setting.
- Be prepared to provide adequate health, safety, and nutrition, but also know how to access other services, such as physical, dental, or social services.
- Help children feel like a part of the family or school group to satisfy the need for belonging and love.
- Provide opportunities for making choices or solving interesting problems so children can learn to trust their own ideas.
- Facilitate children's investigative capacity by accepting a range of solutions to problems and encouraging children to express a range of feelings and ideas.

COMPANION WEBSITE 4.6 To add a child development product to your developing portfolio, go to *Journal: Constructing Your Professional Portfolio* in Chapter 4 of the Companion Website at http://www.prenhall.com/jalongo.

From these theorists, we learn that there are many approaches to understanding children's development. We also learn that no single theoretical perspective tells us all we would like to know. Knowing about multiple approaches to child development enables you to select and use whatever is best for each child at a given time. At this point, it is time to extend your thinking about child development to the teaching portfolio you are constructing.

COMPANION WEBSITE 4.7 To test your knowledge of this chapter's contents, go to the *Multiple-Choice* and *Essay* Modules in Chapter 4 of the Companion Website at http://www.prenhall.com/jalongo. These items are written in the same format that you will encounter in the PRAXIS test to better prepare you for your licensure exam.

Conclusion

Understanding what children are like is a critical first step in promoting their development. Thorough observations of children in all contexts, supplemented with a growing knowledge of typical patterns of development as well a firm grounding in psychological theories, are necessary to meet the needs of all children and to detect exceptionalities as early as possible. These understandings will help you make better professional decisions about your own practice in whatever early childhood setting you might be.

ONE CHILD, THREE PERSPECTIVES

Angelica's Baby Pictures

Angelica is a 4-year-old child who was adopted from Bolivia, South America, at age 2. Angelica lives with her mother, a single parent, in a diverse community near a major city.

Angelica's preschool class was studying about how living things grow and change. On this particular day, Angelica came home from school crying because she couldn't do her homework. Angelica's teacher, Ms. Kane, had sent home a piece of adding machine tape with the following directions: "Cut the paper to the length you were when you were born, and please bring a photo of you when you were a baby, so we can see how much bigger you are now, and how different you look now that you are older."

Angelica had spent her first 22 months of life living with a foster family in South America and came to this country with only the clothes on her body. There were no photos and only a little medical history. Angelica's mother would never know what Angelica looked like when she was a baby, when she said her first word, or when she took her first step.

Because Angelica was so sad, her mother made an appointment to speak with Ms. Kane. Ms. Kane explained that she was having her class make books about themselves, including special information about when they were babies. Ms. Kane seemed to think this was a perfectly appropriate activity for preschoolers and could not understand why Angelica was so upset.

During the course of the conversation between Angelica's mother and Ms. Kane, Angelica's mother shared how this seemingly harmless activity created a series of painful questions between Angelica and her mother about Angelica's past. She could not be told who her birth parents were, why they didn't want to keep her, whether there were pictures of her when she was a baby, what she looked like, or who her friends were. Angelica's mother reminded Ms. Kane that she had filled out the family questionnaire at the start of the school year and reported that Angelica was adopted; she was surprised that Ms. Kane had selected an adoption-insensitive assignment for Angelica and her classmates.

Ms. Kane decided to seek more information about adoption-sensitive assignments, so she talked with the community social worker who served the preschool. During their conversation, Ms. Kane learned that certain typical school projects, such as finding baby pictures, making family trees, exploring family heritage, and making Mother's Day presents, may cause emotional turmoil for children who are adopted. The social worker told Ms. Kane how important it was for her to be sensitive to the needs of adopted children because even though they don't appear to be different, their needs are somewhat unique and to never dismiss an issue as insignificant because, to adopted children, they are not. She also reminded Ms. Kane that children do not like to feel different and that anything teachers of young children can do to affirm who they are contributes to their sense of self. The social worker invited Ms. Kane to talk with the other preschool staff and determine their interest in a staff development seminar entitled "Adoption Awareness in the Schools," which she would be happy to conduct.

REACT	Think about how the perspectives of Angelica's mother, Ms. Kane, and the social worker are alike and different. What might be some reasons? With whom do you identify most in this case? Why?
RESEARCH	Call several adoption agencies and search the World Wide Web to locate information and materials that will help you learn more about what adopted children are like and what they need. A good source is the Center for Adoptive Families, 10230 New Hampshire Avenue, Suite 200, Silver Spring, MD 20903 (Tel: 301-439-2900). What key characteristics of adopted children did you find that apply to child development?
REFLECT	What assumptions about adopted children do Ms. Kane, the social worker, and Angelica's mother hold? Generate some ways you can be adoption-sensitive in your setting, such as having children make gifts for other family members on Mother's Day or Father's Day if children have only one or no parents.

IN-CLASS WORKSHOP

Understanding Inclusion

In the Ask the Expert feature earlier in this chapter, Richard Gargiulo talks about inclusion—the belief "that all young children with exceptional needs should receive intervention and educational services in settings designed for youngsters without those needs, that is, in typical environments such as child-care centers, Head Start programs, or regular classrooms." He urges all teachers of young children to focus on children's abilities, not on their disabilities, because a child is first and foremost a child. If you visit an inclusive early childhood classroom you will notice children with disabilities who are part of a community of learners in a regular classroom; a team of professionals (special and regular education teachers, paraprofessionals, and other support personnel) collaborating to modify and adapt the learning environment for individual children; and teachers who take responsibility for helping all children learn and succeed in the regular classroom.

Early childhood teachers are increasingly being expected to teach in inclusive settings. This movement has been supported by several national associations and is reflected in the position statement shown on page 145 that was developed by the Council for Exceptional Children, Division for Early Childhood in 1993, endorsed by the NAEYC in 1993, reaffirmed by DEC in 1996, and revised in June 2000. Read this position statement to help you (a) explore the ideas behind inclusion, (b) examine your own attitudes toward children with special needs, and (c) think about your beliefs about the capacity of children with special needs to learn in regular early childhood settings. Then respond to the following questions.

The Division for Early Childhood of the Council for Exceptional Children Position on Inclusion.

Inclusion, as a value, supports the right of all children, regardless of their diverse abilities, to participate actively in natural settings within their communities. A natural setting is one in which the child would spend time had he or she not had a disability. Such settings include, but are not limited to, home and family, playgroups, childcare, nursery schools, Head Start programs, kindergartens, and neighborhood school classrooms.

DEC believes in and supports full and successful access to health, social service, education, and other supports and services for young children and their families that promotes full participation in community life. DEC values the diversity of families and supports a family guided process for determining services that are based on the needs and preferences of individual families and children.

To implement inclusive practices DEC supports: (a) the continued development, evaluation, and dissemination of full inclusion supports, services, and systems so that options for inclusion are of high quality; (b) the development of preservice and inservice training programs that prepare families, administrators, and service providers to develop and work within inclusive settings; (c) collaboration among all key stakeholders to implement flexible fiscal and administrative procedures in support of inclusion; (d) research that contributes to our knowledge of state of the art services; and (e) the restructuring and unification of social, education, health, and intervention supports and services to make them more responsive to the needs of children and families.

Endorsed by NAEYC, November 1993.

SOURCE: From *Position of Inclusion*, by the Division for Early Childhood of the Council of Exceptional Children, 1993, Reston, VA.

1. What do you think about these ideas? Do any of them cause you concern? If so, name them and try to describe what concerns you.
2. What questions does this position paper raise for you?
3. How do the ideas in this paper relate to those that Richard Gargiulo shared in the Ask the Expert feature earlier in this chapter? Be prepared to share one of your ideas with the whole group.

What Is Inclusion?

There are many reasons to include young children with exceptionalities in the regular early childhood classroom. Inclusion can benefit children with and without disabilities, teachers, and families of all of the children. Based upon your answers to the preceding questions, brainstorm statements that describe what inclusion means and what inclusion does not mean. Use the following example as a starting point and then complete your own comparison chart.

Inclusion Means	Inclusion Does Not Mean
Having children with a disability attend regular early childhood classes	Placing children with disabilities in regular classrooms without the support and services they need to be successful.
Regular education teachers use appropriate strategies for the varied needs of children in the class	Having separate pull-out programs for children according to disability

Once you have completed your chart, think about why inclusion is or is not needed for children with exceptional needs.

CHAPTER 5

Exploring Your Role in Fostering Children's Learning

> **The overwhelming majority of teachers . . . are unable to name or describe a theory of learning that underlies what they do in the classroom, but what they do—what any of us does—is no less informed by theoretical assumptions just because these assumptions are invisible. Behind [teaching practice] is a theory that embodies distinct assumptions about the nature of knowledge, the possibility of choice, and what it means to be a human being.**
>
> **Alfie Kohn, 1993, p. 10**

Meet the Teachers

MRS. SUAREZ teaches toddlers in a local child-care setting. If you visit her class, you will see Mrs. Suarez sitting on an oversized pillow on the floor while reading books to a small group of children, one of whom is sitting on her lap. She is talking to them about the imaginary characters they have seen in their books. Mrs. Suarez believes it is important to talk with and read to children regularly and she helps the children's parents do the same in their homes. She suggests that the parents use short, simple sentences to talk with their children, and helps them find good books to read to their infants and toddlers because, as she says, "Children's brains are being wired for learning from birth."

MS. BURKE teaches in an inclusive, public preschool setting. She is just beginning to use children's interests and questions as a basis for her teaching and wonders about such questions as "Where will I find ideas for next week?" "How can I really plan for children's learning based on their interests and still meet the required standards?" Ms. Burke was asking herself these questions at the same time that her school was being renovated and the children expressed interests about the renovation—the trucks, the heavy equipment, and the demolition that was taking place daily in and around the school. She decided to take her children on a planned tour of the construction site. She and the children photographed the workers and the machinery, created a pictorial timeline that documented the transformation of the building, gathered a variety of picture books about construction, collected tools and toys for the children to use, and read *The Three Little Pigs* to help children extend their concept of building. Ms. Burke noticed that children talked with each other more about the school construction, were less dependent on her for ideas in their play, and needed less adult direction in their learning experiences. Ms. Burke now considers children's needs and interests in her planning, when writing individualized education plans, and in initiating staff referrals because, she says, "I am more in tune with how children's thinking and abilities influence their learning."

MS. DOMBROWSKI uses math journals in her first grade as one way to integrate the national mathematical standards in her curriculum. Ms. Dombrowski has read about writing in mathematics to assess children's mathematical understandings. She uses that knowledge to introduce math journals to her first graders because, she says, "Communication in mathematics helps the children clarify their ideas and helps me to understand how they are thinking, what mathematical knowledge and concepts they possess, and how they express that knowledge." Ms. Dombrowski's first graders write and draw about word problems, counting sequences, and patterns that have to do with such mathematical concepts as missing addends, counting money, telling time, and identifying place value. Sometimes the children write or draw alone, but sometimes they do so with a partner, because Ms. Dombrowski believes "that true understanding of mathematics comes from representing and explaining their ideas in different ways." She shared her students' mathematical progress with other teachers for the primary grades, and they now include journal writing as part of the mathematics curriculum.

Each of these teachers understands the different ways children learn. Using the following questions, consider these teachers' understandings about how children learn, and compare, contrast, and connect them with your own thinking.

COMPARE	What are some similarities in the ways that these three teachers help children learn?
CONTRAST	What do these teachers think about how young children learn? What differences do you notice in the methods they have used to foster children's learning?
CONNECT	What impressed you most about these teachers' views of learning? How do you think you will incorporate these ideas with children? Why?

Now that you have reflected on the perspectives of three different teachers, here is a preview of the knowledge, skills, and dispositions you need to acquire in order to fulfill your role in fostering children's learning.

Learning Outcomes

- ✔ Become familiar with standards for helping all children learn **(NAEYC #1 & 4, INTASC #1 & 4, and ACEI #3a & 3c)**
- ✔ Understand the learning processes in early childhood education
- ✔ Examine the features of authentic learning
- ✔ Explore learner-centered teaching and learning and explain the cycle of learning
- ✔ Describe the major learning theories and their implications for young children
- ✔ Examine the effect of teachers' beliefs on children's learning
- ✔ Consider the central role of play in children's learning

A Definition of Learning

COMPANION WEBSITE 5.1 To learn more about defining your role as a facilitator of children's learning, go to *Journal: Defining Your Role* in Chapter 5 of the Companion Website at http://www.prenhall.com/jalongo.

Picture the difference in yourself when you are learning something new and when you are doing something that you have already learned. In which situation do you feel more confident about demonstrating what you know? Though there are many different theories about what learning is, most agree that learning is the natural process of making sense of information and experience that is fostered through interactions with others. Learning "occurs when experience causes a relatively permanent change in an individual's knowledge or behavior" (Woolfolk, 2007, p. 206). To illustrate, recall what it was like when you first learned to drive a car. You knew it was a natural activity for most teenagers and adults, but you first needed to figure out how to shift to drive forward, reverse, parallel park, brake, and so forth. The more practice you had behind the wheel

DID YOU KNOW...?

Key Facts About Children's Learning

- Learning is a basic, adaptive function of humans. More than any other species, people are designed to be flexible learners and active agents in acquiring knowledge and skills. Learners are most successful if they are mindful of themselves as learners and thinkers.
- Children lack knowledge and experience, but not reasoning ability. Although young children are inexperienced, they reason with the knowledge they have.
- Misinformation can impede school learning, so teachers need to be mindful of the ways in which children's background knowledge influences what they understand.
- By the time a student graduates from high school, he or she will have watched 20,000 hours of television, more than the number of hours spent in the classroom.
- The human brain weighs a mere 3 pounds and is barely larger than an adult fist, yet it is our body's most vital organ. The brain's 100 billion nerve cells (neurons) communicate with one another primarily through biochemical signals (neurotransmitters) traveling at speeds up to 220 mph along a network that involves trillions of synaptic connections.
- About half of 3-, 4-, and 5-year-olds are enrolled in public or private preschool programs, including Head Start.

SOURCES: Bransford, Brown, & Cocking, 1999; Dana Alliance for Brain Initiatives, 2005; Donovan & Bransford, 2005; Lynch, 2005.

with a more experienced driver, the more your experience helped your driving become better each time. Now, a few years later, you can see a permanent change in your driving behavior from the first day you took the wheel.

Recent research in multiple intelligences (Gardner, 1993, 2000), multicultural education (Banks & Banks, 2005), and cognitive and neurosciences (Shonkoff & Philips, 2001) has contributed to our deeper understanding of how all people think and learn. This research has clear implications for early childhood educators because it provides evidence that all children can and do learn regardless of their backgrounds or innate learning abilities.

PAUSE AND REFLECT

About Learning

Think about one of your most successful learning experiences. What made it meaningful, memorable, and enjoyable? Now think about one of your least successful learning experiences. What made it uninteresting, irrelevant, and discouraging? List the characteristics of each and compare and contrast them. What observations do you notice?

Features of Authentic Learning Experiences

People learn best when they believe in themselves and are confident that they can learn (Bandura, 1997, 2001). Authentic learning experiences resemble situations that people naturally encounter outside the classroom and that make sense to them in their interactions with people, materials, and/or ideas (Eggen & Kauchak, 2007). The following scenario involving preschoolers Danielle and Maria illustrates the important characteristics of an authentic learning experience.

Danielle and Maria were building with large, hollow blocks during center time. Together, they decided to build a maze for their animal figures so they could have an animal relay race. They collected blocks; built large enclosed spaces with side openings and lanes to connect each space; wrote signs that said Start, Stop, and Tickets; and gathered a variety of animal figures from the box of accessories nearby. While the girls were concentrating intently on their building and deciding which animals were going to participate in the relay race, their teacher passed by the block building area. Here is what she noticed: Danielle and Maria were (a) measuring space, (b) writing their signs, (c) selecting the correct number of blocks to build each side of their enclosures, (d) using two small blocks to equal one long block (which demonstrated an understanding of equivalency), and (e) classifying when putting away their blocks according to like shapes at the end of their project.

The scenario involving Danielle and Maria shows these children naturally making sense out of their block play. Together, they are engaged in a project that demonstrates what they know about measurement, spatial relations, and early literacy through real, or authentic, learning. **Authentic learning** develops learners who see possibilities, want to know about things, and use what they are learning; nonauthentic learning develops learners who want to give correct answers and do exactly what their teachers want them to do (Daniels & Bizar, 2005; Eggen & Kauchak, 2007; Woolfolk, 2007). Authentic learning experiences for all children share the following features:

1. ***Authentic learning experiences use children's prior knowledge to spark their interest in meaningful, purposeful activities.*** All children learn best by thinking about what they are doing. Merely manipulating objects does not assure that thinking will occur. Take, for example, one of the most well known authentic learning projects, the 1994 building of the Amusement Park for Birds, found in the La Villette School in Reggio Emilia, Italy. The school site attracts lots of birds, which capture children's interest, spark questions, and encourage talk about birds. Children throughout the years have explored the grounds from a "bird's eye view," built interesting birdhouses, and created unusual drinking fountains for the birds in their midst. While the children's interests were sparked by the birds, the teachers' awareness of how to deepen children's curiosity, provide opportunities to choose how to follow their interests in birds, and allow children to work at their own pace provide the cornerstone for authentic learning experiences. You can see two primary grade teachers activating children's prior knowledge of the story of Cinderella and creating interest in the reading of an African Tale like Cinderella in the "Preparing for Teaching" video clip online at the Teacher Prep Website.

TEACHER PREP WEBSITE 5.1

Go to Video Classroom, select Foundations/Intro to Teaching, choose Learners and Development (Module 3), and select Preparing for Learning (Video 2).

2. ***Authentic learning experiences promote strategic thinking.*** Strategic thinking is the heart of good teaching and learning because it teaches specific skills in contexts that the learners need to use. In learning to become better readers, for example, all children need command of how and when to use a variety of strategies. Using picture cues, making predictions, and asking questions for advance organizers all help children apply the skills they need as readers. Strategic thinking allows children to discover new meanings and understandings and to develop the reflective skills to make them independent learners (American Psychological Association, 2005; Eggen & Kauchak, 2007).

3. ***Authentic learning experiences involve some social interactions.*** Vygotsky (1978) believes that learning is a social process and that children first learn new knowledge through social relations with others, which they later internalize. Starting from birth, children's communication with others is essentially social. They use language for different purposes: to ask for something they need, to get things done, to

find out information, or to maintain relations with another (Santrock, 2007; Vygotsky, 1978). Communicating ideas with others promotes improved collective understanding and provokes appropriate higher-level thinking skills.

What makes this an authentic learning experience?

4. *Authentic learning experiences are based on each child's ways of learning and displaying knowledge.* Because learning is individual and developmental, not all children learn in the same way, at the same rate, or have the same interests. Howard Gardner (1993, 2000) suggests that we all construct knowledge through at least eight different intelligences, which provide multiple ways of learning skills, concepts, and strategies. (See Table 5.4 and the In-Class Workshop of this chapter for a description of Gardner's eight intelligences.) Similarly, we demonstrate what we know in different ways. A good example of this is a study of the rain forest by a second-grade class. The children read books about the rain forest, such as *Save My Rain Forest* (Zak, 1992), learned specific vocabulary words related to the rain forest, and wrote stories about tropical evergreens and endangered species. Some children counted and graphed a vast array of evergreens and endangered species, and some made a class mural depicting the different species of plant and animal life. Throughout their study, the second graders transformed their classroom into a rain forest and invited their families to come and experience all that they had learned. Some children read and told stories about the lives of specific organisms in the rain forest; others provided their parents with headphones to listen to their tape-recorded information about life and life cycles. What did the children learn? Aside from vocabulary words, they practiced the reading, writing, oral language, and mathematical and science skills that were expected at the second-grade level in their school district. When you consider children's multiple ways of learning, children at any age can approach almost any topic from a variety of meaningful learning perspectives.

5. *Authentic learning experiences help children apply their learning to other situations.* Research from cognitive and neuroscience suggests that most learners have difficulty appropriately applying knowledge learned in one setting to a different setting (Bransford et al., 1999; Shonkoff & Phillips, 2001). Being able to transfer knowledge, skills, concepts, and strategies from one situation to another is an essential aspect of learning. When younger children learn to use picture cues to "read" a story from one book, they use that strategy over and over again in "reading" other books. When older children learn to read to the end of the sentence to get its meaning before sounding out an unfamiliar word, they are using the context of the sentence to increase their reading comprehension and then use that strategy in other reading situations.

These features of authentic learning highlight how central learners are to the learning process. Because teachers are expected to reach all learners, you will need to plan authentic individual and group experiences for young children.

Your Role as a Facilitator of Learning

Being a facilitator of learning—one who is a partner with children in the learning process—is one way to maximize your significant influence on children's learning. As a facilitator, you view learners as active participants in the learning process (Henniger, 2005; Jackman, 2005), and you view your role as engaging children in learning and promoting their understanding rather than simply transmitting knowledge. With this disposition to learn along with others, you become a lifelong learner who has the capacity to explore, satisfy curiosity, meet new challenges, and love learning. Your commitment to learning helps children value its importance—a message that is as critical as the content you teach. It also honors the reciprocity between you and the learner, and exemplifies the simple but powerful words of Robert Fulghum, "All I ever needed to know I learned from my kindergarten students." Your role in fostering children's learning can be guided by the following principles about learning.

1. ***Teachers' beliefs about learning affect children and their families.*** What you believe about how children learn guides your interactions and relationships with children and their families, your daily schedule, your room arrangement, and the experiences that you plan. Sometimes you may use open-ended questions to probe children's thinking; at other times you may use closed-ended questions that focus on factual information. These interactions reflect not only certain theoretical perspectives, but also your beliefs of how children learn. Your personal belief system greatly influences what you do, constitutes a large part of your teaching, and has a powerful impact on your ability to promote learning (McCombs & Whisler, 1997).
2. ***Teachers create opportunities for co-learning.*** As a partner in learning, you must be skilled at selecting the appropriate learning materials that will help children move from learning with assistance to learning independently. For example, when young children can consistently solve a particular kind of math problem using manipulatives, they next need to try to solve it using pictures, and then finally solve it only in their minds. These different levels of learning indicate the type of support children require to internalize the concepts that lead them toward independence. As a co-learner, planning how and when to use materials to support children's learning at different levels is one of the most challenging tasks you will encounter, because supporting children's learning helps children gain confidence in their own capacity to learn (Bodrova & Leong, 1996, 2005).
3. ***Teachers encourage social interaction and shared experiences to increase learning.*** Because social interaction is central to learning (Vygotsky, 1978), children need many opportunities to share and compare their thinking with that of others. The others can be peers or adults who provide the opportunity to refine and develop thinking. As a facilitator, you can increase learning in your setting with some of the following strategies that rely on social interactions: cooperative learning, peer tutoring, cross-age tutoring, group investigations, sociodramatic play, and sociodramatic play centers. Each of these strategies respects children as resources in constructing their own learning.
4. ***Teachers model and teach lifelong learning skills.*** Lifelong learning skills enable you to engage in continuous learning. The following skills are needed to be a lifelong learner (Berns, 2007): confidence ("I can do it"), motivation ("I want to do it"), effort ("I am willing to try"), responsibility ("I follow through on commitments"), initiative ("I am a self-starter"), perseverance ("I finish what I start"), caring ("I show concern for others"), teamwork ("I work cooperatively with others"), common sense (" I use good judgment"), and problem solving ("I use my knowledge and experience effectively").

COMPANION WEBSITE 5.2 To learn more about fulfilling your role in fostering children's learning and the NAEYC, go to *Web Links* in Chapter 5 of the Companion Website at http://www.prenhall. com/jalongo.

The Importance of Learner-Centered Experiences

Think back to the way you learned in school. Were you mostly concerned with memorizing facts and reciting correct answers to your teachers' questions? Or do you remember having opportunities to ask questions, become involved in answering many of your own questions, and pursue some of your own ideas? Both of these ways of learning are common in schools. While you probably remember what you learned in school, do you also remember how you felt while learning, and how your teachers kept you interested in learning? Based on new advances in the study of learning and learners, educators are changing their understanding of learning from a passive view of learners who accumulate information through a series of reinforcement techniques to an active view of learners who utilize learning strategies to construct knowledge (American Psychological Association, 2005; Daniels, Kalkman, & McCombs, 2001; Gardner, 1993, 2000; Goleman, 1997, 1998; McCombs, 2001; Piaget, 1970; Vygotsky, 1978).

COLLABORATING WITH FAMILIES

What Is a Good Learning Experience?

Children's interests are important sources of good learning experiences; these interests provide opportunities for developing and expanding knowledge and skills. The following example shows one way that you can help families capitalize on children's interests as an important part of their learning.

Ms. Davis sent the following letter to the families of the children in her class. The letter was translated in the different languages the families spoke.

Dear ________________

Please take a few minutes to watch your child's activities at home. Then, answer the following questions and return this paper to school in your child's folder by **Friday.**

1. What activity does your child **spend the most time** doing?
2. What activity does your child **spend the least time doing or does not seem to want to do at all?**
3. List one or two of your child's favorite activities.

This information will help me know your child better, so I can plan learning experiences that will interest him or her. In a few weeks, I will share our activity calendar for next month and will send home an activity that is special for you and your child.

Thank you for your participation.

Beth Davis

Child's Name ________________________________

Adult's Signature ________________________________

As a follow-up, Ms. Davis sent home the following activity to one family:

Dear ____________________:

Thank you for letting me know what Antonio likes to do at home. You told me that he likes to play number games and go on scavenger hunts. So, I am sending some home learning packets that Antonio might enjoy and that support his learning in school.

Home Learning Packet:

- Included are a deck of cards and a pair of dice. Have two people turn over cards or roll dice to see who has the highest or lowest number. This develops number awareness.
- Scavenger hunt: List objects related to the color blue. Have your child record or check the blue objects found at home. This will build print awareness, number sense, and writing.

What can you find that is blue?

— Balls	— Shirts
— Blocks	— Other things
— Shoes	

Thank you for your help.

Beth Davis

A learner-centered focus means that you know how learners come to understand their world (McCombs & Whisler, 1997). This focus takes into account (a) the learning needs of diverse learners, (b) the impact of brain research on learning, (c) lifelong learning, (d) social and emotional learning as well as intellectual learning, and (e) child-initiated and child-directed learning. These five principles are described in the following paragraphs.

Learner-Centered Experiences Meet the Needs of Diverse Learners

All early childhood classrooms have children who differ in how they learn. Yet, many teachers feel uncomfortable with learners from different cultural, language, and economic backgrounds because they believe they learn differently and often blame the children or their families for their failure to achieve in school. Regardless of background, all children bring talent with them that influences their learning. To meet children's diverse learning needs requires your insight about a child's individual abilities, knowledge of the child's cultural background, and skill in creating a responsive learning environment in the classroom (Banks & Banks, 2005; Hernandez, 2001). Knowledge and skill in using a variety of learning models, such as learning styles (i.e., how individuals process thoughts and feelings) and multiple intelligences (i.e., how individuals come to learn content), is essential for addressing the diverse learning needs of students. Notice how Carol Brunson Day's "Ask the Expert" feature answers teachers' concerns about the influence of culture on children's learning, the focus of multicultural education on children's learning, and anti-bias education.

COMPANION WEBSITE 5.3 For more information about how children learn, go to *Web Links* in Chapter 5 of the Companion Website at http://www. prenhall.com/jalongo.

ASK THE EXPERT

Carol Brunson Day on Cultural Influences on Learning and Anti-Bias Education

Carol Brunson Day

How does culture influence how children learn?

Culture operates as a set of rules for behavior, shaping values, beliefs, and ways of being in the world. Every child grows up in an environment governed by cultural rules and learns them in the socialization process. At birth, cultural rules start to shape such things as the ways children express themselves, determining what language they speak and understand; what they regard as important and how they prioritize what they pay attention to—the meanings that are in words or the context that surrounds them. When children enter school—even infant programs—they are already empowered to participate in their own development and learning, through the ways cultural rules have shaped their behavior and expectations. When there is continuity between home and school, their power to develop is enhanced and their development continues to build. But when what they have learned to do and say no longer works, their development is disrupted.

In multicultural education, isn't it better to focus on sameness and not difference?

Developmental theory tells us that children are **simultaneously** human beings, individual personalities, and cultural beings. As human beings, children share some sameness with all other children, as individuals every child is unique, and as cultural beings children share characteristics with members of the group to which they belong—all at the same time. In early childhood education, it is easy for us to talk about meeting children's needs as individuals—in fact we are quite proud of that. Yet cultural differences make us uneasy, not because children are cultural beings, but because in this society racial and cultural bias attach negative value to certain groups. So it is the response to culture that is the problem and thus our multicultural education should have as its goals unlearning negative responses to the differences that culture creates. That won't happen if we only focus on sameness.

If young children are not exposed to bias, doesn't anti-bias education unnecessarily raise negative issues?

It is a mistake to assume that young children either don't notice or aren't exposed to bias. Studies have shown that by age 3 children notice difference in skin color and are learning to attach value to those differences. In fact, children at this age can demonstrate a preference for white images and negative attitudes toward dark-skinned people and objects. Families cannot fully shield children from general societal attitudes. So teachers and parents together must work to introduce nonbiased messages to counteract these influences. Unless there is a deliberate plan to teach positive views about difference, children will absorb society's prevailing attitudes and beliefs.

Carol Day is President of the National Black Child Development Institute.

Learner-Centered Experiences Are Based on Brain Research

New research in medical and cognitive sciences is increasing our knowledge of the brain's role in learning. This research confirms what early childhood educators have always known—that the early years are critical years for building a strong foundation for learning. Figure 5.1 lists four major principles of brain-based learning.

FIGURE 5.1 Principles of brain-based learning.

1. **Functioning.** The brain operates on different levels (for example, conscious and subconscious and in different ways simultaneously). These functions include physiology, thoughts, emotions, imaginations, and predispositions.
2. **Feelings.** The brain is fundamentally social. Human relationships and emotions profoundly influence the ways in which the brain processes information.
3. **Patterning.** The brain searches for meaning through patterns. It identifies the familiar and responds to novel stimuli. It perceives parts and wholes.
4. **Learning.** The brain's tendency to seek greater complexity is enhanced by encouragement and inhibited by threat.

SOURCE: Bransford et al., 1999.

Brain research also illustrates the importance of the first 3 years of life for "wiring" pathways in the brain for a lifetime of learning. These pathways develop from children's positive stimulation with adults, events, and objects. They also affect how children learn, how they interact with others, and what they believe about themselves, all of which they carry throughout life (Commission on Behavioral and Social Sciences and Education, 2001; Gallagher, 2005). Understanding brain research is essential for preparing learners who can learn spontaneously, independently, and collaboratively to maximize their learning.

Anthony Magnacca/Merrill

The brain is impacted by human relationships and emotions.

Learner-Centered Experiences Focus on Lifelong Learning

Educational experiences involve all learners across the lifespan, from birth through old age. In conceptualizing how we learn new knowledge, skills, attitudes, or dispositions, Bredekamp and Rosegrant (1992) propose a cycle of learning that all learners experience. They describe a four-step recursive learning cycle that begins with awareness, moves to exploration, then to inquiry, and finally to utilization. Think about yourself now as you begin to learn to teach young children. You are at the beginning of a new learning cycle about learning to teach. Suppose, for example, that you have observed a smoothly operating early childhood setting where children work at centers, and now you are trying to learn how to manage several small groups of children engaged in different learning tasks at the same time. Your *awareness* might consist of paying closer attention to how experienced teachers orchestrate several groups; your *exploration* might consist of trying it yourself and noticing what

TABLE 5.1 The Cycle of Learning

	What Children Do	What Teachers Do
Awareness	Experience Acquire an interest Recognize broad parameters Attend Perceive	Create the environment Provide opportunities by introducing new objects, events, people Invite interest by posing problem or question Respond to child's interest or shared experience Show interest, enthusiasm
Exploration	Observe Explore materials Collect information Discover Create Figure out components Construct own understanding Apply own rules Create personal meaning Represent own meaning	Facilitate Support and enhance exploration Provide opportunities for active exploration Extend play Describe child's activity Ask open-ended questions—"What else could you do?" Respect child's thinking and rule systems Allow for constructive error
Inquiry	Examine Investigate Propose explanations Focus Compare own thinking with that of others Generalize Relate to prior learning Adjust to conventional rule systems	Help children refine understanding Guide children, focus attention Ask more focused questions—"What else works like this?" "What happens if. . .?" Provide information when requested—"How do you spell . . .?" Help children make connections
Utilization	Use the learning in many ways; learning becomes functional Represent learning in various ways Apply learning to new situations Formulate new hypotheses and repeat cycle	Create vehicles for application in real world Help children apply learning to new situations Provide meaningful situations in which to use learning

SOURCE: Bredekamp & Rosegrant (1992).

happens when you work with several small groups simultaneously; and your *inquiry* might involve further application of what you are learning as well as a comparison with what others are doing with the same skill. At this stage, you adapt your practice based upon what you know about the process and what you have experienced. Lastly, you *utilize* this skill in a way that enhances children's learning and allows you to monitor their learning at multiple levels and on multiple tasks simultaneously. This cycle repeats itself many times over, because once you utilize your knowledge of managing small groups, you develop new awareness about some of the gaps in what you know or do not know about managing small learning groups. The more you revisit the learning cycle, the deeper your knowledge or skill becomes. Table 5.1 illustrates the cycle of learning and the teacher's role in supporting children at each of its recursive stages.

An essential outcome of school for all children is to become knowledgeable, responsible, and caring adults. Learner-centered experiences help children become *knowledgeable* because they naturally motivate children to learn and help them use new information in their lives. They help children become *responsible* by offering them opportunities to make decisions that affect others as well as themselves; and they encourage *caring* behavior by experiencing concern about others as well as themselves. The ability to manage the social and emotional aspects of your life in a complex world is an important yet "different way of being smart" and is a basic responsibility of all educators (Goleman, 1997). Attending systematically to children's social and emotional competence increases academic achievement, decreases problem behaviors, and improves their interpersonal relationships (Kostelnik, Whiren, Soderman, & Gregory, 2006; McCombs & Miller, 2007; Saarni, 2001).

Learner-Centered Experiences Are Child-Initiated and Child-Directed

Learning experiences that help children to assume some responsibility for their own learning are referred to as child-initiated or child-directed. Recall your positive memories about learning. You probably remember being able to pursue ideas that interested you, being given reasons for why you were being asked to learn something, or being trusted to make other meaningful learning choices. These attributes help learners take ownership for their own learning because they foster intrinsic motivation in the learner by sparking children's curiosity and interests (American Psychological Association, 2005; Bodrova & Leong, 2005; Denton, 2005; McCombs & Miller, 2007). Early childhood teachers who use child-directed learning experiences are reflecting Dewey's (1916) theory of progressive education, in which the overarching purpose of schooling is to prepare students for the realities of today's and tomorrow's world. Educators assume that children can make good learning choices, that the process of learning is just as important as the products children produce, and that learning to make decisions is an important skill and a fundamental right in a democratic society. Although child-initiated and child-directed learning is an important part of learner-centered experiences, children need to experience a balance between learner-centered and teacher-centered learning in order to succeed in this complex world.

As teachers, these five principles remind us of our students' central role in learning both content and process. In the next section we focus on the role of play as one of the primary ways young children learn.

Michelle Pearlstein

Adults need to value the importance of children's play.

How Play Contributes to Children's Learning

Understanding how play helps children learn is an important part of becoming a teacher of young children. You might have overheard conversations with parents of young children who say, "But all my child does is play," or ask, "When is my child going to learn something?" How will you respond when you are the child's teacher? Knowing why play is the catalyst for children's learning will help you answer these questions. It will also help you understand that the absence of play in young children is often an obstacle to their capacity for optimal learning.

A Definition of Play

Think about the following scenario in a Head Start classroom where two children are preparing a pretend birthday celebration for the child who plays the role of the mother. When they realize they need a present, one of the children says, "We can ask Mr. Bear."

This is a reference to the book, *Ask Mr. Bear,* by Marjorie Flack (1932), in which Danny tries to find the perfect birthday present for his mother by asking many different animals for suggestions. After the children locate the book in their library center, they take on the roles of the different animals in the book—the goat, the cow, the hen, the goose, and the bear—as they search for a birthday present for their "mother." When they finish the celebration for their "mother," they plan another celebration for their pretend sister. The book has become the content for role-playing, trying out different intonations that might sound like these animals, and talking with each other about how to enact their pretend birthday celebration. This particular scenario illustrates the definition of play as any activity that is freely chosen, meaningful, active, enjoyable, and open-ended (Fromberg, 2002; Frost, Wortham, & Reifel, 2005). Play is an important condition for learning that demonstrates the following unique characteristics.

Play is symbolic and enables children to demonstrate what they know about certain concepts. Symbolic play enables children to represent reality as they mentally think through solutions to problems (a "what if" attitude) and deepen their thinking (an "as if" attitude). For the two Head Start children, the "what if" thinking occurred when they imagined the roles of the animals. The "as if" behavior occurred when the children actually pretended to talk like the animals.

Play is meaningful and helps children make sense out of their experiences. In the preceding scenario, the children were relating what they knew about birthdays to the content of the book they had heard, *Ask Mr. Bear.*

Play is active and is a natural process of doing something both mentally and physically. The children's reenactment of the familiar story demonstrates how they "learned by doing" by exploring the roles of the animals and inventing their own version of a birthday celebration.

Play is pleasurable and supports children's different ways of learning even when the activity is serious. The idea that children's enjoyment can actually enhance their learning is often difficult to understand and accept, yet we know that the two children are enjoying their reenactment and at the same time seriously preparing a birthday celebration for the child who plays the role of the mother.

TEACHER PREP WEBSITE 5.2

Go to Video Classroom, select Early Childhood Education, choose Early Learning (Module 2), and select Intrinsic Motivation–Early Childhood (Video 1).

Play is voluntary and intrinsically motivating, and capitalizes on children's curiosity through personally meaningful and purposeful experiences. The children's initiative in locating the book and establishing the scenario to enact is a good illustration of this characteristic. You can see an interviewer asking a primary-aged boy about what *motivates* him to learn, such as the desire to succeed or for the pure enjoyment of the challenge, in the "Intrinsic Motivation–Early Childhood" video clip online at the Teacher Prep Website.

Play is rule-governed, whether the rules are implied or expressed, and allows children to apply rules to different settings. In play, children establish and sometimes change the rules; nevertheless, there are rules for appropriate role behavior and the responsibilities of the players. These rules organize children's play, as is evident in the roles taken on in the preceding scenario.

Play is episodic in that there are emerging and shifting goals throughout the experience that foster children's strategic thinking. In the *Ask Mr. Bear* play scenario described earlier, the children completed their enactment of the birthday party for the child playing the role of mother and then immediately began to plan another birthday party for their sister, shifting the focus of the play.

In play, children construct understandings of their world, become empowered to do things for themselves, and experience social competence. These are essential learning processes. In addition, the play context contributes to children's learning across all of the domains (Isenberg & Jalongo, 2006; Wassermann, 2000).

The Importance of Play

Most educators do not understand how play or playful ways of knowing help children learn. If you ask teachers of young children what play is, they might say, "It is when children are dressing up and pretending, or using games, or going outside during recess." These views of play are limited mostly to physical activity and do not represent how play contributes to all aspects of children's development, how it helps children construct knowledge, or how it helps children learn.

In the field of early childhood education, play has long been respected as the primary way young children learn. According to Bredekamp and Copple (1997), research and theory across disciplines support the notion that "play gives children opportunities to understand their world, interact with others in social ways, express and control emotions, and develop their symbolic capabilities" (p. 14). The work of Vygotsky and Piaget illustrates the important role of play in the following quotes. According to Vygotsky (1978), play is a "leading factor in development [because] in play a child behaves beyond his average, above his daily behavior; in play it is as though he were a head taller than himself" (p. 102). According to Piaget (1980), "play is a powerful form of activity that fosters the social life and constructive activity of the child" (p. viii). Moreover, through play, children also discover what they can do, test their physical and mental abilities, and compare these with those of their peers. While play is important for all children, it is particularly important for children with exceptional learning needs (e.g., delays in motor skills, speech and language, or social development) and for English language learners (Allen & Cowdery, 2005; Frost et al., 2005). Doris Fromberg, noted expert on play, answers some commonly asked questions about play in the "Ask the Expert" feature that follows.

Scott Cunningham/Merrill

Children need appropriate levels of challenging activities.

Play and Children with Exceptionalities

All children, regardless of their exceptional needs, play. Yet, depending on their exceptionality, some children may play differently and less effectively than their peers without exceptionalities because they are less likely to explore their environments, have less opportunity for social play, or are unable to think symbolically or use language skills like their peers without exceptionalities (Allen & Cowdery, 2005; Frost et al., 2005). Your role in helping children with exceptional needs learn through play is to intervene, encourage, and support their development of play skills. You can support children's learning by providing opportunities for them to practice specific skills, assisting with language development, adapting the play setting to accommodate their needs, and helping them enter a play situation once they have mastered specific skills. The more opportunity for social interaction, the more likely children with exceptionalities will increase the complexity of their play.

ASK THE EXPERT

Doris Pronin Fromberg on the Value of Play

Doris Fromberg

If children play, how will teachers have time to cover the curriculum?

Consider analyzing what you mean by "covering" the curriculum in ways that can "cover" the children. Consider the image of world-to-child as contrasted with child-to-world. Analyze what concepts and tasks you think the world-to-child curriculum intends. It will invariably be less significant than what children can organize if you provide the settings, props, and opportunities. Children's thinking develops in both ways, but their awareness of their own ideas as compared with those of others takes place particularly during sociodramatic play. They learn an enormous amount about how to create oral playwriting as they negotiate sociodramatic play episodes with other children. The feedback that they receive from playing with one another helps them to understand how effectively they communicate their child-to-world thoughts, a precursor to writing and comprehending stories.

When children play, could teachers lose control of the class?

When children play, they are engrossed in what they are doing. In any case, children who seem out of control when they have true choice and autonomy to set the rules of the play may very well be stressed by too much teacher direction and too much sedentary activity. This suggests the need to reevaluate the schedule of a class in order to reduce whole-class times, reduce the number of transitions, and lengthen blocks of time (not less than 45–60 minutes) in which children may select learning centers that include opportunities for all types of play.

If children play, will parents complain that they are not learning in school?

Some parents need to learn that the appearance of children actively engaged in play may mask the reality of their learning. Extensive research indicates that children who engage in pretend and sociodramatic play increase their literacy skills; cognitive development, particularly problem solving; social competence; and capacity to generate new connections in a creative way. Some ways to let parents know what children are learning in a class are the following: (a) save children's drawing and writing samples to show progress over time, (b) with photographic slides, document learning experiences that are active and show the uses of different materials and thematic props at parent meetings, (c) save language experience charts for display, (d) four-for-the-day: send four one- or two-line notes each day to four different parents informing them of something that their children learned that day and how their children participated, and (e) consider creating a collaborative newsletter with other teachers that records children's comments about their school activities.

What are the differences among work, exploration, and play?

Children usually define a particular activity as play if they autonomously choose to do it; they might define the same activity as *work* if the teacher asks them to do it. Philosopher John Dewey suggested a continuum of drudgery—. . . work . . . play . . . fooling— and proposed that a balance between work and play is appropriate for schools. *Exploration* is when we find out what something or someone can do, and *play* is when we see what we can do with it or another. Work, exploration, and play can be satisfying or challenging, but exploration and play are typically self-motivated and pleasurable, even when serious.

Doris Fromberg is a Professor of Education and Chairperson, Department of Curriculum and Teaching, Hofstra University, New York.

COMPANION WEBSITE 5.4 To learn more about linguistic and cultural diversity, go to *Enrichment Content: Research Highlight* in Chapter 5 of the Companion Website at http://www.prenhall.com/jalongo.

Play and Children from Diverse Backgrounds

The ever increasingly diverse population of children mandates that early childhood teachers provide learning opportunities that encourage understanding of others. Adults gain important insights into children's learning by understanding what to look for when children play. Young children's play provides adults with important information about children's cultural experiences. You can learn about special traditions, celebrations, and family values by watching and listening to children at play. One appropriate way to do this is to provide culturally relevant toys and materials for children's play (Frost et al., 2005). Toys such as dolls, games, puppets, puzzles, and motor toys are common to children worldwide and are differentiated only by their decoration or presentation. Through the use of culturally appropriate materials and toys, children have the opportunity to learn about others, practice newly acquired skills, take on new social roles, and "play out" what is already familiar and comfortable to them.

Recall that earlier in this section we defined play as a condition for learning that has unique characteristics. Children learn best when play is linked with other conditions such as social interaction, concrete experiences, and a sense of competence. The characteristics of play (e.g., that it is active, voluntary, and symbolic) support children's learning of specific academic skills across the content areas and growth in each developmental domain. (See Chapter 7 for a full discussion of these content areas.) Table 5.2 illustrates the connections between play and learning.

TABLE 5.2 Play and Learning

Learning Domain	Play Experiences	Skills and Concepts Learned
Cognitive	• sorting objects • playing school at the chalkboard	• problem solving, hypothesis testing • problem solving, mental planning, self-evaluation
Language	• repeating rhymes, using nonsense words, telling jokes and riddles, and chanting jump-rope songs • role-playing a trip to the hospital and maintaining a complex play theme	• using language to organize and maintain their play; understanding multiple meanings; understanding words, sounds, and grammatical structure; exploring the phonological, syntactic, and semantic rules of language • using purposeful verbal interactions with explanations, discussions, negotiations, and commands; exploring the forms and functions of language
Literacy	• pretending to read a book, write a shopping list, read environmental print, and reenact stories	• developing interest in stories and books, comprehending stories and story structure; understanding fantasy in books; and symbolically representing the world
Social and emotional development	• engaging in dramatic and sociodramatic play, reenacting stories, working through conflicts, learning how to enter an ongoing play event, and creating a puppet show	• seeing other perspectives; taking turns; sharing roles, materials, and responsibilities; communicating both verbally and nonverbally for needs and wants; waiting for a turn • developing empathy for others' feelings; expressing one's own feelings and coping with them (helps children think out loud about their experiences so they can cope with them more easily)
Physical	• using various writing and drawing tools (e.g., markers, paintbrushes, pencils) • engaging in running and climbing activities and games	• fine-motor skills • gross-motor skills • body awareness and fitness
Creative	• pretending to have a birthday party; using scraps of material and paper for creating art products; and interpreting familiar roles in new ways	• problem solving, internal imagery, flexible thinking, and alternative responses to situations

SOURCE: Adapted from Isenberg, J. P., & Jalongo, M. R. (2006).

Stages and Types of Play

PAUSE AND REFLECT
About Play

Think back to some of your most pleasant moments when you were invited to "come and play." What characteristics of play were evident in these experiences? How do you think these experiences helped you learn? Relate your experiences to what Doris Fromberg says about how play fosters learning in the Ask the Expert feature in this chapter.

Children's play develops in a sequence that parallels their cognitive and social development. *Cognitive play* reflects children's ages, understandings, and experiences. It includes sensorimotor play, symbolic play, constructive play, and games with rules (Piaget, 1970; Smilansky & Shefatya, 1990). *Social play* describes children's interactions with their peers. It includes onlooker, solitary, parallel, associative, and cooperative play (Parten, 1932). While both cognitive and social play develop sequentially over time, some types of play are more typical of particular periods of children's development. Nonetheless, all types of play occur in different forms throughout one's life. Table 5.3 lists the types of cognitive and social play, provides a definition of each, and supplies an age-appropriate example.

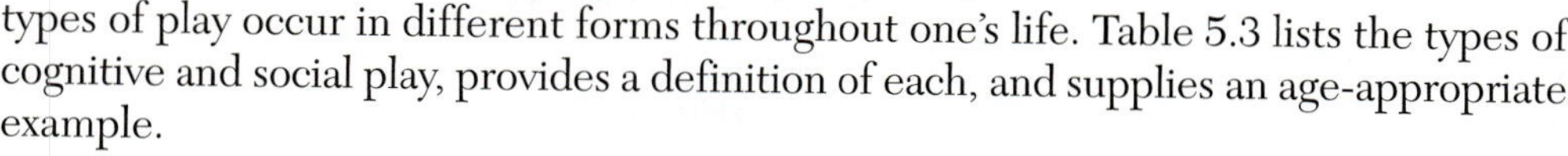

Fostering Learning Through Technology

Today's children live in a technological world. Infants use books and other toys that are computer based and contain synthetic voice output; toddlers manipulate computer software programs using touch screens and large track balls; preschoolers and kindergartners use computer art programs, and school-age children learn through the Internet. With this technology revolution comes the need for all children, including children with exceptional needs learning through assistive technology, to develop technological skills such as digital literacy, new ways of thinking, effective communication skills, and a capacity for higher-order thinking (Swaminathan & Wright, 2003). The challenge to early childhood teachers is to find appropriate ways to use technology as a powerful tool to foster children's learning (Clements & Sarama, 2003; Haugland, 2000). You can see an example of how Katie's printed sportsmanship trophy could enhance her learning by acknowledging her attitude towards school participation in the "Educational Technology–Technology, Media and Learning" student and teacher artifacts online at the Teacher Prep Website.

TEACHER PREP WEBSITE 5.3

Go to Student and Teacher Artifacts, select Educational Technology, choose Technology, Media and Learning (Module 1), and select Personalized Sportsmanship Trophy Printout (K–2), (Artifact 1).

Using Computers to Facilitate Learning

Consider the following scenario in a first- and second-grade multiage classroom. Pairs of children are using the software program Kidspiration (2000) as part of their study of a plant life cycle. The children chose pictures from a "library" of pictures created by scanning in photos of the different stages of a plant's life cycle, placed them in correct order on the cycle, and then wrote about what each stage represented. During this process, the children took turns using the mouse and doing the typing, but consulted one another about which picture came next. In one conversation, one of the children said to the teacher: "I'm doing the odd-number stages, and she's doing the even-number stages."

The teacher in this scenario effectively maximized children's learning by selecting appropriate software (Kidspiration) and integrating it appropriately in the curriculum. Software that meets the learning needs of children enhances their visual thinking, self-expression, persistence, teamwork, and communication skills—the essential technological

TABLE 5.3 Types of Children's Play

Type of Play	Definition	Age-Appropriate Example
Cognitive Play		
Sensorimotor	Repeated movements with or without materials—sensorimotor play is the primary type of play for infants and toddlers.	Infants and toddlers: stacking and unstacking rings on a pole Preschool and kindergartners: repeating a pattern while stringing beads School-age children: practicing jump-rope skills and rhymes
Symbolic	Involves transforming one object into another and later transforming self and object to satisfy needs in dramatic play. Symbolic play emerges around age 2 and dominates in the years between ages 2 and 7.	Infants and toddlers: pretending to drink from a toy cup Preschoolers and kindergartners: pretending to rescue people from a burning building School-age children: using secret codes or made-up languages to communicate
Constructive	Making things from a preconceived plan—constructive play combines sensorimotor and symbolic play.	Preschoolers and kindergartners: constructing a plane from a building set School-age children: creating sets for a story reenactment
Games with rules	Predetermined rules guide acceptable behavior and depend upon reciprocal behavior—games with rules emerge in simple form in infancy but predominate in the school-age years and beyond.	Infants and toddlers: playing peek-a-boo Preschoolers and kindergartners: playing simple singing and circle games School-age children: playing card games, board games, group games
Social Play		
Onlooker	Observing what others are doing, not joining in the play but involved as a spectator. Toddlers engage in a great deal of onlooker play.	Infants and toddlers: watching another child paint at an easel Preschoolers and kindergartners: watching an ongoing play group before deciding to enter School-age children: watching a group game before participating
Solitary	Playing alone and independently, child concentrates on the activity rather than on other children. Solitary play is typical of infants and toddlers and young preschool children, but may be seen in older children as well.	Infants and toddlers: playing alone and showing no interest in others Preschoolers and kindergartners: playing with own toys School-age children: choosing to play alone for privacy or to think about how to elaborate a play theme
Parallel	Playing side by side but not with others, using toys similar to others and sometimes imitating the behavior of other playing children. Parallel play is typical of toddlers and young preschool children.	Infants and toddlers: playing nearby others with little or no interaction Preschoolers and kindergartners: using shared toys but not sharing toys School-age children: using own materials but aware of others using the same materials
Associative	Playing with others in a loosely organized activity with a major interest in being with each other rather than the play itself. Associative play first appears in young preschool children and is often the first attempt at group play.	Preschoolers, kindergartners, and school-age children: playing in the same area with the same materials but for different purposes and different ends
Cooperative	A complex form of play with shared goals focusing on social interaction. Uses negotiation, differentiated roles, and division of labor to create, coordinate, and enact a play theme. Cooperative play is most typical of older preschoolers and school-age children.	Older preschoolers and school-age children: building an airport and deciding how to get there, what to see, and how to build a lounge, air-traffic control tower, hangar, and parking lot

skills for the 21st century (Clements & Sarama, 2003; Haugland, 2000; NAEYC, 1996; Swaminathan & Wright, 2003). Computer drawing programs, such as Delta Draw, Color Me, and Thinkin' Things Collection 3, encourage discovery and the invention of stories. Open-ended software, such as Millie's Math House, Bailey's Book House, Kidspiration, and *KidPix*, encourages children to work together to create a quality product. Problem-solving and inquiry oriented software, such as *Destination: Neighborhood*, *Destination: Time Trip USA*, *Create Your Own Adventure with Zeke*, and *Oregon Trail*, provides children with possibilities to gather information, make decisions, and test their solutions. Computer materials such as Ani's Rocket Ride and Ani's Playground reflect the Reggio Emilia approach to learning and encourage children's intellect, curiosity, social interaction, and interests. Before using any software with young children, review it for quality and for an appropriate match to the child outcomes identified in your early childhood setting. (See the website www.netc.org/ earlyconnections/ index.html for more resources and information on connecting technology with how children learn, selecting appropriate software, and lesson plans on integrating technology into your curriculum across grade levels.)

Selecting appropriate websites is a second consideration. Whether it is an *information site* used to help children gain new knowledge and answer questions; a *communication site*, which puts children in touch with one another in the classroom, center, school, community, nation, or world; or a *publication site* that provides a place to post children's products, these sites must be evaluated as well. You can evaluate websites using specific evaluation tools (Haugland & Gerzog, 1998).

COMPANION WEBSITE 5.5 For more information about technology and early childhood, go to *Web Links* in Chapter 5 of the Companion Website at http://www.prenhall.com/jalongo.

Major Learning Theories

As an early childhood teacher, how you think children learn strongly influences what and how you teach them. Many scientifically tested theories of learning have endured and are used widely. But because learning is so complex, we cannot use one single theory to explain it. Thus, early childhood educators use multiple theories to understand how children learn.

What Is a Theory?

A theory is an organized system of knowledge that describes, explains, and predicts behavior. Theories "guide and give meaning to what we see [and] . . . theories that are verified by research often serve as a sound basis for practical action" (Berk, 2005, p. 7). The fields of psychology, anthropology, and sociology provide early childhood educators with most of the theories of how children learn. From these theories, you will begin to make decisions in your own classrooms about classroom environments, motivation, and appropriate expectations for children's learning.

Some theories suggest that nature, or heredity, exerts the greatest influence on learning; others suggest that nurture, or the physical and social environment, exerts the most influence on children's learning. Most modern views of learning explore how nature and nurture work together to influence learning. In the sections that follow, we examine the major learning theories that influence how teachers approach learning. We describe the key ideas of each theory, identify the primary theorists associated with each theory, and apply each theoretical perspective to early childhood classrooms.

Maturation Theory of Learning

Maturation theory suggests that growth is hereditary and naturally unfolds through a predetermined sequence under the proper conditions. It focuses on predictable patterns of development that are the result of a biological, genetic plan and assumes that efforts to teach behaviors before they naturally occur are unnecessary and may indeed be harmful to children's learning (Santrock, 2007; Woolfolk, 2007). To illustrate, most children begin to sit, walk, talk, play, and read at about the same ages. These early developmental milestones set the stage for learning more complex skills throughout one's life. Even though all children progress through typical sequences of development, they do so at different rates. Consequently, maturation theorists assume that children who are not ready to learn a skill do not benefit from intervention.

Maturation Theorists

ARNOLD GESELL (1890–1961). Arnold Gesell was a physician who studied the process of maturation at the Yale University Clinic for Child Development. Gesell was the first theorist to provide systematic, normative descriptions of children's development in all domains—physical, language, intellectual, and social—through detailed descriptions of children from birth through age 10. His research, commonly referred to as "ages and stages," provides typical characteristics of children by ages that represent a predictable sequence of development for all children regardless of race, culture, or economic status.

Other maturation theorists who have influenced our thinking about learning include Jean-Jacques Rousseau and Noam Chomsky. Rousseau (1712–1778), a French philosopher and author of *L'Emile,* believed that children are inherently good and should be left to develop naturally so their inherent goodness can develop. Rousseau was the first to identify "childhood" as a stage of life. Chomsky (1928–), a noted linguist, emphasizes the important role of maturation in learning language. He suggests that children are "prewired," or biologically endowed, to learn language at a particular time and in a particular way, thus explaining the differences in the capacity for children's language to develop.

APPLYING MATURATION THEORY IN EARLY CHILDHOOD PRACTICE. Maturation theory and research has helped parents, pediatricians, and teachers clarify expected behaviors for children at particular ages and provide age-appropriate learning environments and materials. The following strategies have their roots in maturationist theory.

TEACHER PREP WEBSITE 5.4

Go to Student and Teacher Artifacts, select Early Childhood Education, choose Early Learning (Module 2), and select Jeff (Language Arts–Preschool) (Artifact 3).

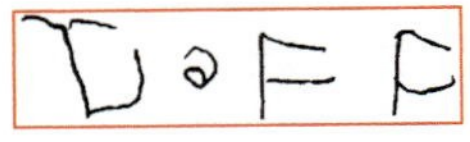

1. ***Use developmental milestones as the basis for your teaching.*** Assess children's progress and plan experiences based on what they can do today and what is anticipated that children will next be able to accomplish. However, be cautious about misusing some of these "ages and stages" data so that you do not label children as delayed rather than identifying their strengths as individual learners as the starting point on the learning continuum. You can see preschooler, Jeff, exhibit his ability to write his name in the "Early Childhood Education–Early Learning" student and teacher artifacts online at the Teacher Prep Website.
2. ***Rely on your own ability to monitor the knowledge and skill acquisition of all children.*** Children develop at different rates in one or more areas. Because there are no fixed criteria for what constitutes delayed development, early childhood teachers must have a clear understanding of how children learn.

3. ***Provide learning experiences at children's present level of ability.*** The notion of readiness has its roots in maturation theory. This concept can sometimes be counterproductive by maintaining children's current level of learning rather than providing them with appropriate levels of challenging learning opportunities. Decisions about the appropriate time to enter kindergarten based solely on age, and waiting to teach children to read until they are mentally ready are still evident in many early childhood settings today.

Behavioral Theory of Learning

Behavioral theory identifies all learning in terms of behavior that can be observed, measured, and recorded. Although behaviorists acknowledge that heredity somewhat limits what people can learn, they view the environment as the most influential element on learning. They suggest that learning is the accumulation of knowledge and responses through selective reinforcement, and that learning occurs when one reacts to aspects of the environment that are pleasurable or painful. From the behaviorist perspective, learning occurs in three different ways: *through association* (classical conditioning), *through reinforcement* (operant conditioning), and *through observation and imitation* (observational learning). Learning through *association* occurs when a person generalizes between events. When a young child says "bird" for all things that fly, adults provide reinforcing responses, such as, "We call that an airplane." Eventually, the child distinguishes birds from other flying things. Learning through *reinforcement* happens when adults try to stop an inappropriate behavior by ignoring it or praise a behavior to ensure its continuance. Learning through *observation* occurs when children watch the behaviors of peers and adults, form mental pictures of them, and later try to imitate those behaviors. How behaviors are reinforced determines how ingrained they become. Because behaviorists consider learners to be passive recipients of stimuli from the environment, they believe that learning results from the adults' shaping and changing children's behavior through the use of cues and reinforcement techniques in a carefully designed external environment.

Behavioral Theorists

B. F. SKINNER (1904–1990). Probably the best-known behavioral theorist is B. F. Skinner, who theorized that all behavior can be modified and that the basic principles of learning apply to all learners, regardless of age. He assumed that specific behaviors can be increased through a range of reinforcers such as smiles and praise, and decreased through punishment, such as withdrawal of special privileges.

Other behavioral theorists who have influenced our view of learning are John Locke, Edward Thorndike, and John Watson. John Locke (1632–1704), a prominent English philosopher, theorized that environment and experience determine learning. He proposed that environment is the primary factor in shaping individual development and learning. Locke's ideas paved the way for future behaviorists.

Edward Thorndike (1874–1949) studied learning through association and suggested the stimulus-response method. From his research on animals, Thorndike concluded that learning depends on associations, which in turn form learned habits. Complex learning is the result of combined associations.

John Watson (1878–1958), an American psychologist influenced by Russian psychologist Ivan Pavlov, is known for his ideas about classical conditioning. In his view, learning depends only on observable behaviors. Watson claimed he could shape the entirety of a person's learning by taking full control of all events of a child's first year of life and by discouraging emotional and social connections between parents and their children.

APPLYING BEHAVIORAL THEORY IN EARLY CHILDHOOD PRACTICE. Behavioral learning theory is among the most influential views of learning today. It has given rise to practices that are orderly, carefully sequenced, and demonstrate change in observable behavior. Behavioral principles of learning have been applied in the following ways.

1. ***Use of behavior modification,*** a behavior management tool that is widely used to eliminate undesirable behaviors and increase desirable behaviors. Many early childhood teachers use external rewards (e.g., stickers, smiley faces, and marbles) to motivate and control behavior. While reward systems do work for some children, you will need to examine how and when they should be used, if at all.
2. ***Incorporate time-out,*** which is removing a child from a situation and ignoring the undesirable behavior. Though this technique promotes automatic responses to specific requests, it does not promote inner or self-control. The use of time-out must be handled very carefully and sensitively.
3. ***Employ some drill-and-practice exercises.*** Memorizing word lists and multiplication tables are typical examples of a behavioral approach to learning. Many teachers rely almost exclusively on this approach to learning. Whereas drill-and-practice exercises promote the learning of discrete facts and skills, they do not provide children with the opportunity to think about "big ideas" or to think conceptually about problems.

Social Learning Theory of Learning

Social learning theory suggests that children learn social behaviors by observing and imitating models, especially those of their parents. It accepts the key behavioral learning principles of conditioning and reinforcement but has expanded them to include how children learn social skills. Social learning theorists view learners as being active in shaping their own learning and believe that observational learning, a cognitive influence on learning, is central to how children learn. They also acknowledge the central role of children's identification with key family members in influencing their learning of language, dealing with aggression, developing a moral sense, and learning socially acceptable behaviors (Santrock, 2007; Woolfolk, 2007). Today, social learning theory is more influential than behavioral learning theory in considering how children learn.

Social Cognitive Theorists

ALBERT BANDURA (1925–). Albert Bandura, a contemporary behaviorist, expanded the principles of behaviorism and conceived the theory of social learning. He recognized that children learn much of their social behavior from imitating or watching others. As a result, modeling became a major principle of learning that has prompted parents and teachers to explicitly demonstrate expected forms of behavior. Bandura's work underscores that how children think about themselves and judge their own expectations about learning strongly influences their behavior and their beliefs about their own abilities to learn.

APPLYING SOCIAL LEARNING THEORY IN EARLY CHILDHOOD PRACTICE. Social learning techniques are widely used to help children develop appropriate behaviors, skills, and approaches to learning. They bridge behavioral theories with cognitive theories by acknowledging the active role children play in their own learning and the cognitive influences on learning (Berk, 2005; Woolfolk, 2007). Among the applications of social learning theory that will influence learning in your classrooms are the following.

Anthony Magnacca/Merrill

Children imitate behavior that they observe.

1. ***Model appropriate skills and behavior.*** When young children have difficulty in getting along with other children, for example, you can model appropriate ways of getting along to change undesirable interactions and understand the reasons for doing so. If a preschooler wants a toy from another child and grabs rather than asks for it, you can model appropriate behavior by encouraging the child to use words to ask for what he or she needs. Second, observational learning occurs in sociodramatic play when young children are asked to imitate behaviors of important adults in their lives (e.g., parents, siblings, teachers) to demonstrate what they would like the children to accomplish; with guided practice, children often can complete the task. Third, model the skills you teach through "think-alouds," to illustrate your thinking, such as helping children see how you read to the end of a sentence to get the meaning of a sentence even if you cannot read all of the words.
2. ***Promote self-efficacy.*** Hearing adults' comments about children's efforts (e.g., "I'm pleased that you didn't give up on that task even though it was hard and frustrating" or "I know you can figure that problem out") helps children view themselves as can-do rather than can't-do learners. Such comments also promote interest in learning through self-efficacy and the development of personal standards and expectations. You can see two digital photos of Megan, a primary grade child, that show her "can do" attitude towards learning mathematics on the "Educational Technology–Computers" student and teacher artifacts online at the Teacher Prep Website.
3. ***View children as active learners.*** Children play an active role in their own learning, particularly in choosing whose behavior to imitate. These models may be significant adults such as parents or teachers, or they may be television heroes. When children spend many hours watching cartoons or adult television programs, for example, they often adopt the behaviors of those characters as their own.
4. ***Promote opportunities for self-regulation.*** Children can participate in appropriately setting their own learning goals, monitoring their progress, and assessing the effectiveness of their efforts with the help of supportive adults. Checklists, choice charts, and conferences can be used to help children develop self-regulation.

TEACHER PREP WEBSITE 5.5

Go to Student and Teacher Artifacts, select Educational Technology, choose Computers (Module 3), and select Digital Images of Megan's Math (K–2) (Artifact 1).

Constructivist Theory of Learning

Constructivist theory focuses on the mental processes children use in thinking and remembering. It views learning as the self-regulated changes in one's thinking that occur from the acquisition of knowledge through which learners seek solutions to cognitive challenges. Influenced by research in the cognitive, computer, and social sciences, constructivism emphasizes the active roles of the learner, prior knowledge, social interactions, and authentic tasks in constructing understanding rather than imposing knowledge (Woolfolk, 2007). Constructivist theory is rooted in the works of Jean Piaget, Jerome Bruner, and Lev Vygotsky and can be viewed from the interrelated perspectives of cognitive developmental and sociocultural theory.

Cognitive Developmental Constructivist Theory

JEAN PIAGET (1896–1980). Piaget, a Swiss biologist and theorist, studied how children acquire knowledge and how thinking and learning develop in children. Piaget assisted in standardizing the first intelligence test at the Binet Laboratory in Paris. While assessing the intelligence of French schoolchildren with this test, he became intrigued with children's incorrect answers to questions. Simultaneously, he noted that children's responses appeared to be age related.

Central to Piaget's cognitive theory is the concept of adaptation. Adaptation, which begins in infancy and continues over a lifetime, is how the mind develops cognitive structures to make sense of the outside world. According to Piaget, learning is the active construction of knowledge through interactions with people and their environment that takes place in stages. It results from the interactions among the reciprocal processes of assimilation, accommodation, and equilibration. From children's interactions with their environment, they organize mental structures that become the foundation for more complex thinking and learning. They do this by taking in new information into existing structures (assimilation) or by changing existing structures to accommodate the new information (accommodation), therefore creating a balance between the new and the old information that makes sense to them (equilibration). Imagine yourself arriving for your first class at your current college or university. You first had to figure out certain features of the building, such as where your room was, how you got from the classroom to the restroom, and perhaps how you could get a snack during a break (assimilation). Familiarizing yourself with the building enabled you to routinely enter the building and find essential places in the future so that you do not have to think each time about how to find your classroom. You changed your mental structures and used accommodation to learn your way around the building. Learning your way around the building is an example of equilibration, the mental need to find ways to maneuver in a new environment. For Piaget, the changes in behavior reflect changes in thinking occurring in distinct stages with unique features that correlate with specific ages of development.

In Piaget's theory, children's minds develop in a series of four stages, each of which is characterized by distinct ways of thinking. Each stage builds upon the preceding one, which becomes the foundation for new ways of thinking about and responding to the world. From birth through age 2, children are in the *sensorimotor stage.* Infants learn about their world by using their senses to solve sensorimotor problems, such as shaking a rattle to hear noise or finding hidden objects. This sensorimotor thinking evolves into the *preoperational stage,* which lasts from ages 2 to 7. During this stage, children use symbolic thinking to show what they know, especially through pretend play and language. Preoperational thinking lacks the logical qualities that are characteristic of the thinking of older children and adults. In the next stage, the *concrete operational stage,* children ages 7 to 11 build upon preoperational thinking and think in more logical ways, but their thinking and learning are tied to concrete objects. Though children organize objects into various categories and hierarchies at this stage, they are not yet ready to think abstractly. From about age 11 on, children in the *formal operational stage* are able to think and reason abstractly in ways that are similar to those of mature adolescents and adults (Berk, 2005).

JEROME BRUNER (1915–). Influenced by the work of Piaget, Jerome Bruner promoted the idea of discovery learning and individual concept learning through the study of the thought processes of perception, memory, strategic thinking, and classification. He promoted the idea of discovery learning and concept development in which children must figure out problems for themselves. Unlike Piaget, Bruner does not propose stages of these thinking capacities; rather, he theorizes that they are simply less well developed in children. Bruner likens learning to a computer, because learning occurs as much from the outside in as from the inside out. Thus, the mind actively codes, transforms, and organizes information as it takes it in. Bruner views children as active learners who organize information into higher and more complex categories and modify their own thinking as it makes sense to them in their environments.

APPLYING COGNITIVE DEVELOPMENTAL CONSTRUCTIVIST THEORY IN EARLY CHILDHOOD PRACTICE. Cognitive developmental theory has fundamentally changed the way we view teaching and learning. It has been applied in the following ways.

1. ***Plan learning experiences that stimulate children's curiosity*** through the use of concrete inquiries, experiments, and discovery learning that mentally involves hands-on use of open-ended materials. In a science study of shadows, for example, younger children might investigate how to make long and short shadows using flashlights and paper; older children might use shadows to determine the size of objects. Both of these experiences enable children to construct knowledge about sources of light.
2. ***Facilitate, rather than direct, learning.*** Your role is to provide meaningful activities and ask questions that promote children's thinking, decision making, and the exchange of viewpoints. By also encouraging children to explain their answers and reasons, you stimulate their thinking.
3. ***Foster exploration, discovery, big ideas, and investigation.*** Early childhood classrooms must include a variety of equipment and materials for children to use each day. Having time to explore and think about materials helps children to build conceptual understanding. To understand the concept that mixing different proportions of colors produces new colors, for example, children need time to experiment with mixing colors, observe the changes that occur, and infer how to match someone else's color mixture rather than having an adult tell them what will happen during this process.
4. ***Connect content to the real world.*** Whatever the topic of study, children construct more meaningful understanding when they make connections to their own world and

Scott Cunningham/Merrill

Children need time to think and experiment.

their own experience. Always ask children what they already know about a topic so that you can provide appropriate learning activities that build upon their current understandings. For example, when *preschool and kindergarten children* study living things, provide a variety of experiences and activities for them to make connections to what is familiar. For instance, in the dramatic play center, add farmer and chef clothes and props and related books so that children can create their own market and act out stories. Or in the construction area, have them use pots, pans, empty seed packs, and rulers to design their own gardens. *Primary children* may germinate seeds to gain first-hand knowledge of the life cycle of plants or care for animals at home and in the classroom to develop foundational concepts of the foundational needs of all living things.

Sociocultural Constructivist Theory

LEV SEMENOVICH VYGOTSKY (1896–1934). Vygotsky, a Russian psychologist, asserted that the social and cultural context strongly influences how children learn. Sociocultural theory is an outgrowth of Vygotsky's studies of educational practices with Russian children with disabilities. Many of these disabilities were caused by years of war, famine, and poverty that beset the Soviet Union early in the 20th century, suggesting that cultural influences strongly impact children's learning.

According to Vygotsky (1978), children learn primarily through their relationships with other people, particularly in dialogue between each child and a more knowledgeable person. These social relationships form the basis for later communication and thinking. Vygotsky emphasizes the importance of family, social interaction, adults and more capable peers, and play as primary influences on learning and believed that as a result, learning occurs first on the social level and then on an individual level.

Three major concepts permeate Vygotsky's sociocultural theory: the zone of proximal development (ZPD), scaffolding, and the role of the adult. First, Vygotsky theorized that a child has an actual and a potential level of learning. The distance between what a child can do independently (actual level) and what that child can do with assistance (potential level) is called the **zone of proximal development** and substantially influences children's learning when they encounter a problem to solve (Vygotsky, 1978). When children work at their potential level, they experience what is possible to do independently before they can actually do it.

Vygotsky's second major concept is **scaffolding,** a support system that enables children to move along the learning continuum by building new competencies. For scaffolding to take place between an adult and a child, the child must be engaged in meaningful, problem-solving situations with mutual give-and-take between the learner and the adult.

Last, Vygotsky ascribed major importance to the **role of the adult** in children's learning. Through the use of the zone of proximal development, supportive adults can guide children's learning in many areas. Vygotsky viewed learning as a socially mediated process—as dependent upon the support that adults and more mature peers provide as children try new tasks.

APPLYING SOCIOCULTURAL CONSTRUCTIVIST THEORY IN EARLY CHILDHOOD PRACTICE. Vygotsky's emphasis on the relationship between culture and learning has given rise to the following early childhood practices.

1. ***Teach to a child's zone of proximal development.*** Adults who take responsibility for children's learning must provide learning experiences that are slightly above the children's level of functioning and assist children's inquiry and investigations in reaching toward the child's upper limit of understanding with assistance. You can support children's self-initiated learning by asking if there is anything you can do to help or by encouraging a child to keep practicing a skill.

2. *Use more capable peers, where appropriate, to guide learning.* Strategies such as cooperative learning activities (e.g., think, pair, share; cooperative learning groups) with a mix of ability levels provide important opportunities for children to learn. Classroom practices, such as multistudent projects and center-based learning, offer children opportunities to solve problems together through verbal exchanges and negotiation. The presence of imaginative play, small-group activities, mixed-age grouping, and children interacting with each other offers additional valuable learning experiences that capitalize on the social aspects of learning.

3. *Create early childhood classrooms that include discovery and guided learning experiences* with many opportunities for dialogue between children and adults. The richer the context for language usage in learning tasks, the more children will develop the knowledge and skills needed for a particular culture (Berk, 2005).

Multiple Intelligences Theory of Learning

HOWARD GARDNER (1943–). Howard Gardner is a psychologist at Harvard University and codirector of Project Zero, a cognitive research project that measures intelligence. He is best known for identifying eight different frames of mind, or intelligences: linguistic, logical/mathematical, musical, visual/spatial, bodily/kinesthetic, interpersonal, intrapersonal, and naturalist. Gardner (1993) views intelligence as more than a single ability that can be enhanced, taught, and changed. For Gardner, each form of intelligence involves unique cognitive skills that can be demonstrated through solving problems and creating products that are culturally valued. Problem solving enables learners to figure out how to reach a stated goal; creating products allows learners to display their knowledge, feelings, and understandings of their world. Grounded in brain research (see Figure 5.1), Gardner suggests that while each of us has certain intelligences that dominate, all of the intelligences work together to help individuals solve problems and accomplish a task. This inclusive view of intelligence differs from the narrower, traditional view that intelligence can be measured as a single entity that is demonstrated outside of one's natural learning environment through standardized testing. Table 5.4 describes each of Gardner's intelligences, and suggests possible learning applications.

APPLYING MULTIPLE INTELLIGENCES THEORY IN EARLY CHILDHOOD PRACTICE. If you consider for a moment the strengths in learning that your friends or family members have, you might notice that some are especially good at getting along with others. According to Gardner's theory, these individuals would have high interpersonal intelligence. Others you know may be especially capable of using language to express their knowledge and understand their world. In this case, they would be high in verbal/linguistic intelligence. Knowing these different capacities helps you to reach all types of learners when teaching skills and concepts so that children have an opportunity to show what they know and understand. Although Gardner's research is still new, it provides insights into maximizing children's potential by connecting classroom learning to real-life experiences. Multiple intelligences (MI) theory asks the question, "In which ways is this child smart?" The following practices represent multiple intelligences theory.

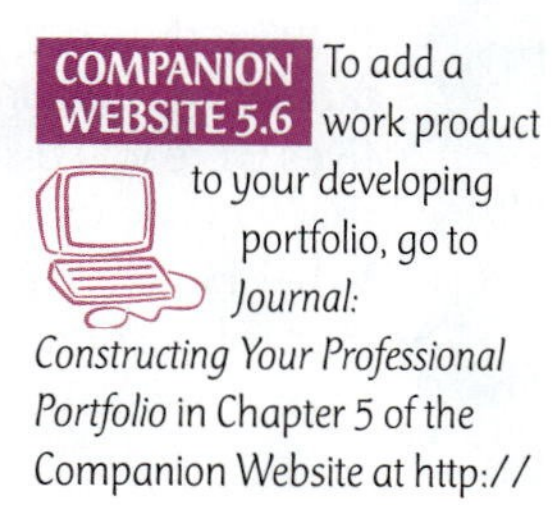
COMPANION WEBSITE 5.6 To add a work product to your developing portfolio, go to *Journal: Constructing Your Professional Portfolio* in Chapter 5 of the Companion Website at http://www.prenhall.com/jalongo.

1. *Incorporate curriculum approaches that tap into different intelligences,* such as journaling, playing games of logic, asking children to visualize an experience and then map it, having children make up songs, encouraging children's imagination and work in

TABLE 5.4 Applying Gardner's Eight Intelligences

Intelligence	Description	Applications
Verbal/linguistic	using language to express ideas and to understand others	writing in a journal, reading a book, listening to a story, telling about an experience
Logical/mathematical	using reasoning to discern numbers, quantities, and abstract patterns (sometimes called scientific thinking)	making projects following a plan, comparing and contrasting objects, graphic organizers, performing calculations
Visual/spatial	forming images of your world in the mind	expressing ideas and feelings with no words (e.g., drawing, making posters, inventing an imaginary character), engaging in pretend play
Bodily/kinesthetic	using all or part of your body to make something or solve a problem	dancing, using movement, enacting a play; dramatic play, pantomime, noncompetitive games
Musical	thinking in music by hearing, recognizing, and remembering tonal patterns; sensitivity to rhythm and beat, humming	creating raps and songs, playing musical instruments, appreciating different kinds of music (folk and classical)
Interpersonal	understanding, getting along, and working well with others; relies on all other intelligences	teams, projects, cooperative group learning, verbal and nonverbal communication
Intrapersonal	knowing who you are and what you can and cannot do	reflecting on own actions, metacognitive activities (e.g., thinking strategies used in reading), writing about self
Naturalist	discriminating among living things (e.g., plants and animals) and developing sensitivity to the rest of the natural world	environmental units, caring for pets and plants, observing and touching real plants and animals outside, asking questions about similarities and differences in plants and animals, categorizing natural materials

SOURCES: Armstrong, (2000); Campbell, Campbell, & Dickinson, 2004.

groups, and creating a naturalist learning center in the classroom. Differentiating teaching in this way acknowledges the different talents that children possess.

2. ***Use assessment strategies that help students show what they know*** in a variety of ways. Authentic assessment such as portfolios and projects give children choices of how to display their learning (e.g., a play, a graph, a song). These strategies are consistent with a multiple intelligences view of learning.

3. ***Personalize teaching to meet children's cultural and learning needs.*** Linking learning to children's real-life experiences and their cultural backgrounds capitalizes on their strengths and maximizes learning potential. Knowing, for example, that many African American children often learn best through interpersonal relations, a teacher might tap into this intelligence through cooperative projects that include experimentation and improvisation. Knowing that many Hispanic children prefer holistic, concrete, and social approaches to learning, a teacher might provide them with opportunities to express their knowledge through art, music, drama, and dance in addition to verbal and linguistic forms to affirm their dominant intelligences (Berns, 2007). Table 5.5 compares the key theoretical perspectives on how children learn.

PAUSE AND REFLECT

About Theories of Learning

Think of a time when you taught something to a younger person. Describe the learner, the time and place, and what and how you taught that person. What theoretical perspectives were you using? Now that you have read this section, which theorists do you relate to? Why? How would these theories inform your own philosophy of learning? Compare and share your responses with a peer.

TABLE 5.5 A Comparison of Theoretical Perspectives on How Children Learn

Theory	Theorist	View of Learning	View of Learner	Role of Adult	Practical Applications
Nativist	Gesell (1890–1961) Rousseau (1712–1778) Chomsky (1928–)	• develops naturally by age-related stages • maturation is the key factor in learning; occurs when children are ready	• passive • emphasis on nature	• nonintervening; allow child's learning to unfold	• readiness—waiting for readiness skills to appear before beginning formal instruction
Behavioral	Skinner (1904–1990) John Locke (1632–1704) Edward Thorndike (1874–1949) John Watson (1878–1958)	• behavior can be observed, measured, and recorded • quantitative increase in learned behavior as children grow older • modeling and conditioning are primary principles of learning	• passive recipient of stimuli in environment	• shapes and changes behavior through cues and reinforcement techniques by direct intervention	• behavior modification • time out • stickers and rewards • behavioral charts • direct instruction
Social Learning	Bandura (1925–)	• results from observation and imitation of significant role models, especially parents • cognition is a strong influence on learning	• active in shaping own learning • how one thinks about one's own experiences influences beliefs about self-efficacy	• models expected behaviors and skills	• modeling • direct instruction
Constructivism: Cognitive Developmental	Piaget (1896–1980)	• mental structures determine how children understand their world • occurs in stages that are distinctly different from one another • new learning depends on prior understanding	• active, not reactive • independent effort to make sense of world by actively constructing knowledge	• presents useful problems to solve that challenge and support children's innate drive to seek solutions to problems • prepares an environment with hands-on learning materials that challenge students' thinking while doing	• discovery and inquiry learning • concrete objects to teach concepts (e.g., manipulatives in mathematics)

(continued)

TABLE 5.5 Continued

Theory	Theorist	View of Learning	View of Learner	Role of Adult	Practical Applications
Constructivism: Cognitive Development (*continued*)	Bruner (1915–)	• active processing of experiences • quantitative increase in perception, attention, memory, and problem-solving skills with age • occurs from the interaction of nature and nurture • cultural context impacts learning • imaginative play helps children separate thought from action, influences learning	• actively processes experiences • active		
Constructivist: Sociocultural	Vygotsky (1896–1934)	• occurs first on a social level and then on an individual level • dialogue and language are critical to learning; self-talk provides guidance and direction to learning	• focus on the social context mediated by dialogue with others • more capable peers and adults influence learning • children internalize the essential social and cultural values, beliefs, and attitudes that guide their behavior	• does not assume a direct teaching role • provides variety of materials to be used in different ways • scaffolds learning to continue to build new competencies when learner is working at the edge of ability • teacher as a partner • asks questions that require investigative thinking and abilities	• cooperative learning • play leads learning activities • assisted learning and performance • shared activities • think-alouds and talk-alouds • discovery learning • children's interests
Multiple Intelligences	Gardner (1943–)	• intelligence has more than one dimension	• active in seeking more than one way of knowing	• provides learning opportunities that use different intelligences in the teaching/learning process	• teaching concepts through different intelligences • learners choose ways to learn • learners choose how to demonstrate knowledge • interdisciplinary curriculum • projects • authentic assessment

Given the vast array of theories on how children learn, it is important that you understand your own perspective on learning as well as that of the learner. The Pause and Reflect about Theories of Learning feature provides a good opportunity for you to think about what it means to learn.

COMPANION WEBSITE 5.7 To test your knowledge of this chapter's contents, go to the *Multiple-Choice* and *Essay* modules in Chapter 5 of the Companion Website at http://www.prenhall.com/jalongo. These items are written in the same format that you will encounter in the PRAXIS tests to better prepare you for your licensure exam.

Conclusion

A review of how children learn best reveals clear relationships between the way teachers approach learning and its lasting impact. Understanding the diverse ways in which young children learn maximizes their learning potential. Teachers, who have the greatest impact on children's learning, relate to children's experiences, connect learning opportunities to real-life situations, foster the acquisition of knowledge by allowing children to be participants in their own learning, provide scaffolding, and love learning themselves. Developing a healthy respect for different ways of learning, knowing, and representing knowledge and skills is necessary in all early childhood settings.

ONE CHILD, THREE PERSPECTIVES

Alexander's Struggle to Learn to Read as an English Language Learner

Alexander is in the third grade in a local public school. This is his first year in school in this country. In Russia, where he came from, Alexander was reading at grade level in Russian, his first language.

In Alexander's school, there are many children whose first language is not English. They are called English language learners. On the school support staff there is an English-as-a-second-language (ESL) teacher and an English-as-a-second-language specialist who assesses children's literacy levels and provides support for both second-language learners and their teachers. Alexander's teacher, Ms. Myers, referred Alexander to the ESL assessment specialist with the following note: "Alexander is not doing well in reading and lacks comprehension in content-area reading. He does not pay attention in reading group, nor does he understand grammar or spelling, show word recognition, or answer questions at the end of a reading assignment. Alexander cannot sit still during reading time, and is often excluded from the group. He has difficulty writing in English in his journal, completing long-term projects, and he has of late become frustrated and decreasingly confident in his ability to read and write even in his first language."

Each day Alexander goes to his ESL class, where the ESL teacher approaches reading and writing in English in a different way. Before beginning to read the text, his teacher formulates questions about the topic, finds out what Alexander knows about it, and assists Alexander through the text by using picture clues and other supports each step of the way. For content reading, the ESL teacher works with Alexander on strategies for gathering and recalling information. According to his ESL teacher, Alexander is making steady progress in English as a second language and is very attentive to the task of learning to read under her tutelage.

Soon after Alexander began having difficulty with reading and was becoming a behavior problem in her class, Ms. Myers called Alexander's parents, who are fluent in English, for a meeting with the ESL team and herself. Alexander's parents expressed surprise when Ms. Myers reported Alexander's lack of progress in learning to read and his lack of interest in school. In Russia and at home, Alexander has not been a problem. He reads a variety of things in Russian, his first language, and shows none of the behaviors Ms. Myers reports. Ms. Myers suggests that Alexander's parents stop using Russian at home and speak only English to Alexander. The ESL specialist suggests that he spend more time in her class using her ESL strategies. Alexander's parents do not want him to stop using his Russian. They end the meeting without arriving at an agreement on what to do for Alexander.

REACT	Think about how the perspectives of Ms. Myers, the ESL teacher, and Alexander's parents are alike and different. What might be some reasons? With whom do you identify most strongly in this case, and why?
RESEARCH	Search the ERIC website and read several articles on teaching reading to young children who are English language learners. What are the key learning principles that apply to this topic?
REFLECT	What assumptions about learning to read in a second language do Ms. Myers, the ESL teacher, and Alexander's parents make? Generate some key strategies for teaching reading to English language learners.

IN-CLASS WORKSHOP

Learning Environments for Multiple Intelligences

When you think about creating the best learning environments for children, you surely want to consider Howard Gardner's theory of multiple intelligences (MI) discussed earlier in this chapter. MI theory suggests that people have many forms of intelligence that are unevenly distributed and developed and can be improved through practice. As a teacher of young children, you will want to be aware of which intelligence(s) each individual child uses to best learn, understand, and construct knowledge. One way to do this is to create a balance of learning experiences that tap all of children's intelligences. This approach to teaching helps children to form and express their conceptual understanding through the intelligence(s) of their choice and make personal connections to their learning in all areas of the curriculum. It also provides opportunities to develop their untapped talents.

Using Gardner's theory of multiple intelligences, two first-grade teachers designed and implemented a mental health unit. They used three basic concepts to structure their unit: (a) physical affection can be an expression of friendship, celebration, or a loving family; (b) there is a difference between stressful and relaxing situations; and (c) individuals and the community need to be sensitive to persons with disabilities. Here is how they designed center-based learning experiences to deepen children's understandings (Liess & Ritchie, 1995).

Intelligence	Learning Experiences
Bodily/Kinesthetic	write in Braille by hole punching or gluing peas on a card; assist blindfolded friends around the school
Visual/Spatial	draw pictures of sounds you would miss if you could not hear or sights you would miss if you could not see
Musical/Rhythmic	write songs and raps about disabilities
Verbal/Linguistic	read stories about disabilities; decode sign language and Braille riddles
Interpersonal	select pictures from magazines of people assisting each other
Intrapersonal	reflect on learning in journals on the computer or by drawing
Logical/Mathematical	measure areas of the school for wheelchair use; examine the building to identify what needs to be done for people with disabilities
Naturalist	look for animals with a physical disability and discuss what needs to be done for animals with disabilities

Use the following procedure for incorporating MI as an essential part of the learning environment. When you have finished with this procedure, consider carefully the questions listed in item 6.

Procedure for Developing a Multiple Intelligences Learning Environment

1. **Select a topic or unit of study.** Select a topic or unit of study that your children show interest in or that you are required to teach. This topic can be from any area of the curriculum. Be sure you identify the major concepts or ideas you wish to teach.
2. **Brainstorm possible ideas including room arrangement and the schedule.** Think about all the possibilities for teaching. Make a list or a chart of all of them.
3. **Select activities and learning experiences.** From your list of ideas, select at least two different learning experiences for each intelligence that are most appropriate for children in your own setting. Decide which activities are most appropriate for each intelligence and tell why.
4. **Plan for arranging the learning centers.** Think about how to arrange the room so children can choose different centers. Consider the space, the traffic flow, and the type of materials you will need.
5. **Assess the children's learning.** Decide how you will assess what the children learned. You might consider observation, anecdotal records, photography, interviewing the children, or looking at their journal entries.
6. **Think about the implications by considering these questions.**
   - How does a multiple intelligences approach to teaching foster children's learning?
   - How does it set the stage for further learning?
   - What kinds of planning do teachers need to use this approach?

SOURCE: Adapted from "Using Multiple Intelligence Theory to Transform a First-Grade Health Curriculum," by E. Liess & G. Ritchie, 1995, *Early Childhood Education Journal, 23*(2), 71–79.

CHAPTER 6

Exploring Your Role in Creating High-Quality Early Childhood Environments

> **A warm, nurturing, stimulating environment tells children that they are valued and that they, and their ways of learning, are understood and respected. A dull, disorganized, or barren environment, on the other hand, suggests to children, their families, and the community that children are not valued or respected.**
>
> **Mary Anne Frye and Jacqueline Mumpower, 2001 p. 16**

Meet the Teachers

MS. KOEN is a lead teacher of 2-year-olds. During a recent graduate course, she learned that the "environment is the third teacher." The idea that the environment could be an important teaching and learning tool intrigued Ms. Koen, who was frustrated by the behavior of her toddlers. As she told her colleagues, "My classroom is small and everything seems to wind up all over the floor. The children argue over materials, and often wander aimlessly from activity to activity." After reading about good environments for toddlers, talking with her colleagues, and engaging in some personal reflection, Ms. Koen began to realize that toddlers' behavior is often affected by the classroom and materials provided for play. So, Ms. Koen redesigned her classroom space on paper, starting with the housekeeping area. She created a corner by placing the sink, stove, and refrigerator catty-corner to each other, and she placed the dolls and dress-up materials in separate containers so the children could more easily locate and put away the items. Next, she enlarged the block center to facilitate building, added figures and other materials to extend the toddlers' play, and moved the sand table to a location where it could be easily wheeled onto a drop cloth and four children could use it at the same time. Almost immediately, Ms. Koen noticed a change in the toddlers' behavior from aimless wandering to longer, more sustained play.

MS. ENDO has been teaching in Head Start for over 10 years and knows that her room must be safe, welcoming, and appropriate to meet the needs of all of the children. This year her class includes a child who is confined to a wheelchair as a result of injuries suffered in an automobile accident and a child with a visual impairment who requires teaching modifications using other sensory skills. After consulting with other members of the Head Start team (the nurse, social worker, speech-language therapist, and psychologist) as well as the children's families, Ms. Endo modified parts of the physical environment. She put adhesive-backed Velcro on the bottom of some fine-motor materials to help the child in the wheelchair attach items to the lap tray. She also cleared the pathways to accommodate the wheelchair and increase mobility for the child with low vision. Next, she adapted her classroom by altering the amount of light, distance, contrast, and colors, each of which affects how children process visual information. For example, she painted brightly colored letters on some wooden blocks to make them easier for the child with visual impairment to see. She decided to use storytelling and flannel-board characters, and she located lots of big books with enlarged type and pictures, a molded plastic globe, an abacus, and a clock with a raised face. She even found a book in the library on how to make touch toys and games. Ms. Endo also uses tactile cues, such as marking the child's name on his cubby with a textured sign that can be felt and taping small objects or toys on the outside of bins so that children can identify where each piece of equipment belongs.

MS. MITSOFF teaches first grade in an urban school. Early in the year, she and the children establish simple rules for sharing materials and respecting each other in their first-grade community because she believes that "The relationships children have with one another deeply affect the amount of control they have in their environment. Children need to be able to clearly express their feelings and ask for what they need to live harmoniously in their world and the world in which they will be growing up." Yet even though she takes time to create classroom behavioral expectations with the children, some children have disagreements over materials, space, or taking turns. When this occurs, Ms. Mitsoff expects the children to talk through their problems by themselves and find a solution before she intervenes. One example of this occurred on a day that two first-grade boys were making puppets to dramatize their original stories about the farm. The boys became increasingly silly, boisterous, and disruptive with their puppet making, so Ms. Mitsoff called them aside in a quiet corner to talk about the effect their interactions were having on the others. Each of the boys blamed the other for the noisy behavior. After listening to each child, Ms. Mitsoff said, "Talk to each other until you can figure out how to act appropriately in the puppet-making center so all the children can learn without being disturbed. Then come and tell me how you plan to solve the problem." Ms. Mitsoff uses this strategy to create a responsive learning environment that helps children become self-sufficient, collaborative problem solvers who can live comfortably in a community of respect, choice, and reasonable expectations.

These three teachers know how critical a safe, healthy, and challenging environment is. Use the following questions to compare, contrast, and connect these teachers' views on high-quality environments to your own ideas about establishing such environments for children.

COMPARE	What are some similarities in the ways these three teachers create their environments?
CONTRAST	What differences do you notice in the ways these teachers' environments communicate to children about learning, about using materials, and about a sense of belonging?
CONNECT	What impressed you most about how these teachers set up their classrooms and arranged materials to meet the needs of their children? How could you incorporate some of these ideas in your own teaching?

Now that you have reflected on the perspectives of these three teachers, here is a preview of the knowledge, skills, and dispositions you need to fulfill your role in creating high quality early childhood environments.

Learning Outcomes

- ✔ Become familiar with standards for creating appropriate environments for children **(INTASC #3, NAEYC #1c, and ACEI #5)**
- ✔ Appreciate the influence of the environment on children's behavior and learning
- ✔ Use criteria to select and evaluate materials for play and learning

DID YOU KNOW...?

- Depending on how it is arranged, the physical environment can elicit either aggressive or prosocial behavior. The physical environment of the classroom can contribute to social interactions of preschool children by providing "safe havens" for play within the environment (Martinez-Beck & Zaslow, 2006).
- For most children, outdoor play offers the only opportunity to engage in aerobic activities that enhance fitness—strength, flexibility, and endurance—and help compensate for faulty diets. Children who take time for physical education do at least as well academically as children who devote all their time to academic tasks (Frost, Brown, Sutterby, & Thornton, 2004).
- A disproportionate number of students from culturally and linguistically diverse backgrounds are inappropriately referred to and placed in special education environments. The Individuals with Disabilities Act (IDEA), reauthorized in 2004, seeks to redress the disproportionate number of these referrals.
- In the United States, 68% of 4-year-olds and 39% of 3-year-olds attend preschool, but there is a racial disparity between those attending public versus private preschools. More than 70% of 4-year-olds attending public preschool are either African American or Hispanic compared with 43% of white children attending public programs (Duncan, Cook, & Hedges, 2006).
- Children who attend a full-day public preschool perform better on literacy and math tests than children in a traditional half-day preschool and show continued gains through the end of first grade. High-quality full-day preschool programs narrowed the achievment gap between the privileged and less privileged children (Robin, Frede & Barnett, 2006).
- At least 38 states and the District of Columbia have one or more state-funded preschool initiatives (Barnett, Hustedt, Robin, & Shulman, 2004).

✔ Explore the early childhood educator's role in providing safe, healthy, and challenging environments for children's learning

✔ Apply principles of design to planning and evaluating indoor and outdoor environments

✔ Adapt environments to meet the needs of all children

A Definition of Environment

Imagine entering someone's home and immediately sensing that you are in a special place. There is music playing in the background; the smell of warm apple pie is in the air; there are comfortable places to sit, beautiful wall decorations and plants to admire, and light permeates through the house. Your host and hostess are interested in who you are and engage you easily in conversation. You feel welcome and valued. The attributes that convey this comfortable, homey feeling are the same ones that characterize good early childhood environments. High-quality environments invite children to discover, invent, create, and learn together in a community that is healthy, caring, respectful, and supportive.

By *environment,* we mean all the influences that affect children and adults in early childhood settings (Copple & Bredekamp, 2006; Jackman, 2005; Kohn, 2005; NAEYC, 2005b). These include the planned arrangement of physical space, the relationships

COMPANION WEBSITE 6.1 To learn more about defining your role in creating high-quality environments, go to *Journal: Defining Your Role* in Chapter 6 of the Companion Website at http://www.prenhall.com/jalongo.

between and among the people, and the values and goals of a particular program, center, or school system. Yet, each environment is unique because of how these influences interact. One useful way to think about environment is to consider its different parts: **physical, human,** and **curricular.** The **physical** environment includes such features as the space, room arrangement, equipment, and materials; the **human** environment comprises the social atmosphere and interactions between and among children and adults; and the **curricular** environment includes the content, experiences, routines, schedule, values, goals, and daily organization. Each part must be considered in a high-quality environment.

Features of High-Quality Early Childhood Environments

Creating a high-quality early childhood environment is based on what we know about children's growth, development, and learning. The differences in environments can be found in the types and uses of age-appropriate materials and learning experiences as well as how the teachers and families participate to make that environment unique. The following five research-based principles of environmental design will guide your development of high-quality environments for all children.

High-Quality Early Childhood Environments Are Organized, Challenging, and Aesthetically Pleasing

For children to respond favorably to an environment, it must be predictable, stable, and comprehensible to them (Bredekamp & Copple, 1997; Hendrick & Weissman, 2006; NAEYC, 2005b). Predictable environments have simple routines and rituals that help children to feel secure and safe, and to understand what behaviors are expected of them; predictable environments also have flexible structures that make it easy for everyone to work and be productive. Think back to Ms. Koen, the teacher of toddlers whom you met in the opening scenario. Initially, her environment was not orderly or predictable—indeed, it was quite chaotic! Nor was there a place to keep materials so the children could use them easily to play in a meaningful way. After Ms. Koen reorganized her space, the children knew where to find what they needed and how to maintain a sense of order. She had provided predictability for her toddlers. Moreover, Ms. Koen made clear her behavioral expectations about the use of materials. How you organize your physical environment reflects the needs and developmental levels of the children you teach, your beliefs about teaching and learning, and the goals and values of the community in which you teach (Edwards, Gandini, & Forman, 1998). High-quality environments are also pleasant places to be. They often have living green plants, attractive colors, comfortable furniture, soft lighting and colors, open spaces, and a clean fragrance. A pleasant environment for living and learning invites both adults and children into the learning process.

High-Quality Early Childhood Environments Create a Caring Community of Learners

Early childhood classrooms must support positive relationships between and among adults and children, children and children, and teachers and families. Children need consistent, positive relationships with a limited number of adults and other children in a respectful setting to develop healthy relationships with others, and to learn about themselves and their world (Bredekamp & Copple, 1997; Copple & Bredekamp, 2006). These conditions help children feel like part of their community. Being part of a caring community of learners means including all children in all aspects of classroom life. It also enables children to appreciate individual differences and value the concept that each child is unique and has something to offer. Cultivating a sense of belonging wherever possible is an essential principle of the human part of the environment.

High-Quality Early Childhood Environments Reflect Clear Goals

The goals of every classroom are expressed directly in the arrangement and relationships of the environment. How you relate to children and families, how you arrange physical space and select materials, and how you use space and time reflect the goals of the program and individual classroom. While these goals vary widely because of age, community, culture, and experience, goals are reflected in your environment. If, for example, a goal of your classroom is to nurture children's curiosity and disposition to learn, your environment would likely include regular opportunities for children to engage in individual, small-group, and large-group problem solving and social interactions that offer multiple ways of learning and showing what they know (Fraser & Gestwicki, 2002; Harms, Clifford, & Cryer, 2004). In contrast, consider the American classrooms earlier in this century that had students' desks bolted to wooden floors: Clearly the goal was to have all the children learn the same knowledge and set of skills at the same time and at the same rate. The focus in these classrooms was on whole-group activities during which children were doing the same tasks.

Courtesy of the Library of Congress

Mike Peters/Silver Burdett Ginn

Adult ideas about high-quality environments have changed through the years.

High-Quality Early Childhood Environments Protect Children's Health and Safety

Early childhood environments must support children's physical and psychological safety and health and meet both local and national standards for licensing. At a minimum, physical health and safety needs include adequate space and appropriate entrance and exits. *Physical health and safety needs* also include food, clothing, shelter, rest, medical care, and a balance between active, sensory stimulation and quiet opportunities for reflection. *Psychological health and safety needs* include a consistent, predictable relationship with a caring adult who has high, positive expectations, encourages strong peer acceptance, and supports creative expression, and respects children for who they are. Children know they are in a safe place when they feel welcome and relaxed. This happens when their needs are met and when adults listen to and talk with them in a respectful way. Children who grow up

TEACHER PREP WEBSITE 6.1

Go to Student and Teacher Artifacts, select Early Childhood Education, choose Appropriate Learning Environments (Module 3), and select One-Eyed Creature (Social Development K–2) (Artifact 5).

with their basic physical and psychological needs met are likely to trust themselves and others and rely on inner resources for coping with difficulties. However, children who grow up without having their basic physical and psychological needs met are at a clear disadvantage for becoming successful learners (Carnegie Task Force, 1994; Children's Defense Fund, 2005). You can see the outcome of an environment that supports children's psychological health and safety needs through a primary grade child's drawing of a one-eyed creature on the "Early Childhood Education–One-Eyed Creature" student and teacher artifacts online at the Teacher Prep Website.

High-Quality Early Childhood Environments Provide Access to Age-Appropriate Materials and Equipment

Materials and equipment are learning tools that suggest what children can do. They also support children's physical, intellectual, social, and emotional development. **Materials** are classroom items, such as crayons, paints, and paper, that are regularly replaced or replenished; **equipment** refers to the large, more costly items such as furniture and outdoor structures. The best materials for all children are attractive, have strong sensory appeal, invite children to imagine and create their own ideas and interpretations, and allow for active exploration. These materials are:

- developmentally appropriate and match children's abilities and interests.
- open-ended and offer flexibility, variety, and multiple uses for children of different ages and abilities.
- culturally appropriate and reflect the children's family and community, and promote equality and tolerance rather than perpetuating stereotypical roles.
- safe, durable, nontoxic, well-designed, and have good workmanship.

Infant and toddler environments have unique criteria—as illustrated through the six S's (Lowman & Ruhmann, 1998):

1. **Simplicity**—there are areas divided into large motor, messy, or quiet zones.
2. **Softness**—there are comfortable, homelike qualities and textures.
3. **Seclusion**—there is sensory stimulation.
4. **Sense**—there is sensory stimulation.
5. **Stimulation**—there is a balance that allows children to feel successful yet still provides challenges.
6. **Stability**—there is a slow and careful rotation of centers to provide a sense of security.

PAUSE AND REFLECT

About Features of High-Quality Environments

Think about a college classroom where you are now studying to become a teacher. What principles of design are evident or not evident, and how do they affect your learning? What changes could you realistically suggest to make this classroom setting more powerful for learning? Explain your recommendations.

The Compendium of Early Childhood Resources and Materials at the end of this book suggests basic materials and equipment for infants and toddlers, preschoolers and kindergartners, and school-age children.

Quality early childhood environments hold numerous possibilities for optimizing children's learning and development. If you follow these principles, you will become a teacher who supports children's efforts to become absorbed in learning and make good learning choices (Isenberg & Jalongo, 2006). Table 6.1 describes the key features of high-quality environments, and gives practical applications of each.

TABLE 6.1 Features of High-Quality Early Childhood Environments

Feature	Characteristics	Practical Applications
Ideas	• reflects concrete evidence of the teachers' beliefs about teaching and learning	• children use materials independently or with support from an adult or more capable peer • children may choose activities and materials and take initiative about how plans will be completed • children are encouraged to identify and solve problems
People	• promotes quality interactions between and among adults and children, adults and adults, and children and children • focuses on how adults behave toward children	• adults show delight with children by smiling, listening, and attending • adults respect children and empathize with their feelings • adults support children's learning through probing questions, comments, coaching, and extensions • families and community resources are regular and integral to the program
Time	• the schedule allows children to work at their own pace to complete projects	• long-term investigations, representations, and interdisciplinary experiences are present • there is a balance of large-group, small-group, and individual learning time • outdoor play is a priority • opportunities exist to work one-on-one with an adult, another child, in groups, or alone
Space	• attention is given to the arrangement of the physical environment (and the accessibility of materials)	• children and teachers arrange space as they explore and as interests change • centers are clearly defined by low shelving, carpets, or labels • areas are large enough to accommodate children's real and changing interests • areas contain adequate table and floor space for children to work together comfortably • areas exist where children can spend "alone time" if desired
Resources	• concrete materials, objects, people, and ideas are available for children to explore and solve real problems	• original children's artwork is displayed throughout the room • child- and adult-made materials reflect the children's families, cultures, and interests • materials include real items as well as replicas • transitions occur naturally for children

SOURCE: Adapted from S. V. McLean, (1995).

Your Role in Creating High-Quality Environments

Creating a high-quality environment is an important skill for early childhood educators. Consider the following example of a first-grade teacher, Ms. Schutta, as you think about your role in providing high-quality environments for all children.

The physical environment in Ms. Schutta's first-grade classroom is divided into specific activity areas. There are clear entrances and exits to these areas, pathways within the classroom for the children to move about safely, and tables clustered together where children do their work. Ms. Schutta's classroom is full of plants and has displays of children's work, comfortable and cozy areas, and a few aesthetically pleasing prints and posters on clean, painted walls. The daily schedule begins first thing in the morning with a large block of time (45 minutes) called "breathing out" time, during which children transition from home to school and have time to settle into the school routines (Wassermann, 2000). During "breathing out" time, Ms. Schutta observes from the sidelines and then works one-on-one with children who need specific instruction on a skill or concept. There is also a 2-hour language arts block, during which children pursue individual projects, including a variety of hands-on, small-group experiences, followed by a sharing and debriefing time. During this time, the children choose from among three or four centers. Each center is clearly labeled; materials are accessible and inviting. Some of the centers in this class are a class library that contains collections of books of many different sizes and genres; an art center that has an easel stand with tempera paints and watercolors, a wikki center with a board for wikki sticks (e.g., wax-covered, bendable sticks the size of pipe cleaners that are used for construction and can stick to different surfaces); a game-and-puzzle center where children together or independently work wooden puzzles, Lego blocks, pattern blocks, or unifix cubes or play checkers, dominoes, or board games; and a magnet center filled with a variety of magnetic letters that children put together to make sounds and words that they know. The content taught through Ms. Schutta's centers is based upon county and state standards of learning. One of the first things Ms. Schutta's first graders do upon arrival at school is to select an area for work by hanging a tag on a choice board, allowing them to occupy a space at a particular center. The morning block ends with a sharing time, during which children share important aspects of projects that are meaningful to them.

One of Ms. Schutta's first graders, Jon, a child with learning disabilities, has difficulty with writing. When the class was studying the life cycle of the pumpkin, Jon drew pictures to tell the story of the pumpkin's stages of growth. He explained each stage of his drawing to Ms. Schutta, who wrote down his words so he could share them with his classmates. Chad, however, is receiving services for being gifted and talented in math and reading, but he does not like to write. Ms. Schutta noticed how he loves baseball and provided him with trade books and research formats to learn more about the sport. Chad used the long time blocks to illustrate and write about a baseball book he was reading. He created a baseball diamond, listed baseball facts, and used his love for baseball to develop his writing skills.

To learn more about fulfilling your role in creating good environments for young children's learning and the NAEYC, go to *Web Links* in Chapter 6 of the Companion Website at http://www.prenhall.com/jalongo.

Ms. Schutta is demonstrating several key aspects of her role in creating a safe, healthy, and appropriate environment. Educational researchers have identified the following guidelines for high-quality early childhood environments.

Arrange Space to Meet the Needs of All Learners

One of the very first decisions you will make when you have your own classroom is to determine how to use the space you have. How and where you place the furniture, arrange the materials, and organize space will influence the behavior and learning of your children (Clayton, 2001; Curtis & Carter, 2003; Isbell & Exelby, 2001; Kritchevsky, Prescott, & Walling, 1977). Space must be arranged to accommodate a variety of learning experiences occurring in different-sized groupings and to meet the children's different developmental needs and physical sizes. Finding the right use of space is a challenge for all teachers, both experienced and new; somehow, classrooms never seem to have enough of it. Notice that Ms. Schutta arranged her space into centers, or areas, where children work together on projects in small groups, in pairs, or individually. She labeled each area clearly, and arranged the materials so that the children can access them easily and independently. Figure 6.1 shows Ms. Schutta's room arrangement for

FIGURE 6.1 Room arrangement for school-age children.

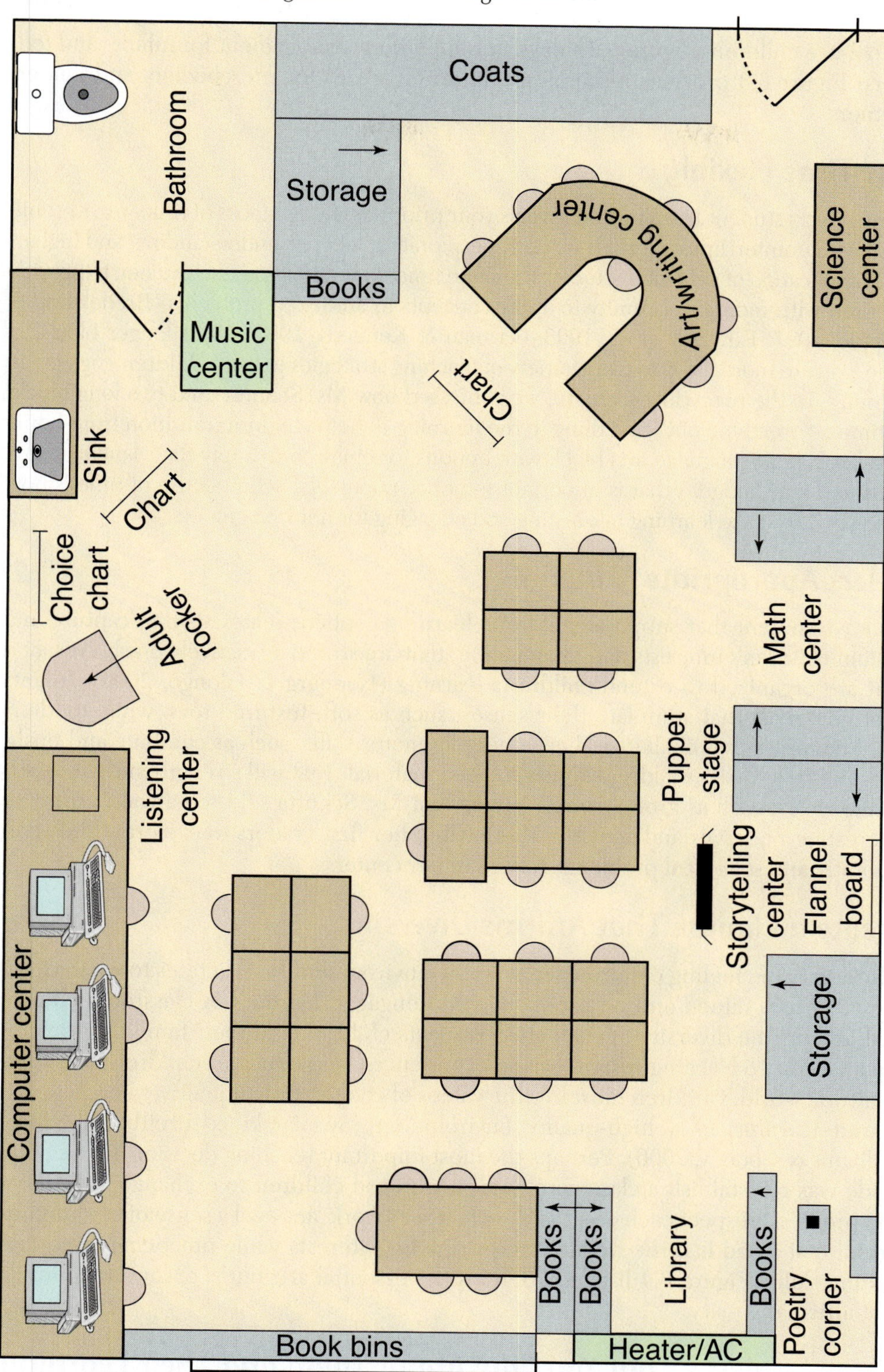

SOURCE: Courtesy of Mary Schutta and Robyn Cochran, Deer Park Elementary School, Fairfax, Virginia.

school-age children. Figure 6.2 shows a sample room arrangement for infants and toddlers; Figure 6.3 provides a sample room arrangement for preschoolers and kindergartners.

Use Time Flexibly

Time affects student learning and reveals your priorities. Long blocks of time provide children with uninterrupted periods for active exploration, deeper understanding, and higher-level application of subject matter. At the same time, they allow you, the teacher, to provide children with more opportunity to apply concepts to authentic problems (Bredekamp & Copple, 1997; Edwards et al., 1998; Garreau & Kennedy, 1991). With longer blocks of time, you are more likely to use a variety of teaching strategies to keep children engaged in learning. In the preceding scenario, we witnessed how Ms. Schutta used two long blocks of time—"breathing out" first thing in the morning to help children transition from home to school, and a language arts block with options for children to apply their language arts skills and knowledge. What is important to notice about Ms. Schutta's use of time is how she uses it to make learning interesting and engaging for her first graders.

Select Appropriate Materials

An environment that supports children's learning contains materials that capture and sustain children's interests and imagination, that are stored attractively on shelves, and that are organized to extend children's learning (Isenberg & Jalongo, 2006). Infants need materials that stimulate their senses, such as soft, textured toys, while toddlers need materials that challenge their emerging motor skills, such as climbing and push-and-pull toys. Older children, however, need materials that will strengthen their minds and muscles, such as group games. Notice that Ms. Schutta selected a wide variety of interesting materials and activities that invited her first graders to explore, think, collaborate, and solve real problems in each of her centers.

Create a Climate That Affirms Diversity

Climate is the feeling children get from the environment that dictates to what extent they will feel valued and be productive and engaged learners. A classroom climate that affirms the diversity of each child respects children and their families, provides equal access to learning resources and experiences, and educates children for a multicultural world. Children must live the values of cooperation, equality, tolerance, and shared learning in a high-quality environment (Swiniarski & Breitborde, 2003; Williams & Cooney, 2006). Perhaps the most important teaching decision Ms. Schutta made was to establish a classroom that encouraged children to exchange their ideas and progress, respect each other and each other's work, and feel a sense of community. Recall that Chad had the freedom to pursue his interests while practicing important writing skills. Figure 6.4 lists and defines the essential attributes of an environment that affirm diversity.

Show Students That You Care About Them and Their Learning

At this point in your preparation to become an early childhood educator, you might feel overwhelmed and uncertain about your ability to create appropriate environments. As you gain confidence in doing so, be certain to show children that you care about them

FIGURE 6.2 Room arrangement for infants and toddlers.

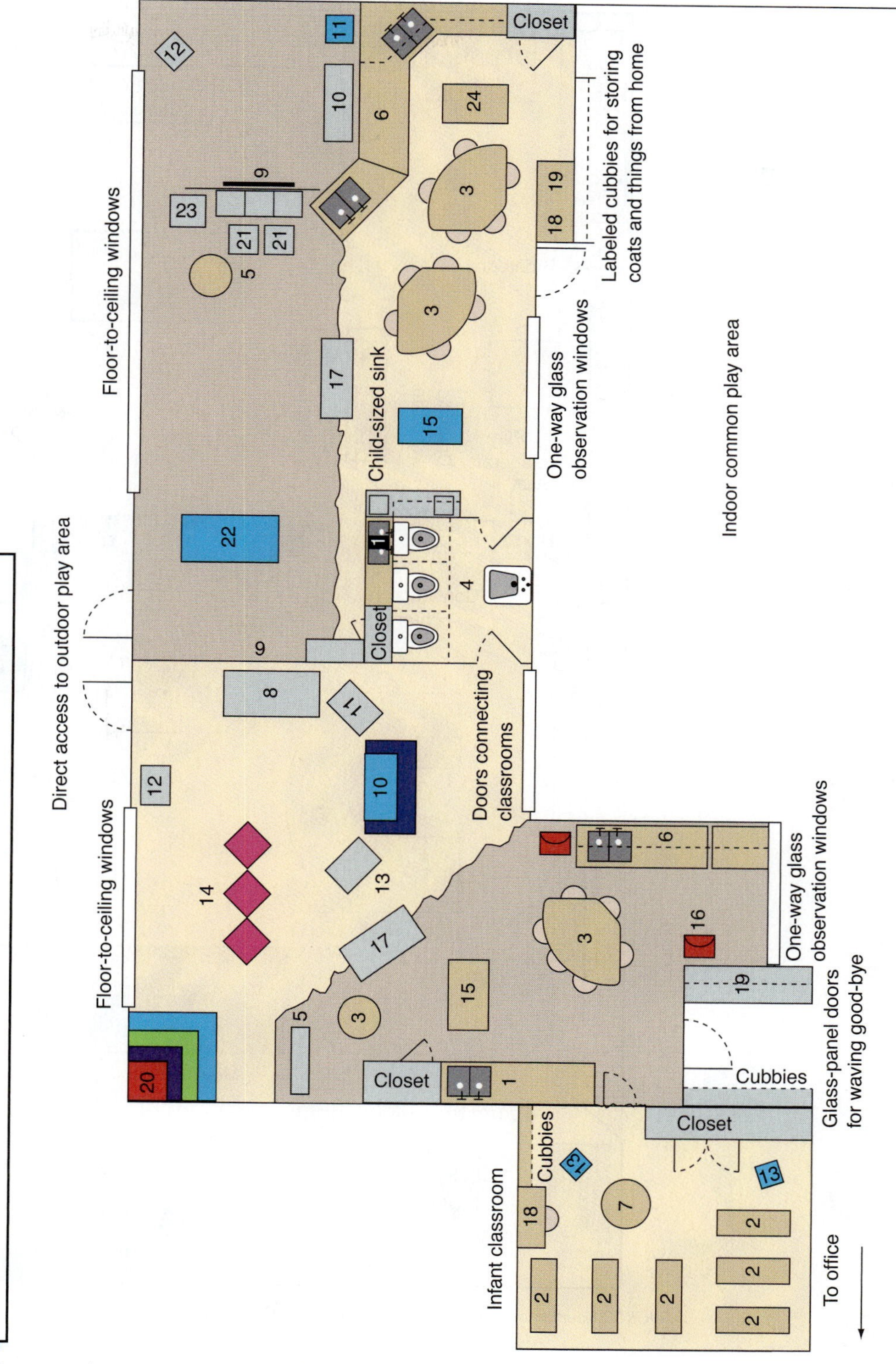

KEY

1. change table with sink
2. crib
3. child-sized table
4. child-sized toilets with individual half-wall stalls
5. home-living furniture
6. food prep/kitchen area
7. rug
8. padded quilt
9. low, mounted wall mirror
10. sofa
11. book shelf
12. music center
13. adult rocker
14. foam blocks (for sitting, stacking, or climbing)
15. media table
16. high chair
17. manipulative/block shelf
18. teacher work space
19. parent sign-in area
20. vinyl-covered foam climbing structure
21. child rocker
22. toddler climbing structure
23. dress-up area
24. double-sided easel with self-help shelving

SCALE

$^1/_8$"=1'

SOURCE: Courtesy of Nelly Adams, Director, Fairfax County Employees' Child Care Center, Fairfax, VA.

FIGURE 6.3 Room arrangement for preschoolers and kindergartners.

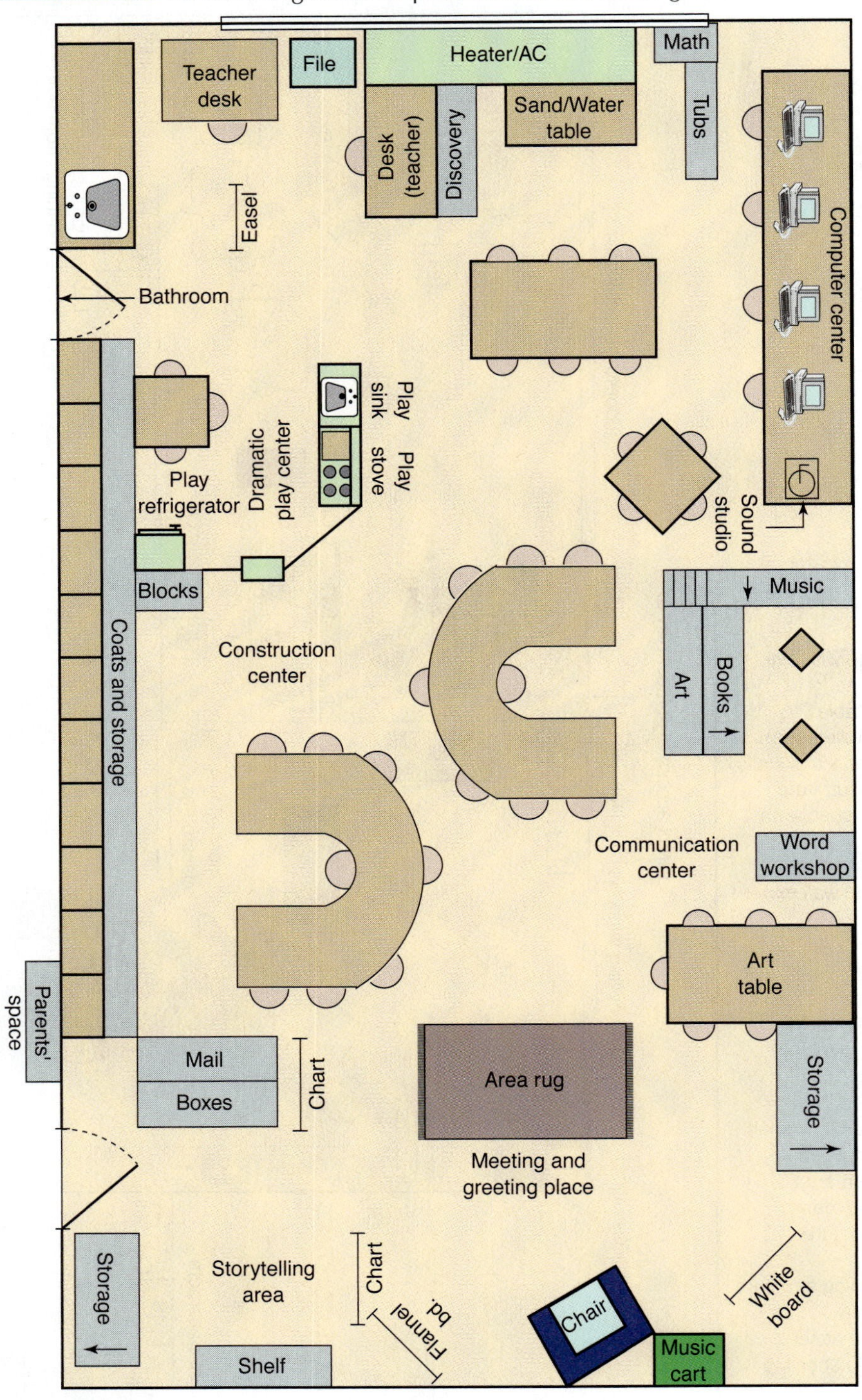

SOURCE: Courtesy of Gall Ritchie, Kings Park Elementary School, Fairfax, Virginia.

FIGURE 6.4 Essential attributes of an environment that affirms diversity.

Security	Children must feel safe enough to take risks as they learn.
Identity	Every child must be valued and appreciated as an individual with unique needs and abilities.
Responsibility	A sense of belonging to a community is felt by the children.
Dignity	Every child should have self-respect and respect for the thoughts and actions of others.
Community	A sense of trust and responsibility is created and supported by the children, families, and teachers.

SOURCES: Adapted from "Making a Good Start," *Education Update, 39*(6), 6, Association for Supervision and Curriculum Development, 1997; and *Educating the Global Village* (2nd edition), by L. Swiniarski, & M. Breitborde, 2003, Upper Saddle River, NJ: Merrill/Prentice Hall.

and their learning. A true spirit of caring is at the heart of high-quality environments. You show caring when you find out about children's interests, and offer them just enough support, structure, and expectation to be self-directed, responsible learners. The ethic of care is aptly discussed by Nel Noddings (1992), who states that "caring for students is fundamental in teaching and . . . developing people with a strong capacity for care is a major objective of responsible education" (p. 678). Ms. Schutta exhibited an ethic of care with both Jon and Chad. She took time to attend to their individual differences (e.g., Chad's love of baseball) and teach them skills in a supportive way through what is important to them (e.g., taking dictation from Jon about a pumpkin's life cycle so he could share his ideas). She provided different kinds of support to each child to increase his or her participation, achieve a sense of belonging, and become better connected with their individual learning and with the classroom learning community.

Connect with the Children's Families

It is a well-known fact that strong families make strong schools. As a teacher of young children, you will want to find many ways to connect with the children's families, because they are an essential part of your classroom environment. Involving families sends the message that you value their children and want to build respectful, two-way communication about their children's learning (Copple & Bredekamp, 2006; NAEYC, 2005b). For example, send home positive notes—you can always find something positive to say about each and every one of your students. Such notes let parents know that you have a vested interest in their children's learning and that you care about their children's progress. (See Chapter 11 for more specific suggestions on the family-school connection.) The Collaborating with Families feature on the next page provides one way to invite families into the experience of learning centers in your classroom.

Why the Environment Is Important

The classroom environment is as important as the role of the teacher because it directly affects how children behave, develop, learn, and form values. Many organizational or behavior problems within early childhood settings can be reduced or eliminated by creating healthy conditions for learning. These conditions make learning safe and

COLLABORATING WITH FAMILIES

Why Use Learning Centers?

Ms. Davis uses a center-based approach to learning. Because parents are often unfamiliar with centers, they may question their purpose and value. Therefore, at the first open house for families, Ms. Davis plans a mini center time, so parents can get a flavor of what and how their children learn at school. On a paper that Ms. Davis prepares for each parent is the following:

> Our classroom is organized around centers that help your child grow, develop, and learn by thinking about what he or she is doing. As your child changes activities, he or she will work with many different groups of children. In this way, your child will learn to talk with others about different ideas and ways to meet and solve problems. Notice that I have prepared activities for you to do tonight in our different centers. You will have 30 minutes to try one or more centers. I hope you will enjoy yourself and leave with a better sense of what your child does during center time. Please write down what you have learned as well as any questions you might have.
>
> Construction Computer Listening Mathematics Science Writing
> Library Art Dramatic Play

Here is what the sign in the **Science Center** said:

Materials: Living Things Area: hermit crab and cage; 5-gallon aquarium with fish; food for critters; a feeding log/calendar; 3 magnifying glasses, a balance scale

Electricity Box: an open box with batteries, wires, switches, small light bulbs, and magnets; a small basket with a variety of familiar objects; an old radio and tools to take it apart; a collection of shells; books on fish, hermit crabs, radios, and magnets; paper, crayons, and pencils

Purpose: The more young children know about and understand their world, the more they become independent, confident learners. The Science Center is designed to encourage children to ask questions, to look for answers, to experiment, and to engage in a scientific method of learning. It conveys a message to children that their interests are important and gives them new ideas to think about. When children finish their investigations in the center, they show what they are learning in pictures, words, writing, or constructions with others.

Task 1: Using the materials in the Electricity Box, figure out more than one way to make the light bulb shine.

Task 2: Observe the hermit crabs. Then feed them and look at them using the magnifying glass. Record your findings in the journal. What questions do you have? Look in some of the books to find your answers.

Conclusion: What did you notice about your experience? What questions do you have?

NOTE: We also have sample activity kits for the hermit crab that your child can bring home. The kit includes:

Hermit crab in small plastic habitat
A picture or a photo story on DVD of related classroom activity
Picture book, *A House for Hermit Crab* (Carle, 1991), and poem about crabs
Journal or observation log to record or draw about experience at home
Directions that include the care of the crab, the procedures to follow at home, and safe return guidelines.

Encourage your child to bring one home!

supportive, and they encourage all children to develop confidence, take risks, work independently, and strengthen their social skills. High-quality environments provide a wide range of authentic learning opportunities whenever and wherever possible. They also contain appropriate materials for individuals and groups of children to use independently; enable adults to observe, support, and meet the learning needs of each child; and support program goals and outcomes.

There is a large body of research that documents the effect of the classroom environment on children's behavior, learning, and development and identifies the importance of key features that reflect high-quality environments (Black, 2001; Bredekamp & Copple, 1997; Cryer & Phillipsen, 1997; Edwards et al., 1998; Lackney, 2002; NAEYC, 2005b. National Academy of Early Childhood Programs, 1998;). These features—ambiance, privacy, size, density, and space—are discussed below.

Ambiance: Light, Color, Texture, and Noise

Ambiance refers to sensory information that increases comfort, understanding, and learning. The sights, sounds, smells, and touches in every environment bring it to life for the present but also become part of long-term memory to be recalled long after one has left that setting (Crumpacker, 1995; Curtis & Carter, 2003). *Light* is one important aspect of early childhood environments. They should have as much natural light as possible through windows and doors. Hanging things in windows and mirrors on the walls creates a spacious feeling. Where this is not possible, a variety of soft lighting, such as desk and floor lamps instead of glaring fluorescent lighting, should be used for a softer effect. *Color* also contributes to the feeling of an environment. Environments for children should have enough color to stimulate but not overwhelm the senses. *Texture* stimulates tactile learning, which is important for all children, especially those with special needs. Quality early childhood environments have many materials with soft textures, such as finger-paints, modeling dough, and stuffed toys, and cozy furnishings, such as beanbag chairs, carpeting, and pillows (Jones & Prescott, 1978); soft and cozy items make children feel safe and secure. *Noise* that comes from children's natural interactions in active learning environments is healthy. However, excessive noise is uncomfortable and negatively affects children's ability to communicate, interact socially, and concentrate, and impedes their ability to learn (Readdick, 2006). In many early childhood classrooms, you will find special spaces designed for children to seek privacy and feel secure by being able to escape from the bustling activity of a classroom filled with engaged learners.

Privacy

Children have different needs for levels of interaction. Some children need time alone and enjoy silent periods; others do not. For children who easily become overstimulated, tired, or upset, places to be alone are important, because they respect children's need to enjoy quiet moments to regain control of their ability to focus on learning. You can create private spaces in safe alcoves that contain soft features such as carpeting and pillows or as part of a loft where children can be quiet but still see the rest of the classroom. Quiet spaces set off by themselves and housed with some books and perhaps a few floor cushions send the message, "Here is a place where I can think, watch, and collect myself in a safe way." Private spaces nurture children's emotional health and also send a message about how to use the area or the materials. There should be space for children to play alone or with a friend, protected in some way from other children, in every classroom (Cryer & Phillipsen, 1997).

COMPANION WEBSITE 6.3 For more information about environments, go to *Web Links* in Chapter 6 of the Companion Website at http://www.prenhall.com/jalongo.

Scott Cunningham/Merrill

Scott Cunningham/Merrill

Which features of high-quality environments are apparent in these classrooms?

Size

Size refers to both numbers of children in a learning group and to areas of the classroom. The best early childhood environments enable children to interact regularly and often in small groups within a small space. Research shows that small-group interactions improve children's attitudes, achievement, social skills, and voluntary participation (Moore & Lackney, 1995). In contrast, extensive large-group interactions have been associated with "decreased attention, lower task performance, behavioral problems, and social withdrawal" (Moore & Lackney, 1995, p. 18). Daily opportunities for learning in small groups allow teachers to use a wider array of interaction patterns with children, learning centers, student learning teams, peer tutorials, and other instructional strategies.

In regard to the size of areas of the classroom, again, smaller is better. Areas provided for small groups mean low numbers of children interacting together or with an adult. Small groups foster family-like feelings of sharing, connection, trust, and support. These feelings are what bind groups of people together. How you create spaces for small-group interaction with the materials and equipment you have will send messages to children such as "This is not a space for a lot of people. We will not be pasting or cutting with scissors here, or doing gymnastics." There are active places as well, which are wide open in the classroom. For example, there is enough room in the block area for children to work together, so that social development and shared thinking are encouraged. The block area has the blocks neatly organized so children can think through what they are doing and what they are planning to do.

Density

Density, the number of children that occupy the square footage of a space, or use available materials, is closely connected to classroom size. Because research shows the positive effects of small, intimate groupings, having environments with very high concentrations of children, adults, or materials would be counterproductive. There are two types of classroom density: *social density,* which refers to how many people are in a space, and *spatial density,* how many square feet is available per child (Trawick-Smith, 1992).

Social Density

From the literature on size, we know that children in large groups interact in less positive ways, regardless of how much space is available to them (Johnson, Christie, & Wardle, 2005; Moore & Lackney, 1995; White, 2006). Having lots of children and adults in one area increases social density. Some studies have shown that social density can restrict peer interactions, verbalization, cooperative behaviors, and fantasy play (Clarke-Stewart, 1987). Smaller groups are more likely to create feelings of comfort and safety and to enable children to acquire independence and social competence when sharing classroom space with a moderate number of other children and adults (Trawick-Smith, 1992).

Shirley Zeiberg/PH College

Spatial Density

Generally, the smaller the space available for each individual, the more likely it is that children will have difficulty with their interaction. The National Academy of Early Childhood Programs (1998) requires an indoor minimum of 35 square feet per child and 75 square feet per child outdoors. Not enough square feet per child can lead to uninvolved, aggressive, and solitary behaviors. Similarly, not enough materials can lead to such undesirable behaviors as teasing, hitting, fighting, and playing alone. Teachers might increase the amount of materials, then, as one solution to problems of negative behaviors. When the environment is small and intimate, but with enough square footage and materials to allow active learning, it can foster the positive behaviors and learning we seek for all children.

What impact can social density have on children?

Space

How materials, equipment, and furniture are arranged in a classroom can critically affect children's self-esteem, security and comfort, autonomy, self-control, and peer interaction (Clayton, 2001; Firlik, 2006; Frye & Mumpower, 2001; Isbell & Exelby, 2001). When teachers divide space into defined interest and learning areas, they protect children from visual and auditory distraction and promote a more intimate setting for learning. Separating the active from the quiet and the messy from nonmessy areas also provides an organizational structure that can enhance children's persistence at tasks and improve the quality of their social interactions.

Learning Centers

Learning centers are well-defined, organized areas of the classroom set aside for specific learning purposes without the teacher's constant presence and direction. They enable teachers to integrate the curriculum, develop cultural awareness, address multiple intelligences, and nurture children's spontaneity and originality (Isbell, 1995; Isbell & Exelby, 2001; Isenberg & Jalongo, 2006). A center arrangement enables children to interact more frequently than they can in large groups. In centers, children are more likely to get immediate responses to their ideas, communication, and work. Centers allow for self-directed activity with opportunities to work individually or with a partner, thereby helping the child to become more independent or learn to work cooperatively.

The versatility of centers makes them an essential part of early childhood classrooms. Some possible learning outcomes for children in center-based learning environments include the following:

- problem-solving ability, by making good learning choices that determine the direction of their play and their work

- responsibility, by selecting, using, and caring for their materials
- persistence, by carrying out plans to completion (Isbell & Exelby, 2001; Isenberg & Jalongo, 2006; Sanoff, 1995)
- learning by working at their own pace and ability level to meet appropriately individualized goals and objectives (Tiedt & Tiedt, 2005)

You must take into account each of these environmental features when planning your own early childhood classroom. We will consider them further in the next sections.

The Culturally Responsive Classroom

A high-quality learning environment is culturally responsive. It reflects both the home culture and group culture of the families of the children and acknowledges the need for culturally diverse students to find meaningful connections between themselves, their learning tasks, and the environment in which they are learning (Gay, 2000; Montgomery, 2001; Villegas & Lucas, 2002). Culturally responsive classrooms invite children into the learning process, take into account the strengths the children bring with them, and improve children's ability to be successful in school.

Children begin to notice differences early; therefore, the classroom environment should reflect the lives of the children and families that it serves. Just as your lifestyle and home suit your needs, culture, and community, so, too, should the setting in which children learn. Such an environment is called *multicultural* or *anti-bias,* because it helps children understand and appreciate their own backgrounds as well as the backgrounds of others. What would a multicultural setting look like? It might include posters on the walls that represent the cultures of the children in the room; a dramatic play center with dolls, toys, and books from a variety of cultures; and a classroom library containing a rich selection of books and music from many cultures (Harms et al., 2004; Jalongo, 2007; Montgomery, 2001; Wortham, 2006).

To learn more about linguistic and cultural diversity, go to *Enrichment Content: Research Highlights* in Chapter 6 of the Companion Website at http://www.prenhall.com/jalongo.

Culturally responsive environments meet the unique needs of individual children (see Figure 6.5). For example, children from some family backgrounds and cultures have many privacy needs. Girls may show a greater need for personal space and may react more negatively than boys to wide-open spaces and classrooms with more teachers per child (Allen & Cowdery, 2005; Hull, Goldhaber, & Capone, 2002; NAEYC, 2005a and 2005b).

Creating High-Quality Early Childhood Environments

Think back to the teachers you met in the Meet the Teachers opening section of this chapter. Recall how Ms. Endo modified her environment so all children could participate and how Ms. Mitsoff believed in the importance of positive relationships between the children. Reread that section and think about those teachers as you explore the nature of both the indoor and outdoor environments.

Preparing the Indoor Environment

The indoor environment is the place in which children acquire skills, concepts, attitudes, and values about the world. It is, in fact, the children's home for learning that occurs each day. Good early childhood teachers create opportunities for children to

FIGURE 6.5 What to look for in a culturally responsive environment.

Classroom Climate

- Children's artwork is visually present and displayed.
- Centers and play areas have ethnically diverse materials.
- Classroom displays represent the families of the children.
- Displays acknowledge and celebrate every child's efforts.

Materials

- Books explore a variety of cultural traditions and a range of culturally diverse literature.
- Toys and materials reflect the cultural backgrounds of the children.
- Content area materials represent the cultural and linguistic backgrounds of the children in your classroom and of other major cultures.
- Learning materials depict a variety of cultures, roles, family lifestyles, and disabilities.

Activities

- Children have rich oral language experiences in their home language.
- Experiences reflect family traditions, such as family recipes, family photos, and cooking utensils used in the home.
- Children are encouraged to learn about others' cultures through such activities as family-facts games, family cookbooks, and video exchanges.
- Children use the Internet to communicate in their native language with children from similar linguistic and cultural backgrounds.

Teacher's Role

- Teachers support children's home language and many different ways to communicate.
- Teachers provide a range of books and songs that represent the children's home language.
- Teachers invite families to share traditions and stories of their home cultures.
- Teachers take time to understand cultures other than their own and plan a variety of multicultural experiences.

SOURCES: Data based on Corson, 2001; Montgomery, 2001; and NAEYC, 2005a and 2005b.

develop self-help skills, make good learning choices, become self-directed, and feel competent and confident. In this way, teachers facilitate children's learning from the home environment to the school environment.

The indoor environment is one of the most visible outcomes of your efforts. A well-planned environment provides a safe, supportive place for children to live, learn, and grow; provides a balance of teacher-directed and child-initiated activities; and invites children to learn in purposeful and meaningful ways (Bredekamp & Copple, 1997; Kontos & Wilcox-Herzog, 1997; Wortham, 2006). Think about the essential features of high-quality indoor environments for children as you read the next section that discusses room arrangement, schedule and routines, and materials and equipment.

Room Arrangement

Your classroom can be arranged in two different ways. The space can be arranged according to children's developmental areas, such as physical, social, or cognitive development, or by curriculum areas, such as writing, reading, science, and art. Regardless of how you arrange it, space should facilitate, not hinder, learning. Your room arrangement should include the following:

- a large area to hold group demonstrations, meetings, and discussions
- small areas for work in small groups, in pairs, and alone
- individual areas to facilitate independent work on projects
- display areas that invite children to look, touch, and converse about instructional materials, reference materials, or their own work
- clearly labeled work areas and easy access to engaging materials to encourage independence (Clayton, 2001; Frye & Mumpower, 2001; Harms et al., 2004)

LARGE AREA. Some teachers locate a large area in the center of the room and have smaller work and play areas around the room; others arrange a quiet corner of the classroom for it; and still others use a large classroom library for this purpose. In the large area of your classroom, you will need an easel for group work such as class news and charts. Within easy reach, you will also want an organized supply of materials, such as markers of various colors, chart paper, scissors, a magnetic board, or a cookie sheet with an assortment of magnetic letters and shapes, sentence strips, and masking tape or other tape.

SMALL AREAS. Teachers often use low bookshelves, tables, and other furniture to create centers or areas where groups of children can work together. Using these as dividers gives the room an open, uncluttered look and gives you an unobstructed view. Dividers can double as a display for instructions, examples of children's work, or storage for reference materials. Small work areas should have enough space, materials, and chairs for the number of children who will typically be working there. Crowded areas frustrate children and make it difficult for them to work together productively. If you have desks in your classroom, you might want to cluster some together to form a worktable.

TEACHER PREP WEBSITE 6.2

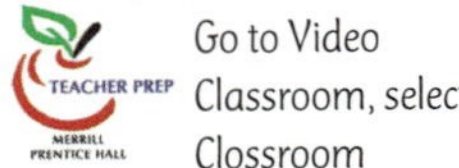

Go to Video Classroom, select Classroom Management, choose Organizing Your Classroom and Supplies (Module 1) and select Arranging Furniture and Materials (Video 1).

INDIVIDUAL AREAS. Every classroom needs to have space for individual projects. Even though children can work independently at a common table, they need enough space for their own materials. Moreover, some individual areas should be quiet places where individuals can work without distraction, thereby providing more psychological than actual separation. You can see the room arrangement of first-grade teacher, Diane Leonard, in the "Arranging Furniture and Materials" video clip online at the Teacher Prep Website.

DISPLAYS. Classroom displays should encourage children to observe, question, and investigate, so you need to be especially mindful of how you use them. Crowded walls that are overstimulating and unplanned *discourage rather than encourage* learning (Curtis & Carter, 2003; Frye & Mumpower, 2001). Displays should be at the children's eye level so they can revisit their work and use reference materials easily. A large display space is best used for a piece of well-loved writing that becomes shared reading the children go back to again and again, or for a classroom mural that many children had a hand in creating. Teachers use displays to allow children to discuss their own work and the work of their classmates, and they point out the positive qualities of all pieces. Displays are changed after they have been appreciated. When walls and dividers are covered with children's work, appropriate posters, and aesthetically appealing art that reflects the cultures of the children, they send the message that the children and families in the group are valued and valuable. However, when walls and dividers are covered with cartoonlike materials or oversized management tools, such as classroom rules, they can be visually noisy and stressful for children.

CLEARLY LABELED WORK AREAS AND EASY ACCESS TO MATERIALS. Most classrooms include a number of learning areas. Some may be permanent centers, such as those for art and writing; others may be changed according to children's interests, needs, and the particular topic under study. These work areas, or centers, have clear pathways so children can safely move in and out, are labeled clearly so the children and teachers know what to do at each center and how many children can be in there at one time, and contain materials that facilitate children's thinking and exploration. Following are some suggestions for making centers work.

- Identify the center with print or an appropriate picture.
- Arrange commonly used materials in clearly labeled baskets or other containers that are accessible from where the children are working independently. Children should know how the materials are used and stored.
- Introduce centers one at a time, explicitly demonstrating and practicing the routines for using each one with the children.
- Have an adequate supply of materials.
- Use a work board to establish routines for participating in centers. The work board can be on an eye-level easel or can lean against a wall. Children can choose and monitor center use through this tool. Figures 6.6 and 6.7 show work boards used

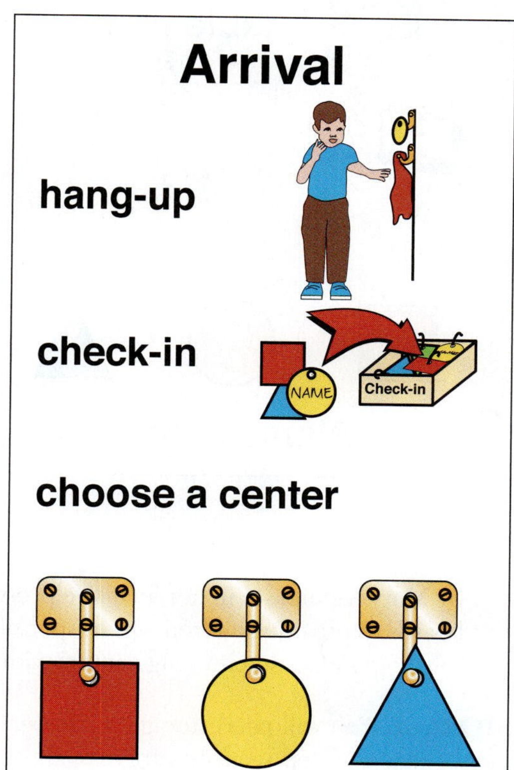

FIGURE 6.6

Example of work board for self-help skills.

SOURCE: Courtesy of Mary Kleinpaste.

FIGURE 6.7
Example of work board for choosing centers.
SOURCE: Courtesy of Mary Kleinpaste.

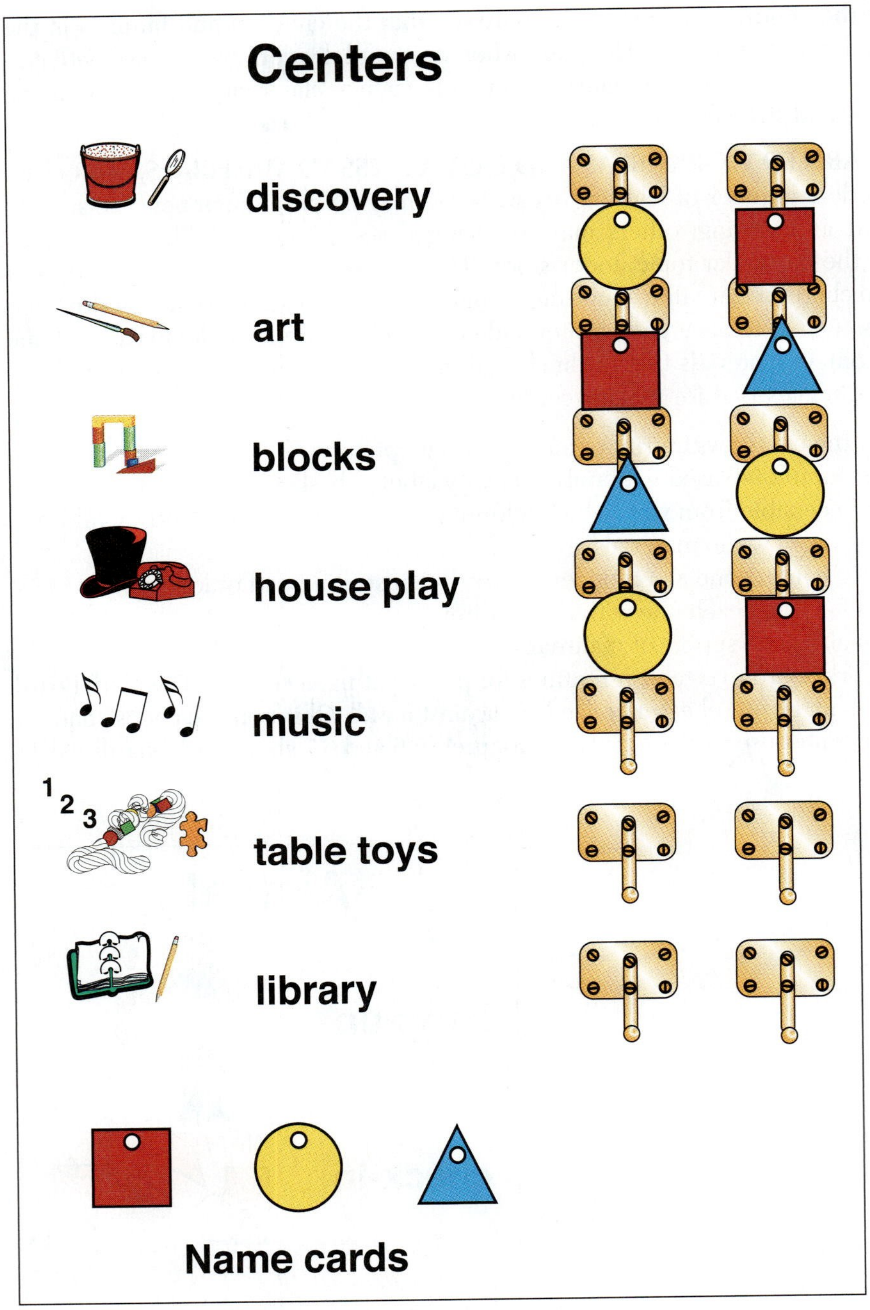

Centers
discovery
art
blocks
house play
music
1 2 3
table toys
library
Name cards

by Mary Kleinpaste in her inclusive preschool classroom. Notice how she uses her boards to provide children with responsibility for developing independent and self-help skills and choosing centers with the aid of pictorial representations.

STORAGE. You will need storage for materials and for children's daily work. Children need space to keep work-in-progress, finished work that will be used to assess their progress, and personal belongings. Materials, supplies, and work can be stored in a variety of ways but should be orderly and aesthetically pleasing. Here are some suggestions:

- Use easy-to-find storage containers that have different and interesting textures, such as berry baskets or decorated boxes.
- Consider balance and design when arranging materials, displays, and furniture.
- Store daily work in a labeled, clear plastic tub or box.
- Use a plastic crate with hanging files for finished writing.
- Try a drying rack for drying paintings.
- Use a plastic shoe rack for storing puppets.
- Cut cereal boxes in half, cover them with contact paper, and have students store their materials in them. These boxes can easily be placed in the center of worktables to designate particular children who should work there.

Schedule and Routines

The schedule and routines in an early childhood classroom must be thoughtfully planned. Each day, you need to provide enough time for a balance of large-group, small-group, and individual activities. Your *schedule* provides consistency for learners so they know what to expect; this gives children control over their day, and conveys a clear message about what you think is important. For example, we know that long blocks of uninterrupted time help children to be more productive, self-directed, and self-expressive, and they send the message that their work is important (Garreau & Kennedy, 1991; Tegano, Moran, DeLong, Brickman, & Ramsisini, 1996). A good place to keep your daily schedule is in your meeting area, where you and the children can review it each morning.

Routines are the regular and predictable activities that form the basis of the daily schedule and ensure effective use of time and space. They help children sense the passage of time (e.g., snack follows cleanup) and help them to anticipate events (e.g., a musical selection marks the end of the day). A consistent but flexible schedule and regular routines provide a strong foundation for high-quality indoor environments. They set the stage for learning and can create an atmosphere that makes your classroom special for every child.

Figure 6.8 provides sample schedules for half-day preschool, full-day kindergarten, and second grade that can guide your planning. One note of caution: Adhering to a rigid schedule can impede children's thinking just as much as not having any schedule at all.

Materials and Equipment

Materials are the tools children use to learn. Developmentally appropriate materials are concrete, real, and meaningful to children (Bredekamp & Copple, 1997). They allow children to investigate, explore, and experiment. Teachers choose materials that can be used by children with a wide range of abilities, are easily manipulated and safe, and meet the needs of the children in the group. All children are responsible for the care and cleanup of the materials. Following are some things to think about when providing good learning tools for children.

Anthony Magnacca/Merrill

Labels help keep active classrooms organized.

FIGURE 6.8 Sample schedules.

Half-Day Preschool

8:45–9:00	Arrival and Greeting
9:00–9:15	Class Meeting
9:15–10:15	Choice and Centers
10:15–10:30	Cleanup
10:30–10:50	Sharing and Snack
10:50–11:20	Outdoor Play
11:20–11:45	Story and Preparation for Home

Full-Day Kindergarten

8:50	Arrival, Greeting, Group Time
9:25	Centers and Work Time
10:45	Whole-Group Sharing and Debriefing
11:00	Gross Motor Activity (indoors or out)
11:30	Lunch
12:00	Whole-Group Story and Discussion
12:30	Integrated Language Arts, Science, Math
2:30	Group Share, Story, Music
3:00	Preparation for Home

Second Grade

8:15	Free Choice
8:30	Investigative Centers
10:00	Cleanup
10:15	Class Meeting
10:30	Outdoors
10:45	Integrated Science and Math
12:15	Lunch and Story
12:45	Integrated Language Arts/Social Studies/Arts
2:45	Music and Preparation for Home

TEACHER PREP WEBSITE 6.3

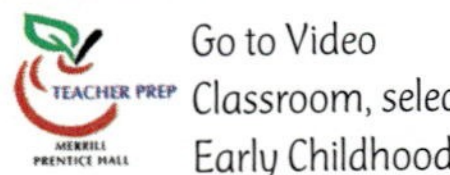

Go to Video Classroom, select Early Childhood Education, choose Appropriate Early Environments (Module 3), and select Environments–Early Childhood (Video 1).

- Have plenty of materials available.
- Include adequate props and materials for play.
- Model the appropriate use of materials when necessary.
- Be creative in finding resources for your classroom. Use recycled materials, ask parents to provide and construct items, and begin your own collection of scraps and inexpensive resources.

It goes without saying that an important aspect of high-quality early childhood environments has to do with the materials available for children's use. You can see examples of developmentally appropriate materials for preschoolers in many areas of the indoor and outdoor environment in the "Environments–Early Childhood" video clip online at the Teacher Prep Website. Table 6.2 provides guidelines for safe and developmentally appropriate materials for children of all ages. In the following sections, we explore how to ensure that indoor environments for all children are safe, healthy, and appropriate.

Creating high-quality environments strongly influences the way learning will happen in the classroom. To support children's learning effectively, the environment has to be created so that children are able to do many routine things for themselves and for each other. Additionally, children also need support and encouragement to be independent and to work with others. "The most enticing, wonderful resources, and the largest, most spacious classroom, will count for nothing unless children

PAUSE AND REFLECT

About Why the Environment Is So Important

Consider one of the floor plans shown in Figures 6.1, 6.2, or 6.3. Describe at least three features of high-quality indoor environments that you notice. Now use the evaluation criteria listed in Figure 6.9 and the comments of expert Thelma Harms on p. 209 to determine its quality. What message does the room convey about the teacher's values? What changes could you suggest to make it more inviting and appropriate for young children?

TABLE 6.2 Guidelines for Selecting Safe and Appropriate Materials for Children of All Ages

Age	Guidelines	Appropriate Materials
Infants (0–1 year)	• equipment should be sized appropriately • too large to swallow • washable • brightly colored • free of small or removable parts • free of sharp edges and toxic material • nonelectric and durable • soft and varied textures • rounded and smooth edges on furnishings	• soft cloth and thick cardboard books, musical toys • push-pull toys, infant bouncers • simple rattles, teethers, sturdy cloth toys, squeeze-and-squeak toys, colorful mobiles, activity boxes for the crib • soft rubber blocks, dolls, animals • soft hand puppets • tactile toys
Toddlers (1–3 years)	• nonelectric • painted with lead-free paint • easily cleaned • cannot pinch or catch hair • too large to swallow • no glass or brittle plastic • suited to child's skills, and the right size and weight • helps child learn new skills and practice learned skills	• simple picture books and poems about familiar places and people • toys to push and pull such as wagons, doll buggies • ride-on toys • low slides and climbers, tunnels for crawling, variety of balls • color paddles, dressing dolls, activity boxes, simple puzzles • stacking toys, sandbox toys, finger-paints
Preschoolers and Kindergartners (3–5 years)	• durable, nontoxic, flame retardant • designed to promote children's large and small muscle development • designed to foster children's interest and skills in literacy • nonelectric • designed to enhance children's interest in adult roles, growing imaginations, and increasing motor skills	• props for imaginative play (e.g., old clothes, hats, cookware) • puzzles • art materials and media • simple board games • wheeled vehicles • woodworking sets (hammer, preschool nails) • sewing materials • bead-stringing materials • picture books, simple repetitive stories and rhymes • climbers, rope ladders, balls of all sizes, old tires • dressing frames, toys to put together and take apart • toys, globe, flashlight, magnets, lock boxes
School-Age Children (6–8 years)	• require involvement and concentration • some electric current but not enough to overheat • expand children's school experiences (e.g., computers, planting) • suited to individual's children's skill level to promote interest	• simple card games • simple board and table games (e.g., Bingo) • collector's items (e.g., shells, rocks) • sports equipment (e.g., for baseball, hockey) • puppets, sand art kits, woodworking and sewing kits

SOURCE: Data based on Isenberg & Jalongo (2006).

are given the opportunity to explore the environment, with the support, encouragement, and extension that adult facilitators can provide. This combination of a *physical environment* that is rich with materials and a supportive *human environment* really creates powerful learning opportunities for young children" (McLean, 1995, p. 171).

A high-quality environment also includes your ability to use your knowledge to create environments that build children's healthy bodies and healthy minds. To help you in this area, in the following section, we discuss the important role of nutrition and fitness in your classroom.

Nutrition and Fitness

Goal 1 of the *Goals 2000: Educate America Act* (U.S. Department of Education, 1994) states that "By the year 2000, all children in America will start school ready to learn." A major objective of this goal is to ensure that children receive the nutrition and care they need to build healthy bodies and healthy minds. The relation between nutrition and development (i.e., how nutrition contributes to children's development and learning) is clear; thus, in early childhood settings, building healthy nutrition and fitness habits is essential to children's optimal learning (NAEYC, 2006). In contrast, poor nutrition and fitness habits place children at serious risk for suboptimal learning. Standards and appropriate learning experiences for healthy nutrition and fitness are available in *Make Early Learning Standards Come Alive* (Gronlund, 2006). Fit Source from the National Child Care Information Center provides access to several fitness and nutrition curriculum and lesson plan resources by age and topic at www2.nccic.org. Two other websites that offer lesson planning and assessment resources are www.mypyramid.gov, supported by the USDA for resources for children in grades 1–4, and www.PEcentral.com. The NAEYC (2006) and the American Alliance for Health, Physical Education, Recreation, and Dance (AAHPERD, 2006) recommend the following hands-on nutrition and fitness activities for all children to develop active, healthy lifestyles that support successful learning:

- Integrate learning activities about nutrition and fitness. Use seed catalogues and real vegetables to explore, taste, and talk about the nutritional value of different vegetables. The class might also want to make vegetable soup. Incorporate health-related fitness activities across the curriculum, such as movement both indoors and outdoors and "brain breaks," to ensure good physical fitness in your early childhood setting (Picar, 2006).
- Learn about diverse cultures. Use the cultural backgrounds of children in your classroom as a theme for the day's snacks, meals, or cooking experiences. Explore the different cultural influences on food. At the same time, engage children in movement and dance activities that also support children's cultural backgrounds.
- Plan a balance of indoor and outdoor physical activities that support and stretch children's control, balance, strength, and coordination, such as jumping, pulling, walking at different paces, playing tag, stretching, reaching, or hanging.
- Visit local markets. Help children become aware of how food is grown and sold in places other than a market.
- Use replicas of healthy food, such as fruits, vegetables, cheeses, and bread, in the dramatic play area that serve as a good model for play related to foods.
- Serve nutritious snacks and meals in an atmosphere that encourages social or self-help skills (Colker, 2005).
- Engage in pleasant interactions during snack and mealtimes that will encourage children to accept new foods and develop healthy eating habits. Snacks and meals are more pleasurable when food is served on a predictable but flexible schedule, when there are small portions of food and drink so children can ask for more, and when the conversation focuses on the children, not the food. Table 6.3 lists some nutritious foods appropriate for children at different ages.

High-quality early childhood environments are safe, secure, and respectful. They include adults who provide plenty of attention to children and who understand them and can meet their needs. High-quality environments also are characterized by consistent,

TABLE 6.3 Nutritious Foods for Children at Different Ages

Age	Nutritious Foods	Foods to Avoid
Infants		
0–4 months	breast milk or formula	
4–6 months	iron-fortified cereals of barley or rice	egg whites, seafood, chocolate, citrus fruits, tomatoes (allergies)
6–7 months	strained fruits and vegetables, fruit juices, teething foods such as crackers, toast	honey, raisins, nuts, peanut butter, pieces of hot dog, and raw carrots (choking)
8–9 months	pureed meats, potatoes, rice, pasta	
10–12 months	finger foods such as cheese cubes, toast strips	
Toddlers/ Preschoolers	sandwiches cut into shapes; finger foods, such as pretzels; cut-up vegetables; fresh fruit, such as apple slices, strawberries, orange and grapefruit sections; dried fruit, such as apples, pears, apricots; milk-group items, such as cheese sticks, frozen yogurt, sherbet; bread-group items, such as bagels, cookies, dry cereals, pretzels, rice cakes; vegetable-group items, such as celery, cucumber slices, green beans; meat-group items, such as hard-boiled eggs, peanut butter	big pieces of hot dog, jelly beans, nuts, popcorn, raisins, raw carrots, seeds, small hard candies, tough meat, whole grapes

responsive caregiving for long periods of time, and by children who feel assured that they will be secure and protected. These environments are especially healing for children who have been exposed to violence. To ensure these kinds of environments, you will regularly need to evaluate your classroom. In the next section we provide guidance on how to evaluate your indoor environment.

Evaluating the Indoor Environment

Periodic evaluation of your indoor environment will help you meet your learning outcomes as well as those of each child. Some early childhood teachers use one of the many observational instruments (Harms et al., 2004; NICHD Early Child Care Research Network, 2002; Pianta, LaParo, & Hamre, 2005) to assess the quality of their environments as related to child outcomes. Whatever criteria you use, when assessing your environment, consider the *physical characteristics,* such as room arrangement, light, time, and relationships; the *social characteristics,* such as the cultural backgrounds and needs of the children; and the *unique qualities of the local community,* such as neighborhood safety, that affect the children. Noted expert Thelma Harms deepens our understanding of evaluating high-quality early childhood environments in the Ask the Expert piece that follows, and Figure 6.9 lists questions you should ask yourself to evaluate your indoor environment to ensure its quality.

Preparing the Outdoor Environment

Although preparing the outdoor environment is as essential as preparing the indoor environment, it often is neglected. Outdoor environments stimulate children's thinking, ability to solve problems, make decisions, socialize, and try new ideas in ways that are often different from those in indoor environments. To maximize children's learning outdoors as

FIGURE 6.9 Evaluating your indoor environment.

Questions to consider: Does the indoor environment

- Have large spaces for the whole group to meet comfortably?
- Provide medium spaces for small-group instruction that are far enough apart to reduce interference?
- Have small spaces where two or three children can work together?
- Offer quiet spaces for individual tasks and privacy?
- Provide space and room arrangement support cooperation?
- Use moveable walls, furniture, or bookcases to divide centers?
- Label interest areas clearly (e.g., dramatic play, writing)
- Have clear pathways and traffic lanes?
- Provide furnishings and materials that contribute to children's learning?
- Have a range of culturally sensitive materials?
- Display children's work attractively at eye level throughout the classroom?
- Provide soft spaces with rugs, pillows, or cushions that make the room warm and inviting?
- Consider safety in available supplies and equipment?
- Have fresh, pleasant smells and living plants?
- Display positively worded signs and messages?
- Provide materials that are easily accessible, aesthetically pleasing and organized, and invite children's exploration?
- Have an ample supply of open-ended materials to challenge thinking and prevent frustration?
- Represent the children's lives and interests throughout the room with work samples, photographs, sketches, and cultural artifacts?

well as indoors, the outdoor environment should be as enriching as the indoor environment. High-quality outdoor environments focus on equipment and materials that hold children's interest over time to promote their motor development, cardiovascular endurance, enjoyment of the outdoors, and their thinking; are safe in their design, construction, and supervision, to minimize the risk of accidents yet also offer motor challenges; and house materials that are easily accessible to children and easily stored for teachers to facilitate their activity and interaction. The outdoor environment should provide children with the following:

- a wide range of diverse activities, such as gross motor activities, pretend play, and group games
- plenty of well-organized space, such as sand and water areas, natural gardens, and pathways for wheeled vehicles
- easy access from the indoor environment
- adult supervision from many vantage points
- unstructured, movable equipment and materials for use in different play areas
- aesthetic surroundings, including plants and well-cared-for equipment
- defined zones or areas for different activities and easy movement between play areas, such as digging and constructing, role-playing and enactment, mixing and pouring, and painting and splashing (Frost et al., 2004; Rivkin, 2002; Wellhousen, 2002)

ASK THE EXPERT

Thelma Harms on Evaluating High-Quality Early Childhood Environments

Thelma Harms

Why should I devote so much time to thinking about my environment?

Quality environments must meet the three basic needs of children for protection of their health and safety, emotional and social support, and meaningful opportunities for learning. When infants, toddlers, and preschoolers spend the majority of their waking hours in out-of-home group settings, including child-care centers, family child-care homes, preschools and kindergartens, the quality of these early childhood environments significantly influences all aspects of their development. Yet many programs focus on only one of the three basic needs of children and largely ignore the other two. For example, offering exciting hands-on activities is part of a high-quality program for children, but it cannot by itself meet children's equally important needs for warm nurturance or protection from illness and injury. That is why the four widely used classroom assessment instruments my colleagues, Richard M. Clifford and Debby Cryer, and I have developed contain items to cover all three basic components of quality: protection, emotional support, and opportunities for learning. These scales, including the Early Childhood Environment Rating Scale (ECERS), the Infant/Toddler Environment Rating Scale (ITERS), the Family Child Care Environment Rating Scale (FCCERS), and the School Age Care Environment Rating Scale (SACERS), are comprehensive process quality assessments.

Are you saying that I need to use a comprehensive assessment instrument to evaluate my own classroom environment?

Early childhood educators can get a more objective picture of the actual quality of their classroom by using a comprehensive assessment instrument, with proven reliability and validity, to guide their observation. There are now a number of classroom observation instruments that teachers can use as self-assessment guides. For example, national quality recognition programs such as NAEYC Center Accreditation and NAFCC Family Child Care Accreditation, as well as CDA Credentialing, include classroom observation instruments. In addition, many early childhood agencies and state governments use instruments such as our Environment Rating Scales (ECERS, ITERS, FCCERS, and SACERS) to improve early childhood practices and for giving higher payment to better programs (tiered reimbursement).

An observation with any of these instruments must be accurate and objective to be helpful. Therefore, in order to get the greatest benefit from a classroom self-assessment, teachers should:

- Get training on the instrument so that they understand and can use the scoring system accurately.
- Read the instrument thoroughly and make sure they understand all the requirements.
- Get someone else–preferably an outsider who knows the instrument well, to observe the classroom at about the same time as the self-assessment is done.
- Compare and discuss their scores and insights with those of the outside observer.

Any additional training resources that offer greater detail than the instruments themselves should be used to improve accuracy. For example, the ECERS and the ITERS each have an "All About" book that is a detailed guide in words and pictures to explain every indicator in the scales. There are also introductory video and/or print training packages for each of our scales.

If I use an assessment tool to look at my classroom, will it help me be a better teacher of children?

In order to improve the daily practices in the classroom, information observed during assessments provides a good basis for planning and implementing change. Many research projects have shown that high-quality classroom practices result in better social and intellectual preparation for children. Since an accurate observation based assessment provides specific information about actual practices, it can serve as a good baseline from which to plan. Instruments that include step-by-step indicators on different levels of quality, from poor to excellent, are particularly useful in planning for change. Thus, the instrument itself provides a blueprint for gradual improvement. Our scales use such a "levels of quality" format and are therefore often used to prepare for accreditation.

Making significant changes in a classroom requires the active involvement of both teachers and administrators. Schedules may need to be modified, new materials purchased, and additional training provided. By getting the whole team working together to reach more immediate short-term goals, an ongoing improvement process is initiated that can result in achieving more challenging long-term goals.

Thelma Harms is Research Professor Emeritus and Director of Curriculum Development, Frank Porter Graham Child Development Institute, University of North Carolina, Chapel Hill, School of Education.

TEACHER PREP WEBSITE 6.4

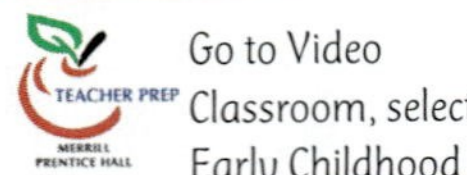

Go to Video Classroom, select Early Childhood Education, choose Child Development (Module 1) and select Physical Development–Early Childhood (Video 5).

All children need outdoor time every day, weather permitting (Frost et al., 2004; Gronlund, 2006). Outdoor play is beneficial not only for children's physical development but also for brain development. Physical exercise and play helps children enjoy vigorous and healthy movement activity; develop large motor skills, such as running, jumping, climbing, swinging, and balancing; and display self-confidence. Outdoor play also benefits children's healthy brain development through frequent opportunities to move (Frost et al., 2004). You can see Acadia and Cody, two preschoolers, exhibit interest, enjoyment, and self-confidence on the playground in the "Physical Development–Early Childhood" video clip online at the Teacher Prep Website.

For young children, long blocks of carefully planned and supervised outdoor periods each day are important for their total development. Older children usually have scheduled recess for an entire grade or grade level, and many primary-grade teachers use the outdoors to teach specific lessons in social studies and science. The rules of a classroom community should apply outdoors as well.

According to research on children's health and fitness, we are seeing a decline in children's physical fitness, an increase in childhood obesity and related diseases, more sedentary activity, and a decrease in recess and physical education (Frost et al., 2004). Read the Ask the Expert feature on page 212, which recounts Joe Frost's views on children's play and playgrounds and why children need a well-planned outdoor play environment. Notice his mention of playground design, safety, and the appropriate role of the adult in the outdoor environment.

Evaluating the Outdoor Environment

As with indoor environments, ongoing evaluation of your outdoor environment will help you meet your learning outcomes. You will want to consider the *space,* such as play zones, groupings, surfacing, and shade; *materials,* such as active, quiet, flexible usage, and variety; *experiences*, such as interactions, gross motor, fine motor, and cardiovascular; and

FIGURE 6.10 Evaluating your outdoor environment.

Questions to consider: Does the outdoor environment

- Provide appropriate spaces for individuals and small groups of children according to their ages, physical sizes, interests, and abilities?
- Have places for games and paths for wheeled toys?
- Contain interesting and challenging play spaces for climbing, swinging, and balancing?
- Offer a pleasant area to enjoy the natural elements and a visually appealing look?
- Provide varied ground surfaces such as hardtop for games and vehicles, grass, soft mulch, or sand?
- Offer easy access to coats, toilets, and drinking fountains?
- Have shaded areas, benches, tables, and support materials for group activities?
- Promote independent and creative use of flexible materials such as sand and water?
- Provide materials for gross motor and fine motor development?
- Provide for children's interactions with materials, peers, and adults?
- Have adults actively supervising?
- Have accessibility, materials, and equipment for children of all abilities and disabilities?
- Meet the physical and neurological needs of all children?

safety, such as supervision, materials in good repair, cushioning materials, and no litter. Figure 6.10 lists questions you should ask yourself to evaluate high-quality early childhood outdoor environments.

The Inclusive Environment

Today, children with exceptionalities have the same access to public education as all other children. It is likely that you will have children with moderate, temporary, or permanent disabilities in your care. These children need the same type of classroom environments as other children, even though they may have different developmental needs (Division for Early Childhood, NAEYC, and The Association of Teacher Educators, 2000). They may, however, need changes in the amount or arrangement of space and materials, or require a different kind of access to areas in the classroom. For example, lofts may not be appropriate for a child with a physical disability, and using a pictured schedule may help a child with autism negotiate the day more successfully (McWilliams, Wolery, & Odom, 2001).

In planning environments for children's exceptionalities, you will want to make some adaptations by either adding something in the environment that is not there, using something that is already there in a different way, modifying the schedule so that all children can participate, or adjusting adults' usual roles and routines. Before making any modifications, be sure to contact the families about the child, the special need, or the special equipment (Allen & Cowdery, 2005; Flynn & Kieff, 2002; Harms et al., 2004). Following are some suggestions for adapting the environment for children with particular exceptionalities.

ASK THE EXPERT

Joe Frost on Outdoor Environments

Joe Frost

Do children need adult-designed playgrounds?

Today's children do need planned playgrounds to compensate for crowded conditions in urban areas, to provide reasonably safe play areas, and to help ensure that children play. Children reared in rural areas have ample places and opportunities to play in rich natural environments filled with hills, streams, vegetation, and animals. In these environments, there is less threat from the hazards of cities—crime, traffic, and drugs. In urban areas, however, natural play spaces are limited or nonexistent. We must create spaces for urban children, including well-designed environments at schools, in public parks, and in children's museums. *Well-designed* means incorporating many of the advantages of the countryside into these built environments.

Must national playground safety standards result in uninspired, boring playgrounds?

The growing emphasis on national safety guidelines and standards for playground equipment *can* contribute to "cookie-cutter," boring playgrounds, which were the norm throughout the last half of the 20th century. The mentality that focused on limited conceptions of play in earlier periods unfortunately is alive and well today, but a growing number of contemporary playgrounds are light years ahead of those of even a decade ago. The most authoritative national play equipment guidelines and standards apply to standard equipment, for example, climbers, slides, and swings. The elements that most influence creative play—nature areas, gardens, storage facilities, building materials, pets, and water and sand areas—are virtually untouched by playground standards. Continuing revision of national safety standards and state regulations is resulting in inconsistencies between national and state requirements, growing complications in interpretation and litigation, and contributing to the decline of school recess. Playground safety standards at all levels sorely need reexamination, simplification, and clarity.

What is the appropriate role of adults in children's play?

Several European countries, notably England, Sweden, and Denmark, surpass the United States in understanding how adults can best contribute to children's play. Over the past decade, they moved from the concept of "play leader" (one who leads children in play) to the present conception of "play worker" (one who interacts with children in a play atmosphere of cooperation and respect). The basic premise for play work is that children's play is free—freely chosen by the child, yet supported by adults who ensure that children have many opportunities for play in rich, reasonably safe environments. Adults provide the materials and places for play, allow ample time for play, and interact cooperatively about play, leaving the lead in play roles to children. Perhaps the most fundamental requirement for adults in enhancing children's play is that they value and understand play and allow children freedom to shape their own play worlds.

Joe Frost is Parker Centennial Professor Emeritus, University of Texas.

Adapting Environments for Children with Limited Motor Abilities

Limited motor ability applies to children whose ability to move negatively affects that child's participation in an activity. This could be the result of cerebral palsy, spina bifida, or a child in a wheelchair either temporarily or permanently. These children need access in the classroom. The following are suggestions for adapting the environment for children with limited motor abilities (Best, Heller, Bigge, 2005; Diener, 2005):

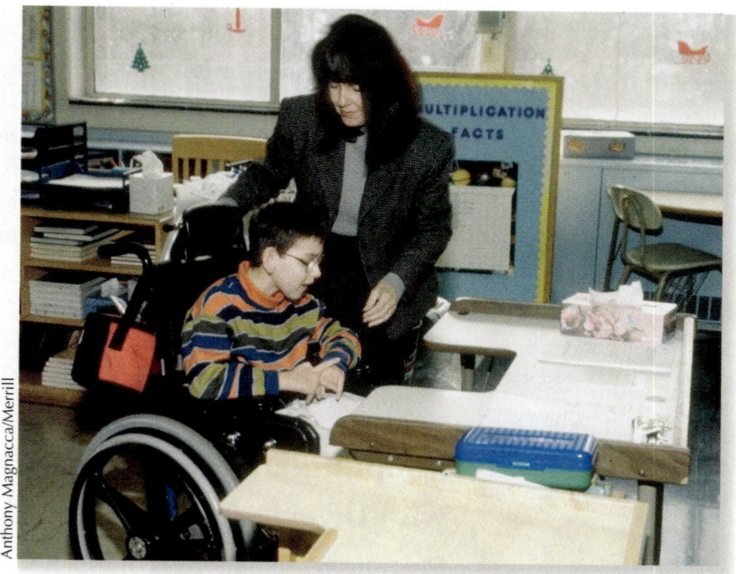

Anthony Magnacca/Merrill

This teacher knows how to adapt the classroom environment to accommodate children with special needs.

- **Access.** Be sure children can enter the building and classroom through wide paths, doorways, and walkways. Have low sinks, water fountains, and table surfaces for a child in a wheelchair. Put lever-style handles on faucets and doors for simpler operating movements than those required by traditional knobs and faucets.
- **Circle Time.** Children with limited motor abilities often have difficulty finding a place to sit and see. You can have all children sit on chairs at circle time, keeping everybody's eye level the same and making the child in a wheelchair feel "less different."

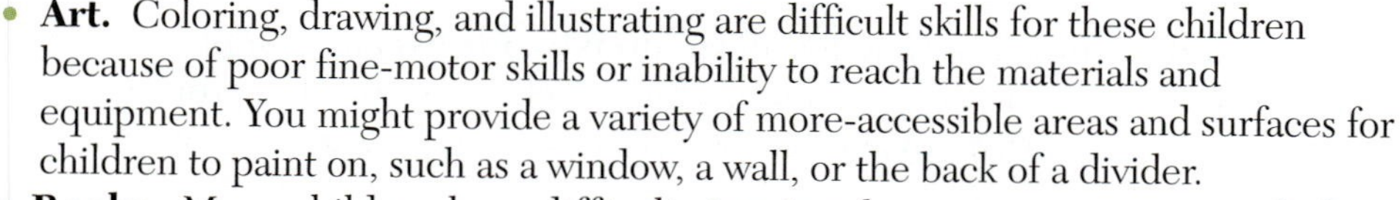

- **Art.** Coloring, drawing, and illustrating are difficult skills for these children because of poor fine-motor skills or inability to reach the materials and equipment. You might provide a variety of more-accessible areas and surfaces for children to paint on, such as a window, a wall, or the back of a divider.
- **Books.** Many children have difficulty turning the pages or cannot reach the books from the bookshelves. You can arrange shelves at different levels so the books are accessible to everybody; provide headphones and tapes so children can listen to the stories; or provide books in several areas of the classroom, especially if your regular classroom library is in a loft or other inaccessible place.
- **Computers and Technology.** Technology for children with limited motor abilities is often an easy way to adapt your environment. Try touch-sensitive computer screens, hand-held devices, and voice-input computers; place stickers on keyboard keys for a particular program to help children locate keys more easily, or set a template over the keyboard so only certain keys show.
- **Space.** Entrances to centers need to be wide and free from materials for children who are in wheelchairs or who need a walker. Table height can be adjusted so a wheelchair can fit underneath. Adjusting legs on large pieces of equipment, such as an easel, will make activities accessible to more children.

COMPANION WEBSITE 6.5 For more information about

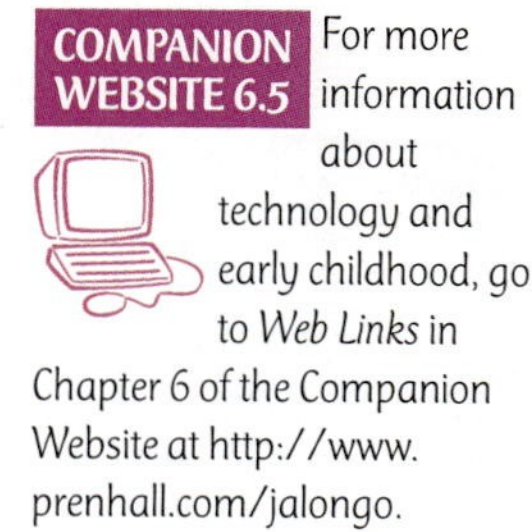

technology and early childhood, go to *Web Links* in Chapter 6 of the Companion Website at http://www.prenhall.com/jalongo.

COMPANION WEBSITE 6.6 To add a professional development product to your developing portfolio, go to *Journal: Constructing Your Professional Portfolio* in Chapter 6 of the Companion Website at http://www.prenhall.com/jalongo.

Adapting Environments for Children with Sensory Impairments

Children with sensory impairments need multisensory experiences to feel like a part of the learning environment. Wald, Morris, and Abraham (1996) and Diener (2005) suggest the following adaptations that provide a more inclusive environment.

- **Vision.** Use brightly colored boxes to hold objects for discussion. Illustrate main events of the day on your daily schedule. Use tactile and auditory cues for children to find their way around the room.
- **Hearing.** Vary the tone of your voice and the pace of your talk. Make sure you have audiotapes of sounds in children's natural environments such as the cafeteria or the school bus. Check for a blinking light on the fire alarm in case of emergency.
- **Touch.** Use a "talking wand," a small tube held by the child who is speaking and then passed on to others so that the speaker is clearly identifiable. Make sure you introduce all new materials before adding them to the centers for children's exploration and use.
- **Smell.** Add scented items to containers with perforated tops and have a "smell and tell" instead of "show and tell" on some days.

TEACHER PREP WEBSITE 6.5

Go to Strategies and Lessons, select Early Childhood Education, choose Appropriate Early Environments (Module 4), and select Transitions (Item 20).

Adapting Environments for Children with Diverse Academic Needs

Every early childhood classroom has children with a range of academic abilities. Following are some suggestions for meeting the diverse academic needs of each child.

- **Space.** Have a quiet place for children who are easily distracted or need to calm themselves down.
- **Time.** Allow sufficient time for all children to process and complete their play and work. Some may need more time to clean up, finish a project, or move from one activity to another before beginning preparation for the next activity.
- **Transitions.** Moving from one activity to another or from one space to another creates difficulty for some children. Some may need specific instructions and practice with transition behaviors, such as where to put away materials and how to move quietly from one area to the next. Others may need you to reiterate what the next activity will be. You may need to give several notices that the next activity will soon end before using an abrupt transition warning such as a light or bell. You can read more about appropriate transitions for all children at the "Appropriate Early Environments–Transitions" online at the Teacher Prep Website.

Adapting the environment to include all children is essential. The efforts you make to modify your environment can result in a new level of learning for all children and adults in the environment.

COMPANION WEBSITE 6.7 To test your knowledge of this chapter's contents, go to the *Multiple-Choice* and *Essay* modules in Chapter 6 of the Companion Website at http://www.prenhall.com/jalongo. These items are written in the same format that you will encounter in the PRAXIS tests to better prepare you for your licensure exam.

Conclusion

High-quality early childhood environments are spaces where all children learn to live, grow, and learn together. Within these spaces, children need to become increasingly independent and feel safe, comfortable, and valued to become confident and competent learners. Creating environments that engage all children's minds and bodies requires not only a substantial collection of concrete resources and equipment but also a great deal of skill, knowledge, and sensitivity on your part. A teacher who creates and evaluates high-quality environments establishes a climate that invites children to explore, learn, and develop.

ONE CHILD, THREE PERSPECTIVES

Creating a Sensory-Rich Environment for Robert

Robert is in the 4-year-old class at a preschool that he has attended since he was 2. He is a quiet child who goes willingly to preschool, usually plays by himself, and does not often participate in group activities. His teacher, Ms. Green, has been teaching preschool for more than 20 years. At one of Ms. Green's conferences with Robert's mother, Ms. Green shared her concerns about Robert's difficulty in listening, paying attention, calming down, approaching his peers to play, focusing on some academic tasks such as making patterns, and attending to and following directions, such as when building a tower. She also mentioned his underdeveloped fine motor coordination that makes his handwriting look very immature. Ms. Green suggested that Robert's mother arrange some play dates to help his social development and work on some fine motor tasks at home, such as clipping clothespins on a paper plate.

Ms. Green's conference caused Robert's mother to address some of Robert's behaviors that she knew were not quite age appropriate, but she was unsure of how to help her son. She certainly did not want to interfere with Ms. Green's experience as a preschool teacher but did want to give Robert every chance to be successful in his preschool. She knew that Robert played alone often at preschool but did not know why. She also knew that when Robert turned 3 and then 4, he did not want to have a birthday party and rarely liked to go home after school in anyone else's car. Robert still sucked his fingers, walked on his toes, and did not speak clearly. When Robert was 3, his mother took him for an evaluation at "Child Find," the county office for children with special needs, because his speech appeared delayed for his age. Results from his assessment indicated an average speech delay and no intervention was recommended. Now, Robert was turning 5 and Robert's mother still had concerns. So, she read books, talked to her friends, searched the Internet, and talked to Ms. Green, Robert's teacher, who suggested that she try "Child Find" again.

Meanwhile, Robert's mother talked again to her pediatrician about her concerns about Robert's toe walking and eventually took him for physical therapy to strengthen his leg muscles. When physical therapy did not completely stop the toe walking, the physical therapist (PT) referred Robert to an occupational therapist (OT), who evaluated him thoroughly. She identified Robert with Sensory Processing Disorder (SPP), a complex disorder of the brain which makes children misinterpret everyday sensory information, such as touch, sound, and movement. This can lead to behavioral problems, difficulties with coordination, and other issues.

Robert then began weekly occupation therapy sessions during which he engaged in sensory-rich activities involving touch, pressure, and movement activities in a safe and comfortable environment to help his body properly learn how to "read" sensory information. The OT also suggested that Robert's mother read *The Out-of-Sync Child: Recognizing and Coping with Sensory Integration Dysfunction* (Kantrowitz and McGinn, 1998). Robert's mother also contacted the county Child Find office again to schedule another evaluation based on new information. Following a comprehensive assessment, here is what Robert's mother learned.

Robert is of high average academic ability but has difficulties with attending to tasks and becomes anxious when he cannot do a task or thinks he cannot do a task. He does well on tasks when he feels confident. The Child Find team did raise concerns about Robert's social and emotional development. As noted by his mother and preschool teacher and now by independent evaluators, Robert has difficulty playing with peers. One day he told his mother, "I am lonely on the playground." His delayed social development clearly is interfering with his ability to interact with his peers and his ability to feel confident in himself. Those feelings qualitatively impact his ability to learn and be successful in school. His difficulty in attending to tasks appears as if he were not cooperating or not understanding when in reality, he needs assistance in organizing or planning his task. Personal or small-group instruction where each step of the expected task is clearly stated and demonstrated, if possible, will keep Robert from becoming overwhelmed and allow him to learn the components of the project, which he can then internalize and draw on for future use. Over time, in kindergarten and beyond, Robert's behavior could lead to his teachers believing that he cannot do a task when he simply needs specific strategies to be applied. For Robert, the Child Find eligibility team, consisting of a child psychologist, physical therapist, social worker, and special education teacher, recommended that an IEP be developed and a preschool resource teacher be assigned to observe Robert weekly in his preschool setting, to offer suggestions to Robert's teacher and mother, and to provide enough intervention and support for Robert to develop the social and emotional skills necessary to be successful in school. Robert's private OT also recommended a balance of sensory activities, such as a variety of tactile experiences like using small table blocks and eating foods with different textures; motor experiences such as swinging, climbing, and crawling through tunnels; spatial awareness experiences such as playing catch, wheelbarrow walking, or hammering nails into tree stumps or golf tees into thick Styrofoam; visual experiences such as playing flashlight tag, tossing beanbags, and playing board games; and auditory experiences such as dancing, drawing to music, humming, or whistling. The OT also recommended that sedentary activities such as TV, video games, and the like should be greatly limited.

As a result of the OT and special education consultations and conferences with Robert's mother, Ms. Green realized that she needed to create an environment for Robert that supported his attempts to interact with others, to be successful with academic tasks, and to give directions in a way that Robert could attend to. That meant spending more time observing Robert and making sure that the activities she planned were appropriate for him. Ms. Green first worked on lowering the noise level in the classroom to keep background noise from interfering with instruction and to provide a calmer atmosphere. To address Robert's hesitancy in peer interaction, she read books to the class about how to be a good friend, and during free-play sessions and stations, Ms. Green created small groups instead of letting the children divide themselves into groups. She noted that her discussion of friendships and grouping children with peers they may not have chosen to play with greatly reduced the "cliques" in class and enriched the experience of many other children as well. While Ms. Green made sure that either she or her assistant were available to help Robert get started on a new task or activity, she also wanted to work on purposeful play and planning with the entire class. She used the "Plan, Do, Review" method (Hohman & Weikart, 1995) that involved having the whole class talk about the next activity, such as going to a learning station, *plan* what they wanted to do, *do* the activity, and then *review* it as a class to see if they really did what they had planned to do.

Ms.Green's determination to find out what kind of environment and materials Robert needed to be successful also allowed her to more effectively meet the needs of the other children. She believed that every child had the same opportunities to learn and grow in her classroom. Following a "Let's find out what's best for you" approach to meeting Robert's needs, Ms. Green expanded her own understandings about how the environment influences children's behavior. She took the challenge Robert and his mother presented and grew with it.

REACT	Think about how the perspectives of Ms. Green, Robert's mother, and the occupational therapist are alike and different. What might be some reasons? With whom do you identify, and why?
RESEARCH	Interview at least two different teachers about how they plan their environments for children with exceptionalities. For example, find out how they encourage children's social and emotional interactions with one another. How do they respond to children who appear not to focus and attend to directions? Compare the responses of the teachers you interviewed with the key features of high-quality environments described in Table 6.1. Chart your findings and draw one major conclusion from your research.
REFLECT	What assumptions about children who need support in making friends and initiating and maintaining peer interactions do Ms. Green, Robert's mother, and the occupational therapist make? Using the data gathered from your interviews, generate some ways you can more appropriately respond to children like Robert in your class.

IN-CLASS WORKSHOP

Creating a High-Quality Environment

Read the feature "Ask the Expert: Thelma Harms on High-Quality Environments" presented earlier in this chapter. Respond to the following points that Harms makes about high-quality environments by answering the two questions that follow. Then, share your responses with a partner.

- High-quality environments must meet three basic needs of children: protection of their health and safety, emotional and social support, and meaningful opportunities for learning.
- Early childhood educators can get a more objective picture of the actual quality of their classroom by using a comprehensive assessment instrument, with proven reliability and validity, to guide their classroom. To improve daily practices in the classroom, information observed during assessments provides a good basis for planning and implementing change.

1. What do you think of these ideas?
2. How do you think you could implement them? Discuss why or why not.

CHAPTER 7

Exploring Your Role as a Curriculum Developer

> ***If we continue teaching the planned curriculum as if nothing is happening on the part of the learner, out of fear that we will lose sight of our goals, we risk encountering a far greater and ultimately more tragic problem—losing the learner and leaving him behind.***
>
> Beverly Falk, 2000, p. 105

Meet the Teachers

YVETTE EAGLE has been a child-care provider for 7 years and is now the new owner and director of a child-care center in a rural area of her state. One of Yvette's first tasks as director was to develop the curriculum. At a recent conference, Yvette was sharing her new role with her colleagues: "At this point, I must implement a curriculum with an existing staff that is not used to planning. How will I get my teachers to view curriculum as a plan to guide children's learning and not as a series of unrelated, cute activities?" Yvette believes that curriculum for young children should be organized to reflect their physical, social, emotional, language, and cognitive needs. She sees her biggest challenge as convincing her teachers that curriculum development is an important responsibility. At this point, Yvette is overwhelmed, but not discouraged, with the idea of developing an effective curriculum for her center.

MS. ORNSTEIN teaches a full-day kindergarten class. If you visit her classroom, you will notice children working on different projects. When Ms. Ornstein's kindergartners arrive at school, they choose two activities to work on for the day and immediately begin completing unfinished work from the previous day. Ms. Ornstein believes that "Children can be trusted to select activities that interest them and to develop the habit of completing work they have started." An important part of Ms. Ornstein's curriculum is having her kindergartners record and chart their completed work to share with the group each day. On one particular day, Lukas was constructing a plane from his woodworking plan, Juan was recording his favorite part of *Peter Rabbit* after listening to the story on audiotape, and Elena had drawn a picture of the solar system that looked like a puzzle she had just completed and was recording the names of the people who helped her. Ms. Ornstein encourages children to record and chart their work each day because it "offers children an important way to communicate their ideas to others and to make sense of their experiences to themselves."

MS. BUSCOVICH is a third-grade teacher who describes her class as "quiet, organized, and well-planned with lots of whole-group teaching for basic-skills instruction." While taking a graduate class on curriculum in early childhood, she learned that teaching mathematical skills in isolation can be confusing to many children and that children need to apply mathematical operations to real-life situations. So, Ms. Buscovich decided to provide opportunities for children to learn math by doing math. She began by developing small-group activities with pattern blocks. Children observed, experimented, and discovered answers to questions about particular characteristics of the pattern blocks. They shared their findings with their peers and reused the pattern blocks in different ways after listening to classmates' ideas. The more Ms. Buscovich used authentic strategies for teaching math concepts, the clearer it became to her that all students were better able to connect what they were doing to larger mathematical concepts. For Ms. Buscovich, learning new ways of teaching mathematics helped her feel more confident and less overwhelmed.

All of these teachers are using three important principles to guide their curriculum decisions. First, the teachers are considering what their children are like and then developing experiences to match those characteristics. Next, the teachers are noting which particular experiences influence children's learning and behavior. Finally, the teachers are showing respect for the different ways children learn (Kostelnik, Soderman, & Whiren, 2007).

COMPARE	What do these three teachers know about children that guides their curriculum decisions?
CONTRAST	How do these teachers think about the curriculum, or what happens in the classroom? What are some commonalities and differences among them?
CONNECT	What aspects of curriculum do you think you will look for when you begin observing teachers of young children? Why do you think so?

Now that you have reflected on the perspectives of three different teachers, here is a preview of the knowledge, skills, and dispositions you need to acquire to fulfill your role as a curriculum developer.

Learning Outcomes

- ✔ Become familiar with your role as a curriculum developer **(NAEYC #4c, INTASC #1 and ACEI #2a, 2i)**
- ✔ Define and describe high-quality early childhood curricula
- ✔ Explore the early childhood educator's role as a designer and collaborator of curricula
- ✔ Identify major issues and trends in early childhood curricula
- ✔ Understand curriculum theory and the process of curriculum evaluation
- ✔ Define, describe, and create developmentally appropriate and effective practices for all children
- ✔ Understand areas of the curriculum and ways to integrate subject matter

A Definition of Curriculum

The **curriculum** is the pathway of education; it is what children actually experience in schools from arrival to departure and reflects the philosophy, goals, and objectives of the program, classroom, or school district. According to Bredekamp and Rosegrant (1992), a curriculum is "an organized framework that delineates the *content* that children are to learn, the *processes* through which children achieve the identified curricular goals, what teachers do to achieve these goals, and the *contexts* in which teaching

DID YOU KNOW...?

- The majority of our schools are underfunded, especially those in low-wealth school districts. Children in these schools lack adequate instructional materials and access to technology, and they are often housed in buildings that fail to meet the safety codes of their states. They are usually taught by less-qualified personnel (Thomas & Bainbridge, 2002).
- Children of color represent 45% of all U.S. schoolchildren, and this percentage is expected to grow over the next decade (U.S. Census, 2004). The most common countries of origin for immigrant parents with young children are: Mexico at 39%, followed by India at 2.8%, and the Philippines at 2.7% (Capps et al., 2005).
- Qualified teachers manage to produce better achievement regardless of which curriculum materials, pedagogical approach, or reading program they use (Allington, 2002).
- More than a million children—about 20% of the population—are now in public preschool programs and there is increased accountability for these schools. Sixteen of the 39 states that fund public preschools have standards for preschool in place, and 6 of those states—California, Connecticut, Georgia, Maryland, Michigan, and Washington—require that preschool programs adhere to those standards (Edwards, 2002; Lewin, 2006; Stipek, 2006).
- The Head Start reauthorization bill requires the development of educational performance standards so that children are being prepared academically to be successful in school (Lewin, 2006; Stipek, 2006).
- Multiculturalism refers not only to race and ethnicity, but also to class, religion, sex, and age. The multicultural, multiracial, and multilingual nature of our society mandates that we teach tolerance and understanding of differences as an ongoing process involving self-reflection and self-awareness, increasing knowledge, and developing relevant skills (Morrow, 2005).

and learning occur" (p. 10). In other words, a curriculum is a plan for what children need to learn in schools and suggests ways to teach it. All children experience curriculum in an environment that influences what they learn.

Curriculum decisions include what children are expected to learn (content), how children will learn it (instruction), and when the material is best learned (timing) (Henson, 2006; Jackman, 2005; Katz & Chard, 2000). Simply stated, what we teach differs from how we teach it and how children experience it. Early childhood professionals incorporate research and theory about children's development and learning, best practices, different program models, and standards in their definition of curriculum. Ultimately, however, the curriculum should help children develop the knowledge, skills, values, and dispositions they will need to become productive members of society.

Why the Curriculum Is So Important

It is common to think of curriculum only as standards and academic content, but there are other important dimensions. Although there are some local, state, and national curriculum standards that teachers are expected to follow, differences in teaching practices, differences in implementing legislated policies, and differences in testing emphasis lead to great variations in the quality of curriculum for children. A visitor could observe

COMPANION WEBSITE 7.1 To learn more about defining your role as a curriculum developer, go to *Journal: Defining Your Role* in Chapter 7 of the Companion Website at http://www.prenhall.com/jalongo.

several early childhood classrooms in which the same lesson is being taught and notice considerable variations in ways of teaching as well as clear differences in what and how children are learning. What makes the difference is not the required content, but the way in which each teacher interprets and implements the curriculum. To fully understand the curriculum, a teacher needs to consider not only the curriculum standards and content, but also the intent of schooling and all of the experiences children have while they are in school. In other words, there is a written curriculum (documents and standards), a taught curriculum (the teacher's interpretation and practices), and a tested curriculum (the assessments used to evaluate children's progress or overall program effectiveness). Some experts have even argued that there is a "hidden curriculum" (Jackson, 1968), meaning all of the lessons that children learn about school and society.

Suppose, for example, that you are teaching a lesson on shapes to a group of kindergartners. You decide to focus on the basic shapes of circle, triangle, square, and rectangle. You begin the lesson by saying to the kindergartners, "What is a shape?" and "Name some shapes that you know." One child responds that a star is a shape. But you are not expecting that answer and, without considering the child's point of view, reply, "No, that is not one of the shapes we are studying." It could be argued that the lesson the child learns from this interaction has very little to do with the curriculum standards or the subject matter. Instead, the child may have learned that being a "good" student means guessing what is on your mind because you are the teacher or that conformity is the goal of education. The child actually may be learning to dislike school rather than learning to identify basic shapes, which was the intended goal. Thus, children not only learn content, they also learn about what school is and what it means to become an educated adult. When curriculum is viewed in this way, it becomes virtually everything that occurs under the auspices of the school. Teachers interpret curriculum according to their beliefs about teaching and learning. Thus, providing for individual differences, flexibility,

Scott Cunningham/Merrill

What curricular objectives are apparent in this classroom?

and continuity in learning are important criteria to consider in your curriculum. Even though there is a local curriculum that you will be expected to follow, there are also social, political, and economic changes that will strongly influence how you teach. We discuss these influences next.

Influences on the Curriculum

Throughout history, early childhood professionals have been challenged by factors that have influenced the way curriculum is taught. These factors reflect social, political, and educational changes that place heavy demands on teachers and have an enormous impact on what and how children learn (Glatthorn, Boschee, & Whitehead, 2006; Henson, 2006). Some of the trends currently influencing the early childhood curriculum are briefly discussed next.

Social Influences

The curriculum is greatly influenced by the changing social issues and values—such as diversity, home-schooling, parental engagement, poverty, and technological literacy—that shape and reshape how schools educate children. At times, these influences send conflicting messages about effective curriculum, and it is up to the teacher to reconcile such contradictions. All teachers need to comply with their local, state, and national curriculum, consider the program's goals, conform to the school administrator's policies, respond to input from families, rely on their professional training, and refer to the recommendations of various professional organizations when teaching their currirulum. Early childhood professionals put the needs of children and families first and use them as guiding principles in response to prevailing social influences. Maintaining this focus helps teachers to function as child advocates who not only teach but also support and defend all children in their care. Parents can be quite forceful in impacting the curriculum. They might advocate for more rigorous academic courses, be concerned about poor student performance on tests, request that their children opt out of certain topics of study, or ask for more attention to diversity issues in materials, activities, and lessons. For example, because the United States is so culturally diverse, the curriculum must reflect different cultural values and interests. This divergence often leads to controversies over curriculum content and conflicting calls for reform.

Political Influences

The curriculum is also affected by changing political influences such as national reform reports and related federal funding. Since 1983, with the publication of *A Nation at Risk: The Imperative for Educational Reform* (National Commission on Excellence in Education), reforming American education has been a front-and-center topic for the American public. Early reform goals focused on raising educational quality by requiring more testing of students and evaluating teachers' performance. Later reform efforts in the late 1980s and 1990s focused on school improvement through increased accountability and addressing issues facing children of color. Today's focus builds on past education reform agendas. It emphasizes high-stakes student assessments, standards, and accountability of each state to report the annual yearly progress (AYP) of each public school in increasing the percentage of students scoring proficient in reading and math and in narrowing the achievement gap.

Educational Influences

Federal, state, and local governments influence curriculum through their judicial decisions, legislative actions, and funding for education. For example, in 2001, the passage of the No Child Left Behind (NCLB) Act significantly changed the curricular landscape by creating a high-stakes testing culture and requiring states to develop and measure standards. States are now creating state standards, curriculum guides, and frameworks for all of their public schools to follow, which has led to a narrowing of the curriculum and an increased emphasis on tests and testing. While NCLB does not explicitly mandate testing for young children, it has influenced the early childhood curriculum at all levels. For example, the new Head Start policies and the National Reporting System test require using a standardized test with 4- and 5-year-olds (Meisels & Atkins-Burnett, 2004; Raver & Zigler, 2004). In addition, although NCLB does not require students to be tested until third grade, early childhood curricula are affected by policies that increase accountability in schools and student achievement (Hyun, 2003; Seefeldt, 2005b; Wortham, 2006). Early childhood curriculum is also affected by the federal requirement to utilize scientific, research-based reading programs for children in grades K–3. Finally, early childhood curricula are influenced greatly by the media and commercial early childhood materials. Without a doubt, most teachers structure classroom lessons and plans around textbooks that provide teachers with teaching objectives, learning activities, tests, audiovisual aids, and other supplements to help them meet local, state, and national standards. Textbooks play an important role in student learning, and the people who select them play an important role in shaping the curriculum.

Todd Yarrington/Merrill

These teachers are modifying the state's curriculum guidelines to meet the needs of their community.

Regardless of the many influences on the curriculum, it is important to remember that the key ingredient for any curriculum is the learner. Early childhood professionals can look to the NAEYC position paper *Developmentally Appropriate Practice in Early Childhood Programs* (Bredekamp & Copple, 1997) for guidance on making informed curriculum decisions for young children.

Developmentally Appropriate Practice and the Curriculum

Developmentally appropriate practice is not a curriculum. Rather, it is a set of key ideas that center on what children know and can do. Adults who work with children can take into account children's needs and characteristics as they make thoughtful and appropriate decisions about early childhood curriculum. Everything that has been learned through research and formulated into theory about how children develop and learn is used to create a curriculum that matches children's abilities and needs. Developmentally appropriate practice is based on the following three elements:

1. Developmentally appropriate practice is based only on what is presently known and understood about children. It is not based on what adults wish children were like, or hope they will be like, or even expect they might be like.
2. Developmentally appropriate practice is characterized by planned learning experiences that take into account children's strengths, interests, and needs. This means that adults must recognize that children learn in different ways and at different rates.
3. Developmentally appropriate practice incorporates family needs, values, and cultural backgrounds. Treating children and families with respect is essential to making learning relevant to all learners, especially those children with diverse needs and from linguistically and culturally different backgrounds (Bredekamp & Copple, 1997; Copple & Bredekamp, 2006). Figure 7.1 compares developmentally appropriate practice with less developmentally appropriate practice.

FIGURE 7.1 Comparison of developmentally appropriate practice to less developmentally appropriate practice.

Appropriate

- low adult–child ratios
- staff are trained in the curriculum
- authentic assessment measures are used to design appropriate activities
- individualization is occurring
- children have some choice of their learning experiences
- teachers use different methods to facilitate children's learning
- learners are actively engaged in varied, interesting learning experiences
- active learning experiences dominate in all developmental domains
- emphasis is on balance of process and product
- subjects are integrated
- concept development is emphasized
- children's ideas are recognized and valued
- teachers value and reward self-discipline through positive guidance
- family participation is valued

Less Appropriate

- high adult–child ratios
- inadequate staff training
- test scores predominate
- all children do the same activity
- children are generally assigned tasks
- teachers rely heavily on direct instruction
- learners are passive and are expected to sit still and listen most of the time
- learning experiences are narrowly focused on cognitive development
- emphasis is on correct products
- subjects are taught separately
- skills and memorization are emphasized
- children's have no input into the curriculum
- teachers rely heavily on extrinsic rewards and/or punishments to control behavior
- communication with families is minimal and perfunctory

SOURCES: Data adapted from Bredekamp & Copple (1997); Copple & Bredekamp (2006); Hyson, Copple, & Jones (2006).

A curriculum based on these three elements of developmentally appropriate practice helps early childhood teachers to provide a realistic range of experiences, materials, and activities. Such variety is needed to meet the needs and interests that each child brings to the group learning experience. Note what Sue Bredekamp says about developmentally appropriate practice in the Ask the Expert feature on page 227.

What Does Research Say About Appropriate and Effective Early Childhood Curricula?

Studies of programs and practices that produce successful results for all children suggest the following agreed-upon principles for appropriate curricula (Bredekamp & Copple, 1997; Carnegie Corporation of New York, 1996; Copple & Bredekamp, 2006; Landry, 2005; NAEYC, 2001). These principles of practice apply not only to school-based and child-care settings, but also to adults who interact with children in other educational settings such as scouting or recreational programs.

Anthony Magnacca/Merrill

A successful curriculum provides a balance of support between home cultures and languages and the shared culture of the school.

Appropriate and effective curricula provide for all areas of a child's development: physical, emotional, social, cognitive, linguistic, and aesthetic. Early childhood curriculum focuses on the "whole child" (Bredekamp & Copple, 1997; Bredekamp & Rosegrant, 1995; Copple & Bredekamp, 2006; NAEYC, 2001). For example, the curriculum supports children's physical development through movement, climbing, or cutting experiences; social and emotional development through learning how to solve conflicts over materials, working cooperatively in groups, caring for each other and for materials and building predictable and trusting relationships with adults; and cognitive development through acquiring the skills of reading and writing, solving mathematical problems, and posing and answering questions about their world. Children's early learning experiences affect their performance in schools and beyond. Research on brain development, for example, indicates that during the first 10 years of life, a child's brain has already formed most of its lifetime connections (Commission on Behavioral and Social Sciences and Education, 2001; Levine, 2002).

Appropriate and effective curricula include content that is worth knowing and meaningful. All young children need to learn content that does not trivialize learning. Content that is worth knowing builds on big ideas, and fosters deep understanding. While some early childhood teachers would shudder at the thought of teaching physics to young children, in fact, the content of physics, which includes the study of motion, can be made appropriate. To illustrate, at the simplest level, children can explore how objects move and what makes them move. When preschool children experiment with the effect that changing the incline has on a ball, they are doing physics on a level that they understand. The same is true of children in the primary grades who place drops of colored water and oil in a pan and carefully tip the pan at different angles, speeds, and directions, then observe differences in the moving circles. Both of these activities are

ASK THE EXPERT

Sue Bredekamp on Developmentally Appropriate Practice

Sue Bredekamp

Does developmentally appropriate practice mean watering down or oversimplifying what is taught to young children?

The NAEYC's 1987 publication on developmentally appropriate practice may have inadvertently contributed to this misconception because it was written in the context of a "push-down curriculum," in which next-grade expectations are routinely pushed down to younger children. Because the NAEYC opposed rote drill and practice on isolated academic skills and the overuse of whole-group, teacher-directed instruction with very young children, some people interpreted the statement to mean that in developmentally appropriate classrooms, children are not expected to learn anything. Nothing could be farther from the truth. To be developmentally appropriate, a curriculum must be intellectually challenging and engaging, because young children are naturally curious and eager to learn just about everything there is to know about their worlds. It is somewhat ironic, in fact, that one of the most developmentally appropriate programs in the world—the early childhood program in Reggio Emilia, Italy—is also among the world's most intellectually challenging and enriching.

If I use developmentally appropriate practice in my classroom, does that mean I cannot do any direct teaching?

If we base our practices on what children need to develop their full potential, adults have to be highly involved and even directive. Young children do need opportunities to explore and make discoveries on their own, but they can do this best in contexts in which adults provide care, guidance, information, and a host of other things that adults, but not young children, know and are able to do.

Do developmentally appropriate practice principles apply to children with exceptional needs?

One of the most well-known principles of human development is that there is a wide range of individual variation on every dimension; therefore, it is impossible to be developmentally appropriate without also being individually appropriate. These are not mutually exclusive terms. Because each child in a developmentally appropriate program must be viewed as an individual for whom teachers assess, plan, and adapt the curriculum and teaching, developmentally appropriate programs are ideal environments in which to include children with disabilities or special learning needs.

Is developmentally appropriate practice sufficiently sensitive to and responsive to cultural and linguistic diversity of children and families?

The very idea that any set of practices could be called developmentally appropriate for all children is criticized because it assumes that there are universals of development irrespective of cultures. This particular concern led to the most important modification in the NAEYC's 1997 revised edition of developmentally appropriate practice—a fundamental clarification of the definition that takes into consideration at least three important pieces of information: age-related human characteristics (predictions about what is age-appropriate), knowledge of the individual children in the group, and knowledge of the social and cultural context. Because all development occurs in and is influenced by social and cultural contexts, early childhood programs cannot be developmentally appropriate unless they are also culturally appropriate.

Sue Bredekamp is Director of Research, The Council for Professional Recognition, Washington, DC.

designed to help children discover information about their physical world by conceptualizing how objects move (Chaille & Britain, 2003; NAEYC, 2001).

Appropriate and effective curricula are culturally relevant. Culturally relevant curricula support children's home culture and language while also developing all children's abilities to participate in the shared culture of the school. Children's first languages and their cultural values are essential to good early childhood practice. For example, when teachers use stories written in a child's home language and then retell them in English, they are conveying an important message about the value of another language. Moreover, early childhood classrooms should display signs and labels in other languages; display children's writing; and incorporate culturally appropriate songs, dances, and drama to affirm children's culture and language (Gay, 2004; Tiedt & Tiedt, 2005).

Appropriate and effective curricula have clearly stated outcomes. Outcome-based curricula are results oriented and expect all learners to show improved short-term and long-term gains. Studies show that children from low-income families who participated in such programs were less likely to drop out of school, be placed in special classrooms, or engage in criminal activity (Barnett, 1995; Lazar & Darlington, 1982; National Study Group for the Affirmative Development of Academic Ability, 2004; Schweinhart & Weikart, 1996). Moreover, an extensive body of research supports the conclusion that it is important for teachers to believe that all children can learn. Rosenthal and Jacobson conducted the classic study that reinforced this idea in 1968. This study, as well as many that followed it, demonstrated that children would rise or fall to the level of the teachers' expectations for them (ASCD Advisory Panel on Improving Student Achievement, 1995; Carnegie Corporation of New York, 1996; NAEYC, 2001). If, for example, teachers expected you to read well, you probably did. If, however, teachers thought you would not learn to read well, you probably did not.

Appropriate and effective curricula are developed by teachers who believe in themselves and their practice. Over and over again, research has indicated that the best teachers believe in their power to influence children's lives for the better (Ayers, 1996; Bandura, 1997; Raines & Johnston, 2003). They are confident that they can exert a positive influence on children's lives despite the complex challenges that characterize teaching today. Confident teachers do not blame the school, the family, or the child when learning is difficult. Instead, they do everything in their power to improve the situation so that all children can reach their full potential.

These five research-based principles form the foundation of the early childhood curriculum. They make clear why it is important for teachers to develop curriculum so that all children can learn.

PAUSE AND REFLECT

About a Developmentally Appropriate and Effective Curriculum

In your own words, how would you define a developmentally appropriate and effective curriculum? Include what characteristics you would look for in an early childhood classroom, what kinds of activities you might see, and what kinds of activities would be of concern to you. Now, compare your responses to the five principles of practice just described. Share one of your responses with a partner and tell which principle of practice it met and why.

Your Role as a Curriculum Developer

Your role as a curriculum developer is an exciting one. You can shape what children should learn and how they should learn it. Simply stated, you are the link between the child and the content. In John Dewey's (1933) words, "Teachers are the agents through which knowledge and skills are communicated and rules of conduct enforced" (p. 18).

As a teacher, you will develop curriculum both formally and informally. Formally, you may serve on a textbook adoption committee or actually work on writing your district's curriculum. Informally, in your own classroom, you will interpret and adapt the official curriculum to best meet the needs and interests of your children and most likely supplement the prescribed curriculum with your own materials.

In developing curriculum, you will be offering children experiences that help them develop knowledge, skills, cultural values, and appropriate behaviors. You can do this by asking yourself the following questions:

- "What will I teach?"
- "To whom will I teach it?"
- "How will I teach it?"
- "Why am I teaching it?"
- "When and for how long will I teach it?"

A curriculum that is engaging to children relies as much on your own personal experiences and beliefs as on your subject-matter knowledge and methodology. To create a developmentally appropriate and effective curriculum for young children, you need to have understanding and skill in the following five areas.

1. ***Understand and use knowledge of children's growth and development to plan and enhance learning.*** A primary principle of curriculum development is teaching the whole child. This means using your knowledge of children's typical developmental patterns, their needs and interests at different ages, and their different ways of learning best so that each child can learn optimally. We know, for instance, that preschool children have high energy levels, so teachers plan short group times that offer children many opportunities to talk and move. Likewise, we know that peer relationships are very important to children in second or third grade, so teachers provide many opportunities for children to learn with and from each other (Hendrick & Weissman, 2006; Jackman, 2005; Wortham, 2006).

2. ***Understand and use the content you teach to create a curriculum worth teaching.*** All early childhood teachers must have specialized knowledge in the subject areas they teach in order for content to have integrity. Thus, you must know the key concepts, facts, principles, and processes for each discipline, because they provide a coherent means of organization. In addition, you will want to make sure that the subject matter adequately represents authentic, real-life experiences so that children have a way to solve problems. To illustrate, suppose you were teaching key concepts about measurement to young children. You might have preschool children pour and measure sand and water, but second graders might weigh the containers to see which weighs the most (NAEYC, 2001; Wortham, 2006). In this way, you would tailor a key concept from mathematics to the age and experience level of your students while teaching children accurate and interesting ideas.

COMPANION WEBSITE 7.2 To learn more about fulfilling your role as a developer of curriculum and the NAEYC, go to *Web Links* in Chapter 7 of the Companion Website at http://www.prenhall.com/jalongo.

Today's teachers often feel pressured to add more rigorous content from later grades into early childhood settings; this is sometimes referred to as the "push down" curriculum. The expectations for such a curriculum are often unattainable because they include excessive amounts of paper-and-pencil, abstract experiences for children. We know, for example, that preschool and kindergarten children need concrete experiences with real people and objects to make sense of their learning. Engaging young children in meaningless experiences, such as memorizing tables of mathematical facts or copying

Scott Cunningham/Merrill

Young children need concrete experiences, not just paper-and-pencil activities.

TEACHER PREP WEBSITE 7.1

Go to Video Classroom, select Foundations/Intro to Teaching, choose Curriculum and Instruction (Module 6), and select What are Students Learning (Video 1).

words from the chalkboard, only adds to frustration and a negative disposition toward learning (Bredekamp & Copple, 1997; Copple & Bredekamp, 2006).

3. ***Understand and use teaching strategies that help children become successful learners.*** Knowing content is different from knowing how to teach the content (strategies). Sometimes called *pedagogical content knowledge,* teaching strategies simply are how teachers present content to children so they can use it. Knowledge of a wide range of teaching strategies is not a recipe book but rather a repertoire of ways to help teachers pace instruction to maximize all children's learning. You can see Sue Brush, a second-grade teacher, demonstrate a wide range of strategies to teach graphing in the "What Are Students Learning" video clip online at the Teacher Prep Website. Given the rapid increases in knowledge, it is imperative that you provide children with the skills to keep up with the ever-expanding knowledge explosion. Some appropriate methods you might use are hands-on learning, investigations, thematic units and projects, choice of learning experiences, coaching or guiding children with skill acquisition and use of reference materials, demonstrations, modeling, role-play, or problem solving. Your knowledge of how and when to use different strategies also includes what misunderstandings, challenges, and prior knowledge children bring to their learning (Bredekamp & Copple, 1997; Jackman, 2005). You will put your own imprint on curriculum by selecting illustrative examples, explaining how to accomplish tasks, monitoring children's activities, and revisiting topics to make the children more readily understand the material.

4. ***Understand and use curriculum for diverse populations.*** Your curriculum should reflect the diverse families, cultures, languages, and socioeconomic status of the children in your class. When studying a topic, be sure to include the cultures of the children in your class. Be certain also to be sensitive to family environments that affect your children and provide support to children no matter what type of family environment they live in. As was discussed in number 3, pay attention to the various strategies you use with diverse populations. If, for example, you use mostly methods that rely heavily on memorizing verbal material, you will meet with limited success when working with diverse groups of young children. A heavy reliance on words and recall inhibits positive teacher–child communication, particularly when the child's ethnic background or first language differs from the teacher's or when the child has a language delay or disorder. If, however, you use methods that utilize direct involvement with real materials, you have a much better chance of helping children make sense of their experiences because children learn best with concrete, real experiences that involve direct participation rather than through abstract ideas.

5. ***Realize that your curriculum reflects your own personal experiences, values, beliefs, and expectations as much as your knowledge of content and pedagogy.*** Your experiences with schools, teachers, and learning up to this point affect how you

view curriculum. These experiences are what will make you a unique teacher of children, and at the same time will influence how you implement the how, why, and what of your curriculum. It is important for you to be in touch with your own personal life experiences, which will influence your role as a curriculum developer. One of the first steps you might take is to reflect on the culture and ethnicity of your own family and your own experiences. As you explore your own background, you might also begin to explore the way you feel about children and families who differ from you. This personal journey will help you support the children and families through the curriculum that you develop because teachers teach who they are (Palmer, 1998).

While your role in developing curriculum is focused on planning quality learning experiences for children, you must also be focused on the relationship between the planned experiences and how you will teach them to maximize children's learning. In the next section, we will explore two different types of curricula—the written curriculum and the taught curriculum—and what these types of curriculum mean for early childhood teachers.

Understanding the Written Curriculum

The **written curriculum** is a comprehensive document for each grade level that contains the general goals or outcomes that all children should meet, the specific objectives that all children should master, a sequence of study for selected topics, and suggested learning activities. The written curriculum can be *general,* usually developed by a state curriculum office for use across that state, or *specific,* usually developed by a local school district or provider, a specific school, or a particular program. The main purpose of the written curriculum is to standardize the learning expectations using local, state, or national standards to guide teachers' decisions and to determine what children should know and be able to do at a particular grade level. Most early childhood educators believe that high academic standards and high teacher expectations lead to higher achievement when the curriculum is personally relevant, meaningful, and interesting.

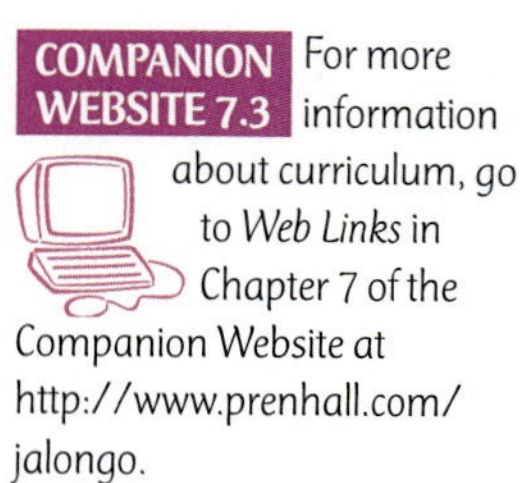

For more information about curriculum, go to *Web Links* in Chapter 7 of the Companion Website at http://www.prenhall.com/jalongo.

Standards-Based Curriculum

How do we know what children are supposed to learn at different grade levels? A **standards-based curriculum** specifies what children should learn, focuses on practices that meet those standards, and continually assesses children to see if the standards have been met. It is one way to ensure that all children have the same opportunity to achieve excellence and equity in their education. To meet this new demand, most states have adopted state standards that define what children should know and be able to do in each subject area. Additionally, almost all states have identified early learning standards for preschool children below kindergarten age (Gronlund, 2006). Early learning standards describe expectations for children's learning and development in all domains and developmental stages that provide the foundation for later learning. And Head Start has developed a Child Outcomes Framework. Curriculum standards enable teachers to know what to teach and how to assess what is being taught. When we talk about curriculum standards, we mean both content standards and performance standards (Bowman, 2006; Bredekamp & Rosegrant, 1995; Gronlund, 2006; NAEYC, 2001, 2003; Seefeldt, 2005b).

Content Standards

Content standards state what learners should know and be able to do in the subject areas at specific grade levels. Content standards include the knowledge, skills, and dispositions toward learning that children need to develop. For example, in a science study of plants, children at different levels might know the following: names of plants, different parts of plants (e.g., leaves, stems, blossoms, and roots), how plants grow, and the particular botanical techniques that keep plants healthy and alive. Children would also need to know and use some of the scientific processes, such as inquiry, observation, systematic description, and hypothesis testing, to gather and evaluate information and to communicate that information to others. The depth of this knowledge would differ for children according to their age, experience, and interest level (Bowman, 2006; Squires, 2005).

As a result of the standards movement, the early childhood profession has developed its own curriculum guidelines that address the most important curriculum content questions that affect children's learning. All teachers need to be able to answer the following curriculum questions in a positive way in order to realize positive child outcomes. "Is the content meaningful and relevant to the children I am teaching?" "Is the content accurate according to the standards of the subject area?" "Is it reasonable to teach specific skills and knowledge at this time or would children benefit from learning it at a later time?" These questions are typical of those raised in the 20 guidelines for curriculum content that are published by the NAEYC (Bredekamp & Rosegrant, 1995). Figure 7.2 lists these Guidelines for Curriculum Content, which have been adopted by the profession.

Performance Standards

Performance standards differ from content standards by showing what children can actually do in a particular subject area or a particular developmental domain, such as using age-appropriate social skills. For example, in evaluating the writing of kindergarten children, teachers need to know what constitutes mastery along the literacy learning continuum. One child might be using drawings for writing; another might be stringing letters together; yet another might be writing conventionally. These indicators are essential in determining what children can do in particular content areas (Bowman, 2006; NAEYC, 2001, 2003; Squires, 2005).

Early childhood professionals are very much a part of the standards movement. While high content and performance standards are necessary, they are not sufficient by themselves. Standards are primarily used to set the direction for the teacher. Fundamentally, it is the way the teacher implements the curriculum—the quality of teaching—that in the end actually makes the difference in children's learning (Bredekamp & Rosegrant, 1995; NAEYC, 2001, 2003; National Board for Professional Teaching Standards, 2001; Wortham, 2006).

Content Areas of the Early Childhood Curriculum

What is appropriate content for young children? By *curriculum content,* we mean those key concepts, ideas, skills, and processes that are unique to the specific subjects of language and literacy, math, science, social studies, technology, the arts, health, and physical education. For example, some key concepts in mathematics include number sense,

FIGURE 7.2 NAEYC guidelines for curriculum content.

Curriculum . . .

1. uses a theoretical and research base that supports how children learn.
2. achieves learning for children in all domains and enables them to participate in democratic living.
3. teaches knowledge and understanding, skills and processes, and attitudes and dispositions.
4. includes varied subject matter that is interesting and relevant to children.
5. specifies age-appropriate, realistic learning goals.
6. reflects the needs and interests of particular groups of children and incorporates varied teaching strategies and learning experiences to accommodate individual differences.
7. respects children's home culture and language and builds positive relationships with families.
8. builds on and extends what children already know and can do.
9. uses broad concepts to organize learning experiences to meet individual learning needs, abilities, and interests.
10. integrates subject-matter knowledge through units themes, and topics of study that allow for rich conceptual development and meaningful connections.
11. uses the standards of the subject-matter areas to provide content that has intellectual integrity.
12. provides content that is meaningful and worth knowing.
13. engages children actively in learning through meaningful choices.
14. values children's errors as a necessary part of the learning process.
15. develops children's thinking, reasoning, decision making, and problem-solving abilities.
16. values social interaction as integral to the learning process.
17. protects children's physical and emotional safety needs.
18. strengthens children's competence by ensuring successful learning experiences.
19. adapts to individual or group needs where appropriate.

SOURCE: Adapted from the National Association for the Education of Young Children (1995).

estimation, and geometry. Having a deep understanding of this content as well as knowledge of what discipline concepts are appropriate for children at different ages to learn is essential because content makes up a large part of the early childhood curriculum. You can see how a second grader represents numbers from 1–1000 in the "Early Childhood Education–Curriculum Planning and Program" student and teacher artifacts online at the Teacher Prep Website. Table 7.1 lists the content areas of the early childhood curriculum, defines them, and identifies key national standards for each content area that have been developed by each specialty association.

For a searchable database for standards for all of the curriculum areas, go to the website for the Mid-Continent Regional Education Laboratories (McREL): www.mcrel. org/standards-benchmarks/.

All teachers must have a deep understanding of the content that they teach and an appreciation of the unique concepts, processes, inquiry tools, and applications to real-world settings of the knowledge in those areas to develop appropriate curriculum for

TEACHER PREP WEBSITE 7.2

Go to Student and Teacher Artifacts, select Early Childhood Education, choose Curriculum Planning and Program (Module 4), and select Numbers to 1000 (Math K–2) (Artifact 2).

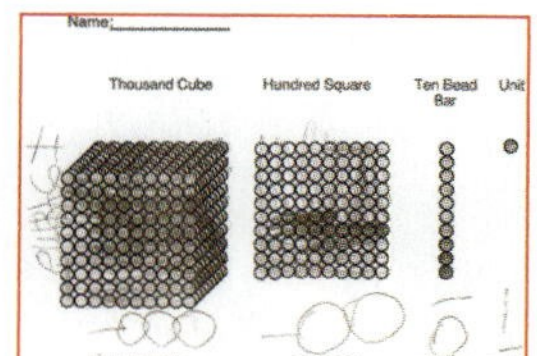

TABLE 7.1 Overview of Content Area Standards in the Early Childhood Curriculum

Content Area	Definition	National Standards	Professional Association
Language and Literacy	The ability to be active, critical users of not only print and spoken language but also of visual language of film and television, commercials and political advertisements, and photography Goal: Literacy	**Reading Standards:** 1. Print-sound code 2. Getting meaning 3. Reading habits **Writing Standards:** 1. Writing in diverse forms and content 2. Writing for different audiences and for diverse purposes 3. Language use and conventions **Listening Standards:** 1. Active listening to recall, interpret, evaluate, and respond to information from a variety of sources **Speaking Standards:** 1. Communicating for varied purposes and to varied audiences in a variety of contexts **Viewing and Representing Standards:** 1. Viewing, understanding, and using nontechnical visual information and representation for critical comparison, analysis, and evaluation	International Reading Association (IRA) *www.ira.org* and National Council of Teachers of English (NCTE) *www.ncte.org*
Mathematics	The search for sense and meaning, patterns and relationships, and order and predictability Goal: Mathematical Literacy	**Process areas:** 1. Problem solving 2. Communication 3. Reasoning and proof 4. Connections 5. Representation **Content areas:** 1. Number operations 2. Algebra 3. Geometry and spatial sense 4. Measurement 5. Data analysis and probability	National Council for Teachers of Mathematics (NCTM) *www.nctm.org*
Science	The application of science to problems of human adaptation to the environment Goal: Science Literacy	1. Unifying concepts and processes 2. Science as inquiry 3. Physical science 4. Life science 5. Earth and space science 6. Science and technology 7. Science in personal and social perspectives 8. History and nature of science	National Science Teachers Association (NSTA) *www.nsta.org/standards*
Social Studies	The development of knowledge, attitudes, values, and skills believed necessary for citizens to participate, continually improve, and perfect society Goal: Social Sciences Literacy	**Geography Standards:** 1. The earth is the place we live 2. Direction and location 3. Relationships within places 4. Spatial interactions 5. Regions **History Standards:** 1. Time 2. Change 3. The continuity of human life 4. The past 5. The methods of the historian **Economic Standards:** 1. Scarcity: The awareness of difference between needs and wants 2. Understanding contributions of those who produce goods and services 3. Career choices and roles 4. Decision making about resources	National Geographic Society *www.nationalgeographic.com/education/xpeditions/standards/matrix.html* National Council for Social Studies (NCSS) *www.ncss.org*

TABLE 7.1 Continued

Content Area	Definition	National Standards	Professional Association
		Social Relations/Civics: 1. Participate as members of a group 2. Recognize similarities among people of many cultures 3. Learn principles of democracy 4. Respect for all others	
Technology	A tool to help children live, learn, and work successfully in an increasingly complex and information-rich society Goal: Technological Literacy	1. Basic operations and concepts 2. Social, ethical, and human issues 3. Technology productivity tools 4. Technology communications tools 5. Technology research tools 6. Technology problem-solving and decision-making tools	National Educational Technology Standards for Students and Teachers (ISTE) *www.cnets.iste.org*
Health	The capacity of individuals to obtain, interpret, and understand basic health information and services and the competence to use such information and services in ways that enhance health Goal: Health Literacy	1. Concepts related to health promotion and disease prevention 2. Health information and health-promoting products and services 3. Health-enhancing behaviors that reduce health risks (most applicable for preschool health education) 4. Influence of culture, media, technology, and other factors on health 5. Personal, family, and community health 6. Interpersonal communication skills to enhance health	National Health Education Standards with Association for the Advancement of Health Education (AAHE) and American Public Health Association (APHA) Alliance for Health, Physical Education, Recreation, and Dance (AAHPERD) *www.aahperd.org*
Physical Education	The acquisition of sequential movement skills and increased competency based on the unique development level of the individual	1. Movement forms 2. Physically active lifestyle 3. Physical fitness 4. Responsible personal and social behavior in physical active settings 5. Respects self and others in physically active settings 6. Physical activity for health, enjoyment, challenge self-expression, or social interaction	National Association for Sport and Physical Education (NASPE) *www.naspe.org* Alliance for Health, Physical Education, Recreation, and Dance (AAHPERD) *www.aahperd.org*
Music	Acquisition of song and melodic understanding	**For preschool children:** 1. Singing and playing instruments 2. Creating music 3. Responding to music 4. Understanding music **For kindergartners and school-age children:** 1. Singing alone and with others; a varied repertoire of music 2. Listening to, analyzing, and describing music 3. Performing on instruments, alone and with others, a varied repertoire of music 4. Reading and noting music	National Association for Music Education *www.menc.org*
Visual Arts	The ability to create visual images and interpret images that others have made Goal: Arts Literacy	1. Media techniques and processes 2. Choosing and evaluating a range of subject matter 3. Knowledge of structures and functions 4. Visual arts in relation to history and cultures 5. Characteristics and merits of own works and works of others 6. Connections between visual arts and other disciplines	Consortium of National Arts Education Associations (NAEA) *www.org/compendium/standard.asf*

COMPANION WEBSITE 7.4 For more information about technology and early childhood, go to *Web Links* in Chapter 7 of the Companion Website at http://www.prenhall.com/jalongo.

children (Bredekamp & Rosegrant, 1995; NAEYC, 2001; National Board for Professional Teaching Standards, 2001). Table 7.2 describes the goal for each content area and suggests appropriate learning experiences for toddlers, preschoolers and kindergartners, and school-age children.

Organizing the Written Curriculum

Once you understand the content of the written curriculum, you can use it to organize how you will teach it. There are many ways to organize your curriculum—by developmental domains or by content area, for example. In addition, you may also organize your curriculum as integrated, emergent, or culturally responsive. A description of each follows.

Developmental Domains

Kostelnik et al. (2007) suggest using areas of children's development, called developmental domains, to design and develop curricula for young children. Such an approach is truly learner centered; teaches the whole child; and allows children to integrate their developing knowledge, skills, abilities, and dispositions as the teacher decides what, how, and when to teach certain concepts and skills. Developmental domains provide a broad view of curriculum and a balanced view of the whole child and help teachers to match content to each child's capabilities to achieve positive outcomes. When content is beyond a child's abilities, the result is often failure. Table 7.3 lists each of the six domains and provides the purpose of each.

Content Areas

Organizing your curriculum by content areas provides a different focus from organizing it by developmental domains. Because a large portion of the curriculum comes from the specialized knowledge of each content area, this approach to the curriculum makes sense to many teachers, school boards, and curriculum developers. Content area knowledge helps children to "learn about the world; describe what is learned; structure the knowledge; test assumptions and challenge understandings; and define and solve problems" (Bredekamp & Rosegrant, 1992, p. 69). Let's look at four of the content areas and see what a content approach looks like in the early childhood grades.

TEACHER PREP WEBSITE 7.3

Go to Video Classroom, select Reading Methods, choose Emergent Literacy (Module1), and select Interactive Writing (Video 1).

In literacy, children develop basic concepts of print and then begin to experiment with reading and writing. Very young children become aware that "Print carries a message"; preschoolers and kindergartners develop the basic concept that "Books contain stories and information that can be retold"; and primary-grade children develop the understanding that "Print can be read and written as they gain skill with reading and writing simple stories with increased fluency and independence" (Morrow, 2005). You can observe a group of K–3 multilingual children composing and transcribing sentences about a lady bag in the "Interactive Writing" video clip online at the Teacher Prep Website.

In mathematics, children develop basic concepts of number, counting, geometry, and measurement through active physical and mental interaction with materials, peers, and supportive adults in order to make sense out of ideas (Charlesworth & Lind, 2007). In geometry, for example, preschool and kindergarten children can build their concepts

TABLE 7.2 Goals of Content Areas and Age-Appropriate Experiences

Content Area	Goal	Age-Appropriate Experiences
Mathematics	To develop a conceptual understanding of quantitative, logical, and spatial reasoning to understand the relationship between and among pieces of information To represent mathematical ideas with symbols and utilize appropriate mathematical procedures and processes to compute and solve problems	**Topic: Classification** **Toddlers:** Sort blocks by shape in a sorting box **Preschoolers and kindergartners:** Simple classifications by sorting objects that are alike (e.g., in shape, color, size) in one place **School-age children:** Multiple classifications by sorting objects into two or more groups (e.g., by color and size)
Language and Literacy	To help children communicate using both oral and written language	**Topic: Writing** **Toddlers:** Opportunities for making random marks on paper, chalkboard, and other surfaces **Preschoolers and kindergartners:** Let children set the purpose for communicating by choosing to communicate through pictures and letters; provide an environment rich with print including class lists, murals, group stories, song charts, and children's labeling of their own work using sound spelling **School-age children:** Utilize different forms of writing such as diaries, editiorials, journals, and stories
Health	To understand basic health concepts and develop lifelong healthy skills and attitudes related to nutrition, safety, personal hygiene, and exercise	**Topic: Nutrition** **Toddlers:** Provide healthful food snacks such as fruits and vegetables; taste and name foods **Preschoolers and kindergartners:** Provide healthful cooking activities such as making stuffed celery or fruit salads, or spreading cheese on crackers **School-age children:** Categorize food into food groups through class and individual books, displays, or food charts; identify source of food products
Visual Arts	To develop the ability to express ideas and feelings using the senses	**Skill: Making Art** **Toddlers:** Make marks on large paper using large, sturdy markers, crayons, or paint; use soft play dough for rolling and modeling **Preschoolers and kindergartners:** Draw and paint using brushes of various widths and markers of different styles (e.g., chisel, fine point), experiment with making different kinds of lines (e.g., wavy, curly, zigzag) **School-age children:** Draw or paint on different textures and surfaces (e.g., transparencies, fabric, wall paper) using different tools (e.g., yarn, tubes, marbles) to create different results
Physical Education	To develop lifelong, positive habits of fitness	**Skill: Body Awareness** **Toddlers:** Use different body parts (e.g., feet, hands, legs) with movement activities to respond to music with different tempos **Preschoolers and kindergartners:** Switch body parts in movement activities such as "Skip, skip, skip to my Lou" changed to "Hop," "Jump," or "Crawl to my Lou" **School-age children:** Improvies and match movement to the beat of music (e.g., clap in time, march to a different beat) and engage in simple folk dances

(continued)

TABLE 7.2 Continued

Content Area	Goal	Age-Appropriate Experiences
Social Studies	To help children become effective participants in a democratic society	**Topic: Families** **Toddlers** Look at pictures of own family; identify people **Preschoolers and kindergartners:** Explore roles and functions of family members (e.g., provides basic shelter and food; provides model for nurturing and support of interactions among family members; provides model for solving problems in emergencies); draw pictures of family roles and function; make a class poster or mural depicting different roles of family members **School-age children:** Create a timeline of special celebrations of the families represented in the class; gather and organize data chronologically; write names of families that observe special celebrations and invite those children and families to share them with the class

TABLE 7.3 Developmental Domains as a Curriculum Organizer

Domain	Purpose
Aesthetic	To build awareness of, appreciation for, participation in, and responses to the expressive arts: art, music, dance, drama, and other sensory experiences
Affective	To develop self-awareness and self-esteem and to learn to handle powerful emotions
Cognitive	To acquire knowledge of math and science, develop basic skills, build understanding of complex concepts, and develop information-processing and problem-solving skills
Language	To develop listening, speaking, reading, and writing abilities, and foster enjoyment of and response to high-quality children's literature
Physical	To build gross motor and fine motor skills, foster care and respect for the body, and encourage positive attitude toward physical health and activity
Social	To develop social attitudes, learn social interaction skills, appreciate and respect cultural and individual differences, as well as enhance social studies content

SOURCE: Adapted from Kostelnik, Soderman, & Whiren (2007).

of shape and size by drawing and cutting shapes; by reading books about shapes, such as *Shapes, Shapes, Shapes* (Hoban, 1986); by comparing seeds from different plants; by moving their bodies into various shapes; and by experimenting with shapes from different materials. Primary-grade children build spatial understandings through making symmetrical designs, reading books such as *Rosie's Walk* (Hutchins, 1968), constructing figures, and making body movements to show positional words such as *in*, *on*, *over*, and *under* (Charlesworth & Lind, 2007).

In science, children learn scientific concepts through problem solving and inquiry such as "Change is all around us" and "Things move in different ways." They also learn to use science process skills to test hypotheses through observing, comparing, classifying, and communicating—skills that lead to the development of knowledge and concept development in science. All children develop scientific understanding through teacher-developed and child-generated problems and investigations (Charlesworth & Lind, 2007).

In social studies, children at all ages learn history concepts, such as the concept of time. Young children's concepts of time are more intuitive than conventional, but their intuitive knowledge is necessary for meaningful understanding of the concept. All children enjoy learning about their own lives, which helps them gain understanding of the passage of time. A personal history book with pictures, stories, notes, and growth chart records helps them understand time concepts. Through active questioning, experiences, and conversations that describe events and routines in a sequence, they use methods of the historian such as thinking about cause-and-effect relationships, analyzing records of the past, and drawing conclusions (Seefeldt, 2005a).

Using a content approach to the curriculum, however, causes some concerns for early childhood educators. Because it is expert based, much of the content is difficult for children to understand. Making specialized knowledge accessible to children at their varying levels of understanding often leads to a watered-down, inaccurate, or confusing curriculum and places primary responsibility on the learner to make connections within and across the content areas (Bredekamp & Rosegrant, 1992). Moreover, content by itself is not adequate enough because it often leads to "fragmented, isolated skill development or the exclusion of other kinds of knowledge and skills essential to children's ultimate success in society" (Kostelknik et al., 2007). Early childhood teachers need the knowledge, skill, and understanding to teach subject matter in age-appropriate ways to all children. Knowing how to organize your curriculum in different ways reflects what you know and believe about teaching and learning.

Integrated Curriculum

The word *integrated* means "joining all parts of something together to make a whole." Sometimes called *interdisciplinary teaching*, an **integrated curriculum** teaches skills and concepts from the different developmental domains and content areas based on the study of a broad concept or theme, and on the developmental needs of the learners. An integrated curriculum has the following characteristics (Fleener & Bucher, 2003/2004; Morrow, 2005; Wortham, 2006).

- It helps children connect their past experiences to what they are currently learning by focusing on processes and concepts within each content area and connecting them to the other content areas.
- Emphasizes children's actual experiences or interests, their interactions with each other, with materials, and with ideas; and promotes active learning through hands-on and minds-on experiences with materials and people.
- Provides ample time for children to experiment and explore ideas that promote all aspects of children's development along with their developing knowledge, skills, and dispositions.

An example of using literature to integrate curriculum is a primary class studying about trees. The children might start with hearing the book *Tell Me Tree: All About Trees for Kids* (Gibbons, 2002) and then help create a graphic organizer to make connections with the text and learn about the types of trees, the parts of trees, and how to identify trees. As children read or hear the story, they can complete sections of the graphic organizer. Figure 7.3 shows how to use children's literature as a starting point for integrating the curriculum.

FIGURE 7.3

Integrated curriculum graphic organizer for study of trees using Gail Gibbon's book *Tell Me Tree: All About Trees for Kids.*

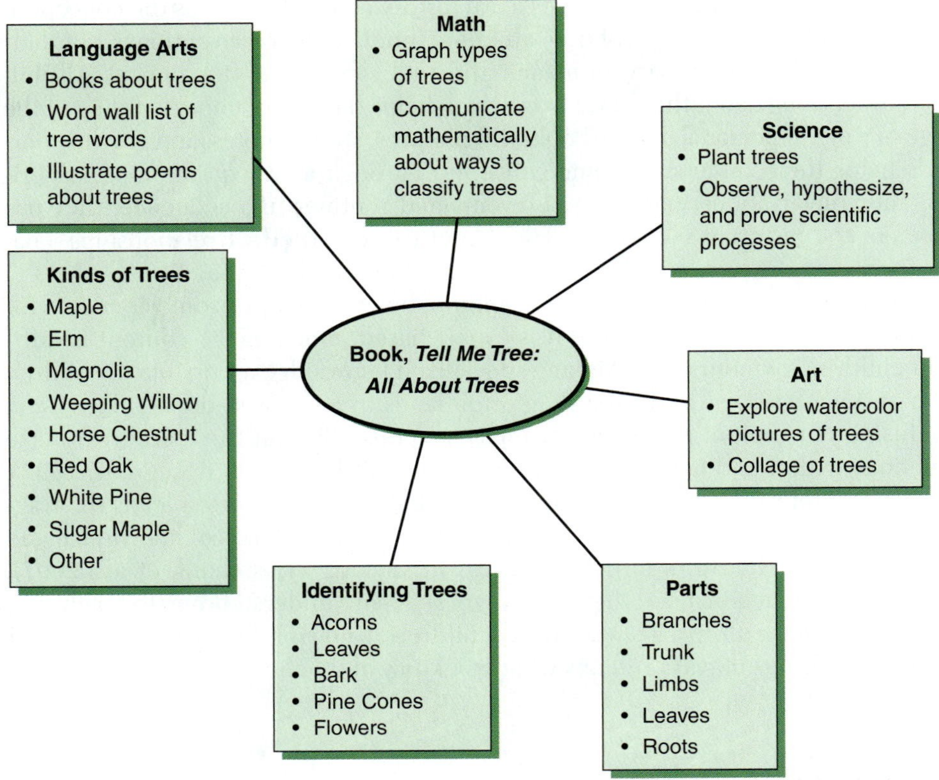

In this case, children can be answering questions they asked, such as "What do trees need to live?" "What kinds of food come from trees?" or "Why do people and animals need trees?" In art, children will want to explore the large watercolor pictures in the book and perhaps make collages of leaf patterns; in science, they may chart the types of trees and animals they learned about or perhaps plant a tree for their class; in language and literacy, they could make a tree identification book, or develop a word wall list of tree words. They might also illustrate other stories or poems about trees, read other literature about trees (such as *Trees, Leaves, and Bark* [Burns, 1995]), and perhaps create advertisements for their favorite tree. Through a variety of learning experiences related to the topic of trees that combine different subject areas and developmental domains, children deepen their knowledge and skills.

The idea of integrated curriculum is not new; it has its origins in the ideas of John Dewey (1938), William Kilpatrick (1936), and Jean Piaget (1965). These respected thinkers suggested that curriculum for children should be holistic, that knowledge should be integrated and include some child-directed activity, that children and teachers should decide together what to learn, and that content should be learned through the study of themes and larger ideas. Learning is more meaningful for children when they make connections among concepts, experiences, school, and life to what they know. Notice how Diane Dodge answers important curriculum questions about young children in the Ask the Expert feature on the next page.

ASK THE EXPERT

Diane Dodge on Early Childhood Curriculum

Diane Dodge

What does curriculum mean in early childhood education?

Today, we have an impressive body of knowledge about child development, learning theory, and principles of pedagogy. Decades of research confirm the value and long-term positive effects of early childhood programs that emphasize active learning and social competence. I believe that an early childhood curriculum should offer educators a vision of what an age-appropriate program looks like and a framework for making decisions about how to achieve that vision.

Why would people who work with infants and toddlers need a curriculum?

Caring for babies should occur in a safe and healthy environment. It should also take advantage of the unique learning opportunities that occur during this period. The brain development that takes place in the first 3 years of life is astounding. These are critical years for emotional, social, and language development. According to Erik Erikson, infants and toddlers are discovering whether the world is a place they can trust and whether they can assert their independence and feel capable. They develop trust and autonomy in the context of relationships. A curriculum for programs serving infants and toddlers must reinforce relationships as the focus of decision making.

Is a preschool curriculum also appropriate for kindergarten?

There should be many similarities between a preschool curriculum and a curriculum for kindergarten. Because kindergartners are, in many ways, closer to preschoolers than they are to primary-grade children, the physical environment of the kindergarten classroom should look very much like a preschool classroom. Children should have daily opportunities to work in interest areas where they can explore, try out their ideas, create representations of what they have learned, and share ideas with others. Long-term studies provide a way for teachers to integrate learning of content. While social competence should still be a major focus, children ages 5 to 6 are capable of higher-level cognitive work and the academic content of the curriculum would be more advanced, with particular attention to literacy and math.

Why talk about curriculum in the primary grades when teachers are required to follow subject-matter curriculum guides adopted by their schools?

Curriculum guides and textbooks offer teachers direction about what to teach in each subject, but classroom teachers must find a way to make the curriculum effective and meaningful for their children. Because every group is different and every child is unique, teachers build curriculum around the interests of the children while still covering the material required by their districts. It is the individual teacher, with the input and involvement of parents, who knows the children well enough to make informed decisions about what each child needs to become a competent learner. The teacher has to plan how to teach.

Diane Dodge is Founder and President, Teaching Strategies, Inc., Washington, DC.

Emergent Curriculum

When teachers consider children's needs, prior knowledge, cultural backgrounds, and interests in developing their curriculum, it is referred to as **emergent curriculum** (Benham, 2006; Jones & Nimmo, 1994; Katz & Chard, 2000; Seitz, 2006). All children learn best when what they are learning interests them, means something in their personal lives, and builds on their prior knowledge. Emergent curriculum involves children in planning and evaluating projects and activities as well as having a general objective, hypothesizing what could happen with this particular group of children, and documenting children's learning. But what happens if children show no interest in what the class is studying? A child may not be interested in learning about magnetism, for example, unless he or she has experienced magnets, read books such as *Amazing Magnets* (Rowe & Perham, 1994) or *The Science Book of Magnets* (Ardley, 1991), and experimented with different objects to see which ones are attracted to magnetic force. When children have such experiences, they are more likely to show interest in the content to be studied. In addition to children's interests and initiation of ideas, teachers and other adults in the environment may spark curriculum ideas because of their particular passions, interest, and experiences. The emergent curriculum is based on the belief that the characteristics of the learner and the way children learn are the most important considerations in curriculum. The schools in Reggio Emilia, Italy, provide the model for emergent curriculum. The Reggio model is discussed in Chapter 2.

Culturally Responsive Curriculum

Did you know that by the year 2020, school-age children of color and English language learners will represent 48% of all U.S. schoolchildren (Banks & Banks, 2005)? For early childhood teachers, understanding how culture and learning affect curriculum is very important.

To learn more about linguistic and cultural diversity, go to *Enrichment Content: Research Highlights* in Chapter 7 of the Companion Website at http://www.prenhall.com/jalongo.

A culturally responsive curriculum acknowledges diversity in the classroom and accommodates it in the curriculum in three ways (Eggen & Kauchak, 2007; Tiedt & Tiedt, 2005). First, a culturally responsive curriculum accepts and values differences by communicating to all children that they are welcomed and valued by giving them time, showing interest in their families, and finding ways to involve all of them in quality experiences. Second, it accommodates different learning styles by using a variety of effective approaches, teaching strategies, and tools that "span a continuum from child-initiated to teacher-directed learning and from free exploration to scaffolded support or teacher modeling" (NAEYC, 2001, p. 18). And third, a culturally responsive curriculum builds on children's cultural backgrounds by using this knowledge to promote personal pride and motivation in children, to promote a more positive sense of self-esteem, and to develop respect for others (Tiedt & Tiedt, 2005).

Whichever approach or combination of approaches you use to organize, your curriculum must reflect what we know about how children learn and develop. If your school system or program typically organizes curriculum by content areas, you might try to match some of its goals, outcomes, and activities to the domain areas. If children need opportunities in one or two domains, it would be beneficial to supplement activities for them by developmental domains. You may also integrate two or more subject areas, use children's interests, and capitalize on the children's cultures as you organize and prepare to teach your curriculum.

Understanding the Taught Curriculum

The **taught curriculum** is *what* someone sees the teacher and children doing in the classroom. It is *how* you make the written curriculum meaningful to a particular group of children. Meaningful curriculum is relevant to that particular group of children and considers their developmental needs and interests, the environment and culture in which they live, and the ways to include all children. Meaningful curriculum also promotes active learning of subject-area knowledge that is age-appropriate for a particular group of children (Bredekamp & Rosegrant, 1995; NAEYC, 2001; Scully, Seefeldt, & Barbour, 2003; Wortham, 2006).

Characteristics of Meaningful Curriculum

There are four distinguishing characteristics of meaningful curriculum, as follows.

1. *A meaningful curriculum teaches content that is worth knowing.* The content that children learn must focus on key concepts and relevant ideas that are presented to children in a unified way. Curriculum that is relevant links children's learning to their real-life experiences, interests, and knowledge. Consider, for example, a first-grade class studying homes. A meaningful curriculum might have children reading books about homes such as *A House Is a House for Me* (Hoberman, 1978), *Noah's Ark* (Spier, 1978), or *The Village of Round and Square Houses* (Grifalconi, 1986); writing stories and drawing pictures about their own homes; or taking inventories of what is in each room of their own homes. Children might also take a field trip to look for different types of houses and notice the materials used to build those houses. In social studies, children might investigate houses that people lived in long ago, and in math, they might make blueprints of houses and then construct them from blocks using different shapes. In science, they might explore homes for different animals such as turtles and hermit crabs. These learning activities are *meaningful* because they build on and extend what children already know. Contrast this type of curriculum with one in which a first-grade class is studying the same topic of homes but the children primarily complete teacher-created worksheets about homes and listen to the teacher's facts about homes, about which they may or may not have prior knowledge. When teachers consider children's experience and interest level in curriculum, children utilize higher-order thinking skills to wrestle with real issues and problems (Bredekamp & Rosegrant, 1992; NAEYC, 2001; Scully et al., 2003; Wortham, 2006). Moreover, when children plan some of their learning, it is more likely that their needs, interests, backgrounds, and abilities will be taken into account. Joint planning bridges what is personally meaningful and relevant for the child to what content needs to be taught. It allows for varied learning activities at different levels to occur simultaneously in the classroom.

2. *A meaningful curriculum is culturally responsive.* Culturally responsive curricula capitalize on the diverse backgrounds of the children in each early

childhood classroom. Using a variety of culturally sensitive methods and materials—such as pictures, books, music, technology, and language—represents the different cultures of the children you are teaching. For example, you might want to include different cooking materials, such as a wok or tortilla press, in the home living center. Or you might find out about the children's after-school activities and their holiday customs so that you can connect with children's families and other caregivers and use them as resources in celebrating the cultural practices of the children in your class. You may also want to emphasize values, such as courtesy and respect, that cross all cultures so that all the children notice different yet acceptable ways of demonstrating these cross-cultural values in school. Creating a literacy corner with books and writing materials that appeals to all children and introduces children to other cultural practices and backgrounds is a powerful way to build a culturally responsive curriculum. See the References and the Compendium of Resources at the end of this text for further recommendations of appropriate resources for creating a culturally responsive curriculum.

3. *A meaningful curriculum is inclusive.* Including all children in the curriculum promotes feelings of belonging on the part of all learners. An inclusive curriculum must be adapted to meet the needs of individuals and their families who differ in some way from the average or typical student. In addition, all teachers must be able to develop, implement, and evaluate curriculum that demonstrates how each child can perform in all academic areas for which they are responsible. The benefits of an inclusive curriculum are increased opportunities to interact with typically developing peers, participate in experiences that enable children with disabilities to use their skills in typical early childhood activities, and interact with competent peer models to build new social and communication skills. Children without exceptionalities also benefit from increased opportunities to develop positive attitudes about children with exceptionalities and to develop caring and unselfish behaviors (Hull, Goldhaber, & Capone, 2002; Montgomery, 2001).

4. *A meaningful curriculum promotes active learning.* Active learning occurs when children are mentally involved in direct experiences that help them connect the information and skills they are learning to their own lives. For example, if a second-grade class is studying living things, children may choose to read books on a topic that interests them or take a walking field trip through the neighborhood to identify living things unique to their school building, and practice literacy skills as they read, write, and draw about what they are learning. Active learning experiences encourage children to demonstrate true understanding by explaining, finding evidence, generalizing, applying, and representing the topic in a new way (Piaget, 1965; Vygotsky, 1978). Teachers create active learning environments by respecting children's ideas; modeling strategies such as thinking aloud, problem solving, and problem posing; and helping them see familiar ideas in new ways (NAEYC, 2001; Ryan & Cooper, 2007, Scully et al., 2003).

PAUSE AND REFLECT
About Meaningful Curriculum

Think back to the curriculum that you experienced in elementary school. What was most meaningful to you and why? What was least meaningful to you and why? How do you think your experiences affect how you would like to teach?

In today's schools, some school districts and programs believe that teachers should teach the curriculum exactly as it is written or in a prescribed way. Others believe that teachers should have more say in interpreting the curriculum as long as they teach the key concepts and skills that have been prescribed. What do you believe, and why?

1. Brainstorm a pro and con list for teaching a prescribed curriculum.
2. List three different ways you could teach a prescribed concept by making it meaningful to the children in your classroom.

Scott Cunningham/Merrill

Learning is more meaningful for children when they make connections among concepts, experiences, school, and life to what they know.

Building a Meaningful Curriculum

There are many different ways to build a meaningful curriculum. However you develop your curriculum, the best curriculum for children is created around broad concepts that reflect the content and standards you need to teach, the processes unique to those content areas, appropriate strategies, and thoughtful consideration of the children's development, families, and community. The two primary approaches typically used by early childhood teachers to build meaningful curriculum are units of study and projects, as described next.

Unit Approach

Units are related learning experiences organized around key concepts or ideas about a particular topic of study and last over a period of time. They use a variety of experiences in more than one content area and are relevant and interesting to children. Units help children link their learning from many different subject areas, generalize knowledge and skills from one experience to another, and connect what they are learning to real life (Heroman & Copple, 2006; Jackman, 2005; Tomlinson & McTighe, 2006).

Units can take different forms. Some may center on a certain type of literature, such as the study of fairy tales. In this type of unit, the children may read and listen to different fairy tales, talk about their characteristics (e.g., royalty, magic, a setting in a faraway time and place, and commoners finding great riches and power), and perhaps write or enact fairy tales using those characteristics. Other unit approaches focus on a topic that links several content areas, including music, art, play, mathematics, social studies, and science. For example, the topic of farms in a unit may drive the curriculum decisions. In this case, children would ask questions about what they wanted to find out about farms, and then read, write, and illustrate their findings. Skills would be taught where appropriate. Suppose, for example, in the study of farms, that children decide to plant individual and

COLLABORATING WITH FAMILIES

Building Connections with Families About the Curriculum

Ms. Davis's children have been studying fairy tales. Each week, she invites a child to select a take-home pack (PAK) that contains a related activity to be completed by the child and an adult in the home. Families with limited English literacy skills may complete the activity and the feedback form verbally on a cassette tape. Following is an example of a PAK for *The Gingerbread Man*.

Materials Needed

One-gallon plastic bag, canvas bag, or small knapsack

A copy of *The Gingerbread Man* with cassette tape

A recipe for gingerbread cookies and cookie cutter

An Activity Card

A Feedback Form

Gingerbread cookie mix (optional)

Format of Activity Card

Name of Activity

Cooking Activity

What the Child Will Learn

Measuring skills (math, science)

How to use the senses of smell, taste, touch, seeing, and hearing (sensory/physical skills)

How substances (dough) change when baked (science)

How to use small-motor skills (physical skills)

How to count ingredients as added (math)

How to describe steps taken to make the cookies (language)

What to Do

- Ahead of time, gather the ingredients, directions, and utensils necessary to make the cookies.
- Read *The Gingerbread Man* with your child (or listen to the cassette tape and follow along with the book). Ask your child, "Why was the fox so interested in the gingerbread man? Can cookies become real?"
- Then, suggest that, together, you make some gingerbread cookies and talk more about the story. Follow the directions by allowing your child to "read" the pictures on the recipe, make the cookies, and then enjoy!
- Clean up supplies and answer the questions on the Feedback Form.
- Send the PAK back to school.

Feedback Form

Did you complete the activity with your child? Yes No

Did your child "read" the recipe? Yes No

Did your child talk about measuring ingredients? Yes No

Did your child think cookies can come alive? Yes No

What did your child like best about the activity?

____

____

What did you like best?

____

____

Signature ____________ Date ____________

classroom vegetable gardens. They may make a classroom bar graph on the growth of the seedlings (mathematics), write or draw about the progress of the seedlings in journals (literacy), and illustrate and categorize the different plants in a class mural (art). Still other units may be organized around multiple intelligences. (See the Chapter 5 In-Class Workshop for an illustrative example.) Whatever form you use, a unit approach to teaching must include children's ideas and interests as a part of the entire study.

The teacher, the children and teacher together, or the children by themselves may select topics to study. When making decisions about topics for units and themes, teachers should consider the children's previous experiences and knowledge that is worth knowing (Katz & Chard, 2000). Units may be based on topics we know interest most children, or they can be based on something interesting happening in the school, in a child's family, in the community, or in the world. Figure 7.4 provides a list of commonly used early childhood topics. Chapter 8 provides detailed information on planning for teaching with units.

A unit approach to curriculum also helps teachers make decisions that support the 10th NAEYC curriculum content guideline (Bredekamp & Rosegrant, 1995). This guideline states "curriculum allows for focus on a particular topic or content while allowing for integration across traditional subject-matter divisions by planning around themes and/or learning experiences that provide opportunities for rich conceptual development" (p. 16). According to Katz and Chard (2000) and Heroman and Copple (2006), to meet this guideline, effective units should enable children to do the following:

1. build on what they already know, stimulate questions they want to answer, and relate information to their lives
2. understand basic concepts and processes from the subject areas rather than focusing on isolated facts
3. learn accurate facts and information related to the theme
4. integrate content and processes from all the subject areas
5. engage in hands-on activities as they inquire about the theme
6. grow in each of their developmental domains
7. use the same content in more than one way and at more than one time
8. capitalize on interests, because that is what motivates learning

To illustrate these principles, consider an example of a second-grade study of outer space during which children learn concepts and facts about the planets, sun, moon, and space exploration. In *math*, the children compare temperatures of the planets or measure distances between the sun and other planets; in *social studies*, they relate life on other planets to their own lives or illustrate life in a spacecraft; in *science* they study different moon and cloud formations, or explore what life might be like on other planets; and in *language arts*, they write about their knowledge of space or learn phonics skills from the books they are reading on space; this helps children to integrate the content and processes from all subject areas, participate in hands-on activities to inquire about the topic, and use the same content in more than one way and at more than one time.

Project Approach

Projects are focused, in-depth studies of something that children, in collaboration with teachers, initiate, direct, organize, and develop. These deep investigations can take different forms, such as the project approach (Katz & Chard, 2000), emergent curriculum (Edwards, Gandini, & Forman, 1998), and long-term studies (Dodge, Colker, & Heroman, 2002). A project approach supports children's natural ways of learning, provokes their thinking by making learning meaningful, and sparks their curiosity by challenging their abilities. Teachers who use the project approach to curriculum believe in children's capacity to pursue their own ideas and represent them through different media. Thus, teachers facilitate and document children's progress while ensuring their learning of skills, content, and processes in different subject areas. Projects have their roots in Dewey's (1938) and Kilpatrick's (1936) ideas that experience-based learning

FIGURE 7.4 Commonly used early childhood units and themes.

The following commonly used units, organized around big ideas or concepts, encourage meaning making for children. Though they are categorized by subject area, notice that many topics fit into multiple categories, making it ever so important to integrate your curriculum so it is engaging, relevant, and interesting to children you are teaching.

Social Studies
My Family and Me; My Neighborhood; Jobs and Work; Friends; Transportation and Vehicles; Homes; The Food We Eat; Explorations; Familiar Things in Our World; Feelings; Celebrations; My World, Working and Learning Now and Long Ago; Children Now and Long Ago; People Who Make a Difference; Beginnings: People, Places, and Events

Science
Environmental Studies (recycling, pollution); Caring for Pets; Endangered Species; The Rain Forest; Living Things; Light and Shadows; Water; Animals; Seasons; Weather; Things That Grow; Exploring Space; The Physical World (magnetism, light, color, sound, weather, seasons); Ways to Communicate; The Natural World; How Things Work (machines, faxes, copy machines, computers), Sea Life; Mysteries and Secrets; Natural Science; Change and Continuity

Mathematics
Patterns; Opposites; Colors and Shapes; Numbers; Time; Measurement; Stores; Space

Literacy
Fairy Tales; Fables; Folk Tales; Poetry; Author Study; Chants and Rhymes; Chapter Books

Interdisciplinary Study
Transformations; Old and New; Near and Far; Above and Below; Patterns, Containers; Fasteners; Ways of Communicating; Diversity; Intergenerational Relationships; Cycles and Systems (light, heat, life, food); Clothing; Health and Wellness; Interdependence; Natural Science; Community Institutions (museum, aquarium, bowling alley, zoo); Stores (department, farm stand, grocery, ice-cream parlor, shoe, bank, bakery, garden); Public Service (police, fire, library, dump, town hall, hospital, highway); Offices and Factories (bank, school, constriction site, veterinarian, clothing); Similarities and Differences

Themes for Toddlers and Preschoolers
Self-Awareness; My Family and Me; Music and Movement; The Five Senses; Vehicles; Home-living

Resources for Unit Teaching

Alleman, J., & Brophy, J. (2001). *Social studies excursions K–3 Book One: Powerful units on food, clothing, and shelter*. Portsmouth, Heinemann.

Allen, D., & Piersma, M. (1995). *Developing thematic units: Process and product*. New York: Delmar.

Altheim, J., Gamberg, R. Hutchings, M., & Kwak, W. (1988). *Learning and loving it: Theme studies in the classroom*. Portsmouth, NH: Heinemann.

Herr, J., & Larson, Y. (2000). *Creative resources for the early childhood classroom* (3rd ed.). Albany, NY: Delmar. (Also available in a Spanish edition)

Herr, J., & Swin, T. (2002). *Creative resources for infants and toddlers* (2nd ed.). Albany, NY: Delmar.

Jackman, H. (2005). *Early childhood curriculum. A child' s connection to the world* (3rd ed.). Albany, NY: Delmar.

Kostelnik, M. (Ed.). (1991). *Teaching young children using themes*. Glenview, IL: Good Year.

Raines, S., & Canady, R. (1989). *Story stretchers*. Mt. Rainier, MD: Gryphon House.

Roberts, P. (1993). *A green dinosaur day: A guide for developing thematic units in literature-based instruction, K–6*. Boston: Allyn & Bacon.

Seefeldt, C., & Galper, A. (2006). *Active experiences for active children: Social studies* (2nd ed.). Upper Saddle River, NJ: Merrill/Prentice Hall.

forms the foundation of education. More recently, the schools in Reggio Emilia, Italy, have used the project approach successfully with the entire preschool community. You can see how one child's detailed drawing illustrates that child's knowledge and understanding of Under Sea Life based on a long-term study called the Project Approach in the "Early Childhood Education–Curriculum Planning and Program" student and teacher artifacts online at the Teacher Prep Website.

TEACHER PREP WEBSITE 7.4

Go to Student and Teacher Artifacts, select Early Childhood Education, choose Curriculum Planning and Program (Module 4), and select Deep Sea (Science K–2) (Artifact 4).

Projects can last for a day, a week, a month, or even a year and are characterized by five features: individual and group discussion, field trips, representations of children's knowledge, investigations, and displays of learning. The following example of a pet store project created by kindergartners illustrates some of the key principles of the project approach.

Ms. Ornstein's kindergartners began the year studying about themselves and their interests. These activities and conversations prompted extensive group and individual discussion about the children's pets, what they knew about them, and questions they had about caring for pets. The children regularly brought pictures of their pets to school, and many pets visited the classroom. From this expressed interest, Ms. Ornstein took the children's lead and added books and pictures about pets to her classroom library. The children's questions sparked an interest in planning a field trip to the local pet store to see what it included. Ms. Ornstein created a large word-and-picture chart for children that asked the question "What do you think we will see?"

Ms. Ornstein's kindergartners used a checklist to record which animals and pet toys they expected to see and then compared those data with what they actually saw after the trip. Planning the field trip sparked children's investigations of their pet study. They generated lists of what they already knew about pets and what they needed to know, read several more books about all kinds of pets, and planned specific questions to ask during the field trip to the pet store. The children represented what they already knew and what they were learning about pets by creating fact folders, drawing what they saw during their field trip, illustrating stories they read and stories they wrote, and making diagrams and sketches of the block and dramatic play area where they had created their own pet store, and they learned the basic economics of buying and selling through enactment of pet store scenarios. Small groups, called committees, planned and developed other experiences such as a final sale for the other kindergarten and first-grade classes in the school and an open house for the parents and families to celebrate the children's accomplishments. Some children displayed their learning by explaining with confidence and assurance the key aspects of their pet store, while others shared their writings, labeling, and artwork. In this project, the kindergartners used math skills by classifying pets; science processes by using charts, graphs, and written reports to record scientific data; art skills by sketching, drawing, and painting pictures of real and imaginary pets; and writing skills by labeling, copying, and making signs for the displays.

Michael Newman/PhotoEdit Inc.

The children's interest in pets prompted a field trip to a pet store.

Planning the Visit
We are going to visit a pet store. What do you think we will see?
guinea pigs
parrots
fish
rabbit
lizards
snakes
cats
~~puppies~~
~~porcupine~~
insects
frogs
gerbils
rats
bones for dogs
cages
pet toys
water bowl
bedding
food
clothes
~~chipmunk~~
~~turtle~~
mice
We checked off what we saw at the pet sotre.

abcdefghijklmnopqrstuvwxyz
Here are some things we saw that were not on our list
centipede
eel
scorpion
hermit crabs
ferrets
hedge hog
chinchilla
South American Caiman
sugar gliders

abcdefghijklmnopqrstuvwxyz
Drawing what we saw...
Tom
Sue
Jill
Billy
Travis

Favorites
Ted Rabbit
Jodi Turtle
Robby Scorpion
Billy Snake
Travis Beetle
Cory Parrot
Tristen Kittens
Ross Mice
Christen Gerbil
Tom Ferret
Steve Fish
Sarah Puppies

This example clearly illustrates how projects help children acquire new knowledge and skills while developing dispositions toward learning and creating feelings of competence (Katz & Chard, 2000).

Whatever approach to curriculum you use, your curriculum should be informed by one or more theoretical frameworks. Such an orientation can help you choose how to help your students learn best, guide your daily practice, and explain why your curriculum is the way it is. In the next section, we examine five major theoretical perspectives on curriculum.

COMPANION WEBSITE 7.6 To add a professional development product to your developing portfolio, go to *Journal: Constructing Your Professional Portfolio* in Chapter 7 of the Companion Website at http://www.prenhall.com/jalongo.

Curriculum Theories

Have you ever wondered about the behavior of certain animals, the nature of rainstorms, or why some things are easy for you to learn and others are not? These speculations are based on certain assumptions you make about those things and are called theories. A theory is knowledge that is systematically organized, applies to a wide variety of circumstances, and can explain or predict a set of phenomena. Consequently, you can prove or disprove a theory as you deepen your knowledge about it.

The idea that many theories of curriculum reflect different assumptions about children, teaching, and learning is important for all teachers. The theoretical perspective that underlies your curriculum provides a window into your thinking about how children learn, what knowledge is worth knowing, how content should be taught, and how learning should be evaluated (Bredekamp & Rosegrant, 1995; Glatthorn et al., 2006; Katz & Chard, 2000; Posner, 2004). Differing assumptions have spawned many theories about what and how children should learn. While each theory offers its own perspective about curriculum, together, they serve us well in providing the most effective curriculum for children.

George Posner (2004), noted curriculum theorist, suggests five theoretical perspectives that shape curriculum: traditional, knowledge-centered, experiential, behavioral, and constructivist.

A *traditional* perspective views curriculum as the study of a common body of knowledge and skills ideas. Traditionalists advocate teaching the same information and content to all children and view a core body of knowledge as essential for all learners. This orientation has led to the development of a core knowledge curriculum for preschool through high school. Traditionalists consider knowledge as unchanging and view their primary role as passing on that essential knowledge to all children.

A *knowledge-centered* perspective assumes that content determines the curriculum and that each subject area has its own way of conducting inquiry. For example, in science, the scientific process skills of observation, hypothesis or prediction, and verification are used to learn science concepts. From a knowledge-centered perspective, curriculum should help children develop several different "modes of inquiry" (Posner, 2004, p. 57) about those subjects. It not only emphasizes children's active participation in inquiry in each subject area but also emphasizes multiple ways of knowing. Teachers who have this view of curriculum need a deep conceptual understanding of all of the subjects they teach in order to teach them well. They also need to be able to organize ideas and make connections among ideas, ways of thinking, and beliefs about modes of inquiry that characterize a discipline.

TEACHER PREP WEBSITE 7.5

Go to Video Classroom, select Social Studies Methods, choose Teaching Citizenship/Civics (Module 2), and select Sunnyville (Video 1).

A third perspective, *experiential* or *learned* curriculum, emphasizes what children actually experience and learn. This perspective views knowledge as constantly changing and seeks to develop a curriculum that is relevant to each learner at his or her level of understanding. Teachers with this perspective facilitate learning rather than transmit knowledge and view their curriculum as a vehicle for fostering learning communities that engage in problem solving. They utilize experience-based learning matched with students' needs and interests as the source of curriculum. You can see an example of an experiential curriculum as first graders interact with one another to create classroom rules together and learn about citizenship in the "Sunnyville" video clip online at the Teacher Prep Website.

TABLE 7.4 Key Curriculum Theorists and Theoretical Perspectives

Theorist and Perspective	Goal	Source of Knowledge	Teacher's Role	Methods
Traditional E. D. Hirsch	intelligent citizens acquisition of knowledge and cultural heritage	specialized facts and vocabulary of each academic discipline	disseminate factual information and teach basic skills through direct instruction	worksheets, workbooks, seatwork, drill and practice, isolated teaching
Knowledge-Based Jerome Bruner	development of thinking skills	manipulation of objects, ideas, and information using higher-order thinking skills	develop children's critical and creative thinking; and learning through solving problems	experiences using the following taxonomy of thinking skills: knowledge, comprehension, application, analysis, synthesis, evaluation
Experiential (Learned) John Dewey	each child learns at his or her level of understanding in all subject areas	children's real-life experiences, needs, and interests; child development; cultural values of individuals and groups	connect children's learning with past experiences and stimulate their interests and ideas to increase their understanding and learning	self-directed learning; learning contracts; problem-solving experiences; experience-based, child-centered practice
Behavioral B. F. Skinner	student achievement for clearly specified, observable, and measurable objectives mastery learning	predetermined standards and goals; precise objectives; carefully sequenced objectives in the content areas	efficient and effective means to achieve specific ends	scope and sequence of learning tasks; reinforce correct responses; modeling; guided practice; independent practice
Constructivist Jean Piaget	development of internal mental ability and cognitive processes	meaning and understanding in learning content and in learning different ways to think about their world	facilitate children's thinking and concept development in all areas of development in learning to make sense of their world, focus on child outcomes	group experiences and projects using real, active, and purposeful learning experiences related to thinking, reasoning, and problem solving

SOURCES: Based on data from Eggen & Kauchak (2007); Glatthorn, Boschee, & Writehead 2006 and Posner (2004).

The *behavioral* perspective is an efficient view of the curriculum quite common in American schools. In a behavioral orientation, the curriculum is predetermined to reach the same measurable outcomes for all students. It utilizes behavioral objectives to measure changes or test students' achievement in particular skill areas and assumes that curriculum standards must be explicitly stated, taught, and tested. A behavioral curriculum looks at the behaviors that children should learn as opposed to the content teachers want to teach or the experiences that teachers want children to have.

Finally, a *constructivist* perspective emphasizes that individuals actively construct knowledge and understanding and that adults encourage children to explore their world, discover knowledge, reflect, and think critically. Constructivists believe that learning occurs when learners tie new information to what they already know and understand. Constructivists put learners at the center of the curriculum and believe that children develop their own understanding rather than having it dictated by another.

How you view curriculum theory greatly influences your role as a curriculum developer. Table 7.4 lists the key theorists and aspects of their five theoretical perspectives.

Conclusion

Developing effective curriculum for children poses great challenges to early childhood professionals. The trend in curriculum toward an integrated, meaningful curriculum is accompanied by simultaneous pressure for increased accountability and higher standards. These pressures are resulting in more high-stakes testing, more standardized and subject-centered curricula, and more scripted teaching lessons (Raines & Johnston, 2003). If you talk to experienced teachers today, you might hear them say, "There is so much to teach and so little time to teach it." Teachers will tell you that the combination of daily distractions, a fragmented schedule, local and state curriculum mandates, and parental pressure allow little time for exploration of topics in depth. Whatever the reason for teachers' concerns over not having enough time to teach what they must in the way they wish, the results are the same. When less time is spent on a topic, there are fewer opportunities to explore a topic in depth. Curriculum expectations that are too high are frustrating to children and lead to false labeling as immature, disruptive, and unready for school. However, a curriculum that is not challenging enough leaves many children bored and disinterested while leading to wasted learning opportunities. The organizations for each subject area support a curriculum that provides children with ample opportunities to explore the discipline subjects in more depth.

COMPANION WEBSITE 7.7 To test your knowledge of this chapter's contents, go to the *Multiple-Choice* and *Essay* modules in Chapter 7 of the Companion Website at http://www.prenhall.com/jalongo. These items are written in the same format that you will encounter in the PRAXIS tests to better prepare you for your licensure exam.

ONE CHILD, THREE PERSPECTIVES

Benjamin's School Play

Benjamin is in kindergarten at a school where the teachers plan an elaborate annual kindergarten play. In this year's performance, *About the Presidents*, each child was assigned the part of a U.S. president. Benjamin was the 31st president, Herbert Hoover.

The teachers asked parents to go to the library with their child and help them find three or four interesting facts about the presidents their children were studying and to try to dress their children for the performance in clothing that represented their presidents' time period. In school, the children practiced their parts, which consisted of facts they researched and memorized with the help of their parents, and sang songs about George Washington and Abraham Lincoln. Benjamin's teachers believed that having parents help their child research interesting facts, practice their parts, and prepare special clothing was a worthwhile way to involve them in their children's learning.

Benjamin's mother, a single, working parent, first heard of her son's kindergarten play through a written notice from the teachers. When she learned that she had to go to the library with her son to help him research facts, Benjamin's mother was excited. But she soon discovered that Benjamin had little or no understanding of Herbert Hoover, of what a president is or does, of wars, or of what it means to be a humanitarian. Furthermore, the library books about Herbert Hoover were not written so a 5-year-old could understand them. The more Benjamin's mother explained to Benjamin about Herbert Hoover, the more frustrated she became, because Benjamin was not interested in this president. He only wanted to be "George Washington," a name that had some familiarity to him. Thus, preparing Benjamin for his part in the school play became his mother's project.

On the day of the performance, the kindergartners were seated in a semicircle on the stage, the microphone was in the center, and the teachers were at each end coordinating the children's spoken parts. Some of the children spoke so softly they could hardly be heard; others looked frightened and stiff but said their parts. One boy, who spoke too close to the microphone, received an electrical shock to his mouth and burst into tears. He never did get to say his part. Three months later, Benjamin cannot recall any of the facts about Herbert Hoover, but he can tell you which of his friends played certain presidents. He does enjoy watching the videotape his mother took of the performance and singing the class songs.

This profile of Benjamin, his mother, and the kindergarten teachers raises a number of issues about developmentally appropriate curriculum. What is appropriate content for children? How can teachers make that content accessible to young children? How should children represent that content to each other and to their families?

REACT	Think about how the perspectives of Benjamin, Benjamin's teachers, and Benjamin's mother are alike and different. What might be the underlying reasons? Which perspective do you identify most strongly with and why? Why should the lives of children's family members influence teachers' expectations for their involvement?
RESEARCH	Read about the appropriate roles of social studies in early childhood settings. Go to the website for the National Council on Social Studies (www.ncss.org) and look at its standards for all of the social studies. Read and discuss these with your classmates. Which of these ideas will affect the kinds of social studies experiences you develop for children?
REFLECT	What values, attitudes, and dispositions about living in a diverse and democratic world do all children gain from using drama to teach social studies? Generate a portrait of what appropriate drama for kindergarten children should look like in order to develop such values and attitudes.

IN-CLASS WORKSHOP

Brainstorming with Curriculum Webs

Curriculum webs are tools for planning. Webs can be used to brainstorm with other teachers and with children to develop a curriculum that is most relevant to the children whom you are teaching. Brainstorming, a method of problem solving in which all members of the group spontaneously contribute ideas, is a useful tool because it allows many ways to develop your curriculum.

Using the ideas discussed in "Ask the Expert: Sue Bredekamp on Developmentally Appropriate Practice," which was presented earlier in this chapter, brainstorm a developmentally appropriate topic of study for a particular age group. Here are some steps to follow while brainstorming:

1. Choose a topic to explore by examining your school or school district's curriculum.
2. Brainstorm with the children what they already know about the topic and what they want to know about the topic.
3. Brainstorm with your colleagues about the concepts or big ideas to be learned, the topics to be covered, and the activities and lessons to be integrated into each curriculum area or domain.
4. Organize your ideas into the form of a web. **Figure 7.5** provides an example of a brainstorming web for a kindergarten study of animals, and **Figure 7.6** illustrates a third-grade study of Greece.
5. Select resources and a means of assessment.

Then, construct a curriculum web by doing the following:

1. Brainstorm the possibilities related to a developmentally appropriate topic for the age level you are teaching (see Figure 7.5 for a list of suggestions).
2. Think of key words or terms and appropriate activities associated with your topic.
3. Group some of the ideas together by a common category to form a few broad categories.
4. Search for information, resources, and a broad range of reference materials to support the categories.
5. Finalize the web by selecting the major concepts to be learned and identifying the possible connections among the web strands created.

Finally, ask yourself, "How does this web compare to the characteristics of a developmentally appropriate curriculum?"

FIGURE 7.5 Brainstorming web for kindergarten about the study of animals.

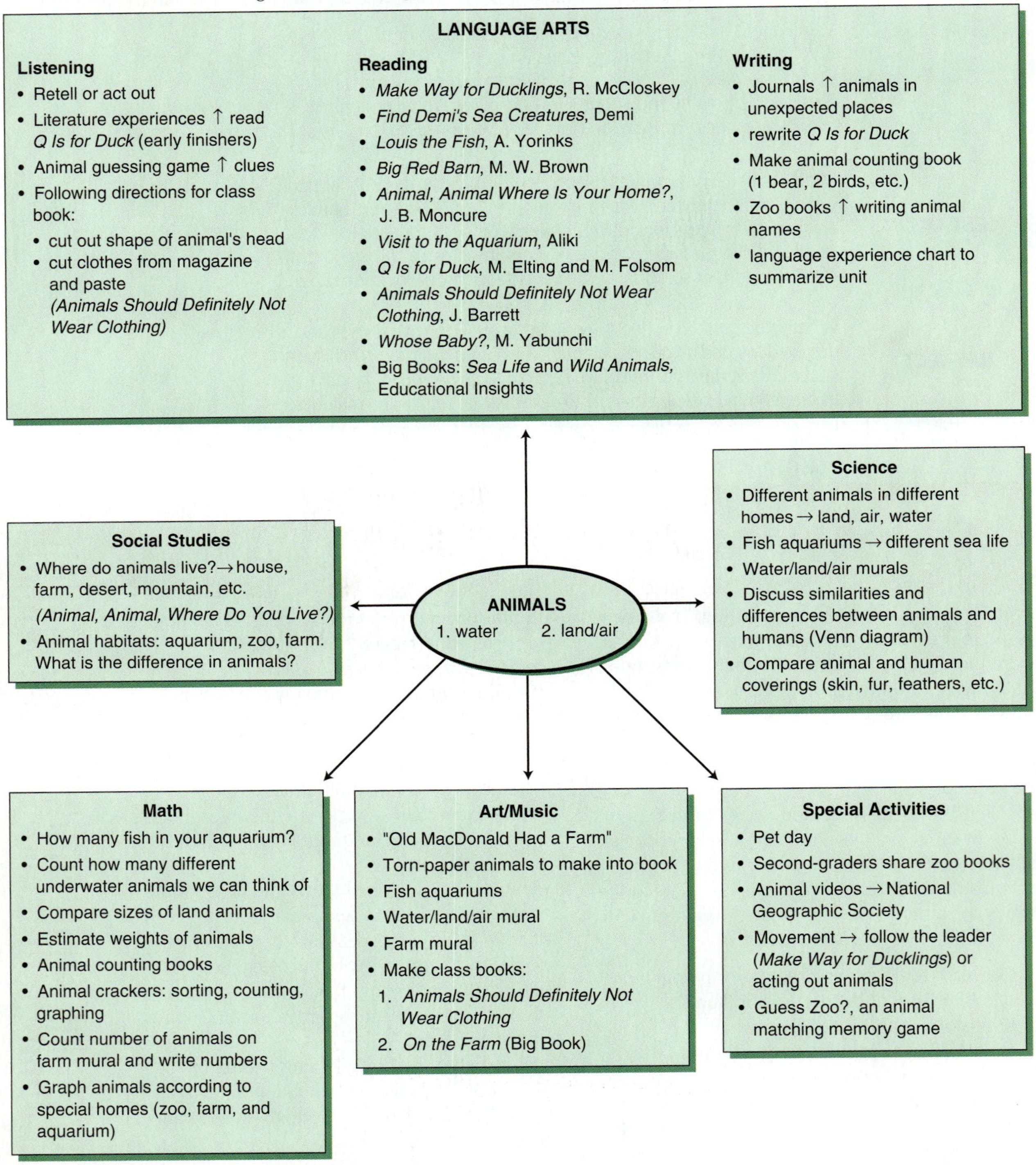

LANGUAGE ARTS

Listening
- Retell or act out
- Literature experiences ↑ read *Q Is for Duck* (early finishers)
- Animal guessing game ↑ clues
- Following directions for class book:
  - cut out shape of animal's head
  - cut clothes from magazine and paste *(Animals Should Definitely Not Wear Clothing)*

Reading
- *Make Way for Ducklings*, R. McCloskey
- *Find Demi's Sea Creatures*, Demi
- *Louis the Fish*, A. Yorinks
- *Big Red Barn*, M. W. Brown
- *Animal, Animal Where Is Your Home?*, J. B. Moncure
- *Visit to the Aquarium*, Aliki
- *Q Is for Duck*, M. Elting and M. Folsom
- *Animals Should Definitely Not Wear Clothing*, J. Barrett
- *Whose Baby?*, M. Yabunchi
- Big Books: *Sea Life* and *Wild Animals*, Educational Insights

Writing
- Journals ↑ animals in unexpected places
- rewrite *Q Is for Duck*
- Make animal counting book (1 bear, 2 birds, etc.)
- Zoo books ↑ writing animal names
- language experience chart to summarize unit

ANIMALS
1. water 2. land/air

Social Studies
- Where do animals live?→ house, farm, desert, mountain, etc. *(Animal, Animal, Where Do You Live?)*
- Animal habitats: aquarium, zoo, farm. What is the difference in animals?

Science
- Different animals in different homes → land, air, water
- Fish aquariums → different sea life
- Water/land/air murals
- Discuss similarities and differences between animals and humans (Venn diagram)
- Compare animal and human coverings (skin, fur, feathers, etc.)

Math
- How many fish in your aquarium?
- Count how many different underwater animals we can think of
- Compare sizes of land animals
- Estimate weights of animals
- Animal counting books
- Animal crackers: sorting, counting, graphing
- Count number of animals on farm mural and write numbers
- Graph animals according to special homes (zoo, farm, and aquarium)

Art/Music
- "Old MacDonald Had a Farm"
- Torn-paper animals to make into book
- Fish aquariums
- Water/land/air mural
- Farm mural
- Make class books:
  1. *Animals Should Definitely Not Wear Clothing*
  2. *On the Farm* (Big Book)

Special Activities
- Pet day
- Second-graders share zoo books
- Animal videos → National Geographic Society
- Movement → follow the leader (*Make Way for Ducklings*) or acting out animals
- Guess Zoo?, an animal matching memory game

SOURCE: Courtesy of George Mason University interns.

FIGURE 7.6 Brainstorming web for third grade about the study of Greece.

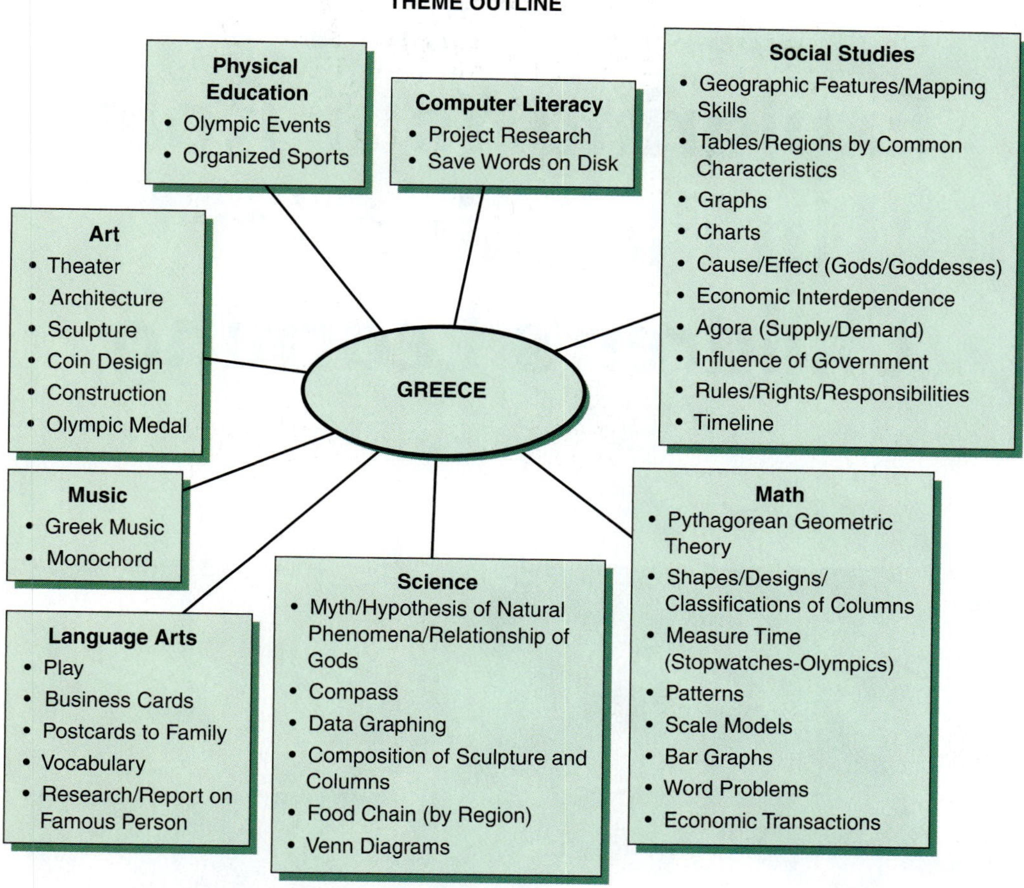

SOURCE: Courtesy of George Mason University PDS8 interns.

CHAPTER 8

Exploring Your Role in Planning for Children's Learning

> **Teacher planning is the thread that weaves the curriculum, or the what of teaching, with the instruction, or the how of teaching. The classroom is a highly interactive and demanding place. Planning provides for some measure of order in an uncertain and changing environment.**
>
> Freiberg & Driscoll, 2005, p. 22

Meet the Teachers

MS. BURKE is a preschool special education teacher who is intrigued by the beliefs and principles of the schools of Reggio Emilia. She has learned the importance of responding to children's interests as part of planning her curriculum. She says, "Teachers need to know that finding out about children's interests is a key tool for planning. I know children stay engaged in small- and large-group activities when they are of interest to them. In many ways, using children's interests in planning my curriculum allows children to operate on many different developmental levels and at their own pace. Many teachers I know think that brainstorming ideas around a seasonal theme or a subject that they choose is the best way to inspire learning. I say, 'The theme is just the big umbrella under which different types of learning occur.' "

MS. KIM is teaching in an inclusive first-grade classroom for the first time. Although she includes a read-aloud time at some point each day, many of the children do not seem interested in the books she is reading. She concluded that, "Children with special needs have short attention spans." Yet after talking with a colleague in the lunchroom about her concern, Ms. Kim realized she was not planning her read-aloud time in the same way she was planning in other areas. She was reading whatever books were available, which is not how she was taught to read aloud to children. So, Ms. Kim started to plan more carefully for her read-aloud time each day by first reviewing *The Read Aloud Handbook* (Trelease, 2006). Next, she carefully selected short picture books, informational books, and poetry that would be of interest to first graders. She also made sure that she invited children's comments more often as she read to them and that she had good conversations with the children after reading the book. Finally, Ms. Kim placed the read-aloud book for each day in the classroom library so that children could reread it alone or look at it with others following the read-aloud time. Ms. Kim says, "By more carefully planning my read-aloud time, I am providing my children with a meaningful reading experience that increases their appreciation of literature. Planning has also boosted my confidence as a teacher."

MR. PEARLMAN has just completed his student teaching in a third-grade classroom. In his final journal, he wrote, "I learned that I can plan in advance, although what I plan may not be what I do. I love to research—to look for activities—to create my own lessons because I think I can better meet specific needs of the children. This takes so much time, and requires so many modifications, that I learned I couldn't do it constantly. I was surprised by how much time planning consumed, and I was afraid of failing, of teaching poor lessons, or of losing the children." Mr. Pearlman simplified his plans well in advance of actually teaching them, "tried them on" in his imagination as he watched his cooperating teacher teach, and then talked through his ideas with her. That strategy led directly to better planning, better teaching, and better learning outcomes for children.

These three teachers know how important planning is for positive child outcomes. Use the following questions to think about the key elements of planning. Compare, contrast, and connect these teachers' views about planning to what you know about planning for all children's learning.

COMPARE	What are some similarities in the ways these teachers plan for children's learning?
CONTRAST	What differences do you notice in how these teachers plan?
CONNECT	What surprises you about how these teachers plan for positive child outcomes? What idea do you think will be most useful to your planning? Why?

Now that you have reflected on the perspectives of three different teachers, here is a preview of the knowledge, skills, and dispositions you need to acquire in order to fulfill your role as a planner.

Learning Outcomes

- ✔ Become familiar with your role as a planner **(NAEYC #4b & 4d, INTASC #7, and ACEI #1)**
- ✔ Define and describe types of planning
- ✔ Investigate the purpose of planning and its role in positive child outcomes
- ✔ Apply principles of planning to lessons, integrated units, and projects
- ✔ Develop daily, weekly, monthly, and quarterly plans that meet standards
- ✔ Plan for individual needs and abilities of diverse learners

A Definition of Planning

COMPANION WEBSITE 8.1 To learn more about defining your role in planning for children's learning, go to *Journal: Defining Your Role* in Chapter 8 of the Companion Website at http://www.prenhall.com/jalongo.

Think about some of the best parties you have ever attended. Before those parties, your hosts or hostesses needed to think about whom to invite, what kind of party to have (e.g., barbecue, cake and ice cream, dinner), when to have it, how long it should be, and any special items that were needed (e.g., paper plates, hats, gifts, games). During those parties, the hosts or hostesses made sure the food was ready, the guests were comfortable, and the gifts were opened at the appropriate time and place. And after the parties were over, the hosts or hostesses probably thought about what they might do or might not do again for another party. To have a successful party, then, there has to be planning.

Planning is the ability to think ahead and anticipate what is likely to make an event run smoothly. Just as there is a need to plan for social events, so too there is a need for teachers to plan. Planning for teaching and learning involves making decisions before actually teaching. As a teacher, you will decide about the content you will teach, the experiences you will prepare, the way you will engage children in the learning process, how you will group children for learning, what materials you will need, how you will assess children's learning, and how you will manage the learning process. Planning also includes creating and arranging teaching events in your mind and continually thinking and rethinking them. Planning helps you manage time and instruction and make decisions

DID YOU KNOW...?

- New teachers plan differently from experienced teachers. They spend more time writing down specific details of their lesson plans to help them understand the complexity and demands of daily teaching. Planning helps new teachers begin to reflect on what it means to teach and what they have learned in their teacher education programs, such as having a classroom management plan, planning for transitions between lessons, and pacing activities (Shambaugh & Magliaro, 2006).
- Competence is not tied to any particular language, dialect, or culture. Teachers should never use a child's dialect, language, or culture as a basis for making judgments about the child's intellect or capability (Woolfolk, 2007).
- The transition to formal schooling is a landmark event for millions of children, families, and educators. But recent research by the National Center for Early Development and Learning (NCEDL) and other investigators indicates that the transition practices commonly used in schools may not be well suited to the needs of children and families (NCEDL, 2002). It is predicted that in the next 10 to 20 years, public schools will be the primary agency for meeting the child-care and learning needs of 3- and 4-year-olds. Yet there is remarkable variability across states in the way in which pre-K programs are being implemented (Pre-K Education in the States, 2005).
- The United States is one of the few industrialized nations that does not offer public support for universal preschool programs. "Today's business leaders see that early childhood education is important to future U.S. economic competitiveness and a worthwhile investment. More than 80 percent of business leaders agree that public funding of voluntary prekindergarten programs for all children would improve America's workforce" (Committee for Economic Development, 2006).
- Although about 3 million children are born each year, up to 40 million Americans move in that same period, making mobility an important concern of teachers. Many teachers have 22 students in the fall and 22 in the following spring, but 20 out of 22 are different students (Hodgkinson, 2001). Student residential mobility could be a possible cause of the significant achievement gap that exists among white students, African American students, and Latino students because these children have less access to school supports than do less-transient students (Ream, 2005).

that will benefit each child. It also includes troubleshooting, the ability to predict what might be confusing or require additional time or practice (Arends, 2007).

To maximize positive outcomes for children, you need to answer questions about planning before, during, and after each lesson or activity. Before teaching, ask yourself: "What do I want children to know and be able to do? Why and who should learn what I am planning? When and how can I meet the needs of both individual children and the group? How will I evaluate and assess children's learning?" During teaching, ask yourself: "Is what I planned really engaging the children? Do I need to make any adaptations or adjustments to my plan?" And after teaching, ask yourself: "What parts of this plan worked and what parts need to change? Why do I think so?" To answer the questions about *what, why,* and *for whom* planned learning occurs, you need to assess what children already know, and what is worthwhile and appropriate for an individual child or a group of children to learn. To answer the questions about *when and how* requires careful planning to achieve your intended outcomes.

When teachers discuss planning, they refer to different types of planning, different ways of planning, and different purposes for planning. You will need to plan for the following parts of your day: developmentally effective curriculum in both the content areas and areas of development; a high-quality environment; the routines, procedures,

Krista Greco/Merrill

Time spent in planning is essential to a well-run early childhood classroom.

and transitions that provide the predictability of the day; and for children's interests and special needs (see Chapters 6 and 7 for more specific details). Otherwise, learning is left to chance.

Time spent in planning is essential to a well-run early childhood classroom. Good planning at every level is the roadmap that connects meaningful curriculum to the overall goals and outcomes of the program or school district. The decisions you make during planning will deeply influence what your students will know and be able to do. In the next section, we describe different types of planning that all teachers do.

Types of Planning

Teachers engage in two basic types of planning: long term and short term. Most prospective teachers cannot wait to start planning lessons and activities for children. What they sometimes fail to realize is that they will be teaching in a program or school district that has predetermined objectives and outcomes for the children to meet. Even though there may be mandated content and skills to teach, as a teacher, you are continually shaping and reshaping lessons and activities because teaching is a dynamic, interactive process. In many ways, you are like an architect of your own classroom world (Hansen, 1995), a professional decision maker who plans for children's learning based on both child development and curriculum knowledge. All planning, regardless of type, includes the essential elements of purpose, content, methods, and assessment (Feeney, Christensen, & Moravcik, 2006).

Long-term planning is very general and serves as a framework for later planning efforts. It includes yearly, semester, or quarterly planning, and unit or project planning. While each has its own purpose, each is connected to the other. Yearly plans are very general and should contain the overall knowledge, skills, and attitudes to be taught (e.g., caring, tolerance, respect), topics of study (e.g., understanding self and others, literary genres, change), and cycles of the school year (e.g., grading periods, holidays, best times to introduce new units of study) that will influence your planning over the course of the year (Arends, 2007). Semester, quarterly, unit, and project plans contain more specific goals, objectives, concepts, and skills that you hope children achieve during that particular period of time. Long-term planning helps you decide the content and topics to cover (the *what* and *why* of planning), the sequence in which those topics will be taught (the *how* and *where* of planning), the amount of time to spend on each topic (the *when* of planning), and the way in which you will assess the children's learning (the *how, what, why, when,* and *where* of planning). In many cases, the school district, state, or program in which you are working will already have made some of these decisions. Even so, your long-term planning will review and fine-tune such decisions to meet the individual learning needs of your students (Kauchak & Eggen, 2007).

Long-term planning guides your development of children's learning that is based on their prior experiences; it helps you think through the topics that you might want to introduce during a semester or year. Once you have a general idea of what you are going to teach, you can begin to gather materials and plan field trips that will enhance children's learning. You will also be able to share your long-term plans with families so that they have advance notice of events that call for participation and a better understanding of what their children will be learning. Long-term plans should be flexible to meet the changing needs, interests, and abilities of your children. When your planning is flexible, you can capitalize on unanticipated learning opportunities or "teachable moments," align your planning with state standards, develop reasonable goals for each child, determine the extent to which each child will be expected to achieve those goals, and implement meaningful ways to assess student learning (Feeney et al., 2006; Freiberg & Driscoll, 2005). Figure 8.1 provides a sample of a yearly plan for a kindergarten and Figure 8.2 provides long-range plans, organized by topic, for first grade. Notice how the teachers have developed their own methods for long-term planning.

Short-term planning is more specific and detailed than long-term planning because it addresses the day-to-day decisions that you will make as a teacher. It includes weekly and daily plans that identify the activities, experiences, and lessons to be used in the classroom. *Weekly plans* identify the activities for each day of the week. Again, you will need to plan in the way that works best for you or that your school requires. Some teachers write weekly plans in a brief calendar format; other teachers like to be very specific and detailed about each activity in their weekly plans; and still others like to include adaptations for certain children each week. *Daily plans*, on the other hand, are what most teachers refer to when they talk about planning. Some schools require teachers to write daily plans and follow a prescribed format; other schools allow more flexibility for teacher planning each day. Regardless, weekly and daily planning take a variety of forms and contain a variety of detail. Whatever form your plans take, they often contain key concepts, specific objectives or anticipated child outcomes of lessons and activities that are related to long-term goals. Short-term plans contain the schedule, sequence, and mode of assessment of lessons and activities. As you prepare your daily plans, consider which skills, concepts, and attitudes children need to develop throughout the days and weeks ahead. Your planning will also include ways to organize your learning environment and your time, how best to integrate the subject areas (e.g., math, literacy) across your units of study, how to best meet individual children's needs, and how to sequence and assess children's learning. Short-term planning also includes detailed lesson planning for particular parts of each day, such as transition times and opening and closing the day (Arends, 2007; Feeney et al., 2006). Figure 8.3 provides a sample daily plan for infants and toddlers. Figure 8.4 provides a sample daily plan for full-day child care

FIGURE 8.1 Yearly plan for kindergarten.

FT–Fairy Tale Unit
FLE–Family Life Education Optional Lessons
G/T–Gifted and Talented Required Lessons
POS–Program of Study
(oval)–Teacher's Key Options

	"My World and Welcome to It"			"Windows to the World"	
Months/Themes	**September** Start School I Am Special Shapes/Colors	**October** We Are Special Change Seasons Properties	**November** Community Food/Nutrition Animals Changes	**December** Nursery Rhymes Fairy Tales* Number Concepts	**January** Senses Winter Patterns
Language Arts/ Verbal/ Linguistic	Intro. Roberts & ABC books Intro. Journals Apple book 1st qtr. interviews	Intro. —work folders —take-home books Pumpkin book Intro. blending activities (cont.)	Fall and animal poetry Intro. syllables—use names	Reading conferences See POS K4 Pocket chart poetry Minibooks (What are letters and words?)	Winter poetry Begin alphabet dictation Writing conference Story retelling
Math/Logical-Mathematical	Shapes Colors Physical properties Intro Tool box	Begin Days of Kindergarten graph Sort Classify Map symbols and directions	Play money and HM math money Inventory #4	Number concepts (What are numbers?)	Intro. Venn diagram (*The Mitten*) Patterning Inv. # 3 & 5
Science/ Naturalist	Explore Science table Rainbows, sun, shadows	Pumpkins and Apples (What's happening outside?)	Animals Adaptations (Squirrels)	*Three Little Pigs* House Experiments (Which house will not blow down?)	(What are the senses?)
Social Studies/ Interpersonal	Citizenship Making friends Classroom community	Friends and family project (What is a neighborhood?)	Careers, Jobs, Helpers Thanksgiving Veteran's Day	Geography connection to fairy tales (Where do fairy tales come from?)	Martin Luther King (Who was MLK?) Chinese New Year
Health G/T	Safety Telephone numbers Business numbers G/T - 5 & 6 Faces and vehicles FLE - K.9(911)	FLE K.5 Working and playing with others K1.2.3 Families G/T 8 & 9 Sorting	Food and Nutrition project Helpers Changes Animal homes Substance abuse	(How does food keep me healthy and help me to grow?)	G/T Patterns Smell

FIGURE 8.1 Continued

"Discovering the Natural World" (February–March) · "Look How We've Grown" (May–June)

February Magnets Germs/Health Comparing	**March** Weather/Water Geography Measuring	**April** Ecology Spring Sequencing	**May** Ants No. Experiments Rhyming	**June** Summer We Are Special (Revisit)
Weather poetry Five Senses books Intro R & W charts	Journal and Reading conferences *Read Aloud* *Rhymes for the Very Young* by Jack Prelutsky	3rd qtr. interviews Assessments Science experiment Write all letters and numbers you can	Paul Revere poem Rhyming poetry Journal and Reading conferences	(How many words can I write?)
Comparing (Rice table, mitten matching) HMV–c Inv. #2	Measuring: –length –height –weight –temp	Sequencing Inv. #6	Number experiments (What is . . . 5, 7, 9?) Consult POS	Revisit Days of Kindergarten graph
Magnets (How do magnets work?) Project - Five senses	Weather Water –erosion –sink/float –bubbles Peanuts	Growing plants Water table Butterflies –life cycles Recycling project	Ants/Insects (project) (How do plants and animals grow and change?)	Summer
Valentine's Day Love I like . . . Presidents' Day Chinese New Year	G.W. Carver Harriet Tubman Geography	Earth Day Conservation (Who cares about the world?)	Memorial Day	Booker T. Washington We Are Special (revisit) Flag Day—Betsy Ross
FLE K.4 Keeping healthy	G/T #1 Weather hazards (What causes weather?)	G/T #2 Planting machines	FLE Keep Safe G/T Pets	

(*continued*)

FIGURE 8.1 Continued

FT–Fairy Tale Unit
FLE–Family Life Education Optional Lessons
G/T–Gifted and Talented Required Lessons
POS–Program of Study
⬭–Teacher's Key Options

	"My World and Welcome to It"			"Windows to the World"	
Months/Themes	**September** Start School* I Am Special Shapes/Colors	**October** We Are Special Change Seasons Properties	**November** Community Food/Nutrition Animals Changes	**December** Nursery Rhymes Fairy Tales* Number Concepts	**January** Senses Winter Patterns
Computer	Explain programs Children, children who do you see? Kid Pix	Alphabet book Dr. Seuss	Sammy's Science House Thankful book	Math I Bugs in a Box	Patterning
Music/ Musical	I Am Special We All Live Together Rainbows	Mary Wore a Red Dress If You Are Happy and You Know It	Piggy Bank Squirrel song	FT chants and songs Where has the gingerbread man gone?	Five Senses songs and poems Rhythm –patterns (What patterns can I copy or create?)
P.E./Bodily-Kinesthetic	Play dough Imagination station and puppets Body parts	Magnetic letters Five Little Pumpkins	Grocery store (What will I be when I grow up?) Connect with our people	Play dough numerals FT props & puppets (Who can I pretend to be?)	Pass the Mitten game Texture patterns Senses –experiments
Visual/Spatial	Buildings, pod, neighborhood Blocks Monthly poster	Apple prints Fall people from natural materials	Wreath of thankfulness	FT Neighborhood in pod Candyland	Snowflake patterns Texture painting
Intrapersonal	I Am Special Intro. Kinds of Smart	Feelings (How do I fit in?)	Needs/wants (What am I thankful for?)	Favorite character Voting	(What if I were . . . blind, etc.?)

FIGURE 8.1 Continued

February Magnets Germs/Health Comparing	March Weather/Water Geography Measuring	April Ecology Spring Sequencing	May Ants No. Experiments Rhyming	June Summer We Are Special (Revisit)
	"Discovering the Natural World"		"Look How We've Grown"	
Computer valentines	(Individual Books) *Green Eggs and Ham*	Wind stories	*Down by the Bay* (Songbook) Old Lady (sequencing)	
New Year Bells Health songs	Irish music Follow the drinking sound	Taping selves singing Can I sing? Ecology songs	I Know an Old Lady Down by the Bay No More Pie Jamberry Star Spangled Banner	
Magnet –experiments	Experiments –leprechauns –water	Ecology experiments	Outdoor sports Hopscotch	Physical fitness test What did we learn this year?
Multimedia valentines	Construction Weather Maps Artwork	Block map of classroom	Ant pathways Sand art	End of Year poster Revisit "What We Did" posters
Personal habits of cleanliness	Are leprechauns real?	Environmental stewardship "Giving Tree"	What have I learned this year?	Portfolio conferences MI goal setting

SOURCE: Courtesy of Gail Ritchie, Fairfax County Public Schools, Virginia.

FIGURE 8.2 Long-range plans for first grade.

Subject	September	October	November	December	January
Social Studies	Families I Am Special All About Me rules Citizenship	Families I Am Part of a Family Christopher Columbus	Families Thanksgiving Veteran's Day Children of long ago	Families Traditions and celebrations Needs and wants	Families People of the World Martin Luther King Jr.
Reading	Reading Assessment Text levels Letter identification	Shared language: pumpkins, fall, trees	Shared language: families, homes	Shared language: *Gingerbread Man* Celebrations	Shared language: winter, snow
Writing	Writing assessment	Ongoing assessment is used to determine the needs of individual students and plan instruction accordingly. Scope of instructional emphasis includes •Using multiple strategies to attach meaning to print •Sentence structure •Word usage •Capitalization •Punctuation			
Math*	Investigating numbers: patterns, comparing number relationships	Addition sentences Counting on measurement: nonstandard units	Numbers 11–15 Shapes Subtraction	Numbers 16–19 Measurement: weights (nonstandard), money	Equal groups problem Solving with + Combinations Facts: zeroes, doubles
Science	Five senses	Leaves Adopt a tree Fall	Parts of a Tree Leaves	Evergreens	Seeds Recording plant growth Winter
Health	School safety Bus safety	Fire safety Police officer	Poison Pharmacist Mr. Yuck	Medicines Controlled substances	Nutrition
Handwriting	Formation of letters Fine motor skills	Formation of letters Fine motor skills	Formation of letters Fine motor skills	Formation of letters Fine motor skills	Formation of letters

February	March	April	May	June
Families The World: different types of families Chinese New Year	Families How the environment affects how we live Maps/Geography	Families Local community	Families Community Economics	Families Review
Shared language: national celebrations Plants	Shared language: plants, weather	Shared language: weather, flowers	Shared language: seasons	Shared language: summer
•Spelling •Structural analysis •Letters and sounds •Building vocabulary •Story structure •Author's craft •Writing in different forms •Using informational sources in the classroom •Planning before writing •Self-monitoring strategies •Initiating writing •Revising to help clarify or expand meaning •Developing oral language •Collaborating with others for the purpose of writing				
10's and 1's Place value Time duration On the hour	Measurement: length Solid shapes Subtraction sentences	Relating addition and subtraction Counting on/ counting back Money	Measurement: capacity, weight 2-digit numbers	Area Fractions Multiplication Division
Propagation: growth without seeds	Clouds Tree growth	Flowers	Grass Plants Flowers	Flowers
Nutrition Dental health Personal Hygiene	Nutrition	Emergencies	Strangers Safety procedures	Playground and pool safety
Formation of letters	Formation of letters	Formation of letters	Formation of letters	Formation of letters
*Graphing Calendar Activities integrated throughout the year.				

SOURCE: Courtesy of Diana Sparrgrove, Parklawn Elementary School, Fairfax, Virginia.

FIGURE 8.3 Daily planning form for infants and toddlers (partially complete).

Teacher Brenda Day/Date Tues 9-22

Theme Families Age group: Walkers (10-15 mos.)

	Child: Corey	Child: Mandy	Child: Mateo	Child: Lori
A.M. Language—books, pictures, conversation	Family picture collage Who Is That? game "Gamma"	Ma Ma, Daddy, baby	Point To game (family members from pictures)	Bubba (brother) Telephone dialogue
Large and small muscle activity	Play pat-a-cake Cruise activity area	→→→→ Arrange and climb, soft blocks	→→→→ Play stand up and sit down by ballet bar	→→→→ Arrange and climb, soft blocks
Creative—art, blocks, music, dramatic play				
Learning—size, nature, colors, numbers, five senses, shapes				
P.M. Language—books, pictures, conversation				
Large and small muscle activity				
Creative—art, blocks, music, dramatic play				
Learning—size, nature, colors, numbers, five senses, shapes				

Notes: Mateo's mom reports he often cries standing at the rail of his crib. He needs help to get down. Corey's grandmother is visiting for a week.

FIGURE 8.4 Daily plan for full-day child care for 4- and 5-year-olds.

Time	Activity
7:15	Arrival: Quiet Area choices (manipulatives, books, art/tactile media available) and/or dramatic play and block areas are prepared and available
8:15	Breakfast offered, children bathroom as needed. Set timer/clean-up
8:40	Early morning storytime
8:45	Gross motor play (playground/multipurpose room)
9:40	Circle: group gathering for music, movement, and/or language arts activities
9:55	Small-group activity/children plan
10:15	Choice time: all areas open/snack offered
11:20	Set timer/clean-up/recall time in small group
11:30	Storytime
11:40	Lunch Children: bathroom, brush teeth, and choose a book
12:20	Book and stories on cots
12:30	Soft music and lights off for rest time
2:30	Children begin to awaken; bathroom Afternoon choice time/snack offered (continuation of earlier projects and new activities)
3:30	Set timer/clean-up
3:45	Circle: group gathering—music/science
4:00	Playground or other gross motor activity (Multipurpose Room available 4:30–5:00)
5:00	Activities—games/stories/exploration
5:45	Departure/Staff prepare for next days events

SOURCE: Courtesy of Nelly Adams, Fairfax County Employees' Child Care Center, Fairfax, VA.

for 4- and 5-year-olds, and Figure 8.5 provides a sample daily plan for first grade. A sample weekly plan for half-day preschool is shown in Figure 8.6. Again, notice the different formats that teachers use to plan.

A word of caution is needed about planning. While planning is essential to children's learning, becoming too rigid about continuing on with a plan regardless of children's interest in it limits learning. Good planning provides for a variety of self-selected activities within carefully prepared alternatives that are related to the needs, interests, and cultural backgrounds of particular children. Planning begins before the school year and continues until the children leave at the end of it.

FIGURE 8.5 Daily plan for first grade.

Tuesday

Date: ______________________

Special Information for today: ____

9:00–9:30 **Morning Choice Time/Announcements/Attendance**

- hang up backpacks and check job chart
- each child chooses an activity (read books; play games on rug; computer; explore manipulatives from math center; use writing center, art center, or listening center)
- morning announcements and pledge—about 9:15 A.M.
- take attendance after announcements; messengers take it to office

9:30–10:00 **Morning Meeting**

- children are on the rug, calendar helper fills in and reads calendar, schedule; does weather chart, number of days in school, ABC chart
- read poem: ____October______;

  Choose two children to share news; write news on white board
- Focus Lesson: *Interactive writing—What we will learn later about October*

10:00–10:45 **Writing Workshop** Program of Study Link: ______________

- Fill out individual calendars and weather graphs
- Writing activity: ____________________________ or journals
- Group 1: ___________ *Emari's: Kitty & the Birds/Tom Is Brave* ________
- Group 2: ___________ *Jeremy's: Uncle Bunde/Our Granny* ________
- Group 3: *Ali's Little Brother/Me Magnetic letters: Practice their names*

10:45–11:30 **Reading Workshop**

- Shared Reading: ___________ *Health-Fire Safety—Jennifer* ________
- Reading Response: ___________ *Stop-Drop-Roll* ___________
- Small Group ____
- Quiet Reading from Book Boxes
- Sharing Circle

11:30–11:50 Outdoor break, then bathroom break before lunch

11:50–12:20 Lunch (pick up children at door by main stairs)

12:20–12:30 Bathroom Break

12:30–12:50 Storytime and Discussion Sharing

FIGURE 8.5 Continued

	Book: Finish Picking Apples and Pumpkins
12:50–1:40	**Math**
	Program of Study Link: ______
	Developing Number Sense: *Math Happening**
	Concept Lesson: *Addition/Problem solving*
	Activity: *Ways to make 5—use cut-paper squares to record, in groups of three*
	Small Groups: ______
1:40–2:00	**Free Choice or Outdoor Break and Snack**
2:00–2:30	**Library**
2:30–3:15	Mrs. Prince every other week/Science (2:30–3:15 or 3:00–3:30)
	Concept Lesson: ______
	Activity: ______
3:15–3:30	**DEAR Time** (Drop Everything and Read) (independent reading or buddy reading) only when science ends at 3:15
3:35–3:45	**Prepare for Dismissal**
	• stack chairs, pick up things off floor, tidy centers
	• check cubbies and pack bags
3:45	**Dismissal** (children gather by door and sit on the floor)

*A Math Happening is an authentic math problem that occurs in children's natural daily activities (e.g., How many snacks are needed for the children after counting those who are absent and subtracting that number from the number of children in the class).

SOURCE: Courtesy of Diana Sparrgrove, Parklawn Elementary School, Fairfax, Virginia.

Your Role as a Planner

Planning is one of the most important skills of successful early childhood teachers. You are responsible for what happens when children are with you, for selecting and establishing appropriate goals and methods, setting the pace for learning, and evaluating and assessing children's progress. How well you plan can diminish or enhance children's learning and well-being. Consider the following example of five student teachers

FIGURE 8.6 Weekly plan for half-day preschool.

Teacher's Name ____________

Week of ____________

	Monday	Tuesday	Wednesday	Thursday	Friday
Morning Meeting **—Greetings** **—Calendar** **—Weather**	Talk about water and its uses.	Discuss field trip to pond and ask children to take paper and crayons. Have clipboards to share.	Have children write in their News Books today. What might they write?	Remind children about store. Give out play money.	
Art	Add new collage materials.	Only in afternoon. Add new paint.	Sponge art.	Make sculptures for store.	
Literacy	Have books and posters on water (e.g., rivers, oceans).	Have books and posters on water (ponds, creeks, waterfalls).	New books. Miss P. will help.	Begin pricing for store.	Have blank books available (use colored paper) with markers.
Blocks	Add blue colored paper so children can make rivers.	Add pencils and paper so children can make plans for bridges.	Teacher supports bridge building.	Add boats and people.	
Dramatic Play	Include doctor and sailor props.	→→→→	Books about water and bridges.	Put rocker/boat in areas with sailor hats.	→→→→
Sand/Water	Use plastic tubing, funnels, measuring cups, spice containers.	→→→→	Put boats in water table.	Add cars, plants, and boats.	→→→→
Manipulatives	Introduce new lotto game. Teacher will join group.	In afternoon, play lotto again.	Remove stones from sorting tray.	Begin pricing new items for store.	Have buttons for sorting.

Outdoors	Take water table outside. For building bridges, use stones.	Water table outside in afternoon.	Free play. Nature walk.	Set up balance beam.	Balance beam.
Group Time	Music—Mrs. Z. will play guitar and teach songs. Story: *Cloudy with Chance of Meatballs.*	Flannel-board story: *Swimmy*	Group story on visit to the pond.	Read *Riptide.*	Read *Swimmy.* Play Who Is Hiding?
Other Activities	Snack—make carrot sticks at square table in afternoon.	Visit local pond.	Collect wood on nature walk.	Mary's birthday—cupcakes for snack.	Cooking—make fruit salad for afternoon snack.

Theme/Unit: Water

TO DO:

Remember to send home note about trip to bridge. Invite parents to come.

Ask Jo's aunt to help with News Books time on Wednesday.

Send note to Mrs. Z.—Thank her for guitar playing.

Mary has birthday on Thursday.

planning an integrated social studies unit on The Family for kindergarten. It included the mandated state and local social studies standards and goals and the specific content that is required of kindergartners. As you read about these student teachers' planning process, think about your role as a planner.

The student teachers began their collaborative planning for an integrated social studies unit The Family by first reviewing the information about their schools and students, which reminded them of the diversity of the student population. After looking at the national, state, and local standards, they created a general statement about how to make the topic of families relevant to the lives of kindergartners. They stated that studying the family was important because kindergartners are beginning to build a strong sense of self and to understand their relationships with others. Through discussion with one another, the student teachers agreed on three major goals of the social studies unit on families: students would be able to (a) identify historic events that happened while a family member was living, (b) experience a family member's work, and (c) understand where they live in relation to the school and their classmates. The student teachers identified the school district goals in each of the content areas (e.g., language arts, math, science, social studies, and the arts) that applied to their unit on families and that would guide their choice of activities. They also used the key concepts of self, others, needs, family, and responsibility that were described in their school district's curriculum guide to make decisions about the lessons and activities to prepare.

Guided by the content goals and national and local standards, the student teachers located books, poetry, multimedia, and websites appropriate for their student population. They chose nonfiction books such as *I Love My Family* (Beal, 1991); picture books such as *Tell Me Again About the Night I Was Born* (Curtis, 1996); technology books such as *Just Grandma and Me* (Mayer, 1994); and professional resources such as *Social Studies for the Preschool/Primary Child* (Seefeldt, 2005a), *Active Experiences for Active Children: Social Studies* (Seefeldt & Galper, 2006), and *Social Studies: A Way to Integrate Curriculum for Four- and Five-Year-Olds* (Gryphon House, 2005), a multimedia tape for integrating social studies across the curriculum areas. They also examined numerous websites for teaching and learning about social studies, such as the NAEYC's website at www.journalnaeyc.org/btj/200509, to learn as much as they could about available resources. The student teachers noticed that many of the books and resources they located naturally formed categories such as What Is a Family? Family Traditions, Family Changes, Where Families Live, and Family Roles and Responsibilities. These categories helped them brainstorm the topics, which led to a conceptual web they hoped to use during

A unit on the family needs to show sensitivity to nontraditional family groups.

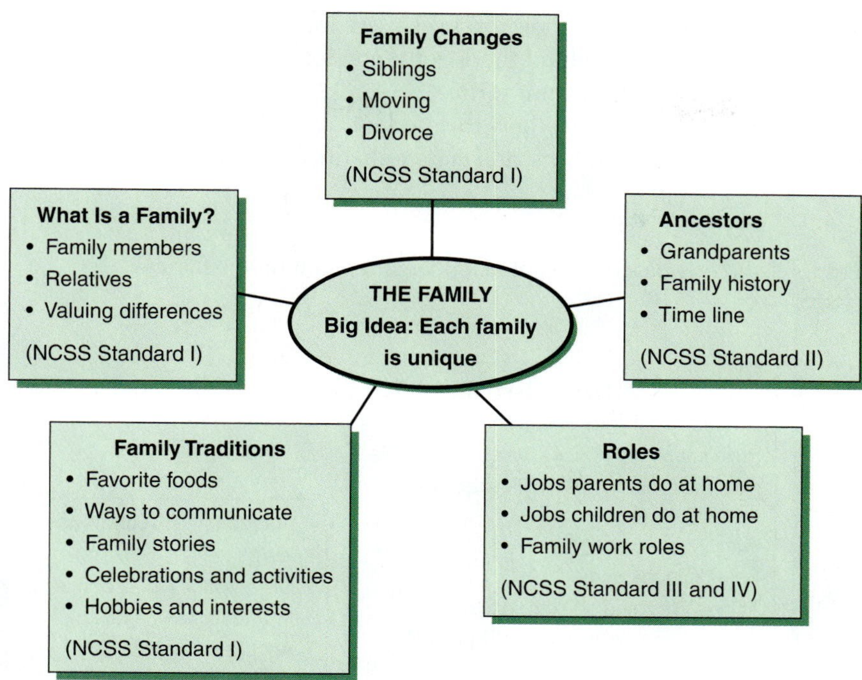

FIGURE 8.7
Concept web for standards-based kindergarten unit on families.

the unit. Figure 8.7 shows the concept web linked to National Social Studies standards they used to start planning for their unit The Family.

With their web created, the student teachers planned to find out what the children already knew about families as a starting point for their unit. They decided to assess children's prior knowledge during a class meeting on the first day of the unit by asking children, "What do you already know about families?" and "What would you like to know about families?" This inquiry strategy allowed the children to have input into the learning and provided the student teachers with a starting place for the individuals in their classes (Kauchak & Eggen, 2007). The student teachers planned a variety of teacher- and child-selected activities that would meet their goals, enhance the children's self-esteem, and build respect and understanding for others and their families. For example, in language arts, the children would read and write stories about their own families and homes; in math, they might create a class graph about the children's family members and class pets; and in science, they might identify special sounds in their homes. The student teachers also developed integrated learning centers focusing on family-centered activities, such as cooking and carpentry; a library center with special books on the topic, including books children would make; and career roles of the family members in the class. To do this, they needed to ensure that the rooms were arranged to accommodate different centers and the diverse needs of the learners.

COMPANION WEBSITE 8.2 To learn more about fulfilling your role as a planner for children's learning and the NAEYC, go to *Web Links* in Chapter 8 of the Companion Website at http://www.prenhall.com/jalongo.

After the student teachers organized the topics to be covered, they turned their attention to developing meaningful activities. They identified special vocabulary terms (e.g., adoption, divorce, single-parent, and extended family) associated with the study of family that were characteristic of some of the children in their classes. They talked about these terms' meanings to develop sensitivity for children who are members of these kinds of families. This helped them get ready for the questions they anticipated children would ask about family unit terms.

Look at Figure 8.8 and notice how the student teachers planned assessment techniques, resource persons, field trips, and classroom displays that met the Guidelines for

FIGURE 8.8 Selected experiences for standards-based, integrated kindergarten unit on the family.

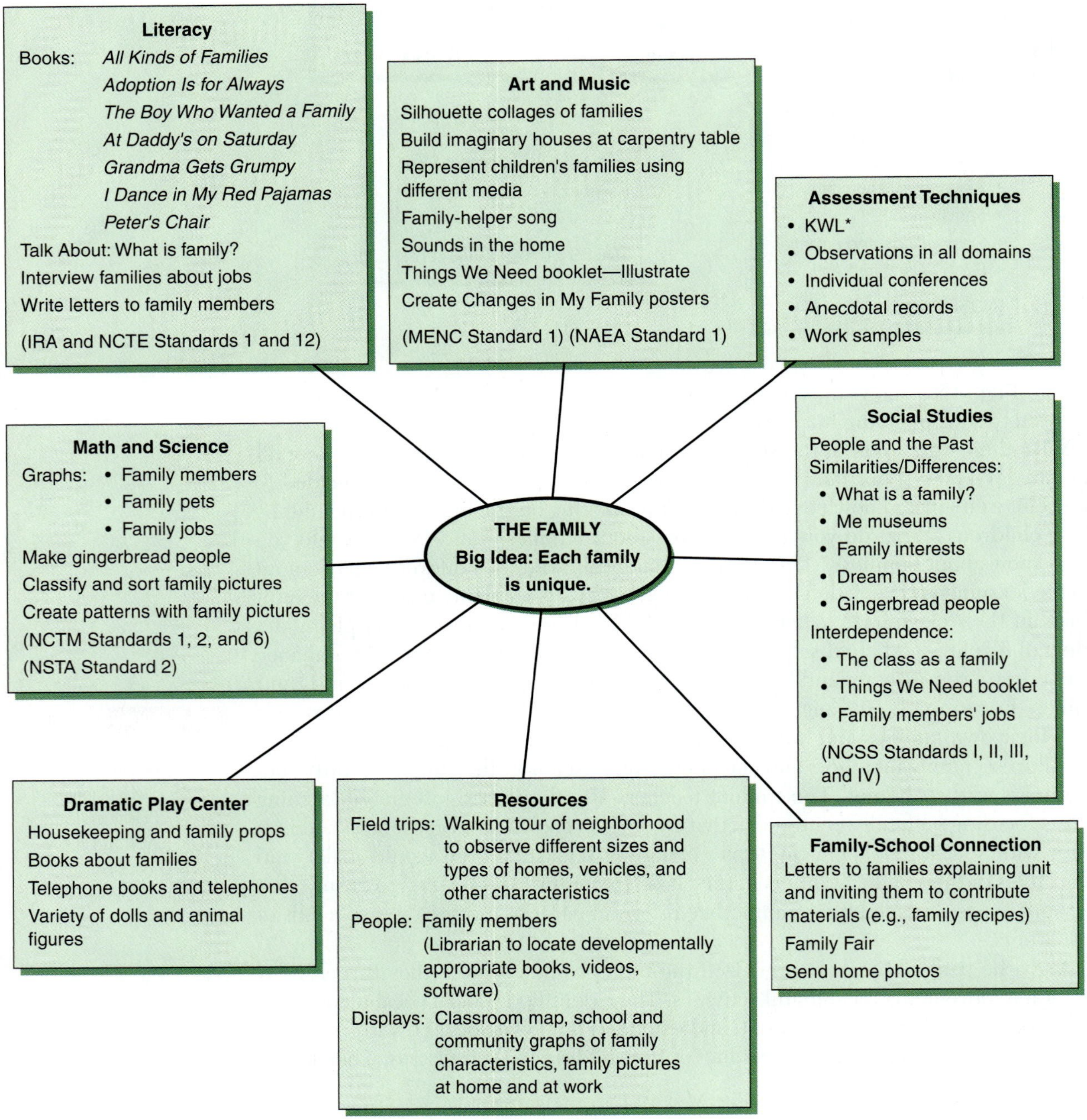

THE FAMILY
Big Idea: Each family is unique.

Literacy

Books: *All Kinds of Families*
Adoption Is for Always
The Boy Who Wanted a Family
At Daddy's on Saturday
Grandma Gets Grumpy
I Dance in My Red Pajamas
Peter's Chair

Talk About: What is family?
Interview families about jobs
Write letters to family members
(IRA and NCTE Standards 1 and 12)

Art and Music

Silhouette collages of families
Build imaginary houses at carpentry table
Represent children's families using different media
Family-helper song
Sounds in the home
Things We Need booklet—Illustrate
Create Changes in My Family posters
(MENC Standard 1) (NAEA Standard 1)

Assessment Techniques

- KWL*
- Observations in all domains
- Individual conferences
- Anecdotal records
- Work samples

Math and Science

Graphs:
- Family members
- Family pets
- Family jobs

Make gingerbread people
Classify and sort family pictures
Create patterns with family pictures
(NCTM Standards 1, 2, and 6)
(NSTA Standard 2)

Social Studies

People and the Past
Similarities/Differences:
- What is a family?
- Me museums
- Family interests
- Dream houses
- Gingerbread people

Interdependence:
- The class as a family
- Things We Need booklet
- Family members' jobs

(NCSS Standards I, II, III, and IV)

Dramatic Play Center

Housekeeping and family props
Books about families
Telephone books and telephones
Variety of dolls and animal figures

Resources

Field trips: Walking tour of neighborhood to observe different sizes and types of homes, vehicles, and other characteristics
People: Family members (Librarian to locate developmentally appropriate books, videos, software)
Displays: Classroom map, school and community graphs of family characteristics, family pictures at home and at work

Family-School Connection

Letters to families explaining unit and inviting them to contribute materials (e.g., family recipes)
Family Fair
Send home photos

*What I Know, What I Want to Know, What I Learned.

Developmentally Appropriate Curriculum and Assessment (Bredekamp & Rosegrant, 1995) as a benchmark of the choices they were making. Figure 8.9 illustrates week 1 of their multiweek kindergarten family unit. These student teachers have demonstrated the essential components of good planning (Feeney et al., 2006; Freiberg & Driscoll, 2005; Gordon & Williams-Browne, 2007; Seefeldt, 2005b; Woolfolk, 2007) that are described in the following paragraphs.

Know the Children, Families, and Community for Whom You Are Planning

Successful planning begins with the children themselves as well as their families. Developmentally appropriate practice (DAP) is an important principle of practice in early childhood education. It requires that teachers make decisions based on three important kinds of knowledge: (a) child development and learning; (b) individual needs, abilities, and interests; and (c) social and cultural contexts in which children live (Bredekamp & Copple, 1997; Copple & Bredekamp, 2006). Understanding typical growth and development is the foundation for age-appropriate planning and is necessary to understand individual needs, abilities, and interests. Considering children's ages, developmental levels, uniqueness, and social and cultural backgrounds will greatly enhance your planning. Younger children need large blocks of time for play and spontaneous exploration; older children do more project-oriented and structured planning to more accurately represent their learning (Feeney et al., 2006). Notice how the unit on the family planned by the student teachers took into account the characteristics of 4- to 6-year-old children by providing many meaningful activities for them to work in small groups and expand their academic skills across the subject areas. Notice also how the unit addressed the children's cultural backgrounds through the resources identified, connection with the children's families, and the activities planned.

Michelle Pearlstein

Know the children for whom you are planning.

Be Knowledgeable About the Content and Concepts You Plan to Teach

Each professional subject-area organization for teachers has identified key standards, content and concepts considered essential to learn at different ages (Arends, 2007; Bredekamp & Rosegrant, 1995). (Many of these concepts are listed in Table 7.1 in Chapter 7.) One of the first sets of questions you will ask yourself in order to make content accessible to your children is "What content and concepts will I be teaching? What do the children already know and how can I build on that? What are the most effective age-appropriate ways to teach this content?" This kind of planning focuses on results and

FIGURE 8.9 Weekly plan for kindergarten unit on the family.

Week of ____________________

Week 1 of Multi-Week Kindergarten Social Studies Unit, "The Family"

Time	Monday	Tuesday	Wednesday	Thursday	Friday
8:30–9:30 12:15–12:45	Center Choice Family books, puppets, block people, carpentry	Center Choice	Center Choice	Center Choice	Center Choice
9:30–9:55 12:45–1:10	Morning Meeting Calendar, pledge, attendance, Morning Message, Share Time Intro. topic: "What Is a Family?" with KWL*	Morning Meeting Venn diagram: Family Pets	Morning Meeting Family recipes	Morning Meeting Read *Bread, Bread, Bread*	Morning Meeting Prepare for classroom visitor
9:55–10:10 1:10–1:25	Movement Family in the Dell	Movement Pantomime Pets	Movement Simon Says	Movement Heads, Shoulders, Knees, and Toes	Movement Carnival of the Animals
10:10–10:40 1:25–1:55	Snack/Recess	Snack/Recess	Snack/Recess	Snack/Recess	Snack/Recess
10:40–12:00 1:55–3:15	Read-aloud All Kinds of Families Centers Family Center: Class book: *My Family*	Read-aloud *Your Family, My Family* Centers Family Center: Graphing Family members	Read-aloud *The Relatives Came* Centers Family Center: Cover for recipe book	Visitor: Mr. Ramos will cook tortillas Centers Family Center: Making tortillas	Visitor: Grandmother Centers Family Center: Family crests
12:00–12:15 3:15–3:30	Class meeting	Class meeting	Class meeting	Class meeting	Class meeting

*What I Know, What I Want to Know, What I Learned.

SOURCE: Courtesy of George Mason University PDS8 Interns.

positive child outcomes. To see a teacher reading Eric Carle's book, *Pancakes, Pancakes* to make learning about the past and changes over time interesting and meaningful, view the "Life in the Supply Chain" video clip online at the Teacher Prep Website. Children want to know many things about their world. They are particularly interested in knowing about themselves, about their families and communities, about how things work, and about the natural and physical aspects of their environment. You will want to plan experiences that are meaningful, challenging, and will extend children's thinking, but that also help them to be successful learners. Whatever content and concepts you teach must have integrity and be worth knowing, or they will be of little value (Katz & Chard, 2000). In the unit on the family previously described, we saw how the student teachers selected books on topics directly relevant to 5-year-olds and planned graphing activities using children's family members and pets to teach math concepts. Notice, too, that most of the activities they planned were worth knowing and doing.

TEACHER PREP WEBSITE 8.1

Go to Video Classroom, select Social Studies Methods, choose Connecting to Literature (Module 5), and select Life in the Supply Chain (Video 1).

Plan a Variety of Experiences to Meet the Needs of Diverse Learners

Good planning consists of varied experiences that maximize all children's learning. Planning for children from diverse cultural and linguistic backgrounds, children who are "at risk" for school failure, and children with exceptionalities is important because not all children learn in the same manner (Price & Nelson, 2003). The abilities, interests, and backgrounds of children even of the same age vary, so activities must be open-ended and flexible enough to be used by a number of children with a variety of skills and abilities. Instead of working with one set plan for all children, stretch yourself to incorporate the different types of intelligences into your planning (Gardner, 1993; Silver, Strong, & Perini, 2000). This effort recognizes that students learn differently and allows them to express themselves in their own ways. You can see that the student teachers planned a variety of authentic activities, which met different learning styles. For example, they included graphing for those who prefer patterns, writing stories for those who prefer words, cooking and carpentry for those who like spatial activities, and individual activities for children to do alone as well as activities to be done in a group. In this way, their plan was to work from children's strengths and to choose teaching strategies that use multiple modes of representation of performance (Price & Nelson, 2003; Silver et al., 2000; Tiedt & Tiedt, 2005).

Planning a variety of experiences also takes into account children's interests. Most children have particular interests and enjoy pursuing them. That usually leads them to find out more about their interest and to gain skill and expertise in it—sometimes lasting a lifetime. This can also lead to children being exposed to other interests, which in turn leads to other competencies. For example, exposing kindergarten children to different family occupations may spark an interest in a particular career option in one or more children in the class.

COMPANION WEBSITE 8.3 To learn more about linguistic and cultural diversity, go to *Enrichment Content: Research Highlights* in Chapter 8 of the Companion Website at http://www.prenhall.com/jalongo.

Plan Appropriate Methods of Assessing Children's Learning

How will you know what children have learned? An important responsibility of all early childhood teachers is planned, ongoing assessment of children's learning. Serious assessment leads to better understanding of children and better planning. Note that the methods of assessment planned by the student teachers who developed the unit on the family show evidence of good planning. They planned to assess children's prior knowledge

TEACHER PREP WEBSITE 8.2

Go to Student and Teacher Artifacts, select General Methods, choose Teaching Strategies for Concepts (Module 8), and select Weather (Artifact 3).

through the KWL strategy (What I Know, What I Want to Know, What I Learned), which will enable them to start the unit by building on children's prior knowledge and increasing their understanding from that point. You can see an example of a KWL from second grader, Tom, who showed what he knew and learned about trees in the "General Methods–Teaching Strategies for Concepts" student and teacher artifacts online at the Teacher Prep Website. Teaching for understanding means children can do "a variety of thought demanding activities with a topic-like explaining, finding evidence and examples, generalizing, applying, and representing the topic in a new way" (Perkins & Blythe, 1994, pp. 5–6). The student teachers also planned for ongoing observations in all domains, using work samples for portfolios, and conducting individual conferences. Each of these assessment strategies is tied to the unit goals and reflects the importance of unifying goals and assessment from the outset.

Plan to Reflect on Your Teaching

Reflection is part of every teacher's planning process. Thoughtful teachers reflect on questions about student learning and their own teaching methods. Ask yourself: "What have my students learned?" "What evidence do I have that shows they are learning?" As you think about the outcome of your planning, identify the aspects of your teaching that worked and those that did not and why that was so. Look at the part of the lesson or activity that did not work as well as you would have liked. What can you change about it to improve it? You will need to think about your teaching every day to improve it in order to optimize children's learning (Hiebert, Morris, Berk, & Jansen, 2007).

Allow Plenty of Time to Plan Ahead

Your best teaching will occur when you plan well in advance of the teaching day so you have enough time to gather materials, make contacts, and think through how to implement your

David Young-Wolff/PhotoEdit Inc.

Teachers need to be lifelong learners, too.

ideas. You will want to find a regular planning time for yourself, and with your teaching team, to ensure the best planning. Writing down your daily, weekly, unit, and project plans gives you the flexibility you need to implement them. You might also consider planning extra or optional activities, even if you do not use them. Some of these extra or optional activities can be planned to include families, as described in the following Collaborating with Families feature. Additional planning will make you feel more confident in case your planned activities take less time than expected or are just not engaging the children as you had hoped.

PAUSE AND REFLECT

About Your Role as a Planner

Think about your role as a planner in relation to the unit on the family described in this section. What did you realize about planning when you read about these student teachers' plans? What questions do you have from reading this description? What do you agree and disagree with? Can you think of ways to connect these ideas with ways to communicate with families, as is demonstrated in the accompanying Collaborating with Families feature?

COLLABORATING WITH FAMILIES

Communicating with Families About Meaningful Activities at Home

Each month, Ms. Davis sends home a calendar of activities for children and families to do that are related to what the children are learning at school. Following is a *portion* of one of her February calendars. Suggest some other activities that would be appropriate for families to do with their children.

February Home Activities

Monday	Tuesday	Wednesday	Thursday	Friday
2 Ask me what *communicate* means.	3 Read with your child the picture message or rebus chart brought home today.	4 Write a rebus message about what you did after supper tonight.	5 Sing *Little Cabin in the Woods* with and without words—just hand signs!	6 Select and make a recipe from the *Home-to-School Cookbook*.
9 Collect 20 old envelopes with stamps on them—15 for home and 5 to take to school.	10 Have your child sort the 15 envelopes. How many ways did your child sort the envelopes?	11 Make a valentine to send to someone special. Address and stamp the envelope.	12 Take the valentine to the mailbox or post office.	13 Read *A Letter for Amy* by Ezra Jack Keats.
16 Finish the picture phone book with your child. Call a friend in the new phone book.	17 Take turns acting out activities you do during the day. Can you guess what they are doing?	18 Select four or five Pictures of your child at various ages. Play a sequencing game to see if they can order the pictures from babyhood to present.	19 Give your child a hug and say "I love you." How many ways can you tell each other "I love you"?	20 On a piece of paper write the word *communicate*, then find pictures in magazines that show ways to communicate. Make a collage.

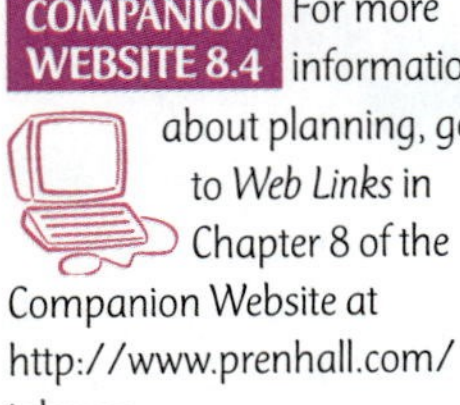

For more information about planning, go to *Web Links* in Chapter 8 of the Companion Website at http://www.prenhall.com/jalongo.

Why Is Planning So Crucial to Successful Teaching?

There is considerable evidence that planning is an essential aspect of successful teaching. Throughout your career as an early childhood teacher, you will be engaged almost continually in some kind of planning. You will also be developing your own style of planning that will allow you to establish your own teaching style. It will occur in each phase of the teaching process—before teaching (e.g., making decisions about the purpose for learning, identifying child outcomes, and writing down the specific steps to take through the teaching-learning activity), during teaching (e.g., making necessary changes with your procedures, materials, and the content as you are teaching as you notice children's responses and level of engagement), and after teaching (e.g., assessing your teaching in terms of its outcomes, thinking about what will affect your teaching for the next day or week, and noting changes you want to make). Although each of these phases of planning has a different focus, they are very interrelated. Note also that in each of these planning phases you will be making decisions about accountability to local, state, and national standards; individual and group learning; and assessing each learner's success. These three fundamental principles of planning are discussed in the following paragraphs.

Planning for Accountability to Standards

TEACHER PREP WEBSITE 8.3

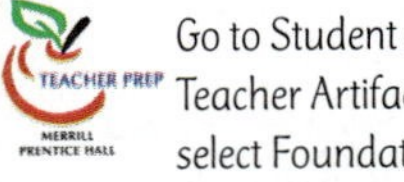

Go to Student and Teacher Artifacts, select Foundations/Intro to Teaching, choose Curriculum and Instruction (Module 10), and select Math (Artifact 6).

Why do you need to be so clear about standards for students? Most states have standards that clearly state what children should know and be able to do in kindergarten through third grade. Moreover, many of these states have developed or are developing standards for preschool children. Head Start has adopted specific learning outcomes for children to reach by the end of preschool. In addition to state standards, professional organizations have also identified outcomes in content areas that children should achieve at particular grade levels (Copple & Bredekamp, 2006; Gronlund, 2006). In this era of high accountability, it is essential that you use state and local standards in your planning. In many schools and programs today, you probably will be asked to teach specific units of study and will most likely be given standards and benchmarks, goals, objectives, and a prepared curriculum guide to follow. It is likely that you will be given one or more of the following: a list of competencies that students are expected to achieve, specific textbooks to use to teach certain subjects, and perhaps some curriculum kits. You can incorporate these standards and materials into your curriculum, provided you can state how your own goals and outcomes for the children's learning mesh with other mandates such as local and state curriculum standards. In this way, you will have more control over what you plan and how you teach. When you are clear about your own goals and objectives, you have the means to incorporate any mandate into your program (Arends, 2007; Gordon & Williams-Browne, 2007; Price & Nelson, 2003; Woolfolk, 2007). You can see an example of how a child's math subtraction story artifact relates to national and state standards in the "Foundations/Intro to Teaching–Curriculum and Instruction" student and teacher artifacts online at the Teacher Prep Website.

Quality early childhood programs and practices readily accept the principle of accountability. Accountability means that you assess student progress frequently and make plans for each child's future learning.

Planning for Individual and Group Learning

When you understand and appreciate students' unique needs, you take into account what each child brings to your classroom. You also recognize that no two children and no two groups of children come into the classroom in quite the same way. Children bring their own experiences, attitudes, skills, interests, questions, and problems with them to school. Only the teacher—knowing the children, their families, and the school environment—makes a deliberate effort to differentiate instruction to meet individual children's needs (Kostelnik, Soderman, & Whiren, 2007; Silver et al., 2000; Woolfolk, 2007). When you are responsive to the wide range of abilities and learning styles of the children in the classroom, you demonstrate to children that accepting and responding to differences are important democratic values. The opposite approach assumes that all children respond equally to one particular teaching method and is often less effective for meeting individual needs.

One good way to facilitate individual learning is through a variety of grouping practices. Basically, there are four types of groups that you will regularly use: large groups, small groups, one-on-one interactions, and individual. Generally, children learn more readily if they experience a variety of instructional groups. Grouping should be flexible and vary in size consistent with the learning activity, allow for child-initiated activities, foster self-esteem and social and emotional learning, and have appropriate pacing of activities to enhance learning (NAEYC, 2005). Table 8.1 lists and describes the different types of grouping patterns for children.

TABLE 8.1 Grouping Patterns for Children

Type	Description	Appropriate Uses
Large Groups/ Whole Class	• includes 10 or more children • is economical with time • invloves children generally as passive participants	• share common experiences • singing, story time and read-alouds • demonstrations, classroom visitors • group games • class meetings and discussions • group conferences
Small Groups	• provides opportunity for social interaction and leadership skills • involves 2–10 children to develop skills, concepts, and ideas with others • involves negotiation, interaction, and support	• peer teaching and tutoring • multiage groups • flexible skill groups (short term) • activities that require teacher assistance (e.g., literacy and math skills) • cooperative groups • interest groups • social or random groups • centers, stations, choices
One-on-One Interactions	• involves focused adult-child interaction, generally to help a child acquire a skill or concept or pursue a need or interest • capitalizes on spontaneous learning and teachable moments encouraging dialogue and questioning	• observation and assessment of skill level and adaptive teaching based on observational data • concentrates on children's learning
Individual	• helps a child to explore an idea on his or her own (e.g., insects, water, printing, building) • maintains control within the child • pursues interests and continues learning after instructional activities have ended	• hands-on, interactive learning opportunities (e.g., books, interactive bulletin boards, replicas to explore, centers) • contracts, centers, stations • peer tutoring, volunteers • choices and projects

Planning for Each Child's Success

Teachers have a responsibility to optimize each child's chance to be successful in school. Planning for each child's learning needs at every level depends to a large extent on the outcomes that you select, the strategies that you use to reach those outcomes, and the ways that you interact with individuals and groups of children (Kauchak & Eggen, 2007). Consider the way in which the three teachers you met in the chapter opener try to ensure success for each learner: Ms. Burke said, "Teachers need to know that finding out about children's interests is a key tool for planning"; Ms. Kim now uses a variety of age-appropriate books and read-aloud strategies to better engage the children in her inclusive classroom; and Mr. Pearlman talked through his mental and written plans with his classroom teacher to better meet the needs of his students.

Scott Cunningham/Merrill

Teachers plan all the time, not just the night before a lesson.

Building a planning repertoire that includes multiple effective instructional strategies is important for beginning teachers and others who want to improve their teaching and facilitate children's learning. While it is beyond the scope of this book to present in-depth instructional strategies to address students' diverse needs, the general guidelines presented in Figure 8.10 are appropriate for teaching all learners with the goal of success.

Good planning also has other benefits, ranging from providing a snapshot picture for a day, week, month, or quarter, to making content accessible to the children, to using time wisely and productively, to asking higher-level questions. Each of these functions empowers your teaching in the most positive way (Freiberg & Driscoll, 2005).

Research on Teachers' Planning

Research on teachers' planning supports what most experienced teachers have concluded: that planning plays a critical role in teaching and school learning (Clark & Dunn, 1991; Cooper, 2006; Kauchak & Eggen, 2007). When do teachers plan? Contrary to the notion that teachers don't start planning their instruction until the night before they must teach it, researchers have found that teachers are constantly engaged in planning. In reality, teachers plan their instruction all the time—while driving home from school, while grocery shopping, standing in the shower, and sitting on the beach.

PAUSE AND REFLECT

About Why Planning Is Crucial to Your Success as a Teacher

Reread the opening section, Meet the Teachers. Now that you have read about the importance of planning, discuss how these teachers might have planned differently. What would be the advantages and disadvantages of alternative approaches?

FIGURE 8.10 Strategies for meeting needs of diverse learners.

Planning for Culturally and Ethnically Diverse Learners

1. Incorporate the home culture into the classroom and curriculum.
2. Encourage active participation from families.
3. Capitalize on students' backgrounds.
4. Use culturally relevant curriculum materials.
5. Identify and dispel stereotypes.
6. Demonstrate concepts and use manipulatives.
7. Create culturally appropriate learning environments.
8. Use various grouping patterns and provide opportunities for children to work together.

Planning for English Language Learners

1. Integrate teaching experiences.
2. Use multiage and peer tutoring.
3. Incorporate units and projects.
4. Have two or more children at a computer at a time to enhance communication.
5. Use language that invites children's participation and that they can understand.
6. Simplify your language.
7. Bring the child's home language and culture into the classroom.
8. Provide books written in the various languages in the classroom library.

Planning for Children with Exceptionalities

1. Provide the consistency and structure that children with special needs require to thrive.
2. Use audiotape materials for children who cannot read successfully.
3. Provide visual reminders (e.g., pictures, graphs, maps, charts) for children who have difficulty attending.
4. Give directions in small steps.
5. Discover the special interests and strengths of each child and capitalize on them in the classroom.
6. Provide a circle time space for every child, such as a small rug or mat.
7. Demonstrate new materials, equipment, and activities.
8. Be sensitive to what prevents children from learning.

SOURCES: Data based on Peregoy & Boyle (2005) and Salend (2005).

We know from research (Arends, 2007; Berliner, 1986; Borko, Bellamy, & Sanders, 1992; Clark & Peterson, 1986; Cooper, 2006; Kauchak & Eggen, 2007; Lawler-Prince & Jones, 1997) that there are major differences in the planning process between new teachers and their more experienced counterparts. For example, experienced teachers have more pedagogical and subject-matter knowledge than new teachers; they also have more highly developed mental systems for organizing and storing this knowledge and use different strategies for solving problems. Consequently, experienced teachers process information more efficiently than new teachers do during each of the phases of teaching.

Experienced teachers are better able than new teachers to use their knowledge of children, content, and pedagogy to plan in their heads, making mental maps to guide their teaching and support children's learning. Their plans are more detailed and more richly connected to learning than those of novices. Experienced teachers include a greater number of student actions, teacher instructional moves, and routines for common classroom activities (Borko et al., 1992). Figure 8.11 compares and contrasts the differences between experienced and new teachers' planning.

FIGURE 8.11 Planning characteristics of experienced and new teachers.

Experienced Teacher	New Teacher
Before Teaching	**Before Teaching**
1. Has system for teaching successful lessons matched to unit and lesson topics previously used and modified (e.g., folders, files)	1. Focuses on detailed, written lesson plans and gathering resources
2. Uses extensive planning based on more pedagogical and content knowledge and better-developed conceptual organizers	2. Has limited mental plans and experiences to draw upon
3. Keeps lessons flowing through detailed mental planning to guide the direction of the learning	
During Teaching	**During Teaching**
1. Uses an extensive variety of teaching strategies to teach activities and lessons	1. Uses a limited repertoire of teaching strategies
2. Has well-defined beliefs about student learning and outcomes	2. Has untested and undefined pedagogical beliefs about student learning and content
3. Uses a great number of instructional and management routines and procedures, leading to more efficient responses	3. Uses a limited number of routines and procedures, causing extensive thinking and a focus on surface features of events
After Teaching	**After Teaching**
1. Uses an extensive array of teaching strategies to make content accessible to learners of varying abilities and backgrounds	1. Has a limited number of ways to make content accessible to learners of varying abilities and backgrounds
2. Attends to children's performance and interests	2. Attends primarily to children's interests

Elements of Effective Planning

A beginning teacher recently said to us, "Planning is the hardest thing I do. Be sure your preservice teachers learn how to plan well so they can have more control over their teaching in their own classrooms and with their planning teams." This teacher has a good insight into an important aspect of best practice: being able to articulate what she wants to do and how she will accomplish it. She will need this information in addition to various planning tools necessary to implement good learning experiences for children. In this section, we provide you with practical information on how to design purposeful long-term plans (e.g., integrated units and projects) and short-term plans (e.g., activities or lessons). We begin first with basic elements of both types of planning.

There are five key elements of appropriate planning: goals and objectives, processes and procedures, activities and lessons, assessment and evaluation, and differentiation. Each is important to the total planning process (Arends, 2007; Cooper, 2006; Jackman, 2005; Jensen & Kiley, 2005) and will be discussed in the following paragraphs.

TEACHER PREP WEBSITE 8.4

Go to Student and Teacher Artifacts, select Early Childhood Education, choose Curriculum Planning and Program (Module 4), and select Dear Mr. Lincoln (Social Studies K–2) (Artifact 5).

Dear Mr. Lincoln.
you were a great presadent. I'm glad you fre-d the slaves is it fun up there in hevin

Yours truly,
Jared

1. ***Goals and Objectives.*** Goals are broad purposes for learning (e.g., in science and math, a goal is to build on children's natural interests in the world), whereas objectives define the specific behavior, skill, or concept you wish the child to attain. Goals take into account learners' needs, the content to be learned, and the community values and interests. Whatever your goal, clearly identifying the purpose of a lesson or activity is necessary so you think about what children will learn. To view Jared's letter to Abraham Lincoln that illustrates his teacher's goals and objectives, look at the "Early Childhood Education–Curriculum Planning and Program" student and teacher artifacts online at the Teacher Prep Website. Objectives are specific behaviors that children will show as a result of their learning. They should answer the question, "What should children know and be able to do when this lesson, activity, or integrated unit is finished? Goals and objectives can be based on children's needs, abilities, or interests; they can also be based on curriculum standards and outcomes or can result from your observations and assessment.
2. ***Processes and Procedures.*** *Processes* are ways of thinking about and making sense of information. For example, children use the scientific processes of observing and classifying and the mathematical processes of measuring and counting to understand information; they use the reading processes of predicting and inferring to gain meaning from text. These basic process skills are necessary for conceptual understandings. *Procedures* are the steps you plan to take to teach a lesson. They include how you will introduce the lesson to access children's prior knowledge and gain their interest, how you will develop a lesson including the teaching strategies you will use to teach the content in an age-appropriate way, how you will group children, how you plan to meet individual children's needs, and how you will end the lesson to see what learning has occurred. Procedures should also include a way to help children transition to the next experience.
3. ***Activities and Lessons.*** These are specific learning experiences, designed by the teacher or together with a child or children, to meet the intended outcomes, goals, and objectives. The term *activity plan* is most commonly used at the prekindergarten level; the term *lesson plan* is most commonly used in the elementary grades. Whatever term is used, the activity or lesson should be worth doing and meet a particular outcome. For example, writing responses to literature in language arts, graphing family members in mathematics, and formulating hypotheses about plants in science are typical lessons and activities in early childhood. Effective planning requires that activities and lessons are age appropriate and match the abilities and skills of individual children in a group (Bredekamp & Copple, 1997). It also requires identifying resources and materials needed and deciding how to present these learning experiences to children (e.g., procedures and methods to be used). You can see first grade teacher, Susan McCloskey, using real materials from the book, *If You Give A Mouse A Cookie,* to enhance children's comprehension in the "Celebrating Learning" video clip online at the Teacher Prep Website.

Go to Video Classroom, select Classroom Management, choose Planning and Conducting Instruction (Module 3), and select Celebrating Learning (Video 1).

4. ***Assessment and Evaluation.*** These are methods and criteria you will use (e.g., rubrics, observation checklists, format for anecdotal record) to assess your stated objective(s) to determine what and how well children are learning. The methods used should provide a way to determine what children know and can do following the lesson or activity. The results of your assessment will help you to determine the next steps you will take and to revise your instruction based on children's performance and responses.

5. ***Differentiation.*** **Differentiation** is the way you adapt the activity or the lesson for individual learners based on assessment data that you have collected. It involves planning for children's different levels of interest, ability, and styles of learning in any given activity. To keep children engaged in the learning process, you will also want to be responsive to children's needs for more practice, more challenge, more independence, or a more active approach to learning (Tomlinson & Cunningham-Eidson, 2003).

Effective planning is an important part of your role in helping all children learn. In the next section, we discuss both long-term and short-term planning. We will also show you some models of different planning tools so that you have an idea of what these elements look like in a plan prepared by new teachers.

Long-Term Plans

There are primarily two kinds of long-term plans: integrated units of study and projects. Because these are extended plans, many teachers like to begin their planning by brainstorming possibilities using a web as a planning tool. Webbing is a way to brainstorm possible key concepts, ideas, and learning experiences and then connect them through a pictorial or graphic representation (Feeney et al., 2006; Jones & Nimmo, 1994; Katz & Chard, 2000). You may create a web around a topic (e.g., plants), subject areas (e.g., language arts, science), or program or school district goals (e.g., multicultural education, critical thinking). Figure 8.12 illustrates curriculum webs organized around "The Self" for preschool and kindergarten children; Figure 8.13 illustrates concept webs organized around "Famous Americans" for primary-grade children. Note that both webs are organized around concepts and subject areas. The following paragraphs describe planning specific to integrated units and projects.

Planning for Integrated Units

Integrated units involve a variety of planned learning experiences around a core concept. A core concept is a big idea, question, or problem that helps children make connections and further their understanding of the world around them. It has intellectual integrity, is relevant and meaningful, and represents in-depth thinking and problem solving that can be studied at different age or grade levels. Examples of core concepts include human relationships, patterns, processes of change, traditions and celebrations, and communities. How a concept is studied changes with the age, interests, background, and grade level of the children.

Unit planning should include both teachers and children. You will be using your knowledge of children (e.g., their interests, their prior knowledge, and their learning styles); you will also be utilizing your knowledge of curriculum (e.g., choosing content and learning experiences; selecting appropriate products) as well as your knowledge of teaching (e.g., using a variety of teaching strategies). Inviting children into the planning

FIGURE 8.12 Standards-Based, integrated concept and subject-area webs for preschool and kindergarten children.

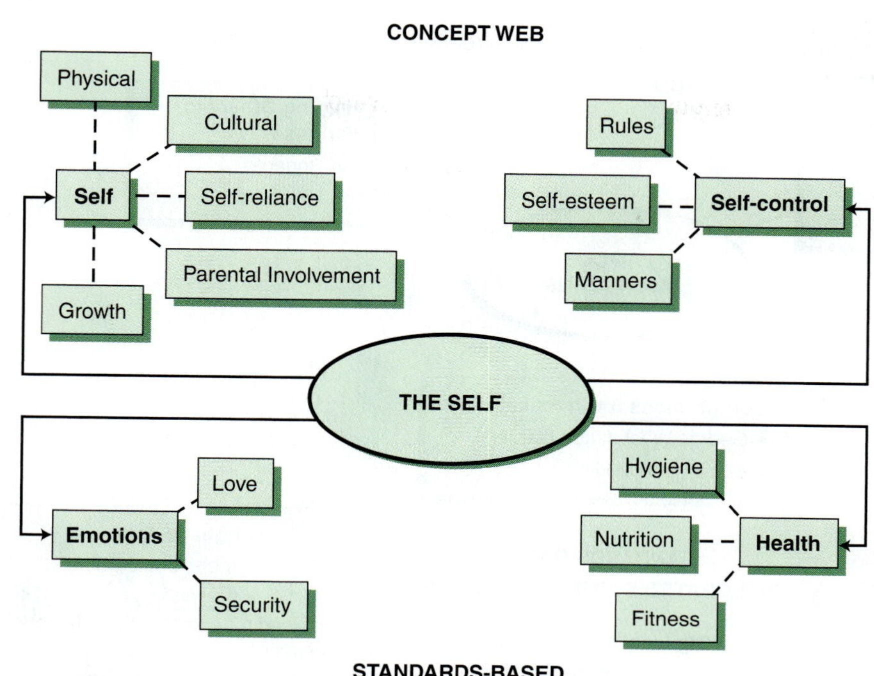

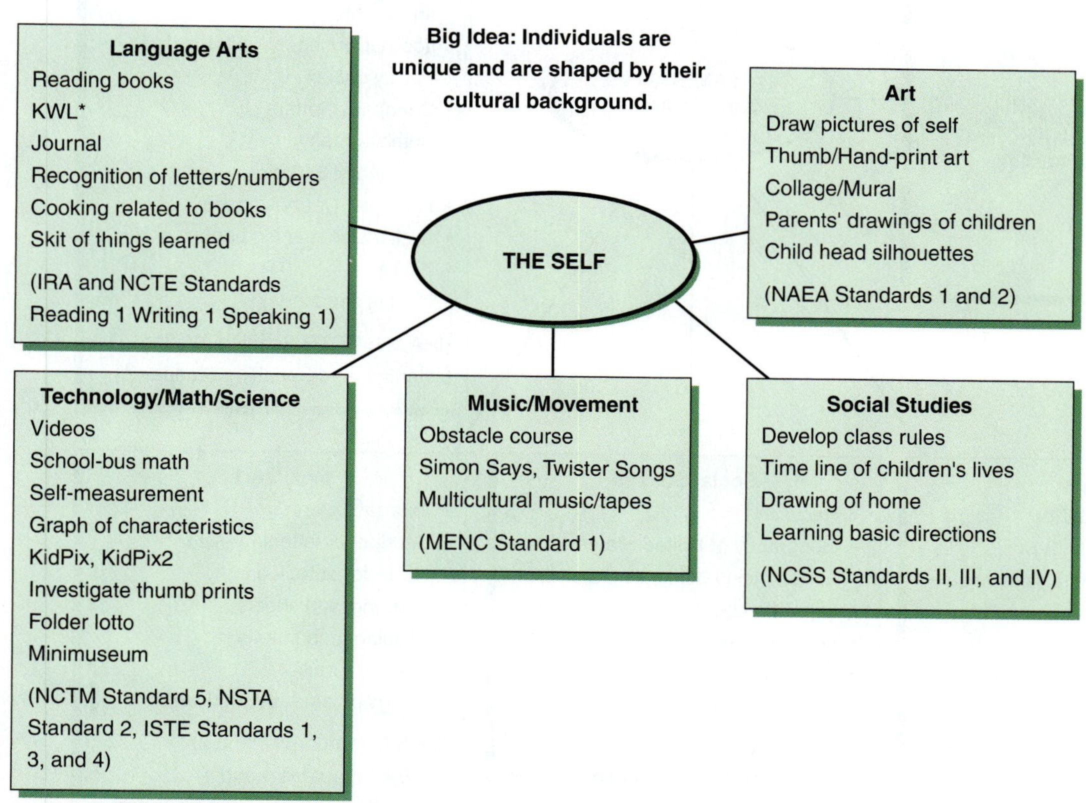

* What I Know, What I Want to Know, What I Learned.
SOURCE: Courtesy of George Mason University PDS interns.

FIGURE 8.13 Standards-Based, integrated concept and subject-area webs for primary-grade children.

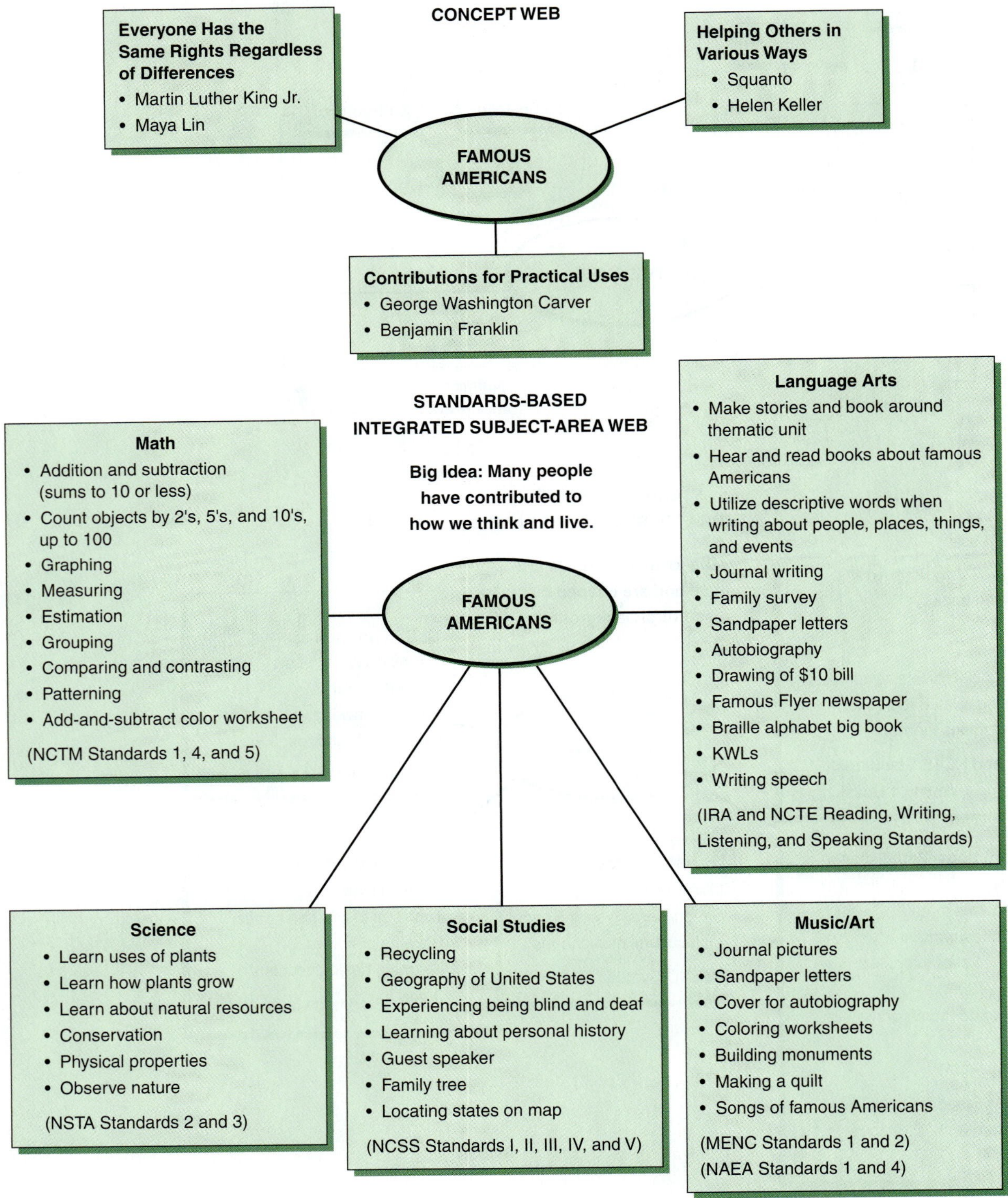

SOURCE: Courtesy of George Mason University PDS interns.

can lead to more meaningful activities, to the formation of a healthy learning environment, and to more active learning (Keefe & Jenkins, 2002).

The Ask the Expert feature by Marjorie Kostelnik answers questions about thematic units. (Recall, too, that Chapter 7 provided an extensive discussion of organizing a curriculum around concepts and themes.) Figure 8.14 provides an outline of the questions teachers should ask themselves to help them plan meaningful integrated units; the questions are answered in the context of the theme, Famous Americans, for which concept webs were provided in Figure 8.13. Figure 8.15 on pages 296–297 is a unit overview of a primary social studies unit developed to teach the concept of Past and Present.

Planning for Projects

Projects are planned, in-depth investigations of a topic worth learning about. The investigations are usually undertaken by a small group of children within a class, sometimes by a whole class, and occasionally by an individual child, about a topic posed either by the children, the teacher, or the teacher working with the children (Katz & Chard, 2000). The goal of a project is to learn more about the topic by applying higher-level thinking skills rather than to seek right answers to questions posed by the teacher. It epitomizes the collaborative nature of teaching, during which teachers and children think, plan, and evaluate together.

In the Ask the Expert feature on page 304, Jeanette Allison answers questions about the difference between thematic units and projects, selecting topics, and getting started on projects. For even more information and project approach examples for preK–K and grades 1–3, visit the website www.project-approach.com.

The following are steps to use when planning projects.

Phase 1: Getting Started

- Have several discussions to select and refine the topic. Topics must be (a) closely related to the children's experience, (b) integrated across subject areas, and (c) have enough depth to be explored for an extended time period.
- Brainstorm ideas with the children and make a web of the possible topics and subtopics for study. Invite children to ask questions they want to find answers to through investigation.

Phase 2: Field Work

- Provide many opportunities for direct investigation of the topic through field trips to places and for investigations of objects and people. In these investigations, children are learning from observing, constructing models, recording findings, predicting, discussing, and dramatizing their new understandings (Katz & Chard, 2000).

Phase 3: Culminating and Debriefing Events

- Children and their teacher(s) prepare and present the results of their investigations in the form of displays of findings and artifacts, talks, dramatic presentations, and/or guided tours of their constructions.

Planning for project work is not a one-time event. As children's needs and interests change and deepen, you can rebalance your curriculum by including project work

FIGURE 8.14 Steps to planning an integrated unit on Famous Americans.

1. **What is the core concept or big idea?**
   Many people have contributed to the way we think and live today.

2. **What standards will be addressed?**

   NCTM: Standards 1,4,5
   NSTA: Standards 2,3
   NAEA: Standards 1 and 4
   NCSS: Standards 1,2,3,4, and 5
   MENC: Standard 1 and 2
   IRA and NCTE: Reading, Writing, Listening, and Speaking Standards

3. **What is topic or unit focus?**
   The topic is Famous Americans. This is a required unit of study to meet state standards. The social studies goals are to increase student awareness of historically significant deeds from past generations. Children will learn about Martin Luther King Jr., Helen Keller, George Washington Carver, Benjamin Franklin, Maya Lin, and Squanto.

4. **What content areas will be integrated? What concepts will be explored?**
   The content areas are language arts, mathematics, science, social studies, art, and music.

   Other concepts are helping others and rights and responsibilities. Skills in each content area will be taught.

5. **What materials, resources, and field trips are needed?**

   Materials: peanuts and plants, Braille alphabet, books on these famous Americans, magazines, pencils, crayons, markers, scissors, glue, journal books, bandana, ear muffs, tag board and sandpaper, clay and play dough

   Resources: children and their families, guest speaker (person who uses Braille), school specialists, and community members; child- and teacher-made displays (e.g., class monument, sand letters, Earth friends made from recycled materials, and quilt replica)

   Multimedia: videos (Black Americans of Achievement series, *Squanto and the First Thanksgiving,* and *Franklin, What's the Big Idea?*)

   Software: Kid Pix, Make a Map

   Websites: Ben Franklin
   www.pbs.org/benfranklin

   Squanto and the Pilgrims' First Year in America
   http://www.bv229.k12.ks.us/vp_pilgrims/NEWWORLDWebsite.htm

   Martin Luther King Jr.
   http://www.lib.lsu.edu/hum/mlk/sns217.html

   Maya Lin
   http://www.greatbuildings.com/architects/maya_Lin.html

   Field Trips: National Museum of American History, neighborhood nature walk

FIGURE 8.14 Continued

6. **What is the culminating activity?**
Minimuseum containing exhibits of Braille alphabet letters and words, materials made from peanuts and sweet potatoes, kites with a key, map of places where Martin Luther King Jr. lived and visited

7. **How will the unit be introduced?**
KWL: Ask, "What makes a person famous?" "Whom do you know who is famous?"

8. **How will children's learning be assessed? How will the teacher's teaching be evaluated? How will the unit meet individual needs?**

Assessment Techniques: observation, recording, and documentation; anecdotal records; work samples and work folders; participation in project; skills tailored to individual needs

Teacher Self-Evaluation: reflective notes in journal, daily review of lessons and activities that are adapted for the next day

Differentiation: Children who exhibit particular interests may pursue those interests

periodically so that it reflects those changes. Additionally, be prepared to learn along with your children. Figure 8.16 on pages 299–301 provides an outline for a primary-grade project on gardening.

Short-Term Plans

Planning for daily or weekly learning experiences is what we refer to as short-term planning. Activity or lesson plans focus on a single teaching episode. In most preschool programs, the term *activity* is used for planning; in most primary and elementary grades, the term *lesson* is used. Both, however, have similar components. The term *activity* is preferred for younger children because it implies a less formal and rigid approach to learning. In this text, we make the distinction by age only.

PAUSE AND REFLECT
About Appropriate Planning

Read both Ask the Expert features in this chapter and then search the Internet for suggestions for projects and units. What did you find that would be useful to you in planning? What criteria will you use for judging the worthiness of units and projects located on the Internet? What questions do you still have?

Planning for Activities and Lessons

Activity and lesson plans provide the working documents of a program or classroom. At a minimum, the activity and lesson plans describe what is planned for that day, including the goals and objectives for the activities, the time frame within which they are to be carried out, and a means of assessment and evaluation. In addition, activity and lesson plans provide information about which teacher will be in charge of the activity, in what part of the classroom each activity is to be carried out, and what materials are needed. Although activity and lesson plans can take many forms, they should be complete enough so that any teacher can pick one up and know for any given day what is

FIGURE 8.15 Overview of social studies unit for primary grades.

TOPIC: Where we are in place and time
UNIT TITLE: *Schools—Past and Present*
FOCUS SUBJECT: Social Studies
LEVEL: Primary
BIG IDEA: People, places, and things change over time.
UNIT OBJECTIVE: SWBAT demonstrate knowledge that people, places, and things change over time.
UNIT STANDARDS: VA History Standard 1.1 and NCCS II.a

CULMINATING ASSESSMENT: Venn Diagram Quilt

	Day 1	**Day 2**	**Day 3**	**Day 4**	**Day 5**
Daily Topic, Theme, or Question	What is a school?	Why do we go to school?	Who makes our school work?	Old Fashioned School Day	School Architecture
Daily Objective	Students will be able to illustrate and label the elements that make up a school.	SWBAT attribute skills needed in society to skills they learn in school.	SWBAT explain the roles of the different people who make up our school.	SWBAT will describe elements in the past classroom that differ from their current classroom.	SWBAT produce representations of past and present school buildings.
Instructional Activity and SS Materials	KWL Chart Introduce Word Wall Picture sort—example and nonexample	Whole-class discussion and review of jobs in the community Think-Pair-Share of skills learned in school needed for jobs in the community.	Brainstrom with the class who makes up a school (must include students and teachers). Interview people around the school (head of school or principal, nurse, custodian, lunchroom staff, office staff).	Simulation of a penmanship lesson incorporating classroom practices including seating.	MM presentation on school buildings then and now. Picture sort of school buildings then and now.
Daily Assessment	Draw and label a school and at least 3 of its elements.	Oral presentation on at least 3 skills learned in school needed for jobs in the community.	Jigsaw interview findings and use anecdotal notes to record.	A *reflective* journal entry on 3 things students experienced that are different from the present classroom.	Create 2 quilt squares representing past (blue) and present (yellow) school buildings.

FIGURE 8.15 Continued

	Day 6	Day 7	Day 8	Day 9	Day 10
Daily Topic, Theme, or Question	Field Trip: Historical Schoolhouse	Artifacts	Schoolyard Games	Schools in Time	Wrap-Up and Reflection
Daily Objective	SWBAT identify features of school buildings in the past.	SWBAT locate and describe pictures of school artifacts.	Content: SWBAT differentiate between games children played in the past, games they play now, and games played in both eras. Process: SWBAT demonstrate the ability to participate in several schoolyard games.	SWBAT group people, places, and things on a timeline. SWBAT demonstrate an understanding of the past and present by reflecting on and choosing what would go into a time capsule.	SWBAT create a Venn diagram quilt that represents how people, places, and things change over time.
Instructional Activity and SS Materials	Photo scavenger hunt.	Opening of old time capsule. Read: A Country Schoolhouse. Locating pictures of old artifacts in the classroom library.	Large-group game (Simon Says). Game centers (marbles, jacks, hopscotch, and rock school).	Sort pictures and create a timeline. Students will *choose* 3 items to draw and drop in the time capsule.	Create and assemble Venn diagram quilt.
Daily Assessment	Photo display of features of school buildings in the past.	Present and describe findings to class.	Content: Worksheet that distinguishes between past, present, and games common to both. Process: Participation in the games.	Create a timeline showing past and present, including at least 1 person, place, or thing. Write a sentence describing each part of the timeline. Score time capsule item on appropriateness using checklist.	Quilt squares and teacher checklist.

SOURCE: Courtesy of George Mason University Fast Train Students (2006).

ASK THE EXPERT

Marjorie Kostelnik on Teaching Young Children Using Thematic Units

Marjorie Kostelnik

How do teachers choose topics that will make good themes?

Themes represent concepts. Concepts, such as children come from different types of families or plants grow from roots and stems, are big ideas supported by smaller bits of information such as terms, facts, and principles. Topics that do not meet these conceptual criteria lack substance and depth. This is exemplified by weekly plans centered on a letter of the alphabet, such as ***B.*** Since ***B*** is not a concept, it is a poor choice for a theme.

In addition to being *conceptual,* themes must be *relevant.* Relevant themes are directly tied to children's real-life experiences. Themes such as foods, night and day, homes, and backyard birds are relevant because they help children make sense of their lives and expand their understanding of life around them. Conversely, ancient Rome, the rain forest, and penguins are less relevant because these topics fall beyond most children's firsthand experiences.

Do teachers have to make every activity relate to the theme?

Some teachers have the mistaken impression that every activity must relate to the theme. This can be problematic for several reasons. First, not everything worth learning is theme related. Children need a wide array of learning opportunities; some of these easily fit the theme of the moment, others stand apart. Both kinds of experiences benefit children. Second, when the classroom is overly saturated by a given topic, the theme loses its appeal for children and adults alike. Youngsters, initially excited by the theme, grow weary of dealing with it at every turn, and children less interested in the topic have a hard time finding activities that genuinely excite their curiosity. To avoid these drawbacks, several non-theme-related activities should be interspersed throughout a unit plan. The most effective unit plans are ones in which children have several theme-related activities from which to choose each day as well as some other experiences that cover content or processes not addressed by the overall topic under study.

Can teachers plan a whole year of units in advance?

Planning units too far ahead overlooks an important criterion for effective planning: timeliness. Activities are timely when they build on children's current interests. Thus, units should take advantage of teachable moments. Children who discover an anthill on the playground and become curious about it are ripe for a unit on insects. Likewise, discovering that several children in a class will become older brothers and sisters during the year could prompt a unit on babies. The chance to tap children's interests as they become evident is lost if all the topics are mapped out for the year. It is reasonable to have a few standard themes or units to cover annually. However, it is also important for teachers to leave time for topics particularly suited to the children with whom they are currently working.

Many teachers use holidays to plan their thematic units. What do you think about this approach to planning?

Several potential problems accompany holiday themes. First, holiday themes run the risk of being little more than a convenient backdrop for classroom decorations and craft projects. Children usually come away from such experiences without having expanded their concepts or increased their

skills across the curriculum. This is not effective teaching. Second, there are many opportunities for children to learn holiday lore at home and through the community. The same cannot be said for other concepts such as spiders, homes, friends, or storytelling. Limiting holiday themes allows more attention to be paid to those concepts for which early childhood teachers can add richness, variety, and experiences not so easily obtained elsewhere. Third, the religious or cultural significance of certain holidays may be lost. For instance, the true importance of Easter may be overlooked in a flurry of bunny images and Easter baskets. Such simplistic approaches promote stereotypes and assume that every family celebrates particular holidays and that their celebrations are similar. None of these assumptions is in keeping with the cultural and religious sensitivity that early childhood professionals strive to achieve. Holiday activities may appropriately comprise some of the non-theme-related concepts in a given unit, such as family traditions or "people living together." These concepts are inclusive, not exclusive. They support children's growing awareness of the similarities as well as differences among people.

Marjorie Kostelnik is Dean of the College of Education and Human Sciences, University of Nebraska, Lincoln, Nebraska.

FIGURE 8.16 Outline for project on gardening for primary-grade students.

I. Project Title: Gardening (with a focus on the arts)

II. Objectives: Children will

- use the arts to communicate ideas about gardens and gardening
- use constructive, analytical, problem-solving, literacy, and oral-language skills
- explore a variety of materials and discuss their potential for making art associated with gardens
- develop interpersonal intelligence through collaborative and cooperative experiences

III. Planning Web

IV. Phase 1: Getting Started

Goal: To develop children's knowledge about and experiences with gardening and gardens

- Teacher-initiated KWL on gardens and gardening
- Books, poetry, and songs about gardens
- Artworks of gardens by other children and artists
- Paint own gardens
- Children interview families about types of gardens they have seen or had
- Journal writing about the kinds of gardens children would like to start
- Authentic props relating to gardens
- Visit gardens with class and families

Questions to assess prior knowledge:

- What does a garden need to grow?
- What animals would you expect to see in a garden?
- Who has a garden? Why?
- What else would you see in or near a garden?

FIGURE 8.16 Continued

Phase 2: Finding out about gardens through investigative activities

Field Visits: Field visits to community gardens (involve families); look for evidence of animals, identify types and purposes of gardens, observe and confirm predictions of gardens and surroundings, generate own questions and find out the answers

Classroom Activities:

Visual Arts:

- Use watercolors to imitate impressionists' paintings of gardens
- Use a variety of materials (e.g., Popsicle sticks, pebbles, bark) to construct a three-dimensional representation of each group's garden
- Observe and note details in paintings of gardens by several different artists
- Explore works of art featuring gardens from around the world via books, videos, photos, posters, and the Internet
- Provide authentic props (e.g., soil, water, pots, seeds, watering can) to create own minigardens

Construct:

- Decide where and how to construct a minigarden in the most suitable place
- Design and build birdbath for the garden
- Plan for obstacles (e.g., rain, lack of wind, unwanted pests)

Drama:

- Sing garden songs and create appropriate movements
- Retell stories through puppetry, miming, and readers theater
- Listen to garden sounds and enact them

Math:

- Graph numbers of each type of plant the class is growing
- Count how many pennies, nickels, dimes, and quarters children need for purchasing seed packets of their choice
- Sort seeds by color, size, and type

Science:

- Conduct experiments to see what happens when plants go without water
- Observe garden growth
- Examine plants to learn about their parts: leaves, stems, roots
- Observe an earthworm making its way through soil
- Reroot plant clippings in water and in soil to observe changes

Classroom Visitors and Resources:

- Local artists, museum curator, and resources on impressionist paintings
- Garden-shop employees, nursery employees, produce employees
- Architects and gardeners in the community to discuss upkeep
- Musicians from local community to explore musical movement through gardens
- Families and other resources on personal gardens that are different, have different needs and purposes
- Local community member who enjoys gardening
- Local farmers

Phase 3: Culminating Event (Choose from these possibilities)

- Field trip to a nearby farm to observe how gardens are constructed and maintained
- Family luncheon to view projects developed (e.g., minigardens), enjoy a tasting of fruits and vegetables planted, and exchange recipes of tasty dishes

FIGURE 8.16 Continued

- Family picnic during which families can view student art displays, seed-sorting graphs, slide show of children at work in their garden, displays of student-conducted experiments, and hear a retelling of *Stone Soup* by Ann McGovern

Assessment Strategies: (Choose from these possibilities)

- Share constructions
- Question individuals about projects
- Anecdotal records of children's participation during investigations
- Videotape and display children's work from projects
- Observe participation during culminating event with families
- Have children describe what they liked and did not like about planning and growing a garden
- Have children complete a participation chart (e.g., I Turned the Soil, I Picked Weeds, I Watered Plants) and graph responses

Children's Books:

Anderson, L., & Bjork, C. (1988). *Linnea's windowsill garden.* New York: R & S Books.
Carle, E. (1987). *The tiny seed.* Saxonville, MA: Picture Book Studio.
Chevalier, C. (1991). *Little green pumpkin.* New York: Bradbury.
Cole, H. (1995). *Jack's garden.* New York: Greenwillow.
Cooney, B. (1982). *Miss Rumphius.* New York: Viking.
Ehlert, L. (1988). *Planting a rainbow.* New York: Harcourt Brace Jovanovich.
Ehlert, L. (1994). *Red leaf, yellow leaf.* New York: Harcourt Brace Jovanovich.
Ernst, L. (1991). *Miss Penny and Mr. Grubbs.* New York: Bradbury.
Florian, D. (1991). *Vegetable garden.* New York: Harcourt Brace Jovanovich.
Ford, M., & Noll, S. (1995). *Sunflower.* New York: Greenwillow Books.
Krause, R. (1989). *The carrot seed.* New York: Harper Trophy Books.
Lionni, L. (1960). *Inch by inch.* New York: Astor-Honor.
McGovern, A. (1987). *Stone soup.*
Ryder, J. (1989). *Where butterflies grow.* New York: Dutton.
Zion, G. (1959). *The plant sitter.* New York: Harper & Row.

Teachers' References:

Bauer, K., & Drew, R. (1992). *Alternatives to worksheets K–4.* California: Creative Teaching Press.
Hart, A., & Mantell, P. (1996). *Kids garden! The anytime, anyplace guide to sowing and growing fun.* Charlotte, VT: Williamson.
Kite, P. (1995). *Garden wizardry for kids.* New York: Barron's Educational Series.
Muhlberger, R. (1993). *What makes a Monet a Monet?* New York: Viking.
Munro, E. (1961). *The encyclopedia of art.* New York: Golden Press.
Optical Data School Media. (1994). *Kinder ventures user guide for laser disc multimedia program.* One of five modules. "Out and about: Exploring plants, animals, and the environment." Warren, NJ: Author.
Raboff, E. (1987). *Art for children: Renoir.* New York: Harper & Row.
Roalf, P. (1993). *Looking at paintings: Flowers.* New York: Harper & Row.
Steele, M. (1989). *Anna's garden songs.* New York: Greenwillow.
Venezia, M. (1988). *Getting to know the world's greatest artist: Van Gogh.* Chicago: Children's Press.

NOTE: This project was developed by a group of early childhood Professional Development School interns. They were asked to develop a project with a focus on the arts.

FIGURE 8.17 Short and long forms of activity or lesson plans.

Short Form for a Lesson or Activity Plan

I. Activity or Lesson Plan	(What is the name of what you will teach?)
II. Lesson Overview	(What are the standards, goals, concepts, or skills you will teach?)
III. Teaching Procedures	(What will you do before, during, and after teaching?)
IV. Materials	(What materials, resources, and space do you need?)
V. Assessment	(How will you know what the children learned? How will you evaluate your own teaching?)
VI. Other Comments	(Is there anything specific you need to do for this lesson or activity?)

Long Form for a Completed Lesson or Activity Plan

I. Lesson Topic: Social Studies, Time and Place

II. Lesson Overview

A. *Concept:* People, places, and things change over time.

B. *Objectives:* The student will:
- identify elements of school buildings as past or present
- categorize school buildings as past or present

C. *Standards*:
- **VA history 1.1** . . . compare everyday life in different places and times, and recognize that people, places, and things change over time.
- **NCSS Standards II. a** . . . use correct vocabulary associated with time such as past, present, future, and long ago; identify examples of change.

III. Materials
- Photographs of school buildings, past and present, cut in half
- PowerPoint presentation with different types of school buildings past and present (downloaded from Internet)

IV. Procedures

Introduction (15 minutes)
- Gather students to review yesterday's lesson.
- Access prior knowledge about classroom practices in the past and how they differ from the present.
- Introduce topic of school buildings and architecture.
- Talk about school buildings and architecture, focusing on features of present and past school buildings and their similarities or differences.

Instructional Strategies

Activity 1 (8–10 minutes):
- Show PowerPoint presentation of past and present school buildings. Invite students to identify some elements of past school buildings (e.g., one-room

FIGURE 8.17 Continued

schoolhouse) through questions about the size and features of school buildings in the past/present.

Activity 2 (8–10 minutes):

- Provide each child with half a picture of a school building and have them find the person with the other half of their picture. Each pair must talk about and be prepared to tell the class why they believe that the building belongs to the past or present and describe at least two elements of old school buildings.
- Post their composite picture on the appropriate area of the board (past or present).
- Evaluate each other's work by deciding if the buildings have been categorized correctly.

Summary:

- Have children imagine past life in a one-room schoolhouse. Suggest elements of a schoolhouse in the past that would help with their imagery (e.g., lack of electricity, smell, discomfort of uniforms).
- Compare that with their experiences in their present school building. Use that experience for introduction during tomorrow's lesson.

Extensions:

- Categorize pictures of school buildings into past and present.
- Use Venn diagrams to organize similarities and differences between past and present school buildings. Use the classroom library to do research.

V. Assessment (15–20 minutes)

- Note children's knowledge of elements of past and present using anecdotal records.
- Note children's use of correct vocabulary related to time and understanding of changes over time.

VI. Differentiation

Students with more advanced writing skills can write sentences describing their school building. Students with less advanced writing skills can orally describe their school building and the teacher can scribe for them.

SOURCE: Courtesy of Anne Eileen Gomez, George Mason University, Fast Train Program, Fairfax, VA.

planned and why it is planned. Figure 8.17 shows two lesson planning forms. The first is a very short form providing the basic information; the second is a longer, standards-based form that contains all elements of effective planning as discussed earlier in this chapter. Both forms can be used for different purposes.

COMPANION WEBSITE 8.5 To add a professional development product to your developing portfolio, go to *Journal: Constructing Your Professional Portfolio* in Chapter 8 of the Companion Website at http://www.prenhall.com/jalongo.

Planning for Diverse Learners

All early childhood teachers must plan for the needs of diverse learners. Classrooms today include children from a variety of cultural, linguistic, and ethnic backgrounds, children with exceptionalities, children who are at risk for school failure, children who are

ASK THE EXPERT

Jeanette Allison on the Project Approach

Jeanette Allison

What is the difference between projects and units?

This is the most frequently asked question, because projects and units appear to be similar. However, understanding the uniqueness of both approaches provides for more effective project work. Units have overlapping characteristics with projects and therefore can be natural stepping stones to project work. Projects and units differ in how much emphasis is placed on: investigation, inquiry, conceptual understanding, children's questions and input, problem solving, real-life artifacts, internal motivation, self-control, choice, creativity, time, and flexibility. For example, projects allow for more inquiry, understanding, curiosity, choice, and time investigating phenomena. Units have more predetermined outcomes and timeliness that the teacher monitors closely. Units are often implemented similarly each year and usually on a predictable schedule each month, while projects change yearly. Another distinction between projects and units is that units tend to emphasize activities more than the children. Projects cause children to question deeply and examine thoroughly real-world, "right-here" phenomena.

How do you suggest that a teacher start a project?

The first step in starting a project is choosing a topic. Find out what children want to investigate. Notice their interactions, activity preferences, and conversations. During group time, consult with children about things they would like most to explore. Together, decide on major milestones and events and initial plans. For example, I implemented a project with children that originated from a construction site next to the school. Daily, children scampered over to the windows and monitored the site. When I observed them closely, I began to appreciate their curiosity, and I asked, "Would you like to find out what is happening at the construction site?" From there, our project began. Within 5 weeks, the project's focus changed from construction site to house to post office to laundromat to hospital. The overall focus, then, was on a community. Our major theme was structures.

How do you choose topics?

It is crucial to base topics on what children want to investigate. When the project approach is new to teachers, it may be helpful to begin with starter topics with which the teachers feel comfortable. But it is imperative that teachers quickly move away from teacher-determined topics. True benefits of project work cannot be realized until children are integral to the process from the outset. Their topic preferences are linked directly to the long-term motivation needed to sustain project work. Teachers must choose topics that focus on *concepts,* such as underlying meaning and ideas, rather than primarily on facts and trivia. Instead of randomly studying about pets, for example, begin with a more focused idea, such as "people who take care of pets," guided by the overall theme of interdependence, or "what pets need to survive," centered on the theme of survival. Finally, topics must relate to children's lives because learning is determined largely by what they know and want to know.

Is the project approach unstructured?

At first glance, projects appear chaotic and goalless. Projects are less structured than traditional teaching because they follow the natural and necessary shifts in children's interests and learning. If a teacher does not begin with a concept-based theme, such as systems or communication, and consider

major goals ahead of time, the project can be rather rocky. The goals and purposes of the project approach help children develop useful knowledge, skills, and attitudes about their world. Project activities help children understand their roles in the world and what the world has to offer them. Children develop research skills throughout a project's three main phases. Each phase's length depends on what is being investigated, children's wonderments, and teachers' resources and responsibilities.

Jeanette Allison is a consultant in early childhood education and intervention and resides in Visalia, California.

coping with undue amounts of stress, and children who have special gifts and talents. All children, regardless of background, must develop academic skills and learn to become full participants in the day-to-day life of the classroom. Although the way this is accomplished and developed will vary from child to child, all teachers must have high expectations of their students, believe that all children can learn, and plan to meet the needs of diverse learners. See Figure 8.10 in this chapter for specific planning strategies to meet the needs of culturally and ethnically diverse learners, English language learners, and children with exceptionalities.

The decisions you make when you plan will greatly affect child outcomes and your behavior in the classroom. Keeping these strategies in mind will increase your success as a planner for diverse learners. You will have the opportunity to examine some types of planning in the In-Class Workshop at the end of this chapter.

Conclusion

Planning provides the framework for teaching and learning and will probably require many adaptations along the way. Planning for the education of children should be based on a blend of theory and practice that reflects how children grow and learn. It should always acknowledge children as active and creative learners (Arends, 2007; Bowman, Donovan, & Burns, 2000; Kauchak & Eggen, 2007; National Association of Elementary School Principals, 1998). Planning well makes the uncertainties of teaching easier to handle. To achieve the best outcomes for children, you must become skilled in the various techniques of planning. When planning, always ask yourself: "Why am I asking children to do this activity or lesson?" "How will what I am doing help my children become better learners?" and "Will this lesson or activity help children learn a concept, skill, or strategy, or will they simply be completing a task?" Having high yet realistic expectations for each child is the hallmark of effective planning that leads to positive outcomes for young children.

COMPANION WEBSITE 8.6 To test your knowledge of this chapter's contents, go to the *Multiple-Choice* and *Essay* modules in Chapter 8 of the Companion Website at http://www.prenhall.com/jalongo. These items are written in the same format that you will encounter in the PRAXIS tests to better prepare you for your licensure exam.

ONE CHILD, THREE PERSPECTIVES

Shayna Goes to Kindergarten

Shayna was a kindergartner who was curious and quick to learn but had difficulty adjusting to large groups of children and large-group activities. Shayna's teacher had been teaching for 25 years in a rigorous, skills-based kindergarten program with lots of group work. Each day, the children completed many papers. According to Shayna's teacher, the more papers they completed, the more it meant that everything was running smoothly. Shayna, who was already reading and speaking two languages, was spending her days coloring pictures, cutting them apart, and gluing them in sequence. She also spent large amounts of time circling pictured objects beginning with the same letter, and then coloring all the pictures.

One day, as usual, Shayna's kindergarten teacher had given the children ditto sheets and workbook pages to complete and she insisted that the children remain quiet while they worked on them. Suddenly, Shayna started to chant softly, "*Boring, boring, boring*" and one of her classmates began to tap in rhythm to the words with a fat crayon. Soon, every child took up the chant, and like penitentiary prisoners, "BORING, BORING, BORING" grew louder and louder. The teacher was incensed! Shayna was marched down to the principal's office and her parents were called, because Shayna had "started a kindergarten revolt"!

In a conference between Shayna's teacher and parents, Shayna's parents questioned why Shayna was doing these activities that seemed meaningless to her. Shayna's teacher reminded them that Shayna needed to conform to the kindergarten program and that these activities were expected of all kindergarten children; Shayna's behavior in the group was simply unacceptable, she said. Her parents were concerned that Shayna, already labeled the class clown, would lose interest and enthusiasm for kindergarten and learn that school was boring.

If Shayna's teacher had planned her curriculum with Shayna's needs, interests, and abilities in mind, she might have planned some meaningful activities for Shayna to do: Her planning decisions should have been different. Shayna's teacher should have planned for Shayna in three different ways. Before each activity, she should have considered what Shayna brought with her to school—her culture, her family background, the influences of her community, and her prior experiences—and what kind of grouping pattern would work best for Shayna. During each activity, Shayna's teacher should have noticed Shayna's reactions and interactions with the work and with her peers. After the lessons, Shayna's teacher should have evaluated Shayna's intellectual, behavioral, and attitudinal outcomes, as well as unintended effects. Taken together, that would constitute the whole of what we mean by planning.

But Shayna's teacher assumed that it was her job to get Shayna ready for first grade by teaching her with small, digestible pieces of information. Shayna's teacher felt obligated and pressured to cover the material and get every child on track by conforming to the demands of the written material. She believed that if her students were quiet and diligent, they would fit in with the school culture in which she worked.

REACT	Think about how the perspectives of Shayna, her parents, and Shayna's teacher are alike and different. What might be some reasons? With whom do you most closely identify, and why?
RESEARCH	Shayna's teacher is using the direct instruction model of teaching. Compare this way of teaching with the strategies for meeting the needs of diverse learners listed in Figure 8.10 and the use of units and projects as described by Marjorie Kostelnik and Jeanette Allison in the Ask the Expert features in this chapter. How could Shayna's teacher have planned to better meet Shayna's needs and still hold true to her beliefs that she was covering the material and getting Shayna ready for first grade? Search the Internet and find support for your rationale.
REFLECT	What alternatives does Shayna's teacher have in planning to meet Shayna's needs and keep her engaged in learning?

IN-CLASS WORKSHOP

Planning for Diverse Learners

Planning for diverse learners requires the teacher's thoughtful attention to expected outcomes for all children. All teachers must be able to adapt their instruction to accommodate the needs of diverse learners, such as attending to children's cultural and linguistic backgrounds; children's special gifts, talents, and exceptionalities; and children who are at risk of school failure. Thus, a "one size fits all" approach to teaching will clearly be ineffective, as will writing individual learning plans for each child. What, then, does a teacher do to plan for diverse learners?

Think about an activity or lesson you have taught or have seen taught as part of a larger unit and complete a planning matrix for that lesson. Divide a sheet of paper into two columns. Label the left-hand column **"What was done well"** and the right-hand column **"What can be done more effectively to meet diverse learning needs."** Now, use the guidelines discussed in the section "Your Role as a Planner" on page 273 of this chapter and the strategies for meeting needs of diverse learners in **Figure 8.18** to examine the following planning elements and discuss each of the categories. In small groups, discuss (a) the strategies you used in initial planning, (b) strategies designed to meet the needs of specific diverse learners (e.g., children who have difficulty maintaining attention, children who are English language learners, children who are academically gifted, or children who are academically challenged), and (c) any information that you have that does not fit on the chart. Finally, discuss the strategies you might use to compile your planning matrix into a classroom chart that allows for easy access to implementation. How do you think a planning matrix contributes to improving the learning of all children? Explain why you believe your adaptations are likely to be helpful to the learners.

FIGURE 8.18 Planning matrix.

Grade Level ______________________________

Lesson Topic ______________________________

Unit Topic ______________________________

Planning for Lesson or Activity Components

A. Planning for Learners

1. Consider the interests, developmental abilities, and cultural backgrounds of your group of children.
2. Consider developmental milestones and learning sequences.
3. Think about children who have difficulty remaining engaged.
4. Nurture the child's self-identity within the context of the group activity.
5. Account for children who have difficulty beginning or completing tasks.
6. Note children who have difficulty organizing themselves and/or their thinking.

B. Planning the Content and Objectives

Be sure that the **content**:

1. Is worthwhile.
2. Provides for cultural diversity.
3. Allows for student choice and student interests.

Be sure that your **objectives**:

4. Are connected to a key concept.
5. Are meaningful to your students and have real-world applications.
6. Describe appropriate learning outcomes.

C. Planning Learning Experiences

1. The experiences support student learning.
2. The materials help children work independently and in small groups.
3. Some materials utilize technology.
4. The activities incorporate cultural information.
5. The activity is sensitive to the needs and values of the children and families of the children in that classroom.
6. Materials and equipment are in ample supply and meet the developmental level of the children being served.

D. Planning for Assessment, Evaluation, and Documentation

1. The objective or outcome for the lesson has a means of assessment.
2. The assessment lets you know what the children know and can do.
3. The assessment lets you know what misconceptions still remain.
4. There is documentation of children's understanding of the big ideas, skills, and attitudes.

E. Planning for Differentiation

1. Consider children's readiness to learn the content.
2. Consider children's interests as a motivator.
3. Consider the way children learn best.
4. Make adaptations for individual learners.

CHAPTER 9

Exploring Your Role in Documenting and Assessing Children's Learning

> The movement for standards-based education has had a powerful impact on policy and practice. But it has done little to address the primary mission of schools—the preparation of the young for success in childhood, adolescence, and adult life. To function adequately across the life span, children and youths need formative experiences that aid their growth and development along the physical, social-interactive, social-emotional, moral-ethical, linguistic, and cognitive pathways. . . . The standards movement focuses primarily on teaching subject matter, on achievable outcomes as measured by test scores, and on accountability sanctions; it does not stress development.
>
> James P. Comer, 2006, p. 59

Meet the Teachers

LAURIE NICHOLSON is a nursery school teacher who works with 3-year-olds. When Nam Sun, a newly immigrated child, enrolled in her class, she sought to welcome him into the group and to communicate with him despite the fact that he did not speak English. At the end of the day, when children were leaving, Laurie would often kneel down, give them a hug, and say, "See you tomorrow!" But Laurie was sensitive to the fact that hugging the teacher was not a part of Nam Sun's school departure ritual. One day when Nam Sun's mother came to pick him up after school, he paused in the doorway and bowed to Laurie. Laurie bowed back. The 3-year-old's face registered great surprise and delight, and he dashed to his mother's side, smiling and speaking in a very animated way. Then he paused, turned around, came slowly back to his teacher, raised his open arms, and looked at her. Laurie bent down and hugged Nam Sun, to his obvious delight. About this incident, Laurie remarked, "I will remember forever the day we learned to say good-bye in two languages" (Jalongo & Isenberg, 1995).

MAGGIE POMPA is completing the second half of her student teaching internship in a first-grade class. One of her insights was that she needed a better system of assessment than what she observed in others. In speaking with her university faculty supervisor, Maggie said, "Most teachers seem to depend on their recollections, paper-and-pencil tests, and children's products to determine how a child is doing. I need a more systematic approach to collecting such information. What happens if records are not kept on a consistent basis and there is a parental question or a legal issue? I need the sort of documentation that will give me confidence in whatever I am reporting." Fortunately, she was able to visit with several teachers who had such systems in place and were willing to share their ideas. The system that appealed to her most is multifaceted and includes observational notes, checklists, interviews, formal assessment, and carefully selected samples of students' work.

MR. DEMARINES, the principal of an elementary school, called a staff meeting last year to discuss a schoolwide assessment plan. Although many of the teachers were maintaining purposeful, well-organized collections of children's portfolios, Mr. DeMarines thought it would be useful to have reading and writing portfolios that would accompany children as they progressed from one year to the next. The goals of a schoolwide literacy portfolio system would be to inform others about what each child can do and to build students' skills in self-assessment. After a year of hard work, the principal speaks with pride about the system now in place: "It gives teachers a clearer idea of what children can do with language than a test score ever could. It also prepares teachers to conduct informative and well-planned conferences with parents and families."

COMPARE	What are some commonalities among the assessment practices of these three educators, even though the first is focused on a single child, the second on her overall assessment practices, and the third on a schoolwide program?
CONTRAST	How do these educators think about assessment? How would you characterize the outlook of each one?
CONNECT	In these scenarios, what made the greatest impression on you, and how will you incorporate this into your teaching?

Now that you have reflected on the perspectives of three different teachers, here is a preview of the knowledge, skills, and dispositions you will need to acquire in order to fulfill your role in assessing young children's learning and documenting their progress.

Learning Outcomes

- ✔ Become familiar with national standards and guidelines governing the early childhood educator's role in assessment of children's learning and program effectiveness **(NAEYC #3, INTASC #8, and ACEI #4)**
- ✔ Examine assessment issues and practices affecting young children
- ✔ Understand the purposes of assessment and delineate ways of sharing assessment information with families
- ✔ Develop skills for observing, recording, and analyzing information about children's learning and development
- ✔ Identify and describe the principles of performance assessment
- ✔ Understand the components of a balanced assessment program

Assessment Defined

Suppose that you were going to apply for a $10,000 scholarship and the application procedure required a 1,000-word essay about your reasons for pursuing a career in early childhood education. Think about what you would want to know before beginning to write your essay. You would probably be wondering about the following things:

COMPANION WEBSITE 9.1 To learn more about observing, documenting, and evaluating children's learning, go to *Journal: Defining Your Role* in Chapter 9 of the Companion Website at http://www.prenhall.com/jalongo.

Competition: How many people usually apply?
Standards: What criteria will be used to evaluate the essays?
Format: How is the final copy of the essay to be prepared?
Support: Is there a previous recipient of the scholarship I can talk with to get some pointers?
Outcomes: When and in what way will the applicants be notified of the results?

Similar questions about competition, standards, format, support, and outcomes are raised when young children enter school. Parents wonder, "How is my child doing in

DID YOU KNOW...?

- The current preoccupation with standardized testing in the United States began in the 1980s with reports, such as *A Nation at Risk,* claiming that U.S. education was in decline (Rotbert, 2001).
- According to a national poll, 81% of parents believe that students achieve only a small part of their potential (Rose & Gallup, 2007).
- The best predictor of student achievement in reading and mathematics is the level of teacher preparation and certification of the teachers (Darling-Hammond, 2000).
- "Summer loss"—the decline in children's achievement after the summer break—is greatest for children of low socioeconomic status (SES). While middle- or high-SES children tend to engage in varied learning experiences (e.g., museums, fairs, parks, sports, camping, private lessons), the out-of-school resources for low-SES children are not adequate to support their achievement (Alexander, Entwisle, & Olson, 2001).
- In 2001, President George W. Bush signed the No Child Left Behind (NCLB) Act. This law launched the national standards and testing movement (U.S. Department of Education, 2004). NCLB now requires children to be tested every year in third through seventh grade.
- "NCLB has placed a special burden on early childhood education—for it is widely believed that academic careers are made or broken in the early grades, when a child either learns to read well, poorly, or not at all. The standards movement has resulted in a barrage of testing; millions of teacher-hours spent aligning curriculum to standards and tests, and a huge range of remediation packages in both traditional and online formats" (Tolbert & Theobald, 2006, p. 271).
- NCLB subjects schools that do not perform well on the national tests to sanctions. In some cases, low-performing schools will be "taken over" and operated from a business model, called a charter school, in an effort to solve the problem of academic standards and standardized tests. Thus far, this has occurred in several large urban districts (Neill, 2001).
- A national study of early childhood education reported that 16 states and the District of Columbia require diagnostic/developmental tests for pre-K programs, and 17 states plus The District of Columbia require diagnostic tests for kindergarten students (Editors of *Education Week,* 2002).
- In one study of an ethnically diverse group of parents, Diamond, Reagan, and Bandyk (2000) identified three clusters of skills necessary for kindergarten success: (1) listening, feeling confident, following directions; (2) counting, reading, and writing; (3) enthusiasm, effective communication, and appropriate behaviors.
- Different linguistic and cultural groups should be involved during a test's development. In addition, the examiner's manual should provide both separate scoring scales for specific groups and suggestions for modifying the assessment/interpreting the results in ways that consider the cultural or linguistic backgrounds of children (McLean, 2000).

comparison to other children? Will the teacher evaluate my child fairly? What types of information and work samples will be used to assess my child's performance? If my child is experiencing difficulty, what assistance is available? How will I be kept informed about my child's progress?" These concerns of parents and families not only have educational implications, they also have social and ethical consequences for the child. That is why assessment is such an important issue for you as an early childhood educator.

What is assessment in early childhood? The National Association for the Education of Young Children defines assessment in early childhood as "the process of observing, recording, and otherwise documenting the work children do and how they do it, as a basis for a variety of educational decisions that affect the child" (Bredekamp & Rosegrant,

Anthony Magnacca/Merrill

Learning to say "good bye" in two languages is an example of an appropriate anecdotal assessment.

1992, p. 22). Teachers use assessment procedures to determine the degree to which an individual child possesses a particular attribute (Gullo, 2006b, p. 139).

Assessment should not be used to label children, categorize them, define them as failures, or deprive them of intellectually stimulating opportunities. At its most basic level, "assessment is the ability to see children, to perceive what they can do in the hope of understanding how they learn" (Brainard, 1997, p. 163). At its best, assessment should help to inform instructional decisions, result in benefits to the child and family, and relate to what the child is learning in school. Four main purposes for assessment in early childhood are to *plan instruction for individuals and groups of children*, to *communicate with parents and families* about the progress of individual children, to *identify children and families* who need specialized programs and support services, and to *evaluate the effectiveness and quality* of early childhood programs and services. Figure 9.1 describes the purposes of assessment in greater detail.

Early childhood assessment is fulfilling its purpose when it: (1) has a specific and appropriate purpose, (2) the assessments are reliable and valid, (3) the assessment tasks are suited to the young child's developmental level in both content and means of data collection, (4) the assessment takes children's linguistic and cultural differences into

FIGURE 9.1 Purposes of assessments.

Overarching Goals of Assessment

- to better understand children's overall development
- to monitor children's progress through the curriculum
- to identify children who are at risk for academic failure or who may need special education services (Gullo, 2006a)

For Children and Families

- to assess the value or worth of the program
- to determine whether program goals are being met
- to make planning decisions
- to report to parents on the progress of individual children or the school
- to make decisions about support services for children
- to help children build skills in self-evaluation

For Early Childhood Practitioners

- to obtain feedback on ways to improve teaching
- to gather, organize, and interpret information about children's abilities and interests
- to identify steps to meet individual needs

ASK THE EXPERT

Sue Wortham on Assessment

Sue Wortham

Should standardized tests be used with young children?

There are circumstances when standardized tests can be used appropriately with young children. Children who have developmental disabilities or a lack of experiences with concepts and language might need to be assessed using a standardized test. There are individual tests to determine if a child needs to be served in an intervention program in the preschool years. Other strategies, such as observation and parental reporting, should be part of the evaluation process. It should be remembered, however, that most children in the preschool years should not be administered standardized tests, particularly to determine if a child is accepted for a preschool program or is screened to determine if she can move to the next level or be retained in a prekindergarten or kindergarten program. There is national concern about the practice of placing young children in transitional or junior first-grade classes because a standardized test has determined that they are not "ready" for first grade. Preservice teachers need to remember that standardized tests can have weaknesses and cannot necessarily be relied on to measure individual student development and achievement. The younger the child, the more likelihood that results of a standardized test are inaccurate.

What are some appropriate assessment strategies that can be used with young children?

Observation is a primary source for assessing young children. This is because watching children at play or working on classroom tasks can reveal much more about their development than a formal test. Teachers can observe all domains of development while children are engaged in daily activities. Teachers can use checklists and interviews with children to acquire information about their understanding of concepts and topics being studied in the classroom. They can also collect samples of the children's work and organize the work into portfolios. This can provide the teacher, student, and parent with a longitudinal record of a child's progress through writing samples, artwork, photographs of projects, and other examples of the child's accomplishments.

What is performance assessment?

Performance assessment is evaluation of what a student can both understand and use. For example, if a teacher gives a student a work page on simple addition and the student answers the problems correctly, then the teacher knows the student understands how to complete addition problems. But if the student is asked to refer to a grocery ad and correctly determine how much would be spent purchasing the items on a shopping list, then the child has demonstrated both knowledge and application. There are different types of performance assessments. A student who demonstrates how to conduct a science experiment or shows a group of peers how to arrange puzzles and construction toys on a shelf correctly is demonstrating both understanding and application. With young children, observation, work samples, and project products are some possibilities for performance assessment. Performance assessment can also be called authentic assessment because the student is being assessed in a real-life or purposeful activity.

What is the connection between assessment and instruction?

The common understanding of assessment has been as a tool to determine student achievement and progress. However, it has been perceived as a way to determine how well students have learned in order to give grades on a report card. It is sometimes not understood that the primary reason for assessment is

to guide the teacher in planning for classroom activities and instruction. All assessments, including performance and portfolio assessments, should be used to determine a child's progress and to plan experiences that will further that progress. The assessments should reflect how well instruction and classroom activities assisted the child in accomplishing learning objectives designed by the teacher. If a variety of types of assessment have been used, the teacher, parents, and child should be able to understand and describe how the child has demonstrated development and learning.

Sue Wortham is Professor Emerita of Early Childhood and Elementary Education, University of Texas at San Antonio, Texas.

PAUSE AND REFLECT

Assumptions About Early Childhood Assessment

What ideas do you have about assessment? Is it possible that your ideas reflect those of the general public rather than those of a professional educator? Before you read on, make a list of your assumptions about assessment during early childhood. After reading the chapter, revisit this list and consider how the newly acquired information has affected your thinking.

account, (4) the results are used to benefit the child, and (5) the process values families and effectively communicates assessment data to them (Gullo, 2006).

Your Role as an Evaluator

One of the worst things that anyone could say about you as a teacher is that you identify favorite children in the group who receive preferential treatment. At first, this might seem out of the question, because you imagine a blatant instance of favoritism, such as a teacher's pet. But unfair assessment practices can creep into your practice in unanticipated ways. It might consist of expecting more from children who live in a wealthy neighborhood and less from children who live in housing projects. It might be allowing a few more seconds for one child to respond to a question and jumping in sooner for another child. Or, inequity might be expressed by giving a second chance to a child whose family is very vocal and involved in the school program while immediately reprimanding a child whose family is uninvolved in school events. Effective early childhood educators have a strong commitment to equity and fairness. It is this conviction that forms the foundation for assessment practices.

COMPANION WEBSITE 9.2 To learn more about your role as an observer and evaluator and the NAEYC, go to *Web Links* in Chapter 9 of the Companion Website at http://www.prenhall.com/jalongo.

As a teacher, your assessment practices should be "a means to find out what children know, can do, and care about" (Smith & Goodwin, 1997, p. 117). Early childhood teachers are expected to be competent in a number of areas related to assessment practices (McAfee & Leong, 2007); these are discussed in the following paragraphs.

Recognizing Unethical, Illegal, and Otherwise Inappropriate Assessment Methods and Uses of Assessment Information

Confidentiality is an important aspect of assessment (Mindes, 2007). Clearly, it is entirely inappropriate for a teacher to sit in the lunchroom with colleagues and remark about a child, "What can you expect? He got the lowest score on the reading readiness test in the entire class . . . and everyone knows what his family is like." Such public pronouncements are likely to taint everyone's opinion of that child's abilities and do irreversible reputational damage to the family. When the child moves on to the next grade level, his teacher probably will recall some of these negative remarks and expect to experience difficulty with the child. If such negative remarks were overheard

Alan Oddie/PhotoEdit Inc.

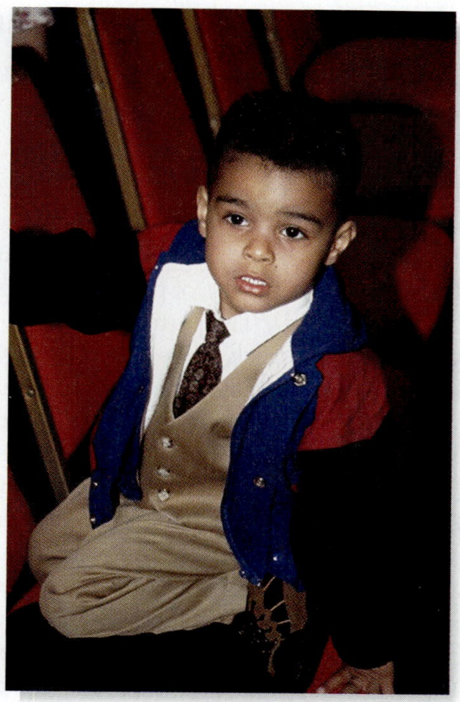
James L. Shaffer

Effective teachers try not to let a child's appearance influence expectations for achievement.

in conversation outside the school, it would be even worse, and it would reflect unfavorably on the teacher and on the entire school. Part of becoming a professional is knowing when to keep quiet and protect confidentiality. A useful guideline in making these decisions is to ask yourself how you would feel about a member of your family being treated in this way. If your sibling or child had scored low on a test, would you want it known by anyone who happened to pass by in the grocery store or broadcasted to every teacher in the school? Without a doubt, professional information can be shared in unprofessional ways with colleagues and with other members of the community; you must guard against such unprofessional behavior in yourself.

Choosing and Developing Appropriate Assessment Methods

Early childhood educators must carefully consider children's rights, the purposes for assessment, and the corresponding methods (Puckett & Black, 2000). Take, for example, the assessment of children's visual acuity. It is important to be well informed about different types of visual impairments, corrective measures, and, for impairments that cannot be corrected, ways of adapting materials and the curriculum to accommodate children's needs. Yet it is not cost-effective to subject every child to an exhaustive vision evaluation. Under these circumstances, most schools conduct a vision screening. The purpose of a screening is to detect the presence or absence of a problem and, if a problem exists, to make recommendations for more in-depth evaluation. Thus, children are given several different vision evaluation tasks administered by trained volunteers and are then referred to eye-care professionals if the quick screening instrument suggests that there might be a problem. This is an example of choosing an appropriate assessment method. It has the children's best interests at heart, it serves the purpose of making appropriate referrals to eye-care specialists, and it uses an efficient and cost-effective method of providing the needed level of service to all children.

Administering, Scoring, and Interpreting the Results of Various Assessment Methods

Teachers are notorious for carrying tote bags full of students' work back and forth between home and school. If you could look inside student teacher Tina Hidalgo's bag, you would see illustrated math problems that her first graders invented by working with a partner. They used the folktales and nursery rhymes with which they were already familiar to develop math sentences, then they represented them pictorially. One pair of children drew three bears, three bowls of porridge, three chairs, and three beds along with the equation $3 + 3 + 3 + 3 = ?$ The partners were also responsible for figuring out the correct answer, writing it on the back of the page, signing their names, and evaluating their number sentences using a simple ☺ or ☹. As Tina analyzes these papers, she does much more than mark the answers right or wrong and hand out stickers or stars. Rather, she analyzes children's errors, makes notes about what to teach next, and plans for minilessons with small groups of children who share the same misunderstandings. Just think of how much more Tina knows about her students' abilities than the teacher who gives a timed test on math facts! Not only can she see their mathematical reasoning from concrete drawings to abstract equations, but she also can tell if they are learning to use mathematical symbols and even find out something about their literacy skills, because the problems are based on the class's prior knowledge of stories. Varied assessment methods developed and evaluated by teachers make significant contributions to knowledge about what children can do independently or can do with assistance. They also suggest appropriate next steps for teaching.

Using Comprehensive Assessment Data to Make Decisions About Individual Students, Instructional Planning, Curriculum Development, and Programmatic Improvement

TEACHER PREP WEBSITE 9.1

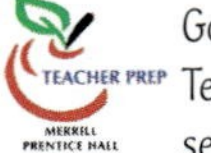

Go to Student and Teacher Artifacts, select Special Education, choose Assessment (Module 7), and select Tory's Psychoeducational Report (Artifact 3).

Evaluation Summary

REFERRAL AND BACKGROUND INFORMATION

A schoolwide cumulative student work portfolio enables teachers to plan for instruction. It also points out areas of the curriculum that can be strengthened and ways to improve the portfolio system. One of your roles as an early childhood practitioner is to make certain that assessment is ongoing, comprehensive, and put to good use. You can see a summary of various formal assessment methods contained in a psychoeducational report on a three-year old child named Tory, in the "Special Education–Assessment" student and teacher artifacts online at the Teacher Prep Website.

Communicating Assessment Results to Students, Parents, Educators, and Other Audiences as Appropriate

Information gathered over time allows teachers to document children's effort and progress in ways that are more understandable to laypersons than are technical, statistical terms, such as stanines, percentile ranks, and normal curve equivalents.

With children in kindergarten and the primary grades, *student-led conferences* may become part of the assessment process. Instead of hearing about the results of parent/teacher conferences second hand, the children are active participants in the conferences with the adults. Students are prepared for their role in the conference, first by reflecting on learning goals they had set for themselves. Some examples of kindergartners' self-selected goals include "I want to make a big book and read it to the whole class," "I want to make a picture book about collecting Beanie Babies," and "I want to learn to spell all my friends' names." Next, the teachers can send home brief surveys to parents and families asking them about their goals for their child's learning. Some examples are, "I hope that he learns to like reading," "If she can learn her alphabet, we will be very pleased," and "We want him to learn to count and add." The last outgrowth of student-led conferences is an opportunity to set goals for the child's future learning.

Anthony Magnacca/Merrill

Consider using student-led conferences as part of your overall assessment plan.

Involving Children and Families in the Assessment Processes

Think about your experiences with assessment as a child. Perhaps your parents or guardian met for 5 or 10 minutes with the teacher once or twice a year. They probably had to sign your report card and return it to the school. But assessment practices in some schools have changed in several significant ways. First of all, many schools and centers provide parents and families with more-detailed written reports.

Contemporary parents and families are likely to be directly involved in setting goals for children, particularly those with special needs. A good example of this is the individualized educational plan (IEP). Developing an IEP for a child typically includes a goal-setting meeting in which the parents/family, teachers, and various specialists all participate. For younger children, ages birth through 3 years, the plan is called the individualized family service plan (IFSP). If this team agrees upon a goal, such as supporting the ability of a child with a physical handicap to feed himself or herself, each adult at the meeting would bear responsibility for carrying out this plan. The teacher would be responsible for helping the child to become more independent during meals served at school, the physical therapist would suggest some adaptive strategies to facilitate self-help skills (e.g., a special spoon, a bowl with a suction cup on the bottom, a stainless steel wheelchair tray with high edges), and the family members would agree to reinforce this learning during meals served at home by cosigning an IEP document with school and support services personnel. Figure 9.2 summarizes your multiple roles in early childhood assessment.

In fulfilling these roles, your first and most important responsibility is to be fair. When asked to explain fairness, most people say something like, "Everyone being treated the same." But equity is far too complex a concept to be explained by identical treatment at all times. To illustrate, imagine that a teacher is leading children in a rhythm band and has in her class a child with an attentional disorder who begins to wander around the room, a child who is hitting another child with the tambourine, and a child who keeps striking the triangle without trying to coordinate his efforts with the group. If you were interacting with these children, it would not be fair to treat them exactly the same way and would be even worse to assess them without considering their individual differences; rather, you would need to observe thoughtfully and think about what would enable each child to experience success at some level. You might, for example, invite the child who is playing the triangle to come forward and strike it only when the group claps, remind the child who has the tambourine of its proper use, and invite the child who is wandering around the room to rejoin the group by speaking softly in her ear and leading her back to the circle.

COMPANION WEBSITE 9.3 For more information about documenting and assessing learning, go to *Web Links* in Chapter 9 of the Companion Website at http://www.prenhall.com/jalongo.

FIGURE 9.2 Your multiple assessment roles.

Evaluating the Learning Environment

- analyzing a good environment for learning
- noting what children can learn from different areas of the classroom
- observing what children learn through outdoor activities

Evaluating Children's Work

- evaluating the progress of individual children
- communicating assessment information to families, educators, and professionals in other fields
- protecting children's confidentiality
- planning individualized learning

Evaluating Program Effectiveness

- determining the success of the lesson
- evaluating the curriculum in various areas
- participating in large-scale evaluation of the total program

Evaluating Professional Performance

- documenting your own professional growth
- assessing the performance of colleagues
- developing skill in self-evaluation and to becoming a better observer of children

Approaches to Assessment

Appropriate assessment requires documenting, recording, and interpreting children's behaviors and performances (Johnston & Rogers, 2002; Popham, 2002).The ultimate goal of assessment is to optimize children's learning and to improve classroom practice. The next section examines major approaches to assessment and the advantages and limitations of each approach.

Norm-Referenced (Standardized) Tests

Of all the assessment tools used in America, group-administered tests are the most familiar. Tests are samples of behavior in a particular area or domain (e.g., reading readiness, mathematics achievement). In today's educational climate, standardized test scores often are considered by policymakers to be the only thing that "counts" as evidence of children's learning (Groark, Mehaffie, McCall, & Greenberg, 2006). When using tests, educators need to appreciate that they are not simply applying a scientific tool. Even standardized tests have to be interpreted and are influenced by the values, beliefs, and language of all parties—children, families, and educators. Test results have consequences, not only for children's learning, but also for teachers' pedagogical approaches and classroom practices (Johnston & Rogers, 2001).

Standardized tests—also called *norm-referenced tests*—are rooted in a comparative concept of assessment. The procedure is to administer the test to a large group of children who become the normative group to which later test takers are compared. Thus, if you were developing a standardized test for kindergartners, you would write the items, try them out, revise them, write standard instructions for administering the test, identify a group of kindergartners, give the test, and calculate the scores. Children who later take the test would have their scores compared, or referenced back, to those of the normative group. This is where the terminology *norm-referenced* comes from. Usually, this comparison will tell you where a child ranks. For example, if a child has a percentile rank of 93%, this does not mean that the child got a score of 93 out of 100. Rather, it means that 93% of the normative group, that first reference group, scored lower than this child on that particular test.

The advantages of published, formal, norm-referenced tests are that they are efficient, inexpensive, convenient, and considered by the general public to be objective (Educational Testing Service, 2003). Standardized tests are often used to

- *compare and categorize* people, educational institutions, and problems according to abstract, impersonal, and generalizable rules
- *measure the performance* of students and educators using a consistent "yardstick" to provide information to policymakers and bureaucrats
- *determine opportunities* on the basis of objectives, qualifications, or merit (Madaus & Tan, 1993)

The disadvantages of norm-referenced testing are numerous, however. Perhaps the most obvious failing of these tests is that they provide virtually no guidance in planning instruction. After the test scores arrive in the mail, the teacher has a number on a piece of paper for each child rather than any direction about what to teach next or how to present it.

Cautions About Standardized Testing with Young Children

Too often, a single test score becomes the basis for making important decisions (Wortham, 2005), such as deciding who will be admitted to a program (e.g., qualifying for a gifted and talented program), which programs will survive (e.g., determining how much money to allocate to Head Start), or which children will gain access to support services (e.g., deciding which infants are "at risk" and qualify for intervention services). Where young children are concerned, the dangers of overreliance on testing are even more acute. First of all, young children are at the very beginning of their lives as learners, and errors in assessing their abilities can have profound consequences. If significant adults are told that the child is lagging far behind peers or has a learning disability, for instance, they may lower their expectations for the child and offer fewer intellectually challenging activities. Research on the human brain suggests that challenges are essential for optimal neural development (Jensen, 2006), so children who are labeled as deficient in some way are further deprived of the very things they need to learn.

What is worse, the probability of making huge errors in assessing young children's performance and potential is very high. As Meisels (1995) points out, "Group-administered tests focus on the acquisition of simple facts, low-level skills, superficial memorization, and isolated evidence of achievement. The tests hold great power, and that power can be abused. Of greatest concern is that they rob teachers of their sense of judgment about how to help children develop to their optimal potential" (p. 1).

Because very young children cannot perform paper-and-pencil tests or, if they can, cannot attend to such a boring task for long, many of the assessment tools for young children rely on motor skill tasks to make predictions about success in school. An infant might be asked to drink from a cup, a toddler to construct a tower out of three wooden blocks, and a preschooler to copy a triangle shape. Yet when these children are older, virtually all of the standardized tests will emphasize verbal and, to a lesser extent, mathematical skills. None of the skills measured by the tests are directly related to the criteria used to measure school success later on. This situation makes tests given during the early childhood years poor predictors of later school achievement; if these long-term predictions are accurate no more than about half the time, the tests are not much more useful (and more time-consuming and much more expensive) than the toss of a coin.

Additionally, young children do not understand testing procedures and the importance of tests. Common errors of naive test takers include not responding at all even when they know the answer, losing their place in a test booklet and getting most of the subsequent answers wrong, becoming distracted from completing the task, talking to one another, and copying from someone else's test paper. For all of these reasons, young children are notoriously poor test takers, and their test scores are not necessarily a reflection of their true abilities.

A basic principle of assessment is *content validity*, meaning that there is a clear connection between what is taught and what is assessed. A major part of early childhood education is teaching children self-help skills such as feeding and dressing themselves and learning social skills such as taking turns and sharing materials. Young children also have experiences in play, art, music, and drama, which do not lend themselves to evaluation through tests (Jalongo & Stamp, 1997). The range of abilities that is (or can be) evaluated through traditional tests is also a major limitation in testing. It would be difficult to imagine a group-administered, easy-to-score, paper-and-pencil test that could measure all the important outcomes of a high-quality early childhood program. For all of these reasons, assessment in early childhood must be fair, focus on what children can do, examine a range of behaviors, and optimize every child's learning potential.

Despite all of these concerns, standardized tests are very much with us in early childhood education. The reputation of teachers, programs, schools, and districts can rise or fall on the strength of these numbers. The predictable response is "teaching to the test"—meaning that time is devoted to practicing the very types of tasks and questions that children are apt to encounter. Figure 9.3 highlights issues to be considered in test preparation and in reducing test anxiety in young children.

Criterion-Referenced Tests

Many professional organizations have issued position statements on assessment (International Reading Association/National Council of Teachers of English, 1995; NAEYC & National Association of Early Childhood Specialists in State Departments of Education, 2003; Perrone, 1991). A synthesis of several of these general standards challenges the long-standing purpose of testing: to sort, measure, and determine opportunities for people. Contemporary views of assessment argue for a very different set of goals. Critics of norm-referenced tests for young children argue that assessment should do the following:

- Improve student learning, be fair to all students, and have beneficial consequences for children

FIGURE 9.3 Test preparation and test anxiety.

Disadvantages of Teaching to the Test

Test preparation can reduce instructional time with new material or other activities that benefit children (e.g., outdoor play, art, music, social studies).

Repetition of the same work frequently results in boredom and burnout, particularly for students who have already mastered the basic material.

Intensive preparation for the test may actually heighten students' fears and test-anxiety problems.

Both the teacher and student can become highly frustrated as the classroom environment, where learning and critical thinking are supposed to take place, becomes completely focused on test taking.

Labeling can result from in-class preparation tests as some children catch on quickly and are viewed as "helping" the individual teacher, the school, and the district while those who struggle are treated as a "drain" on the higher test scores that will determine funding and reputation of the teacher, program, and school.

Ways to Minimize Test Anxiety

Test anxiety refers to an array of cognitive and physical responses that are aroused when people feel that they are being personally evaluated.

- *Focus learning away from the test.*
- *Explain the nature of the tests.*
- *Select culturally relevant tests.*
- *Appreciate students' cultural backgrounds.*
- *Be aware of influences on student learning.*
- *Choose tests that correspond to curricular goals.*

SOURCES: Cizek & Burg, 2006; Garcia, 2002; Kirylo, 2006.

- Promote processes that involve multiple perspectives on the child's learning that are supported by various data sources collected in different contexts
- Be systematic, regularly reviewed, and continuously improved
- Communicate regularly and clearly to and with all stakeholders: students, parents, teachers, administrators, policymakers, and the public
- Enable teachers to critically analyze the curriculum and instruction
- Recognize that teachers play a crucial role in comprehensive assessment
- Invite family and community participation
- Support collaboration between and among educators and other professionals dedicated to working with young children

Criterion-referenced tests have been proposed as a better way of addressing these issues. Unlike norm-referenced tests, which compare one child's performance with that of a reference group of peers, criterion-referenced tests analyze in considerable detail each child's attainment of objectives that are deemed reasonable and appropriate for young children. With toddlers, a criterion might be naming a pictured object; with preschoolers, an objective might be identifying and naming the basic colors; with children in the primary grades, a criterion might be writing a paragraph that would be scored using a very detailed rating scale called a *rubric.* It is easy to see how the results of criterion-referenced assessment would provide more helpful information about what to teach next. In fact, most of these tests result in individual profiles of student performance that are designed to keep track of children's attainment of generally agreed-upon objectives.

Some disadvantages of criterion-referenced assessment are that these instruments are very detailed, have to be administered individually, and are therefore more time consuming. In addition, educators need to be trained in how to use criterion-referenced assessment to monitor and facilitate children's progress, and, because the general public is oriented toward competition, single test scores, and comparisons, many adults are reluctant to accept criterion-referenced assessment.

Even though tests are the type of assessment tool that is most familiar to students, parents, and educators, tests—whether norm- or criterion-referenced—are not the only approach to comprehensive assessment. Increasingly, early childhood educators are using a variety of alternatives to tests.

Principles of Performance Assessment

In everyday use, the word *perform* refers to executing a task or process and bringing it to completion. Given this definition, learners' abilities are assessed as they produce work of their own by drawing upon their knowledge and skills, considering the context, and responding to a task (Wiggins, 1998). The difference between a traditional paper-and-pencil test and performance assessment is like the difference between taking a test on math facts and running a cash register at a department store in a shopping mall. Although it is important to master basic math in order to be a cashier, that knowledge is not adequate when one is called upon to make change, deduct coupon amounts, and process credit card transactions. In other words, there is a difference between *knowing about* something and *knowing how* to do something. In performance assessment, children are called upon to produce something rather than merely select the correct answer from several choices. These tasks are more similar to those that they are likely to encounter outside the classroom. Because of this emphasis on practical application of skills, performance assessment is sometimes referred to as *authentic assessment,* and, because it is a departure from traditional testing methods, performance assessment is sometimes called *alternative assessment.* Many educators believe that performance/authentic/alternative assessment is a better means of developing and documenting higher-level thinking skills in students. Advantages of performance assessments include that they:

- Focus on the developmental and achievement changes in children over time
- Focus on the individual child rather than on groups of children
- Do not rely on a "one chance" opportunity for the child to demonstrate competence
- Do not interrupt the process of curriculum implementation
- Help children better understand their own learning, as children reflect in conjunction with the teacher or other children
- Provide concrete information to share with families (Gullo, 2006, p. 143)

TEACHER PREP WEBSITE 9.2

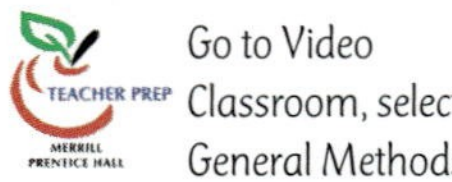

Go to Video Classroom, select General Methods, choose Learner Assessment (Module 10), and select Performance Assessment (Video 2).

To better understand performance assessment and student portfolios, watch the video on learner assessment with Kay Burke. Figure 9.4 summarizes different categories and levels of assessment.

Performance assessment questions (adapted from Glickman & Alridge, 2001) include:

1. What should virtually all students know and be able to do prior to leaving my classroom and our early childhood setting?

FIGURE 9.4 Categories and levels of assessment in early childhood.

FOUR CATEGORIES OF ASSESSMENTS

A **developmental screening assessment** is a brief procedure designed to identify children who—because of a possible learning problem or disability—should receive further diagnostic assessment.

A **diagnostic assessment** is a process used to definitely identify those children with a disability or specific area of academic weakness.

A **readiness assessment** is a brief achievement test designed to determine a child's relative preparedness to participate in a particular classroom program or area of the curriculum (e.g., reading).

An **achievement test** assesses the extent to which a child has acquired certain information or skills that are identified as curricular objectives.

Large-scale Assessment

Federal- and state-mandated assessments	*Examples:* • National Head Start evaluation • Accreditation of early childhood programs by the National Association for the Education of Young Children • On-site evaluation for state licensure in child care or area of the curriculum (e.g.,reading)
District-, school-, and program-wide assessments	*Examples:* • Assessing the development of toddlers prior to their entry into a program • Evaluation of all early childhood classrooms in a school using a rating scale • Requiring all kindergarten children to take a reading readiness test

Individual Assessment

Child	*Examples:* • Teacher's anecdotal records of behavior and events • Parent/family questionnaire data • Notes taken on home visits
Teacher	*Examples:* • Portfolio produced by the individual teacher to document attainment of competence • Self-assessment of attainment of lesson plan objectives • Observations of preservice teachers by an experienced teacher and college supervisor

SOURCES: Gullo, 2006a, 2006b; Meisels & Atkins-Burnett, 2005; Wortham, 2005).

2. What student work samples should be used as the basis for determining these students' knowledge, understandings, and abilities?
3. Who else should participate (e.g., other faculty, staff, parents, peers, community members) in reviewing and assessing various types of student work? Why?
4. What set of criteria should be used to assess the work?
5. How will the overall quality of the child's products and the processes used to achieve those products be determined?

Effective teachers are constantly documenting how their students are doing, gathering evidence of progress, identifying problems, and adjusting instructional plans accordingly (Project Zero, 2003). Controversies about whether to rely on traditional tests or to incorporate a wider variety of assessment strategies persist. Parents and families are familiar with test scores, letter grades, and comparisons of one child's abilities with another's (Popham, 2000). As a result, they often express a preference for these methods of explaining how a child is doing at school. Administrators are understandably concerned with how a program, grade level, or school system is doing in comparison with others. As a result, they are often insistent on large-scale measures and are uninformed about or nonsupportive of teachers' efforts to amass detailed profiles on each child. Likewise, teachers themselves may regard alternative forms of assessment as too much work that is given too little consideration by other colleagues, supervisors, families, and the community at large. One workable solution to this controversy is to stop thinking of assessment as *either* standardized tests *or* teacher-developed methods. It should be both. Just as a medical doctor is interested in community health as well as the health of the individual patient, educators at all levels need to consider the overall learning successes of a program as well as the learning of each child.

Remember that "assessment is more than just the collection of information, it is collection with a purpose" (Salvia & Yesseldyke, 1995, p. 3). In essence, assessment is research about children's abilities. Tests, both those that are professionally published and those that are teacher constructed, are plentiful in schools. The challenge, then, is to balance traditional means of assessment with performance-based methods of evaluation. Performance assessment rounds out the assessment picture by examining student performance in many contexts over a long period of time; reducing the gap between assessment, diagnosis, and teaching methods; and obtaining the most valuable data on individual effort, progress, and achievement (Chard, Katz, & Genishi, 1996). The sections that follow address the two major categories of performance assessment: evaluation of individual children's progress and overall program evaluation.

Evaluating Individual Children's Progress

The basic question answered by observation of individual children is, "How is this child doing?" "Observing students in diverse contexts across the curriculum calls on teachers to take a closer look at themselves, their practices, their students, and their students' learning. In doing so, the details of the learning process are revealed, clarifying the kinds of environments and practices that support different learners to learn in different ways. Rather than 'teaching to the test,' teachers are supported to 'teach to the child'" (Falk, 2001, p. 126). Figure 9.5 provides an overview of the observation process.

FIGURE 9.5 Observation processes and methods.

THE PROCESS

Perception →

What you notice, based upon sensory input, prior experience, individual ways of reacting to experience, the cultural context, teacher education, beliefs about children, educational values, personal ethics, and society.

Description →

What you capture, in words, on tape, or on video and use to characterize the settings, events, and verbal and nonverbal behaviors based on direct observation or inferences from the data collected.

Interpretation

How you make sense of the behaviors and events you perceived. This process typically includes noting patterns, generating hypotheses, and making recommendations.

METHODS FOR OBSERVING AND RECORDING

- **Anecdotal records:** a narrative (storylike), factual account recorded after behavior occurs. Often used to obtain details on a child's behavior (e.g., early reading efforts) and plan appropriate learning experiences.
- **Specimen records or running records:** anecdotal information gathered during a specified time (e.g., during outdoor play) or over a period of time (e.g., a record of the verbal interactions with other children of a newly immigrated child who is learning English). Often used to discover causes and effects of behavior by studying what precedes and follows an event.
- **Time sampling:** tallies or other coding system used to show the presence or absence of a behavior during specified time periods (e.g., observing children's patterns of interaction at lunchtime).
- **Event sampling:** used during a particular event (e.g., charting children's questions in response to a read-aloud). Often used to get baseline data, information on how frequently a particular behavior occurs prior to an intervention strategy (e.g., a toddler crying when brought to child care).
- **Checklists:** charts of information that record yes/no, presence or absence of a behavior (e.g., a list of developmental tasks completed by the child's family with items such as "knows basic colors and color words").
- **Rating scales:** charts of information that add a dimension of kind or amount (e.g., an item such as "Prints name without adult assistance: Usually/Sometimes/Not Yet").
- **Observation using mechanical means:** audiotapes, videotapes, and photographs used to record observations (e.g., audiotaping circle time to make decisions about music instruction, videotaping a puppet play so that the children and teacher can critique it, or taking photographs of children working in groups to document a class project).
- **Interviews:** questions used to gather children's perceptions, ideas, and feelings about a topic or situation (e.g., interviewing children to determine their reading interests or asking them to provide explanations of friendship prior to beginning a unit on friends).
- **Children's drawings:** analyzing children's artwork and inviting them to talk about their work as a way of better understanding their concerns, interests, and lives (e.g., asking children to draw happy and sad things prior to a discussion).

David Mager/Pearson Learning Photo Studio

Teacher observation is a major method of assessment.

TEACHER PREP WEBSITE 9.3

Go to Student and Teacher Artifacts, select Special Education, choose Early Childhood Special Education/ Early Intervention (Module 6), and select Nolan's Visit Notes (Artifact 4).

Observations are sometimes written as anecdotes, or short, written descriptions of behavior and events (Power, 1996). As Strickland (2006) notes, effective teachers are

> keen and competent observers. They study what students do every day in various situations. They observe to determine what students can do independently with success. They note areas of growing competence and areas of difficulty. They use what they learn to inform their plans for intervention and curriculum adjustment. Teachers gather information through anecdotal records, checklists, personalized conferences, formal and informal observations, and by systematically collecting work samples. They examine the information to determine how learners are progressing. (p. 82)

You can see an example of a speech therapist's observational notes on an infant that were gathered during home visits, in the " Special Education–Early Childhood Special Education, Early Intervention" student and teacher artifacts online at the Teacher Prep Website.

Shirley Tertemiz, a student who was observing a teacher at work in a kindergarten classroom, wrote this anecdote:

> Tchr. presented a lesson on colors. Ch. mixed food coloring and water to produce diff. colors. Ch. were instructed to use all eight colors in their crayon boxes to produce colorful pictures. Tchr. questions/comments: "How many diff. colors did you use?" "I see words in your picture, could you read them to me?" "Did anyone experiment with mixing colors?" "I noticed that you made shapes." "Could you tell me more about your picture?" To J., tchr says, "I like those railroad tracks" and walks away. J. says to E., "The tchr. didn't even know that it's a sidewalk!"

Note how she wrote just enough to jog her memory and described objectively what the children were doing in art, just as the experts suggest. Figure 9.6 identifies major errors that are commonly made when teachers first begin observing young children. Be certain to study this information carefully before you begin gathering observational data.

FIGURE 9.6 Major errors in observation.

- **Error:** Being overly judgmental
  Example: "She's probably just lazy."
  Why Not? Judging children does not solve anything. If you judge them, you merely absolve yourself of responsibility for facilitating changes in behavior that will serve them better, both now and in the future.
  Alternative: Be careful about describing behavior, saying, for instance, "Janine sometimes moves from center to center without engaging in the activities there. We have found that it is important to invite her into the ongoing activities and get her started."

- **Error:** Overgeneralizing
  Example: "He never finishes any of his work."
  Why Not? It is not accurate to say that someone *never* finishes *anything*. This is clearly an overstatement.
  Alternative: Be precise, saying, for instance, "At the end of the day, Xi frequently has several activities that he has begun but not finished."

- **Error:** Labeling
  Example: "He is sloppy."
  Why Not? It is not fair to characterize someone's entire personality with a word.
  Alternative: Describe an actual behavior, saying, for instance, "Krish has a tendency to rush through his work, particularly when it involves handwriting."

- **Error:** Stereotyping
  Example: "These children from the housing projects aren't like other children."
  Why Not? It is prejudicial to categorize a group of children in this way based on family income.
  Alternative: Say what needs to be addressed and be a child and family advocate, saying, for instance, "It is often the case that these toddlers arrive at school without much prior experience with lap reading of picture books. We have been collaborating with the public library to use the bookmobile as a way to offer toddler story times and to provide greater access to high-quality literature."

- **Error:** Blaming
  Example: "The way she keeps acting out, it's clear that she doesn't get any discipline at home."
  Why Not? You have no basis in fact for making such an assumption. It could even be the case that the child is disciplined severely at home and that she is acting out at school as a cry for help.
  Alternative: Work to find out what might be causing the behavior, for instance, conferring with a parent or other family member and saying, "I am concerned that Sean has been giving other children karate chops and pushing them down on the playground. Can you think of any reason why he might be behaving in this way?"

- **Error:** Making long-term predictions
  Example: "He's never going to amount to anything. I wouldn't be surprised to find out he's in trouble with the law while he is still in junior high school."
  Why Not? Teachers cannot see into the future, and making dire predictions only results in lowered expectations that are communicated to children and may have a self-fulfilling prophecy effect.
  Alternative: Note what the child is doing right, saying, for instance, "I noticed that Lucien really helped out when Adrianna fell at the bottom of the slide by comforting her and going to get help."

- **Error:** Comparing children to peers and adults
  Example: "He's the best artist in the class. He draws even better than most adults."
  Why Not? Teachers need to focus on what children can do, and it is better to encourage them than to praise them. The difference is that praise tends to say, in effect, "Just keep doing what you are doing to please me and stay ahead of the others." Encouragement, however, lets children know that their efforts are recognized and that they bear responsibility for self-evaluation.
  Alternative: "Monroe frequently chooses to go to the art table first. I have noticed that he is interested in trying different media to produce pictures, including not only crayons, but also paints, chalk, colored pencils, and a variety of materials and tools."

COMPANION WEBSITE 9.4 To learn more about linguistic and cultural diversity, go to *Enrichment Content: Research Highlights* in Chapter 9 of the Companion Website at http://www.prenhall.com/jalongo.

FIGURE 9.7 Materials for recording observations.

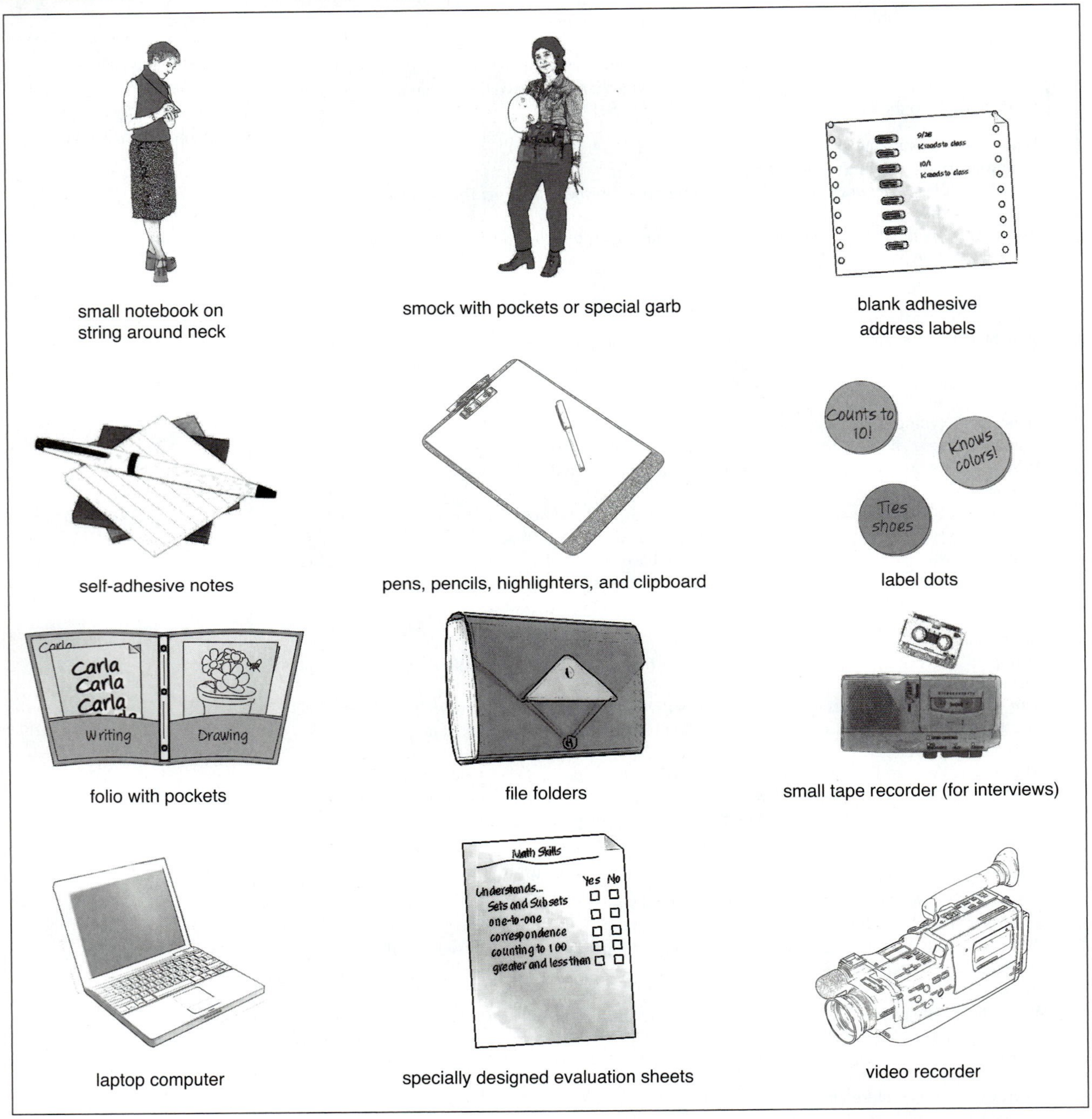

small notebook on string around neck

smock with pockets or special garb

blank adhesive address labels

self-adhesive notes

pens, pencils, highlighters, and clipboard

label dots

folio with pockets

file folders

small tape recorder (for interviews)

laptop computer

specially designed evaluation sheets

video recorder

After you have collected many pieces of information about a child or your program for evaluation purposes, the next step is to compile that information. Figure 9.7 suggests some materials for collecting observations and organizing them in useful ways.

Student work portfolios are purposeful collections of children's work that document achievements and provide data on the processes involved in products. If traditional testing is like a snapshot, then portfolio assessment is more like a photo album—a collection of

ASK THE EXPERT

Deborah Leong on Assessment, Development, and Technology

Deborah Leong

Is assessment the same thing as testing?

Assessment is more broadly defined than testing and encompasses many different ways of measuring the behavior of young children. Assessment may include testing, observations of children, samples of their work, interviews, and the performance of a skill or the solving of a problem. Sometimes the term *assessment* is used to avoid the negative connotations of the word *testing*. Testing usually refers to standardized tests or paper-and-pencil tests through which teachers elicit specific responses from children and the children's responses are scored in a numerical fashion.

Why do I need to assess more than once?

The primary purpose of assessment is to help children in their efforts to learn. If assessment is to be used to help teachers make decisions about learning in the classroom, then assessing a child only once a year or even twice a year is not enough. The purpose of beginning and end-of-year assessment is to sum up the child's performance. However, the real strength of good assessment information is that it helps the teacher really decide what will be the optimum steps in the teaching-learning exchange.

How can assessment help me teach?

Assessment can help the teacher identify a child's zone of proximal development (ZPD). The ZPD is the area that encompasses the skills that are just on the edge of emergence. Thus, scaffolding or supporting learning within the ZPD is most beneficial for later development. Through assessment, the teacher can discover the boundaries of a child's ZPD, what the child can do without help and what the child can do with assistance. Assessment can also help you monitor a child's progress on important goals and objectives. As a growing number of early childhood programs, such as Head Start, developed specific performance outcomes, teachers had to document progress and attainment of those outcomes.

How will technology help me assess children in the future?

One of the most exciting developments today is the way that computers will support assessment in the future. Scanners and optical recognition programs make direct input of data into the computer possible so that teachers can easily process their own notes, which they ordinarily take while observing students. Voice recognition and graphic tablets, while they have limited application today, will someday enable even young children to assess themselves while interacting with a computer. The computer can keep records straight and track progress on skills as diverse as math facts and literacy. Computers can make the saving of images of children's work easy and can help teachers weave these together with coherent parent reports of child progress. With the advent of artificial intelligence, computers can spot error patterns, provide profiles of individuals, and provide alternative means of analysis of information. Computers will never be able to replace the experience and knowledge of an expert teacher, but they can make the management of assessment information easier.

Deborah Leong is a Professor of Psychology, Metropolitan State College of Denver, Denver, Colorado.

pictures showing growth and change over time (McTighe, 1997). A portfolio is an organized, purposeful compilation of evidence documenting a child's development and learning over time. Portfolios reveal to the child and others the experiences, efforts, progress, and accomplishments of that child (Dale-Easley & Mitchell, 2003; McAfee & Leong, 2007).

To seen how the process of documentation is used in the Reggio Emilia approach, watch the preschool video "Reggio Emilia Documentations" video clip online at the Teacher Prep Website.

PAUSE AND REFLECT
About Systems of Assessment

In most classrooms today, teachers continue to use folders, files, and paperwork to gather assessment information. Read the Ask the Expert feature on page 331, and then search the Internet for information about computer systems for storing student work portfolios. What systems do you expect to have in place by the time you are finished with your teacher preparation program? (For a detailed plan, see Power [1996] and Nilsen [1999].

Evaluating Program Effectiveness

TEACHER PREP WEBSITE 9.4

Go to Video Classroom, select Early Childhood, choose Documentation (Module 5), and select Reggio Emilia Documentations (Video 1).

Program evaluation answers the question, "Am I providing a quality program?" Of course, program evaluation depends on who is responsible for deciding about program quality. A child enrolled in a program may view it differently from how a parent views it, and a trained external evaluator might regard a program differently from how the director of the program views it. Thus, it is important to consider program quality from multiple perspectives, as described in Figure 9.8.

One way of assessing program quality is through the process of documentation (Fleet, Patterson, & Robertson, 2006; Project Zero, 2003). *Documentation* is often used to capture the essence of a class or schoolwide project (Carter & Curtis, 1996; Curtis & Carter, 2000; Helm & Helm, 2006). The process of documentation "allows us to see and understand better the children and ourselves, as well as to enable others to do the same, so that we can

Scott Cunningham/Merrill

Schoolwide projects create exciting assessment and program evaluation opportunities.

FIGURE 9.8 Perspectives on program evaluation.

Katz (1993) suggests that there are five different perspectives on program quality. In order to provide a high-quality program, each of these perspectives must be considered simultaneously.

- ↘ The **top-down perspective** examines easily observed and measured characteristics. Top-down program characteristics set the stage for effective instruction to occur. Is the classroom space adequate? Are there sufficient toys and equipment in the room? Are there enough adults to work with the number of children in the class? These top-down considerations influence effective instruction by providing educators with the basic resources to establish a learning environment.
- ↗ The **bottom-up perspective** focuses on the quality of the daily experience of the child in the program. Does the child feel valued, accepted, and successful? Are there interesting activities for children to pursue? Are children's special needs and circumstances addressed appropriately? Is school a place that children want to be?
- → The **inside perspective** deals with the working conditions experienced by teachers. Are their basic needs being met through adequate salary and health-care benefits? Are they treated with respect by colleagues and supervisory personnel? Is there support for their ongoing professional development?
- ↔ The **outside-inside perspective** emphasizes the relationship between early childhood educators and families. Do parents and other family members feel welcome at the school? Is there regular communication between teachers and families? Can families rely upon the educational system for support?
- ← The **outside perspective** deals with the relationships among the educational program, the community, and the larger social context in which it operates. How is the kindergarten program viewed in our community? How is the program regarded in our country? Is there a general belief among community members that the program is supporting children's development and preparing them for more productive lives?

COMPANION WEBSITE 9.5 For more information about technology and documenting and assessing learning, go to *Web Links* in Chapter 9 of the Companion Website at http://www.prenhall.com/jalongo.

continue to see, reflect, interpret, and understand over time that which took place" (Vecchi, 2001, p. 159). Methods used for documentation are selected with these goals in mind: enhance children's learning, respect children's ideas and work, involve children in planning and evaluation, foster parent participation, and make the learning process visible (Chard, 1996; Gandini & Kaminsky, 2004). Documentation has the following features:

- It begins with a guiding question—something about which children are genuinely curious—and maintains a focus on children's ways of learning.
- It uses words and pictures—diffferent media—to provide breadth and depth of a learning experience.
- It approaches the topic from multiple perspectives and uses collaboration to strengthen the process of analysis, interpretation, and evaluation.
- It results in public sharing as children and adults reflect upon, revisit, and refine their work and share it with different audiences.
- It shapes curriculum as teachers use children's work to guide their efforts and design future learning experiences (Kroeger & Cardy, 2006; Rinaldi, 2004; Seidel, 2003).

The schools in Reggio Emilia, Italy, are known worldwide for their documentation practices (New, 2003). In these schools and in the traveling exhibits of children's work that have come out of Reggio Emilia, you can see beautiful displays of children's work at various stages, photographs that chronicle the progress of projects, written comments on the children's work from teachers and parents, and transcripts of discussions with children about their work.

Large tables, display cases, and three-dimensional bulletin boards are all ways in which the life cycle of a class project can be communicated to others.

General Indicators of a Balanced Assessment Program

COMPANION WEBSITE 9.6 To add a product that demonstrates your competence in observing and documenting children's learning to your developing portfolio, go to *Journal: Constructing Your Professional Portfolio* in Chapter 9 of the Companion Website at http://www.prenhall.com/jalongo.

Balanced assessment

> provides teachers with important knowledge of students and their growth as learners, informs ongoing curricular and pedagogical practice, is a basis for helping students reflect on their own learning, and serves as a window for parents into the power of the teaching-learning exchange that involves their sons and daughters. (Perrone, 1997, p. 305)

How will you know if your assessment plan is balanced and working well? One indicator is *student motivation to learn.* When learners understand why learning is important, know what is expected, and are confident that they will be treated fairly, they are much more likely to produce work that is of high quality. In a balanced early childhood assessment program, teachers realize that learning is far more complex than memorizing information. The connections between and among a child's knowledge, skills, attitudes, and values are recognized and respected. Think about yourself as a student trying to produce a lesson plan. If you understand that careful planning will enable you to become a much more effective teacher, if you see examples of outstanding lesson plans, and if you know that your instructor will work with you to improve instead of merely grading what you have turned in, then you are going to adopt a more positive attitude and work harder than you would if these conditions were not met. The same holds true for children. They learn better when adults believe in their abilities, show them how something is done, provide guided practice, and set clear performance standards.

Another indicator that an assessment program is well balanced is *child and family participation in assessment.* A teacher we know of who sought to build her second graders' self-assessment skills in writing invited them to complete questions such as, "I already know how to. . . ." "Right now I am learning how to . . ." and "Next, I want to learn . . ." Similarly, when this teacher sent home a questionnaire to parents, she asked them to set literacy goals for their children with questions such as, "This year, I hope that my child learns. . . ." In both instances, the teacher was setting goals and encouraging families and children to develop a vocabulary of assessment.

A third indicator of a balanced assessment program is *recognition that errors are part of the learning process.* If evaluation takes the form of accurately guessing what is on the teacher's mind, young children will experience frustration and failure. A young child's thinking isn't merely less sophisticated or in-depth than an experienced adult's, it is qualitatively different. Children are relative newcomers to the world. They attribute human qualities to inanimate objects, as when they converse with a toy and believe it can eat or sleep as they do. They hear words and interpret them literally, as in thinking that "warm mittens" somehow give off heat like tiny furnaces. If they try to explain a complex phenomenon, such as the images on a television, they will probably resort to the idea that miniature people are inside the box. For all of these reasons, errors are an inevitable part of childhood. They are not easily eradicated, because the child's naïve theories about the world have to be replaced by more accurate ones, and this takes time, experience, and the ability to truly understand. Telling children the "right" answer—even getting them to memorize an answer and recite it back—is not sufficient to develop new concepts.

TEACHER PREP WEBSITE 9.5

Go to Student and Teacher Artifacts, select Early Childhood Education, choose Families and Community (Module 7), and select Letter "T" Homework (Artifact 4).

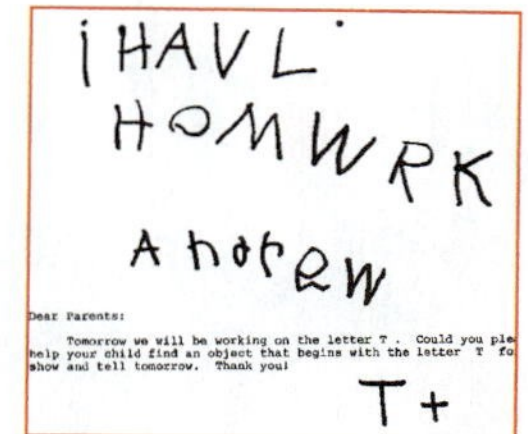
i HAVL HOMWRK A horew

Dear Parents:

Tomorrow we will be working on the letter T . Could you ple help your child find an object that begins with the letter T fo show and tell tomorrow. Thank you!

T +

Balanced assessment programs also *provide varied opportunities for children to demonstrate what they have learned.* The concept of one-to-one correspondence is a good example. It is possible for a child to demonstrate understanding of this correspondence on a worksheet by drawing lines from a set of five dogs to a set of five food dishes. It is also possible for a child to demonstrate that understanding by putting one napkin, cracker, and cup of juice at each child's place at snack time; by enacting examples with toys and pieces of string; or by creating flannel-board shapes for one-to-one correspondence examples. In other words, mastery of a concept can be determined via daily routines and playlike activities rather than relying exclusively on worksheets. One type of teacher assessment is homework. Take a look at an example of a kindergarten child's homework with the letter "T" in the "Early Childhood Education–Families and Community" student and teachers artifact online at the Teacher Prep Website.

A balanced assessment program also *recognizes the limitations of measurement.* Clearly, all forms of measurement are flawed in some way. A published, standardized test that arrives in neat little plastic-wrapped stacks along with a booklet that specifies all of the administration and scoring procedures certainly seems more official and objective than one teacher's anecdotal records, but it may not be truly reflective of what children can do under normal circumstances. The same child who has difficulty matching a clock face to the time written in numerals on a test can have a clear idea of his daily schedule at home and at school, including lunchtime, bedtime, and so forth. However, one teacher's anecdotal notes on the children in a class will not say much about how that child is functioning in comparison with peers. The underlying issue here is how educators pose problems to the learners. When problems are highly structured for the learner, the trade-off is that the learning being tested might not have much use in everyday experience. Even though a child can circle the letter that a pictured word begins with, that skill does not necessarily translate into reading words. When the problems are less well defined (as they more often are in real life), comparing one person's response to another's is far more difficult. If several toddlers are figuring out how to push and pull toys, a teacher can observe them as they struggle to solve this less-structured problem, but a standardized testing of their abilities would be virtually impossible.

Finally, a balanced assessment program *does not confuse measurement with curriculum and instruction.* The mere fact that data on a child or program are collected is no substitute for really teaching. Just as taking a patient's temperature and recording it on a chart doesn't improve that person's medical condition unless it is coupled with appropriate treatment, evaluating children's work doesn't enhance learning unless these data are used to provide an appropriate curriculum and instruction. When the total curriculum (written), daily learning experiences (taught), and methods of evaluation (tested) are aligned across the child's educational experiences, children are far more likely to increase their understanding and improve their skills (Kagan, Carroll, Comer, & Scott-Little, 2006). Assessment and curriculum need to be bound together:

> Central to the curriculum development enterprise is knowledge of assessment, which allows the teacher to monitor where students are, individually and collectively, in their understanding and development at the beginning of a teaching segment, so that the

right entry points can be chosen and the right scaffolds for learning constructed; to identify what and how students are learning, so that teaching can be continuously adapted to students' emerging needs; to instantiate goals for learning in performance assessments that can guide both learning and teaching; and to provide careful feedback to students so they can strengthen their own performance and improve their work through revision.(Darling-Hammond, 2006, p. 96)

In your role as an early childhood practitioner, keep in mind that the goal of early childhood assessment is to gain valid, reliable, and useful information about children, to translate that information into improved instruction for young children, to enhance services for children and their families, and, when necessary, to design appropriate interventions (Fewell, 2000; McConnell, 2000).

COLLABORATING WITH FAMILIES

A Question-and-Answer Session with Parents on Portfolios

Read the following script of an actual conversation that took place between a teacher and a group of parents on Back-to-School Night, where parents had an opportunity to raise questions concerning the new school year.

Parent A: I noticed you said that you will be using portfolios to grade the children. What's wrong with tests and regular grades?

Teacher: I have used both approaches—portfolios, and tests and grades—in recent years and I have found that the children learn more about the subject matter and themselves with the use of portfolios. The problem that I see with relying exclusively on tests and grades is that children are placed in a competitive situation with their classmates.

Parent B: But competition is what the *real* world is about. You should be preparing our children to compete, not make school a warm, fuzzy place!

Teacher: Actually, I have wrestled with that point about helping children to develop skills that they will use throughout life. Business and industry tell us that teamwork is important. How do I reconcile teamwork and competition? I tell the children that they must compete with *themselves* to try to do better than they have done before. I also help them to realize that sometimes the best way to do a better job is to work with others and share ideas.

Parent A: Can't you grade them on tests and homework assignments? My child has been working on a project for 2 weeks and I don't see any workbook pages or practice sheets. How do I or you know if she is learning anything?

Teacher: Children can show us what they know in so many ways—by telling us, by writing a story, by drawing a picture, by performing a play they have written, by building with blocks, and so many others. Portfolios give me a means to document what a child has learned in a way that is meaningful to him or her. The children and I have many opportunities to discuss their work, and they select with me what they want to include in their portfolios. Think about your jobs. If the only information that was given about your work performance was a letter grade, you would probably feel that a grade alone would not adequately describe your capabilities. The same holds true for children in school. I want your children to control their own learning and to take responsibility for self-evaluation. When they reflect on their accomplishments, evaluate their work, plan revisions, and set goals, they are also developing their competence.

Parent C: But how do you evaluate their work?

Teacher: I use their work to assess their progress in achieving the standards of learning and the skills and knowledge within the school system's curriculum. I look for problem-solving skills and evidence that the child is really thinking. Portfolios may contain a variety of information, including such things as writing samples, a reading list, a spelling file, a video of a play, a recording of an original song, and so much more.

Parent B: What can I do to help my child?

Teacher: When you talk with your child about what he or she is learning at school, ask challenging questions, such as "Why do you think that happened?" or "What might have happened if you had . . .?" Help your child to understand that real learning is a thinking process, not just memorization of some facts.

Weekly Practice

Encourage children to learn to reflect on their own learning and communicate that learning to their families. Have children routinely reflect on their learning by establishing a weekly time to do so.

At the end of the week, discuss with the children the activities and learning that took place that week. Then, have each child draw or write about one thing they did and what they learned from this activity. Let the children take their pictures home and discuss the learning with their families. Allow room for parent comments and ask them to return the paper to school. At conference or report time, you will have a collection of children's and families' reflections on progress through the year that you can review together. Families can see the child's growth and compare it to the skill development expected for a child in that age range. During this conversation, make the connection between the learning activity and standards.

Conclusion

As a teacher, you will find that you are expected to exert a powerful, positive influence on children's learning as well as on their motivation to continue to learn. The pressure to do this today is intense:

> These are hard times for public education, which increasingly is characterized by a mean-spirited and hostile discourse, one with little respect for teachers and the young people they teach. Currently, the most common buzzwords in education are borrowed shamelessly from the business world: The school is a "market," students and families are "consumers," and teachers are "producers." In this discourse, "accountability" is proposed as the arbiter of excellence, teacher tests as the answer to "quality control," and high-stakes tests are the final judge of student learning. (Nieto, 2005, p. 4)

If you contend, "We offer high-quality care for infants at this center," "These children are learning to read," or "This is a good program," you should expect that the standard response from parents, families, colleagues, community members, school administrators, and professionals in other fields will be, "How do you know?" "Show us that these children really are learning," or "Convince us that this is true." In your assessment role with the very young, your goal is to document that significant contributions were made to children's learning. This means that what they achieved with your guidance and support was appreciably better than what one would expect from normal maturation. The most fundamental question in early childhood assessment is one of "value added"—how did the learning activities that you designed and the educational programs for which you are responsible improve the child's learning and life? When you can document that value has been added, you have fulfilled an essential dimension of your role as an early childhood educator.

COMPANION WEBSITE 9.7 To test your knowledge of this chapter's content, go to the *Multiple-Choice* and *Essay* modules in Chapter 9 of the Companion Website at http://www.prenhall.com/jalongo. These items are written in the same format that you will encounter on the Praxis test to better prepare you for your licensure exam.

ONE CHILD, THREE PERSPECTIVES

Damien, a Drug-Exposed Child

On a tour of a program for preschoolers at-risk, the program director said to a visiting early childhood professor, "I guess we should warn you. There is a crack-exposed child in the preschool classroom we will be visiting next. I know this is terrible, but he has kicked and bitten and thrown things so often that we call him 'the attack child.' He needs a full-time aide. Fortunately, he's a lot better now than he was at the beginning of the year. Our new principal, who was just transferred here from the high school, expelled the boy for 3 days. A lot of good that did! Everyone knows that this kid lives in a crack house. How is spending more time there supposed to solve his problems?"

They entered a classroom to see and hear a first-year teacher reading Eric Carle's picture book *The Very Hungry Caterpillar* aloud. A biracial boy with light brown ringlets and hazel eyes was seated on a young woman's lap. This was Damien, the child the visitor had been forewarned about.

When the children were actively involved in listening to the story and playing a game, Damien participated enthusiastically. But when they were assigned to color, he began to race around the room and scream. Then he swept a shelf of toys and a puzzle rack onto the floor with his arm while the other children watched him uneasily. His aide, a frail-looking young African American woman who appeared to be fresh out of high school, managed to catch Damien and attempted to restrain him by speaking softly, leading him to another area of the classroom, and encircling him with her arms. Damien struggled at first and then he relaxed.

It was time for free play. Damien sat down, opened up a miniature barn, and took out the toy animals, people, and farm equipment stored inside. The other children kept their distance. It was as if a magnetic field had been created, with Damien repelling every other person. All of the adults, including his aide, were positioned on the other side of the room.

The visitor approached Damien cautiously and knelt down on the carpet. He was making the plastic tractor and the wagon attached to it go around in a circle, over and over again. The visitor picked up a plastic spotted cow, waddled it over toward the roly-poly farmer who was positioned in the driver's seat, and said in a goofy voice, "Hi, Damien. I want to go for a ride. Can I, please? Huh? Huh? Can I please?" Damien peered at the cow intently, then at the visitor, his jaw dropping in amazement. He nodded affirmatively. The play continued in this way with different plastic toys sometimes leaping over fences, screeching into the barn, losing a passenger, or giving Damien a noisy kiss on the cheek. Some of the other children stopped by to watch and ask what Damien was doing and why he was laughing. What they were really wondering, the visitor concluded, was whether it was safe to play with Damien.

Later that day when all of the adults had an opportunity to talk, the teacher, aide, and program supervisors wanted to know what the visitor thought about Damien. "I would capitalize on the fact that Damien has the services of a full-time aide. Her time might be better spent in one-to-one playful interaction rather than in attempting to control Damien during group time. As long as everyone is wary of Damien and tends to keep away, his social development will be arrested. I think the most pressing issue is Damien's acceptance into the group. You need to give yourselves permission to treat him differently, to focus on furthering his social and emotional development, rather than being overly concerned about making sure that he covers the content." The aide shared her frustration with the situation and reported that they had been working with social services to try to have Damien removed from his mother's custody. So far, all of their efforts had been futile (Jalongo, 1996).

REACT	In what ways are the perspectives of the program director, the visiting professor, and the aide in the class alike?
RESEARCH	Investigate the subject of prenatal drug exposure and identify the major issues and recommendations. What beliefs did the adults in this situation seem to be acting upon? How did their responses to Damien compare with the recommendations you found?
REFLECT	Which perspective do you identify most strongly with, and why?

IN-CLASS WORKSHOP

Designing Portfolios of Children's Work

Now that you have seen what might go into a child's portfolio, work in a group to invent a different type of portfolio. You could, for example, design a portfolio for all areas of the curriculum (MacDonald, 1997; Nilsen, 1999) or for one curricular area, such as the arts (Jalongo & Stamp, 1997). You might prepare a portfolio that documents the life cycle of a project (Borgia, 1996). There are also three general types of portfolios, one of which you may want to develop. A permanent portfolio is a very selective sampling of work from each year that is advanced to the next grade to communicate with the child's new teacher (Gullo, 2005). The other two types of portfolios are a work-in-progress portfolio of what a child is currently working on in school and a current-year showcase portfolio that documents accomplishments chosen by teacher and child (Gullo, 2005).

Goals of Student Work Portfolios

Keep in mind the main goals of student work portfolios as you work in your groups:

- **Portfolios should incorporate actual classroom work.** The systematic collection of student work throughout the year helps to document student progress and achievement. The student work serves as a lens through which the faculty can reflect on their successes and adjust their instructional strategies.
- **Portfolios should enhance students', teachers', and families' participation in the assessment process.** Students accept more responsibility for their own learning and take pride in their achievements when they share their accomplishments and evidence of growth with others. School-family-community communication is enhanced when laypersons can really see evidence of effort, progress, and achievement.
- **Portfolios should meet the accountability concerns of school districts and funding agencies.** Portfolios are unlikely to replace large-scale assessment efforts in schools, districts, and programs, but they can do much to complete the assessment picture in ways that provide in-depth information. Large-scale assessment is like a telescope; portfolios are like a microscope on the same programs (Gullo, 2005).

How to Develop Portfolios

Use the following steps and resources to develop your portfolio plan (Genishi, 1996).

1. **Why?** What do you want to assess? Why create a portfolio for each child? What is it that you are trying to learn or reveal via this

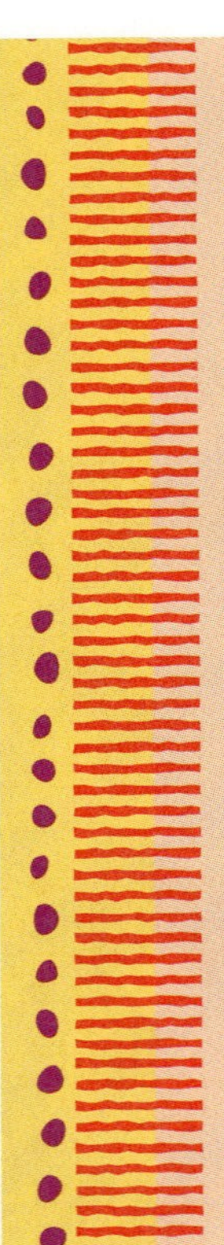

portfolio? Refer to Figure 9.1 for a list of purposes for assessment.

2. **What?** Which documents best demonstrate development? Which work samples are typical of the child's play or work? Which samples show what is unique about the child's work? What products document the attainment of curricular goals?
3. **How and When?** How will you schedule the collection of samples of children's work? (For example, would you compare a sample taken the first and last months of school, or would you take the child's choice of three best examples?) How will you obtain child input? (For example, through individual interviews, small-group contacts, or coaching children how to select and discuss their choices of products for the portfolio?) (See Benson and Smith [1998] for an example of a first-grade portfolio.)
4. **Where?** Where will work samples be stored? (In a plastic crate, in a file drawer, or in magazine files?) In what formats? (Folders, videotapes, audiotapes, photographs, or binders?) How will they be organized? Who will need access to them?
5. **What Else?** Determine whether there are gaps in the profiles for each child or in the "developmental story" of your class or program. If so, what other work samples could you collect to make the information more comprehensive?
6. **Who?** Will what you have collected tell a clear story to the intended audience? Decide how to share the portfolio and with whom (e.g., parents and other family members, administrators, future teachers of the child, other children).

Presenting Your Plan

Make a list, chart, web, or sketch of your portfolio plan on the chalkboard, an overhead transparency, newsprint, or computer that can be shared with the total group. As each group presents its portfolio plan, evaluate it using the goals and questions in this workshop.

CHAPTER 10

Exploring Your Role in Guiding Children's Behavior

> Until the mid-20th century, the primary focus of most early childhood and kindergarten programs was "socialization"—the process through which a young child adopts and internalizes the values and behaviors of society. . . . Over the last decade, an increasing emphasis on standards and accountability has led to a greater tendency in kindergarten to teach academic subject matter such as literacy and mathematics, to assess children's progress, and to focus on the types of social and emotional skills that allow young children to benefit from instruction, such as self-control, curiosity, self-direction, and persistence. At the same time, school populations have become increasingly diverse. Children today need the types of social and emotional skills that allow them to value and get along well with peers from a wide variety of backgrounds.
>
> Martha B. Bronson, 2006, p. 47

Meet the Teachers

CHARLES works in a child-care program at the local hospital. His job is to work with medical personnel to determine each child's physical condition and limitations, then plan appropriate activities for the children in the playroom. He also works with families to help them get things back to normal as much as possible when the child is well and ready to return home. Over the years, he has found that after a hospital stay, young children often resist separation from their parents while parents tend to become rather permissive. As Charles sees it, "A big part of my role is to help the adults consider the child's point of view, give additional support when needed, and set reasonable limits for the child's behavior."

MRS. DAVIS runs a group child-care program for low-income families supported by the county. She cares for a mixed-age group of five preschool children in her home. The general rule in her classroom setting is that nobody owns any of the toys or materials; children are expected to share. But when a toddler brought his favorite teddy bear to school and didn't want to share, Mrs. Davis felt that he was entitled to cling to his toy and say, "It's mine!" She decided to read several children's books during the week about "attachment objects" (blankets, soft toys, and other items that young children form a connection with) and then talk with the children about the toys that most of them still sleep with or fondly remember. Mrs. Davis was surprised by the children's idea to modify the rules about very special toys. They decided that, "Other kids can look at them, but not take them away" and that, "Sometimes, you don't have to share."

MS. PETTIT has a child in her class this year who is well-known throughout the school and community. Tonya lives with her chronically ill mother and 3-year-old brother in a remote rural area. As a result, Tonya has responsibilities far beyond her eight years at home for cooking, cleaning, and babysitting. Although she is a bright and competent child, Tonya's school performance has been poor, because she frequently arrives at school tired, hungry, and neglected. Despite the research against retention at grade level, the professional staff members decide to keep Tonya in first grade for another year. Ms. Pettit describes what happened during the first few weeks of school: "Other children arrived with new school supplies, and Tonya, who can be quite persuasive, started to make deals with her classmates in which they ended up with the bad end of the bargain—such as Kim's new backpack being traded for a set of markers that were going dry. Then I received an angry telephone call and a note from parents asking me what was going on. My first reaction was to punish her, but instead, I explained to her that it wasn't right for her to make unfair trades. Then I used my $100 allocation from the local parent group to equip several backpacks with writing and drawing supplies so that children could borrow them. That solved the problem, because now, Tonya has access to the materials that she needs."

COMPARE	What are some commonalities among these three teachers?
CONTRAST	How do these teachers think about teaching? How would you characterize the outlook of each one?
CONNECT	What made the greatest impression on you, and how will you incorporate this into your teaching?

Now that you have reflected on the perspectives of three different teachers, here is a preview of the knowledge, skills, and dispositions you will need to acquire in order to fulfill your role in guiding children's behavior.

Learning Outcomes

- ✔ Become familiar with national standards and guidelines concerning the early childhood educator's role in guiding children's behavior and classroom management **(NAEYC #1, INTASC #6, and ACEI #3d & 3e)**
- ✔ Learn how to establish a community of learners in your classroom
- ✔ Understand children's rights and needs and the ways in which those rights and needs shape a child guidance philosophy
- ✔ Understand aggressive behavior in children and appropriate responses to it
- ✔ Define conflict, common types of conflict, and ways to resolve conflict in the classroom
- ✔ Develop greater confidence in your ability to function as a mediator and teach children self-regulation
- ✔ Acquire more skillful ways of communicating with children when difficult issues arise

Children's Needs and Rights

Any discussion of child guidance or children's inappropriate behavior must begin by considering their basic needs as human beings. What is it that children have a right to expect? First and foremost, children have a right to caring relationships. They deserve adults who take time, listen to their concerns, support their efforts, treat them with

DID YOU KNOW...?

- Most beginning teachers consider themselves to be inadequately prepared to handle classroom management (Martin, Chiodo & Chang, 2001; Silvestri, 2001). Just 17% of teachers report feeling adequately equipped to deal with diverse student populations.
- Preservice teachers quickly discover that rather than relying on formulas for classroom management, they need to respond to concerns about specific situations on a case-by-case basis (Martin et al., 2001).
- A teacher's child guidance approaches appear to be very consistent with his or her overall philosophy, goals for students, and teaching style (Richardson & Fallona, 2001).
- Educators tend to rely on punitive methods (e.g., losing privileges, threatening to contact parents or the principal) when they are confronted with children's challenging behavior (Maag, 2001). Yet research supports more productive techniques, such as discussion of problems, rewards for good behavior, and student involvement in decision making (Kaiser & Rasminsky, 2006; Lewis, 2001).
- In a study involving 21 elementary schools, students reported that their teachers react to misbehavior with increased coercive discipline (Lewis, 2001).
- Time-out, in which the child is isolated from the group following misbehavior, has been criticized for being used excessively as well as for confusing young children who don't necessarily make a connection between their behavior and forced separation from the group (Wein, 2006). Time-out relies on blame and shame to control and modify behavior (Gartrell, 2001).
- When teachers provide choices of activities and encourage children to reflect on their actions, this tends to increase self-regulatory behaviors in children (Zaslow & Martinez-Beck, 2006).
- Variables that exert a powerful influence on children's emotional self-regulation include the development of the frontal lobes of the cerebral cortex, cognitive and language development, a firmer self-concept, and the patient guidance and reasonable expectations of adults (Berk, 2006).
- Children with highly emotionally reactive temperaments have greater difficulty regulating their feelings, and they require extra adult support (Berk, 2006).
- ADHD occurs in 3 to 5% of school-age children, making it the most common psychiatric disorder among children (Sherman, Rasmussen, & Baydala, 2006, p. 196).
- Boys usually have more dopamine in their bloodstream and they process more blood flow in the cerebellum, the part of the brain that controls physical action; therefore, boys often prefer to be more active. A boy's corpus callosum, the tissue connecting the brain hemispheres, is up to 25% smaller than a girl's; therefore, it may be easier for girls to multitask. Brain scans show that when boys are at rest, their level of brain activity is less than girls'; therefore, boys should be allowed to move a little, draw, or hold a squeeze ball when attempting to concentrate in class to stay alert (Gurian & Stevens, 2005).
- In an increasing number of cases, children with behavioral problems are being expelled from classrooms (Zaslow & Martinez-Beck, 2006). Boys are five times more likely to be expelled from school than girls (Gartrell, 2006).

dignity, and protect them from harm. Human beings remain helpless longer than any other species and therefore require a tremendous investment of love, care, and attention from families, educators, and other professionals, as well as from the communities in which they live. The following story about a child we know helps to illustrate why there is no effective substitute for nurturing.

Unlike several of his kindergarten classmates, Jason adjusted readily to a full-day kindergarten program when school started in September. Later on in the school year, however,

COMPANION WEBSITE 10.1 To learn more about defining your role in child guidance, go to *Journal: Defining Your Role* in Chapter 10 of the Companion Website at http://www.prenhall.com/jalongo.

Anthony Magnacca/Merrill

How many of these children will be home alone until parents return from work?

Jason started to cry, not at the start of the school day, but in the afternoons shortly before the buses arrived. His teacher was sympathetic at first but eventually lost patience with him and complained to anyone who would listen that Jason's crying was "driving her crazy." In desperation, she resorted to the behavioristic approach recommended by a more experienced teacher, convinced that if she ignored the crying it would eventually stop. Yet as the winter began, Jason's tears and protests became, if anything, even more intense.

Clues to the puzzling pattern of Jason's behavior began to emerge after a concerned neighbor reported the child's situation to Children and Youth Services. Jason's mother had abandoned the family during the summer, and his father, who had a demanding job and a long commute, suddenly had sole responsibility for the boy. Monday through Friday, 5-year-old Jason was getting off the school bus, unlocking the front door, and staying home alone until his father arrived around 7:00 P.M. When the social worker spoke with Jason, the kindergartner confided that he had been frightened by some advertising for a horror movie that he saw on television and was terrified to stay by himself when it was dark outside. (Isenberg & Jalongo, 2005, p. 9)

We begin with this story because it reminds us that adults in crisis, such as Jason's father and teacher, sometimes make bad decisions in the absence of appropriate support. Such errors in judgment occur when adults disregard the child's needs or neglect their collective responsibility to care for the child. As Valora Washington (1996) reminds us, in a society that truly values children,

> *Every child should be*
> *cherished in families,*
> *supported by communities,*
> *considered holistically,*
> *nurtured with care.* (p. 136)

All human beings have fundamental needs for such things as food, shelter, clothing, adequate rest, and freedom from threat (Maslow, 1968). Yet with nearly half of America's children living in poverty, many children arrive at school without even these basic needs having been met (Children's Defense Fund, 2002). When a child is hungry, it is cruel to berate the child for not paying attention in class. When a child's father is in jail, it is inconsiderate to sponsor a father-son event. When a child has witnessed a drive-by shooting, it is disrespectful to act as if nothing has happened. As an intervention specialist puts it, "Children carry their home lives to school as easily as the books and papers in their backpacks" (Krahl & Jalongo, 1998). Any teacher who overlooks this is failing to really *see* children.

In addition to the basic needs, all human beings have fundamental personal and social needs, including (a) *autonomy,* the need to exert an influence on decisions and events rather than feeling powerless and the victim of circumstance; (b) *relatedness,* the need for love, affirmation, and a sense of connectedness with others and belonging to a group; and (c) *competence,* the need to accomplish new things, acquire new skills, and successfully put these learnings to use (Deci & Ryan, 1985; Rodgers, 1998). In fact, some experts on guiding children's behavior believe that all children are striving to belong and that when they cannot feel like a valued part of the classroom community, they resort to antisocial behaviors such as seeking attention, exerting their power, trying to even the score through revenge, or resisting passively by withdrawing from adult demands (Dinkmeyer & McKay, 1989). Aggressive behavior (behavior intended to inflict physical or psychological harm) can be its own reward through the outcomes it brings about, such as when children use aggression to get a desired object (e.g., a toy), to get an opportunity (e.g., a turn on the swing), or to retaliate against perceived wrongdoing (McDevitt & Ormrod, 2007). You can watch a preschool teacher as she redirects a child's behavior, in the "Managing Behavior" video clip online at the Teacher Prep Website.

TEACHER PREP WEBSITE 10.1

Go to Video Classroom, choose Special Education, select Emotional and Behavioral Disorders (Module 7), and choose Managing Behavior (Video 1).

Strategies that promote a sense of community include:

- Welcoming children into the room by labeling cubbies and hooks with their names
- Using class meetings to encourage group discussions, social problem solving, and sharing of ideas and information
- Bringing each child's home culture and language into the shared culture of the classroom
- Developing classroom rules with children
- Planning ways for children to work and play together collaboratively

"Creating a community of learners in the classroom has a significant impact on how children work together, how they feel about school, and the relationships that are built with them as individuals and as a group" (Heroman & Copple, 2006, p. 61). Children also have the right to expect certain things from their educational experiences, as described in Figure 10.1. Additionally, every child has a right to hope—to have a sense of moving forward, making progress, and anticipating a brighter future. Some ways that

FIGURE 10.1 Children's rights.

Children have a right to . . .
be greeted warmly every day
be noticed in positive ways
exercise choices throughout the school day
enjoy their educational experiences
be heard and responded to by adults and peers
be allowed to converse with their peers
gain competencies, skills, and confidence
have their abilities recognized and regarded
think and solve problems
learn about their world
expect daily and weekly routines
learn the skills of independence
give and receive compliments
establish warm and supportive relationships with adults
have adventures that involve new challenges or risks
expect fairness in class rules, policies, and procedures
give and get help
learn to resolve conflicts
understand how to make, keep, and be a friend
be accepted into the classroom community and make contributions to it
be able to make mistakes, break a rule, or act wrongfully and then make amends, repair, and recover their place in the group

SOURCE: Based on ideas in *Teaching Children to Care: Classroom Management for Ethical and Academic Growth, K–8,* revised ed., by Ruth Sidney Charney, 2002, Greenfield, MA: Northeast Foundation for Children.

teachers build hope include communicating the following important messages to every child (Gannon & Mncayi, 1996):

People like me here; I can come back.
I have my own space here; I can leave my stuff and it will be safe.
Nice things happen here; I can depend on good things happening again.
I might not get finished today, but I can work on it some more later.
There are nice people here; I can become like them.
I am getting better at this, and I can learn new things.
What I want and think matters; I can make responsible choices.
I don't have to depend on others all of the time; I can do some things well all by myself.
My work matters to me and to the group; I can do outstanding work.
What I am learning at school works in other places and at other times, too.
There are so many choices, I can try and succeed at new things.

When you see a child misbehave, ask yourself what might be motivating him or her. William Glasser (1992) argues that there are just four fundamental motivations for doing something: love, power, freedom, or fun—or some combination of these. Consider something as simple as brushing your teeth. You do it because you want to avoid dental fillings and pain (freedom) and enjoy good food (fun). You also do it because others will be more attracted to you than if your teeth were decayed (love), and because they may hold you in higher esteem if you have a dazzling smile (power). Likewise, children behave as they do, good or bad, in response to one or more of these motivating factors. The great majority of the time, young children strive to please adults and comply with their requests. The rest of the time, you will need to dig deeper to learn what might be causing a behavior. Some underlying causes of children's behavior include:

- Physical environment e.g., the child may be new to an environment and unfamiliar with procedures; there may not be enough materials to go around, and this leads to disputes; the classroom layout may be poor and fail to clearly demarcate quiet and noisy areas; the room may not be arranged in ways that encourage children to access materials and put them away independently
- Child's basic needs are unmet e.g., the child may be neglected, abused, ill, tired, or hungry; may feel inadequate or incompetent; may feel unaccepted by peers and/or adults
- Curriculum problems e.g., the academic demands may be unrealistic for the child's age or stage; an inflexible schedule might cause the child to act out; the child may be generally unchallenged and disinterested in the required activities
- Cultural differences e.g., and family may feel overwhelmed by the adaptive demands of a new culture; may not have mastered the language well enough to make his or her needs known; may have suffered traumatic experiences in the process of immigrating; the family's values may conflict with certain school or class policies and procedures
- Special needs e.g., the child may be abused or neglected, subjected to physical harm, sexual molestation, emotional maltreatment, or a disregard of the child's basic needs; may have attention deficit disorder, characterized by a child's inability to concentrate on a task long enough to process information or accomplish a goal; may be autistic, a severe impairment of two-way verbal or nonverbal social interaction in

which the child's activity is dominated by repetitive and ritualistic behaviors; may have a behavioral disorder, characterized by a difference from the norm in the *amount* and *intensity* of the child's reactions; may have a learning disability, a variety of problems manifested as difficulty with verbal or mathematical skills, with fine or gross motor skills, or with visual, auditory, and tactile perception (adapted from Paasche, Gorrill, & Strom, 1990).

COMPANION WEBSITE 10.2 To learn more about your role in guiding children's behavior and the NAEYC, go to *Web Links* in Chapter 10 of the Companion Website at http://www.prenhall.com/jalongo.

Your Role in Child Guidance

Teachers confront many situations in which young children's behavior does not meet their expectations. Yet when a child misbehaves, it is difficult for most adults to avoid rushing to the question of how to stop the behavior. Before you assume that the child is at fault, you will need to consider whether what we expect is necessary, productive, fair, and age appropriate (Kohn, 1996). "Our first question should be 'What do children need?'—followed immediately by 'How can we meet those needs?'—and from that point of departure we will end up in a very different place than if we had begun by asking, 'How do I get children to do what I want?' " (Kohn, 1996, p. xv).

One way to get the behavior that you hope for from children is to take a positive, schoolwide approach (Elementary Educators, 2006). Focus on coaching children in how to interact more successfully rather than reprimanding and punishing (Severson & Walker, 2002; Walker, Ramsey, & Gresham, 2003/2004). Have a few simple rules and repeat them often. Remember that in order to succeed in school, young children need to be able to follow directions, participate in group activities, express their needs and ideas, conform to classroom rules, and interact appropriately with adults and peers. You can observe a class discussion on the first day of school in which the teacher establishes classroom rules with the children, in the "Classroom Rules" video clip online at the Teacher Prep Website.

TEACHER PREP WEBSITE 10.2

Go to Video Classroom, choose Educational Psychology, select Classroom Management (Module 12), and choose Classroom Rules (Video 1).

Is It Necessary? A day-care provider who works with 3-year-olds insists that every child lie down and take a nap in the afternoon. For the children who are in the habit of taking an afternoon nap, this procedure is fine. For those who are unaccustomed to naps, it is a constant struggle. She spends much of her time leading them back to their cots or saying "Shhhh!" loudly and frequently. The real question is not whether children are napping or not but whether a nap is necessary. If the nap is designed to keep children from getting overtired, and some children clearly are not tired, then who is the nap for? Wouldn't it be sufficient to have a quiet time instead of attempting to enforce a nap? Might the naptime be more for the teacher's benefit than the children's?

Is It Productive? In a Head Start classroom, all of the 4-year-olds are required to assemble in a circle and seat themselves on pieces of masking tape placed on the carpet. The circle time lasts for nearly 30 minutes, and every time a child moves from the tape, the teacher sends the child to a "growing-up chair." By the time the large-group session is over, about a third of the children are or have been placed in chairs as punishment for failing to sit still. In fact, by the end of this excessively long and boring circle time, it almost looks like a game of musical chairs! If you talk with the teacher, she will tell you that the children come from poor families and "just don't know how to behave." What she really needs to do is to rethink group time. Ironically, what she considers to be a punishment (moving to chairs) is actually a momentary escape from the tedious work she repeats day after day.

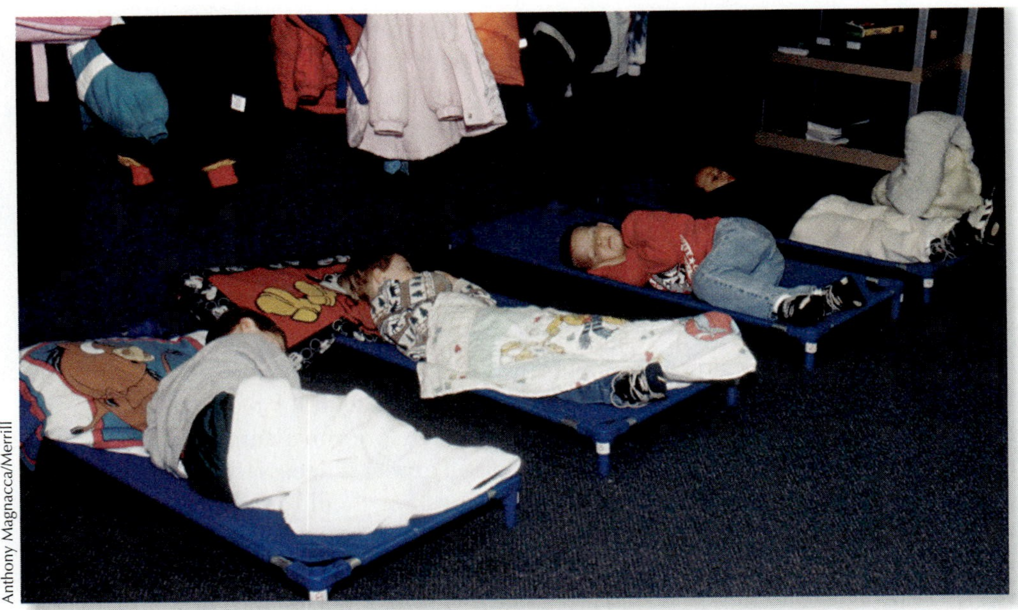

Anthony Magnacca/Merrill

Does every child need a nap at the same time? What alternatives can you suggest?

Is It Fair? A second-grade teacher has attended a workshop on assertive discipline, and one of the recommended strategies is to list the names of children who misbehave and place a checkmark next to the child's name with each new incident of violating classroom rules. She decides to do this on the chalkboard so that everyone can see who the offenders are. After a child accumulates three checkmarks, that child loses a privilege. A regular visitor to the classroom asks about the names on the board and says, "I just wondered. I see the same names up there all the time." Afterward, the teacher thinks about what the visitor said and wonders to herself, "How can I say that this system is working if none of the children who need to learn self-control are improving?"

Is It Age Appropriate? A private nursery school in a wealthy suburb has high tuition and a long waiting list. The director knows that parents and families send their children there in the hopes that their children's development will be accelerated, so she pressures the teachers to "get more out of" the children to build her program's reputation for developing precocity in children. Because the competition for the available slots in each class is keen, the director decides to institute more-stringent policies about entrance requirements and a more academic focus. The curriculum is deliberately "pushed down," so that toddlers are now expected to do what was once part of the program for 3-year-olds, the 3-year-olds do what was once part of the program for 4-year-olds, and so forth. When several of the toddlers do not sit quietly during stories, memorize songs and fingerplays, or paste shapes cut out by the teachers in the correct way, the director invites the parents in and asks them to remove their children from the program to make room "for those who can benefit." There is undeniable damage done by such practices because they cause parents/families to begin to wonder and worry about their child's capabilities. Guiding young children's behavior is a complex and challenging task, particularly when adults have different expectations and beliefs (Shore, 2003).

Does It Respect the Natural Behavior of Young Children? A 5-year-old boy comes running into the classroom and slides onto the floor with all the intensity of a baseball player stealing first base. He went to the library yesterday and was given a temporary tattoo as a prize for reading 10 books. With that, he lifts up his t-shirt to show his friends, commenting "Yeah, it makes me look tough!" When the teacher approaches, he says proudly "I'm only 5 and I already look like a man!" How would you handle such a situation as a teacher? Sadly, many teachers would take this boy aside and speak with him harshly, put him in time out, or reprimand him in front of his peers. A better approach would be to emphasize what is right and notice the rest: "Wow, Darnell! Ten books! Good for you! Yes, I see that tattoo. How long do they last?" and then, quietly, just for him to hear, "I can see why you are so are excited but don't forget about no running. I don't want you to slip on the floor and get hurt." It is possible to gently remind children of rules intended to protect them without quashing the joy a child is feeling if you bear in mind that somber, quiet, tightly controlled environments are not suitable for the very young:

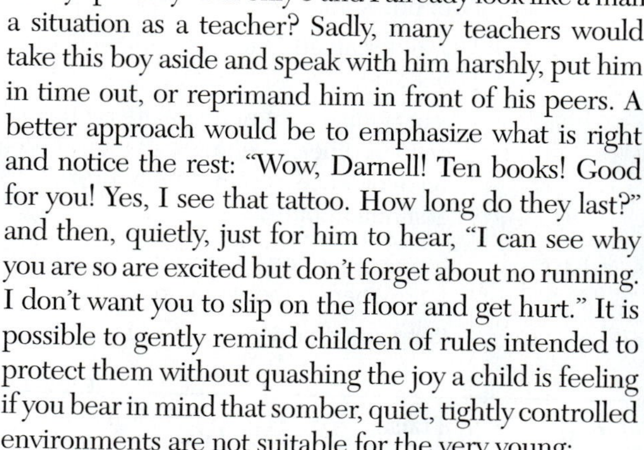

> energetic classrooms, rich in nurturing and encouragement, are good for all children. Let's face it: classrooms in general (particularly in light of the obesity epidemic) need to be less like Sunday school and more like summer camp—which of course would make them more developmentally appropriate and healthier . . . young people—boys *and* girls—learn through movement (Gartrell, 2006, p. 93).

PAUSE AND REFLECT
About Discipline

Which of the following did you experience as a child? How did you feel about such statements? What connections do you see between these statements and the children's rights listed in Figure 10.1?

- "All of you will sit here and miss recess until the person who broke the rules comes forward."
- "If everyone gets 100% on the spelling test on Friday, we will have a popcorn party."
- "You know the rules. Now you have to write 'I will not throw snowballs' 500 times."
- "I like the way that Heather is working. Look at Heather's picture, everyone."

Discipline and Child Guidance

What is "old-fashioned" discipline? Usually, it consists of some combination of rewards and punishments. Punishments are unpleasant or painful experiences that are imposed upon others to "teach a lesson" and enforce compliance, as in, "Go sit by yourself in time-out. I asked you twice to clean up the toys and you did not do it." Corporal punishment is physical pain inflicted to force compliance, as in spanking; in most states, corporal punishment is against the law. Threats are warnings about the punishments that will occur if compliance with the rules is not forthcoming, as in, "If you do not finish your work on time, you will miss recess." Rewards are pleasant experiences that are held out to recognize compliance, as in, "Those of you who did well on your papers get a sticker." Bribes are promises of future rewards, as in, "If you work quietly for the next 10 minutes, we will get to make play dough this afternoon." The trouble with these methods is that they require constant group surveillance (Kohn, 1996; Wein, 2006). Figure 10.2 compares/contrasts discipline with child guidance and compares/contrasts praise with encouragement. See Majorie Field's suggestions on child guidance in the Ask the Expert feature.

COMPANION WEBSITE 10.3 For more information about child guidance, go to *Web Links* in Chapter 10 of the Companion Website at http://www.prenhall.com/jalongo.

A student teacher who had been told that the best way to manage children's behavior was to "catch them being good" decided to put a chart on each of her first graders' desks. As she walked around the room, she would stamp stars on the charts of children who were working quietly. After accumulating five of these stamps, a child was permitted

FIGURE 10.2 Child guidance versus discipline.

Contemporary Child Guidance	**"Old-Fashioned" Discipline**
Child is encouraged to . . . exercise self-control over emotions and override impulses distinguish what is right, just, and good from what is wrong, unfair, and bad internalize a code of conduct recognize others' feelings and consider the consequences of behavior cope with powerful emotions and act autonomously engage in problem solving and consider underlying motives	*Child learns to . . .* yield to impulse in the absence of a threat of punishment wait for an adult to pass judgment on behavior fear punishment or negotiate for rewards dismiss others' feelings and focus instead on avoidance of punishment or attainment of rewards repress emotions temporarily and retaliate later when authority figure is absent keep score of who wins and loses
Encouragement	**Praise**
Teaches children to evaluate their own efforts **Examples:** *"Was that fun?" "Are you glad you tried to . . . . ?" "You seem pleased about . . . ."*	Teacher is the judge of what is good and bad **Example:** *"You have been very good today, so here is a sticker for you."*
Does not judge children or their work **Examples:** *"I noticed that you were . . ." "Which of your paintings do you like best?"*	Judges children and their work **Examples:** *"What a great story!" "You had the best idea."*
Focuses on the process rather than the outcome **Examples:** *"How did you use the software to do this?" "It looks like you are working on your sign." "I see you are enjoying . . . . "*	Focuses on the outcome **Examples:** *"I am putting the best papers up on the bulletin board." "Who has their work finished?"*
Is a **private** event that does not embarrass children in public or compare them with each other **Examples:** *"Thanks for helping to clean up today." "I appreciate that you . . . ," "Aren't you pleased that you were able to . . . . ?"*	Is a public announcement or event **Examples:** *"Room 5, you have been very good today." "Look at Sheri's paper, everyone. She did it correctly." "The winners of the contest are . . . . "*

SOURCE: Adapted from "Discipline in Early Childhood" by L. Porter, 1999, *Landscapes of Development: An Anthology of Readings* (pp. 295–308), L. E. Berk (Ed.), Belmont CA: Wadsworth.

ASK THE EXPERT

Marjorie Fields on Effective Child Guidance

Marjorie Fields

If you don't punish or reward children, how do you get them to obey?

Helping children to learn personal responsibility for their behavior and to judge between right and wrong is a much higher goal than teaching obedience. Many people fear that children will run wild unless adults force them to obey, but teaching children personal responsibility creates people who monitor their own behavior and don't require policing from others. If we use punishments and rewards to get desirable behavior, the only time we can count on good behavior is when someone is there to give out the punishment or reward. Asking only for obedience is asking for far too little.

We are told to respond to the cause of misbehavior, but how can we figure out why children act inappropriately?

The best way to determine the cause of a child's behavior is to observe the child carefully and record your observations. You need to know a lot about a child to plan effective discipline. You need to note whether this is usual or unusual behavior, and also under what circumstances it occurs. What do you know about the child's home routine, health, or family situation that might provide some clues?

Never overlook the possibility that you may have caused a discipline problem. Unfortunately we often see teacher expectations and school environments that are not appropriate for children's levels of development, individual temperaments, or cultures; in these cases the teacher causes discipline problems.

Unmet needs also cause inappropriate behaviors. These may be physical needs such as hunger or tiredness or they may be emotional needs such as trust, attention, personal power, friendship, or self-esteem. Missing social skills or communication skills account for much of the negative interactions between children; teaching these skills will improve the behaviors. Punishment will not.

If we focus on building relationships with children, won't that get in the way of teaching them to mind adults?

Building relationships with children doesn't mean being their buddy and letting go of your adult role. It means making sure that each child knows you care about him or her. Unless a child knows you care, and unless that child is concerned about maintaining a relationship with you, there is really no reason for the child to pay attention to what you ask. If you don't have a caring relationship with a child, your only recourse is punishment or reward—with their ultimately negative impact on behavior.

Caring relationships require investing some time listening respectfully to children and having other pleasant interactions with them. This investment will pay off during a behavior crisis.

Marjorie Fields is an Early Childhood Education Professor Emerita, University of Alaska, S.E.

to get a piece of candy from a jar. Stamps could also be crossed off for inappropriate behavior. After experimenting with this system, the teacher recognized several drawbacks:

- Distributing candy was against the new policy of the school intended to address the childhood obesity problem. It specified that only healthful foods were to be distributed or consumed at school.
- Instead of talking with the children about what they were doing, she was preoccupied with scanning the room for good and bad behavior.
- Children started to tattle more, particularly after she had been out of the room or when they were under someone else's supervision at music, art, library, gym, or recess.
- A parent complained that her daughter's dentist found an unusually high number of cavities; the parent blamed the sugary treats that were given almost daily to her well-behaved daughter.
- The student teacher had little money, and it was becoming expensive to keep the candy jar filled with treats.
- The children who had been well behaved previously continued to be the "winners," while those who had difficulty complying with classroom rules continued to be "losers," except on rare occasions.
- The custodian complained that hard candy was being spit out and trampled into the carpet.

Anthony Magnacca/Merrill

Guiding young children's behavior requires a strong commitment to communicating effectively.

Notice that the student teacher did not question her own behavior at all. She operated on the assumption that children needed to do whatever she asked. This is one of the great fallacies of working with children—the assumption that whatever adults request is appropriate and that the only legitimate role for the child is to obey. A more useful definition of discipline is quite different: Discipline is "helping children to learn personal responsibility for their behavior and to judge between right and wrong for themselves" (Fields & Boesser, 1998, p. 5).

The basic minimum requirement for any appropriate way of guiding young children's behavior begins by building a relationship with them and depends upon effective communication. Effective communication occurs when teachers do the following:

- Demonstrate understanding, respect the child's point of view, and identify with the child's situation.
- Use a pleasant, calm, and normal tone of voice.
- State clear, simple, polite, and firm expectations in a positive way.
- Offer appropriate suggestions and alternatives for behavior.
- Enjoy and verbally appreciate children's appropriate behavior.
- Express feelings, especially anger, in an appropriate and constructive manner.
- Use humor and see the funny side of situations to reduce tension.
- Be consistent and predictable in responses to children's behavior.

- Use positive, affectionate nonverbal communication such as smiles, nods, hugs, or laughter. (Lerman, 1984; Rodd, 1996). You can see a teacher guiding children in the primary grades in resolving their own conflicts, in the "Resolve Conflict" video clip online at the Teacher Prep Website.

TEACHER PREP WEBSITE 10.3

Go to Video Classroom, select Classroom Management, choose Maintaining Appropriate Student Behavior (Module 5), and select Empowering Students to Resolve Conflict (Video 1).

Violence, Aggression, and Conflict

Parents, educators, and professionals in related fields are expressing concern about the escalation of violence in children's lives. There are three broad categories of violence that exert a powerful influence on children's lives (Groves, 1996). *Media violence* refers to the aggressive acts that children see depicted in television programs, newscasts, videos, movies, newspapers, and magazines. On television alone, the average child sees 12,000 acts of violence each year (Dietz & Strasburger, 1991). Television violence is deceptive, because it "sanitizes" violence, seldom showing the pain, anguish, suffering, or even the blood that results from violence (Simmons, Stalsworth, & Wentzel, 1999). More often than not, the "bad guys" simply fall down and die instantly. One type of media violence that is frequently overlooked by adults, because it does not involve real people, includes the brutal acts of cartoon characters who magically spring to life after being cut up, run over, dropped from a cliff, and so forth. *Family violence* refers to the injuries, both physical and emotional, that children suffer as a result of abuse or neglect, as well as the acts of violence that children witness between and among adults and other family members. Increasing numbers of children watch the hostility that comes from a bitter divorce or witness abuse of people and pets in their homes. *Community violence* refers to the violence that children witness in their communities, such as fights, stabbings, and shootings. Children and families who live in high-crime areas often do not have the financial resources to leave the area. As a result, they live in fear for their lives.

Many Americans would like to think that violence is exclusively an urban problem or a racial problem that exists among certain ethnic groups, but the reality is that media violence is present in virtually every home, with 99% of American families owning at least one television set (Comstock & Strasburger, 1990). Likewise, domestic violence can erupt anywhere without regard to race, class, or ethnicity, although families who do not live in crowded areas may be better able to maintain secrecy than others.

The effects of an increasingly violent society are evident in children's responses to conflict in early childhood settings (Carter, 1992; Eisenberg, 1992; Stone, 1993). Young children's aggressive behavior is on the rise, and incidents that used to involve an exchange of words now often result in an explosion of anger and a resort to hitting, kicking, and biting (Levin, 2002). As one teacher put it, "It used to be that an angry child would storm off or a frightened child would cry. Now they are more apt to lash out, not by knocking over blocks or throwing down a toy, but by being aggressive toward one another."

Thus, the teacher's responsibility for helping young children to acquire skills of self-regulation have increased. A review of the research reported that:

- Of kindergarten teachers, 46% consider nearly half of their students to lack sufficient levels of self-regulation.
- Problem behaviors, such as kicking or threatening others, occurred once a day for 40% of the children.
- There were six or more instances of problem behaviors for 10% of the children in a day. (Zaslow & Martinez-Beck, 2006)

Figure 10.3 identifies goals, strategies, and activities to promote self-regulation.

FIGURE 10.3 Goals, strategies, and activities to promote self-regulation.

GOALS

Control Impulses

- demonstrate patience
- manage difficult situations
- verbalize feelings
- resist tempting objects

Follow School Routines

- follow rules
- organize school materials
- accept evaluative comments
- make classroom transitions

Manage Group Situations

- maintain composure
- appraise peer pressure
- participate in group activities
- describe effect of behavior on others

Manage Stress

- adapt to new situations
- cope with competition
- tolerate frustration
- select tension-reducing activities

Solve Social Problems

- focus on the present
- learn from the past
- anticipate consequences
- resolve conflicts

STRATEGIES TO PROMOTE SELF-REGULATION

Techniques to promote self-regulation include:

- ***Provide visual reminders,*** such as social interaction rules posted in the classroom, lists of tasks to be done, or the tracking of strategies used to solve problems.
- ***Focus on the process.*** Pose exploratory questions to get children engaged in the task. Connect with their interests and natural curiosity.
- ***Take a positive approach.*** Use reinforcement and carefully planned classroom management strategies and encourage children to reflect on them.
- ***Create a positive climate*** that reflects the enthusiasm, enjoyment, and emotional connection that the teacher has with the children as well as the nature of peer interactions (Martinez-Beck & Zaslow, 2006, pp. 243–244).
- ***Provide choices*** in activities so that children regulate where they want to go and what they want to do; supply open-ended materials.
- ***Model social-emotional problem solving.*** Use either videos or stories and pictures and provide practice in using the strategies in a variety of settings, such as class meetings.
- ***Address naturally occurring disagreements*** to teach about social problem solving and to model self-regulation.
- ***Design appropriate activities.*** Create activities that help children learn academic content and incorporate elements of self-regulation (Zaslow & Martinez-Beck, 2006).

ACTIVITIES TO PROMOTE SELF-REGULATION

- Place marble mazes (or other exploratory activities) in the science area that can be played by two or more children. Encourage verbal discussion as well as problem solving.
- Introduce a variety of books that deal with perspective taking, feelings, and emotions in the literacy corner.
- Arrange the housekeeping area to include a doll house with people of many cultures represented.
- Provide rainbow ribbons in the music area so children can come together in dance to express themselves.
- Place giant floor puzzles in the manipulative area so that children can work together toward a common goal.
- Play a parachute game where cooperation is necessary during large motor times.
- Promote helping skills and acts of kindness by setting up opportunities in the dramatic play area, such as a pet hospital.
- Follow a simple recipe and share the food.
- Include open-ended materials in the block area.
- Facilitate play groups for those reluctant to join in.
- Set up bath time for baby dolls in the sensory table. Model caring and helping behaviors.
- Supply paint, brushes, and a very large piece of paper for the whole class to make a mural in the art area.
- Display children's work in the classroom at their level.

SOURCES: French, 2004; Henley, 1996; Preusse, 2006; Zaslow & Martinez-Beck, 2006.

Conflict refers to competing wishes, desires, or behaviors that evoke powerful emotions. It is, of course, possible for a person to have conflicting inner emotions (e.g., "Should I cheat on the test to get a good grade or should I be honest and suffer the consequences of not studying?"). Conflict also occurs when two or more people are on opposite sides of an issue (e.g., Child: "I was sitting there first, it's *my* chair." Sibling: "But you got up, so now *I'm* sitting here. If you get up, it's not your seat anymore.").

One of the most important things that any adult responsible for the care and education of young children can do is to try to prevent behavior problems before they occur. Figure 10.4 provides an overview of prevention strategies.

Anthony Magnacca/Merrill

Established teaching routines can prevent behavior problems.

Aggression refers to a deliberate act that is designed to harm or diminish another person in some way. Aggression is a common response to conflict, a situation in which the needs or desires of one individual or group are at odds with the needs or desires of another individual or group. Research on children's aggressive behavior has revealed some interesting results, including the following:

Aggression Is in the Eye of the Beholder. A group of 3-year-old children is seeing how Silly Putty stretches as well as placing it on the Sunday newspaper comic strips to make imprints of the colored-ink pictures. One of the boys grabs all of the Silly Putty, stretches it out, and then presses it onto the face of another child while saying, "Put Caitlin's face on here." Is this an innocent experiment or an act of aggression? Does it depend, to some extent, on Caitlin's reaction? If Caitlin's feelings are hurt and she feels violated or humiliated, most teachers would say that it is an act of aggression. But what if she laughs and says, "I asked him to try it"? Clearly, what counts as an act of aggression is influenced by the social situation.

Consider the Child's Needs. Visit Rashid's first-grade classroom on any given day, and you are likely to see him in time-out. Because Rashid is repeatedly isolated from the group, his peers treat him as untrustworthy and reject his overtures of friendship. Children like Rashid, who are less adaptable, more distractable, and more intense, really need to learn how to adjust to new circumstances, concentrate, and calm themselves. None of these things can be learned in isolation. Child behavior that disrupts ongoing play and elicits negative responses usually leads to even stronger feelings of isolation, anxiety, and hostility. Knowing this, it is particularly important for teachers to guide children's behavior rather than merely judge it or police it.

Work with the Total Group. When invited to talk about "kids who are bad," 5-year-old David said, "Kalessha is *really* bad. She moved away and I'm glad. 'Cause one time, I was trying to write in my journal and she was holding my arm so I couldn't even write! And Oliver, he's really bad too. One time the teacher made him go to the principal's office because he was kicking other kids." Social conflict does not belong to a child; it is a consequence of relationships. Intervention efforts, such as those used with troubled youths at Boys' Town, are more effective when they concentrate on the group,

FIGURE 10.4 Preventing behavior problems.

Focus on General Goals

1. Create order so that the group can function effectively and so that all children can learn.
2. Teach children to take responsibility for their own actions and to acquire self-discipline.
3. Teach children to handle powerful emotions and express their feelings in socially appropriate ways.
4. Foster cooperation between and among children and adults.
5. Teach children the social responsibility and ethical principles necessary to function as citizens in a democratic society. (adapted from Porter, 1999)

Coach Children in Ways to:

- Approach others positively
- Express wishes and preferences clearly
- Assert personal rights and needs appropriately
- Avoid intimidation by bullies
- Express frustration and anger appropriately
- Collaborate with peers easily
- Participate in discussion and activities
- Take turns
- Show interest in others
- Negotiate or compromise with others
- Accept and enjoy people of diverse backgrounds
- Employ appropriate nonverbal greetings and communications (Mindes, 2006, pp. 108–109)

Build Positive Interactions

- Treat children with dignity.
- Be fair.
- Engage in one-to-one interactions with children.
- Communicate warmth and respect.
- Get on the child's level for face-to-face interactions.
- Use a pleasant, calm voice and simple language.
- Provide warm, responsive physical contact.
- Follow the child's lead and interest during play.
- Help children understand classroom expectations.
- Redirect children when they engage in challenging behavior.
- Listen to children and encourage them to listen to others.
- Acknowledge children for their accomplishments and effort.
- Promote positive peer interactions. (adapted from Ostrosky & Jung, 2007)

Know students' abilities and limitations. For example, it is not fair to expect a child with attention deficit disorder to stay "on task" for the same amount of time as peers without this problem. You may find that adaptive equipment is needed to help a child with sitting upright, feeding herself, or helping himself to paint at the easel. Try to foster independence so that children's frustrations are reduced. Avoid rushing children, as this usually results in stress and acting out. Avoid leaving children waiting with nothing to do, such as lining them up too early to go to the cafeteria. Time pressures (too little, too much) frequently erupt into problems.

Have a well-organized classroom and established routines. If everyone decides that the blocks go on the shelf, for example, that makes it clearer what is expected when the blocks are to be put away. Engage as many senses as possible when teaching routines. For instance, if a child is supposed to be responsible for watering the plants, announce that in the morning by placing cards with the helpers' names on them next to a picture of a flowerpot, have a stick-person poster near the plants to show what he or she is expected to do, and establish an auditory signal for helper time. Demonstrate how to water the plants. Ask children to repeat the instructions before they actually perform the task. In this way, children with special needs can get the message in several different ways.

Discuss rules and consequences. Remind children of the rules that they have helped to set and keep those rules simple and clear, such as "No water on the floor." Make consequences clear too, such as, "If you spill water on the floor, you have to mop it up." At times, there may be natural consequences of children's actions that it may be better for them to experience directly. For instance, a child in the primary grades might have a very messy desk and be unable to find things when needed. Rather than criticizing the child, this situation could be used to help him or her see the value of organizing materials.

Teach, model, and review appropriate behaviors. Trust children and believe in them. They are not trying to make you look bad or being difficult deliberately. Young children are inexperienced and may not know rules and procedures. For example, if teachers do not wash their hands but require it of children, then children will wonder why they are supposed to do this. Instead of *telling* children what they should not do, *show* them what they should do.

Learn to be a troublshooter. Be alert to signs of difficulty and anticipate situations that will require special support. Realize that young children often are doing something—such as cutting shapes out of the middle of a piece of paper—for the very first time.

Walk them through difficult tasks. The "matching law" suggests that if a behavior is rewarded every 5 times it occurs (e.g., giving in to a temper tantrum,) and prosocial behavior is reinforced only every 15 times it occurs (e.g., praising a polite request), then, on average, aggressive behavior will be chosen five times more frequently than prosocial behavior (Snyder, 2002). Sometimes a corrective measure is viewed very differently by a child. For example, if a teacher sees a child pinching another child and says, "Come and sit by me," that child might think it is a privilege.

Think before you speak. Do not threaten children, saying, for instance, "You will have to stay after school if you don't get your work done" when the child rides the bus and there is no way this will happen. Learn to say what you mean and mean what you say.

Choose your battles. Don't feel that you have to respond to every inappropriate behavior but don't be afraid to change something when things are falling apart, either. Beginning teachers who are striving to be liked by children will sometimes smile sweetly at virtually any behavior. It is better to project a serious, concerned facial expression when difficulties arise rather than being afraid of taking steps to stop a behavior.

Use children's literature. Children's books are a rich source of examples of children who engage in inappropriate behaviors, the consequences of those behaviors, and different ways of "trying on" solutions.

SOURCES: Adapted from Nelsen, Erwin, & Duffy, 1995; Rief, 1993.

demonstrate the desired behavior through role-play, and discuss the role-play situation afterward (National Educational Service, 1996). Instead of calling out the offender's name over and over again, a teacher should clearly demonstrate what the child needs to do in order to be accepted by the group.

Aggressive Behavior Is Affected by the Social Context. "We're the Baywatch guys! Look out, we're coming through in our powerboats." With this announcement, a group of 4-year-olds comes running through the housekeeping area leaving dishes, plastic food, and babydolls in their wake. Research suggests that groups of aggressive children, clustered together, are frequently responsible for as much as a third of aggressive acts (Perry, Kussel, & Perry, 1988). Often, this aggression is related to media violence that is reenacted in the classroom, as in superhero play. One intervention that a teacher can institute is to form flexible groups that will create new alliances and social networks.

Physical Aggression Can Be Reduced by Verbal Expression. The rate of openly aggressive acts depends to some extent on a child's ability to use words rather than actions to express emotions. For example, two toddlers are ambling about the child-care center when one stops, watches the actions of the other's pull toy, and grabs the toy away. The first toddler retaliates by biting the offending arm that took the toy away, then they both begin to cry. Although many adults would cite this as evidence that children are cruel, these toddlers are no more cruel than adults; they simply express their hostility in more concrete ways (Daros & Kovach, 1998). Whereas adults in a traffic jam have access to a repertoire of aggressive acts, such as cutting one another off, blowing the horn, shouting insults, and even making obscene gestures, the

Anthony Magnacca/Merrill

A quiet moment when a child is at play is often a good time to approach the child and gain acceptance.

young child's repertoire of aggressive responses is often limited to inflicting physical harm on another. Therefore, coaching children in socially acceptable ways of expressing anger and frustration—learning to "use their words"—is particularly important.

Teachers Sometimes Intervene Too Quickly When Aggression Occurs. Although it is important for every child to feel safe and protected from harm, children need to be taught to work out some of their problems. Teachers who cast themselves in the role of judge and jury soon will find that tattling increases. For example, two children in the dress-up corner reach for an old bridal veil at the same time, and a tussle ensues. This is a good example of an incident that can be negotiated. Rather than rushing in and quickly dispatching a solution, the teacher can "narrate" the argument with statements such as, "I see that Lisa and Shawneen both want to play brides," "How can you play brides if there is just one veil?" or "It wouldn't be much fun to play brides all by yourself." Whenever possible, skillful teachers encourage children to use their own problem-solving resources rather than always playing the role of referee. Your job is to help children develop the social skills they will need for a lifetime. In fact, your intervention in children's conflicts may be thought of as a continuum, ranging from most to least invasive or direct.

Positive Guidance Strategies

What can early childhood educators do to guide children's behavior? Begin by learning something new rather than resorting to what you already know (e.g., Adams & Baronberg, 2005; Marion, 2007). Far too many teachers defend their practices on shaky grounds, saying, for example, "That's what my parents did to me and I turned out okay," "I always heard that you were supposed to make an example out of the ones who break the rules," or "All the teachers I know use stickers to get the children in their classes to cooperate." It is the rare educator who admits that, "In the face of inappropriate behavior my job is to create a change in order to effect a change. I may change the structure of the classroom, the method of instruction, the peer interaction, my actions or thoughts or expectations, or I may simply command change in the actions of the child. Of these, the last is the least effective" (Tobin, 1991, p. 38).

Anthony Magnacca/Merrill

When should an educator intervene in children's disputes?

Walk by any number of classrooms and you can hear teachers relying upon these least-effective methods with statements such as, "Shari, pay attention," "Brian, remember to raise your hand," "We always take turns in preschool," "I'm going to have to call your mother if you don't settle down," and "One more time, Carlos, and you are going to the principal's office." How do teachers begin to change this talk and replace it with something that will actually *teach* children how to get along with others? Five basic precepts follow.

1. ***Learn to Identify with the Child, Not with the Label.*** It is possible to see that a child *has* a problem without seeing that child *as* the problem. Approach a child who is acting out with the goal of understanding that child rather than with the goal of obtaining instant obedience, as difficult as that may be when disruptions occur. Maintain sufficient curiosity to find out why a child might act in a certain way and realize that in that quest, the child is your best teacher. In other words, you must see yourself in the child and truly identify with him or her so that you can reach and teach that child (Strachota, 1996). Suppose that a toddler is very high-spirited. He dashes to the carpet when you offer to read a story, pushes down another child, and handles the book roughly. Try thinking to yourself, "When do I get carried away? When was I reprimanded for this as a child? How did it feel?" Then firmly, but gently, guide behavior and speak directly to that child: "Slow down, Terry. Gina wants to hear the story too and she doesn't like to be pushed down. I'll make sure that everyone gets to see the pictures."
2. ***Focus on the Child's Needs Rather Than on Fear of Failure.*** Put aside your worries about appearing inept and losing face. Think about the child and realize that the child's behavior may be invoking exactly the opposite of what that child truly needs from adults. Second-grader Marjorie is a good example. When the teacher directed everyone to draw pictures of their families, Marjorie grew sullen and refused to comply. The more the teacher pressed, the more adamant Marjorie became, and her teacher saw it as open defiance. What her teacher did not realize is that Marjorie's father had abandoned the family to move in with his new girlfriend. Marjorie was mourning the loss of her father and had overheard her mother talking about being without money. The second grader was terrified that they would be poverty-stricken in the desperate ways she had seen portrayed in movies. Finally, Marjorie relented and drew the picture, but when she arrived at home, she cried bitterly about the fact that she "lied at school," because her picture depicted the entire family "even though I know Daddy doesn't live with us anymore."
3. ***When Confronted with the Most Difficult Teaching or Learning Situations, Go Back to the Basics.*** What is truly basic for young children is what they respond to naturally from the beginning: sensory experiences, play, and enactment. Newborns are soothed by sensory experiences such as being touched and listening to pleasant sounds; toddlers enjoy active play such as pushing, pulling, emptying, and filling; and 3-year-olds typically take delight in enacting familiar routines such as pretending to sleep, eat, or care for a baby. These are the things that mark a return to the basics for young children and are usually a good starting point for reaching a child who seems difficult to reach. For example, it is well known that children who are successful at joining in other children's play have learned to merge with the activity that is taking place rather than disrupting it or simply asking, "Can I play?" A quiet moment when the child is at play is

often the most opportune time to gain acceptance from that child. Particularly when children are aggressive, adults often treat these quiet moments as a "breather" and ignore the child at the very time he or she is most approachable. Co-playing, or merging with the child's spontaneous play, is a way to build trust between an adult and a child, because it is less intrusive, less threatening, and less controlling than other types of teacher-student interactions.

4. ***Don't Expect That You Can Make It All Better.*** We are teachers, not miracle workers. Admitting that we cannot set everything right, however, is no excuse for ignoring what is right for the child. We are powerless to make it all better, yet we have tremendous power to make our corner of the world, our classrooms, better places for children. Stephanie, a private nursery-school teacher, was deeply frustrated and saddened by the painfully slow process of trying to remove a child who was being sexually abused by her adoptive father from his custody. This teacher punished herself because she could not be a rescuer, yet she had done everything within reason by discussing it with the program director, reporting it to a social service agency, and discussing the evidence with a psychologist. Sometimes, the best we can do as teachers is to make our classrooms a safe haven while children are in our care.
5. ***Learn How to Talk with Children About Inappropriate Behavior.*** Beginning teachers often do not know what to say when a child's behavior is inappropriate and surprising. The In-Class Workshop at the end of this chapter will give you practice in speaking with young children in ways that promote appropriate behavior yet do not damage children's self-esteem.

Conflict Resolution and Classroom Communities

Beaty (1995) defines conflict as "interpersonal encounters needing a positive emotional resolution" (p. 5). Ideally, conflict is resolved through a form of cooperative negotiation that leads to a mutually acceptable solution. A classroom community has clearly understood goals, a sense of belonging to the group, effective communication, fair treatment, agreed-upon standards for behavior, opportunities to deal with ideas and values, care and concern for all members, and dynamic, interactive learning (Boyer, 1995; Jalongo, 1992). Research on the human brain suggests the following about human emotions (Sylwester, 1994):

1. ***Emotions simply exist, and they are resistant to change.*** A frequently overlooked part of learning to handle powerful emotions is acknowledging that they exist in the first place. Everyone feels jealous, angry, wronged, or uncooperative at times. The issue is how such feelings are expressed. Students *can* learn how and when to control emotions, but it is often useful to allow children to vent their feelings before attempting to teach them to override their emotions using rational thought processes. Too often, teachers try to repress intense emotional responses in children to avoid unpleasantness. Often, the outcome is that these emotions erupt later with greater force, undermining the sense of community that is being built.
2. ***Activities that enable students to talk about their emotions,*** listen to their classmates' feelings, and think about the motivations of others teach children how to articulate emotions through words rather than lash out physically. One frequently recommended approach for talking about feelings is the class meeting (McClurg, 1998). Figure 10.5 offers some guidelines for making group decisions via a class meeting.

FIGURE 10.5 Making group decisions.

KEYS TO KEEPING CHILDREN ENGAGED IN THE PROCESS

- **Respect and Tolerance.** Be tuned in to children's interests and concerns. Teach them to be considerate of others.
  Example: If there is a new classroom pet, everyone is thinking, "Will I get a turn to feed the bunny? When can I expect a turn?"
- **Timing and Patience.** Adjust time devoted to discussion to children's developmental levels. Teach them to try to stick with a topic long enough to discuss it.
  Example: For preschoolers, just 5 minutes may be long enough. For third graders, it might be as much as 15 or 20 minutes.
- **Imagination and Leadership.** Use props to focus children's attention and harness their imaginations.
  Example: Allow a child to use play binoculars to scan the room for a problem area when children have failed to clean up. Give the group leader an object to wear (e.g., a special scarf) or to hold (e.g., a yarn pompom).
- **Cooperation and Communication.** Use activities that build a sense of cooperation and group unity.
  Example: Have children play a game in which everyone grasps the edge of a round plastic tablecloth or a blanket and works together to bounce a ball in the center; hold hands and sway to the music while singing a spirited song together; invite children to demonstrate a new skill (such as skipping or whistling) and clap for them.

GENERAL PROCEDURE

1. **Explain what a decision is.** Offer some concrete examples, such as choosing what to wear or eat for breakfast, then ask children to give some examples. Start with simple decisions, such as where to put a poster or what song to sing. Progress to more challenging decisions whereby children may need to give up something in order for things to work out, such as allocating computer time.
2. **Brainstorm and record ideas.** Keep a written record of what each child contributes to the discussion. It could be a list, a web of ideas, a prioritized list of activities, or a chart on an overhead transparency. Try breaking the group into smaller discussion groups that meet with an aide or parent volunteer so that everyone has a chance to speak.
3. **Decide what most children want to do.** Strive to arrive at agreement, but consider also that there usually are ways to keep some children from getting hurt feelings or being left out. For younger children, you may want to just look around to see if most children agree. For older children, you may want to take a vote. Teach children to respect one another's special talents, interests, and limitations.
4. **Follow through with the plan.** Let children implement their group decisions immediately so that they can see the positive outcomes of the group planning process.

SOURCE: Adapted from "Making Decisions as a Group," by E. B. Church, 1994, *Scholastic Early Childhood Today, 8*(8), 40–41.

3. ***Emotional responses are affected by the context;*** thus, situations that draw out emotions and engage the entire body in lifelike situations, such as simulations, role-play, and cooperative projects, are most likely to help. When students practice the skills of community in real-world situations, they are actively constructing their knowledge about how to get along with others in a social situation.
4. ***Emotionally stressful school environments are counterproductive*** because they interfere with students' ability to learn. Learners must have a sense of control over their environment and develop self-esteem in order to maximize their learning power. Conversely, "a joyful classroom atmosphere makes students more apt to learn how to solve problems in potentially stressful situations" (Sylwester, 1994, p. 61).

Coping with Different Types of Conflict

If teachers can guide young children's behavior and help them to feel empowered, then children will no longer have a need to do unkind things to others to bolster self-esteem. Psychologist Rollo May (1994) contends that "Deeds of violence are performed largely by those who are trying to establish their self-esteem, to defend their self-image, and to demonstrate that they, too, are significant" (p. 23). Thus, a relationship exists among self-esteem, conflict, and conflict resolution.

In the following paragraphs, we list basic types of conflict and provide recommendations for responding to each of these common situations (see Beaty, 2006).

TEACHER PREP WEBSITE 10.4

Go to Student and Teacher Artifacts select Assessment, choose Informal Classroom Assessment (Module 2) and select Group Participation and Work Habits (Artifact 3).

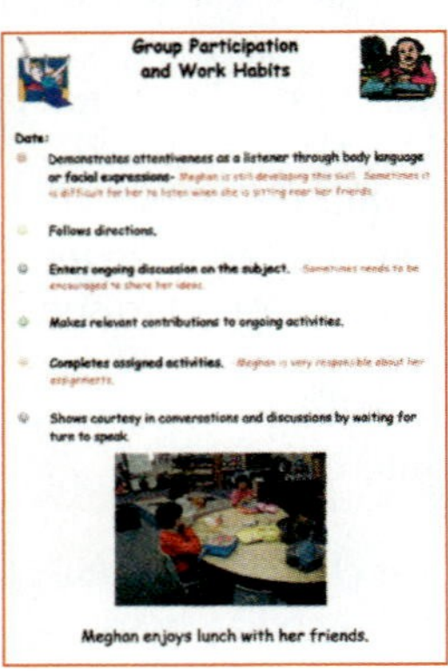

Group Participation and Work Habits

Date:

- Demonstrates attentiveness as a listener through body language or facial expressions- Meghan is still developing this skill. Sometimes it is difficult for her to listen when she is sitting near her friends.
- Follows directions.
- Enters ongoing discussion on the subject. Sometimes needs to be encouraged to share her ideas.
- Makes relevant contributions to ongoing activities.
- Completes assigned activities. Meghan is very responsible about her assignments.
- Shows courtesy in conversations and discussions by waiting for turn to speak.

Meghan enjoys lunch with her friends.

Possession Disputes

Possession disputes occur when arguments arise over ownership. This is the number-one reason for conflict between children. Many teachers grow weary of intervening in these arguments and of the aggressive behaviors that sometimes accompany them. Here are some suggestions for avoiding possession disputes:

Analyze the Materials, Equipment, and Organization of Your Classroom. If a material is in short supply (e.g., one new wagon) you can *prevent* disputes from happening by establishing a policy in advance, such as having a sign-up sheet for turns, setting an egg timer for the length of the turns, and so forth.

Remember That Children Live and Play in Other Environments Where Materials Are Not Shared All That Much. They may be regularly prohibited from playing with an older sibling's toys, for example, because they are "too little" to know how to use them. When children who are accustomed to such prohibitions arrive at school, they may welcome the opportunity to assert their possession over items in the classroom. Take the time to actively build children's understanding that the materials in the classroom are for everyone to use and enjoy and communicate with families about their child's behavior in school. See an example of this at the "Assessment–Informal Classroom Assessment" student and teacher artifacts online at the Teacher Prep Website.

Discourage the Practice of Bringing Items That Children Will Not or Should Not Share to School. Parents sometimes send in an expensive toy or family heirloom, and then become upset if it is damaged. Likewise, children may bring in *transition objects,* items they are particularly fond of that usually offer some sort of tactile stimulation, such as a blanket or a stuffed toy. These items are called transition objects because they are a nonsocial substitute for the primary caregiver's physical closeness and are often used by children at bedtime or stressful times (Jalongo, 1987). Children should not be required to share these items; rather, they should learn to respect one another's right to have something that is not community property.

Attention Getting

COMPANION WEBSITE 10.4 To learn more, go to *Enrichment Content: Research Highlights* in Chapter 10 of the Companion Website at http://www.prenhall.com/jalongo.

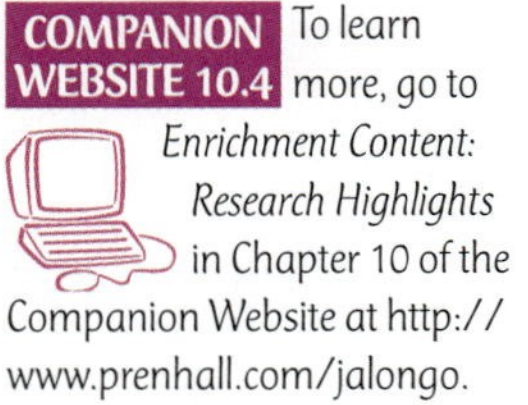

Attention getting refers to using aggressive or inappropriate behavior to demand attention. At first, it might be difficult to imagine that *inappropriate behavior* would be used to gain attention, but negative responses may be preferable to no response at all to the child who is generally overlooked. Yet if children are told that they are bad or stupid or will never amount to anything, they may accept these pronouncements, internalize these low expectations, and act in ways consistent with the negative labels. Remember that children who want attention probably need it.

Greet Every Child Personally Every Day. Say hello and good-bye to every child every day. When you talk with children, let them hear their names in positive ways throughout the day, saying, for example, "Kayla is making a very interesting dinosaur out of clay," "Tyler, you really like this book, don't you? Would you like to take it home and read it again?" or "Let's sing Carmy's verse for our song." Do not use children's names as a shorthand way of correcting inappropriate behavior by saying "Jenny!" to mean "no" or "stop" (Kostelnik, Stein, & Whiren, 1988).

Listen to What Children Say and How They Say It. Make it a habit to have at least one extended interaction with every child every day, even if that means chatting with them at recess or at lunch. Because young children are fairly inexperienced users of language, it is essential to listen not only to children's words, but also to the feelings that underlie those words (Jalongo, 1996). Be patient when the communication is not completely clear and give the child as much undivided attention as possible. Make comments that really let the child know you have understood and care about what he or she has to say.

Identify the Behavior That Is Unacceptable and Why It Is Occurring. Early childhood educators need to develop more skillful ways of talking to young children, such as, "Cherie, keep the blocks on the floor. We do not throw blocks in preschool because someone could get hurt," "Terri and Sheila, please figure out a way that Min can join the hopscotch game" and "Miguel, no hitting in preschool. Look at Crystal's face. You hurt her. Remember our rule: No one is allowed to hurt anyone else in this class." Try to be matter-of-fact about these things and state them plainly and concretely. The teasing sarcasm that peers may find humorous is entirely inappropriate for the young child. If you say, "Oh, *that* was a really great idea" when a child does something wrong, the child is apt to be confused by the inconsistency between your words and the situation.

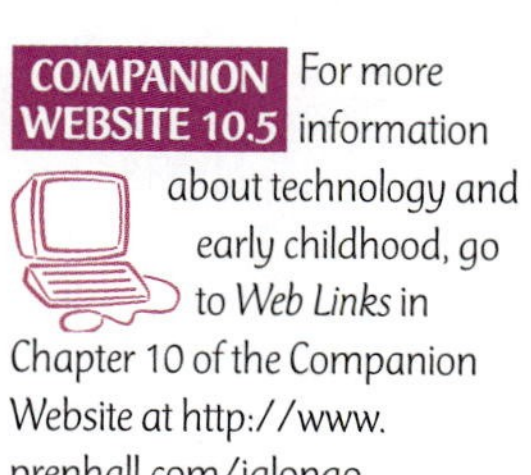

For more information about technology and early childhood, go to *Web Links* in Chapter 10 of the Companion Website at http://www.prenhall.com/jalongo.

Power Struggles

Power struggles refer to conflicts that result when children want to be first or to compel others to play "their way." Remember that children are inexperienced in negotiating and that part of your job is to teach them how to negotiate.

Make Suggestions That Lead to a Mutually Beneficial Outcome. If two children are arguing because they both want to play the mother and neither wants to play the baby, you might suggest that they *both* be mothers and use dolls as babies.

Give Everyone a Turn. Often, children's insistence on being first comes from repeated experiences with the teacher discontinuing an activity before everyone has a turn. Even though it is necessary to stop an activity before children get bored with it, you can let them know that the activity will be available during free play or repeated throughout the week.

Keep Track of Privileges. Busy teachers often forget who had a certain privilege and, if they call on the same person again, the children may protest, "But he already got to feed the guinea pig!" One way to avoid this situation is to make a set of magnetic cards with the children's names on them and use them to keep track of turns when it seems particularly important to do so. You will probably want to use a bulletin board to indicate whose turn it is to water plants, distribute snacks, and so forth. If you want to monitor the number of children at a learning center, a choice board that puts their names next to a drawing that represents each center can help to manage the flow of traffic to and from centers.

TEACHER PREP WEBSITE 10.5

Go to Student and Teacher Artifacts, select Early Childhood Education, choose Guiding Behavior (Module 6), and select Meghan's Friend (Artifact 2).

Personality Clashes

Personality clashes occur when children reject one another because of incompatible temperaments or jealousy. One typical personality clash that occurs often in early childhood settings is conflict between a group of children who want to play quietly and a group of children who want to be more boisterous. Often, the boisterous children will interrupt play, knock down a block structure, or leave the scene of quiet play in disarray. Personality clashes also occur when children differ markedly in their ways of interacting, as in when a child protests, "She always wants to be the boss." You can view an example of a young child's perspective on friendships, at the "Early Childhood Education–Guiding Behavior" student and teacher artifacts online at the Teacher Prep Website.

Be Scrupulously Fair in Everything That You Do. Avoid competitions and prizes that leave some children feeling like winners and others like losers. Young children do not clearly understand games with rules and can be expected to react with tears or frustration to competitive situations. When working with the very young, it is better to emphasize participation and effort rather than competition, which leads to jealousy.

Clearly Designate Quiet and Noisy Areas of Your Classroom. Use bookcases or other large objects to demarcate a quiet area and prohibit wild chasing throughout every corner of the room. Do not assume that children will understand the rules by words alone. Try role-playing. For example, you can ask a child to get on a tricycle, then whisper in his ear to yell and ride through the family living area; this is followed by a group discussion about why this behavior is not acceptable.

Set Up Situations in Which the Children's Differences in Personality Represent an Advantage. For example, a timid child might be paired with a more outgoing child on a field trip so that more questions are asked and ideas are discussed. Dramatizations that enable children to "try on" different personalities, such as play with puppets, can also help them to identify with classmates whose characteristic style of interaction is quite different from their own. Don't be surprised if a shy child delights in assuming the persona of a sassy and mischievous puppet!

Group-Entry Disputes

Group-entry disputes occur when children try to join the ongoing play of another group. Well-known kindergarten teacher, author, and researcher Vivian Paley (1992) considered the following to be one of the most important rules in her classroom: "You can't say you can't play." In her book by the same title, Paley discusses how she instituted this rule to deal with the problem of insiders and outsiders and to counteract prejudice.

Make It Clear That Everyone Is Expected to Get Along with Everyone Else. Children can identify with being excluded because they are "too little" to do something. Children's books, such as *Bailey Goes Camping* (Henkes, 1985), *You'll Soon Grow into Them, Titch* (Hutchinson, 1983), and *Much Bigger Than Martin* (Kellogg, 1976), can be used to spark a conversation about the pain and anger that are caused by exclusion. Using this universal experience of young children can then serve as a basis for making it clear that it is not acceptable to treat anyone in the class as an outcast. Accompany a child who has been excluded, saying brightly, "Make room for Juanita! She wants to play house too," or "Don't forget, no closed games in second grade."

Model the Correct Way of Approaching a Group That Is Playing. Research suggests that the most successful strategy is to join in without disrupting the ongoing play or asking permission. With preschoolers or primary-grade children, you may want to involve them in role-play situations that will give them practice in avoiding group-entry disputes.

Aggressive Play

Aggressive play is conflict that is caused by boisterous play, such as superhero play. Young children are attracted to superheroes because these figures are supremely powerful, and young children are not. Virtually all of the important decisions in a young child's life are made by others—what to do, where to go, when to do various things—so it is not surprising that superhuman characters who are even more powerful than adults are particularly appealing to children.

COMPANION WEBSITE 10.6 To add a reflective practice product to your developing portfolio, go to *Journal: Constructing Your Professional Portfolio* in Chapter 10 of the Companion Website at http://www.prenhall.com/jalongo.

Set Reasonable Limits on Play. If children engage in a persecutor-victim theme such as wild animals chasing their prey, and the child identified as the prey is clearly unhappy about it, then it is time to intervene.

Temporarily Disband Aggressive Groups. Three preschoolers who decided that they wanted to give karate chops and kicks to others started running through the Head Start classroom during free play, a time when children are free to choose centers and materials. Within moments, three children were crying or shouting. Their teacher knelt down next to the boys and said calmly, "I see that your friends do not want karate chops and kicks. I want each one of you to choose a different center . . . . Okay, Rickie has chosen to observe our class rabbit and draw in the journal. That leaves . . . . What will you choose, Kayla?" and so forth.

Teasing and Name Calling

Teasing and name calling are disputes that result when names that are hurtful or embarrassing to one child are used by another (NAEYC, 1996). Although some insensitive teachers dismiss such behavior as an inescapable part of growing up, remember that you are a significant adult in children's lives and, as such, you can influence children for the better.

Model Respect, Caring, and Patience. As everyone knows, children are more influenced by the behaviors they observe in others than by their words. Simply saying, "That's not very nice" is not sufficient, because it does not specify what is objectionable. Be concrete: "Jason, calling people names like 'stupid' and 'fat' makes them sad. Please do not use those word when talking to our friends in this class."

Use Children's Literature That Depicts Teasing and Bullies. Many children's books model how children can cope with these difficult situations and resolve conflict (see Luke & Myers, 1994).

Shifting Blame

Shifting blame occurs when children deny responsibility for their actions and try to shift the blame to someone or something else.

Encourage Children to Tell the Truth and Admit to Mistakes. Young children are at the stage of moral development where they want to avoid punishment. If your punishments consist of setting things right and making restitution rather than harsh discipline, this will tend to support the development of self-discipline. It also is helpful to admit to your own mistakes and say how you will correct them.

About Children's Need to Feel Significant

Now that you have examined different types of conflict that typically occur in classrooms, try to explain how each one is a child's effort to say, in effect, "I am important."

Request an Explanation Before Rendering a Decision. Ask children to offer suggestions about what might solve the problem. For example, "I see that there are Cuisenaire rods all over the floor where Kahlesha and Nicole were working on their math problems. What could the two of you do to have the materials ready for the next math class?" For more practical suggestions on conflict resolution see the Ask the Expert feature on the next page.

Guiding Children to Appropriate Behavior

When you begin teaching, you will no doubt wonder what your colleagues who have such well-behaved classes do to make this happen. Yet even if you were afforded the opportunity to observe in these classrooms, your questions about discipline might remain unanswered because everything is running smoothly. Mainly, teachers fear such conflict situations for one of several reasons:

- **Teachers fear a loss of control over the classroom environment.** A classroom that is chaotic is obvious to anyone who happens to pass by and the report that someone's classroom is completely out of control can spread through the building quickly, damaging the reputation of both the teacher and the group of students. A chaotic classroom is the nightmare of teachers, both figuratively and literally. As one of our students expressed it, "I couldn't sleep the night before school started. I had a dream that I was teaching and the kids weren't listening to me at all. They were running around the room, throwing things and screaming. Did you ever have a nightmare like that?" The answer is "Yes!" Even experienced teachers have anxieties about children's behavior in school. Teachers are correct in assuming that an unruly group of children will reflect unfavorably on them in the culture of the school, where maintaining order and quiet frequently is prized.
- **Teachers fear that they will say the wrong thing.** When a tearful child says, "My grandmother doesn't have any hair. She gets chemo. She has cancer," what should a teacher say? Many teachers are so uncomfortable dealing with tragic situations that they change the subject, say nothing, or offer some formulaic response, such as, "Don't worry, she'll be all right." The first thing to remember with young children is that it may not be necessary to *say* anything. It might be better to gently study the child's face, give a sympathetic look, be a little more understanding throughout the day, and talk over the situation with the family and a counselor rather than trying to give a speech. You might also simply help the child with words that describe the emotions he or she is apparently experiencing: "You seem worried about your Grandma."
- **Teachers fear a loss of face with the group.** Suppose that a child is directed to sit down and completely ignores the direction. Many teachers worry that such defiance will be contagious and infect the rest of the group with a spirit of rebellion when they see a classmate "getting away with" noncompliance. Many teachers find it helpful to get down to the child's eye level, make eye contact, and speak directly to the child. Until you are certain that the child has heard and understood, you should not assume defiance.

ASK THE EXPERT

Edyth Wheeler on Conflict Resolution

Edyth Wheeler

Don't I have to *prevent* children from engaging in conflicts in order to create a peaceful classroom environment?

Most teachers will agree that conflicts occur naturally among young children. Some may be surprised to know that children actually learn important social and cognitive skills as they engage in conflicts with peers. During these interactions, they develop logical thinking, perspective taking, and problem solving, and they practice rich and often complex language. When teachers begin to think of conflict as a natural phenomenon and of children's ability to manage conflict as a developing capability, they will approach this area just as they do other areas of children's development, such as language and motor ability. The teacher's goal, then, is to support children's learning as they work through conflict situations.

Won't conflicts lead to aggressive behavior?

Conflict is an interaction in which children object to each other's actions; in other words, confilt is a mutual opposition or disagreement. Generally, children engaged in a conflict are trying to resolve the issue at hand. Most conflicts do not involve aggressive behaviors. However, aggression, which is defined as an unprovoked attack, can precipitate retaliation. Conflicts, too, can develop in different ways. As teachers observe children's conflicts, they will decide whether the interaction is a constructive conflict, through which children learn, or a destructive conflict, which escalates in intensity as tempers flare and frustration rises.

How can teachers create a peaceful classroom and help children resolve conflicts?

It has been pointed out that "peace is not the absence of conflict" (Wichert, 1989, p. xi). A peaceful classroom depends on two conditions: first, that children want to resolve conflicts; and, second, that they have the ability to do so. The first condition can occur in a classroom that is a caring community where adults and children value and demonstrate cooperation, kindness, respect, and concern for others. Teachers can create the second condition by providing children with words to use in conflict situations and by adding curriculum experiences that encourage children's collaboration, perspective taking, and generation of alternative solutions to problems. In other situations, teachers may need to help children toward a solution.

When should I step in to guide children, and when should I allow children to work things out on their own?

Children are often able to resolve conflicts without adult help. There are two things teachers can look for as they decide whether to intervene: If children have been playing together before the conflict begins, and if they are using reasoning and negotiation during their conflict, they are more likely to settle their dispute agreeably. Teachers who observe these conditions would be wise to give children the opportunity to manage the conflict themselves.

How can teachers create a caring classroom where conflicts are resolved agreeably?

I suggest an approach that I call "a three-layer cake." The bottom layer, the foundation, is the teacher's commitment to a peaceful classroom. The middle layer is made up of curriculum ideas and activities that promote prosocial behavior and conflict resolution. The top layer contains strategies for children and teachers to use when conflicts occur. The icing on the cake is the family–school connection.

Here are a few suggestions for making your "three-layer cake." First, the bottom layer: Demonstrate your commitment to a caring classroom. Model prosocial behavior. Adults can be powerful models of both positive and negative words and actions. Be aware of the pervasive prosocial and empathetic behavior that happens naturally among children. I ask teachers and parents or caregivers to watch for acts of caring and kindness. Acknowledge these acts to children with words of encouragement.

The middle layer: Curriculum elements to build a caring classroom community include morning meetings, peer sharing and supportive routines in classrooms, cooperative activities and games, and discussions of good children's literature. We often see words such as ***respect*** and ***consideration*** on posters in classrooms, but without discussion of exactly what these words mean to children and how they are to act to show respect and consideration, the posters on display have little meaning.

The top layer: Begin by observing children in conflict and resist the temptation to step in right away. Allow for as much child control of the outcome as possible. Respect children's mutual decision making, even if it is not the solution you would have recommended. You may want to encourage children to use more complex reasoning and negotiation through scaffolding. If you observe a conflict that is escalating and may lead to violence, do intervene and allow children to calm down before guiding them to resolution.

The icing on the cake: Remember the importance of ongoing family–school communication to develop a mutual understanding of conflict issues and strategies and to provide continuity from home to school. Additional strategies include school visits from family and community members and joint workshops for families and teachers.

Are these expectations for conflict-resolution skills for all children?

Very young children are capable of empathy and understanding for others. As they learn to communicate effectively, they can resolve conflicts. Children as young as 3 years old have intervened as spontaneous peer mediators to help others. In inclusive and diverse classrooms, guiding children to resolve conflicts is a powerful tool. Experiences with those who are different in some way from themselves help children develop the perspective taking needed for conflict resolution. In turn, the perspective taking learned through conflict helps children understand others. In supporting children's learning about conflict resolution, teachers need to be aware of culture, language, and socioeconomic factors. Concepts of sharing and ownership, interaction and language styles, and social and cognitive development play a part in the issues, strategies, and outcomes of children's conflicts. As with any area of learning and development, teachers will provide appropriate guidance for individual children according to their particular needs and abilities. In some schools, a few children are selected to become peer mediators. It is important for teachers to communicate a belief that all children can, and should, be peacemakers.

Will what we do in classrooms carry over to the world outside the classroom?

Young children live in a world of widespread violence. They witness angry reactions to disagreements among family members, friends, strangers, and nations. They are exposed to violence through first-hand experiences and through the pervasive presence of the media. Teachers, parents, and caregivers can play a vital role in helping children work toward peaceful resolution of their conflicts. In schools and classrooms, there is a growing movement to incorporate peace education and violence prevention. In your own school, share your caring classroom approach so that children may continue to practice peaceful conflict resolution from one year to the next. Strong family–school partnerships will help children bring their conflict-resolution skills from the classroom to the neighborhood. Communities can work to support prosocial children's television programming and nonviolent toys. As early childhood professionals, we face a critical, challenging, and yet promising undertaking, an opportunity to help children make a difference in their world, both now, as children, and later, as adults.

Edyth Wheeler is an Associate Professor of Early Childhood Education, Towson University, Maryland.

These common concerns help to explain why teachers view conflict so negatively. Actually, conflict is like stress in that it is inherently neither good nor bad. Stress results from anything that requires an extra effort of adaptation, including good things such as a job promotion and getting married. Likewise, conflict can be viewed as an opportunity to learn about one's self in relationship to others (Beaty, 1995, p. 2). Learning to deal with conflict in a calm, confident manner is an important part of becoming an early childhood practitioner.

After reading this section on coping with conflict, you might have some reservations about or objections to the approach. Your first thoughts might be that it is too permissive, too time consuming, and too dependent upon verbalization skills. Why not just demand obedience and reprimand children to show them that you are a strict teacher? Why not just take the often-repeated advice of "Don't smile until Christmas," as the old saying goes? The real reason for taking the time and investing the effort is because this method teaches children how to get along with others, so it will become a way of life.

One of the more controversial aspects of conflict resolution has to do with young children's capacity for responding to other children's suffering. Many educators who have some familiarity with Jean Piaget's cognitive-developmental theory would argue that young children are too embedded in their own perspective—too egocentric, to use Piaget's terminology—to take the perspective of another child. But Patricia Ramsey (1991), a leading expert on young children's peer relationships, argues that "because even very young children resonate to others' emotions, children can empathize and communicate on an emotional plane before they are consciously aware of others' perspectives" (p. 18).

Beginning teachers often are too permissive. This sometimes occurs because the teacher draws upon his or her knowledge of being responsible for one child, such as experience with babysitting. Kurt really enjoyed being in the company of children and decided to work as an aide in the summer to gain more experience. He interacted with the children in the same way that he had previously, cheerfully teasing them with remarks such as, "Hey, buddy! C'mon over here. Where'd you get that haircut? Are you having a bad hair day? I think so!" and then tousling the child's hair or roughhousing with the children, particularly the boys. Kurt was completely shocked when the other teachers asked to speak to him about his unsatisfactory work performance and the gender bias that was evident in his behavior. Clearly, Kurt had selected the wrong "script" for how to interact with young children in a child-care center. This does not mean that he was incapable of becoming an effective caregiver, only that he would have to make significant changes in his customary way of responding to the children in order to become their teacher. He would have to learn to resist acting like one of the children himself. Fortunately, Kurt was able to admit that his current style was "headed for disaster," because the children had begun to test the limits of how far they could go and some had insulted and even hit him. Kurt had to begin all over again and set new standards for behavior that were not so permissive. He was able to do so with time, training, and experience.

Conclusion

There is little question that violence is escalating in the United States and that some children live in places that adults would find frightening. Interestingly, "the word violence comes from the Latin word *vis,* meaning 'life force' . . . in violence, the thrust of life is making itself visible. It would be a mistake to approach violence with any simple

COLLABORATING WITH FAMILIES

Common Conflict Scenarios

The Big D—Discipline

One definition of discipline is to guide or to teach self-control. To better explain how I guide children's behavior in my class, I will describe a common conflict scenario. Then I will look at two different responses and what the child might learn from each one.

Scenario: Bill, Robbie, and Samantha are playing a board game together. The game requires children to take turns. Whoever gets to the last space on the gameboard first is the winner. After several turns, Robbie finds that he is falling behind the other two players. At that point, he overturns the gameboard and sends the pieces flying. "That's a stupid game!" he yells out. Bill and Samantha are confused and upset. As the teacher, I approach the table. What would you do?

> ***Response #1:*** Robbie is told that he is not using the materials correctly and is to blame for stopping the game. He is told that his behavior is wrong and that he has to pick up the pieces and apologize to his friends.

What would this action teach? (a) Adults are in charge of all the rules, so children always need to turn to adults to be the referees; (b) feelings that caused the outburst are not discussed; (c) saying that you are sorry settles conflict (even if you don't mean it); and (d) Robbie has lost by being declared the troublemaker, so he will probably try to find an opportunity to be the winner (for example, by tattling on someone else), or he will accept the idea that he is basically bad and make little effort to change that judgment.

> ***Response #2:*** The adult approaches the children and calmly asks what has happened while she gathers them together into a small circle. Each child is given a turn to say what he or she thinks happened and how he or she felt about it. The adult summarizes the comments and states the problem, "You were all playing the game and now the game is over with all the pieces on the floor. It seems that Robbie wanted to stop the game because he decided that he didn't like it and didn't know what to do." The adult then asks if there are other ways to solve this problem. The children suggest that you could leave the game just by saying you wanted to leave, removing your game piece, and going on to another activity. That way, the other children who liked the game could continue. The children also decided to pick up the pieces and restart the game. Bill and Samantha asked Robbie if he wanted to play this time.

What would this action teach? (a) Everyone has feelings, which should be respected; (b) there are many solutions to a problem, and some are better than others; (c) adults are not the only ones who can solve problems; children can participate in and practice this process; and (d) adults can be counted on to guide children's problem solving.

Young children need to learn that feelings are okay, but that how you express your feelings is not always okay. They need to develop skill and confidence in their ability to handle their own problems in socially acceptable ways rather than being branded as "bad." They need to learn how to live with others and work things out instead of constantly running to adults to serve as judge and jury. Think about how you might apply the second type of response to some of the behaviors that you like least. Imagine a long car trip during which two siblings are fighting about space in the back seat. How might the first response actually fuel the arguments? How might the second response build a better relationship?

Teacher Reflection

Use a small, square cardboard box with the numerals 1 through 4 on each side. Roll the box and read the discussion question on the corresponding reflection card. Within your group, brainstorm possible solutions, share ideas, and think about new ways to approach difficult situations. Choose a recorder for your group to take notes on comments, thoughts, points, various views, and so on. Be prepared to share with the total group.

Reflection Card 1. Reflect on terminology. What words come to mind when you think about discussing children's behavior problems? What terminology would you avoid, and why?

Reflection Card 2. Reflect on breaking the news. What reaction do you think you'll get if you tell a parent that his child is experiencing difficulty in her social interactions?

Reflection Card 3. Reflect on personal experience with behavior problems. Tell your group members about a time when your teacher reported something negative about you, a family member, or a child you know well. How did this affect the child's behavior?

Reflection Card 4. Reflect on concerns. What is something you'd like to learn about or discuss when communicating with parents? Explain why this is important to you.

idea of getting rid of it" (Moore, 1992, p. 126). As an early childhood educator, your role is to guide children in finding socially constructive outlets for that "life force." Far too often, children arrive at school with a long list of negative labels that are based on the situations of their families, their communities, or both. But children do not get to choose to whom they are born, and even the most dedicated educator cannot alter the desperate life circumstances in which increasing numbers of young children in America live. As Marian Wright Edelman (1992), the director of the Children's Defense Fund, reminds us, "We need to stop punishing children because we don't like their parents. The truth is we are punishing ourselves in escalating welfare, crime and lost workers and productivity by failing to value, invest in and protect all of our children" (pp. 45–46). When teachers and families become frustrated by children's misbehavior, there are four common responses that do little to teach children more productive behaviors:

- Do nothing, just wait until children become more mature and hope they'll "grow out of it."
- Label the behavior, diagnose it, and medicate.
- Institute the "three strikes and you are out" rule in early childhood education classrooms and expell children from school if they do not behave.
- Attempt to change the parenting practices, and if all else fails, blame the parents. (Martinez-Beck & Zaslow, 2006, p. 210)

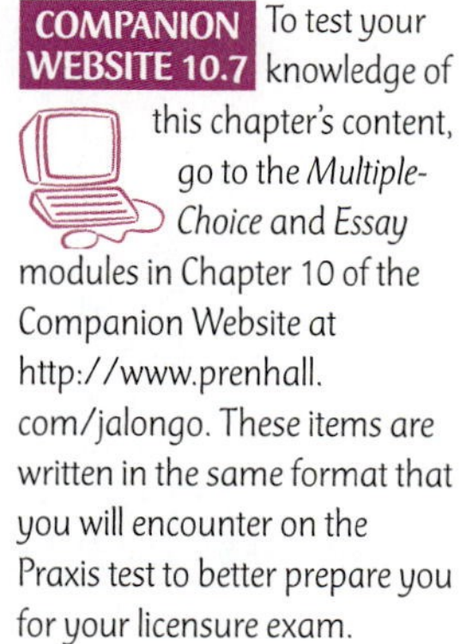

COMPANION WEBSITE 10.7 To test your knowledge of this chapter's content, go to the *Multiple-Choice* and *Essay* modules in Chapter 10 of the Companion Website at http://www.prenhall.com/jalongo. These items are written in the same format that you will encounter on the Praxis test to better prepare you for your licensure exam.

Early childhood practitioners *do* have the power to make centers and schools a haven, a safe community where children can feel accepted and learn valuable lessons. One of our most important roles is to help children understand who they are and how they can become admirable human beings.

ONE CHILD, THREE PERSPECTIVES

Earl's Disruptive Behavior

Earl is a first grader who already has a police record. It seems that he was standing in his front yard pitching rocks as cars passed by, and one of the rocks hit a driver's windshield and broke it, causing an accident. At school, Earl is frequently in trouble despite the fact that he has the attention of the school psychologist, a foster grandparent, a social services caseworker, his teacher, and a student teacher. Within a 1-hour period, the following observational notes were taken about Earl.

E. arrives at school in blue jeans, cowboy boots, and a house key chained to his belt. He is excited about a badge his father gave him that reads, "Kiss me if you love truckers." E. sits down at the desk, looks at the girl sitting next to him, and remarks, "Your eyes are really blue. Do you wear contacts?" The girl frowns and says, "No!" Then she turns away. E. says, "Well, I do. See?" and blinks his eyes rapidly. Then he says, "Look, I can stick this pin in my skin and not bleed—want to see me do it?" "No. That's disgusting," the girl responds. With that, E. slides the point of the pin under his skin and demonstrates that the pin is now attached to his finger. "Want to see me do it again?" E. asks. Again, a no. At this point, the teacher takes the pin away from E. and puts it in her desk drawer.

Time for partner reading. Children go to various corners of the room, arrange plastic tub chairs side-by-side, or stretch out on the floor. Most settle down and begin reading. E. stacks chairs on top of a table, and just as he is ready to climb on, the student teacher stops him, reminding him that chairs stay on the floor. E. walks to the restroom and on the way sees two boys absorbed in a book. "Hey, man! Get out of my chair," E. says to the boys. The boys look at him blankly and E. continues, "If you ain't outta my chair when I come back, you and me's gonna have words." E. takes a few steps away, then walks back, saying, "I mean it, man. That's my favorite chair." When E. emerges from the restroom, he challenges the boys to a fight. The student teacher directs E. to wash his hands and sit down. E. complies, then walks up to the teacher's desk, puts on some hand lotion, and pulls the desk drawer open to look at his badge. The teacher asks what he is doing and E. replies, "Nothing."

Time for the children to write in their journals. E. stares at the paper, then begins to wail loudly that he doesn't know how to write, puts his head down on the desk, and moves his head and shoulders slightly as if sobbing. He glances around to see if anyone has taken notice. The student teacher kneels down next to E. and reminds him of some of the things that he might write, such as his name, letters of the alphabet, words such as stop, no, and so on. With that, E. brightens. He says, "I want to copy the words off the badge that my dad gave me. My dad is a trucker. When he's on the road, I can take care of myself."

- Earl's teacher says, "Earl is a troublemaker. I have to watch him like a hawk. When he was absent for a couple of days, my classroom was peaceful. I have tried everything to get him to behave, but nothing seems to work," while Earl's student teacher says, "Based upon comments that Earl has made, he is left by himself much of the time since his mother abandoned him. I know that he is hurting and wants so much to be accepted, but he is often rejected by his peers."

- The social worker says, "We are currently investigating Earl's case, and it is clear that Earl is neglected. If this situation continues, Earl's father may lose custody."
- The foster grandparent says, "Earl is a very needy little boy. I hear all of these horror stories about him, but whenever I work with him one-to-one, he never gives me any real problems. I enjoy the time we spend together."

REACT	In what ways are the perspectives of these adults alike? How do their approaches to meeting Earl's needs vary?
RESEARCH	Read several articles at the library about children with difficult family circumstances. What recommendations were made?
REFLECT	What might be the underlying reasons for the differences in the responses to Earl's situation? Which perspective do you identify most strongly with, and why?

IN-CLASS WORKSHOP

Role-Playing Ways of Talking with Children

Following are some examples of early childhood professionals speaking with young children in ways that can effectively guide their behavior. Try writing several of your own examples and role-playing them for the class.

- "I noticed that you were sharing the trucks today" or "It was great to see you playing together with the blocks."
- "I'm glad to see the sand staying inside the box" or "You were right to make room for Juanita."
- "I hear shouting," "There are seven people at this center and only four are allowed at one time," "I see clay all over the table," or "Remind me, Elise, of the rule about the woodworking center."
- "Stop throwing the blocks right now," "You cannot leave the playground; there are cars going by," or "Everyone who played with the puzzles has to help put them away. Darien, you were playing here."
- "What happened here?" "Do you think that is fair?" or "Who can help me hang up these paintings?"
- "Who has an idea about what to do when everyone wants to pet the rabbit?" "Is there a way that you could both play with the new wagon?" or "What could we do to keep your blocks from being knocked down?"
- "The table is all sticky from snacks. It needs to be washed with a sponge," "That's enough Power Rangers for today. Jenny and Rick, choose a center," or "Maybe Ms. G. (the aide) could help you glue your wood sculpture back together."
- "You can make your snack as soon as you come in in the morning, or you can wait until you are hungry" or "Everyone has to help clean up the room. You may work at the water table or in the block corner."
- "Tomorrow when you come to preschool, we will put the shopping cart away. The cart is not for crashing into other people" or "You were late coming in from recess again today. Let's make a plan so that this won't happen tomorrow."
- "Now someone has slipped and fallen on the floor. Tanya and Michelle, please go and get the broom and sweep up the sand that you

spilled," "Everyone can play hide and seek. Give Weiwei a turn," or "Lisa is crying because you pushed her off the swing. Help her up and go get a wet paper towel for her elbow, Melissa."

- "Don't worry, everyone will get a turn. I will put the new baby carriage in the family living area for everyone to use. Remember, only five people at a time in the center."
- "Look at Gita's face, Charley. I don't think she likes to get bear hugs and being squeezed so hard, do you? Let's see if we can think of a better way to let Gita know that she is your friend."
- "Second graders, you all know that even though we have new gravel on the playground, it is not for throwing. Why?"
- "Yes, you can write your own name on your painting, Erica. But Kira is only 2 years old, and she needs help writing her name."
- "Tony, when the other third graders made their model of a zoo out of boxes and paper, they did not want anyone to ruin their work. How can you help them feel less angry with you for messing up their project?"
- "Trish, please don't yell across the room. Walk right up to your friends and speak softly."
- "On this walk, we will be looking for signs of fall. It will be very important for everyone to stay together and hold your partner's hand. That way, nobody will get lost."
- "Our custodian, Mr. Lowell, was very disappointed to see our classroom so messy yesterday when school was over. He had to work much harder cleaning our room and was very tired. How can we do better today? What could we do to let Mr. Lowell know that we are sorry?"
- "Please stay in our story circle until story time is over. Lamont, you are part of our group. Come back and join us."
- "I noticed that Jerry and Sandy were at the computer watching DVDs. Now it is time to put the DVDs back in the holders and place them on the shelf until tomorrow."
- "Brad, I can't let you kick other people, even if you are playing. Remember our rule? It's not okay to kick. How can you still play ninjas without hurting anyone?"
- "Wipe your brush on the side of the jar, like this. That way your paint won't run down your picture when you are at the easel."
- "I know that it is hard to wait for your turn, Bahar. Let's look at the list on the wall together. You just had a turn to go get the milk. We can mark on the calendar the day that it will be your turn again, but don't forget that there are lots of different jobs to do in first grade."
- "Remember the rule about using the slide: one person at a time gets to stand on the top step."
- "I put the apple juice in this little plastic measuring cup so that you can pour your own. Pour it very slowly, like this, and watch to see how much will fill the cup. Who would like to try it?"
- "I see that your art project is starting to fall apart. Can I help you fix it?"
- "Some children were playing at the water fountain and got the floor all wet. Who has a good idea about how to solve this problem?"

Applying What You Have Learned

In *So This Is Normal Too?* Hewitt (1995) identifies several common developmental issues that early childhood educators typically encounter. For each of the following incidents, consider everything that you have learned from this chapter and try to formulate a response with your group.

1. **Separating from Parents and Caregivers.** A teenage father brings his 4-year-old son to class on the first day of nursery school. When the child begins to cry, the father says, "Stop being such a wimp! You're embarrassing me. Be a man."
2. **Seeking Attention and Tattling.** A teacher is on playground duty and hears the following comments from children. Gerri calls out while on climbing equipment. "Teacher, look at me! Ms. B., look at what I can do. I can pump my legs and swing really high."

   "Ms. B., didn't you tell us not to climb the fence? Look at Jason and Miguel. They're climbing the fence."

   "It was my turn next on the seesaw and Charlene pushed in front of me."

3. **Telling Tales.** Cheryl is talking to her kindergarten classmates about what she did over the summer. She says, "Me and my mama went to Disneyworld and we saw Mickey and Donald and then we ate french fries and ice cream and. . . ." "Uh uh," says Denny, "I live on her street and she didn't go nowhere this summer. She was right here all the time."
4. **Taking Turns and Sharing.** Two toddlers are playing on the carpeted floor of their day-care provider's home. They both want to use the toy vacuum cleaner at the same time, and one child slaps another child's face.
5. **Having Tantrums and Swearing.** A group of first graders is singing together, and the teacher asks if there are any special requests. Geoff wants to teach the group a song and begins to sing "Frosty the Snowman," but he forgets the lyrics. When the other children grow restless, he becomes increasingly frustrated. He scowls, turns bright red, and then screams loudly, "Just shut up, all of you. I can't think." Then he stomps away from the group and yells over his shoulder, "Assholes!"
6. **Behaving Aggressively.** Within a first-grade classroom, children are busy working at learning centers. Suddenly, screams are heard from inside the restroom. As the teacher scans the room, she notices that Danny is nowhere in sight. She approaches the restroom door and asks, "Danny are you in there? Are you okay?" In response, she hears screeches of laughter and Danny's voice singing, "D-A-N-N-Y, Danny! Danny! Danny!" The teacher recalls the previous week, when Danny bit a fourth grader, and two days earlier, when he decided to "be a bowling ball" and roll down the hallway ramp. She knocks on the door again, saying, "Danny, please come out. Other children need to use the restroom. You are missing your play time." Silence. Soon the first-grade teacher hears scribbling, followed by a tearing sound. She unlocks the door to find Danny standing in the newly decorated restroom, surrounded by crayon drawings and strips of masking tape that he has put all over the new wallpaper (Conrad, 1997).
7. **Toileting or Eating Problems.** A professional couple brings their son to preschool to meet his teacher. The boy is 3 1/2 years old but is not toilet trained. When they discuss this issue, the parents say that they do not want to toilet train him until he is ready. While they are talking, their son goes over into the corner, squats down, and has a bowel movement in his diaper. He then sticks his finger inside his diaper to show the parents that his diaper needs to be changed. Later, when the boy begins at the preschool, children begin to ridicule him for still wearing diapers.
8. **Gaining Acceptance from Peers.** Twila is a very bright child with high academic achievement. She is also obese. Lately, she has been tormented on the bus and arrived in the classroom crying after a bully took her lunch away, saying "You don't need it anyway because you're a big fat hog."

A Problem-Solving Strategy for Practitioners

Now try applying the following problem-solving strategy (Tobin, 1991) to each of the situations just described. Work in small groups, then be prepared to share your ideas with the total group.

1. What bothers you about the behavior?
2. Does it seem like typical behavior or something unusual?
3. What are your hypotheses about possible reasons underlying the behavior?
4. On your own, consider possible teacher responses, both good and bad. Then try to formulate a statement that reflects a skilled way of talking to the child and his or her family.
5. As a group, choose the most effective statement.
6. What might be the intended or unintended outcomes of your choice?

CHAPTER 11

Exploring Your Role in Supporting Families and Communities

Co-authored with Laurie Nicholson,
Indiana University of Pennsylvania

> Early childhood educators need to identify with and respect families despite the fact that perspectives on childhood may differ drastically; we need to collaborate with families in ways that place children's needs uppermost and optimize growth and learning socially, physically, emotionally, cognitively, and artistically; and we need to build mutual trust and respect, particularly for those families who have had negative experiences with the educational system. To accomplish these goals, we must confront our own biases, embrace diversity, respect the knowledge that families have about children, and willingly share power. In every situation early childhood educators face, the overarching purpose is how to respond in ways that serve children's best interests.
>
> Nancy L. Briggs, Mary Renck Jalongo, and Lisbeth Brown, 1997, p. 56

Meet the Teachers

THEO SPEWOCK has been responsible for coordinating a program in her school district for many years, and she has become convinced that they need to establish communication with parents and families *before* children are struggling in school. She coordinates a Title I program—a national, federally funded initiative that provides learning support services to children who are experiencing difficulty with reading and mathematics. One of Mrs. Spewock's many brainstorms was successful in connecting the family and school more closely: She decided to initiate contact with parents as soon as the babies were born, while the mothers were still in the hospital. After that, she communicated directly with the family every year on the child's birthday until the child entered school. Each year, all of the families in the school district received a birthday packet containing information about the child's development, appropriate learning activities, local services and agencies, and—with some financial support from the community—a picture book to begin building a home library for the child.

MS. COLE is a teacher in a program for infants and toddlers with vision impairments. She works on a team consisting of the child's parent(s), the program director, an infant development specialist, and an eye-care professional to conduct a thorough assessment of each child. The team wrote learning outcomes for Kirsten, an 18-month-old who is blind. As Ms. Cole astutely observed, "Over the years, I have worked with dozens of parents who are grieving about their children's visual impairments and who feel helpless. This program offers much needed support." Some of the outcomes that have been identified for Kirsten include teaching her to feed herself, move around the classroom safely, and develop listening skills through recorded music. All of these goals are combined with a course of action, periodic review, and parent reports of progress into a document called an individual family service plan (IFSP).

MR. BREWER is a second-year kindergarten teacher at a large school in a southern city. He is fortunate to work with colleagues who share information with parents about children's progress through newsletters, workshops, home visits, and a lending library of audio- and videotapes about the classroom that have been translated into different languages. Mr. Brewer wrote a grant proposal to fund a family partnership training program that matches parents/families of prekindergartners with parents/families of kindergarten students. For example, a newly immigrated family from Korea was paired with a family that had been in the United States for several years so that they could communicate freely. Likewise, the family of a prekindergartner with a hearing impairment was paired with a family with a kindergarten child with vision problems so that the more experienced family could share information about support services. Mr. Brewer's goal is to introduce families to others in the community who are familiar with some of their major concerns. He is dedicated to the notion that all families, no matter their economic status or structure, want what is best for children and that families can help one another to successfully navigate the support services of the school and community.

COMPARE	What are some commonalities among these teachers, even though they are working with different families and in different situations?
CONTRAST	How do these teachers think about families? How would you characterize the outlook of each one?
CONNECT	What made the greatest impression on you, and how will you incorporate this view of families into your teaching?

Now that you have reflected on the perspectives of three different teachers, here is a preview of the knowledge, skills, and dispositions you will need to acquire in order to fulfill your role in collaborating with families and communities.

Learning Outcomes

- ✔ Become familiar with national standards and guidelines governing the early childhood educator's role in working effectively with diverse families **(NAEYC #2, 4, INTASC #10, and ACEI #5c)**
- ✔ Be introduced to parent involvement traditions in the field of early childhood education
- ✔ Examine goals and models of home–school communication, collaboration, and support
- ✔ Recognize the early childhood professional's unique role in promoting home–school collaboration
- ✔ Learn general techniques and practical strategies for building mutual trust and respect with families
- ✔ Apply knowledge of school–community partnerships to various early childhood settings
- ✔ Identify exemplary practices in communicating with parents/ families, conducting conferences, and supporting young children's learning and development

Understanding Contemporary Families

What is a family? When most Americans hear the word *family,* they think of a mother, a father, and a child or children. The majority of families in America, however, do not fit this pattern. In fact, the most common family structure in the United States is a

DID YOU KNOW...?

- Though living in a household with two married parents has been associated in research studies with more favorable academic and social outcomes for children, the percentage of children under 18 living in such an environment fell from 73% in 1990 to 67% in 2005 (Children's Defense Fund, 2006).
- In 1975, just 47% of mothers with children under 18 were in the workforce. That figure rose to 71% in 2004 (Children's Defense Fund, 2005).
- In 2005, 57% of children ages 3 to 5 spent some of their day in center-based early childhood care and education programs, while 47% of children in grades K–3 participated in some form of nonparental care on a regular basis before or after school. Of children in grades 4–8, 53% also participated in a regular schedule of nonparental care (Childstats.gov, 2006).
- Full-time child care for just one child can cost between $4,000 and $11,000 a year—at the high end, this represents almost 50% of two parents' full-time minimum wage salaries (Sachs, 2005).
- The quality of child-care options available to low-income families often is uneven and some of these arrangements may compromise children's development (Ceglowski & Bacigalupa, 2002). Many families in poverty rely on free care by relatives or friends. Dependence on multiple providers results in frequent changes in child-care arrangements.
- When parents distrust the caregivers of their children they question the quality of the care and education that their children receive and usually disenroll their children from the program in question (Gonzales-Mena 2006; Mensing, French, Fuller, & Kagan, 2000).
- Generally speaking, parents and families decide to participate in their child's education if and when: (1) their participation is necessary or important, (2) their involvement will promote their child's academic achievement, and (3) their contributions are welcomed by educators (McDevitt & Ormrod, 2007).
- Families with children account for 40% of the nation's homeless population (Children's Defense Fund, 2006).
- In the United States, more than 900,000 children were abused and neglected in 2003. This equates to one episode of abuse or neglect every 35 seconds (Children's Defense Fund, 2006). Children who are at the greatest risk for maltreatment in families often began life as premature infants, are young, have disabilities, and have difficult temperaments (McDevitt & Ormrod, 2007).
- The number of medically uninsured children in the United States has reached 9 million. Hispanic families have the highest rate of children without medical insurance—21% (Children's Defense Fund, 2006).
- A food insecure household is one in which the supply and quality of food necessary to support adequate nutrition is not reliably available. The number of children under 17 who go hungry (classified as "food insecure households" by the U.S. Department of Agriculture) rose to 19% in 2004 (Childstats.gov, 2006).

single-parent mother with one or more children. Many other children live in blended families formed by remarriage. Some children reside with family members from different generations, such as grandparents, aunts and uncles, or older siblings. Others live with certain family members at different times of the year and stages in their lives. Still others reside with no family member, such as those in foster care or from international adoptions. Artificial reproductive technology offers yet another definition of what constitutes a family member by making it possible for a child to be conceived outside the human body or for a biological child to be borne by someone else, with none, one, or both of the biological parents' heredity (Hanson & Gilkerson, 1996). Thus, it no longer makes sense to think

COMPANION WEBSITE 11.1 To learn more about supporting families, go to *Journal: Defining Your Role* in Chapter 11 of the Companion Website at http:// www.prenhall.com/jalongo.

> **PAUSE AND REFLECT**
> **About the Influence of Your Family on Your Expectations**
>
> Many preservice educators remember "playing" school, being read to regularly, going to the library, and an array of other experiences that built curiosity and positive disposition for learning. Think about your own family's involvement in this process. List the ways your own family was involved in your early learning experiences and with your teachers in elementary school. How are these ways similar or different from those suggested in the preceding guidelines? Which of these ideas could you try? Talk about your experiences with a classmate. Now reflect on the statistics in the Did You Know? feature that began this chapter. What surprises did you find in this information? What assumptions do you need to change?

of families strictly in terms of traditional legal guidelines of relationships formed by blood or marriage. As a first step in connecting with families, early childhood educators need to seriously broaden their definition of a family.

David Elkind's (1995) definition of family addresses both social and biological influences. He defines the family as "a social system characterized by a kinship system and by certain sentiments, values, and perceptions"(p. 11).

Of particular importance to early childhood professionals in the 21st century is the shift to the postmodern family. Elkind (1994) contends that the family has shifted away from children's needs and moved toward the needs of adults, who are seeking fulfillment. In the past, for example, it was common for unhappy couples to stay together "for the children's sake." Today, however, they would be more likely to separate or divorce, based on the belief that adults are entitled to a satisfying relationship. There are many new lifestyle options such as single-parent families, blended families created by divorce and remarriage, adults returning to higher education and training programs, gay couples with children, and shared custody arrangements. Despite such differences, the general finding has been that strong, successful families share three traits: valuing togetherness, encouraging individual differences, and adjusting effectively to change or stress (U.S. Department of Health and Human Services, 1990). Characteristics of families that are functioning well include:

- **Communication**—clear, open, frequent discussions between and among family members
- **Cohesiveness**—feelings of closeness and connectedness; appreciation for the uniqueness of each family member while advocating a commitment to the family as a unit
- **Adaptabllity**—an ability to adjust to predictable changes as well as to overcome situational stress; seeking outside help when needed
- **Clear roles**—definite, yet flexible roles and responsibilities; fairness for family members and a balance of power
- **Shared time**—quantity and quality of time together in which rituals and traditions abound
- **Shared values**—common core of beliefs, service to others, a sense of spirituality
- **Social support**—connectedness to extended family members, friends and neighbors, and the larger community; effective use of available services and resources

The Family as a Social System

Early childhood educators who view families as part of a larger social system understand that all members of a family affect each others' lives (Kantor & Lehr, 1975). To reach and teach children, early childhood teachers must acquire insight into their students' lives outside of school. When discussing family relationships, most adults first consider the many ways that parents and families influence children. What is sometimes overlooked is the

UPI/Corbis/Bettmann
Lawrence Migdale/Lawrence Migdale/Pix
Skip Nall/Getty Images, Inc.—photodisc

American families have changed dramatically over the last half-century.

fact that this influence is reciprocal. New parents who assume that their lives won't change that much with a new baby in the house are in for a big surprise. As any parent or guardian can attest, every imaginable aspect of life changes with the addition of that new human being. Children affect parents and families in other significant ways, too. A parent who has a child with a learning disability, for example, may become more patient over the years in the process of adapting to a child with special needs. The parent–child relationship also influences the many social contexts in which the parent operates: the role of spouse, relationships with extended family members, relationships with friends and coworkers, and connections to the larger community.

Take, for example, the situation of Mrs. Mason, a child-care provider for a classroom at the YMCA in a small town. She decides to participate in a program sponsored by the Salvation Army. The goal is to fulfill some of the Christmas wishes for a low-income family by creating a gift basket. When she receives the description of her family, however, the description is so distinctive that she realizes it is one of the families in her class—two

PAUSE AND REFLECT
About Family Configurations

Use index cards to draw pictures, one for each person in your family. Pets can be included! Don't worry about your artistic talent, just sketch something that represents your family members on the cards. Write your first name and last initial on the back of each card. Then spread the cards out on the floor and take a look at the different family groupings. Try some different activities with the cards, such as making a class graph of different family sizes, grouping by relationships (e.g., all the grandparents), talking about different kinds of families, or inventing categories (e.g., family with the most sisters, family with the youngest children, family with the most generations). Consider the factors that make your family unique that others might use to describe it (e.g., the family with twins, the family with all girls, the family with three generations living on the same street). Then think about how you might use a similar activity with young children or a group of parents/guardians to send the message that there are many different family configurations (Berry & Mindes, 1993).

sisters who are divorced and are living together to raise their preschool children, a boy and a girl. Mrs. Mason had no idea that their economic circumstances were so difficult until this happened. She keeps the information confidential and discretely suggests that it might be best for her class to work with a different family.

As this situation illustrates, there is an undeniable "ripple effect" that occurs when something happens to another family member. If a parent loses a job, is chronically ill, or suffers injuries in an automobile accident, these changes affect children's lives. Young children cannot leave their problems at the door when they arrive at school, and the fact that they do not fully understand adults' problems does not necessarily make these situations any less troubling for children. A father can say to his son, "I lost my job," but what does that mean to a child in preschool or the primary grades? Mostly, young children build their understandings of such ideas through concrete consequences. Some consequences might be, as some children we have known over the years have put it, "Now we have to go on vacation in the backyard instead of Disneyland," or "My dad watches TV all the time and my mom yells at him," or "I get my clothes at yard sales." Early childhood teachers must be keenly aware of such comments from children and strive to help families gain access to needed resources in the community that will support them in adjusting to their changed circumstances.

The Family in the Larger Social Context

The family is embedded in the larger social system. Consider, for example, the challenge of finding adequate, affordable housing. While American real estate prices have soared over the past 3 years, many Americans have reported selling their homes at two to three times their original purchase price. But what about the impact of this housing trend for families working at minimum-wage jobs? Depending on their geographic location, affordable housing may be truly out of reach. A report from the National Low Income Housing Coalition (2004) indicates that the wage a worker needed to earn to afford a two-bedroom home at market value rose to $15.37 hourly, a 38% increase since 1999. This figure is more than twice the current hourly minimum wage, so even two full-time minimum wage earners cannot afford the fair market rent in 48 states and the District of Columbia. Consequently, families may have few choices in living arrangements, often moving in with other relatives or having to settle for less-than-adequate housing in a potentially unsafe area simply because of affordability. In 1999, 35% of households in the United States with children had one or more of the following housing difficulties: physically inadequate housing, crowded housing, or housing costs greater than 30% of the total family income (Children's Defense Fund, 2006). To see a young child draw and discuss her neighborhood,

TEACHER PREP WEBSITE 11.1

TEACHER PREP MERRILL PRENTICE HALL

Go to Video Classroom, select Child Development, choose Family, Culture, and Community (Module 3), and select Neighborhood, Part I (Video 1).

watch the "Neighborhood Part I" video clip online at the Teacher Prep Website. Lack of affordable housing is also the leading reported cause of homelessness. While many assume that runaways, addicted persons, or individuals who have somehow slipped through the cracks of emotional and behavioral health supports are the ones who are homeless, families constitute 40% of the homeless population in the United States. And the need for affordable housing continues. Homelessness impacts children's educational and care experiences in negative ways, often forcing families to move frequently in search of temporary housing. Attendance may be a problem for children who are constantly changing residence, and catching up on missed learning experiences in the classroom can be overwhelming. Children may also suffer from anxiety or depression because of housing insecurity. Additionally, they may have difficulty forming lasting friendships, an important element of the early childhood years. The Better Homes Fund (1999) reports that 21% of homeless children may repeat a grade, not because of inability, but because of missed learning opportunity.

Michael Newman/PhotoEdit Inc.

How will you communicate respect for diverse families?

A teacher from West Philadelphia learned this first hand. She collaborated with the school librarian and public librarian to present a Saturday workshop on the importance of reading aloud to children. The group of parents and families was lively and attentive and the evaluations suggested that the session was well-received. Yet as the teacher began to gather up her materials, she noticed one young mother who had stayed behind. The mother said softly, "I wanted to say something about the reading to kids. I see what you are saying but you gotta understand. Reading sort of falls through the cracks when you're worried about a roof over your head. That's all." The teacher felt her face flush, embarrased by her ignorance of other people's circumstances. "I . . . I see" she stammered. She later found out that the mother was residing at the homeless shelter with her two preschool children.

Even if a family does not have to resort to shelter life, inadequate housing can be detrimental to children's health at a very basic level. Lead poisoning, exposure to asbestos, radon, and high levels of mold—and a significantly higher rate of childhood asthma—are much more prevalent in homes that low-income families can afford. Almost 5 million children have asthma, a figure that more than doubled between 1980 and 1994. While childhood asthma can be successfully managed, families in stress may have difficulty

PAUSE AND REFLECT

About the Concept of "Home"

Think about your own early years and what it meant to arrive home after a day at school. What were some of the routines that you came to expect? Now consider the impact of living in an unsafe neighborhood, or moving frequently in search of affordable housing.

1. What opportunities were there for after-school play in your neighborhood? If you had lived in a community characterized by violence, how might your parents have changed this routine?
2. How was homework handled? When and where was it done? How did your family support you? Now consider how homework routines would be affected by cramped housing conditions, parents working multiple jobs to pay the bills, or residing in a homeless shelter. How will you take such situations into consideration when assigning homework?

FIGURE 11.1 The educational rights of homeless children.

The McKinney-Vento Homeless Assistance Act of 2002 provides the guidelines that states and school districts must work within to serve children and families who are homeless. Essentially, this legislation provides that:

- Schools must ensure that homeless children meet the same state academic achievement standards required of all students.
- Homeless children must receive access to the same kinds of education programs and services that other students receive.
- Homeless children have a right to transportation to and from school; Title I programs (help for low-income students); special education (help for students with disabilities); programs for students who do not speak English well; vocational or technical programs; programs for students who are gifted and talented; public preschool programs; and school nutrition programs.
- Homeless children may receive transportation to public preschool programs if the school district provides transportation to other children.
- School districts appoint a staff person who will assist homeless children in attending school. This "liaison" assists the school and family in communicating with each other.
- The liaison also ensures that the parents and guardians of homeless children are told about educational opportunities available to their children.
- The liaison additionally assures that parents know how to participate in their children's education. (Adapted from the Education Law Center, 2004, *www.elc-pa.org*)

Additional Resources

National Association for the Education of Homeless Children and Youth:
763-545-0064; *www.naehcy*.org/

National Center for Homeless Education:
800-755-3277; *www.serve*.org/nche/

National Coalition for the Homeless:
202-737-6444; *www.nationalhomeless*.org/

National Law Center on Homelessness & Poverty:
202-638-2535; *www.nlchp*.org/

National Network for Youth:
202-783-7949; *www.nn4youth*.org/

COMPANION WEBSITE 11.2 To learn more about your role in supporting families and the NAEYC, go to *Web Links* in Chapter 11 of the Companion Website at http://www.prenhall.com/jalongo.

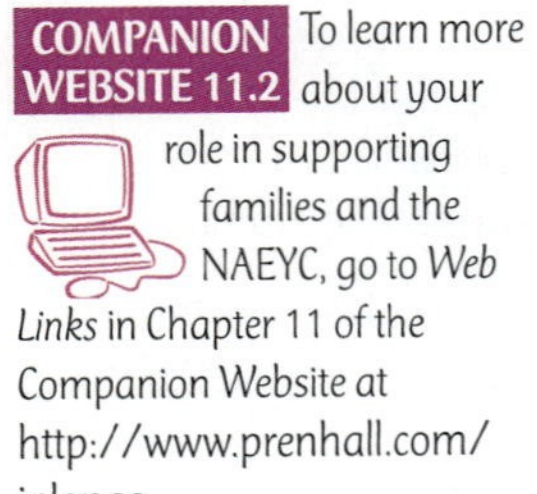

getting treatment for children, leaving a myriad of problems related to missed days of school for the child, missed days of work for the parent who cares for the child, and a home environment that may contain environmental irritants that will simply begin the cycle again. Figure 11.1 is an overview of the guidelines that schools are to follow in supporting the education of homeless children. Kevin Swick's Ask the Expert feature provides additional suggestions on working with families that are homeless.

Respecting Diversity in Families

Grace Anderson steps off the bus at the corner of 4th and Miller, on her way to a conference with 5-year-old Roman's kindergarten teacher. Grace enters the classroom where two chairs are arranged at a round table. "Mrs. Anderson, I'm so glad to see you!" Ms. Everly smiles as she comes over, "Roman has told me so much about his 'MawMaw.'" At 63, Grace Anderson did not expect to be Roman's primary caregiver. But Grace's daughter, divorced since Roman was 3, became addicted to painkillers after sustaining a serious injury in a car accident; his father is a Marine sergeant stationed overseas. The grandparents' modest two-bedroom house is Roman's home now. Grace and her husband R.J. joke that the lively 5-year-old is "keeping them young," but both of them worry about raising a child so late in life.

ASK THE EXPERT

Kevin Swick on Homeless Children and Families

Kevin Swick

Why is homelessness such a major problem in lives of young children and their families?

Over the past 30 years homelessness among young children and families has increased dramatically. A conservative estimate is that 1 to 3 million children in the United States are homeless. The causes of homelessness among children and families are diverse, but major issues are: economics, illiteracy, and abuse/violence in the family. In addition, natural disasters also cause many families to be homeless. On a global scale, war, famine, and disease have affected millions of children and parents.

Key myths about children and families who are homeless

There are some misconceptions or "myths" about children and families who are homeless. One such myth is that homeless parents are lazy and do not work. In fact, over 65% of homeless parents work part time or full time. Many parents who are homeless ask for services such as child care so they can get training and go to work.

Another myth is that parents who are homeless do not care about their children. Nothing could be further from the truth. Research shows that homeless parents are more often involved in the care of their children than parents who are not homeless but at risk for poverty-related problems. Ellen Bassuk of Harvard University found that homeless mothers took better care of their children than peers who were doubled up but not technically homeless.

A myth that is especially damaging is that homeless children do not do their schoolwork. Just the opposite has been noted. Indeed, homeless students do their work quite well when they have the needed support and materials.

The roots of homelessness among children and families

The sources of homelessness in children and families are in three areas: violence, crises in the family of origin, and consistent problems with mental illness and/or drug abuse. While the situation of each homeless family is unique, in most cases violence in the family, some prior trauma in the parent's family of origin, and chronic problems in social and emotional relations prevail and negatively impact the family.

Implications for early childhood professionals

First, develop and use a holistic view of the family's situation. Take into account the many stressors that influence their lives.

Second, exhibit positive and supportive behaviors with children and families. Show parents and children some hope, show them that there are helpful and nurturing people in their lives.

Third, engage parents in being an important part of their children's lives.

Fifth, empower parents through helping them strengthen their educational competence.

By understanding the complexities of what homeless families experience we can be more responsive to the challenges impeding their lives. For example, family literacy and adult education strategies have been successful in empowering parents, both educationally and economically. Providing basic services such as child care and transportation can make a powerful difference in how families work and interact in the world. We need to realize that we indeed are powerful people in the lives of homeless families. We do make a difference when we make it possible for them to open up to new possibilities in their lives.

Kevin Swick is a Professor of Early Childhood Education at the University of South Carolina, Columbia.

U.S. Census data for 2000 indicate that 4.5 million children in America were living in grandparent-headed households, an increase of 30% since 1990 (Jehlen, 2006). While you might assume that low-income, minority grandparents constitute the bulk of this population, this is not the case. Grandparents across the economic spectrum may find themselves in this role after their adult child can no longer care for their grandchild or children. Grandparents often are cast in the role of parents once again after their child dies, is divorced, is incarcerated, or becomes disabled. Many times children have been removed from the family home prior to grandparents being aware of the issues or stepping in to assist, and this can create more stress for the family.

Grandparents face some unique challenges in child rearing. They may have difficulty providing medical insurance for a grandchild, unless they complete a legal adoption. The unexpected responsibility for a child may challenge the income and earning power of older adults who have planned carefully for a time when their out-of-pocket costs were expected to be less, not more (Jehlen, 2006). Older adults also face the obstacle of potentially decreased energy or find it hard to network with the younger adults who are parents of their grandchild's age-mates. Grace remarked, "His classmates' parents are all young, like our daughter. They don't have things in common with us."

Grandparents also may feel out of touch with contemporary youth and their collective fascination with technology or expectations to engage in activities such as sleepovers, birthday parties, and travel. Roman's grandfather chuckles at the memory of a family workshop at school where some of the parents were discussing the video games on their children's wish lists. R.J. felt entirely disconnected from the conversation, and spent the next Saturday morning at Wal-Mart, having a young saleswoman demonstrate a couple of the games to him.

Grandparents raising children may also experience degrees of social isolation from their retirement-age peers. The network of friends that the Andersons socialized with through the years has dwindled since Roman came to live with them. "We can't just take off for an evening; he's our first consideration. While we know that our friends still care, our life is very different now."

In working with this growing population, early childhood educators need to be aware of print resources such as *Parenting the Second Time Around* (PASTA), a curriculum for grandparents produced by Cornell University, and *Project Healthy Grandparents* produced by Georgia State University, as well as online resources (e.g., American Association of Retired Persons Grandparent Information Center, www.aarp.org/families/grandparents; Generations United, www.gu.org; Grands Place, www.grandsplace.com; KINship Information Network, www.kinsupport.org; National Aging Information Center, www.aoa.dhhs.gov; National Committee of Grandparents for Children's Rights, www. grandparents-forchildren.org).

Support groups are another resource. Roman's teacher located a group for grandparents raising children that meets once a month in a community just a half hour away. "It's made a huge difference to us," reports R.J. "It's a chance for Grace and me to share our concerns, and to laugh and cry a little with others who are going through this." Rather than clinging to nostalgic ideas about families borrowed from the 1950s, teachers need to recognize families' strengths and avoid the common tendency to compare, judge, or criticize families that differ from their own. The Head Start program has focused on parent/family involvement since its inception. To learn more about the types of activities used to support children and families, watch the "Head Start" video clip online at the Teacher Prep Website.

TEACHER PREP WEBSITE 11.2

Go to Video Classroom, select Early Childhood Education, choose Families and Communities (Module 6), and select Head Start (Video 1).

Teachers' Concerns About Working with Parents/Families

Beginning teachers often feel overwhelmed when working with families. First of all, the focus of new teachers understandably has been on teaching the children, and those who choose to spend their lives in the company of the very young may not be as confident or relaxed in the company of adults. Moreover, new teachers who are not parents themselves may feel that their knowledge about children is dismissed as "book learning" and lacks authority in the parents' eyes. The more candid among our undergraduate students have sometimes admitted that they don't know what to say to parents or that they feel awkward around them. Instead of worrying about whether parents will judge you as less skillful because you are not a parent, simply acknowledge when they are the experts in this area. If you know nothing about toilet training, do not fake it! When asking parents for help, try something like, "I know about early childhood education, but I don't know much about toilet training. You've toilet trained three children. Can you offer some advice?" This approach acknowledges that you are not the only or best source of information on all topics related to children's development.

Another worry of preservice educators is that their relationships with families or parents will become adversarial. Most traditional-age students in teacher education programs have no experience as parents, and they may find themselves in an "Us vs. Them" mind-set, rather than an "Us, together" mind-set. Your behavior must be governed, first of all, by a commitment to each child's learning (Powell, 1991). Expect that you will need to go well beyond the typical role of providing in-class instruction. Teachers need to view parents as equal partners in education, support parents' efforts to help children learn at home, attend to children's basic needs when the family cannot (e.g., supplying breakfast at school), and refer families to the many school and

Scott Cunningham/Merrill

Collaboration with other professionals is often necessary to find appropriate options for helping young children and their families.

community resources that can provide support. Guidelines for making referrals include:

1. Recognize when you are in over your head and need to gain additional support.
2. Look upon this need for additional support as a professional response rather than a personal defeat.
3. Know the agencies, organizations, and services in your area.
4. Identify competent people in those groups with whom you can work.
5. Make referrals to these specific individuals, not just a general referral.
6. Secure family members' agreement that they will participate.
7. Ask family members to predict what might prevent them from participating and get them to identify ways to overcome obstacles to participation.
8. Check out the family's progress on proposed solutions and have alternative resources available in case difficulties arise.
9. Plan for a follow-up meeting to determine how the referral is benefitting the child. (D. M. Rosenthal & J. Y. Sawyers).

Maintaining a strong home–school connection with multiple cultures is a concern of many soon-to-be teachers. Christenson and Sheridan (2001) remind us that in 2001, 19% of all children in the United States had at least one foreign-born parent. This leads to the possibility that the families we work with may or may not have experience with the school structure, organization, and policies with which we are so familiar. Additionally, this may mean that the foreign-born parent's receptive and/or expressive language skills may be a challenge to school–home communication. Usually, schools and centers with a high percentage of families who speak a language other than English (e.g., Spanish in the Southwest) already have forms, notices, and other written materials translated into the home language of these families. Be sure to ask for them if they are not automatically provided. If your school does not provide this service, or if the home language of a family is not commonly spoken in your community, enlist the help of another parent or an international student at a university who can translate for you. Sending home bilingual notices communicates a welcoming message to parents and families who speak languages other than English. Additionally, get into the habit of regarding these families as important resources who can share "cultural items like magazine pictures, family recipes, dramatic play props, family experiences, stories, and artifacts" (Swick, Boutte, & van Scoy, 1995, p. 2).

When a child has a disability, parents and families frequently look to teachers and schools for support. Often, parents of children with disabilities need additional services and resource materials to meet the special challenges. As a future teacher, you must be sensitive to the special needs and dynamics of parents of a child with a disability.

Having enough information and background about families increases the likelihood of establishing good rapport and a good working relationship with the child and family. Swick and Hooks (2005) found that parents of children with special needs wanted to be valued, to be sought out for feedback on how things were going with their child, and that they appreciated having an important part to play in the parent/family–teacher partnership.

What Parents and Families Expect from Teachers

A Carnegie Foundation for the Advancement of Teaching survey found that the top-ranked expectation parents/families have for a teacher is the ability to motivate their child to learn (Boyer, 1995). This, then, is a good starting point. Begin by sharing the interesting activities in which the child has participated. Parents want to:

- know that the teacher knows their child as an individual.
- work with competent early childhood professionals who deliver the services effectively and in ways that truly meet their needs.
- be regarded as an effective member of their child's education team.
- be heard and take part in shaping the agenda that impacts them.
- be sought out for feedback.
- have their ideas recognized and used in creating quality programs.
- form a close relationship with early childhood professionals that is collaborative and communicative. (Swick, 2004, Swick & Hooks, 2005)

TEACHER PREP WEBSITE 11.3

Go to Student and Teacher Artifacts, select Early Childhood Education, choose Families and Community (Module 7), and select Isabelle's Math Progress and select (Artifact 1).

Informal communication is an important way to build rapport with parents/families. To see an example of a preschool teacher's note about a child's progress in math, look at the artifact in "Early Childhood Education–Families and Community" student and teacher artifacts online at the Teacher Prep Website.

Lawrence-Lightfoot (2003) emphasizes that parents are powerfully affected by how early childhood professionals relate to their children. She states:

> When parents hear the teacher capture the child that they know, they feel reassured that their child is visible in her classroom—that the teacher actually sees and knows him or her—and they get the message that she really cares. (p. 114)

One way to achieve this is to learn to share *small accomplishments and meaningful interactions that children have while in your care* (Swick, 2004b). When the child attempts to help a newcomer to the class, he is demonstrating kindness and compassion. Such acts can be a source of great parental pride if they are noticed and shared in a timely fashion (Knopf & Swick, 2007). Acknowledging special talents is another way to bond with parents/families.

As teachers validate parents by involving them in meaningful partnership roles, numerous benefits emerge:

- Teachers see parental involvement in more positive and diverse ways.
- Families involved in school activities tend to develop more positive attitudes in general regarding school and teachers (Lundgren & Morrison, 2002).
- Parents gain confidence in themselves as partners with teachers and view teachers and the program in positive ways (Swick, 2004a).
- Parents and teachers have more meaningful involvement with the children and each other.
- Children may gain greater social competence when their parents gain confidence through volunteering in the classroom, attending workshops, or being involved in policy councils.
- Families may begin to aspire to higher educational goals for their children (Pena, 2000a, 2000b).

Promoting Parent/Family Engagement in Education

Parental involvement in children's education is not a new strategy. On the contrary, since the beginning of civilization, parents have been the first teachers and socializers of their

COMPANION WEBSITE 11.3 For more information about families and communities, go to *Web Links* in Chapter 11 of the Companion Website at http://www.prenhall.com/jalongo.

children, passing on the skills, customs, and laws of their cultures, intentionally or unintentionally, so that their children would be able not only to meet their own basic needs but also to be productive citizens and carry on their cultural traditions (Berger, 2004).

Family involvement efforts over the past several decades have been widely criticized for being inflexible, superficial, and gender biased. Parents were invited to school at the school's convenience, for example, with conferences scheduled during the day or one evening per year. Often, when parents did volunteer time, they were given menial tasks to do such as cleaning up the classroom. Moreover, the focus was on homemaker mothers who could bake cookies, plan party games, accompany children on field trips, or assist at book sales (Henderson, Marburger, & Ooms, 1992). Frequently, there were few ways for fathers to participate without feeling like outsiders (McBride & Rane, 1997). Fathers, both custodial and noncustodial, need to be included in our communications, our celebrations, and our efforts to support children.

> Female teachers share the gender experience with the mothers of their students and as such they have some insight into how other women have developed into the role of mother. It is not as easy for female teachers, the overwhelming majority of early childhood educators, to relate to fathers. Teachers can maximize the participation of fathers in the school experiences of young children by understanding how men learn what it means to be a father, being sensitive to working fathers, trying to involve absent fathers, and encouraging positive parenting skills. (Friedman & Berkeley, 2002, p. 209)

Parent education programs were the next wave of initiatives to involve parents. Here the idea was to teach parents the skills that they needed in order to parent effectively and support their child's learning. However, many of these programs have been criticized for making the assumptions that: (a) learning flows only from school to parent to child; (b) learning occurs only in formal, school-like contexts; and (c) learning that reflects white, middle-class values is preferred (Briggs et al., 1997). Gradually, the field of education has come to the realization that expecting parents to "help out" at school or participate in "canned" programs to train parents have numerous drawbacks.

Instead of large-group gatherings for which parents are expected to leave work, arrange for child care, come to school, and sit and listen to a lecture about effective parenting, new models of home–school collaboration are being implemented. These programs, called *family resource* or *family support programs,* recognize and respect the fact that while all families share many of the same needs, they do not all need the same type of information or service at the same time. The major goal of such programs is to provide services that will enhance family life, thereby improving the personal, social, and academic development of children and empowering families to help themselves (Davies, 1991; Kagan, Powell, Weissbourd, & Zigler, 1987). Family support programs are a definite departure from the 1950s concept of parental involvement as being mothers working as volunteers or assistants to classroom teachers. Contemporary approaches to allying with families are moving toward a comprehensive services model. Suppose that you were the parent of a child with a hearing impairment. In the past, you would have traveled to and worked with a wide variety of individuals and organizations: an audiologist, a speech/language pathologist, a sign-language tutor, the school, and the National Speech, Hearing and Language Association. If you had relocated to another area of the country, you would have started all over again. Increasingly, today's families are seeing a sort of "one-stop shopping," whereby, for example, support services for a child with a hearing impairment are all coordinated at the school.

The issue of family support needs to be addressed as a national public policy issue so that a more coordinated effort can be put into action (Galinsky, Shubilla, Willer, Levine, & Daniel, 1994). Comprehensive family support programs require a great deal of political action.

Today, we are at a crossroads. Early childhood educators cannot "do it all" while an increasing number of families cannot provide for children's basic needs, much less their educational ones. Although some families may state that they expect schools to assume virtually all responsibility for formal learning while they attend to more basic needs, there is an undeniable "protective potential" of parent involvement in children's education and care (Fantuzzo, McWayne, & Perry, 2004, p. 467). The postmodern era demands that educators, policymakers, and society at large ask more questions about what families need, what assists them most effectively in supporting their children's learning, and how satisfied they are with the level of shared communication between school and home. Moving from the traditional modes of stay-at-home moms assisting with classroom parties, Christenson (2004) suggests that educators must view families as "essential partners" rather than as "desirable extras" in the educational life of the child (p. 87). It is irrefutable that the quality of family–school relationships exerts a profound effect on children's success in school (Fantuzzo et al., 2004). The child's risk is lowered if the relationships between child and family, as well as family and school are functional; and if the home and school communicate and supply consistent, congruent messages (Christenson & Sheridan, 2001). We also know that when families support learning at home by supervising activities, monitoring homework, and engaging in conversation about school tasks, their children show higher achievement in reading, mathematics, and writing, and higher grades on report cards (Fantuzzo et al., 2004).

As early childhood educators, we have the first opportunity to engage families in the educational experience of the child. It is up to us to assist families in knowing how to work as our partners in the critical work of starting children's educational journey. See Eugenia Berger on Communicating with Families in the Ask the Expert feature.

PAUSE AND REFLECT

About What Family Involvement Means

What does family involvement mean to you? First with a partner and then in a group, discuss the actions and activities that would suggest an involved parent. Then discuss the goals and approaches to family involvement that are summarized in Figure 11.2 (Christenson, 2004). How did your group's ideas compare?

Toward More Effective Interactions with Parents/Families

We recommend that those entering the early childhood field recognize the following basic guidelines for working effectively with families.

Respect the Fundamental Differences in Teachers' and Parents'/Families' Perspectives. In the field of early childhood education, it is common to speak of partnerships between families and schools. For a true partnership to exist there must be mutual respect, shared decision making, and appreciation for the contributions made by each person. Hayes (1987) suggests that educators treat parents and guardians as professional child rearers who have extensive on-the-job experience. Family members know children in ways that the school can never know them. Usually, family members have been with children over extended periods of time and have witnessed many developmental milestones. The adults in a child's family typically have been involved with the child on a one-to-one

FIGURE 11.2 Communicating effectively with families.

General Guidelines for Working Effectively with Families

- Be aware that schools are expected to meet more than the academic needs of today's students.
- Confront your own biases about families.
- Recognize that educators are in a unique position to identify children's needs and establish interaction with families.
- Appreciate the importance of effective communication and professionalism in your interactions with families.
- Be aware that teachers bear responsibility for reaching out to parents, families, and communities.
- Explore the many dimensions of your role in working with families and communities.

In interactions with families, strive to:

- Ease families' concerns.
- Keep professional jargon to a minimum.
- Make it easy for families to stay informed.
- Provide opportunities to meet informally and network.
- Schedule meetings at various times.
- Communicate in a variety of ways (e.g., conferences, open houses, musical or dramatic performances by children, parent information board or center, newsletters and websites, "good news" notes, home visits, telephone calls, and special events such as picnics, book exchanges, and field trips).
- Strive to identify with and meet families' special needs and concerns.
- Be sensitive to individuals' discomfort in the school setting.
- Problem solve instead of blame.
- Focus on *all* families.
- Allow parents to contribute in their own ways.
- Know your limits and seek outside assistance when needed.

Correspond with Parents/Families About the Curriculum

- Write a letter that is succinct and jargon-free.
- Make the note or letter short—no more than one page.
- Be certain that the letter is completely free of errors and ask one or more colleagues to read it before you send it out.
- Choose a learning activity with relevance for families, convey enthusiasm for it, and build family interest in participation.
- Use the format for a friendly letter—include the date, a closing, and a signature.
- Address the letter to the parents, family, or guardian of the child.
- Be upbeat and positive rather than demanding or negative.
- Do not assume that all parents and families have resources (e.g., markers, paste, other materials) in their homes.
- Do not impose last-minute requests on parents and families.
- The letter should include:
  The purpose for the activity and what children will learn.
  Ways the parents/families could participate or support at home.
  How to get in touch with you if they have any questions.

basis in a wide variety of contexts, such as in the backyard, at the grocery store, at religious ceremonies, at the shopping mall, in the swimming pool, at family reunions, or at a family vacation spot.

However, educators know the child as one of many other children who are her or his age. They are trained to see evidence of the child's growth in all areas: physical, cognitive, social, emotional, and creative. Teachers also have insights into the child's progress relative to the progress of a child's peers, because they work with children of the same age all of the time. When viewed in this way, it is easy to see why families' and educators' views of the same child are different yet complementary, with each contributing pieces to the puzzle of who a child is, how he or she is doing, and what might be causing a particular behavior.

ASK THE EXPERT

Eugenia Berger on Family Involvement

Eugenia Berger

Are parents truly interested in their children's education?

If schools are "family friendly," parents will feel welcome. When they feel welcome, they are able to express their interest. It is the school's attitude that enables parents to participate.

Most parents want their children to succeed, to achieve academically, and to be confident, positive, and able throughout their school experiences. Those who have marginal jobs hope that their children will be able to use academic success as a way to a better life. Some parents may have a negative or reluctant attitude toward participating in their children's schools as a result of their own life experiences. Perhaps they were unsuccessful in school, or for other reasons they may fear or want to avoid school contact. But when they come to view the school as wanting to help their children they feel more comfortable, and they are able to participate. Schools need to reach out to these parents.

Parents may work with schools at many levels. Most important is the family's basic belief in the school, support for the teacher, and encouragement of and positive interaction with their children. Parents may also become involved by tutoring, assisting in the classroom, being a paid or a volunteer aide, participating in the parent-teacher-student association, or participating in decisions and governance. This higher level of parent involvement is positive, but most important of all is the productive, caring connection between family and school. Schools want children to succeed; so do parents.

Does involvement of parents really help the child's education?

Although we are now in the 21st century, Goal 8 of Goals 2000 has not been achieved and is still essential. It states, "By the year 2000, every school will promote partnerships that will increase parental involvement and participation in promoting the social, emotional, and academic growth of children." This goal was added because it was recognized that it takes more than the school to help all children become literate adults who are able to promote their own well-being and contribute to the overall good of the nation. Research and examination of successful schools support the value of parent involvement. It is particularly essential for at-risk children. If you look at schools with high success rates, you will find schools in which parents are involved, not always, but sometimes actively working in the schools.

How can teachers work with parents?

When I teach a course on parents as partners, I include quite a number of sessions on communication as well as sessions on activities that connect parents and teachers. Sometimes, students ask how they can work with parents, as if parents were a different species! The same communication skills that are positive with children and adults are appropriate when talking with parents. I tell students to remember that their mothers and fathers were parents, teachers are often parents, and they may be or may become parents. They should treat parents as they would like to be treated. A caring environment is necessary for children and families. Parents and teachers can work together to reduce and eliminate actions that exclude, threaten, and bully children. When parents are culturally different from a teacher, the teacher should attempt to understand the differences and, most important of all, treat all parents with care and respect. Parents should also treat teachers with the same care and respect.

Should teachers find that in spite of their positive overtures, parents are unhappy with them or their classrooms, it helps to let the parents explain what it is that makes them dissatisfied. Teachers must listen to parents' protests, let them express their concerns, and be considerate of their feelings

and insights. Although it may be difficult, teachers should not be defensive. They should listen, let parents vent their concerns, and then try to come to an understanding and a plan of action together.

Teachers need to plan activities that encourage parents to connect with the school. These may include a note of introduction with the teacher's photo sent prior to the beginning of school, an early open house, or a breakfast for all parents, especially those who work outside the home. Other things to consider are family-friendly newsletters, weekly telephone calls (with something positive to relate), "up slips" and "happy grams," calendars with home activities that reinforce the curriculum, and home visits. If possible, parents should have telephone access to teachers or tutors and be provided with homework hotlines. Teachers need to set aside ample time for conferences, be aware that they can learn more about children when they listen to the parents, and make conferences a sharing, caring time. Monthly parties, planned by teachers for families, are a wonderful way to connect. Examples include pumpkin measuring and decorating in October, book making in November, winter-holiday celebrating in January, multicultural sharing in March, reading in April, and celebrating spring in May.

Teachers need to remember that parents are partners in the education of children. They were children's first educators, and they continue to be team members.

Eugenia Berger is a Professor Emeritus, Metropolitan State College of Denver, Denver, Colorado.

Meet Standards for Working with Parents/Families. Today, the major accrediting agencies for higher education have made working with parents/families a prominent part of teacher preparation. Instead of fearing this role, seek out every opportunity to interact with parents and families so that you can approach this with confidence when you begin to teach. Programs that facilitate and encourage preservice educators to share information through newsletters or websites, assist with family workshops, and participate in preparation for children's progress conferences all can assist in dispelling myths related to stereotypes and overgeneralizations (Baum & McMurray-Schwarz, 2004). Figure 11.3 is a summary of the national standards and guidelines for working with parents and families.

Confront Your Own Biases About Families. It is not uncommon for those entering the teaching profession to use their own family experiences as a sort of yardstick for evaluating the families of others. When personal experience is used as the standard, a teacher can find other families lacking, use derogatory labels, or even use families' situations as the reason for failing to teach. Too often, schools respond to families only when there is a crisis or take a "We'll contact you if and when there's a problem" stance (Christenson & Sheridan, 2001). There is also a tendency to make thoughtless, destructive comments such as, "Well, he comes from a broken home, you know. What can you expect?" and "That's not her husband, that's her live-in boyfriend," and "Can you imagine? Seven people in that little house!" Statements such as these reflect a bias against diverse families. Even complimentary comments, such as "They're such a nice family," can cause children who never hear any positive comments about their families to feel ashamed of their family situations. It is far better to make specific, nonjudgmental comments that recognize the care and attention that families give to their children, such as, "It looks like somebody braided your hair for you," or "I see that you brought in some leaves for the collection," or "Mmmm. Somebody packed a good lunch for you," or "I noticed that you are wearing your warm scarf and gloves today." Teachers need to "be always in the process of examining their own attitudes and values about issues of difference. In other words, teachers cannot raise parents' awareness about injustice and inequalities if they are not exploring their own attitudes in this area" (Kendall, 1996, p. 68).

FIGURE 11.3 National standards and guidelines for collaborating with parents/families.

The federal government, professional organizations, and leading authorities have identified parent involvement as an "essential ingredient" for high-quality early childhood programs (Seplocha, 2004).

Federal Mandates

No Child Left Behind

- Calls for more structured modes of communicating children's progress, their test scores, and the performance of their school in comparison to other schools in the district and state.
- Provides parents with more flexibility in exercising choice if their child's school is not performing adequately over time. For additional information regarding No Child Left Behind, consult *www.ed.gov/parents/academic/involve/nclbguide/parentsguide.html.*

Goals 2000: Educate America Act, Goal 8

- Directed every school to promote partnerships that would increase parental involvement and participation in enhancing the social, emotional, and academic growth of children.
- Acknowledged that parents are partners in their children's education, and that all teachers must assume a role that facilitates such partnerships.
- Recognized the need for all early childhood settings to create family-friendly policies that truly support today's families.

Association for Childhood Education International/National Council for the Accreditation for Teacher Education

Standard 5.3 Collaboration with Families—Candidates know the importance of establishing and maintaining a positive collaborative relationship with families to promote the intellectual, social, emotional, and physical growth of children. Colleges and universities that prepare early childhood educators must show evidence through students' documented class work and field experiences that students know multiple strategies for involving families that encompass a broad range of traditions, beliefs, values, and practices *(www.acei.org/rubrics, 2002).*

National Association for the Education of Young Children

NAEYC Code of Ethical Conduct—Ideal 1-2.4 of this document states that the early childhood professional has an ethical responsibility "to respect families' childrearing values and their right to make decisions for their children."

NAEYC Guidelines for Developmentally Appropriate Practice

Guideline Number 5—"Teachers and parents share their knowledge of the child and understanding of children's development and learning as part of day to day communication and planned conferences. Teachers support families in ways that maximally promote family decision-making capabilities and competence" (Bredekamp & Copple, 1997, p. 22).

Six Types of Parent/Family Involvement

As noted by Epstein et al., (2002):

1. **Parenting**—helping all families establish home environments that support children as students.
2. **Communicating**—designing and conducting effective forms of communication about school programs and children's progress.
3. **Volunteering**—recruiting and organizing support for school functions and activities.
4. **Learning at home**—providing information and ideas to families about how to help students with schoolwork and school-related activities.
5. **Decision making**—including parents in school decisions.
6. **Collaborating with the community**—identifying and integrating resources and services from the community to strengthen and support schools, students, and their families.

Instead of rushing to rate families as "good," "average," "poor," or "dysfunctional," keep an unswerving focus on the child's needs. It is true that increasing numbers of children arrive at school without even their basic needs for food, shelter, and clothing having been met. This is a reason for early childhood educators to help.

Learn More About Cultural Differences. "Culture is commonly thought of as the customs, practices, and traditions that characterize, distinguish, and give stability to a group . . . it is knowledge of shared norms and rules" (Bullough & Gitlin, 2001, p. 112).

FIGURE 11.4 Frequently observed characteristics of various cultures.

Although there is a wide range of learning styles in all cultures, Diaz (2001) suggests that teachers become aware of some cultural information that may assist them in communicating more effectively with parents/families.

African Americans may

- Value spirituality
- Emphasize emotions and feelings
- Value individual and personal expression
- Value a tradition of oral expression
- Learn best through physical movement and kinesthetic instruction
- Value close teacher–student relationships
- Tend toward intuitive as opposed to analytical learning

American Indians may

- Prefer self-testing in private before demonstrating competency on a task
- Prefer visual, spatial learning over verbal learning
- Learn better privately over publicly
- Prefer small groups over large groups

Asian Americans may

- View schooling as a serious endeavor
- Tend to be hard working and high achieving
- Demonstrate a strong work ethic
- Value academic skills over music, the arts, and sports
- Consider modesty and humility to be virtues (tend not to like to volunteer in class)
- Place high value on family

Hispanics may

- Prefer to work with others on a common goal
- Be sensitive to the feelings of others
- Learn by doing
- Do well in warm, friendly, nurturing classrooms
- Tend to be extrinsically motivated
- Prefer concrete presentations to abstract ones

Sometimes parents and teachers have different expectations regarding discipline, timeliness, or celebrations. Some mannerisms, such as touching, can unintentionally offend culturally diverse families. Even something seemingly innocuous, such as food, can become an issue. For example, three first-grade teachers who planned a pizza party were careful to order vegetarian pizza, but the Muslim children and mothers still refused to eat. It was not until one of the mothers explained that because the same knife had been used to cut all of the pizzas and had touched the pork, their religious beliefs prevented them from eating it.

In another situation, a child from Italy arrived at school with red leather sandals and was teased about wearing "girls' shoes" by peers. Figure 11.4 is an overview of some of the cultural differences that are sometimes observed in different cultural groups.

Expand Your Definition of Caring to Include Out-of-School Contexts. In the teachers' lounge a student teacher is having lunch with her mentor teacher. They are delighted that 95% of the parents/families participated in the open house that was held at the school from 4 P.M. until 8 P.M. the previous day. Another teacher is complaining loudly about the parents' poor turnout for her open house and says, "It doesn't matter when we have this or how long we stay. I've said it before and I'm right! We never see the parents we really need to see!" Kira's mentor teacher has 13 years of experience in a school where over 80% of the children qualify for free lunches, yet she has maintained a positive attitude. She turns to Kira and says, "Always remember that families don't need to be 'fixed,' they need to be supported! They will pick up on negative attitudes in a heartbeat and once their feelings have been hurt, it is so hard to win them back."

Teachers often perceive the failure of families to participate in parent/family involvement programs or in other school functions as evidence that parents are not interested in their child's education (Lawrence-Lightfoot, 2003). The stereotype that "parents do not care" is rooted in teachers' perceptions of what "caring" parents do to support their child's education and classroom functioning. It also may reflect a "school-centric" view that considers neither how parents view the partnership nor their role in it (Lawson, 2003). Sometimes parents do not feel welcome or comfortable in the school because of previous negative experiences or anxiety about discussing their children's progress. Some families do not know how to access resources; others fear that if they ask questions or complain, it will be "taken out on" their children later. Whenever you are tempted to say that a parent does not care, bear in mind that expressions of care and concern are most fully realized in environments that we trust and when we feel valued and empowered (Swick, 2004b). You can overcome this barrier by building mutual trust and by offering a wide range of ways for families to participate both at home and at school (see the Collaborating with Families feature at the end of this chapter).

Many parents have difficulty finding the time and transportation to attend conferences and meetings during the workday. Parents, particularly those who work at the minimum-wage rate, frequently have more than one job in order to provide the bare necessities. Schools and centers committed to families set up carpools, provide babysitting, and create a space where parents can meet informally. Some parents have difficulty dealing with other adults in authority. They may deny that a problem exists, become aggressive when challenged, or become overly protective about their children. In all cases, seeking joint solutions is essential. Informal communication is an important way to build rapport with parents/families. To see an example of a preschool teacher's note to families, view the "General Methods–Classroom Management" student and teacher artifacts online at the Teacher Prep Website. Try to remember that parents love their children, and may just need to be reassured occasionally that they have chosen a high-quality program for their children (Gennarelli, 2004). Figure 11.5 offers practical suggestions on ways to build rapport with families.

TEACHER PREP WEBSITE 11.4

Go to Student and Teacher Artifacts, select General Methods, choose Classroom Management (Module 5), and select Dear Parents (Artifact 3).

Recognize That Early Childhood Educators Are in a Unique Position to Identify Children's Needs and Inaugurate Families' Interactions with Schools. As soon as Lizzie arrived in second grade, it was clear to her teacher that she needed medical attention. The child's teeth were black with decay and the infection was upsetting her stomach. When the teacher called the home to speak with Lizzie's mother, the grandmother answered and said that her daughter was at the beauty shop having her hair done. Lizzie's teacher hung up the telephone, bristling with anger and ready to march down to the teachers' room to tell this story to her colleagues. On further thought, however, she realized that an indictment of the second grader's family would not do the family or the child any good. Wouldn't it be better, she reasoned, to try to resolve the problem using the organizations and resources of the community? Although the teacher confided in her husband and a good friend who taught in another state to let off steam, she resolved not to discuss the incident at all in the community out of her care and concern for Lizzie.

PAUSE AND REFLECT

About Conferences

Think about a child you know and love—your child, a sibling, a niece or nephew, a cousin, or another child with whom you have a close bond. Now consider how you would feel if you were told that the child is "having problems at school" and were asked to meet with the principal, the teacher, and other school personnel. What initial thoughts and emotions might surface? How might the particular nature of the problem influence your response? What behaviors on the part of school personnel might cause you to feel angry or defensive? What actions would you take if your view of the child and the situation was completely different from that of the school personnel? If you felt you had to protest a decision, how would you approach it and how far would you take it?

FIGURE 11.5 Practical ways to build rapport with parents/families.

- **Try to ease families' concerns about children's adjustment.** Orientation days are opportunities for children to become familiar with school and school routines before officially beginning school. Many schools use a buddy system, in which, for example, current kindergartners are paired with incoming kindergartners to help ease new students' transition to school.
- **Strive to communicate by keeping professional jargon to a minimum and speak in ways that the family understands.** One way to stimulate a family's interest in and a child's answer to the age-old question "What did you learn in school today?" is an Ask-Me-About badge. These are short sentences written on paper badges that invite parents to talk with their children about particular activities or experiences that they had in school or at the center. The badges supply information to parents and also provide children with opportunities to recall and describe particular learning activities, such as having a guest storyteller or going on a walking field trip.
- **Keep it easy for the family to stay informed.** Newsletters that feature children's work and are sent to the home let parents and families know about classroom experiences, open the door to two-way communication, and invite parents into their children's learning. Newsletters can cover a variety of topics, such as an upcoming family night, special projects under study, and good books to read. Computer software makes it increasingly easy to produce a professional-looking newsletter. This is a great way to have parents help out as well. No matter how confident you are about your writing skills, however, be certain to have others help you proofread the finished product. Other possibilities for contacting parents include a homework hotline, e-mail, and a home page on the Internet.
- **Offer opportunities for families to gather informally and network.** School-sponsored family gatherings, such as a summer picnic before school begins or a noncompetitive family game night, offer opportunities to make connections. A parent who has a child with Down syndrome may feel that contacts with other families who are raising children with special needs offer a particularly beneficial type of support. When families are closely tied to the community, children's adjustment and development are enhanced. Social events enable families and educators to get to know one another as people.
- **Schedule meetings at various times so that more families can participate.** Meetings scheduled at different times and locations meet the particular needs of families and invite more participation. For example, working parents could come to see a display of the children's work and be served a light breakfast by the children. Meetings could be scheduled on an evening or a Saturday morning, with child care provided.
- **Use a variety of strategies to enhance communication with families.** Be sensitive to the fact that not all parents have English as their first language or take time to read written messages from school. Some ways to let parents know how their children are doing at school that don't depend on the family's reading skills include messages in different languages recorded on the telephone about upcoming classroom events; videotapes of school events, such as the children singing, that can be circulated or viewed at home or at the library; and audiotapes of a child reading aloud. Rinaldi (2000) reminds us that documenting children's progress is really "visible listening," a valuable component of sharing information about children.
- **Strive to identify with and meet the special concerns of families.** Each family has a unique set of circumstances that influences how parents and families respond to teachers' efforts to work with them. For example, when children have physical handicaps, families can be excessively protective, and when children are chronically ill, families sometimes fail to set reasonable limits on children's behavior. In such situations, families often appreciate an information sheet about appropriate learning games to play at home, a professional magazine article, or an informational brochure written especially for parents. Some excellent materials are those published by the Consumer Information Center in Pueblo, Colorado; professional association brochures (e.g., those published by the Association for Childhood Education International, the National Association for the Education of Young Children, and the International Reading Association); and a wide variety of literature from community and social service agencies and organizations.
- **Be sensitive to some family members' discomfort in the school setting.** Not all parents have had positive prior experience with schools or helpful interactions

FIGURE 11.5 Continued

with teachers and administrators. Home visits or meetings held at a location other than the school, such as the public library or the neighborhood community center, are sometimes more appealing to families.

- **When difficulties arise, keep a problem-solving focus instead of blaming.** During a parent conference, it is sometimes tempting to blame the parent for a child's behavior at school. One way to bring up a difficult issue, such as a child who seldom completes activities at school, is to first ask the parent to share his or her views on the child's work habits at home. Often you will find that parents are already aware of the difficulty and are willing to collaborate on a mutually agreed-upon solution.
- **Focus on all families instead of being satisfied with the participation of a few with higher income levels or more leisure time.** Very often, you will hear teachers say that the parents whom they really want to see never come to school for conferences or school events. Making everyone feel welcome is the teacher's responsibility. For example, an evening when children share their accomplishments and every child has an equal opportunity to participate encourages all family members to participate (Liess, 1995).
- **Give parents the latitude to contribute in their own ways.** Some teachers develop a family questionnaire to find out about parents' jobs, hobbies, cultural specialties (e.g., songs, games, recipes), or travel pictures, or their interest in helping provide recycled materials, participating in special events such as birthdays, or volunteering in the classroom (see Collaborating with Families feature on page 406). Invite parents at various times throughout the year to demonstrate a skill, tell a story, or play a musical instrument.
- **Admit it when you need to seek outside assistance.** Part of the skill of being a teacher is to know the limits of your professional preparation. If, for example, you are faced with a child whose mother was killed in an automobile accident or a child who is having difficulty adjusting to the birth of a new sibling, seek the advice of other professionals who work with young children.

Early childhood educators are in a key position to lead the way in restructuring efforts to work with families because they are in contact with families at a time when parents are most receptive to becoming involved in their children's educational experiences. Additionally, they are the community professionals who see children and their families on the most consistent basis throughout the year (Chavkin, 1990). The early childhood educator can also serve as an advocate for families, referring them to appropriate agencies to satisfy their family needs, or speaking out to get needed services in the neighborhood (Allen, Brown, & Finlay, 1992).

Appreciate the Importance of Effective Communication and Professionalism in Interactions with Families. Krista was a 6-year-old who had been in first grade for 2 weeks when her mother called the school and asked to see the teacher. The purpose of the meeting was to find out why Krista was not reading independently yet. When Krista's teacher heard this, her first reaction was to be defensive and say, "Give me a chance! School just started!" Instead, she arranged an appointment and listened carefully, not only to what Krista's mother said, but also "between the lines" to her underlying concerns. It seemed that Krista's father had a reading disability, and her parents were very worried that their daughter might be affected, too. Because the teacher really *heard* what Krista's mother had to say, an angry confrontation was avoided and a positive plan of action was put into place. Krista's mother left with books and ideas instead of frustration, because the teacher had sought to communicate effectively and professionally instead of defending herself. Communicating with parents/families is crucial to effective teaching.

Reach Out to Families and Communities. One colleague with whom we work has a sign posted in the classroom where she teaches undergraduate preservice teachers.

The sign reads *"Remember . . . Teachers are NOT in private practice!"* There is little place in contemporary society for the teacher who closes the door and has virtually no contact with families and the larger community. Instead of sitting behind the desk and waiting for parents to attend conferences, many early childhood educators are going where the parents/families are. For example, one teacher from a rural area discovered that many of the children, their parents, and families gathered on Saturday mornings at a bank parking lot where a farmers' market was held throughout late summer and early fall. She used this venue to distribute information, display children's artwork, and present musical performances by the class. In doing so, she changed the impression of many parents that school personnel had less care and concern for the children of farm laborers.

It is clear that old ways of involving families are not adequate to face today's challenges. A partnership model emphasizes the contributions that both parents and teachers make to promote children's success in school and society. Figure 11.6 explains one-way, two-way, and three (or more) -way forms of collaboration. An effective parent/family involvement program includes all of these approaches to meet the individual needs of families.

Conferencing: Inviting Communication

Conferencing with parents and families is "one of a teacher's most important responsibilities" (Seplocha, 2004, p. 96). Conferences are an important vehicle for significant adults in children's lives to exchange information about their learning and development. Conferences provide an opportunity to support home–school partnerships through a free exchange of insights and observations about a particular child. They can be routinely scheduled (e.g., semiannually) or can be spontaneous, as when you chat with families informally while you are waiting for the bus or out in the community.

In order to maximize attendance and participation at conference events, make certain that you advertise conference opportunities well in advance, in multiple forms, and in ways that all families can access. Consider these early childhood educators' ideas.

COMPANION WEBSITE 11.4 To learn more about linguistic and cultural diversity and families, go to *Enrichment Content: Research Highlights* in Chapter 11 of the Companion Website at http://www.prenhall.com/jalongo.

- Claire Tate realizes that many of her second graders shop at the Muñez Market, so she stops by the market on her way home and asks Mr. Muñez, the proprietor, if she may post colorful posters reminding families about upcoming parent/teacher conferences. The storekeeper is particularly pleased to display the signs, which have been prepared in both Spanish and English. While Ms. Tate does not speak Spanish fluently, she used the Babel Fish Translation website to create a rough draft, and then had the middle school's Spanish teacher proofread and offer corrections before making a final copy.
- Tim Bonn is in his second year of teaching but he remembers that many parents could not attend conferences due to their work schedules and carpooling. This year, Mr. Bonn has asked his principal if he may hold conference times on Saturday at the Community Center, which is just a block from the factory where many of his students' parents and grandparents work the 3 P.M. to 11 P.M. shift. His principal agrees, Mr. Bonn makes arrangements to use the space for 3 hours on Saturday morning, and participation in the conferences increases dramatically over the previous year.
- Mr. Yong teaches third grade at a school located near a large university. This year, he has two internationally adopted children and the children of four graduate students and faculty members who are new to the United States. He noticed at the first open house of the year that these parents had some unique concerns, many of

FIGURE 11.6 Ways of communicating with families.

Strides Forward: Three-Way and Many-Way Collaboration

- Home visits
- Student-led conferences
- Establishing parent resource rooms
- Contacting parents/families on a regular basis to convey good news
- Functioning as a family advocate in the community
- Building a personal knowledge base of families' and community members' interests, occupations, and affiliations
- Providing opportunities for families to improve their situations
- Involving parents and families in decision making at school

Intermediate Steps: Two-Way Communication

- IEP and IFSP meetings
- Language translators to facilitate communication
- Parent-teacher conferences
- Open houses
- Potluck dinners
- Sending children's work home and asking for comments back
- Workshops in which parents/families acquire new skills
- End-of-year celebrations

Initial Steps: One-Way Communication

- Newsletters, school calendar
- Notes, tapes, and videos sent home
- Grades or progress reports sent home
- Announcements of events
- Contacting parents/families when problems arise
- Requesting parent volunteers
- Guest speakers

them centering on what to expect from U.S. schools. After Mr. Yong obtained photo releases from parents/guardians, he decided to work with an intern from the Communications Media Department to develop a video that would capture the essence of third grade. The video included clips of various activities, special events, and interviews with the children talking about their goals for this year. Mr. Yong also created a script that could be used as voiceover narration to the recording and made multiple copies on VHS and DVD for families to borrow. Parents/families have both the right and the need to know how their child is progressing in school.

COMPANION WEBSITE 11.5 For more information about technology and families, go to *Web Links* in Chapter 11 of the Companion Website at http://www.prenhall.com/jalongo.

COMPANION WEBSITE 11.6 To add a product that documents your role in supporting families to your developing portfolio, go to *Journal: Constructing Your Professional Portfolio* in Chapter 11 of the Companion Website at http://www.prenhall.com/jalongo.

Some schools include children with their parents/families during conferences while others do not. Either way, make sure that all of the communication regarding conferences clearly outlines whether children are to be present or not. When children are included in conferences, teachers need to plan ahead with them, help them select appropriate work samples to discuss, and ensure adequate participation from them. Including children in conferences helps them take more responsibility for their own learning by enabling them to contribute insights about their progress in all developmental areas. Some teachers have students lead conferences and share their goals and accomplishments. It is equally important to prepare parents for conferences at which children are present. If you do not set their expectations, some parents may assume that the purpose of meeting with you is for them to demonstrate to you that they are strict disciplinarians who can demand obedience and get it by reprimanding their children in your presence. Even if children are not included in conferences, it is a good idea to share some things about the conferences with them after the conferences have taken place. For additional guidelines on conducting conferences, see Figure 11.7.

FIGURE 11.7 Your role in conducting a conference.

All productive conferences with families have several features in common (Seplocha, 2004):

Flexible conferencing schedule—Too often, conference times are provided with only the traditional school day in mind. Broaden the perspective to consider the parent who works the night shift, has to have child care for a younger sibling, or requires public transportation. If possible, offer several windows of opportunity for conferences at different times of the day. Suggest several times for the conference, let the parent select, then confirm by making sure the parent knows the time, date, place, and length of the conference.

Enough time for the conference—Physicians are taught never to place their hands on the door knob of the examining room to leave while still finishing a conversation with a patient. "Hand on the door" medicine is to be avoided, as is "hand on the door" conferencing. Be present with the parent or family member for the entire conference time. Remember to build in a few buffer minutes between conferences so that you can bring closure to a conference, rather than just stopping the meeting because the next parent has arrived.

A prepared child—Ask the child what information he or she wants to share with parents or family members. If there is a particular piece of work, drawing, or favorite activity area that the child would like to have highlighted, take the time to include that information in the conference.

A welcoming atmosphere—Consider the earlier scenario of Grace Anderson. The classroom was arranged for an informal conversation, the teacher met her at the door with a smile and a greeting, and there were refreshments. Consider the best of what you know about making guests feel welcome. Arrange an inviting environment, and get all the children involved in preparing the classroom for visitors. Establish rapport by welcoming the parent to the room and stating your pleasure in seeing him or her. Eliminate distractions. Give the parent you are speaking with your undivided attention. Sit beside the parent, not at or behind your desk.

Teacher preparation and organization—Be prepared. Know what you are going to say and what evidence of the child's progress you are going to share. Have a written outline, if needed. Be as specific as possible. Have student work samples ready in a folder and be ready to explain how and what that child is learning.

Cultural appropriateness and sensitivity—Understand that vocal tone, inflection, body posture, and eye contact are cultural features that vary with ethnicity. Explore information about the ethnicity of each student's family prior to conference time so that you may be prepared for the interaction.

Positive opening to the conference—Begin by commenting on the child's interests, strengths, and abilities. Point out a displayed piece of work, share a story from yesterday, show a photo of a project or a picture of the child working with others.

FIGURE 11.7 Continued

Encouraging family members to share their perspectives—Listen to what the parents, grandparents, or guardians have to say. Much can be learned from their impressions of the child's experience, and his/her comments at home regarding school. Listening enables you to gain new information and help solve problems.

Restraint—If a parent becomes hostile or confrontational, remain professional and do not respond in kind. Remain calm and professional. Tactfully end the conference and schedule another time to meet and talk.

Avoidance of jargon or "teacher talk"—Phonemic awareness, cognitive processing, and motor skills may all be terms with which you are familiar. However, remember your audience. Make sure that you communicate in ways that are direct and accessible without talking down to families.

Shared suggestions for at-home activities—Why not provide a take-home sheet for parents? A list of a few activities that can be done in the car as they travel to school, shopping together in the market, or preparing a meal at home can be a very useful tool for parents and other family members. Rather than focusing on drilling school activities, encourage families to use their time together in fully integrated ways.

Positive closure to the conference—Thank the family member for coming and share one more strength, skill, or interest of the child as a closing remark. In this way, the conference ends on an upbeat note, and the opportunity for continued partnership and ongoing communication is fostered.

Reflection and documentation—Take a moment while ideas are fresh to record any concerns that the parent expressed, any questions that were asked, and any ideas that you could use to improve the next conversation. Utilize these notes to improve your ability to conference effectively as well as to document particular points regarding each child's development and progress.

Your Role Following the Conference

- Make a note of important points discussed during the conference or agreements that were reached so that you can refer to them later.
- Review conference notes and share them with other school personnel, if needed and appropriate.
- Summarize follow-up responsibilities, who is responsible for what, and how participants will know they have fulfilled their agreed-upon obligations. Make plans for monitoring progress toward goals.
- Tell the child about the conference so that he or she will know areas in which you have reached agreement.
- Send the parent a thank-you message for participating—a note, a telephone call, e-mail, or some other sign of appreciation.

Evaluating Your Role in the Conference

Use conferences as opportunities for reflecting on your role as a professional early childhood educator. Following conferences, ask yourself these questions, and try to assess honestly the areas where you have grown and where you need continued work.

- Did I share a positive anecdote about the child?
- Did I start by stating the purpose of the conference and how I planned to conduct it?
- Did I share information about the child's strengths or what the child *can* do?
- Did I share the child's work samples, to demonstrate specific points, arranged to highlight progress and effort?
- Did I encourage parental information and questions?
- Did I ask open-ended questions that invited discussion?
- Did I listen to what the parent had to say about his or her child?
- Was I alert to nonverbal cues and the way that things were said rather than focusing on the words alone? Did I "listen between the lines"?
- Did I suggest ways the home and school can collaborate? Did we agree upon a plan of action? Did we set goals together for the child?
- Did I summarize the conference and end on a positive note?

COLLABORATING WITH FAMILIES

Coping with Conflict and Conducting Home Visits

An important part of professional development is learning how to interact with parents and families in ways that build mutual trust and respect. Keep in mind that any information shared with you during home visits is privileged and confidential. As you work with families, realize that their attitudes toward authority figures and gender may affect their interactions with you. Kendall (1996) points out that many cultures see schools and teachers as authority figures and therefore unapproachable. In some cultures, men refuse to deal with female authority figures and a father may not be willing to talk with a female teacher. There may be times when you can compromise and others when you cannot. In the case of a father who does not want to speak with a woman, the teacher might bring a male colleague to participate in the first few conversations to help the father recognize that it is in the best interest of the child for him to work with the teacher. On the other hand, if a parent directs you to use corporal punishment with his or her child, you will have to make it clear that this is not an option. You will need to explain that you cannot agree by saying, for example, "I understand what you are saying but it is against our school rules and our laws in this country for teachers to hit a child. We will have to find another way, a way to encourage good behavior, rather than punish misbehavior." One way to diplomatically disagree is to use "feel/felt/found" (Garmston, 2005):

- Accept the **feelings** expressed by the person: *"Many people feel as you do. . ."*
- Identify with the concern personally, acknowledging that you once **felt** this way (if that is true): *"I used to have some of those same concerns. . ."*
- Show the progression of how your changed your ideas, what you **found**: *"But now that I have worked with many, many young children, I have found. . ."*

Now, take a look at the following scenarios that depict a conflict between a parent and a teacher. Remember that your goal is to build mutual trust and respect. Try using the feel/felt/found strategy in response to discussing each issue.

Scenario 1

Gender Issues

A Japanese father stopped by the preschool and was horrified to see his son in a dress, high heels, and an apron standing at the toy stove and pretending to cook. I tried to explain that it was just pretending but the father disagreed and repeated, several times, "Don't want no gay boy!" Now what do I do? Should I restrict the boy's play choices or should I continue to allow the boy to pursue his play interests and run the risk of another confrontation with the father?"

Scenario 2

Memories of Curriculum

A teacher said, "Many of the parents pressure us to offer the curriculum that they experienced as children, one that celebrates Halloween, Thanksgiving, Christmas, Valentine's Day, and so forth or, as one parent stated, 'The way we remember school.' If teachers resist, parents are disappointed, suspicious, or angry with us for not responding to their wishes. I wonder if we should just give in and give up on a multicultural approach."

Scenario 3

A Misunderstanding

A parent said, One day my daughter came home and said that the school was having a food festival and that we were to bring a food item from our native country. We went to the Indian food store to get all of the ingredients so that she could take a traditional Indian sweet to the festival. When school was over, my daughter went directly to her room—this is what she does when she is upset—and didn't want to talk about it. Finally, later that evening, she told me what was wrong. "The children wouldn't eat our food and the teacher threw it in the garbage can." I was outraged! How could the teacher be so insensitive? I thought the whole purpose of the event was to teach acceptance of other cultures. I spoke with the head teacher about it but it may have made things even worse for my daughter. I don't think the teacher likes her.

About Home Visits

Home visits are a way to build rapport. Here is one example of a form you might use or adapt when conducting home visits.

Interviewer: *CK* Date: *Oct. 7*
Child's Name: *Jesus Martinez* Grade: *2nd*
Parents' Names: *Miguel and Yolanda Guiterrez*
Siblings: *1 younger sister, 1 older sister*
Language(s) used: *English and Spanish*
Address: *1 Sonoma Lane, Phoenix, AZ*
Telephone: *602-357-2417*
E-mail: *Guiterrez@hotmail.com*

1. What are your child's interests? (art, sports, hobbies, activities)
   J. likes animals, computers, numbers—can do math in his head. Reads to younger sister. Likes stepfather to read to him. Watches Wheel of Fortune. Saving his money for a cat. Rides bike and swims. Loves Net surfing.
2. How does your child seem to feel about going to school?
   Moved in July and does not know many neighborhood kids. Wants to make friends and exchange phone numbers and e-mail addresses. Does not want to go to school because of "homework he doesn't know."
3. What do you expect your child to accomplish this year?
   Oral language in English needs improvement. He's more fluent in Spanish.
4. What signs of progress were you pleased to see over the summer?
   More confident with numbers, can figure out calorie and cholesterol counts in his head to help stepfather with a special diet! Started to play word games and use rhyming words.
5. Are there any concerns that you have about your child?
   May not be challenged in math at school. Expressed concern about husband's new job and the long hours worked—J. is very close to stepfather.
6. What have you discovered about your child's particular ways of learning?
   Looks for patterns in numbers and can do some of this with letters and words.
7. What is the most important thing your child could learn this year?
   To build his confidence in speaking English. (But he wants to learn to play soccer.)
8. What hopes and dreams do you have for your child in the future?
   Has a head for numbers and math—maybe an accountant or an engineer? Dream of him working at NASA—very good at problem solving.
9. Is there anything else that I should know as I work with your child?
   J. is very sensitive and feelings are hurt easily. Has a food allergy to seafood and is allergic to bee stings.

Thank you for your time and for inviting me to your home.

Conclusion

A few years ago a neighborhood in Pennsylvania was selected by a national organization as one of the best places in America to raise a child, based on such variables as school achievement, crime rate, parent involvement in the schools, and so forth. Perhaps surprisingly, this was not one of the wealthiest neighborhoods. The houses are in an old section of Pittsburgh, but they are well maintained. When residents were interviewed

COMPANION WEBSITE 11.7 To test your knowledge of this chapter's content, go to the *Multiple-choice* and *Essay* modules in Chapter 11 of the Companion Website at http://www.prenhall.com/jalongo. These items are written in the same format that you will encounter on the Praxis test to better prepare you for your licensure exam.

by reporters and asked why the community had been so honored, one of them replied, "Maybe it's because everyone around here is nebby [western Pennsylvania slang for *nosey*]. We look out for one another and ask questions or pick up the phone if something doesn't look right. And, you pay attention to all of the kids here, not just your own."

As Madeline Grumet (1988) asserts, there can be no community until educators begin to develop a sense of responsibility for everybody's children. It is not until families, educators, and other community members accept nothing less for every child in the program than they would for their own children that genuine progress can be made. Three things are needed for social reform: a knowledge base, a public will, and a social strategy (Richmond & Kotelchuck, 1984). Where family support is concerned, American society certainly has a knowledge base and research support for greater home, school, and community collaboration (Roberts, Wasik, Casto, & Ramey, 1991). The thing that is lacking is a public will to act upon that knowledge (Lewis, 1991). You can make a difference. Fulfilling your role as an early childhood educator requires you to care about all the children for whom you are responsible and all of the families they come from, however different they are from your own. By working effectively with children, families, and the community at large, you are much better equipped to make a significant difference in the lives and the learning of the children entrusted to your care. Today, more than ever, families need help in ensuring that their children develop the values, attitudes, and behaviors that will help them succeed in school and beyond. Communities, schools, and programs must all recognize and accept that "yesterday's strategies will not be able to address tomorrow's realities or meet the needs of tomorrow's children" (Kagan, 1990, p. 272). As a result, one of the most persistent themes in the current school reform movement has been the strengthening of the connections among families, schools, programs, and communities—the issue of parental engagement in children's care and education.

ONE CHILD, THREE PERSPECTIVES

David, a Newly Immigrated Child

While there are many kinds of families, people have strong opinions about the ability of single parents to provide the appropriate environments in which to raise children. Much of the concern centers around whether or not single parents can appropriately raise a well-socialized child who will become a productive and contributing citizen. Increasingly, however, women who have never married are choosing to become parents and adopting children to create a family. The case of David is a good example.

David was adopted from a Russian orphanage at 26 months of age. His never-married adoptive mother, Marsha, had invested 18 months of working intensively with a social worker through extensive interviews, a personal history, financial statements, fingerprinting, evaluations by a psychologist and a psychiatrist, and a series of parenting classes. Next, Marsha worked with adoption agencies until a child was identified as a good match. She spent 2 weeks in Russia getting to know David and preparing to bring him home. Although Marsha knew very little about David's birth history, she did learn that he had been in the orphanage since he was 2 weeks old.

The orphanage was well maintained and had a staff of female teachers and doctors. In David's group, there was a large, open room with areas designated for play and small tables and chairs for eating together. The children spent time each day going outside but never left the property. David's basic physical needs had been met and his daily routine was very structured, with meals and bathroom time strictly controlled. However, the food supply was limited, and David's treat for the day and primary means of getting milk was a yogurt shake. David was extremely shy, frightened, and withdrawn. One of David's teachers described him as the runt of the litter and thought he might be retarded because he had not begun to talk at 26 months.

When David came to the United States, he still had no language. He exhibited fear of unfamiliar people and things (e.g., animals, males, bathtubs, strangers), could not walk steadily without support nor climb stairs, did not smile, and was very small for his age. In his first week in this country, he vomited in the car until he became used to the motion and sounds, clung to his new mother, or sat in one place with one toy until he was encouraged to move or to try another. He was also fascinated with looking at himself in the mirror, having never seen his own image. Still, no language or smiles.

At his new home, David experienced a stimulating, warm, and nurturing environment. He had his own room, a space for toys and books, friends to visit, and daily opportunities to explore toys and talk about what he was doing. Even though he did not speak, David's mother talked to him throughout the day as they were getting dressed, eating meals, or getting ready for bed. While in the car, she pointed out interesting objects, such as school buses and traffic lights, and remarked on them. As he grew older and more comfortable at home, David's mother had clear expectations for him in the home such as setting the table and recycling paper.

David's mother enrolled him in a local child-care setting upon a recommendation from her friend, an early childhood educator. With the director's encouragement and confidence, Marsha visited the center with David at different times of the day and stayed with him until he felt comfortable. Adapting to the life and culture of a new country was a challenge.

Each day, David cried and cried as his mother left him in the arms of Miss Gail, his caring and sensitive teacher, and his mother struggled with the question of what would help both David and her adjust to this new setting. David eventually became attached to Miss Gail, who welcomed him every day with open arms and soft, comforting words while he made the very difficult transition from home to school.

David's mother and teachers talked to him every day and read stories to him regularly. At school, David had a regular routine with teachers who cared about children's socialization, comfort level, and learning. David had opportunities to work alone, in small groups, and in whole-group experiences, and he engaged in many different kinds of learning activities. His teachers supported his efforts to adjust to his new school through conversations, pictures, and regular communication with David's mother. After a while, David began to say a few words, then a phrase, then a sentence, and eventually, he could connect thoughts together. When David was 4 years old, he still could not produce certain sounds or say certain words but was communicating easily about his needs and played with others in his child-care group and at home. Several people expressed concern about his language and suggested that David be referred to Child Find, a public program that identifies and serves children with exceptionalities at an early age. Others suggested that David be left alone and that his speech be allowed to develop naturally. His mother, always seeking what was in her child's best interests, struggled with the conflicting information and recommendations. She opted to wait and continue the supportive care and education. This obviously was a wise decision, because David is now a nonstop talker with clear speech and an enormous vocabulary that he uses to make his needs, ideas, and wishes known. Those who never knew David when he first arrived in this country would find it hard to believe that his first words were not uttered until he was almost 3 years old.

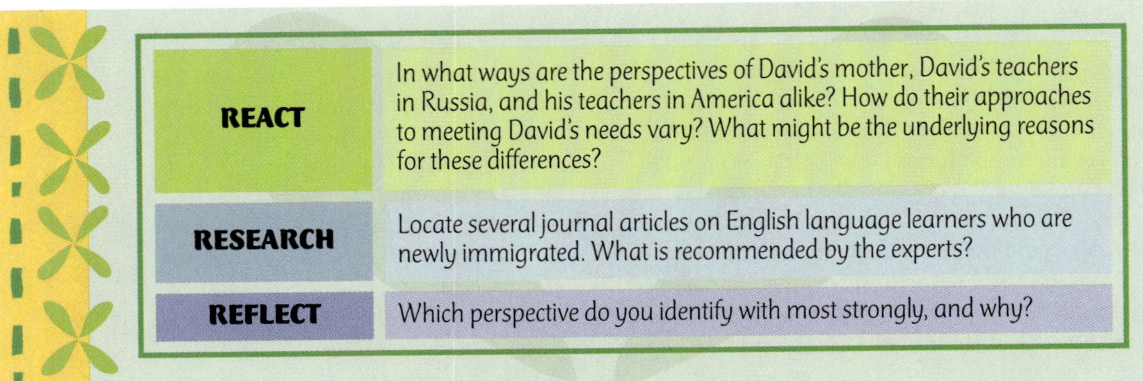

IN-CLASS WORKSHOP

Creating an Informational Brochure on a Topic of General Interest to Parents

When you teach, you will find that it is important to communicate with parents and families in a variety of ways. One way of informing parents about important ideas is to create a tri-fold brochure on a topic. Examples of the titles for brochures that our students have developed for parents have included the following:

Books for Babies
What Does a Baby Know?
How Toddlers Learn
Guiding Children's Behavior
Understanding Developmentally Appropriate Practice
Why Children Need to Play
Ten Reasons to Read to Your Child
Summertime Activities for Preschoolers
How to Raise a Creative Child
Homework: How You Can Help
Questions Parents Ask About Starting School
There's Always Something New at the Library
Learning Mathematics Through Everyday Experiences
Where to Find Help: Services in Our Community

Procedure for Developing a Brochure

1. **Locate examples of brochures.** Collect and examine several brochures written for parents. Some good sources include professional organizations (e.g., the National Association for the Education of Young Children, the International Reading Association, the National PTA, Association for Childhood Education International). Places where you can usually find brochures include pediatricians' offices, shopping-mall displays, schools or child-care centers, mental health associations, and women's shelters. Also check the organizations in the Compendium of Resources at the end of this book. Bring at least one example of a high-quality brochure written for parents to class.
2. **Analyze the way that the material is written for parents.** Read publications such as *Parent's Magazine, Our Children* (published by the National PTA), *Working Mother Magazine,* and *Children Today* or the columns written for parents in popular magazines such as *Redbook* and *Family Circle.* Some of the leading authors who write for parents include T. Berry Brazelton, Penelope Leach, Eda LeShan, and John Rosemond.
3. **Research your topic.** Locate several authoritative sources on your topic using professional journals and books. Gather sufficient information to support the points that you will be making in your brochure, and identify other articles, books, software, or information about organizations (name, address, telephone number, website) that relate to your topic. Before you begin writing, formulate a rationale that states the reasons

why you are bringing families and this information together. State specifically how the information will benefit children and those who care for them.

4. **Make a draft of your brochure.** Remember that your information will need to be clear, concise, and logically organized. Experiment with different arrangements, headings, formats, and illustrative materials until you discover the best way to get your message across. Advances in computer software and desktop publishing have made it possible to design high-quality brochures. If you or someone in your group has the necessary skills and access to this type of software, consider using these resources in producing the final copy. If not, type the text of the brochure and sketch or cut-and-paste art or photographs that have been enlarged or reduced to the appropriate size. Use samples of children's work and comments, if appropriate. Include bulleted lists of important points or ideas from experts in the field. Intersperse short, thought-provoking direct quotations from authoritative sources in the text. Be certain to list the full names of all of the people who worked on the project directly on the brochure. When your draft is complete, seek the feedback of other parents and professionals before making your final copy.
5. **Complete the final, edited version.** Be sure to run a spell check on the text and proofread carefully. Ask someone with good editorial skills to read it one last time before the final copy is produced.

Evaluation Criteria

A high-quality brochure for parents

- focuses on ideas that are important for parents and families to understand
- provides a rationale and how this information will benefit children and families
- effectively synthesizes and translates material from a variety of professional sources into language that is understandable to general audiences
- offers a clear, concise explanation supported by concrete examples (e.g., children's comments, samples of children's work, common situations parents can identify with)
- makes appropriate use of the work of leaders in the field of education (e.g., brief quotations from experts, bulleted lists of recommendations compiled from various sources, all work cited appropriately)
- presents material in an original, engaging, and visually appealing way
- supplies a complete list of references in APA style as well as agencies, organizations, or companies that can serve as resources
- has been carefully proofread and edited to make certain the writing style is conversational and the text is error free
- uses the strategies that professional publishers use to invite readers to take the time to read it, such as an interesting title and a question-answer format, a self-test, or other ways to display the material (one of our students made the back of the brochure into a growth chart; another used a calendar format for summertime activities)

CHAPTER 12

Exploring Your Role as a Professional in the Field of Early Childhood Education

> **Effective teachers learn to live with high levels of ambiguity. To steer a course through contradiction requires that the teacher engage in a complicated balancing act among interests and teaching demands. A strong sense of self, knowledge of where you stand ethically, and clarity of purpose are among the teacher qualities necessary for skilled balancing, the sort of balancing that keeps student learning front and center, and not control or self-preservation, both of which can produce a classroom environment that is uncomfortable for students and less than fully productive of learning.**
>
> **Robert V. Bullough and Andrew David Gitlin, 2001, p. 134**

Meet the Teachers

MS. HUONG has just begun working with toddlers at a private infant-and-toddler care facility in the program director's home. When she accepted the position, she "had no illusions that the center was top quality." Yet she decided to work there, partly to gain experience, partly because it was in her home town, and partly to make a difference in the education and care for infants and toddlers in the program. She knew from talking to the director that the center wanted to earn a credential from the Academy of the National Association for the Education of Young Children (NAEYC), and this seemed like the perfect time to initiate improvements in the program. First, Ms. Huong consulted numerous resources on infant-and-toddler programs. She made a copy of a photo essay on the credentialing process from the journal *Young Children* (Cryer & Phillipsen, 1997), and she located expert advice on quality in infant-and-toddler programming in *Dimensions of Early Childhood, Early Childhood Education Journal, Child Care Information Exchange,* and the online Education Resources Information Index (ERIC). Ms. Huong also visited the NAEYC website at www.naeyc.org/naeyc and printed out the most up-to-date material on the credentialing process. Then she organized all of the information by topic, and when issues were discussed at staff meetings, she "just happened" to have some very useful resources on hand. Later, when the center was accredited by the NAEYC, Ms. Huong's colleagues kept saying, "We never could have done it without you!"

This year has been, by **MS. WILDEN'S** own description, her "most challenging experience in 5 years of teaching third grade" in an urban setting. Ms. Wilden realized early in the year that two of the boys in her class were experiencing serious difficulty in learning to read and sought help from her fellow teachers, the reading specialist, and the school psychologist, as well as information from national organizations, to deepen her understanding of dyslexia. She was surprised to discover that colored overlays—sheets of plastic that look like tinted transparencies—were very helpful to one student, while the other made the greatest progress with the recorded-book method (Carbo, 1997), in which he listened to an audiotape of the book as he looked at the words. Ms. Wilden remarked, "I was delighted to discover that there are some research-based strategies that enable dyslexic children to experience greater success in learning to read. I also wonder, though, what might have happened to the two boys if I hadn't taken the time to investigate dyslexia."

MS. RENZULLI has been teaching kindergarten for 25 years. Although she was always regarded as a good teacher by her coworkers and in the community, over the last 5 years, she felt a growing dissatisfaction with the way she was teaching kindergarten. "I used to be the worksheet queen," Ms. Renzulli admitted. "When I first started teaching, everybody accepted lots of paperwork for kindergarten children as proof that they were learning. Now I have a poster outside my classroom door that reads, 'Real learning isn't measured by the weight of your child's backpack!' I couldn't really say that there was any outside pressure to change. It's just that I saw that my methods weren't working well with my students. Also, I was inspired by the many excellent student teachers who came into my classroom full of enthusiasm and bursting with ideas that they wanted to try. I would let them go, let them do things in their own way, and sometimes marvel at how successful they were. So, I revolutionized my teaching, had a great burning of the busywork from my files, and I love teaching again."

COMPARE	What are some commonalities among these three teachers, even though they work in different settings and are at different stages in their careers?
CONTRAST	How do these teachers think about teaching? About learning? How would you characterize the outlook of each one?
CONNECT	Reflective teachers are *open minded,* willing to admit or consider that they are wrong; *responsible,* willing to look at the consequences of their actions; and *wholehearted,* willing to accept all students and to practice what they preach (Grant & Zeichner, 1984). What evidence did you see of these characteristics in the three teachers profiled? How will you go about becoming more wholehearted, responsible, and open minded in your teaching?

Now that you have reflected on the perspectives of three different teachers, here is a preview of the knowledge, skills, and dispositions you will need to acquire in order to fulfill your role in becoming a professional early childhood educator.

Learning Outcomes

- ✔ Become familiar with national standards and guidelines concerning the early childhood educator's professional growth and development **(NAEYC #5, INTASC #10, and ACEI #5a & 5d)**
- ✔ Define professional culture and professional development
- ✔ Reflect upon the stages in teachers' professional growth
- ✔ Develop strategies for managing personal and professional growth
- ✔ Understand the value of a research base to support teaching practice
- ✔ Document growth as an educator through a professional portfolio

COMPANION WEBSITE 12.1 To learn more about professionalism in the field of early childhood, go to *Journal: Defining Your Role* in Chapter 12 of the Companion Website at http://www.prenhall.com/jalongo.

DID YOU KNOW...?

- According to a national survey conducted by the National Center for Early Development and Learning (NCEDL, 2000a, 2000b), there are more than 1200 early childhood educator preparation programs in U.S. higher education institutions. Less than half award a bachelor's degree in early childhood education. The average number of faculty in these programs is 3.4; most of the faculty are female, Caucasian, and non-Hispanic; and 54% of the faculty are part-time staff.
- When is a bachelor's degree required? Fifty-one states require it of kindergarten teachers; 21 states require it of prekindergarten teachers; and only 1 state requires child-care teachers to have a bachelor's degree (Editors of *Education Week,* 2002).
- In terms of teacher preparation, less than half of the states (23) require preschool teachers to have a bachelor's degree, and only 29 states require preschool teachers to have specialized preparation in teaching young children (Barmett, Hustedt, Robin, & Schulman, 2004).
- A review of research suggests that caregivers with higher levels of education and specific skills training are more apt to engage in the types of caregiver–child interaction that lead to more positive outcomes for children (Martinez-Beck & Zaslow, 2006).
- Congress mandated that at least half of teachers in center-based Head Start classrooms must have an associate's degree or higher with specialization in early childhood education or a related field by September 2003 (Zaslow & Martinez-Beck, 2006).
- The average teacher spends 50 hours a week on all teaching duties, more than those in many other professions, and gets an average of 32 minutes for lunch. On average, they spend nearly $500 a year of their own money for classroom supplies, and their salaries are less lucrative than those of other professionals requiring similar credentials (National Education Association, 2003).
- Experienced teachers who resign cite many reasons for their resignations, including high job stress, increased accountability, increased paperwork, negative student attitudes, lack of parental involvement, unresponsive administration, low starting salaries, and the low status of the profession (Hale-Jinks, Knopf, & Kemple, 2006; Tye & O'Brien, 2002).
- Child-care workers earn, on average, about $7.40 per hour; private preschool teachers earn about $9.40 per hour. The average annual salary for child-care workers is slightly above that of parking-lot attendants, slightly below that of maids and housekeepers, and significantly lower than that of bus drivers. Only public school elementary teachers earn a salary that is comparable to that of people who manage property—about $20.00 per hour (Editors of *Education Week,* 2002). In addition, other benefits such as insurance, paid vacations, and training opportunities are extremely limited for child-care providers (Hale-Jinks et al., 2006).
- Ingersoll and Smith (2003) report that nationally, 15% of new teachers leave the field within the first year and another 15% change schools. A typical school annually would lose 30% of its newly hired staff, thus creating continuous disruption and discontinuity (Smith & Ingersoll, 2003, in Johnson, 2006, p. 12).
- In a survey of 1,100 teachers, 88% reported some form of collaboration with colleagues, 90% said that they could turn to colleagues to support them in trying new ideas at least some of the time, and 93% said that they rely on fellow teachers for good advice (Little, 2001).
- The No Child Left Behind Act of 2001 requires that all teachers employed by local school districts be "highly qualified" by 2005–2006 (Johnson, 2006).
- A teacher's formal education is not finished with the completion of a 2-, 4-, or even 5-year program and initial certification. Nearly every state in the United States requires teachers to earn additional credits in order to maintain certification; many states require training every 5 years (Editors of *Education Week,* 2002).
- The National Board for Professional Teaching Standards (NBPTS) is a group in the United States to which outstanding teachers can apply to be accredited at the national level. Applicants are expected to develop extensive portfolios documenting their work and are rigorously evaluated (see *www.nbpts.org*).
- Based on research, teachers' learning is situated (meaning that it is influenced by the specific circumstances and context), social (meaning that interpersonal interaction supports learning), and distributed (meaning that different people know more or less than others about various things) (Putnam & Borko, 2000).

A Definition of Professional Development

Professionalism refers to an intrinsic code of ethics, values, commitments, and responsibilities that guide thoughts and actions. Professionalism is what keeps a teacher striving for excellence and working hard to help every child learn, even when no one is observing or evaluating. Developing as a professional depends upon your commitment to continue to learn, even after you have completed your initial or advanced preparation program (Lieberman, 1995). (To review the National Association for the Education of Young Children's Code of Ethical Conduct, see the Compendium of Resources at the end of this book.)

Generally speaking, there are five dimensions that differentiate a professional role from other types of occupations (Darling-Hammond & Sykes, 1999; Darling-Hammond, Wise, & Klein, 1999; Saracho & Spodek, 1993).

1. *A defined* ***body of specialized knowledge*** *not possessed by the general public.* Figure 12.1 highlights the types of professional knowledge that teachers are expected to master.
2. ***Control over licensure,*** *certification, entrance requirements, and standards for responsible practice that are monitored by the professionals themselves.*
3. ***Autonomy of practitioners*** *to apply their professional knowledge in diverse situations, make decisions, and exercise judgment in their workplaces.*
4. ***High prestige and economic standing*** *in the larger community.* This means that professionals earn respect for their specialized skills and training and receive adequate compensation for their work.
5. ***Altruism and service to society.*** Professionals are expected to go beyond merely "putting in their time." They are expected to adhere to a code of ethical conduct, to consider more than self-preservation or self-interest, and to contribute to the greater good (altruism).

Anthony Magnacca/Merrill

Most people don't realize the special talents required to work with young children.

Considered from these five dimensions, it is debatable whether or not teaching qualifies as a profession in the same way as law or medicine. Although many early childhood educators are altruistic and dedicated to service, most people do not appreciate the special talents that are required to work effectively with the very young and assume that this type of work is fun and easy. Control over the standards of the profession is often external, emanating from federal, state, and local policies rather than from experts in the field of early childhood. Frequently, the early childhood educator's authority to make decisions is limited. Moreover, it is widely known that early childhood educators, particularly those in child care, are underpaid and held in low regard by the general public. Child caregivers, for example, have an annual turnover rate of between 35% and 50%, partially as a result of low salaries. In 1989, Ellen Galinsky reported that "seventy percent of child care workers earn less than poverty wages" (p. 108), and the situation has not changed much. If one also considers that caregivers rarely receive

FIGURE 12.1 Types and content of professional knowledge.

The Content of Professional Knowledge

Early childhood educators are expected to know about:

Child development—physical, social, emotional, cognitive

Curriculum planning/educational programming

Children's health, safety, and nutrition

Working with parents, parenting, and social services for families

Classroom or behavior management

Program administration

Working with staff

Child abuse and domestic/family violence

Substance abuse

Stress reduction

Play

Child assessment and evaluation

Multicultural education, diversity, and inclusion

Information related to the specific educational program

- **Case knowledge**—acquired through direct experience with actual cases that become part of a teacher's "case files." Teachers return to these cases, sifting through them to find similarities to new cases they encounter.

Example: Making adaptations in the physical environment to meet the needs of a child. The teacher may be working with a young child with cerebral palsy for the first time and, in preparation, will refer to all prior personal experience with making adaptations in the environment to offer guidance in this unfamiliar situation. The teacher may also "borrow" a case file from a more experienced colleague or professional in another field in order to respond appropriately to the child's needs.

- **Episodic knowledge**—gained from personally meaningful, deeply affecting events.

Example: A teacher whose neighbor lost a child to Reyes' syndrome obtains literature on this life-threatening illness and writes an article for the school newsletter alerting parents to the symptoms of this devastating illness.

- **Procedural knowledge**—the physical sequence of events associated with a particular task.

Example: A teacher who has learned the proper procedure for taking children on a field trip, including such things as permission forms, adequate adult supervision, safety procedures on the bus, and so forth.

- **Propositional knowledge**—terminology, facts, concepts, and underlying principles learned through reading and study. Propositional knowledge is brought to bear on experience when teachers use it to more thoughtfully observe, analyze, and discuss real-world teaching.

Example: A beginning teacher who has experienced difficulty during large-group circle time experiments with some of the strategies that were presented in class such as sitting close to a child who has difficulty with self-control, making group times more active and interactive, keeping large-group sessions short, providing a small carpet square to keep each child's space distinct, and restating the rules. The teacher institutes these changes, observes, adapts them to the situation, and shares the results with student-teaching seminar participants.

- **Emotional intelligence**—the ability to perceive accurately, appraise, and express emotion; to access and/or generate feelings in an effort to think better; to understand emotion and emotional knowledge; and to reflect on, manage, and regulate emotions to promote emotional and intellectual growth.

Example: An angry parent arrives at the kindergarten class on Monday morning. She demands to know why her son earned a low score on number knowledge when he can count up to 100. The teacher realizes that the parent is acting out of fear that her child is going to fail the system. Rather than arguing with her, the teacher takes a "conspiratorial," "we're in this together" approach. She explains several of the number activities that she has planned for the boy to do with a college student and tutor and provides his worried mom with a list of activities that they can do together at home to build the boy's concept of number.

SOURCES: Adapted from Berliner, 1994a; Martinez-Beck & Zaslow, 2006; and Mayer & Salovey, 1997.

retirement or medical benefits, it is amazing that there are any child-care professionals at all (Gharavi, 1993). For all of these reasons, the professional status of teaching in general and the early childhood field in particular is a controversial topic.

Teaching has some unique characteristics that differ considerably from those of other professions (Farris, 1996; Swick & Hanes, 1987):

1. Unlike most other professionals, teachers seldom have any say about who their "clients" will be, and, under normal conditions, their work involves hundreds of hours in the company of those clients.
2. The test of a teacher's professional abilities is performance oriented and situation specific. Effectiveness is determined by the skills the teacher demonstrates in particular classrooms at particular times.
3. Teacher education, while ostensibly focused on adults, is actually intended for children. Teachers have responsibility not only for their own learning but also for the effects of that learning on children's learning.
4. Unlike many other professions, in teaching, reciprocal emotional ties between the professionals and the clients are accepted rather than discouraged. It is a breach of professionalism when a psychologist becomes emotionally involved with a patient, while it is perfectly acceptable for young children to love their teachers and for their teachers to say that they love children.
5. Teaching is the only profession that virtually every person in America has had ample opportunity to observe, at least from the other side of the desk. The average high school graduate has spent more time in the company of teachers than on any activity other than sleeping and watching television (Ryan, 1986).

COMPANION WEBSITE 12.2 To learn more about your role as a professional and the NAEYC, go to *Web Links* in Chapter 12 of the Companion Website at http://www.prenhall.com/jalongo.

> Thus, a career dedicated to the care and education of children, while commonplace, is unique among the professions. Teaching is also characterized by complexity and challenges. Three in particular stand out. First, learning to teach requires new teachers to understand teaching in ways quite different from their own experience as students. . . . Second, learning to teach requires that new teachers not only learn to "think like a teacher" but also to "*act* like a teacher." . . . Teachers need to *do* a wide variety of things, many of them simultaneously. Finally, learning to teach requires new teachers to understand and respond to the dense and multifaceted nature of the classroom. . . . They must learn to deal with this "problem of complexity," which derives from the nonroutine and constantly changing nature of teaching and learning in groups. (Darling-Hammond, 2006, p. 35)

Figure 12.2 identifies four elements of complexity in learning to teach.

Your Role as an Early Childhood Professional

An experienced third-grade teacher had saved for many years to travel to Australia. The study of Australia was part of her social studies curriculum, and the teacher was seeking both personal and professional development through travel. She described her reason for pursuing this goal by saying, "In this job you have to take care of yourself." The idea that a teacher should be in charge of his or her own professional development may be a rather startling concept. Educators are, as a group, very altruistic; most people would expect a great teacher's life to be a path of self-sacrifice rather than a plan for self-fulfillment. But becoming a masterful teacher is not a choice between attending to our professional growth and the needs of others; it is doing both (Sparks & Hirsh, 1997). The belief that dedicated teachers deny their needs and attend exclusively to the needs of students is a destructive myth. No matter how supportive the institutions in which early childhood

FIGURE 12.2 What makes teaching so complicated?

Knowledge-Base Challenges
Teachers need to engage in a continuous cycle of learning, enactment, assessment, and reflection in order for their knowledge to grow and become more usable (Snow, Griffin, & Burns, 2005).

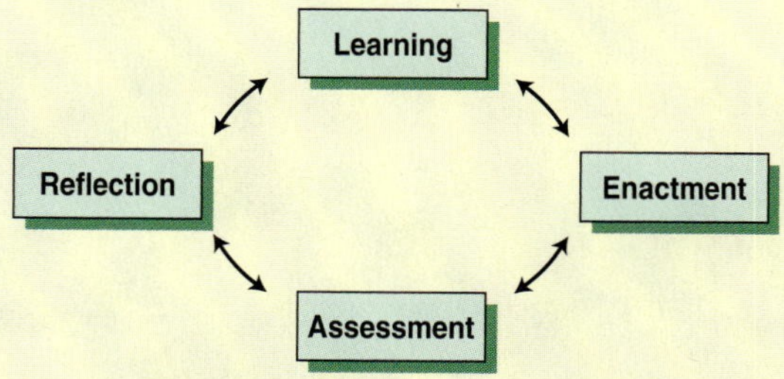

Declarative Knowledge
The student pursuing an education major or certification program is learning from books, lectures, and so forth and gaining the ability to answer questions about what one should do in various situations.

Situated, Can-Do Procedural Knowledge
At this stage, teachers begin to apply what they have learned. For example, a teacher may know something about child development but the challenge here is to use that knowledge to select the best instructional approach for meeting a particular child's needs.

Stable Procedural Knowledge
A teacher with declarative and procedural knowledge should be able to plan instruction that will work for the majority of the class, maintain order and implement the planned instruction, assess child progress, and make some adaptations of instruction. However, when children are experiencing difficulties, new teachers often need support to teach effectively.

Expert, Adaptive Knowledge
With additional practice and reflection, teachers gain facility in addressing a wide array of instructional challenges, seek out helpful and research-based information, and integrate new learning into an expanding repertoire.

Reflective, Organized, and Analyzed Knowledge
Master teachers are able to analyze educational issues, trends, and approaches, to evaluate them as useful or well-founded (or not). Master teachers often bear responsibility for the next generation of professionals as they work with student teachers, colleagues, and college/university personnel (Snow et al., 2005).

Four Elements of Complexity in Teaching

1. *Teaching is never routine.* Teachers must cope with changing situations, learning needs, challenges, questions, and dilemmas.
2. *Teaching has multiple goals* that must be addressed simultaneously. At the same time teachers are teaching content, they are also attending to children's individual needs and considering students' social and intellectual development.
3. *Teaching is done in relationship to diverse groups of students* who differ in cultural background and prior experience as well as learning needs, strengths, areas of challenge, and range of abilities.
4. *Teaching requires the integration of multiple kinds of knowledge.* For instance, to advance the learning of all their students, teachers must constantly integrate their knowledge of child development, subject matter, group interaction, students' cultures and backgrounds, and their particular students' interests, needs, and strengths.

SOURCES: Adapted from Darling-Hammond, 2006; Lampert, 2001; Snow et al., 2005.

educators work may be, it is up to teachers to identify their needs for professional growth and to monitor their own progress toward the goal of becoming better teachers.

Teachers who learn to take care of themselves professionally are smart rather than selfish. As architects of their professional growth, they recognize how their level of satisfaction with teaching influences relationships with colleagues and ultimately affects children's learning. The three timeless questions that guide professional development are

- Who am I?
- What do I need?
- How can I get help? (Clark, 1996, p. 125)

Anthony Magnacca/Merrill

What obstacles face men who want to work with young children?

Sonia Nieto (2005) highlights some of the burning questions that prospective and practicing teachers must ask themselves: "Why do people choose teaching as a career? What is it that entices them to spend their days engaged in learning with other people's children? Why do they decide to go into what are frequently demanding situations, sometimes in poorly funded and rundown schools? Why do they choose teaching rather than other professions that would give them better compensation, higher status, and more respect?" (p. 1). Effective teachers realize that, if they are to improve rather than decline in competence over time, they need to have an unwavering commitment to supporting children's learning and to continually seek professional development. Although they may be well aware of the flaws and foibles of education, their determination to work within the system as advocates for children, families, colleagues, and community is what "keeps them going" (Nieto, 2003). To hear and see three kindergarten teachers discussing how the role of the kindergarten teacher has changed, watch the "Kindergarten" video clip online at the Teacher Prep Website.

TEACHER PREP WEBSITE 12.1

Go to Video Classroom, select Early Childhood Education, choose Professionalism (Module 7), and select Kindergarten Classroom (Video 1).

The first assumption of any effort at professional development is that it is "a complex, human task. It requires a climate conducive to learning and change. . . . It is promoted by the effective use of diverse resources. It includes opportunities for field-testing, feedback, and adjustment. All of these things take time to achieve" (Wood, Thompson, & Russell, 1981, p. 88). There are three key components of professional development:

- *Education* occurs within a formal education system. This includes teachers' overall level of education as well as their content-specific education.
- *Training* occurs outside the formal education system and does not lead to a degree. Training is sometimes referred to as inservice or informal training and includes such things as workshops at professional meetings at the local, county,

state, national, and international levels; training offered by the employer, the county, the state, or the federal government; and videotapes, teleconferencing, Internet tutorials and online discussion groups, supervision of teaching and feedback, and visits to other educational programs.
- *Credentials* do not clearly fall into either the education or training category because the organizations that grant credentials are typically not the same ones that educate or train. For example, a program at a university awards a degree but the certificate, license, or credential usually is awarded by the state or a national organization (Zaslow & Martinez-Beck, 2006).

The ideal outcome of this education, training, and credentialing process is a teacher with the following attributes:

1. Mission-driven—has a genuine calling to become a teacher.
2. Positive and real—respectful, caring, empathetic, and fair with everyone.
3. Leadership qualities—exerts a positive influence on children, parents, and colleagues.
4. With-it-ness—capable of orchestrating all the demands of the classroom, including organization, behavior management, and engaging students.
5. Style—a distinctive way of teaching that includes humor, creativity, originality, and substance.
6. Motivational expertise—holds high expectations for student behavior and achievement and believes she or he can make a positive difference (teacher efficacy).
7. Effectiveness—selects suitable approaches, applies principles of learning, bases decisions on research, and communicates well with learners.
8. Scholarship—values book learning and understands learning content and outcomes deeply and well.
9. Perceptiveness—reads the context, is politically astute, and listens.
10. Reflective—possesses a rich mental life and is strategic, mindful, communicative, and responsive.

PAUSE AND REFLECT

About Your Own Development as a Professional

1. **What have you learned?** How would you explain the difference between teaching young children and teaching students at other developmental levels to someone who is unfamiliar with the field of early childhood?
2. **What will you do?** How do you plan to go about fulfilling the traditional mission of the early childhood educator: educating the whole child and fostering total learning—cognitive, physical, social, and emotional? If you were asked to draw a path or diagram of your hoped-for career, what would it look like?
3. **Where will you find guidance?** What philosophical or theoretical orientations, powerful ideas, and effective strategies do you use to guide your professional practice? Who are your mentors and role models? What are your future goals?

Professionalism in the field of early childhood has been greatly affected by the belief that working with young children is a natural extension of maternal instincts. Historically, the care of young children has been relegated to women, and, because women and children were generally regarded as property in the eyes of society and the law, females and young children were powerless in a "man's world." Today, many people still assume "that preschool and kindergarten are just preparation for the serious learning of first grade—they are not 'real school.' This same attitude influences pay scales; generally, the younger the children, the lower the status and salary of the educator" (Feeney, Christensen, & Moravcik, 2005, p. 75).

COMPANION WEBSITE 12.3 For more information about professional development, go to *Web Links* in Chapter 12 of the Companion Website at http://www.prenhall.com/jalongo.

Despite all of these obstacles, people all over the world dedicate their lives to the care and education of young children. The best in our profession think this is because we are captivated by the very young—their candor, their innocence, their active imaginations,

ASK THE EXPERT

Marilou Hyson on the Importance of Professional Preparation

Marilou Hyson

How important are degrees for early childhood teachers?

Over the past 10 years, national reports, research studies, and professional organizations have increasingly recommended that teachers of young children have college degrees, preferably bachelor's degrees, with specialization in child development and early childhood education. Can someone be a good teacher without having gone to college? Of course. But formal, specialized education can make a difference in most teachers' abilities to provide good educational experiences for children. This can only happen, though, if the college degree reflects a quality program (the NAEYC participates in accrediting high-quality college and university programs, including associate's degree programs).

Why do babies and toddlers need caregivers who have education and training? Isn't it enough to love the children?

Love is the foundation, but love alone is not enough. The first 3 years of life provide incredible opportunities to build children's language, emotional competence, and cognitive and social skills. This doesn't happen by accident—research indicates that adults hold the keys. Professional development helps caregivers learn more about how to talk with infants, how to develop the kind of secure relationships that predict better development, and how to use everyday routines and active play to teach toddlers essential concepts (even in math and science!). It's not surprising that a number of states are creating specialized positions and training for infant-toddler teachers: This is truly one of the most important and challenging jobs in the early childhood field.

If more education is required for early childhood teachers, won't some good people get left behind?

This is indeed a major concern for the early childhood field, which has prided itself on supporting diversity and open access. Many current and future teachers of young children are not well paid and may have difficulty financing further education. Educational opportunities may be more limited in communities of color, or for teachers whose home language is not English. Fortunately, many promising efforts are underway to ensure that all committed and capable educators have access to high-quality professional development. For example, the T.E.A.C.H. program provides scholarships to child-care workers in more than 20 states. Several projects have concentrated on building the capacity of college faculty to help all students succeed, including adult learners, many of whom may have been out of school for years, but who can be among the best and most dedicated students.

Are there some basic things that everyone who works with children should know?

Absolutely! Most states, and several professional organizations such as the NAEYC and the Council for Professional Recognition, have described what have been called *core competencies, competency standards,* or *professional preparation standards.* The NAEYC, for example, identifies five areas in its standards for early childhood professional preparation: Promoting Child Development and Learning; Building Family and Community Relationships; Observing, Documenting, and Assessing to Support Young Children and Families; Teaching and Learning; and Becoming a Professional—each with key elements or components. In this and other descriptions of core competencies, the idea is that everyone should have some level of knowledge and skill in these areas, but that the knowledge and skill should deepen and become more enriched at different steps on the early childhood career ladder—as someone moves, for example, from an entry-level assistant to a degreed lead teacher, or as someone takes on a specialized role such as a home visitor, a director, or a child advocate.

Marilou Hyson is senior advisor for research and professional practice for the National Association for the Education of Young Children.

and their delight in the world they experience afresh every day. One of the greatest rewards of working with the very young is observing their total involvement in learning. As you work with young children, those consummate novices, you too can keep learning, because each child is unique and every situation is individual. There will be daily challenges to your understanding of child development, teaching methods, and conflict resolution skills, because teaching is perpetually complex and engaging. In the process, you can become not only a better teacher, but also a more caring person. Early childhood education and care are a paradox in that so much is demanded for relatively small financial compensation and such great emotional investment; but that investment is in the greatest of our nation's resources: children.

To learn more about refining your practice as a professional see "Foundations & Intro to Teaching–Developing as a Professional" student and teacher artifacts online at the Teacher Prep Websie.

TEACHER PREP WEBSITE 12.2

Go to Student and Teacher Artifacts, select Foundations & Intro to Teaching, choose Developing as a Professional (Module 13), and select Professionalism and Communication (Artifact 2).

Sat
hat
mat
bat

[illegible] is starting to sound out 3 letter phonetics. She may need some help.

Ways of Supporting Professional Development

What conditions are most likely to foster professional development? Variables that affect teachers' overall job satisfaction and contribute to their professional development are depicted in Figure 12.3.

Preservice or inservice educators may be given information, but it is up to each individual to integrate and use that information. No one can simply tell you how to teach.

FIGURE 12.3 Influences on teachers' professional development.

People

- The establishment of friendly, supportive, and trusting relationships with teachers, student teachers, aides, administrators, families, school support personnel (e.g., clerical, janitorial, bus driver), and other professionals (e.g., nurse, counselor, psychologist, consultant, etc.) that build a sense of community

Programs and Systems

- An emphasis on personal and professional growth and a staff-development system that enables all educators to learn about the best that the field has to offer

Roles

- Clearly defined roles and policies combined with leaders who have clear expectations, plan carefully, function efficiently, and who encourage and support staff
- Fairness and equity regarding promotions, raises, and other rewards

Democracy

- Meaningful staff involvement in decision making and agreement among staff members on goals and objectives

Environments

- Physical environments that are well equipped, maintained, and organized

Innovation and Improvement

- Professionals who have developed the ability to adapt flexibly to new demands and change in ways that continuously improve curriculum, teaching, and learning

Relationships with Families and Communities

- Effective ways of working with families and educating the public to the realities of teaching and learning so that continuous improvement becomes a reality

Consider the people you know who are majoring in education. Can you imagine who is most likely to become outstanding, average, or marginal? One way to predict is to consider how adult learners tend to behave. Teachers who are maturing as professionals:

- pursue information today about what will help them to teach better tomorrow
- learn from tapping into their experiences and reflecting upon them

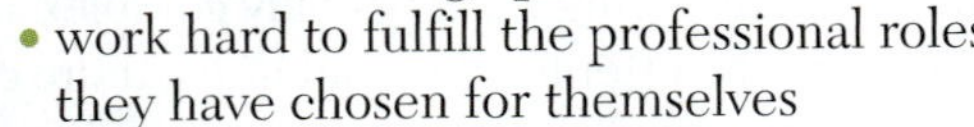

- work hard to fulfill the professional roles they have chosen for themselves
- move from dependence on others to greater self-direction and self-evaluation (Knowles, 1975).

Anthony Magnacca/Merrill

Effective teachers pursue information today that will help them teach better tomorrow.

To illustrate, let's look at Jennifer and Kelly, two college students who are required to observe and participate in a second-grade classroom. Kelly can usually be found sitting at her desk, waiting for the teacher to stop and give her instructions. She is, in her own words, "totally clueless about what to do" during her field assignment, even though a detailed student handbook sits on her desk. When Kelly is confused about something, she complains to anyone who will listen. One requirement is to write in her journal every day, but this is Friday and she has not written anything all week. When Kelly encounters a challenge in the classroom, she panics and protests that she "wasn't prepared" for this particular situation by her teacher preparation program.

In contrast, Jennifer pitches in and suggests a way she might help whenever an opportunity arises in the classroom. She has entered the due dates for each assignment on her calendar and refers to it frequently to pace herself. Jennifer reads the information carefully before formulating a specific question, then she decides who would be the best person to answer that question. When an autistic child joins the class, Jennifer reads several articles about autism, attends a presentation on the topic at the local Council for Exceptional Children meeting, stops by the local mental health association to get information, and speaks with teachers and professors who have training and experience in special education. Jennifer has learned to be self-directed, to use resources to solve problems, and to reflect upon her experiences.

COMPANION WEBSITE 12.4 To learn more about research and your professional growth, go to *Enrichment Content: Research Highlights* in Chapter 12 of the Companion Website at http://www.prenhall.com/jalongo.

Kelly is still entirely dependent upon others, while Jennifer is making steady progress toward her goal of becoming a caring, competent professional who has learned how to evaluate herself (see Black & Davern, 1998, for more on collaborative relationships with other adults).

Stages in Teachers' Professional Development

Every teacher has the choice of seeking growth or resisting growth as a learner: "Professionalism is not an end in itself—a state of being—but an ongoing effort—a process of becoming" (Caulfield, 1997, p. 263). Just as there are stages in child development, there also are stages in teacher development. Knowing these stages may help you to better understand your own experiences on your journey to becoming a teacher of the very young.

Using symbolic language, or metaphors, is one way to talk about stages in teachers' professional development. A metaphor consists of an image or a phrase that symbolizes something else and captures the essence of something profound. For example, a college student who was miserable teaching junior high school and wished that she had pursued early childhood instead chose the metaphor of "a bird in a cage," because anyone could walk by her classroom and see her struggling. All the while she felt trapped, yet obligated to finish the semester. By way of contrast, an early childhood major who was working in a public school prekindergarten for children at risk chose the metaphor of "a covered-dish dinner" to characterize her experience. She worked on an instructional support team consisting of the classroom teacher, a special education teacher, a social worker, and a medical professional to meet with families and make plans for each child. She selected the "covered dish" metaphor because her experience as a teacher thus far had taught her that "everyone brings something important to the experience, and when all of those contributions are combined, the result is wonderful."

In the section that follows, we have synthesized the work of several experts on teacher education to identify the following stages, themes, metaphors, descriptions, and recommended resources (Berliner, 1994b; Katz, 1977, 1995; Swick & Hanes, 1987).

Stage 1: Novice **Theme:** Survival **Question:** Am I cut out to be a teacher?

Metaphors: "Just learning the ropes." "Barely keeping my head above water." "Wondering if I have what it takes to be a teacher."

Description: Garrett Keizer (1988) poignantly characterizes the novice teacher's dilemma when he writes, "I never cared less whether I lived or died than I did my first year of teaching" (p. 1). Most student teachers and even first- or second-year teachers are considered to be novices who are striving to define themselves as professionals. Beginning teachers frequently feel overwhelmed by the daily demands of teaching and ill-prepared for the complexities of the teaching role. "The realization of the great responsibility they have for the group of children, as well as the discrepancy between the success they expect and the reality of the classroom, result in anxiety and feelings of inadequacy" (Essa, 2002, p. 95).

COMPANION WEBSITE 12.5 For more information about technology and the professional development of early childhood educators, go to *Web Links* in Chapter 12 of the Companion Website at http://www.prenhall.com/jalongo.

Many preservice teachers are still in the process of making their career decision about teaching. They usually have the idealism characteristic of their age, but they are also fearful of failure. As they move into their first "survival" year, new teachers are in for a "reality shock" (Messler, 2006). The stamina required of the job, the amount of paperwork, the range and intensity of students' needs, the parents who lack confidence in them, and the lack of support for their efforts within the school and district often are surprising (Ryan, 1986). Early childhood educators at this stage have training but limited experience. Usually, they are relatively immature as professionals and are still under direct supervision, such as a student teacher who works with a veteran teacher and a college faculty member as supervisors, or a first-year teacher who is assigned to a master teacher or mentor. The persistent questions of the beginning teacher usually are "Who am I?" and "What can I do?" (Baptiste & Sheerer, 1997, p. 266).

Recommended Books: For more on first-year teachers, read autobiographical accounts such as Conroy's (1987) *The Water Is Wide,* Kohl's (1967) *36 Children,* Meier's (1997) *Life in Small Moments: Learning in an Urban Classroom,* Kane's (1991) *The First Year of Teaching: Real World Stories from America's Teachers,* and Dollas's (1992) *Voices of Beginning Teachers: Visions and Realities.* Also read

TEACHER PREP WEBSITE 12.3

Go to Getting Your License and Beginning Your Career, select Your First Year of Teaching: Guidelines for Success and Day, Week, and choose Your First Day, Week, and Year of Teaching.

studies of beginning teachers (Clandinin, Davies, Hogan, & Kennard, 1993; LaBoskey, 1994; Reynolds, 1992) or consult handbooks for beginning teachers (MacDonald, 1991; Thompson, 2002; Wong & Wong, 2004).

To review suggestions for successful early teaching experiences, see "Getting Your License and Beginning Your Career–Your First Year of Teaching" online at the Teacher Prep Website.

Stage 2: Advanced Beginner **Theme:** Consolidation **Question:** How can I grow in competence and confidence?

Metaphors: "Putting it all together." "Finding my way." "Hitting my stride."

Description: During the consolidation phase, the teacher begins to focus on specific tasks, individual children, specific behavior problems, and challenging situations. Another hallmark of this stage is developing a more personalized approach to teaching, or a teaching style. The early childhood educator at this stage has completed professional training, worked directly with young children, and made a commitment to the profession. Practitioners at this stage are better equipped to identify possible courses of action, make rational decisions, and predict the consequences of their actions for children, families, colleagues, and professionals in other fields (VanderVen, 1991). "It is not just the availability of classroom experience that enables teachers to apply what they are learning . . . when teachers study and reflect on their work and connect it to research and theory, they are better able to identify areas needing improvement, consider alternative strategies for the future, and solve problems of practice" (Darling-Hammond, 2006, p. 103).

Recommended Books: *Notes from a Schoolteacher* (Herndon, 1985), *Among School Children* (Kidder, 1989), and *One Child* (Hayden, 1980). For research on teachers who are in the consolidation stage of their careers, see Connelly and Clandinin (1988).

Anthony Magnacca/Merrill

Effective teachers are interested in exploring new ideas with colleagues.

Stage 3: Proficient **Theme:** Renewal **Question:** What will I do to improve with experience rather than diminish my effectiveness?

Metaphors: "Avoiding falling into a rut." "Seeking new challenges."

Description: After working for 3 to 5 years, many teachers have gained confidence and effectiveness. The proficient teacher is able to "draw connections to students' prior knowledge and experiences, choose appropriate starting places and sequences of activities, develop assignments and assessments to inform learning and guide future teaching, and construct scaffolding for different students depending on their needs" (Darling-Hammond & Bransford, 2005, p. 176). In order to grow in their proficiency, teachers seek professional enrichment that will bolster their enthusiasm, offer a fresh perspective, enrich their storehouse of ideas, and inspire them to do their best. The teacher at the renewal phase is typically interested in exploring new ideas and resources that will enhance effectiveness. Activities such as collaboration with colleagues; perusal of the professional literature (books, journals, magazines); attendance at conferences, seminars, and workshops; visits to model programs; and the pursuit of an advanced degree are all ways that teachers seek renewal.

COMPANION WEBSITE 12.6 To add a professional development product to your developing portfolio, go to *Journal: Constructing Your Professional Portfolio* in Chapter 12 of the Companion Website at http://www.prenhall.com/jalongo.

Recommended Books: *Qualities of Effective Teachers* (Stronge, 2002), *Finding Our Own Way* (Newman, 1990), *Stirring the Chalkdust: Case Studies of Teachers in the Midst of Change* (Wasley, 1994), *Oops! What We Learn When Our Teaching Fails* (Power & Hubbard, 1996), and *The Case for Education* (Colberg, Trimble, & Desberg, 1996).

Stage 4: Expert **Theme:** Maturity **Question:** What impact has my life had on the lives of children and families?

Metaphors: "Really making a difference." "Taking on the mentoring role."

Description: Teachers who have attained maturity have arrived at a personal and professional teaching style and are most concerned with the long-term consequences of their teaching for learners. Profound and abstract questions characterize their quest to make an enduring contribution to children's learning: "What will their world be like?" "How important is it for children to know this?" and "Which experiences and activities will have the most enduring effect on learning?" It is also during this stage that teachers often assume leadership roles that emanate from expertise in the field, a secure sense of self, and the admiration of colleagues. Remember the veteran teacher, Ms. Renzulli, from the opening scenario? She completely changed her teaching because she regained her focus on the impact of her teaching.

Recommended Books: *The Languages of Learning: How Children Talk, Write, Dance, Draw, and Sing Their Understanding of the World* (Gallas, 1994); *The Transcendent Child: Tales of Triumph over the Past* (Rubin, 1996); *Portraits in Courage: Teachers in Difficult*

PAUSE AND REFLECT

About What Your Metaphor Is

An early childhood administrator had this to say about her role: "I see myself as a change agent, a coach, a mentor, and a facilitator whose job it is to remove obstacles so that people can teach." On her lapel was a button that read "Children First." Early childhood educators use a variety of metaphors or symbols to characterize their professional roles. One teacher from a neighborhood with a high crime rate referred to his classroom as "a safe sector of the city, a haven." A kindergarten teacher described her approach to the curriculum as "like building with blocks—first you make the base, then stack them, one at a time, on top of one another." We also use short statements or mottos that characterize our beliefs, values, and attitudes. Some current examples are "Leave no child behind," "Caring for other people's children," and "Celebrating diversity." What metaphors or mottos do you live by as a teacher of the very young? Give this some thought, then share your ideas with the class.

Circumstances (UNESCO, 1997); *Mentors, Master Teachers, and Mrs. MacGregor: Stories of Teachers Making a Difference* (Bluestein, 1995); and *On Their Side: Helping Children Take Charge of Learning* (Strachota, 1996).

For some fine examples of early childhood educators who have reached maturity, read Carol Hillman's (1988) *Teaching Four-Year-Olds: A Personal Journey;* Mem Fox's (1993) *Radical Reflections: Passionate Opinions on Teaching, Learning, and Living;* or any of Vivian Paley's books, particularly *Wally's Stories* (1981) and *The Girl with the Brown Crayon* (1997). For more on teachers at all of these career stages, read *Teachers' Stories: From Personal Narrative to Professional Insight* (Jalongo & Isenberg, 1995).

Beginning teachers sometimes assume that after they log more hours in early childhood settings, they will automatically become the teachers they aspire to be. Yet experience alone does not necessarily lead to more caring, competent teaching. It is possible to repeat the mistakes of that first "survival" year over and over again and learn little from experience, time after time. Nor will accumulating more formal education or collecting advanced degrees guarantee quality. Becoming an outstanding early childhood educator depends upon the personal investment you make in your learning and teaching, all the while keeping children at the center of your practice. Teachers are required to pass a licensure exam, called the Praxis II, in order to be certified as teachers. To get study tips for the national teacher examination, see "Getting Your License and Beginning Your Career–Passing Your Licensure Exam" online at the Teacher Prep Website.

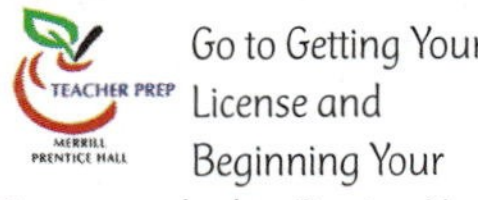

Go to Getting Your License and Beginning Your Careers and select Passing Your Licensure Exam.

Lifelong Learning and the Early Childhood Practitioner

At this stage in your career, you might be dreaming about the day when you have completed your program. That hopeful dreaming might include abandoning your books, tests, and presentations, trading them for exciting lessons, and spending your time in the company of young children. Perhaps you have thought to yourself, "When I get my certificate/degree/first job, I will finally be ready!" The bad news is, no matter how excellent your program is, it is only the beginning. There are several reasons why teacher-preparation programs cannot fully prepare teachers for what they will encounter in a classroom.

Change Versus Status Quo. In every teacher preparation program, your instructors have to deal with the conflict between preparing you for early childhood settings as they are and preparing you for early childhood settings as they should and could be. In other words, your instructors hope that you will go forward and improve education, not merely fit in, as important as that may be, particularly at first. Striving for change can sometimes cause you to feel frustrated with veteran teachers who are satisfied with the way things are. Although you need to respect their experience and acknowledge their strengths, you also have an obligation to improve the quality of care and education for young children.

General Versus Specific. Early childhood teacher-preparation has to prepare teachers for a wide range of possibilities. A student graduating from a 4-year program with a teaching certificate, for example, might be hired to teach third grade in a parochial school, teach prekindergarten in a public school, direct a child-care center, or provide instruction to young children who are ill in hospitals or in their homes. No program can be expected to provide you with guidance on the daily details of how to function in such diverse situations. That is why teachers must continue to be avid learners and develop professionally.

Real Versus Ideal. Even though introductions to the real world of teaching occur more often and earlier through field experiences, no teacher-preparation program can

ASK THE EXPERT

Sharon Lynn Kagan on Public Policy and Teachers' Professional Growth

Sharon Kagan

Some Common Misconceptions About Public Policy and Teachers' Professional Growth

Misconception 1: Policy construction is expected to be rapid and predictable.

We all learn in many ways, but those of us who get to teach learn a great deal from our students and from the questions they ask and the ideas they bring to discussions. For the most part, my students are very, very bright. They have shown some interest in child development and policy because they have taken the prerequisites for the formal courses; those seeking individual guidance (via independent study or thesis advisement) are already quite advanced in their work. They ask good questions, have keen insights, and are in a policy hurry. They want to be policymakers—quickly.

I have been interested that they perceive policy construction as a linear, predictable, and fully knowable process. In their desire to "master" it—to have all the tools in hand before they plunge into the real world—they want it to be rational, to follow a formula. Often, students are mystified that policy is as much about chance, electability, and favors as it is about social justice and equity. They are stunned—and often intrigued—to hear the behind-the-scenes nuances of the policy process. Their surprise and freshness delights me and makes me realize that no work in policy can be complete without a policy practicum. Students constantly remind us, then, that the real work of teaching is to infuse reality without diminishing hope.

In their haste to make waves in the policy world, students often want to move fast. They usually feel that while it is desirable to be theoretically grounded in a discipline, it takes time—and a lot of it. Consequently, many launch into the policy world lacking any empirical understanding of young children and their development, lacking understanding of different theoretical approaches to pedagogy, and lacking any historical exposure to the complexities of the early care and education world. I lament this, because there is simply no substitute for rich empirical, theoretical, and historical understandings—they are the intellectual bedrock of policy work, providing both wisdom and credibility. Many students, therefore, need to learn that there is no substitute for academic training; simultaneously, we need to learn to help them understand the practical value of the empirical, theoretical, and historical perspectives that undergird our discipline.

Misconception 2: Real leadership is simple and effortless.

Beyond being well grounded in practice and theory, students need to realize that real leadership doesn't come easy. Leaders do tend to make leadership look simple: The President waltzes onto the podium and delivers the perfect speech effortlessly; we waltz into our classes and deliver the perfect lectures or seminars; master teachers waltz into their classrooms and seem to magically create the perfect learning environment for children. But behind all this apparent effortlessness are years of hours of work, and countless trials and errors, coupled with some dashed ideals and probably some embarrassing mistakes. We need to let our students know that it isn't all easy and without effort. They need to learn that leadership means having courage and using it; it means having integrity and using it; it means being willing to take risks; it means working hard and sticking to it; and sometimes it means lots of personal sacrifice. My biggest concern and students' most common misconception, then, is that many students perceive child-related policy work to be glamorous, effortless, and somewhat substanceless. My big job is conveying that it is precisely and fully the exact opposite.

Sharon Lynn Kagan is the Virginia and Leonard Marx Professor of Early Childhood and Family Policy, Co-Director of the National Center for Children and Families, Associate Dean for Policy at Teachers College, Columbia University, and Professor Adjunct at Yale University's Child Study Center.

eradicate the feelings of inadequacy during the first year. All professionals enter their profession with some fanciful notions of what their chosen careers will bring. It is surprisingly difficult to keep the right amount of that idealism intact throughout a career rather than deteriorating into a disillusioned or burned-out professional. Teaching well is an expression of who you are as a person and as an early childhood professional. There is no way to become completely prepared to teach, because even if you could be completely prepared for today, tomorrow will bring about changes that will demand new understandings and skills.

TEACHER PREP WEBSITE 12.5

Go to Getting Your License and Beginning Your Career, select Professional Teaching Standards, and choose Association for Childhood Education International and National Association for the Education of Young Children.

Promise Versus Perfection. When you think about it, your instructors are in the business of making predictions about who will become effective early childhood practitioners. When you are a student teacher, they observe you in the context of the college or university classroom and try to imagine how you will perform in various early childhood settings. Then they observe you in someone else's early childhood setting with someone else's students and envision how you will function on your own. Although it may sometimes seem otherwise, your supervisors do not expect you to be perfect in either situation. Rather, they are looking for promise and progress at a level characteristic of other teacher candidates with your level of training and experience.

A good teacher preparation program can inaugurate a teacher's journey as a learner but can never fully prepare you for the realities and complexities of teaching. Each teacher must make the difficult adjustment from college to the real world of the center or classroom. Meeting professional standards in a key responsibility of professional educators. To review the standards of leading organizations, see "Getting Your License and Beginning Your Career–Professional Teaching Standards" online at the Teacher Prep Website. Even when teachers are equipped with a repertoire of effective teaching behaviors, they still have to decide which to use, when and how to use them, and which students to use them with (Clark & Yinger, 1977). Much of what you will need to do and understand as a teacher is learned through on-the-job training. When you become a teacher, you become your own project. Becoming a better teacher is a process that is never finished. There will never come a day when you say to yourself, "At last, I am a perfect teacher!" Rather, there are many aspects of professional practice that every competent, caring teacher addresses throughout life.

The Concerns of Beginning Teachers

Each teacher gradually builds a theory of the world of teaching and continually tests the theory in the classroom. Three experienced teachers were having dinner together when one of them said, "I can tell that I am lacking confidence about something when I have the teaching nightmares I used to have as an undergraduate. In this dream, the children are completely unruly and I can't get them to pay any attention to me at all." Another teacher agreed, saying, "My nightmare is a little different. In it, I find out that I forgot to attend a class and now I can't graduate." A third teacher laughed and said, "Me too! Only in my nightmare, they take back my teaching degree!" Beginning teachers often approach teaching with a mixture of excitement and anxiety. Some of the most common worries of student teachers and beginning teachers include the following:

- **Relationships with children and families.** What should I expect from children of this age? What if they misbehave? How will I respond? Will my response be appropriate? What if children, parents, or families don't like or respect me? What if a child has a problem that I know nothing about how to handle? How will I talk with parents and families during conferences? I've never done this before!

- **Relationships with adults.** What if my supervisors don't like or respect me? What if I make a terrible mistake? What if I am observed on my very worst day of teaching? If my supervisors think that my teaching is bad, what will I do? Will I be encouraged and helped, or simply branded as a bad teacher? What about my grade point average or other types of evaluation? What if my supervisors don't agree on what I should be doing? Will I be caught in the middle?
- **Learning activities.** What if the activity that I have planned turns out to be a disaster? What if children are disinterested or won't cooperate? What if I plan something for half an hour and the children are done in a few minutes? How will I ever find the time to plan adequately for everything I am expected to do? How am I going to assess children's learning? What can I do to make sure that I treat children fairly?
- **Future career.** Will I be able to find a good job? How will I conduct myself during interviews? How will I make sure that prospective employers know what I can do and give me a chance? (MacDonald, 1991)

Figure 12.4 suggests a variety of ways that teachers can contribute to their own personal and professional development.

FIGURE 12.4 Strategies for professional development.

Observing to Learn: paying attention to nonverbal, verbal, and other behavioral responses from children and adults

- In college classes: conducting a case study of a particular child, noticing what classmates plan that is particularly effective, learning from instructors
- In schools and centers: noticing what good teachers do, looking at the work that children have accomplished, analyzing the classroom floor plan, visiting model programs
- In other settings: noticing what other professionals who work with young children and young children's parents do during story time at the library, in a hospital nursery, at a health fair at the mall, at a church fair, at a community playground, at a family reunion picnic, and so forth

Participating to Learn: gaining experience with young children whenever the opportunity arises

- In college classes: working in required student teaching and practicum experiences, volunteering to participate at special campus events for children (e.g., a face-painting booth on homecoming day, a field trip to campus, a "read-in" or a Saturday workshop for parents sponsored by a professional organization)
- In other settings: babysitting for friends and family, volunteering to work with young children in the community (e.g., provide short-term child care for parents attending a meeting), teach a religion class for young children at your church

Writing to Learn: using writing skills to become a reflective practitioner

- In college classes and during teaching: keeping a journal, writing plans, taking notes from teacher resource books, making curriculum webs, communicating with families, documenting what children are learning through bulletin boards, submitting news items to the newspaper, corresponding with a trusted teacher and friend, writing a philosophy statement, creating a portfolio, writing a paper on a topic of interest for a class

Raising Questions to Learn: formulating good questions for yourself and children

- In college classes and during teaching: questioning personal assumptions and biases, raising questions about cultural influences, asking political questions about policies, power, and control issues

FIGURE 12.4 Continued

Collaborating to Learn: combining your skills and abilities with those of other adults to become a more effective early childhood practitioner

- In college classes: forming a study group, working on projects with partners or groups, finding a faculty mentor, joining a professional organization, planning and teaching with another student teacher
- During teaching: coteaching with fellow teachers, working with administrators, parents, families, professionals in other fields, and community members to provide services or plan special events for children
- In other settings: attending workshops and professional meetings, joining organizations that work on behalf of children

Using Resources to Learn: gaining access to a wide variety of materials and people who will support and enhance learning

- In college classes: borrowing children's books, teacher resource books, and scholarly books from the library; using the Internet to locate current information on a topic; consulting experts from other areas of specialization (e.g., talking with a special education teacher about a child's physical handicap); subscribing to professional journals; beginning a collection of children's books; communicating with other professionals or professionals in training through e-mail and the Internet
- During teaching: knowing what support services are available in your community and how to access them to help families; borrowing materials from the public library, school library, or other agencies and organizations; identifying people you can trust in the community to help solve problems (e.g., the Lions Club to assist in getting children eyeglasses, the Shriners to assist with the cost of surgery for orthopedic problems); joining teachers' book clubs; traveling to learn about education in other lands; corresponding with other teachers using e-mail; joining professional discussion groups on the Internet

COLLABORATING WITH FAMILIES

Maintaining Positive Relationships with Families

As a professional educator I understand my commitment to be an excellent teacher. In order to maintain a quality practice for my students and their families, I:

- See myself as a lifelong learner who remains current in not only theory and practice but also cultural and political events and their impact on my students and their families
- Am able to articulate my beliefs about theory and practice in language that is clear to my students' families
- Am respectful and understanding of families' perspectives
- Invite families to become a partner with me in their children's education
- Give families clear explanations about the value and purpose of learning activities in my classroom
- Make it a priority to learn about family and cultural customs, beliefs, and practices as they relate to the students in my classroom
- Extend invitations to families to visit and participate in the classroom at times that are convenient to them and in various aspects of the curriculum and classroom

You will want to document the progress that you make in professional development in your portfolio.

Conclusion

As this chapter has described, there are many misconceptions about what is involved in becoming an effective teacher.

> Most people tend to think of the act of teaching as largely intuitive: someone knows something and then "teaches" it to others—a fairly straightforward transmission model. . . . However, as mountains of research now demonstrate, this notion of transmission teaching doesn't actually work most of the time. The reality of effective teaching is much different: successful teachers link what students already know and understand to new information, correcting misimpressions, guiding learners' understanding through a variety of activities, providing opportunities for application of knowledge, giving useful feedback that shapes performance, and individualizing for students' distinctive learning needs. They do all this while juggling the social and academic needs of the group and of individuals, the cognitive and motivational consequences of their moment-to-moment teaching decisions, the cultural and community context within which they teach, and much more. (Darling-Hammond, 2006, p. 8)

COMPANION WEBSITE 12.7 To test your knowledge of this chapter's content, go to the *Multiple-Choice and Essay Modules* in Chapter 12 of the Companion Website at http://www.prenhall.com/jalongo. These items are written in the same format that you will encounter on the Praxis test to better prepare you for your licensure exam.

Teachers who continue to develop professionally have learned to accept responsibility for their own professional growth, to exercise sound professional judgment, and to use a wide array of human and material resources to foster lifelong learning. Effective early childhood practitioners fully appreciate the paradox that self-development is intertwined with making significant contributions to the care and education of the very young.

ONE CHILD, THREE PERSPECTIVES

Rolando's Mother Gets Involved in Head Start

When Twila, a Head Start teacher, knocked on her door, Mrs. Garcia suddenly realized that she had completely forgotten about the home visit she had scheduled several weeks ago. Mrs. Garcia's infant daughter had just spit up on her, and the house was a complete mess as a result of a family visit over the weekend. As she spoke with Twila, Mrs. Garcia held her front door half-closed and tried to rush through the interaction. Sensing her discomfort, Twila said, "This doesn't seem like the best time to talk. Would you like to reschedule?" With a smile of gratitude, Mrs. Garcia agreed.

After she shut the door, Mrs. Garcia started to think about this opportunity for her son Rolando. Rolando was born with spina bifida: a place in his spine did not fuse together. He moved around by using the upper part of his body to drag his legs across the floor or by using a special wheelchair. What if the other children made fun of Rolando? If they did, then he surely would be better off at home. But the teacher had seemed very kind and had invited Mrs. Garcia and her husband to visit the classroom any time they wished. They even had a special orientation day when Rolando could attend a full day of school with a peer as his guide, and Mrs. Garcia would be permitted to be there throughout the day. She felt hopeful that Head Start would give Rolando a chance to learn and to make friends.

Mrs. Garcia later discussed this with Rolando's father but he was opposed to the whole idea. "What if Rolando picks up all those childhood illnesses? Doesn't he have enough problems to deal with? Besides, you are home all day. It's your job to take care of him."

In the car after leaving the Garcia's home, the Head Start teacher wondered whether this family would agree to participate in the program. "Why would they refuse all of this help for their son?" she thought to herself. "He needs to form good peer relationships as much as strong family ties."

REACT	In what ways are the perspectives of the three adults alike? Which perspective do you identify most strongly with, and why?
RESEARCH	Locate information about spina bifida at the library. What are some ways of helping children with this condition to be accepted by their peers and have successful learning experiences?
REFLECT	Rolando's mother, father, and the Head Start teacher have definite ideas about how to meet this young child's needs. What might be the underlying reasons for the differences in their ideas? How do their approaches compare with what you have read?

IN-CLASS WORKSHOP

Becoming a Valued Colleague

Teachers are often advised to develop the skills of colleagueship. What, exactly, does this mean? A colleague may be defined as a person who accepts responsibility for her or his own actions, yet has a commitment to others and to the mission of the organization. Think about your work with others—in jobs, with your classmates, and in organizations. What makes one person a coworker that you would seek out? Generate a list of attributes, then compare/contrast it with the one that follows.

A valued colleague:

- puts children's and families' needs first
- is committed to equity and fairness
- can be trusted with confidential and important things
- thoughtfully considers other points of view
- volunteers, steps forward
- is filled with energy
- possesses enthusiasm for teaching
- has a sense of humor
- avoids blaming others
- shares success stories that reveal how teachers learn from their students
- realizes when teaching efforts fail and strives for excellence
- notices what you do well
- seeks advice appropriately
- is an avid learner
- develops an ideological map of group members' philosophies
- is dependable and trustworthy
- knows you as a person, not just as a coworker
- listens and carefully considers what you have to say
- shares books, ideas, and other resources
- talks about interests beyond teaching
- has a vision of where he or she is headed personally and professionally
- is candid yet diplomatic
- knows when to take a stand and when to go along
- can disagree without rancor
- dwells on solutions rather than problems
- is willing to take the risks necessary to improve education
- acknowledges mistakes and genuinely strives to do better (adapted from Graves, 2001)

Based on these criteria, how might a responsible colleague respond to the following real-life situations?

Situation 1. Another student teacher has twice asked to "borrow" your lesson plans but never offers to plan with you, share plans, or develop the ones that you gave to him or her. What would you say the third time?

Situation 2. You are sharing a ride with another teacher who has caused you to be late for school twice in the past 2 weeks because the person was not ready when you arrived. Your supervisor has told you that this is unacceptable and must be stopped immediately. What would you say to the other teacher? To your supervisor?

Situation 3. There is a local conference being held on campus on a Saturday and student teachers are expected to attend. A friend asks you to sign in for her so that she can sleep in instead of being there at 8 A.M. How would you handle this?

Situation 4. Two inservice teachers are in the hallway before school starts, engaging in destructive gossip about a family whose children attend the school. They seem to want you to participate and start telling you all about an arrest report that appeared in the paper last night. You are a student teacher in the building. How would you respond?

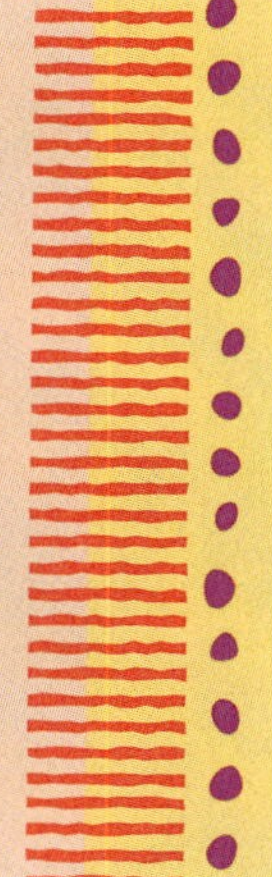

Appendix

Compendium of Early Childhood Materials and Resources

NOTE TO STUDENTS 438

MATERIAL RESOURCES 438

Basic Materials and Equipment by Age Range 438

CURRICULUM RESOURCES 442

Selected Resources for Learning Centers 442

Free and Inexpensive Materials for Teachers 444

Health, Nutrition, and Safety Resources 445

PROFESSIONAL RESOURCES FOR TEACHERS 447

The National Association for the Education of Young Children Code of Ethical Conduct and Statement of Commitment 447

Interstate New Teacher Assessment and Support Consortium (INTASC) Standards 456

Professional Associations, Organizations, Journals, and Materials 456

Ask the Expert: Jerlean Daniel on the National Association for the Education of Young Children (NAEYC) 458

Education Resources Information Center (ERIC) Clearinghouses 462

STORAGE AND ORGANIZATIONAL RESOURCES 463

Finding Materials for a Good Resource File 463

Materials to Include in a Resource File 463

TECHNOLOGY RESOURCES 463

Software Evaluation Criteria 465

HUMAN RESOURCES 466

Community Resources 466

Public School Specialists 468

Public Library–Linked Services for Children and Families 468

Community-Building Strategies 470

CHAPTER-BY-CHAPTER CROSS-REFERENCE OF EARLY CHILDHOOD MATERIALS AND RESOURCES 471

Note to Students

As an *early childhood teacher*, you will always be looking for new ideas. You will gather, identify, evaluate, and use resources that will enhance your teaching and facilitate children's learning. When you begin to teach, you will probably be concerned about the cost and availability of materials and resources to use. That is why we have compiled this beginning collection of resources, many of which can be obtained with little or no cost. As you work with children, remember these resources and use them often. There is an abundance of information, ideas, and materials out there waiting for you.

This Compendium of Early Childhood Materials and Resources lists a wide range of resources that are available from diverse sources for your use. It is intended to provide a starting point for you to obtain information and assistance, add to regularly, and make it work for you; it is *not intended* to be a definitive list of every resource that is available to you. Categorized as either material or human resources, the information is presented in alphabetical order for easy reference.

Material Resources

Children need a large variety of materials. They are the tools with which children explore, experiment, investigate, and understand their world. Gathering materials and creating a resource file is going to make your teaching more efficient. We encourage you to add to this regularly to make it work for you.

Basic Materials and Equipment by Age Range

INFANTS AND TODDLERS (BIRTH–AGE 3 YEARS) *Infants* learn by sensory exploration and social interaction. They need a variety of textured objects to view, hold, and reach for. They also need materials that make sounds, are soft and squeezable, and are simple, realistic, and safe. *Toddlers* are *actively seeking independence* and have a high energy level. They need action toys to take apart and put together and materials scaled to their size that require different kinds of manipulations such as nesting, stacking, and bouncing. Here are some beginning suggestions:

The Arts

music (autoharp, tape recorders), art (brushes, easel, smocks), media (chalk, crayons, play dough, paper of assorted colors), movement and pretend play (props, hats, scarves)

Basic Indoor Equipment

bulletin boards, cabinets, chairs (adult and child-sized), clothes rack, cubbies, file cabinet, infant stroller, safety gates, shelves (high and low), storage bins on rollers, tables (changing table at adult height, other tables at child height), toilet facilities, wastebaskets (covered)

Cognitive

aquarium, blocks, books, floating and sinking pieces, gear-turning toys, nesting toys, number puzzles, plants, shells and rocks, stacking toys, sorting toys

Communication

books, pictures for discussion, feel box, flannel board, language games, puppets

Gross Motor Equipment (Indoor/Outdoor)

apparatus (boxes, climbers), dramatic play (dishes, housekeeping), large-muscle toys (balls, blocks, push toys), sand play (cups, spoons), water play (dump-and-fill containers)

Health and Safety Materials

first aid and toilet supplies, food service (bibs, bottles, flatware), resting facilities (cots, cribs), diapers, sanitation (diaper changing pads), smocks, towelettes, washcloths

Housekeeping Equipment

brooms (adult and child-sized), brushes (bottle, counter, hand), dishpan, dishtowels, disinfectants, hand-held portable vacuum, heating and serving dishes, sponges, towels, trays

Manipulatives

Infants: clutch ball, infant gyms, squeeze toys, teething toys
Toddlers: beads, large-sized stacking and locking sets, giant pegboard, plastic vehicles

Record Keeping

attendance sheets, booklets for observation notes, card file, parent forms, health sheets

Sensory Materials

listening (bells, chimes), smelling (sealed spices), tasting (foods), touching and feeling (textured materials), looking (color paddles)

PRESCHOOL AND KINDERGARTNERS (AGES 3–5) Preschoolers and kindergartners show increasing social ability, fascination with adult roles, growing mastery over their small and large muscles, and interest in pretend play. The materials and equipment for this age group should support their developing social skills and interest in these areas. Here are some suggestions:

The Arts

aprons (plastic or cloth), brushes and holders, chalk, collage materials, containers, newspapers, paint (assorted), paper (assorted), play dough, printing materials, scissors

Audiovisual Equipment

cassette recorder, cassettes, CDs and DVDs, filmstrips, record player, records, tapes

Basic Indoor Equipment

bookcase, bookshelves, bulletin board, cabinets (movable), chairs (adult and child), chalkboard, cubbies, drinking fountain (child height), filing cabinet, rugs, sink, smoke alarm

Building and Construction

blocks (assorted), boards, building sets, carpentry, sand/water play, vehicles, wheels

Dramatic Play

animals, camping, cooking and eating equipment, doctor/nurse, doll equipment, dress-up, family living, furniture for housekeeping, puppets, transportation, traffic signs

General Maintenance

broom, buckets, electrical extension cord and plug, plunger, tool box

Health and Safety

first aid supplies, flashlight, food preparation and service supplies (blender, bottle opener, can opener, flatware), measures, plates, storage containers, tablecloths, trays

Housekeeping Supplies

brooms (push, regular), cleaning cloths, cleansers, dishpan, drying rack (folding), mops, soap, sponges, toilet paper, towels, vacuum cleaner

Language Arts

alphabet letters, books, camera, chart paper, computer, felt board, puzzles, typewriter

Mathematics

counters, food to cut and divide, geometric figures and shapes, matching sets, measuring equipment, money (play, homemade), number games, pegboards, shapes, sorting containers

Music

autoharp, rhythm instruments (bells, maracas, tambourines, triangles, wooden blocks)

Office Supplies and Record Keeping

bulletin board, calendar, computer supplies, file cabinet, manila folders and envelopes, message pads, paper clips, pencils and pens, stationery, thumbtacks, yardstick

Perceptual Development

beads and laces, counting rods, dressing frames, games, linking toys, magnetic board

Psychomotor Development

balls, bars for hanging, bean bags, bowling pin sets, crates, hoops, pails, pulleys, rakes

Science

air experiments, animal foods and types, books about science concepts, food and gardening, light and heat, machines, magnets, picture collections, seeds

SCHOOL-AGE CHILDREN (AGES 5–8) School-age children are refining skills and talents that they prize, are relying more and more on support from their peers, and are becoming more organized and logical thinkers. Materials and equipment for this age group should reflect their need for realistic, rule-oriented, and peer activities. Following are some suggestions:

The Arts

aluminum foil, brushes, chalk, containers, crayons, drying rack, glue, laundry starch, markers, needles, paint, paper, paper cutter, pens, pipe cleaners or wikki sticks, stapler

Basic Indoor Equipment

air conditioner (where appropriate), boards, book racks, cabinets, carpeting, chairs, chart holders, clock (wall), easels, file cabinet, floor pillows, mirror, sink, towels, waste baskets

Consumable Materials

chalk, chalkboard erasers, chart tablets, colored folders, fasteners, markers, metal rings, paper (assorted), paper clips, pencil erasers, tagboard (assorted), transparencies

Health and First Aid

Items available in nurse's or director's office or fully stocked first aid cabinet

Language Arts

alphabet wall cards and sets, bookends, book holder, books, chart tablets, flash cards, letters, pocket wall chart, puzzles, recordings, rubber stamps

Maintenance Materials

brooms, brushes, buckets, dishpan, mops, sponges, towels

Mathematics

blocks, calculators, cash register, chart to 100, clock, counting frames and sticks, dice, flannel board and cut-outs, floor graph, magnetic board, measures, number lines, pegs

Media/Computing

audiovisual player, AV carts, books, book racks, camera, cassette recorder, cassettes, easel for book display, headphones, listening station, VCR/DVD player

Music

autoharp, bell sets, castanets, cymbals, drums, listening station equipment, music books, records, rhythm sticks, sand blocks, teaching aids, tone block, triangles, xylophone

Perceptual Motor

balance beam, balls, bean bags, climbing apparatus, cones for obstacle course, hoops, jump ropes, parachute, records and cassette tapes for movement, slide, tires

Science

ant farm, aquarium, bulbs (garden), cages, cooking equipment, flower containers, garden equipment, magnets, magnifying glasses, microscope, prisms, pulleys, timers

Social Studies

block accessories, blocks, community resource file, construction toys, dramatic play materials, games, globe, magazines, maps and atlas, newspapers, puppets, and puppet stage

Sources: Adapted from *Selecting Educational Equipment and Materials for School and Home*, by J. Moyer (Ed.), 1995, Wheaton, MD: Association for Childhood Education International; *Creative Thinking and Arts-Based Learning: Preschool Through Fourth Grade* (4th ed.), by J. Isenberg & M. R. Jalongo, 2006, Upper Saddle River, NJ: Pearson/Merrill/Prentice Hall; and *Serious Players in the Primary Classroom* (2nd ed.), by S. Wasserman, 2000, New York: Teachers College Press.

Curriculum Resources

Selected Resources for Learning Centers

Carefully designed centers are a valuable resource for teachers and children. They enable teachers to integrate the curriculum, engage in natural and ongoing assessment, be culturally responsive, and teach to all of children's intelligences. Well-designed centers contain an array of materials that are concrete, durable, and real. The following examples are listed below by center.

Art Center Materials

easel
paste
chalk
clay
water, tempera, and finger paint
newsprint, tissue, construction paper
markers, crayons, colored pencils
books related to art topics
paint brushes
tape
hole punches
sponges

Block Center Materials

unit blocks
traffic signs
play vehicles
hardwood hollow blocks
play people and animals
architectural drawings
brick blocks
Legos & Duplos
street signs
books related to building and construction
writing and drawing materials

Dramatic Play Center

kitchen furniture
dress-up clothes
telephone books
cooking utensils, cookbooks, recipes
paper, pencils, food coupons
various dolls
play money
telephone
books, magazines, and newspapers about families
prop boxes containing other theme-related topics such as restaurant, grocery store, transportation, post office
assorted print materials (maps, phone books, coupons) and writing and drawing materials

Library Center

a variety of teacher-made and child-made books, blank books, big books, books on tape, headphones, props to act out stories, pillows, soft chairs, magnetic board and letters, flannel board, flannel board stories, puppets

Manipulatives and Puzzles Center

beads for stringing
pegboards and pegs
lacing cards
dressing frames
parquetry blocks
puzzles
teacher-made and commercial board and lotto games
construction toys (e.g., bristle blocks, star builders, Lincoln Logs, Tinkertoys, Legos)
sorting boards and games

Math Center

nesting cubes
geoboards and rubber bands
play money
abacus and rulers
counters and scales
cash register
playing cards
dice
yardstick
assortment of real objects (shells, rocks, buttons, leaves) for sorting and classifying
books about mathematics, counting, and math themes

Music Center

drums and bells
rhythm sticks
record, tape, and CD players
toy instruments
graduated bottles
instrument-making materials
real instruments
child-made and teacher-made instruments
books about music, musicians, and musical themes

Sand and Water Center

wet and dry sand
sand or water table
bulb syringes, squirt bottles
assorted cups and molds
assorted sticks, strainers
pots and pans, shovels, scoops
colanders, sifters, funnels
small vehicles
flowerpots, flowers
small plastic animals
small garden tools
ice cubes, liquid soap
floating and sinking objects
straws
egg beater, ladle, sponges

Science Center

assorted bolts, nuts, washers, magnets, magnetic letters, buttons, fabric swatches, balls, paper, hand lenses, empty plastic containers, droppers
assorted dried legumes, stones, pebbles, yarn, thread, cord, wire, pipe cleaners
variety of real insects and bugs in covered containers
pets appropriate for a classroom (gerbils, guinea pigs, fish)
plants with and without flowers, seeds, and gardening tools
things to take apart and put together and things to smell
paper, clapboard, and writing supplies
books, charts, posters, magazines, photo word cards about specific topics
instruction cards for completing experiments
small mirrors and flashlights

Woodworking Center

wooden wheels, spools	7-oz. claw hammers and plane	hand drill
7-inch screwdrivers	woodworking bench	safety glasses

variety of rulers, protractors, tape measures
styrofoam for sawing, hammering, and drilling
instruction cards to sequence actions such as hammering a nail into the wood
tools labeled with written words
posters and charts for building furniture, a deck, or shelves
paper and pencils to draw plans

Writing Center

variety of types of paper	alphabet letter stamps	props to enact stories
stapler, hole punch, ink pads	scissors, erasers, glue	books and magazines
book of wallpaper samples	stationery, magic slates	tape recorder, tapes

Source: Adapted with permission from Terri Cardi, Conneaut Lake, PA.

Free and Inexpensive Materials for Teachers

There are many resources and materials that are of little or no cost. Here are some suggestions:

Teaching Tolerance
Provides teachers with copies of its educational kits that promote harmonious classrooms and subscriptions to its magazine free of charge.
400 Washington Ave.
Montgomery, AL 36104
www.teachingtolerance.org

EDUCATORS' GUIDES TO FREE MATERIALS

- Free Teaching Aids
  Provides printed curriculum materials, videotapes, computer resources, and mixed media resources
  www.freeteachingaids.com
- Parent's Internet Sources
  Helps parents make the best use of the online world as an educational tool. To request your free copy, call the U.S. Department of Education's Publication Center (ED Pubs) at 1-800-4ED-PUBS.

HOUSEHOLD AND FOUND MATERIALS A large variety of household and found materials helps children to experiment, imagine, and explore what materials can do and what they can do with materials. These materials help children make discoveries and find answers to their own questions. In this way, they learn naturally how to identify, classify, observe closely, make comparisons, ask questions, describe what they discovered, and make predictions.

Household Materials

buttons, pots and pans, carpentry tools, plastic containers, bottle caps, cooking utensils, real objects that appeal to children's imagination, simple camera, old typewriter, paper and pencils

Natural or Found Materials

sticks, shells, twigs, leaves, rocks, pine cones, sand, mud, water, buttons, candy boxes, cardboard tubing, catalogues, coffee cans, gift wrapping paper, plastic items and containers, ribbon bits, scraps of carpeting and cloth, Styrofoam packing

Local retailers: Try your local retailers for discarded items, samples, and other unwanted items (carpet stores for carpet samples for group meetings; ice-cream shops for discarded displays for dramatic play; wallpaper stores for discontinued wallpaper books for book covers, bulletin boards, and collage material).

Materials Request Form

Dear ________________:

We are studying about ________________. To do our projects, our class needs ________________. If you can help us with any of these materials, please send them to school this week.

Thank you.

Health, Nutrition, and Safety Resources

Health, nutrition, and safety are traditionally parts of early childhood programs that get overlooked. Here are some resources to help you in this area.

ORGANIZATIONS AND ASSOCIATIONS

American Academy of Pediatrics
141 Northwest Point Blvd.
Elk Grove Village, IL 60007-1098
847-434-4000
www.aap.org
TIPP—The Injury Prevention Program (Injury prevention advice is available online at www.aap.org and pamphlets are available)

American Academy of Ophthalmology
P.O. Box 7424
San Francisco, CA 94120-7424
415-561-8500
415-561-8533 (fax)
www.aao.org
(Free eye chart and a variety of pamphlets on eye problems)

American Alliance for Health, Physical Education, Recreation, and Dance (A-PERD)
1900 Association Drive
Reston, VA 22091
1.800.213.7193
www.aahperd.org
Journals: *Journal of Health Education; Journal of Physical Education, Recreation, and Dance*

American Automobile Association
Traffic Safety Department
(Check with local branch office for address)
Pamphlet: *Bicycling Is Great Fun*

National SAFE KIDS Campaign
1301 Pennsylvania Ave. NW
Suite 1000
Washington, D.C. 20004
202-662-0600
202-393-2072 (fax)
www.safekids.org
Pamphlet: *Safe Kids Are No Accident*

U.S. Department of Agriculture
Food and Nutrition Information Center
National Agricultural Library (NAL)
10301 Baltimore Avenue, Room 105
Beltsville, MD 20705-2351
http://fnic.nal.usda.gov

Offers a lending library of curriculum activities and food sets, models, and posters. Check with your local library on how to borrow materials through interlibrary loan with NAL.

Web Resources

www.healthychild.net
An online magazine with articles about child health and safety

www.floridajuice.com
Recipes and nutritional information for children

www.kidshealth.org
Medical information from experts on such topics as immunizations, illnesses, and ADHD

www.kidsource.com
Provides activities for children, answers to questions, and a changing spot with prevention hints

http://cpsc.gov
The national consumer product safety site with information on toy and safety-seat recalls and links to other sites

Professional Resources for Teachers

Knowing where to access appropriate information and resources enhances your ethical responsibility, your accountability to the profession, and your advocacy for children.

The National Association for the Education of Young Children Code of Ethical Conduct and Statement of Commitment

A position statement of the National Association for the Education of Young Children and Statement of Commitment, revised April, 2005; endorsed by the Association for Childhood Education International.

PREAMBLE NAEYC recognizes that those who work with young children face many daily decisions that have moral and ethical implications. The NAEYC Code of Ethical Conduct offers guidelines for responsible behavior and sets forth a common basis for resolving the principal ethical dilemmas encountered in early childhood care and education. The Statement of Commitment is not part of the Code but is a personal acknowledgement of an individual's willingness to embrace the distinctive values and moral obligations of the field of early childhood care and education. The primary focus of the Code is on daily practice with children and their families in programs for children from birth through 8 years of age, such as infant/toddler programs, preschool and prekindergarten programs, child-care centers, hospital and child life settings, family child-care homes, kindergartens, and primary classrooms. When the issues involve young children, then these provisions also apply to specialists who do not work directly with children, including program administrators, parent educators, early childhood adult educators, and officials with responsibility for program monitoring and licensing. (Note: See also the "Code of Ethical Conduct: Supplement for Early Childhood Adult Educators," online at www.naeyc.org/about/positions/ ethics04.asp.)

CORE VALUES Standards of ethical behavior in early childhood care and education are based on commitment to the following core values that are deeply rooted in the history of the field of early childhood care and education. We have made a commitment to

- Appreciate childhood as a unique and valuable stage of the human life cycle
- Base our work on knowledge of how children develop and learn
- Appreciate and support the bond between the child and family
- Recognize that children are best understood and supported in the context of family, culture,[1] community, and society
- Respect the dignity, worth, and uniqueness of each individual (child, family member, and colleague)
- Respect diversity in children, families, and colleagues
- Recognize that children and adults achieve their full potential in the context of relationships that are based on trust and respect

CONCEPTUAL FRAMEWORK The Code sets forth a framework of professional responsibilities in four sections. Each section addresses an area of professional relationships: (1) with children, (2) with families, (3) among colleagues, and (4) with the

[1] Culture includes ethnicity, racial identity, economic level, family structure, language, and religious and political beliefs, which profoundly influence each child's development and relationship to the world. (p. 447)

community and society. Each section includes an introduction to the primary responsibilities of the early childhood practitioner in that context. The introduction is followed by a set of ideals (I) that reflect exemplary professional practice and a set of principles (P) describing practices that are required, prohibited, or permitted.

The ideals reflect the aspirations of practitioners. **The principles** guide conduct and assist practitioners in resolving ethical dilemmas.[2] Both ideals and principles are intended to direct practitioners to those questions which, when responsibly answered, can provide the basis for conscientious decision making. While the Code provides specific direction for addressing some ethical dilemmas, many others will require the practitioner to combine the guidance of the Code with professional judgment.

The ideals and principles in this Code present a shared framework of professional responsibility that affirms our commitment to the core values of our field. The Code publicly acknowledges the responsibilities that we in the field have assumed and in so doing supports ethical behavior in our work. Practitioners who face situations with ethical dimensions are urged to seek guidance in the applicable parts of this Code and in the spirit that informs the whole.

Often, "the right answer"—the best ethical course of action to take—is not obvious. There may be no readily apparent, positive way to handle a situation. When one important value contradicts another, we face an ethical dilemma. When we face a dilemma, it is our professional responsibility to consult the Code and all relevant parties to find the most ethical resolution.

SECTION I: ETHICAL RESPONSIBILITIES TO CHILDREN Childhood is a unique and valuable stage in the human life cycle. Our paramount responsibility is to provide care and education in settings that are safe, healthy, nurturing, and responsive for each child. We are committed to supporting children's development and learning; respecting individual differences; and helping children learn to live, play, and work cooperatively. We are also committed to promoting children's self-awareness, competence, self-worth, resiliency, and physical well-being.

Ideals

I-1.1—To be familiar with the knowledge base of early childhood care and education and to stay informed through continuing education and training.
I-1.2—To base program practices upon current knowledge and research in the field of early childhood education, child development, and related disciplines, as well as on particular knowledge of each child.
I-1.3—To recognize and respect the unique qualities, abilities, and potential of each child.
I-1.4—To appreciate the vulnerability of children and their dependence on adults.
I-1.5—To create and maintain safe and healthy settings that foster children's social, emotional, cognitive, and physical development and that respect their dignity and their contributions.
I-1.6—To use assessment instruments and strategies that are appropriate for the children to be assessed, that are used only for the purposes for which they were designed, and that have the potential to benefit children.
I-1.7—To use assessment information to understand and support children's development and learning, to support instruction, and to identify children who may need additional services.

[2] There is not necessarily a corresponding principle for each ideal. (p. 448)

I-1.8—To support the right of each child to play and learn in an inclusive environment that meets the needs of children with and without disabilities.
I-1.9—To advocate for and ensure that all children, including those with special needs, have access to the support services needed to be successful.
I-1.10—To ensure that each child's culture, language, ethnicity, and family structure are recognized and valued in the program.
I-1.11—To provide all children with experiences in a language that they know, as well as support children in maintaining the use of their home language and in learning English.
I-1.12—To work with families to provide a safe and smooth transition as children and families move from one program to the next.

Principles

P-1.1—Above all, we shall not harm children. We shall not participate in practices that are emotionally damaging, physically harmful, disrespectful, degrading, dangerous, exploitative, or intimidating to children. This principle has precedence over all others in this Code.
P-1.2—We shall care for and educate children in positive emotional and social environments that are cognitively stimulating and that support each child's culture, language, ethnicity, and family structure.
P-1.3—We shall not participate in practices that discriminate against children by denying benefits, giving special advantages, or excluding them from programs or activities on the basis of their sex, race, national origin, religious beliefs, medical condition, disability, or the marital status/family structure, sexual orientation, or religious beliefs or other affiliations of their families. (Aspects of this principle do not apply in programs that have a lawful mandate to provide services to a particular population of children.)
P-1.4—We shall involve all those with relevant knowledge (including families and staff) in decisions concerning a child, as appropriate, ensuring confidentiality of sensitive information.
P-1.5—We shall use appropriate assessment systems, which include multiple sources of information, to provide information on children's learning and development.
P-1.6—We shall strive to ensure that decisions, such as those related to enrollment, retention, or assignment to special education services, will be based on multiple sources of information and will never be based on a single assessment, such as a test score or a single observation.
P-1.7—We shall strive to build individual relationships with each child; make individualized adaptations in teaching strategies, learning environments, and curricula; and consult with the family so that each child benefits from the program. If after such efforts have been exhausted, the current placement does not meet a child's needs, or the child is seriously jeopardizing the ability of other children to benefit from the program, we shall collaborate with the child's family and appropriate specialists to determine the additional services needed and/or the placement option(s) most likely to ensure the child's success. (Aspects of this principle may not apply in programs that have a lawful mandate to provide services to a particular population of children.)
P-1.8—We shall be familiar with the risk factors for and symptoms of child abuse and neglect, including physical, sexual, verbal, and emotional abuse and physical, emotional, educational, and medical neglect. We shall know and follow state laws and community procedures that protect children against abuse and neglect.
P-1.9—When we have reasonable cause to suspect child abuse or neglect, we shall report it to the appropriate community agency and follow up to ensure that appropriate action has been taken. When appropriate, parents or guardians will be informed that the referral will be or has been made.

P-1.10—When another person tells us of his or her suspicion that a child is being abused or neglected, we shall assist that person in taking appropriate action in order to protect the child.
P-1.11—When we become aware of a practice or situation that endangers the health, safety, or well-being of children, we have an ethical responsibility to protect children or inform parents and/or others who can.

SECTION II: ETHICAL RESPONSIBILITIES TO FAMILIES Families[3] are of primary importance in children's development. Because the family and the early childhood practitioner have a common interest in the child's well-being, we acknowledge a primary responsibility to bring about communication, cooperation, and collaboration between the home and early childhood program in ways that enhance the child's development.

Ideals

I-2.1—To be familiar with the knowledge base related to working effectively with families and to stay informed through continuing education and training.
I-2.2—To develop relationships of mutual trust and create partnerships with the families we serve.
I-2.3—To welcome all family members and encourage them to participate in the program.
I-2.4—To listen to families, acknowledge and build upon their strengths and competencies, and learn from families as we support them in their task of nurturing children.
I-2.5—To respect the dignity and preferences of each family and to make an effort to learn about its structure, culture, language, customs, and beliefs.
I-2.6—To acknowledge families' childrearing values and their right to make decisions for their children.
I-2.7—To share information about each child's education and development with families and to help them understand and appreciate the current knowledge base of the early childhood profession.
I-2.8—To help family members enhance their understanding of their children and support the continuing development of their skills as parents.
I-2.9—To participate in building support networks for families by providing them with opportunities to interact with program staff, other families, community resources, and professional services.

Principles

P-2.1—We shall not deny family members access to their child's classroom or program setting unless access is denied by court order or other legal restriction.
P-2.2—We shall inform families of program philosophy, policies, curriculum, assessment system, and personnel qualifications, and explain why we teach as we do—which should be in accordance with our ethical responsibilities to children (see Section I).
P-2.3—We shall inform families of and, when appropriate, involve them in policy decisions.
P-2.4—We shall involve the family in significant decisions affecting their child.
P-2.5—We shall make every effort to communicate effectively with all families in a language that they understand. We shall use community resources for translation and interpretation when we do not have sufficient resources in our own programs.

---

[3] The term family may include those adults, besides parents, with the responsibility of being involved in educating, nurturing, and advocating for the child. (p. 450)

P-2.6—As families share information with us about their children and families, we shall consider this information to plan and implement the program.
P-2.7—We shall inform families about the nature and purpose of the program's child assessments and how data about their child will be used.
P-2.8—We shall treat child assessment information confidentially and share this information only when there is a legitimate need for it.
P-2.9—We shall inform the family of injuries and incidents involving their child, of risks such as exposures to communicable diseases that might result in infection, and of occurrences that might result in emotional stress.
P-2.10—Families shall be fully informed of any proposed research projects involving their children and shall have the opportunity to give or withhold consent without penalty. We shall not permit or participate in research that could in any way hinder the education, development, or well-being of children.
P-2.11—We shall not engage in or support exploitation of families. We shall not use our relationship with a family for private advantage or personal gain, or enter into relationships with family members that might impair our effectiveness working with their children.
P-2.12—We shall develop written policies for the protection of confidentiality and the disclosure of children's records. These policy documents shall be made available to all program personnel and families. Disclosure of children's records beyond family members, program personnel, and consultants having an obligation of confidentiality shall require familial consent (except in cases of abuse or neglect).
P-2.13—We shall maintain confidentiality and shall respect the family's right to privacy, refraining from disclosure of confidential information and intrusion into family life. However, when we have reason to believe that a child's welfare is at risk, it is permissible to share confidential information with agencies, as well as with individuals who have legal responsibility for intervening in the child's interest.
P-2.14—In cases where family members are in conflict with one another, we shall work openly, sharing our observations of the child, to help all parties involved make informed decisions. We shall refrain from becoming an advocate for one party.
P-2.15—We shall be familiar with and appropriately refer families to community resources and professional support services. After a referral has been made, we shall follow up to ensure that services have been appropriately provided.

SECTION III: ETHICAL RESPONSIBILITIES TO COLLEAGUES In a caring, cooperative workplace, human dignity is respected, professional satisfaction is promoted, and positive relationships are developed and sustained. Based upon our core values, our primary responsibility to colleagues is to establish and maintain settings and relationships that support productive work and meet professional needs. The same ideals that apply to children also apply as we interact with adults in the workplace.

A—Responsibilities to Co-workers

Ideals

I-3A.1—To establish and maintain relationships of respect, trust, confidentiality, collaboration, and cooperation with co-workers.
I-3A.2—To share resources with co-workers, collaborating to ensure that the best possible early childhood care and education program is provided.

I-3A.3—To support co-workers in meeting their professional needs and in their professional development.
I-3A.4—To accord co-workers due recognition of professional achievement.

Principles

P-3A.1—We shall recognize the contributions of colleagues to our program and not participate in practices that diminish their reputations or impair their effectiveness in working with children and families.
P-3A.2—When we have concerns about the professional behavior of a co-worker, we shall first let that person know of our concern in a way that shows respect for personal dignity and for the diversity to be found among staff members, and then attempt to resolve the matter collegially and in a confidential manner.
P-3A.3—We shall exercise care in expressing views regarding the personal attributes or professional conduct of co-workers. Statements should be based on firsthand knowledge, not hearsay, and relevant to the interests of children and programs.
P-3A.4—We shall not participate in practices that discriminate against a co-worker because of sex, race, national origin, religious beliefs or other affiliations, age, marital status/family structure, disability, or sexual orientation.

B—Responsibilities to Employers

Ideals

I-3B.1—To assist the program in providing the highest quality of service.
I-3B.2—To do nothing that diminishes the reputation of the program in which we work unless it is violating laws and regulations designed to protect children or is violating the provisions of this Code.

Principles

P-3B.1—We shall follow all program policies. When we do not agree with program policies, we shall attempt to effect change through constructive action within the organization.
P-3B.2—We shall speak or act on behalf of an organization only when authorized. We shall take care to acknowledge when we are speaking for the organization and when we are expressing a personal judgment.
P-3B.3—We shall not violate laws or regulations designed to protect children and shall take appropriate action consistent with this Code when aware of such violations.
P-3B.4—If we have concerns about a colleague's behavior, and children's well-being is not at risk, we may address the concern with that individual. If children are at risk or the situation does not improve after it has been brought to the colleague's attention, we shall report the colleague's unethical or incompetent behavior to an appropriate authority.
P-3B.5—When we have a concern about circumstances or conditions that impact the quality of care and education within the program, we shall inform the program's administration or, when necessary, other appropriate authorities.

C—Responsibilities to Employees

Ideals

I-3C.1—To promote safe and healthy working conditions and policies that foster mutual respect, cooperation, collaboration, competence, well-being, confidentiality, and self-esteem in staff members.

I-3C.2—To create and maintain a climate of trust and candor that will enable staff to speak and act in the best interests of children, families, and the field of early childhood care and education.

I-3C.3—To strive to secure adequate and equitable compensation (salary and benefits) for those who work with or on behalf of young children.

I-3C.4—To encourage and support continual development of employees in becoming more skilled and knowledgeable practitioners.

Principles

P-3C.1—In decisions concerning children and programs, we shall draw upon the education, training, experience, and expertise of staff members.

P-3C.2—We shall provide staff members with safe and supportive working conditions that honor confidences and permit them to carry out their responsibilities through fair performance evaluation, written grievance procedures, constructive feedback, and opportunities for continuing professional development and advancement.

P-3C.3—We shall develop and maintain comprehensive written personnel policies that define program standards. These policies shall be given to new staff members and shall be available and easily accessible for review by all staff members.

P-3C.4—We shall inform employees whose performance does not meet program expectations of areas of concern and, when possible, assist in improving their performance.

P-3C.5—We shall conduct employee dismissals for just cause, in accordance with all applicable laws and regulations. We shall inform employees who are dismissed of the reasons for their termination. When a dismissal is for cause, justification must be based on evidence of inadequate or inappropriate behavior that is accurately documented, current, and available for the employee to review.

P-3C.6—In making evaluations and recommendations, we shall make judgments based on fact and relevant to the interests of children and programs.

P-3C.7—We shall make hiring, retention, termination, and promotion decisions based solely on a person's competence, record of accomplishment, ability to carry out the responsibilities of the position, and professional preparation specific to the developmental levels of children in his/her care.

P-3C.8—We shall not make hiring, retention, termination, and promotion decisions based on an individual's sex, race, national origin, religious beliefs or other affiliations, age, marital status/family structure, disability, or sexual orientation. We shall be familiar with and observe laws and regulations that pertain to employment discrimination. (Aspects of this principle do not apply to programs that have a lawful mandate to determine eligibility based on one or more of the criteria identified above.)

P-3C.9—We shall maintain confidentiality in dealing with issues related to an employee's job performance and shall respect an employee's right to privacy regarding personal issues.

SECTION IV: ETHICAL RESPONSIBILITIES TO COMMUNITY AND SOCIETY

Early childhood programs operate within the context of their immediate community made up of families and other institutions concerned with children's welfare. Our responsibilities to the community are to provide programs that meet the diverse needs of families, to cooperate with agencies and professions that share the responsibility for children, to assist families in gaining access to those agencies and allied professionals, and to assist in the development of community programs that are needed but not currently available.

As individuals, we acknowledge our responsibility to provide the best possible programs of care and education for children and to conduct ourselves with honesty and integrity. Because of our specialized expertise in early childhood development and education and because the larger society shares responsibility for the welfare and protection of young children, we acknowledge a collective obligation to advocate for the best interests of children within early childhood programs and in the larger community and to serve as a voice for young children everywhere.

The ideals and principles in this section are presented to distinguish between those that pertain to the work of the individual early childhood educator and those that more typically are engaged in collectively on behalf of the best interests of children—with the understanding that individual early childhood educators have a shared responsibility for addressing the ideals and principles that are identified as "collective."

Ideal (Individual)

I-4.1—To provide the community with high-quality early childhood care and education programs and services.

Ideals (Collective)

I-4.2—To promote cooperation among professionals and agencies and interdisciplinary collaboration among professions concerned with addressing issues in the health, education, and well-being of young children, their families, and their early childhood educators.
I-4.3—To work through education, research, and advocacy toward an environmentally safe world in which all children receive health care, food, and shelter; are nurtured; and live free from violence in their home and their communities.
I-4.4—To work through education, research, and advocacy toward a society in which all young children have access to high-quality early care and education programs.
I-4.5—To work to ensure that appropriate assessment systems, which include multiple sources of information, are used for purposes that benefit children.
I-4.6—To promote knowledge and understanding of young children and their needs. To work toward greater societal acknowledgment of children's rights and greater social acceptance of responsibility for the well-being of all children.
I-4.7—To support policies and laws that promote the well-being of children and families, and to work to change those that impair their well-being. To participate in developing policies and laws that are needed, and to cooperate with other individuals and groups in these efforts.
I-4.8—To further the professional development of the field of early childhood care and education and to strengthen its commitment to realizing its core values as reflected in this Code.

Principles (Individual)

P-4.1—We shall communicate openly and truthfully about the nature and extent of services that we provide.
P-4.2—We shall apply for, accept, and work in positions for which we are personally well-suited and professionally qualified. We shall not offer services that we do not have the competence, qualifications, or resources to provide.
P-4.3—We shall carefully check references and shall not hire or recommend for employment any person whose competence, qualifications, or character makes him or her unsuited for the position.

P-4.4—We shall be objective and accurate in reporting the knowledge upon which we base our program practices.

P-4.5—We shall be knowledgeable about the appropriate use of assessment strategies and instruments and interpret results accurately to families.

P-4.6—We shall be familiar with laws and regulations that serve to protect the children in our programs and be vigilant in ensuring that these laws and regulations are followed.

P-4.7—When we become aware of a practice or situation that endangers the health, safety, or well-being of children, we have an ethical responsibility to protect children or inform parents and/or others who can.

P-4.8—We shall not participate in practices that are in violation of laws and regulations that protect the children in our programs.

P-4.9—When we have evidence that an early childhood program is violating laws or regulations protecting children, we shall report the violation to appropriate authorities who can be expected to remedy the situation.

P-4.10—When a program violates or requires its employees to violate this Code, it is permissible, after fair assessment of the evidence, to disclose the identity of that program.

Principles (Collective)

P-4.11—When policies are enacted for purposes that do not benefit children, we have a collective responsibility to work to change these practices.

P-4.12—When we have evidence that an agency that provides services intended to ensure children's well-being is failing to meet its obligations, we acknowledge a collective ethical responsibility to report the problem to appropriate authorities or to the public. We shall be vigilant in our follow-up until the situation is resolved.

P-4.13—When a child protection agency fails to provide adequate protection for abused or neglected children, we acknowledge a collective ethical responsibility to work toward the improvement of these services.

STATEMENT OF COMMITMENT[4] As an individual who works with young children, I commit myself to furthering the values of early childhood education as they are reflected in the ideals and principles of the NAEYC Code of Ethical Conduct. To the best of my ability I will

- Never harm children.
- Ensure that programs for young children are based on current knowledge and research of child development and early childhood education.
- Respect and support families in their task of nurturing children.
- Respect colleagues in early childhood care and education and support them in maintaining the NAEYC Code of Ethical Conduct.
- Serve as an advocate for children, their families, and their teachers in community and society.
- Stay informed of and maintain high standards of professional conduct.
- Engage in an ongoing process of self-reflection, realizing that personal characteristics, biases, and beliefs have an impact on children and families.
- Be open to new ideas and be willing to learn from the suggestions of others.

[4] This Statement of Commitment is not part of the Code but is a personal acknowledgement of the individual's willingness to embrace the distinctive values and moral obligations of the field of early childhood care and education. It is recognition of the moral obligations that lead to an individual becoming part of the profession. (p. 455)

- Continue to learn, grow, and contribute as a professional.
- Honor the ideals and principles of the NAEYC Code of Ethical Conduct.

Interstate New Teacher Assessment and Support Consortium (INTASC) Standards

The INTASC standards comprised of a set of 10 standards that includes knowledge, dispositions, and performance expectations for beginning teachers. The teacher

1. understands the central concepts, tools of inquiry, and structures of the discipline(s) he or she teaches and can create meaningful learning experiences from them.
2. understands how children learn and develop, and can provide learning opportunities to support each aspect of their development.
3. understands the many ways students learn and creates learning opportunities that are adapted to learners from diverse cultural backgrounds and with exceptionalities.
4. understands and uses a variety of instructional strategies.
5. creates learning environments that encourage active engagement in learning, positive social interaction, and self-motivation.
6. uses effective communication techniques that foster active inquiry in the classroom.
7. plans instruction based on knowledge of subject matter, children, the community, and curriculum goals.
8. uses formal and informal assessment strategies to ensure continuous growth of the learner.
9. is a reflective practitioner who continually evaluates choices and who actively seeks out professional growth opportunities.
10. communicates and interacts with families, colleagues, and the community to support student learning.

Source: Adapted from *Model Standards for Beginning Teacher Licensing and Development: A Resource for State Dialogue,* by the Interstate New Teacher Assessment and Support Consortium, 1992, Washington, DC: Council of Chief State School Officers. Available online at www.ccsso.org.

Professional Associations, Organizations, Journals, and Materials

Professional Associations, Organizations, Journals, and Newsletters for Early Childhood Practitioners
The following organizations provide information, services, and materials to early childhood teachers.

American Montessori Society (AMS)
281 Park Avenue South
New York, NY 10010-6102
212-358-1250
212-358-1256 (fax)
www.amshq.org

Association for Childhood Education International (ACEI)
(Infancy through adolescence)
17904 Georgia Avenue, Suite 215
Olney, MD 20832
800-423-3563
301-570-2212 (fax)
www.acei.org
Journal: *Childhood Education*

Canadian Association for Young Children
c/o Angie Bothe
302-1775 West 11th Avenue
Vancouver, B.C. V6J2C1
604-731-4631
www.cayc.ca/

Canadian Child Care Federation
201-383 Parkdale Ave
Ottawa, ON K1Y 4R4
1-800-858-1412
www.cccf-fcsge.ca
Newsletter: *Interaction*
Learning Through Play Tool Kit (Free while supplies last)

Council for Professional Recognition
2460 16th Street NW
Washington, DC 20009-3575
800-424-4310
202-265-9090 (fax)
www.cdacouncil.org

CDA credentialing program, Head Start Fellowships, U.S. Military School-Age Child Care credential, and Reggio Children USA.

International Montessori Accreditation Council (IMAC)
IMAC, c/o Lee Havis
912 Thayer Ave. #207
Silver Spring, MD 20910
301-589-1127
e-mail: havis@erols.com
http://trust.wdn.com/ims/IMAC.HTM
Newsletters: *Montessori Observer* and *Montessori News*
Questions and comments: havis@erols.com

National Association of Child Care Resource and Referral (NACCRRA)
3101 Wilson Boulevard, Suite 350
Arlington, VA 22201
703-341-4100
www.naccrra.org

ASK THE EXPERT

Jerlean Daniel on the National Association for the Education of Young Children (NAEYC)

Jerlean Daniel

What makes the NAEYC unique as a large-membership organization?

Founded in 1926, the NAEYC has nearly 100,000 members. It is the nation's largest organization of early childhood professionals and others dedicated to improving the quality of early childhood education programs for children from birth through age 8 years. The NAEYC's primary goals are to improve professional practice and working conditions and to build public understanding and support for high-quality childhood programs.

What kinds of issues does the NAEYC address?

The NAEYC, like other large-membership organizations, faces two major tensions. The *first* pertains to the dual roles of the governing board to serve and to lead the membership. If the governing board acts only in response to the concerns and directives of the membership, then it runs the risk of failing to lead. Leadership requires vision and the ability to anticipate. But leadership without responsiveness to the membership is doomed. The *second* tension revolves around the primacy of children's needs versus the needs of the profession. The majority of the NAEYC's membership affirms the primacy of children's needs. The balancing of the two major tensions, following versus leading and children versus profession, create a synergy, which represent the political realities of progress toward optimal services for children and families. I, for one, see no real competition, but rather an interdependent convergence toward mutually inclusive goals.

How does the NAEYC work to increase standards in the field of early childhood?

An example of the productive convergence of the two major tensions is NAEYC accreditation. In the 1980s, NAEYC accreditation was a leadership vision brought to the membership by the staff and governing board. While the membership had not specifically requested accreditation, the commitment to better standards of early care and education was why people joined the NAEYC. The membership responded positively to the idea, and the organization began a process of consensus building, which created the original set of NAEYC accreditation criteria. Consensus, one of the NAEYC's strengths, is the link between responsiveness and leadership.

Twenty years ago NAEYC accreditation criteria set a high standard for quality. In 2006, NAEYC accreditation was "reinvented" to reflect cutting-edge research across the developmental domains as well as the critical issues related to early childhood teaching and program management. The new standards for program improvement and research-based criteria once again raise the bar for what it means to be a high-quality early childhood program. Because the NAEYC has no authority to require programs to become accredited, the process relies on *voluntary* self-study and subsequent on-site assessment of observable program practices and print documentation.

NAEYC accreditation also balances the second set of organizational tensions. The accreditation criteria set a higher standard for early care and educational programming, establishing the primacy of children's needs. The self-study process enhances professional development, thereby setting a professional standard. Self-study is a valuable, classroom-specific inservice training tool. It allows staff members to cooperatively evaluate their performance, expand their developmental knowledge, make appropriate adjustments, and achieve better-quality job performance. The innovation of NAEYC accreditation continues to generate further clarification of practice in the field in the form of developmentally appropriate practices (DAP).

Why should I belong to the NAEYC or any other professional organization?

The NAEYC, along with many other professional associations, offers a framework for our combined talents to make a difference, to efficiently focus our passion, and to effectively use our knowledge base to advocate for what ought to be. If any reader should think that he or she is not counted among the legions of committed, knowledgeable professionals charged with the responsibility to make early care and education services what they ought to be for young children and their families, I must ask, if not us, together, now, then who, and when?

Jerlean Daniel is a past President of the NAEYC and is currently Deputy Executive Director of NAEYC.

National Association for the Education of Young Children (NAEYC)
1313 L. Street N.W., Suite 500
Washington, DC 20005
800-424-2460
www.naeyc.org
Journal: *Young Children*
Also available: programs supporting teachers and administrators, information resources, position papers, and standards

National Association for Family Child Care (NAFCC)
5202 Pinemont Drive
Salt Lake City, UT 84123
1-800-359-3817
801-268-9507 (fax)
e-mail: nafcc@nafcc.org
www.nafcc.org
Provides technical assistance to Family Child Care Association
Newsletter: *National Perspectives*

U.S. National Committee of the World Organization for Early Childhood Education (OMEP)
1314 G. Street, NW
Washington, DC 20005-3105
1-800-424-4310
http://omep-usnc.org
Journal: *International Journal of Early Childhood*

Child Advocacy Groups

Action for Children's Television
Administration for Children, Youth, and Families
Canadian Day Care Advocacy Association
Child Health Alert
Child Trends
Child Welfare League of America
Children's Defense Fund
Families and Work Institute
National Black Child Development Institute

National Child Care Information Center
Prevent Child Abuse America
Reading is Fundamental
Save the Children
Stand for Children
Society for Developmental Education and Behavioral Pediatrics
The Children's Foundation
UNICEF
Zero to Three

Other Professional Associations and Journals That Publish Some Materials About Early Childhood

The Association for Supervision and Curriculum Development (ASCD)
1703 North Beauregard Street
Alexandria, VA 22311-1714
800-933-ASCD
703-575-5400 (fax)
www.ascd.org
Journal: *Educational Leadership*

The Council for Exceptional Children (CEC)
1110 North Glebe Road, Suite 300
Arlington, VA 22201-5704
888-CEC-7733
TTY: (text only) 866-915-5000
www.cec.sped.org/
http://ericec.org/
Journal: *Exceptional Children*

International Reading Association (IRA)
800 Barksdale Road
P.O. Box 8139
Newark, DE 19714-8139
1-800-336-7323 (READ)
302-731-1057 (fax)
www.reading.org
Journal: *The Reading Teacher*

National Art Education Association (Arts) (NAEA)
1916 Association Drive
Reston, VA 20191-1590
www.naea-reston.org
Journal: *Art Education*

National Association for Bilingual Education (NABE)
1030 15th St. NW
Washington, DC 20005-4018
202-898-1829
www.nabe.org
Journal: *Bi-Lingual Research Journal*

National Association for Gifted Children (NAGC)
1707 L Street NW, Suite 550
Washington, DC 20036
202-785-4268
www.nagc.org
Journal: *Gifted Child Quarterly*

National Council for the Social Studies (NCSS)
8555 16th Street
Silver Spring, MD 20910
www.ncss.org
Journal: *Social Studies and the Young Learner*

National Council of Teachers of Mathematics (NCTM)
1906 Association Drive
Reston, VA 20191-1502
703-620-9840
www.nctm.org
Journal: *Teaching Children Mathematics (PK–6)*

National Science Teachers Association (NSTA)
1840 Wilson Blvd.
Arlington, VA 22201-3000
703-243-7100
www.nsta.org
Journal: *Science and Children (Elementary)*

Other Journals and Professional Magazines Dedicated to Early Childhood Education

Beginnings
The Canadian Journal of Research in Early Childhood Education
Child Development
(Research journal of the Society for Research in Child Development)
Child Care Information Exchange
Children Today
(Published by the U.S. Government Office of Human Development Services)
Dimensions of Early Childhood
(Publication of the Southern Early Childhood Association)
Early Childhood Education Journal
Early Childhood Research Quarterly
(Research journal of the National Association for the Education of Young Children)

Early Childhood Today
Today's Child

Other Journals That Publish Some Articles About Early Childhood

American Journal of Orthopsychiatry
Children
Developmental Psychology
Merrill-Palmer Quarterly of Behavior and Development
Journal of Research in Childhood Education
(Published by the Association for Childhood Education International)
Language Arts
(Publication of the National Council of Teachers of English)
Peabody Journal of Education
Phi Delta Kappan
(Journal of the National Honor Society, Phi Delta Kappa)
Review of Educational Research
(Publication of the American Educational Research Association)
Teacher Research: The Journal of Classroom Inquiry
Topics in Early Childhood Special Education

Book Publishers/Distributors That Feature Early Childhood Materials

Allyn & Bacon
Crystal Springs Books
Gryphon House
Merrill/Prentice Hall
Modern Learning Press
Redleaf Press
SkyLight
Teacher Ideas Press
Zero to Three

Education Resources Information Center (ERIC) Clearinghouses

ERIC, sponsored by the Institute of Education Sciences (IES) of the U.S. Department of Education, produces the world's premiere database of journal and nonjournal education literature that can be accessed online at www.eric.ed.gov.

U.S. Department of Education
National Library of Education
Office of Educational Research and Improvement (OERI)
400 Maryland Ave SW
Washington, DC 20202
800-424-1616
202-401-0552 (fax)
www.ed.gov

Disabilities and Gifted Education
The Council for Exceptional Children
1110 North Glebe Rd Suite 300
Arlington, VA 22201-5704
888-232-7733
703-264-9494 (fax)
www.cec.sped.org/ericec.html

Storage and Organizational Resources

As you create your own personal system for locating, gathering, and using materials and resources, you will need to create a system for organizing them. We have provided suggestions for finding materials and resources to include in your professional resource file.

Finding Materials for a Good Resource File

- Materials distributed from instructors, leaders, and consultants
- Bulletins and publications from your local, state, and federal government; professional organizations; and commercial organizations
- Magazines, pictures, professional journal articles
- Ideas shared by colleagues
- Books from the public library
- Notes taken during workshops; coursework; national, state, and local conferences
- Your own growing file of activities, catalogues, and professional publications

Materials to Include in a Resource File

- Art suggestions (e.g., recipes for play dough, finger paints, materials collection)
- Bulletin board and display ideas (e.g., pictures, themes)
- Drama (e.g., prop boxes, theme-related materials)
- Equipment sources, catalogues, and teacher-made materials
- Field trips and excursions
- Finger plays, songs, records, tapes, CDs, DVDs
- Health and safety information and learning activities
- Literacy information and learning activities
- Math and science suggestions
- Resources
  Children as resources
  Families as resources
  School resources
  Community resources
- Social studies (e.g., ideas for community, understanding the self, rights and responsibilities)
- Thematic unit topics appropriate for a particular age group
- Transition activities and ideas
- Other

Technology Resources

The following websites provide information and ideas about all areas of early childhood. Use this list as a beginning for your own list of useful sites.

Children's Books

Gryphon House Books

www.ghbooks.com
Free activities from resource and children's books by age and content area

www.eric-carle.com
Children's author and illustrator's website

Child Care

National Child Care Information Center
10530 Rosehaven Street Suite 400
Fairfax, VA 22030
800-616-2242
http://nccic.org

Children with Special Needs

www.irsc.org/disability.htm
Information on disabilities

www.dftoys.com
Catalog of toys for children with disabilities

www.newhorizons.org
A general resource for special education

www.dec-sped.org
Division for Early Childhood of the Council for Exceptional Children

Curriculum Resources

http://rite.ed.qut.edu.au/oz-teachernet/projects/book-rap/index.html
An Internet site designed to help children discuss literature with other children

www.inkspot.com/young/
An Internet site where young writers can find resources to expand their writing abilities

www.naeyc.org
NAEYC's home page

Diversity Resources

National Education Association (NEA)
www.nea.org/webresources/diversitylinks.html
Contains links for multicultural curriculum resources, culturally responsive teaching, and other web resources

Science Education for Students with Disabilities
www.sesd.info
Provides teacher resources in science for students at all levels and for specific disabilities

Cornucopia of Disability Information: Children with Disabilities
http://codi.buffalo.edu/children.htm
Provides activities for children with and without disabilities

Lesson Plans
www.teachernet.com
Searchable database of classroom projects and bulletin board ideas for teachers

www.mcps.k12.md.us/curriculum/xocialstd/Curiculum.html
Offers preschool and multicultural lesson plans

www.teachervision.com
Offers many lesson plans from the Learning Network Teacher Channel

Music
www.kididdles.com
Variety of songs for children

Parents and Families
www.zerotothree.org/magic
Offers a series of five booklets, endorsed by the Academy of Pediatrics, that tracks key developmental stages over the first 15 months of life and can be downloaded at no charge

www.familypride.org
Offers information and educational materials, *Opening Doors and Opening More Doors*, to help teachers provide a safe and welcoming school environment for children of lesbian and gay parents

Sites for Student and Teacher Research
www.Edvantia.org
Edvantia, Partners in Education

www.loc.gov/teachers
Library of Congress Information System Database for Teachers

http://cloud1.arc.nasa.gov/intex-na/K6Education.htm
NASA's Internet in the Classroom

www.si.edu
The Smithsonian

Software Evaluation Criteria

Technology has become an integral and accessible part of children's learning. Here are criteria for selecting and using software with young children.

COMPANION WEBSITE A.1 For more information about technology and early childhood, go to *Web Links* in Chapter 8 of the Companion Website at http://www.prehall.com/jalongo.

Technical Features

Are the basic function keys (e.g., delete, return) used appropriately?
Can children easily start, stop, and move about in the program with little or no help?
Can children save or print their work?

Learning Features

Are there visual, auditory, and tactile features that make it easy for the child to understand?
Can the learner control the pace and path of the program (e.g., make it faster or slower)?
Do children receive quick feedback so they stay involved in learning?

Content Features

Do the activities help the child learn new content, processes, or skills?
Can the learner explore concepts on several levels of difficulty?

Developmentally Appropriate Features

Are the content, skills, or processes used appropriate to the age range suggested?
Does the program enable children to be playful or construct elements on their own (e.g., draw pictures, move characters, create stories)?
Is there a range of activities that differ in complexity (e.g., does a mathematics program have activities that include one-to-one correspondence, estimation, simple addition)?
Do children experience success when using this program?

Sources: Adapted from, "Thoughts on Technology and Education," by B. Bowman and E. Beyer, 1994, in J. Wright & D. Shade (Eds.), *Young Children: Active Learners in a Technological Age* (pp. 19–30), Washington, DC: National Association for the Education of Young Children; "Children and Technology," by J. Isenberg and T. Rosegrant, 1995, in J. Moyer (Ed.), *Selecting Educational Equipment and Materials for School and Home* (pp. 25–29), Wheaton, MD: Association for Childhood Education International; "Educational Technology in the Early and Primary Years," by S. Swaminathan and J. Wright, 2003, in J. Isenberg & M. Jalongo (Eds.), *Major Trends and Issues: Challenges, Controversies, and Insights* (2nd ed., pp. 136–150), New York, Teachers College Press; and "Using Technology as a Teaching Tool," NAEYC November 2003, *Young Children*, 58(6).

Human Resources

Human resources involve the services that *people* provide to children, families, teachers, and schools. As an early childhood teacher, it is important that you know what services are available to you to support children's learning and development, and also to help parents access and use them. Keeping track of the many available resources requires some kind of organizational system.

Community Resources

The following community resources are valuable sources of information and assistance in your community. Here is a form to use to identify public and private agencies, consultants, and your own network. Some of the items listed are more useful to child-care workers; others are more useful to teachers of primary children; some are useful to both. These resources provide a beginning list, which will grow with you as you identify other important human resources. You can also use this list to *organize* information, forms, and contact people in one easy location. We have listed community resources in alphabetical order. You might also want to organize these resources by public or private agencies, consultants, or your own personal contacts.

Service	Name/Contact	Address	Telephone No.	Notes
Accounting				
Air Conditioning Service				
Ambulance				
American Red Cross				
Appliance Service				
Arts and Cultural Organizations				
Attorney				
Auditing				
Carpenter				
Center, Chair of the Board				
Center, Director				
Chambers of Commerce				
Child Abuse: Hotline				
Child Abuse: Protective Services				
Child Care: Resource and Referral				
Child Development Clinic				
Cooperative Extension Office				
Dance Studios				
Electric Company				
Family Services				
Fire Department				
Gas Company				
Health Department				
Heating Service				
Hospital				
Information and Referral				
Insurance				
Landlord				
Legal Aid Society				
Museums				
Parks and Recreation				

Service	Name/Contact	Address	Telephone No.	Notes
Physician				
Plumber				
Poison Control				
Police Department, Local				
Police Department, State				
Public Library				
Radio and TV Stations				
Repair Service				
Rescue Squad				
Roofer				
Service Organizations				
Sheriff's Office				
Taxi Service				

Public School Specialists

Most public schools provide support services from specialists who are located throughout the building. Here is a list of some of the specialists who might provide support to you, the children, and families.

Art teacher
Computer teacher
English as a second language (ESL) teacher
Foreign language teacher
Learning disabilities specialist
Librarian
Music teacher
Physical education teacher
Reading specialist
School counselor
School nurse
School psychologist
School secretary
Social worker
Speech teacher

Public Library–Linked Services for Children and Families

Many public agencies and organizations provide various kinds of services to schools and families. As a teacher, you want to be creative in how you use these resources. Figure A.1 is a representation of some ways the public library serves to link the school and community to needed resources.

FIGURE A. 1 Linking libraries with community resources.

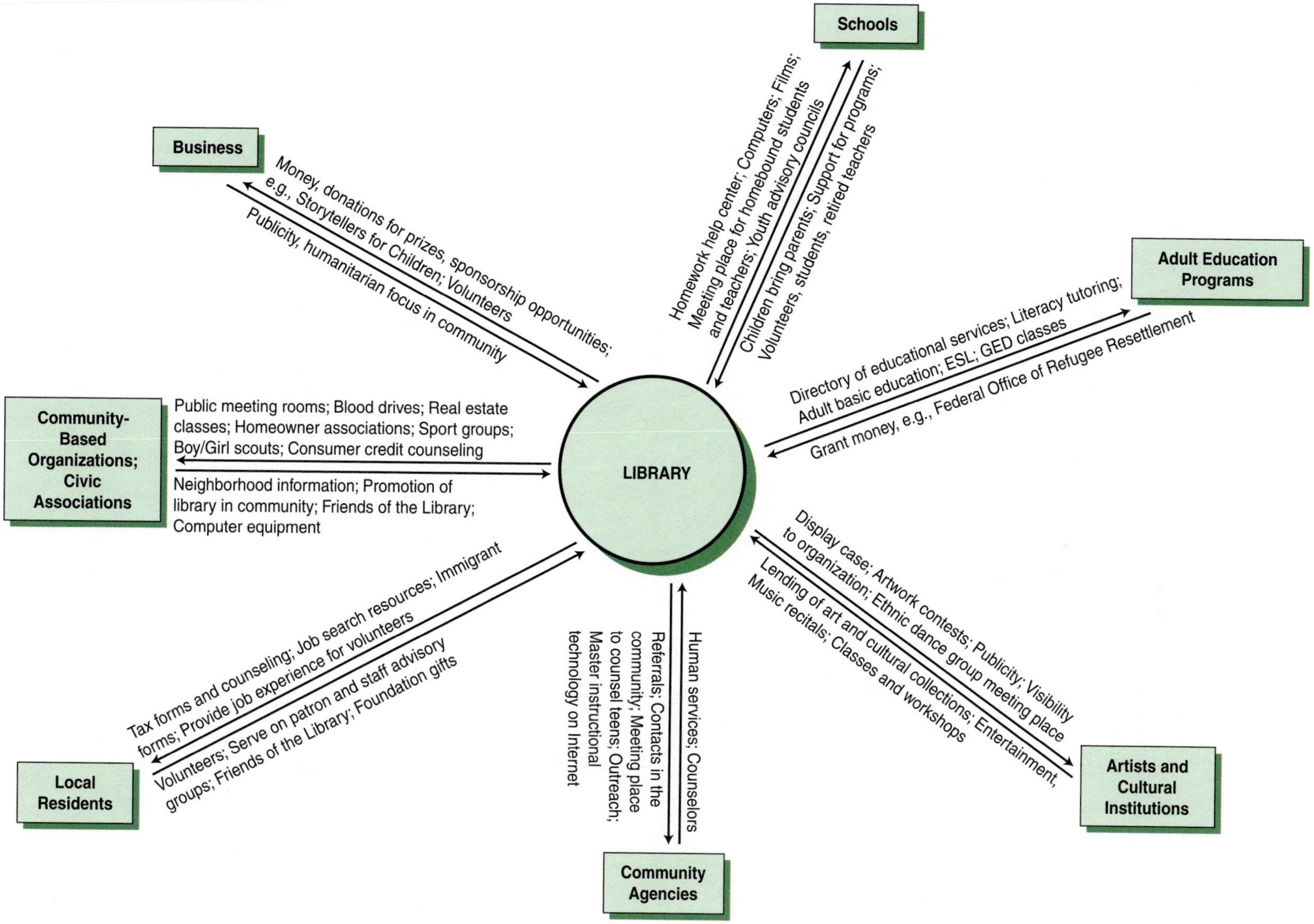

Community-Building Strategies

Most communities provide various types of services to schools and community members. As a teacher, you need to know how to access the many resources your community offers. Table A.1 lists types of services provided, identifies referral agencies often associated with the services, notes typical services provided, and includes questions that you can ask to find out more information.

TABLE A.1 Support Services for Children and Families

Type of Service	Referral Agencies	Typical Services	Information-Gathering Questions
Health Services	Acquired Immune Deficiency Syndrome (AIDS) Hotline Alcohol and Drug Abuse Services American Cancer Society American Heart Association American Lung Association American Red Cross Army Community Services Community Health Centers Dental Hygiene Clinics Food Allergy Network Health Department Home Health Care Juvenile Diabetes Foundation Meals on Wheels Poison Control Center Shriners Hospital	Clinic visits—prenatal/well baby Information and referral In-home services, home-delivered meals Insurance and medical-form counseling Labwork, medications Limited hospitalization Medical, health, and dental care Nutrition information and training Support groups	What do you do? Whom do you serve? What area do you serve? How much does it cost? Is there help to pay for your service? What happens after I call? Is there help for families who don't speak English? What else should I know about your service?
Economic Assistance	American Red Cross Department of Housing and Human Services Salvation Army Shelters Social Security Administration Social Services Temporary Assistance to Needy Families (TANF) United Community Ministries OtherBraces, hearing aids, vision testing	Self-sufficiency: employment services, job counseling, job search, employability skills workshops and training Benefit programs for food stamps, temporary assistance/medical care for children or adults who are disabled or ill Medicaid to cover medical and health care to the elderly, those who are disabled, those who are blind, pregnant women, some needy children, and caretakers Refugee assistance Assistance with hospital bills Temporary cash assistance to families in need	What do you do? Whom do you serve? What area do you serve? How much does it cost? Is there help to pay for your service? What happens after I call? Is there help for families who don't speak English? What else should I know about your service?

TABLE A.1 Continued

Type of Service	Referral Agencies	Typical Services	Information-Gathering Questions
Intervention Services	Association for Retarded Citizens Children and Adults with Attention Deficit Disorder (CHAD) Department of Pediatrics Early Intervention Services Easter Seal Society Family and Early Childhood Education Program Preschool Child Find Public Health Department Public Schools Special Education Services Speech and Hearing Clinics Other	*Americans with Disabilities Act* information Assistive technology services Audiology services Developmental evaluation Equipment and resources Family training, counseling, and home visits Health and nursing services Information and referral Medical services Occupational therapy Physical therapy Psychological services Respite care Service coordination Social work services Speech therapy Support groups Transportation Vision services	What do you do? Whom do you serve? What area do you serve? How much does it cost? Is there help to pay for your service? What happens after I call? Is there help for families who don't speak English? What else should I know about your service?

SOURCE: Courtesy of Marshann Snyder.

Chapter-by-Chapter Cross-Reference of Early Childhood Materials and Resources

The following grid provides a summary and cross-reference for a beginning list of resources for emerging early childhood teachers. The topics covered in the Compendium are matched with the chapters that they support.

Chapter/Topic	1	2	3	4	5	6	7	8	9	10	11	12
MATERIAL RESOURCES												
Basic Materials by Age Range					•	•						
Learning Centers Materials						•	•					
Free, Inexpensive Materials					•	•						
Health, Nutrition, & Safety						•						
Professional Resources for Teachers	•	•					•	•			•	•
Code of Ethics	•											
INTASC, NAEYC & ACEI Standards	•	•	•	•	•	•	•	•	•	•	•	•
National Education Goals											•	
E.C. Professional Organizations		•						•			•	
Child Advocacy Groups		•	•								•	
Other Journals & Organizations											•	
ERIC			•							•	•	
Storage & Resource Organization Information					•	•	•					
Technology Resources	•	•	•	•	•	•	•	•	•	•	•	•
Software Evaluation Criteria						•						
HUMAN RESOURCES												
Community Human Resources		•								•		
Public School Specialists			•	•		•						
School-Linked Services										•		
Support Services for Families										•		

References

Preface

Ayers, W. (Ed.). (1995). *To become a teacher: Making a difference in children's lives.* New York: Teachers College Press.

Hyson, M., & Biggar, H. (2006). NAEYC's standards for early childhood professional preparation: Getting from here to there. In M. Zaslow & I. Martinez-Beck (Eds.), *Critical issues in early childhood professional development* (pp. 283–308). Baltimore: Paul H. Brookes.

Ingersoll, R., & Smith, T. (2003). The wrong solution to the teacher shortage. *Educational Leadership, 60*(8), 30–33.

Isenberg, J. P., & Jalongo, M. R. (2003). *Major trends and issues in early childhood education* (2nd ed.). New York: Teachers College Press.

Johnson, S. M. (2006). *Finders and keepers: Helping new teachers survive and thrive in our schools.* San Francisco: Jossey-Bass.

National Association for the Education of Young Children. (1995). *Guidelines for preparation of early childhood professionals.* Washington, DC: Author.

Chapter 1

Abdal-Haqq, I. (1998). *Professional development schools: Weighing the evidence.* Thousand Oaks, CA: Sage.

Ayers, W. (Ed.). (1995). *To become a teacher: Making a difference in children's lives.* New York: Teachers College Press.

Ayers, W. (2001). *To teach: The journey of a teacher* (2nd ed.). New York: Teachers College Press.

Ball, D. L. (2000). Bridging practices: Intertwining content and pedagogy in teaching and learning to teach. *Journal of Teacher Education, 51*(3), 241–247.

Birmingham, C. (2003). Practicing the virtue of reflection in an unfamiliar cultural context. *Theory into Practice, 42*(3), 188–194.

Bolton, G. (2001). *Reflective practice: Writing and professional development*. London: Paul Chapman.

Boyer, E. L. (1995). *The basic school: A community for learning.* Princeton, NJ: The Carnegie Foundation.

Buchanan, A. M., Baldwin, S. C., & Rudisill, M. E. (2002). Service learning as scholarship in teacher education. *Educational Researcher, 30*(5), 28–34.

Carothers, S. A. (1995). Taking teaching seriously. In W. Ayers (Ed.), *To become a teacher: Making a difference in children's lives* (pp. 23–33). New York: Teachers College Press.

Carpenter-LaGattuta, A. (2002). Challenges in multicultural teacher education. *Multicultural Education, 9*(4), 27–29.

Carroll, S. Z., Conte, A. E., & Pan, A. C. (2000). Advice for student teachers. *Professional Educator, 23*(1), 1–7.

Carroll, T., & Fulton, K. (2004). The true cost of teacher turnover [Electronic version]. *Threshold,* 16–17.

Chilvers, D. (2005). Re-thinking reflective practice in the early years. In K. Hirst & C. Nutbrown (Eds.), *Perspectives on early childhood education* (pp. 163–188). Stoke on Kent, UK: Trentham.

Chokshi, S., & Fernandez, C. (2004). Challenges to importing Japanese Lesson Study: Concerns, misconceptions, and nuances. *Phi Delta Kappan, 85*(7), 520–525.

Copple, C., & Bredekamp, S. (2006). *Basics of developmentally appropriate practice: An introduction for teachers of children 3 to 6.* Washington, DC: National Association for the Education of Young Children.

Cruickshank, D. (1987). *Reflective teaching.* Reston, VA: Association of Teacher Educators.

Csikszentmihalyi, M. (1993). *The evolving self: A psychology for the third millennium.* New York: Harper-Perennial.

Darling-Hammond, L. (2006). *Powerful teacher education: Lessons from exemplary programs.* San Francisco: Jossey-Bass.

Dewey, J. (1909). *How we think.* London: Heath and Company.

Dewey, J. (1933). *How we think: A restatement of the relation of reflective thinking to the educative process.* Boston: Heath and Company.

Eby, J. W., Herrell, A. L., & Jordan, M. L. (2006). *Teaching in K–12 schools: A reflective action approach* (4th ed.). Upper Saddle River, NJ: Merrill/Prentice Hall.

Evans, V. J. (2006). Economic perspectives on early care and education. In M. Zaslow & I. Martinez-Beck (Eds.), *Critical issues in early childhood professional development* (pp. 309–311). Baltimore: Paul H. Brookes.

Fennimore, B. S. (1989). *Child advocacy for early childhood educators.* New York: Teachers College Press.

Fuller, B., Holloway, S. D., & Bozzi, L. (1997). Evaluating child care and preschools: Advancing the interests of government, teachers, or parents? In B. Spodek & O. N. Saracho (Eds.), *Issues in early childhood educational assessment and evaluation* (pp. 7–27). New York: Teachers College Press.

Fuller, F. F., & Bown, O. H. (1975). Becoming a teacher. In K. Ryan (Ed.), *Teacher education: The 47th yearbook of the NSSE, Part II* (pp. 25–52). Chicago: Rand McNally.

Glasgow, K. (1994). A problem of theory for early childhood professionals. *Childhood Education, 70*(3), 131–132.

Glickman, C. D., & Alridge, D. P. (2001). Going public: The imperative of public education in the 21st century.

In A. Lieberman & L. Miller (Eds.), *Teachers caught in the action: Professional development that matters* (pp. 12–22). New York: Teachers College Press.

Gordon, A., & Browne, K. B. (2006). *Beginning essentials in early childhood education.* Clifton Park, NY: Delmar Learning.

Hargreaves, A. (1995). Professional development and desire: A postmodern perspective. In T. R. Guskey & M. Huberman (Eds.), *Professional development in education* (pp. 9–33). New York: Teachers College Press.

Harle, A., & Trudeau, K. (2006). Using reflection to increase children's learning in kindergarten. *Young Children, 61*(4), 101–104.

Hendrick, J., & Weissman, P. (2007). *Total learning: Developmental curriculum for the young child* (7th ed.). Upper Saddle River, NJ: Merrill/Prentice Hall.

Ingersoll, R. (2002). Holes in the teacher supply bucket. *School Administrator, 59*(3), 42–43.

Isenberg, J. P. (1995). Whole language and play in the expressive arts. In S. R. Raines (Ed.), *Whole language across the curriculum: Grades 1, 2, 3* (pp. 114–136). New York: Teachers College Press.

Jalongo, M. R., & Heider, K. (2006). Teacher attrition: An issue of national concern. *Early Childhood Education Journal, 33*(5), 379–380.

Jalongo, M. R., Rieg, S., & Helterbran, V. (2006). *Planning for learning: Collaborative approaches to lesson design and review.* New York: Teachers College Press.

Jones, M., & Shelton, M. (2005). *Developing your portfolio—Enhancing your learning and showing your stuff: A guide for the early childhood student or professional.* New York: Routledge.

Kardos, S. M., Johnson, S. M., Peske, H. G., Kauffman, D., & Liu, E. (2001). Counting on colleagues: New teachers encounter the professional cultures of their schools. *Educational Administration Quarterly, 37*(2), 250–290.

Katz, L. (1972). *Talks with teachers.* Washington, DC: National Association for the Education of Young Children.

Kochendorfer, L. (1994). *Becoming a reflective teacher.* West Haven, CT: NEA Professional Library.

Korthagen, F., & Vasalos, A. (2005). Levels in reflection: Core reflection as a means to enhance professional growth. *Teachers and Teaching: Theory and Practice, 11*(1), 47–71.

Law, N., Moffit, M., Moore, E., Overfield, R., & Starks, E. (1966). *Basic propositions for early childhood education.* Washington, DC: Association for Childhood Education International.

Lee, H. (2005). Understanding and assessing preservice teachers' reflective thinking. *Teaching & Teacher Education, 21*(6), 699–715.

Many, J., Howard, F., & Hoge, P. (2002). Epistemology and preservice teacher education: How do beliefs about knowledge affect our students' experiences? *English Education, 34*(4), 302–322.

McDonald, J. P. (2001). Students' work and teachers' learning. In A. Lieberman & L. Miller (Eds.), *Teachers caught in the action: Professional development that matters* (pp. 209–235). New York: Teachers College Press.

McMullen, M. B., & Dixon, S. (2006). Research in review: Building on common ground: Unifying practice with infant/toddler specialists though a mindful, relationship-based approach. *Young Children, 61*(4), 46–52.

Nieto, S. (2005). *Why we teach.* New York: Teachers College Press.

Noddings, N. (1984). *Caring: A feminine approach to ethics and moral education.* Berkeley: University of California Press.

Noddings, N. (2006). *Critical lessons: What our schools should teach.* New York: Cambridge University Press.

Peters, W. H. (2000). Through the looking-glass portfolio: The journey of preservice teachers in becoming reflective practitioners. Urbana, IL: ERIC Clearinghouse [ERIC Document Reproduction Service No. ED444950].

Poppe, J., & Clothier, S. (2007). The preschool promise: Going to preschool benefits children their entire lives. Can states afford to provide it to all kids? In K. Paciorek (Ed.), *Annual Editions: Early Childhood Education 06/07* (27th ed., pp. 14–17). Dubuque, IA: McGraw-Hill.

Quisenberry, N., McIntyre, J., & Duhon, G. (Eds.). (2002). *Racism in the classroom: Case studies.* Olney, MD: Joint publication of the Association of Teacher Educators and Association for Childhood Education International.

Rand, M. (2000). *Giving it some thought: Cases for early childhood practice.* Washington, DC: NAEYC.

Ryan, K. (1986). *The induction of new teachers.* Bloomington, IN: Phi Delta Kappa (Fastback #237).

Sapon-Shevin, M. (1995). Building a safe community for learning. In W. Ayers (Ed.), *To become a teacher: Making a difference in children's lives* (pp. 99–112). New York: Teachers College Press.

Schon, D. (1987). *Educating the reflective practitioner: Toward a new design for teaching and learning in the professions.* San Francisco: Jossey-Bass.

Schon, D. A. (1983). *The reflective practitioner: How professionals think in action.* New York: Basic Books.

Sparks-Langer, G. M., & Colton, A. B. (1991). Synthesis of research on teachers' reflective thinking. *Educational Leadership, 48*(6), 37–44.

Stronge, J. H. (2002). *Qualities of effective teachers.* Alexandria, VA: Association for Supervision and Curriculum Development.

Surbeck, E., Han, E., & Moyer, J. (1991). Assessing reflective responses in journals. *Educational Leadership, 48*(6), 25–27.

Taggart, G. L., & Wilson, A. P. (2005). *Promoting reflective thinking in teachers: 50 action strategies* (2nd ed.). Thousand Oaks, CA: Corwin.

Tennyson, W. W., & Strom, S. M. (1988). Beyond professional standards: Developing responsibilities. *Journal of Counseling and Development, 64*(5), 298–302.

Whitbeck, D. A. (2000). Born to be a teacher: What am I doing in a college of education? *Journal of Research in Education, 15*(1), 129–136.

Wideen, M., Mayer-Smith, J., & Moon, B. (1998). A critical analysis of the research on learning to teach: Making the case for an ecological perspective on inquiry. *Review of Educational Research, 68*(2), 130–178.

Wilson, K., & Chapman, J. (2003). *Bear wants more.* New York: Margaret McElderry/Simon & Schuster.

Zaslow, M., & Martinez-Beck, I. (Eds.). (2006). *Critical issues in early childhood professional development.* Baltimore: Paul H. Brookes.

Chapter 2

Abelson, R. P. (1979). Differences between belief and knowledge systems. *Cognitive Science, 3,* 355–366.

Anderson, L. (1997). *Argyris' and Schon's theory on congruence and learning* [Online]. Available at *www.scu.edu.au/schools/sawd/arr/argyris.html.*

Aries, P. (1962). *Centuries of childhood.* London: Jonathan Cape.

Barnett, S. W., Hustedt, J. T., Robin, K. B., & Schulman, K. L. (2004). *The state of preschool: 2004 state preschool yearbook.* New Brunswick, NJ: National Institute for Early Education Research.

Barnett, W., Lanny, C., & Jung, K. (2005). *The effects of state pre-K programs on young children's school readiness in five states.* New Brunswick, NJ: National Institute for Early Education Research, Rutgers, the State University of New Jersey.

Birmingham, C. (2003). Practicing the virtue of reflection in an unfamiliar cultural context. *Theory into Practice, 42*(3), 188–194.

Black, S. (2007). Second time around: If repeating a grade doesn't help kids, why do we make them do it? In K. Paciorek (Ed.), *Annual Editions: Early Childhood Education 06/07* (27th ed., pp. 96–98). Dubuque, IA: McGraw-Hill.

Bloch, M. N., & Price, G. G. (Eds.). (1994). *Essays on the history of early childhood education.* Norwood, NJ: Ablex.

Bronfenbrenner, U. (1974). *A report on longitudinal evaluation of preschool programs.* Washington, DC: U.S. Government Printing Office.

Bronson, M. B. (2006). Developing social and emotional competence. In D. F. Gullo (Ed.), *K today: Teaching and learning in the kindergarten year* (pp. 47–56). Washington, DC: National Association for the Education of Young Children.

Brown, D. F., & Rose, T. D. (1995). Self-reported classroom impact of teachers' theories about learning and obstacles to implementation. *Action in Teacher Education, 17*(1), 20–29.

Buchanan, A. M., Baldwin, S. C., & Rudisill, M. E. (2002). Service learning as scholarship in teacher education. *Educational Researcher, 30*(5), 28–34.

Buchanan, T. K., Burts, D. C., Bidner, J., White, V. F., & Charlesworth, R. (1998). Predictors of developmental appropriateness of the beliefs and practices of first, second, and third grade teachers. *Early Childhood Research Quarterly, 13*(2), 459–483.

Bullough, R. V., & Gitlin, A. D. (2001). *Becoming a student of teaching* (2nd ed.). New York: RoutledgeFalmer.

Carbo, M. (1995). Educating everybody's children. In R. W. Cole (Ed.), *Educating everybody's children: Diverse teaching strategies for diverse learners: What research and practice say about improving achievement* (pp. 1–8). Alexandria, VA: Association for Supervision and Curriculum Development.

Cassidy, D. J., & Lawrence, J. M. (2000). Teachers' beliefs: The "whys" behind the "how tos" in child care classrooms. *Journal of Research in Childhood Education, 14*(2), 193–204.

Cassidy, D. J., Mims, S., Lia Rucker, L., & Boone, S. (2003). Emergent curriculum and kindergarten readiness. *Childhood Education, 79*(4), 345–360.

Center for the Child Care Workforce and Human Services Policy Center. (2002). *Estimating the size and components of the U.S. child care workforce and caregiving population* (p. 18). Washington, DC: Center for the Child Care Workforce; Seattle: Human Services Policy Center, University of Washington.

Charlesworth, R., Hart, C. H., Burts, D. C., Mosley, J., & Fleegle, P. O. (1993). Measuring the developmental appropriateness of kindergarten teachers' beliefs and practices. *Early Childhood Research Quarterly, 8,* 255–276.

Cleverley, J., & Phillips, D. C. (1986). *Visions of childhood: Influential models from Locke to Spock.* New York: Teachers College Press.

Cryer, D., & Phillipsen, L. (1997). Quality details: A close-up look at child care program strengths and weaknesses. *Young Children, 52*(2), 51–61.

DeMause, L. (Ed.). (1974). *The history of childhood.* New York: The Psychohistory Press.

Driscoll, A. (1995). *Cases in early childhood education: Stories of programs and practices.* Boston: Allyn & Bacon.

Duch, H. (2005). Redefining parent involvement in Head Start: A two-generation approach. *Early Childhood Development and Care, 175*(1), 23–35.

Education Week. (2002, January 7). *Quality counts 2002: Building blocks for success: State efforts in early childhood education* [Special Issue].

Edwards, C., Gandini, L., & Forman, G. (Eds.). (1998). *The hundred languages of children—the Reggio Emilia approach—advanced reflections* (2nd ed.). Norwood, NJ: Ablex.

Epstein, A. S., Schweinhart, L. J., & McAdoo, L. (1996). *Models of early childhood education.* Ypsilanti, MI: High/Scope Press.

Erwin, E. J. (1996). *Putting children first: Visions for a brighter future for young children and their families.* Baltimore: Paul Brookes.

Estok, V. (2007). One district's study on the propriety of transition-grade classrooms. In K. Paciorek (Ed.), *Annual Editions: Early Childhood Education 06/07* (27th ed., pp. 92–95). Dubuque, IA: McGraw-Hill.

Fang, Z. (1996). A review of research on teacher beliefs and practices. *Educational Research, 38*(1), 47–65.

Feeney, S., Christensen, D., & Moravcik, E. (2006). *Who am I in the lives of children? An introduction to teaching young children* (7th ed.). Upper Saddle River, NJ: Merrill/Prentice Hall.

Glasgow, K. (1994). A problem of theory for early childhood professionals. *Childhood Education, 70*(3), 131–132.

Greenspan, S., & Wieder, S. (1998). *The child with special needs: Encouraging intellectual and emotional growth.* Reading, MA: Addison Wesley.

Gronlund, G. (2006). *Make early standards come alive: Connecting your practice and curriculum to state guidelines*. Washington, DC: National Association for the Education of Young Children.

Grunwald, L. (1996/1997). The amazing minds of infants. In K. M. Paciorek & J. H. Munro (Eds.), *Early childhood education 96/96* (17th ed., pp. 45–50). Guilford, CT: Dushkin/McGraw-Hill.

Hargreaves, A. (2003). *Teaching in the knowledge society: Education in the age of insecurity.* New York: Teachers College Press.

Harms, T., & Clifford, R. M. (1997). *Early childhood environment rating scale* (2nd ed.). New York: Teachers College Press.

Hatch J. A., & Freeman, E. B. (1988). Kindergarten philosophies and practices: Perspectives of teachers, principals, and supervisors. *Early Childhood Research Quarterly, 3,* 151–166.

Helm, J. H., & Beneke, S. (Eds.). (2003). *The power of projects: Meeting contemporary challenges in early childhood classrooms—Strategies and solutions.* Washington, DC: National Association for the Education of Young Children.

Hewett, V. M. (2001). Examining the Reggio Emilia approach to early childhood education. *Early Childhood Education Journal, 29,* 95–100.

Jalongo, M. R., & Isenberg, J. P. (1995). *Teachers' stories: From personal narrative to professional insight.* San Francisco, CA: Jossey-Bass.

Jensen, E. (1998). *Teaching with the brain in mind.* Alexandria, VA: Association for Supervision and Curriculum Development.

Jensen, E. (2006). *Enriching the brain: How to maximize every learner's potential.* San Francisco: Jossey-Bass.

Johnson, S. M. (2006). *Finders and keepers: Helping new teachers survive and thrive in our schools*. San Francisco: Jossey-Bass.

Kamerman, S. B., & Kahn, A. J. (1994). *A welcome for every child: Care, education and family support for infants and toddlers in Europe.* Arlington, VA: Zero to Three/National Center for Clinical Infant Programs.

Kowalski, K., Pretti-Fontczak, K., & Johnson, L. (2001). Preschool teachers' beliefs concerning the importance of various developmental skills and abilities. *Journal of Research in Childhood Education, 16*(1), 5–14.

Kozol, J. (1991). *Savage inequalities: Children in America's schools.* New York: Crown.

Lascarides, V. C., & Hinitz, B. F. (2000). *History of early childhood education.* New York: Falmer Press.

LeFrancois, G. (2000). *Of children* (9th ed.). Belmont, CA: Wadsworth.

Liebovich, B. J., & Adler, S. M. (2007). Teaching advocacy in early childhood teacher education programs. *Early Childhood Education Journal*.

Lillard, P. P. (1996). *Montessori today: A comprehensive approach to education from birth to childhood*. New York: Schocker Books.

Many, J., Howard, F., & Hoge, P. (2002). Epistemology and preservice teacher education: How do beliefs about knowledge affect our students' experiences? *English Education, 34*(4), 302–322.

Mueller, A. (2003). Looking back and looking forward: Always becoming a teacher educator through self-study. *Reflective Practice, 4*(1), 67–84.

National Association for the Education of Young Children. (2007). *Why NAEYC accreditation?* Retrieved January 20, 2007 from http://www.naeyc.org/academy/

Neugebauer, R. (1995, November/December). The movers and shapers of early childhood education. *Child Care Information Exchange,* 9–13.

New, R. S. (1992). The integrated early childhood curriculum: New interpretations based on research and practice. In C. Seefeldt (Ed.), *The early childhood curriculum: A review of current research* (pp. 286–322). New York: Teachers College Press.

New, R. S. (2000). *Reggio Emilia: Catalyst for change and conversation.* Champaign, IL: ERIC/EECE Clearinghouse on Elementary and Early Childhood Education. [EDO-PS-00–15].

Osborn, D. K. (1980). *Early childhood education in historical perspective.* Athens, GA: Education Associates.

Pajares, M. F. (1992). Teacher beliefs and educational research: Cleaning up a messy construct. *Review of Educational Research, 62*(3), 307–332.

Postman, N. (1982). *The disappearance of childhood.* New York: Dell.

Robinson, A., & Stark, D. R. (2002). *Advocates in action: Making a difference for young children.* Washington, DC: National Association for the Education of Young Children.

Rogoff, B. (1993). *Apprenticeship in thinking: Cognitive development in social context.* New York: Oxford University Press.

Roopnarine, J. L., & Johnson, J. E. (2005). *Approaches to early childhood education* (4th ed.). Upper Saddle River, NJ: Merrill/Prentice Hall.

Sameroff, A., & McDonough, S. C. (1994). Educational implications of developmental transitions: Revisiting the 5- to 7-year shift. *Phi Delta Kappan, 76,* 188–193.

Santrock, J. W. (2004). *Children* (8th ed.). New York: McGraw-Hill.

Schickendanz, J. A. (1995). Early education and care: Beginnings. *Journal of Education, 177*(3), 1–7.

Schweinhart, L. J. (1994). *Lasting benefits of preschool programs.* Urbana, IL: ERIC Clearinghouse. [ERIC Digest No. EDO-PS-94–2].

Schweinhart, L. J., & Hohmann, C. F. (1992). The simple but profound approach of the High/Scope K–3 curriculum. *Education Digest, 58,* 4–7.

Sigel, I. E. (1985). A conceptual analysis of beliefs. In I. E. Sigel (Ed.), *Parental belief systems* (pp. 345–371). Hillsdale, NJ: Erlbaum.

Smith, A. B. (1996). Quality programs that care and educate. *Childhood Education, 72*(6), 330–336.

Snyder, A. (1972). *Dauntless women in childhood education.* Washington, DC: Association for Childhood Education International.

Spodek, B., & Saracho, O. N. (2003). "On the shoulders of giants": Exploring the traditions of early childhood education. *Early Childhood Education Journal, 31,* 3–10.

Swick, K., & Brown, M. (1999). The caring ethic in early childhood teacher education. *Journal of Instructional Psychology, 26*(2), 116–121.

Sylwester, R. (1995). *A celebration of neurons: An educator's guide to the human brain.* Alexandria, VA: Association for Supervision and Curriculum Development.

Tanner, L. N. (1997). *Dewey's Laboratory School: Lessons for today.* New York: Teachers College Press.

Tuchman, B. (1978). *A distant mirror.* New York: Alfred A. Knopf.

Vakil, S., Freeman, R., & Swim, T. J. (2003). The Reggio Emilia approach and inclusive early childhood programs. *Early Childhood Education Journal, 30,* 187–192.

Vartulli, S. (1999). How early childhood teacher beliefs vary across grade level. *Early Childhood Research Quarterly, 14*(4), 489–514.

Walsh, B., & Petty, K. (2006, in press). Frequency of six early childhood education approaches: A 10-year content analysis of *Early Childhood Education Journal*.

Whitbeck, D. A. (2000). Born to be a teacher: What am I doing in a college of education? *Journal of Research in Education, 15*(1), 129–136.

Wortham, S. (1992). *Childhood: 1892–1992.* Olney, MD: Association for Childhood Education International.

Wyman, A. (1995). The earliest early childhood teachers: Women teachers of America's Dame Schools. *Young Children, 50*(2), 29–32.

Zaslow, M., & Martinez-Beck, I. (Eds.) (2006). *Critical issues in early childhood professional development.* Baltimore: Paul H. Brookes.

Zigler, E., & Styfco, S. J. (Eds.). (2004). *Head Start and beyond: A national plan for extended childhood intervention* (reissue edition). New Haven, CT: Yale University Press.

Chapter 3

Banks, J. A. (2001). *Cultural diversity and education: Foundations, curriculum, and teaching* (4th ed.). London: Allyn & Bacon.

Banks, J. A. (2004). *Diversity and citizenship education: Global perspectives.* San Francisco: Jossey-Bass.

Barbour, C., Barbour, N. H., & Scully, P. A. (2005). *Families, schools, and communities: Building partnerships for educating children* (3rd ed.). Upper Saddle River, NJ: Merrill/Prentice Hall.

Brazelton, T. B., & Greenspan, S. J. (2000). *The irreducible needs of children: What every child must have to learn, grow, and flourish*. Cambridge, MA: Perseus.

Brown et al. v. Board of Education of Topeka, Sharnee County et al., and Companion Cases, 74 Sup. Ct. 686 (1954).

Children's Defense Fund. (2005). *The state of America's children.* Washington DC: Author.

Cochran-Smith, M. (1995). Color blindness and basket weaving are not the answers: Confronting the dilemmas of race, culture, and language diversity in teacher education. *American Educational Research Journal, 32*(3), 493–522.

Derman-Sparks, L. (1989). *Anti-bias curriculum: Tools for empowering young children.* Washington DC: National Association for the Education of Young Children.

Derman-Sparks, L., & Ramsey, P. G. (2006). *What if all the kids are white? Anti-bias and multicultural education with young children and families.* New York: Teachers College Press.

Duncan, G., & Brooks-Gunn, J. (1997). *Consequences of growing up poor.* New York: Russell Sage Foundation.

Edelman, P., Holzer, H. J., & Offner, P. (2006). *Reconnecting disadvantaged young men.* Washington, DC: Urban Institute Press.

Edmonds, R. (1979). Effective schools for the urban poor. *Educational Leadership, 31*(1), 15–23.

Feeney, S., & Freeman, N. K. (1999). *Ethics and the early childhood educator: Using the NAEYC Code.* Washington, DC: National Association for the Education of Young Children.

Fennimore, B. S. (1989). *Child advocacy for early childhood educators*. New York: Teachers College Press.

Fennimore, B. S. (2000). *Talk matters: Refocusing the language of public schooling.* New York: Teachers College Press.

Gay, G. (2003). *Becoming multicultural educators: Personal journey toward professional agency.* San Francisco: Jossey-Bass.

Goffin, S. G., & Lombardi, J. (1988). *Speaking out: Early childhood advocacy.* Washington, DC: National Association for the Education of Young Children.

Gollnick, D. M., & Chinn, P. C. (2005). *Multicultural education in a pluralistic society* (7th ed.). Upper Saddle River, NJ: Merrill/Prentice Hall.

Gonzalez-Mena, J. (2007). *Foundations of early childhood: Teaching children in a diverse society.* (4th ed.). New York: McGraw-Hill.

Goodwin, A. L. (1997). *Assessment for equity and inclusion: Embracing all our children*. New York: Routledge.

Hout, M. (2002). Test scores, education, and poverty. In J. M. Fish (Ed.), *Race and intelligence: Separating science from myth* (pp. 329–354). Mahwah, NJ: Lawrence Erlbaum.

Irvine, J. J. (2003). *Educating teachers for diversity: Seeing with a cultural eye*. New York: Teachers College Press.

Jensen, A. R. (1969). How much can we boost IQ and scholastic achievement? *Harvard Educational Review, 39*(1), 1–123.

Jensen, J. M., & Fraser, M. W. (2006). *Social policy for children and families: A risk and resilience perspective.* London: Sage.

Johnson, S. M. (2006). *Finders and keepers: Helping new teachers survive and thrive in our schools.* San Francisco: Jossey-Bass.

Koppelman, K. L., & Goodhart, R. L. (2005). *Understanding human differences: Multicultural education for a diverse America.* Boston: Perseus.

Kozol, J. (1995). *Amazing grace: The lives of children and the conscience of a nation.* New York: Crown.

Kumashiro, K. (2004). *Against common sense: Teaching and learning toward social justice.* New York: Routledge-Falmer.

Ladson-Billings, G. (2006). Yes but how do we do it? In J. Landsman & C. W. Lewis (Eds.), *White teachers/divided classrooms: A guide to building inclusive schools, promoting high expectations, and eliminating racism.* Sterling, VA: Stylus.

Meacham, A. N. (2006). Language learning and the internationally adopted child. *Early Childhood Education Journal, 34*(1), 73–79.

National Center for Education Statistics. (2002). *State nonfiscal survey of public elementary/secondary education, 2000–2001, Common core of data (CCD)*. Washington, DC: Author.

Nieto, S. (1999). *The light in their eyes: Creating multicultural learning communities.* New York: Teachers College Press.

Nieto, S. (2005). *Why we teach*. New York: Teachers College Press.

Noddings, N. (1995). Caring. In V. Held (Ed.), *Justice and care: Essential readings in feminist ethics* (pp. 7–30). Boulder, CO: Westview Press.

Noddings, N. (2005). *Educating citizens for global awareness*. New York: Teachers College Press.

Paley, V. G. (1992). *You can't say you can't play.* Cambridge, MA: Harvard University Press.

Pelo, A., & Davidson, F. (2000). *That's not fair! A teacher's guide to activism with young children.* St. Paul, MN: Redleaf Press.

Ramsey, P. G. (2004). *Teaching and learning in a diverse world: Multicultural education for young children* (3rd ed.). New York: Teachers College Press.

Ramsey, P. G., & Williams, L. R. (2003). *Multicultural education: A source book.* New York: RoutledgeFalmer.

Rawls, J. (2001). *Justice as fairness: A restatement.* Cambridge, MA: Belkap/Harvard University Press.

Ritchie, S., & Howes, C. (2002). *A matter of trust: Connecting teachers and learners in the early childhood classroom.* New York: Teachers College Press.

Robinson, A., & Stark, D. R. (2005). *Advocates in action: Making a difference for young children.* Washington DC: National Association for the Education of Young Children.

Roopnarine, J. L., & Johnson, J. E. (2005). *Approaches to early childhood education* (4th ed). Upper Saddle River, NJ: Merrill/Prentice Hall.

Schorr, L. (1988). *Within our reach: Breaking the cycle of disadvantage*. New York: Anchor Press/Doubleday.

Senn, M. (1977). *Speaking out for America's children.* New Haven, CT: Yale University Press.

Snyder, T., & Hoffman, C. (2003). *Digest of educational statistics 2002* (NCES 2003–060). Washington, DC: National Center for Educational Statistics, U.S. Department of Education.

Spring, J. (1994). *Deculturalization and the struggle for equality: A brief history of the education of dominated cultures in the United States.* New York: McGraw-Hill.

Stevens, E., Wood, G. H., & Sheehan, J. J. (2000). *Justice, ideology, and education: An introduction to the social foundations of education* (4th ed.). Boston: McGraw-Hill.

Stone, J. G. (2001). *Building classroom community: The early childhood teacher's role.* Washington, DC: National Association for the Education of Young Children.

Swadener, B. B. (2003). "This is what democracy looks like": Strengthening advocacy in neoliberal times. *Journal of Early Childhood Teacher Education, 24,* 135–141.

Tiedt, P. L., & Tiedt, I. M. (1999). *Multicultural teaching: A handbook of activities, information, and resources* (5th ed.). Boston: Allyn & Bacon.

U.S. Bureau of the Census. (2002). *Profile of the foreign-born population in the United States: 2000.* Washington, DC: U.S. Department of Commerce.

Wasley, P. (2006). Accreditor of educational schools drops controversial "social justice" language. *Chronicle of Higher Education, 52*(41), A13.

Wien, C. A. (2004). *Negotiating standards in the primary classroom: The teacher's dilemma.* New York: Teachers College Press.

Wright, K., Stegelin, D. A., & Hartle, L. (2007). *Building family, school, and community partnerships* (3rd ed.). Upper Saddle River, NJ: Merrill/Prentice Hall.

Chapter 4

Annie E. Casey Foundation. (2006). *Kids count data book.* Baltimore, Maryland: Author.

Banks, J. A. (2006). *Cultural diversity and education: Foundations, curriculum, and teaching* (5th ed.). Boston: Allyn & Bacon.

Bergen, D. (2003). Perspectives on inclusion in early childhood education. In J. P. Isenberg & M. R. Jalongo (Eds.), *Major trends and issues in early childhood education: Challenges, controversies, and insights* (pp. 47–68). New York: Teachers College Press.

Berk, L. E. (2005). *Infants and children* (5th ed.). Boston: Pearson Allyn and Bacon.

Berns, R. (2007). *Child, family, school, and community* (7th ed.). Belmont, CA: Wadsworth.

Brazleton, T. B., & Greenspan, S. I. (2001). *The irreducible needs of children: What every child must have to grow, learn, and flourish.* Cambridge, MA: Perseus.

Bredekamp, S., & Copple, C. (1997). *Developmentally appropriate practice in early childhood programs* (Rev. ed.). Washington, DC: National Association for the Education of Young Children.

Bronfenbrenner, U. (1981). *The ecology of human development.* Cambridge, MA: Harvard University Press. (Original work published 1979)

Children's Defense Fund. (2005). *The state of America's children yearbook.* Washington, DC: Author.

Copple, C., Sigel, I., & Saunders, R. (1984). *Educating the young thinker.* Mahwah, NJ: Erlbaum.

Division for Early Childhood of the Council for Exceptional Children. (2000). *Position on inclusion.* Reston, VA: Author.

Erikson, E. H. (1993). *Childhood and society.* New York: Norton. (Original work published 1963)

Federal Interagency Forum on Child and Family Statistics. (2006). *America's Children in Brief: Key National Indicators of Well-Being.* Washington, DC: Author. [Online]. Available at *www.childstats.gov/america'schildren*

Gallagher, K. C. (2005). Brain research and early childhood development: A primer for developmentally appropriate practice. *Young Children, 60*(4), 12–21.

Goleman, D. (1998). *Working with emotional intelligence.* New York: Bantam.

Guralnick, M. J. (Ed.). (2001). *Early childhood inclusion: Focus on change.* Baltimore: Brookes Publishing Co.

Hallahan, D. P., & Kauffman, J. M. (2006). *Exceptional learners: An introduction to special education* (10th ed.). Boston: Allyn & Bacon.

Individuals with Disabilities Education Act. (1990). Public Law 101–476 (30 October 1990).

Kamii, C. & DeVRies, R. *Group games in early education* (p. vii). Washington, DC: National Association for the Education of Young Children.

Maslow, A. H. (1987). *Motivation and personality* (3rd ed.). New York: Harper and Row.

National Association for the Education of Young Children. (1996). Position statement: Responding to linguistic and cultural diversity: Recommendations for effective early childhood education. *Young Children, 5*(2), 4–12.

National Association for the Education of Young Children. (2001). *NAEYC standards for early childhood professional preparation. Initial licensure programs.* Washington, DC: Author.

National Center for Health Statistics. (2005). *FastStats A to Z.* Hyattsville, MD. [Online]. Available at *www.cdc.gov/nchs*

Piaget, J. (1992). *The origins of intelligence in children.* International Universities Press. (Original work published 1952)

Puckett, M., & Black, J. (2005). *The young child: Development from prebirth through age eight* (4th ed.). Upper Saddle River, NJ: Merrill/Prentice Hall.

Santrock, J. W. (2007). *Child development* (11th ed.). New York: McGraw-Hill.

Shonkoff, J. P., & Phillips, D. A. (2001). From neurons to neighborhoods: The science of early childhood development. In Commission on Behavioral and Social Science and Education (Ed.), *Early childhood development and learning: New knowledge for policy* (pp. 1–20). Washington, DC: National Academy Press.

Springer, M. (1999). *Learning and memory: The brain in action.* Alexandria, VA: Association for Curriculum and Development.

Thompson, R. A. (2001). Development in the first years of life. In R. E. Behrman (Ed.), *Caring for infants and toddlers* (pp. 21–23). Los Altos, CA: The David and Lucille Packard Foundation.

Vygotsky, L. (1978). *Mind in society: The development of higher psychological processes.* Cambridge, MA: Harvard University Press.

White, C. S., & Isenberg, J. P. (2003). Development issues affecting children. In J. P. Isenberg & M. R. Jalongo (Eds.), *Major trends and issues in early childhood education: Challenges, controversies, and insights* (pp. 13–29). New York: Teachers College Press.

Wood, C. (1997). *Yardsticks.* Greenfield, MA: Northeast Foundation for Children.

Woolfolk, A. (2007). *Educational psychology* (10th ed.). Boston: Allyn & Bacon.

Further Reading on Children with Diverse Backgrounds

EDO-PS-94-4. Clearinghouse on Elementary and Early Childhood Education. Urbana, IL.

Feng, J. (1994). *Asian-American children: What teachers should know.* ERIC Digest.

Stewart, E. C., & Bennett, M. J. (1991). *American cultural patterns: A cross-cultural perspective* (Rev. ed.). Yarmouth, ME: Intercultural Press.

Children's Books

Beaumont, K. (2005). *Baby danced the polka.* New York: Dial.

Dewdney, A. (2005). *Llama, llama red pajama.* New York: Viking.

English, K. (2004). *Hot day on Abbott Avenue.* New York: Clarion.

Henkes, K. (2004). *Kitten's first full moon.* New York: Greenwillow.

Hesse, K. (2004). *The cats in Krasinski Square.* New York: Scholastic.

Hillman, E. (1992). *Min-Yo and the moon dragon.* Dallas, TX: Harcourt Brace.

Hooks, W. (1987). *Moss gown.* New York: Clarion.

O'Dell, S. (1960). *Island of the blue dolphins.* Boston: Houghton Mifflin.

Matas, C. (1993). *Daniel's story.* New York: Scholastic.

Sendak, M. (1964). *Where the wild things are.* New York: Harper.

Chapter 5

Allen, K. E., & Cowdery, G. E. (2005). *The exceptional child: Inclusion in early childhood education* (5th ed.). Clifton Park, NY: Thomson Delmar Learning.

American Psychological Association (2005). *Learner centered psychological principles: Guidelines for school redesign and reform* [Electronic version]. Washington, DC: American Psychological Association [Online]. Available at *www.apa.org/ed/cpnewtext.html.*

Armstrong, T. (2000). *Multiple Intelligences in the Classroom* (2nd ed.). Alexandria, VA: ASCD.

Bandura, A. (1997). *Self-efficacy: The exercise of control.* New York: Freeman.

Bandura, A. (2001). Social cognitive theory. *Annual Review of Psychology, 52.* Palo Alto, CA: Annual Review.

Banks J. A., & Banks, C. A. (Eds.). (2005). *Multicultural education: Issues and perspectives* (5th ed.). Hoboken, NJ: John Wiley & Sons.

Berk, L. (2005). *Infants and children.* (5th ed.). Boston: Allyn & Bacon.

Berns, R. M. (2007). *Child, family, school and community. Socialization and support* (7th ed.). Belmont, CA: Thomson Wadsworth. Fort Worth, TX: Harcourt Brace College Publishers.

Bodrova, E., & Leong, D. (1996). *Tools of the mind: The Vygotskian approach to early childhood education.* Upper Saddle River, NJ: Merrill/Prentice Hall.

Bodrova, E. & Leong, D. (2005). Uniquely preschool. *Educational Leadership, 63*(1), 44–47.

Bransford, J. D., Brown, A. I., & Cocking, R. R. (Eds.). (1999). *How people learn: Brain, mind, experience, and school.* Washington, DC: National Academy Press.

Bredekamp, S., & Copple, C. (1997). *Developmentally appropriate practice in early childhood programs* (Rev. ed.). Washington, DC: National Association for the Education of Young Children.

Bredekamp, S., & Rosegrant, T. (Eds.). (1992). *Reaching potentials: Appropriate curriculum and assessment for young children* (Vol. 1). Washington, DC: National Association for the Education of Young Children.

Campbell, L., Campbell, B., & Dickinson, D. (2004). *Teaching and Learing Through Multiple Intelligences* (3rd ed.). Boston, MA: Pearson Education, Inc.

Clements, D., & Sarama, J. (2003). Young children and technology: What does the research say? *Young Children, 58*(6), 34–40.

Commission on Behavioral and Social Sciences and Education. (2001). *Early childhood development and learning: New knowledge for policy.* Washington, DC: National Academy Press.

Daniels, D. H., Kalkman, D. L., & McCombs, B. L. (2001). Individual differences in young children's learning and teacher practices: Effects of learner-centered contexts on motivations. *Early Education Development, 12*(2), 253–273.

Daniels, H., & Bizar, M. (2005). *Teaching the best practice way.* Portland, ME: Stenhouse.

Denton, P. (2005). *Learning through academic choice.* Turners Falls, MA: Northeast Foundation for Children.

Dewey, J. (1916). *Democracy and education.* New York: Macmillan.

Donovan, M. S., & Bransford, J. D. (2005). *How students learn history, mathematics, and science in the classroom.* Washington, DC: National Academy Press.

Eggen, P., & Kauchak, D. (2007). *Strategies and models for teachers: Teaching content and thinking skills* (7th ed.). Boston: Allyn & Bacon.

Fromberg, D. P. (2002). *Play and meaning in early childhood education*. Boston: Allyn & Bacon.

Frost, J., Wortham, S., & Reifel, S. (2005). *Play and child development* (2nd ed.). Upper Saddle River, NJ: Merrill/Prentice Hall.

Gallagher, K. C. (2005). Brain research and early childhood development: A primer for developmentally appropriate practice. *Young Children, 60*(4), 12–21.

Gardner, H. (1993). *Frames of mind. The theory of multiple intelligences* (2nd ed.). New York: Basic Books.

Gardner, H. (2000). *The disciplined mind.* New York: Penguin Putnam.

Goleman, D. (1997). *Emotional intelligence.* New York: Bantam. (Original work printed 1995)

Goleman, D. (1998). *Working with emotional intelligence.* New York: Bantam.

Haugland, S. W. (2000). Early childhood classrooms in the 21st century: Using computers to maximize learning. *Young Children, 25*(1), 12–18.

Haugland, S. W., & Gerzog, G. (1998). *The developmental software scale for websites.* Cape Giradeauz, MO: K.I.D.S. & Computers.

Henniger, M. L. (2005). *Teaching young children: An introduction* (3rd ed.). Upper Saddle River, NJ: Merrill/Prentice Hall.

Hernandez, H. (2001). *Multicultural education: A teacher's guide to linking context, process, and content* (2nd ed.). Upper Saddle River, NJ: Merrill/Prentice Hall.

Isenberg, J. P., & Jalongo, M. R. (2006). *Creative thinking and arts-based learning: Preschool through fourth grade* (4th ed.). Upper Saddle River, NJ: Merrill/Prentice Hall.

Jackman, H. L. (2005). *Early childhood curriculum: A child's connection to the world* (2nd ed.). Clifton Park, NY: Thomson Delmar Learning.

Kohn, A. (1993). *Punished by rewards: The trouble with gold stars, incentive plans, A's, and other bribes.* Boston: Houghton Mifflin.

Kostelnik, M., Whiren, A., Soderman, A., & Gregory, K. (2006). *Guiding children's social development: Theory to practice* (5th ed.). Clifton Park, NY: Thomson Delmar Learning.

Liess, E., & Ritchie, G. (1995). Using multiple intelligence theory to transform a first-grade health curriculum. *Early Childhood Education Journal, 23*(2), 71–79.

Lynch, R. G. (2005). Early childhood investment yields big payoff. San Francisco, CA: WestEd. [Online]. Available at *http:// www.wested/org/online_pubs/pp-05-02.pdf.*

McCombs, B. L. (1993). Learner-centered psychological principles for enhancing education: Applications in school settings. In L. A. Penner, G. M. Batsche, H. M. Knoff, & D. L. Nelson (Eds.), *The challenges in mathematics and science education: Psychology's response* (pp. 287–313). Washington, DC: American Psychological Association.

McCombs, B. L. (2001). What do we know about learners and learning? The learner-centered framework for bringing the educational system into balance. *Educational Horizons, 79*(4), 182–193.

McCombs, B. L. & Miller, L. (2007). *Learner-centered classroom practices and assessment: Maximizing student motivation, learning, and achievement.* Thousand Oaks, CA: Corwin Press.

McCombs, B. L., & Whisler, J. S. (1997). *The learner-centered classroom and school: Strategies for increasing student motivation and achievement.* San Francisco: Jossey-Bass.

National Association for the Education of Young Children. (1996). *Position statement on technology and young children—Ages three through eight.* Washington, DC: Author.

Parten, M. (1932). Social participation among preschool children. *Journal of Abnormal and Social Psychology,* 27(2), 243–269.

Piaget, J. (1970). Piaget's theory. In P. Mussen (Ed.), *Carmichael's manual of child psychology* (3rd ed., Vol.1, pp. 703–732). New York: Wiley.

Piaget, J. (1980). Foreword. In C. Kamii & R. Devries (Eds.), *Group games in early education* (p. vii). Washington, DC: National Association for the Education of Young Children.

Saarni, C. (2001). Emotional competence: A developmental perspective. In R. Bar-On & J. Parker (Eds.), *Handbook of emotional intelligence* (pp. 68–91). Cambridge, UK: Cambridge University Press.

Santrock, J. W. (2007). *Children* (9th ed.). Boston: McGraw-Hill.

Shonkoff, J., & Phillips, D. (Eds.). (2001). *Neurons to neighborhoods. The science of early childhood development.* Washington, DC: National Academy Press.

Smilansky, S., & Shefatya, L. (1990). *Facilitating play: A medium for promoting cognitive, socio-emotional, and academic development in young children.* Gaithersburg, MD: Psychosocial and Educational Publications.

Swaminathan, S., & Wright, J. (2003). Educational technology in the early and primary years. In J. P. Isenberg & M. R. Jalongo (Eds.), *Major trends and issues in early childhood education: Challenges, controversies, and insights* (2nd ed.) (pp. 136–149). New York: Teachers College Press.

Vygotsky, L. (1978). *Mind in society.* Cambridge, MA: Harvard University Press.

Wassermann, S. (2000). *Serious players in the primary classroom* (2nd ed.). New York: Teachers College Press.

Woolfolk, A. (2007). *Educational psychology* (10th ed). Boston: Allyn & Bacon.

Additional References

Dana Alliance for Brain Initiatives (2006). *Brainwork.* Online at *http://www.dana.org/books/press/brainwork*

Hechinger Institute on Education and the Media. (2005). New York: Teachers College Press.

Silver, H. F., Strong, R. W., & Perini, M. J. (2000). *So each may learn.* Integrating learning styles and multiple intelligences. Alexandria, VA: ASCD.

Children's Books

Flack, M. (1932). *Ask Mr. Bear.* New York: Macmillan.

Sendak, M. (1962). *Chicken soup with rice.* New York: Harper.

Zak, M. (1992). *Save my rain forest.* Volcano, CA: Volcano Press.

Software and Websites

www.techandyoungchildren.org/

www.netc.org/earlyconnections/index.html

Kidspiration. (2000). Inspiration Software.

Chapter 6

Allen, K. E., & Cowdery, G. E. (2005). *The exceptional child: Inclusion in early childhood education* (5th ed.). Clifton Park, NY: Thomson Delmar Learning.

Barnett, S. W., Hustedt, J., Robin, K., & Shulman, K. (2004). *The state of preschool: 2004 state preschool yearbook.* New Brunswick, NJ: National Institute for Early Education Research.

Best, S., Heller, K., & Bigge, J. (2005). *Teaching individuals with physical, health, or multiple disabilities* (5th ed.). Upper Saddle River, NJ: Merrill/Prentice Hall.

Black, P. (2001). Review of the research on the relationship between school design, student achievement, and student behavior. *Classroom Leadership Online, 1*(7).

Bredekamp, S., & Copple, C. (Eds.) (1997). *Developmentally appropriate practice in early childhood programs* (Rev. ed.). Washington, DC: National Association for the Education of Young Children.

Carnegie Task Force on Meeting the Needs of Young Children. (1994). *Starting points: Meeting the needs of our youngest children.* New York: Carnegie Corporation of New York.

Children's Defense Fund. (2005). *The state of America's children.* Washington, DC: Author.

Clarke-Stewart, A. (1987). Predicting child development from child care forms and features: The Chicago Study. In Phillips (Ed.), *Quality in child care: What does research tell us?* (pp. 57–59). Washington, DC: National Association for the Education of Young Children.

Clayton, M. K. (2001). *Classroom spaces that work.* Greenfield, MA: Northeast Foundation for Children.

Colker, L. J. (2005). *The cooking book: Fostering young children's learning and delight*. Washington, DC: National Association for the Education of Young Children.

Copple, C., & Bredekamp, S. (2006). *Basics of developmentally appropriate practices: An introduction for teachers of children 3 to 6*. Washington, DC: National Association for the Education of Young Children.

Corson, D. (2001). *Language, diversity, and education.* Mahwah, NJ: Lawrence Erlbaum.

Crumpacker, S. (1995). Using cultural information to create schools that work. In A. Meek (Ed.), *Designing places for learning* (pp. 31–42). Alexandria, VA: Association for Supervision and Curriculum Development.

Cryer, D., & Phillipsen, L. (1997). Quality details: A close-up look at child care program strengths and weaknesses. *Young Children, 52*(5), 51–61.

Curtis, D., & Carter, M. (2003). *Designs for living and learning: Transforming early childhood environments*. St. Paul, MN: Redleaf Press.

Diener, P. L. (2005). *Resources for educating children with diverse abilities* (4th ed.). Clifton Park, NY: Thomson Delmar Learning.

Division for Early Childhood (DEC), National Association for the Education of Young Children (NAEYC), & the Association of Teacher Educators (ATE). (2000). *Personnel standards for early education and early intervention: Guidelines for licensure in early childhood special education* [Online]. Available at *www.dec-sped.org.*

Duncan, G., Cook, T., & Hedges, L. (2006). Evidence of children's achievement. *Institute for Policy Research News, 28*(1). Chicago: Northwestern University.

Edwards, C., Gandini, L., & Forman, G. (Eds.). (1998). *The hundred languages of children: The Reggio Emilia approach—Advanced reflections* (2nd ed.). Greenwich CT: Ablex Publishing Company.

Essa, E. (2007). *Introduction to early childhood education* (4th ed.). Albany, NY: Delmar.

Firlik, R. (2006). Preparing school and classroom environments for active learning. *ACEI Focus on Elementary, 18*(3), 1–4.

Flynn, L., & Kieff, J. (2002). Including everyone in outdoor play. *Young Children, 57*(3), 20–26.

Fraser, S., & Gestwicki, C. (2002). *Authentic childhood: Exploring Reggio Emilia in the classroom*. Albany, NY: Delmar.

Frost, J. L., Brown, P. S., Sutterby, J. A., & Thornton, C. P. (2004). *The developmental benefits of playgrounds*. Olney, MD: Association for Childhood Education International.

Frye, M. A., & Mumpower, J. O. (2001). Lost in space? Design learning areas for today. *Dimensions of Early Childhood, 29*(2), 16–22.

Garreau, M., & Kennedy, C. (1991). Structure time and space to promote pursuit of learning in the primary grades. *Young Children, 64*(4), 46–51.

Gay, G. (2000). *Culturally responsive teaching: Theory, research, and practice*. New York: Teachers College Press.

Gronlund, G. (2006). *Make early learning standards come alive: Connecting your practice and curriculum to state guidelines*. St. Paul, MN: Redleaf Press.

Harms, T., Clifford, R., & Cryer, D. (2004). *Early childhood environment rating scale (ECRS)* (Rev. ed.). New York: Teachers College Press.

Harms, T., Cryer, D., & Clifford, R. (2004). *The early childhood, family day care, infant/toddler and school age environment rating scales* (Rev ed.). New York: Teachers College Press.

Hendrick, J., & Weissman, P. (2006). *The whole child: Developmental education for the early years* (8th ed.). Upper Saddle River, NJ: Merrill/Prentice Hall.

Hohman, M., & Weikart, D. (1995). *Educating young children: Active learning practices for preschool and child care programs.* Ypsilanti, MI: High/ScopePress.

Hull, K., Goldhaber, J., & Capone, A. (2002). *Opening doors: An introduction to inclusive early childhood education.* Boston: Houghton-Mifflin.

Isbell, R. T. (1995). *The complete learning center book.* Beltsville, MD: Gryphon House.

Isbell, R., & Exelby, B. (2001). *Early learning environments that work.* Beltsville, MD: Gryphon House.

Isenberg, J., & Jalongo, M. (2006). *Creative thinking and arts-based learning: Preschool through fourth grade* (4th ed.). Upper Saddle River, NJ: Merrill/Prentice Hall.

Jackman, H. L. (2005). *Early education curriculum: A child's connection to the world* (3rd ed.). Clifton Park, NY: Thomson Delmar Learning.

Jalongo, M. R. (2007). *Early childhood language arts* (4th ed.). Boston: Allyn & Bacon.

Johnson, J., Christie, J., & Wardle, F. (2005). *Play, development and early education*. Boston, MA: Allyn & Bacon.

Jones, E., & Prescott, E. (1978). *Dimensions of teaching—learning environments II: Focus on day care.* Pasadena, CA: Pacific Oaks College.

Kantrowitz, B., & McGinn, D. (1998). *The out-of-sync child.* New York: The Berkley Publishing Group.

Kohn, A. (2005). Unconditional teaching. *Educational Leadership, 63*(1), 20–24.

Kontos, S., & Wilcox-Herzog, A. (1997). Influences on children's competence in early childhood classrooms. *Early Childhood Research Quarterly, 12*(3), 247–262.

Kritchevsky, S., Prescott, E., & Walling, C. (1977). *Planning environments for young children: Physical space.* Washington, DC: National Association for the Education of Young Children.

Lackney, J. A. (2002). *Teacher design principles based on brain-based learning research. Design Share: The International Forum for Innovative Schools* [Online]. Available at *www.designshare.com/research/brain based lessons98.htm.*

Lowman, L., & Ruhmann, L. (1998). Simply sensational spaces: A multi "S" approach to toddler environments. *Young Children, 53*(3), 11–17.

Martinez-Beck, I., & Zaslow, M. (2006). *Critical issues in early childhood professional development*. Baltimore: Paul H. Brookes.

McLean, S. V. (1995). Creating the learning environment: Context for living and learning. In J. Moyer (Ed.), *Selecting educational equipment and materials for school and home.* Wheaton, MD: Association for Childhood Education International.

McWilliams, R., Wolery, M., & Odom, S. (2001). Instructional perspectives in inclusive preschool classrooms. In M. J. Guralnick (Ed.), *Early childhood inclusion: Focus on change.* Baltimore: Paul H. Brookes.

Montgomery, W. (2001). Creating culturally responsive, inclusive classrooms. *Teaching Exceptional Children, 33*(1), 4–9.

Moore, G. T., & Lackney, J. A. (1995). Design patterns for American schools: Responding to the reform movement. In A. Meek (Ed.), *Designing places for learning* (pp. 11–22). Alexandria, VA: Association for Supervision and Curriculum Development.

National Academy of Early Childhood Programs. (1998). *Accreditation criteria and procedures of the National Academy of Early Childhood programs.* Washington, DC: National Association for the Education of Young Children.

National Association for the Education of Young Children. (2005a). Embracing diversity in early childhood settings. *Young Children, 60*(6).

National Association for the Education of Young Children. (2005b). Environments. *Young Children, 60*(3).

National Association for the Education of Young Children. (2006). Nutrition and fitness. *Young Children, 61*(3), 10–58.

National Institute of Child Health and Development Early Child Care Research Network. (2002). *Classroom observation system—1* (COS-1). Washington, DC: Author.

Noddings, N. (1992). *The challenge to care in schools.* New York: Teachers College Press.

Pianta, R. C., LaParo, K. M., & Hamre, B. K. (2005). Classroom assessment scoring system (CLASS). Unpublished measure, University of Virginia.

Picar, R. (2006). Physical fitness and the early childhood curriculum. *Young Children, 61*(3), 12–18.

Readdick, C. A. (2006). Managing noise in early childhood settings. *Dimensions of Early Childhood, 34*(1), 17–22.

Rivkin, M. (2002). Outdoor settings for play and learning. *Young Children, 57*(3), 8–9.

Robin, K., Frede, E., & Barnett, S. (2006). NIEER Working Paper–Is More Better? *The Effects of Full-Day vs Half-Day Preschool on Early School Achievement.* National Institute for Early Education Research, New Brunswick, NJ: Rutgers, The State University.

Sanoff, H. (1995). *Creating environments for young children.* Mansfield, OH: BookMasters.

Swiniarski, L., & Breitborde, M. (2003). *Educating the global village: Including the young child in the world* (2nd ed.). Upper Saddle River, NJ: Merrill/Prentice Hall.

Tegano, D., Moran, J., DeLong, A., Brickman, J., & Ramsisini, K. (1996). Designing classroom spaces: Making the most of time. *Early Childhood Education Journal, 24*(3), 191–194.

Tiedt, P., & Tiedt, I. (2005). *Multicultural teaching* (7th ed.). Boston, MA: Allyn & Bacon.

Trawick-Smith, J. (1992). The classroom environment affects children's play and development. *Dimensions, 20*(2), 27–31.

U.S. Department of Education. (1994). *Goals 2000: Educate America Act.* Washington, DC: Author.

Villegas, A. M., & Lucas, T. (2002). *Educating culturally responsive teachers: A cohort approach*. Albany, NY: State University of New York.

Wald, P., Morris, L., & Abraham, M. (1996). Three keys for successful circle time: Responding to children with diverse abilities. *Dimensions of Early Childhood, 24*(4), 26–29.

Wassermann, S. (2000). *Serious players in the early childhood classroom* (2nd ed.). New York: Teachers College Press.

Wellhousen, K. (2002). *Outdoor play every day.* Albany, NY: Delmar.

White, R. (2006). *The impact of density and the definition and ratio of activity centers on children in childcare classrooms* [Online]. Available at *www.whitehutchinson.com/children/articles.ration.shtml.*

Williams, K. C., & Cooney, M. H. (2006). Young children and social justice. *Young Children, 61*(2), 75–82.

Wortham, S. (2006). *Early childhood curriculum: Developmental bases for learning and teaching* (4th ed.). Upper Saddle River, NJ: Merrill/Prentice Hall.

Children's Books

Carle, E. (1991). *A house for hermit crab.* New York: Simon and Schuster, Inc.

Additional References

American Alliance for Health, Physical Education, Recreation, and Dance (2006a). *Active start: A statement of physical activity guidelines for children birth to five years.* Reston, VA: Author.

American Alliance for Health, Physical Education, Recreation, and Dance (2006b). *Physical activity for children: A statement of guidelines for children 5–12,* (2nd ed.). Reston, VA: Author.

Chapter 7

Allington, R. (2002). What I've learned about effective reading instruction. *Phi Delta Kappan, 83*(10), 740–747.

ASCD Advisory Panel on Improving Student Achievement. (1995). Barriers to good instruction. In R. W. Cole (Ed.), *Educating everybody's children: Diverse teaching strategies for diverse learners* (pp. 9–20). Alexandria, VA: Association for Supervision and Curriculum Development.

Ayers, W. (1996). *To become a teacher: Making a difference in children's lives.* New York: Teachers College Press.

Bandura, A. (1997). *Self-efficacy: The exercise of control.* New York: Freeman.

Banks, J., & Banks, C. (2005). *Multicultural education: Issues and perspectives* (5th ed.). John Wiley & Sons.

Barnett, W. S. (1995). Long-term effects of early childhood programs on cognitive and school outcomes. *The Future of Children, 5*(3), 25–50.

Benham, A. (2006). One teacher, 20 preschoolers, and a goldfish: Environmental awareness, emergent curriculum, and documentation. *Young Children, 61*(2), 28–34.

Bowlby, J. (1999). *Attachment and loss* (2nd ed.). New York: Basic Books.

Bowman, B. T. (2006). Standards at the heart of educational equity. *Young Children, 61*(5), 42–48.

Bredekamp, S., & Copple, C. (Eds.). (1997). *Developmentally appropriate practice in early childhood programs* (Rev. ed.). Washington, DC: National Association for the Education of Young Children.

Bredekamp, S., & Rosegrant, T. (Eds.). (1992). *Reaching potentials: Appropriate curriculum and assessment for young children* (Vol. 1). Washington, DC: National Association for the Education of Young Children.

Bredekamp, S., & Rosegrant, T. (Eds.). (1995). *Reaching potentials: Transforming early childhood curriculum and assessment* (Vol. 2). Washington, DC: National Association for the Education of Young Children.

Capps, R., Fix, M., Ost, J., Reardon-Anderson, J., & Passel, J. (2005). *The health and well-being of young children of immigrants*. Washington, DC: Urban Institute.

Carnegie Corporation of New York. (1996). *Years of promise: A comprehensive learning strategy for America's children.* New York: Author.

Chaille, C., & Britain, L. (2003). *The young child as scientist: A constructivist approach to early childhood science education* (3rd ed.). New York: Longman.

Charlesworth, R., & Lind, K. (2007). *Math and science for young children* (5th ed.). Clifton Park, NY: Thomson Delmar Learning.

Commission on Behavioral and Social Sciences and Education. (2001). *Early childhood development and learning: New knowledge for policy.* Washington, DC: National Academy Press.

Copple, C., & Bredekamp, S. (2006). *Basics of developmentally appropriate practice. An introduction for teachers of children 3 to 6*. Washington, DC: National Association for the Education of Young Children.

Dewey, J. (1933). *How we think.* Boston: D.C. Heath.

Dewey, J. (1938). *Experience and education.* New York: Collier Books.

Dodge, D., Colker, L., and Heroman, C. (2002). *The creative curriculum for preschool* (4th ed.). Washington, DC: Teaching Strategies.

Edwards, C., Gandini, L., & Forman, G. (Eds.). (1998). *The hundred languages of children: The Reggio Emilia approach—Advanced reflections* (2nd ed.). Greenwich, CT: Ablex.

Edwards, V. B. (2002). Quality Counts 2002: Building Blocks for Success: State Efforts in Early Childhood Education. *Education Week 21*(17). [Eric Document: ED 473626].

Eggen, P., & Kauchak, D. (2007). *Educational psychology: Windows on classrooms* (7th ed.). Upper Saddle River, NJ: Merrill/Prentice Hall.

Falk, B. (2000). *The heart of the matter: Using standards and assessment to learn.* Portsmouth, NH: Heinemann.

Fleener, C. E., & Bucker, K. T. (2003/2004). Linking reading, science, and fiction books. *Childhood Education, 80*(2), 76–83.

Gay, G. (2004). The importance of multicultural education. *Educational Leadership, 61*(4), 30–35.

Glatthorn, A., Boschee, F., & Whitehead, B. (2006). *Curriculum leadership: Development and implementation*. Thousand Oaks, CA: Sage.

Gronlund, G. (2006). *Make early learning standards come alive: Connecting your practice and curriculum to state guidelines*. St. Paul, MN: Redleaf Press.

Hendrick, J., & Weissman, P. (2006). *The whole child: Developmental education for the early years* (8th ed.). Upper Saddle River, NJ: Merrill/Prentice Hall.

Henson, K. (2006). *Curriculum planning: Integrating multiculturalism, conservatism and education reform* (3rd ed.). Long Grove, IL: Waveland Press.

Heroman, C., & Copple, C. (2006). Teaching in the kindergarten year. In D. Gullo (Ed.), *Teaching and learning in the kindergarten year.* Washington, DC: National Association for the Education of Young Children.

Hull, K., Goldhaber, J., & Capone, A. (2002). *Opening doors: An introduction to inclusive early childhood education.* Boston: Houghton Mifflin.

Hyson, M., Copple, C., & Jones, J. (2006). *Early childhood development and education.* In A. Reinninger & I. E. Sigel (Eds.), *Child psychology in practice* (6th ed., Vol. 4, pp. 30–56). Hoboken, NJ: John Wiley.

Hyun, E. (2003). What does the No Child Left Behind Act mean to early childhood teacher educators? A call for a collective professional rejoinder. *Early Childhood Education Journal, 31*(2), 119–125.

Jackman, H. L. (2005). *Early childhood curriculum: A child's connection to the world* (3rd ed.). Albany, NY: Delmar.

Jackson, P. (1968). *Life in classrooms.* New York: Holt, Rinehart, and Winston.

Jones, E., & Nimmo, J. (1994). *Emergent curriculum.* Washington, DC: National Association for the Education of Young Children.

Katz, L. G., & Chard, S. C. (2000). *Engaging children's minds: The project approach* (2nd ed.). Stamford, CT: Ablex.

Kilpatrick, W. H. (1936). *Remaking the curriculum.* New York: Newson & Co.

Kostelnik, M., Soderman, A., & Whiren, A. (2007). *Developmentally appropriate curriculum: Best practices in early childhood education* (4th ed.). Upper Saddle River, NJ: Merrill/Prentice Hall.

Landry, S. H. (2005). *Effective early childhood programs: Turning knowledge into action*. Houston, TX: University of Texas, Health Series Center.

Lazar, L., & Darlington, R. (1982). Lasting effects of early childhood education: A report from the consortium for longitudinal studies. *Monographs of the Society for Research in Child Development, 47*(2–3, Serial No. 195). Chicago: University of Chicago Press.

Levine, M. (2002). *A mind at a time.* New York: Simon & Schuster.

Lewin, T. (2006). *The need to invest in children.* New York Times, January 11, 2006.

Meisels, S., & Atkins-Burnett, S. (2004, January). The Head Start national reporting system. A critique. *Young Children Beyond the Journal*.

Montgomery, W. (2001). Creating culturally responsive, inclusive environments. *Teaching Exceptional Children, 33*(4), 4–9.

Morrow, L. M. (2005). *Literacy development in the early years: Helping children read and write* (5th ed). Boston: Allyn & Bacon.

National Association for the Education of Young Children. (2001). *NAEYC standards for early childhood professional preparation: Baccalaureate or initial licensure level.* Washington, DC: Author.

National Association for the Education of Young Children. (2003). *Early learning standards creating the conditions for success.* Joint position statement of NAEYC and the National Association of Early Childhood Specialists in State Department of Education. Executive summary. *Young Children, 58*(1), 69–70.

National Board for Professional Teaching Standards. (2001). *Early childhood generalist standards for National Board certification* (2nd ed.). Arlington, VA: Author.

National Commission on Excellence in Education. (1983). *A nation at risk: The imperatives for educational reform.* Washington, DC: U.S. Government Printing Office. CERIC Document Reproduction Service (ED 279063).

National Study Group for the Affirmative Development of Academic Ability. (2004). The students reaching the top: Strategies for closing the achievement gap [Electronic version]. Naperville, IL: Learning Point Associates.

Palmer, P. (1998). *The courage to teach: Exploring the inner landscape of a teacher's life*. San Francisco: Jossey-Bass.

Piaget, J. (1965). *The moral judgment of the child.* New York: Free Press.

Posner, G. (2004). *Analyzing the curriculum* (3rd ed). New York: McGraw-Hill.

Raines, S. R., & Johnston, J. (2003). Developmental appropriateness: New contexts and challenges. In J. P. Isenberg & M. R. Jalongo (Eds.), *Major trends and issues in early childhood education. Challenges, controversies, and insights* (2nd ed., pp. 83–96). New York: Teachers College Press.

Raver, C., & Zigler, E. (2004, January). Another step back. Assessing readiness in Head Start. *Beyond the Journal NAEYC*.

Ryan, K., & Cooper, J. (2007). *Those who can, teach* (11th ed.). Boston: Houghton Mifflin.

Schweinhart, L. J., & Weikart, D. P. (1996). *Lasting differences: The High/Scope preschool curriculum comparison study through age 23.* Monographs of the High/Scope Educational Research Foundation, no. 12. Ypsilanti, MI: High Scope Press.

Scully, P., Seefeldt, C., & Barbour, D. (2003). *Development continuity across the preschool and primary grades: Implications for teachers* (2nd ed). Olney, MD: Association for Childhood Education International.

Seefeldt, C. (2005a). *How to work with standards in the early childhood classroom.* New York: Teachers College Press.

Seefeldt, C. (2005b). *Social studies for the preschool/primary child* (7th ed.). Upper Saddle River, NJ: Merrill/Prentice Hall.

Seitz, H. (2006). The plan: Building on children's interests. *Young Children, 61*(2), 36–41.

Squires, D. (2005). *Aligning and balancing the standards-based curriculum.* Thousand Oaks, CA: Corwin Press.

Stipek, D. (2006). Accountability comes to preschool: Can we make it work for young children? *Phi Delta Kappan, 87*(10), 740–747.

Thomas, M. D., & Bainbridge, W. (2002). No child left behind: Facts and fallacies. *Phi Delta Kappan, 83*(10), 781–782.

Tiedt, P., & Tiedt, I. (2005). *Multicultural teaching: A handbook of activities, information, and resources* (7th ed.). Boston: Allyn & Bacon.

Tomlinson, C., & McTighe, J. (2006). *Integrating differentiated instruction and understanding by design: Connecting content and kids.* Alexandria, VA, ASCD.

U.S. Census Bureau. (2004). Data set: 2004. American Community Survey. Washington, DC: Author.

Vygotsky, L. (1978). *Mind in society. The development of higher order psychological processes.* Cambridge, MA: Harvard University Press.

Work, B. *Learning through the eyes of a child.* North Carolina State Department of Public Education. Urbana. IL: ERIC Clearinghouse [ERIC Document Reproduction Service No. ED 472193].

Wortham, S. C. (2006). *Early childhood curriculum: Developmental bases for learning and teaching* (4th ed.). Upper Saddle River, NJ: Merrill/Prentice Hall.

Children's Books Cited

Ardley, N. (1991). *The science book of magnets.* New York: Harcourt, Brace, Jovanovich.

Burns, D. (1995). *Trees, leaves, and bark.* Minnesota: Northwood Press.

Gibbons, G. (2002). *Tell me tree: All about trees for kids*. Boston: Little Brown.

Grifalconi, A. (1986). *The village of round and square houses.* Boston: Little Brown.

Hoban, T. (1986) *Shapes, shapes, shapes*. New York: Greenwillow.

Hoberman, M. A. (1978). *A house is a house for me.* New York: Scholastic.

Hutchins, P. (1968). *Rosie's walk*. New York: Simon & Schuster.

Rowe, J., & Perham, M. (1994). *Amazing magnets.* London: Watts.

Spier, P. (1978). *Noah's ark.* New York: Doubleday.

Chapter 8

Arends, R. (2007). *Learning to teach* (7th ed.). New York: McGraw-Hill.

Berliner, D. C. (1986). In pursuit of the expert pedagogue. *Educational Researcher, 15*(7), 5–13.

Borko, H., Bellamy, M. L., & Sanders, L. (1992). A cognitive analysis in science instruction by expert and novice teachers. In T. Russell & H. Mundby (Eds.), *Teachers and teaching: From classrooms to reflection* (pp. 49–70). London: Falmer Press.

Bowman, B., Donovan, S., & Burns, M. S. (Eds.). (2000). *Eager to learn: Educating our preschoolers.* Washington, DC: National Academy Press.

Bredekamp, S., & Copple, C. (Eds.). (1997). *Developmentally appropriate practice in early childhood programs* (Rev. ed.). Washington, DC: National Association for the Education of Young Children.

Bredekamp, S., & Rosegrant, T. (1995). *Reaching potentials II.* Washington, DC: National Association for the Education of Young Children.

Clark, C., & Dunn, S. (1991). Second generation research on teacher planning. In H. C. Waxman & H. J. Walberg (Eds.), *Effective teaching: Current research* (pp. 183–210). Berkeley, CA: McCuthan.

Clark, C. M., & Peterson, P. L. (1986). Teachers' thought processes. In M. C. Wittrock (Ed.), *Handbook of research on teaching* (3rd ed., pp. 198–243). Berkeley, CA: McCutchan.

Committee for Economic Development. (2006, July 25). *Economic benefits of investing in preschool.* Washington, DC: Author.

Cooper, J. M. (Ed.). (2006). *Classroom teaching skills* (8th ed.). New York: Houghton Mifflin.

Copple, C., & Bredekamp, S. (2006). *Developmentally appropriate practice: An introduction for teachers of children 3 to 6.* Washington, DC: National Association for the Education of Young Children.

Feeney, S., Christensen, D., & Moravcik, E. (2006). *Who am I in the lives of children?* (7th ed.). Upper Saddle River, NJ: Merrill/Prentice Hall.

Freiberg, H. J., & Driscoll, A. (2005). *Universal teaching strategies* (4th ed.). Boston Heights, MA: Allyn & Bacon.

Gardner, H. (1993). *Frames of mind: The theory of multiple intelligences* (2nd ed.). New York: Basic Books.

Gordon, A., & Williams-Browne, K. (2007). *Beginning essentials in early childhood education* (6th ed.). Albany, NY: Delmar.

Gronlund, G. (2006). *Make early learning standards come alive: Connecting your practice to state guidelines.* St. Paul, MN: Redleaf Press.

Hansen, D. T. (1995). *The call to teach.* New York: Teachers College Press.

Hiebert, J., Morris, A., Berk, D. & Jansen, A. (2007). Preparing teachers to learn from teaching. *Journal of Teacher Education, 58*(1), 47–61.

Hodgkinson, H. (2001). Educational demographics: What teachers should know. *Educational Leadership, 58*(4), 6–11.

Jackman, H. (2005). *Early education curriculum: A child's connection to the world* (3rd ed). Clifton Park, NY: Thomson Delmar Learning.

Jensen, R., & Kiley, T. (2005). *Teaching, leading, and learning on PreK–8 settings: Strategies for success* (2nd ed.). New York: Houghton Mifflin Company.

Jones, E., & Nimmo, J. (1994). *Emergent curriculum.* Washington, DC: National Association for the Education of Young Children.

Katz, L., & Chard, S. (2000). *Engaging children's minds: The project approach* (2nd ed.). Stamford, CT: Ablex.

Kauchak, D. P., & Eggen, P. D. (2007). *Learning and teaching: Research-based methods* (5th ed.). New York: Allyn & Bacon.

Keefe, J., & Jenkins, J. (2002). Personalized instruction. *Phi Delta Kappan, 83*(6), 440–448.

Kostelnik, M. (Ed.). (1991). *Teaching young children using themes.* Glenview, IL: GoodYear Books.

Kostelnik, M., Soderman, A., & Whiren, A. (2007). *Developmentally appropriate curriculum: Best practices in early childhood education* (4th ed.). Upper Saddle River, NJ: Merrill/Prentice Hall.

Lawler-Prince, D., & Jones, C. (1997). Development of preservice early childhood education teacher's instructional planning. *Journal of Early Childhood Teacher Education, 18*(3), 77–85.

National Association for the Education of Young Children. (2005). *NAEYC Early Childhood Program Standards and Accreditation Criteria: The mark of quality in early childhood education.* Washington, DC: Author. [Online]. Available at *www.naeyc.org/accreditation/next_era.asp.*

National Association of Elementary School Principals. (1998). *Early childhood education and the elementary school principal: Standards for quality programs.* Alexandria, VA: Author.

National Center for Early Development and Learning. (2002). Fact sheet: Transition to kindergarten. *Early Childhood Research & Policy Briefs, 2*(2). Washington, DC: National Institute on Early Childhood Development and Education.

Perkins, D., & Blythe, T. (1994). Putting understanding up front. *Educational Leadership, 51*, 4–7.

Price, K. M., & Nelson, K. L. (2003). *Daily planning for today's classroom. A guide for writing lesson & activity plans* (2nd ed.). Belmont, CA: Wadsworth.

Ream, R. (2005). *Uprooting children: Mobility, social capital, and Mexican American underachievement.* New York: LFB Scholarly Publishing, LLC.

Seefeldt, C. (2005a). *Social studies for the preschool/primary child* (7th ed.). Upper Saddle River, New Jersey: Merrill/Prentice Hall.

Seefeldt, C. (2005b). *How to work with standards in the early childhood classroom.* New York: Teachers College press.

Seefeldt, C., & Galper, A. (2006). *Active experiences for active children: Social studies* (2nd ed.).Upper Saddle River, New Jersey: Merrill/Prentice Hall.

Shambaugh, N., & Magliaro, S. (2006). *Instructional design.* New York: Allyn & Bacon.

Silver, H. F., Strong, R. W., & Perini, M. J. (2000). *So each may learn.* Alexandria, VA: Association for Supervision and Curriculum Development.

Tiedt, P., & Tiedt, I. (2005). *Multicultural teaching: A handbook of activities, information, and resources* (7th ed). Boston: Allyn & Bacon.

Tomlinson, C., & Cunningham-Eidson, C. (2003). *Differentiation in practice: A resource guide for differentiating curriculum. Grades K–5.* Alexandria, VA: Association for Supervision and Curriculum Development.

Trealese, J. (2006). *The read aloud handbook* (6th ed.). New York: Penguin Group.

Woolfolk, A. (2007). *Educational psychology* (10th ed). New York: Allyn & Bacon.

Additional References

NAEYC. (1998). Linguistic and cultural diversity position statement.

National Association for the Education of Young Children, 2005

Social studies: A way to integrate curriculum for four- and five-year-olds. VHS. Beltsville, MD: Gryphon House.

Children's Books Cited

Beal, K, (1991). *I love my family.* Boston: Addison Wesley.

Curtis, J. L. (1996). *Tell me again about the night I was born.* New York: Harper Collins.

Mayer, M. (1994). *Just Grandma and me.* New York: Random House.

Chapter 9

Alexander, K. L., Entwisle, D. R., & Olson, L. S. (2001). School achievement and inequality: A seasonal perspective. - *Educational Evaluation and Public Policy Analysis, 23*(2), 171–191.

Benson, T. R., & Smith, L. J. (1998). Portfolios in first grade: Four teachers learn to use alternative assessment. *Early Childhood Education Journal, 25*(3), 173–180.

Borgia, E. (1996). Learning through projects. *Scholastic Early Childhood, 10*(6), 22–28.

Brainard, M. B. (1997). Assessment as a way of seeing. In A. L. Goodwin (Ed.). *Assessment for equity and inclusion* (pp. 163–180). New York: Routledge.

Bredekamp, S., & Rosegrant, T. (Eds.). (1992). *Reaching potentials: Appropriate curriculum and assessment for young children.* Washington, DC: National Association for the Education of Young Children.

Carter, M., & Curtis, D. (1996). *Spreading the news: Sharing stories of early childhood education.* St. Paul, MN: Redleaf Press.

Chard, S. C. (1996). Documentation: Displaying children's learning. *Scholastic Early Childhood Today, 11*(1), 56–58.

Chard, S. C., Katz, L., & Genishi, C. (1996). A profile of every child. *Scholastic Early Childhood Today, 11*(1), 55–62.

Cizek, C. J., & Burg, S. S. (2006). *Addressing test anxiety in a high-stakes environment: Strategies for classrooms and schools.* Thousand Oaks, CA: Corwin.

Comer, J. P. (2006, January 5). Our mission: It takes more than tests to prepare the young for success in life. *Education Week,* pp. 59–61.

Curtis, D., & Carter, M. (2000). *The art of awareness: How observation can transform your teaching*. St. Paul, MN: Redleaf.

Dale-Easley, S., & Mitchell, K. (2003). *Portfolios matter: What, where, when, why and how to use them.* Markham, Ontario, Canada: Pembroke.

Darling-Hammond, L. (2000). Teacher quality and student achievement: A review of state policy evidence. *Education Policy Analysis Archives, 6*(1), 162–183.

Darling-Hammond, L. (2006). *Powerful teacher education: Lessons from exemplary programs.* San Francisco: Jossey-Bass.

Diamond, K. E., Reagan, A. J., & Bandyk, J. E. (2000). Parents' conceptions of kindergarten readiness: Relationships with race, ethnicity, and development. *Journal of Educational Research, 94,* 93–100.

Editors of *Education Week.* (2002, January 10). *Quality counts 2002: Building blocks for success* [Special issue].

Educational Testing Service (ETS). (2003). *Understanding standards-based assessment*. Pathwise series. Princeton, NJ: Author.

Falk, B. (2001). Professional learning through assessment. In A. Lieberman & L. Miller (Eds.). *Teachers caught in the action: Professional development that matters* (pp. 118–140). New York: Teachers College Press.

Fewell, R. R. (2000). Assessment of young children with special needs: Foundations for tomorrow. *Topics in Early Childhood Special Education, 20*(1), 38–42.

Fleet, A., Patterson, C., & Robertson, J. (2006). *Insights: Behind early childhood pedagogical documentation.* Castle Hill, New South Wales, Australia: Pademelon.

Gandini, L., & Goldhaber, J. (2001). Two reflections about documentation. In L. Gandini & C. P. Edwards (Eds.).

Bambini: The Italian approach to infant/toddler care (pp. 124–145). New York: Teachers College Press.

Gandini, L. & Kaminsky, J. A. (2004). Reflections on the relationship between documentation and assessment in the American context: An interview with Brenda Fyfe. *Innovations in Early Education: The International Reggio Exchange, 11*(1), 5–17.

Garcia, E. (2002). *Student cultural diversity: Understanding and meeting the challenge.* Boston: Houghton Mifflin.

Genishi, C. (1996). Portfolios: Collecting children's work. *Scholastic Early Childhood Today, 11*(1), 60–61.

Glickman, C. D., & Alridge, D. P. (2001). Going public: The imperative of public education in the 21st century. In A. Lieberman & L. Miller (Eds.), *Teachers caught in the action: Professional development that matters* (pp. 12–22). New York: Teachers College Press.

Groark, C. J., Mehaffie, K. E., McCall, R., & Greenberg, M. T. (2006). *Evidence-based practices and programs for early childhood care and education.* Thousand Oaks, CA: Corwin Press.

Gullo, D. F. (2005). *Understanding assessment and evaluation in early childhood education* (2nd ed.). New York: Teachers College Press.

Gullo, D. F. (2006a). Alternative means of assessing children's learning in early childhood classrooms. In B. Spodek & O. N. Saracho (Eds.), *Handbook of research on the education of young children* (2nd ed., pp. 443–456). Mahwah, NJ: Erlbaum.

Gullo, D. F. (2006b). Assessment in kindergarten. In D. F. Gullo (Ed.), *K today: Teaching and learning in the kindergarten year* (pp. 138–147). Washington, DC: National Association for the Education of Young Children.

Head Start Bureau. (2003). The Head Start child outcomes framework. *Head Start Bulletin, 76,* 21–32. [Online]. Available at *www.headstartinfo.org/pdf/Outcomes.pdf.*

Helm, J. H., & Helm, A. (2006). *Building support for your school: How to use children's work to show learning.* New York: Teachers College Press.

International Reading Association/National Council of Teachers of English. (1995). *Standards for the assessment of reading and writing.* Newark, DE: International Reading Association.

Jalongo, M. R. (1996). Editorial: Looking beyond the labels. *Early Childhood Education Journal, 23*(3), 187–188.

Jalongo, M. R., & Isenberg, J. P. (1995). *Teachers' stories: From personal narrative to professional insight.* San Francisco, CA: Jossey-Bass.

Jalongo, M. R., & Stamp, L. N. (1997). *The arts in children's lives: Aesthetic experiences in early childhood.* Boston: Allyn & Bacon.

Jensen, E. (2006). *Enriching the brain: How to maximize every learner's potential.* San Francisco: Jossey-Bass.

Johnston, P. H., & Rogers, R. (2001). Early literacy development: The case for "informed assessment." In S. B. Neuman & D. K. Dickinson (Eds.), *Handbook of early literacy research* (pp. 377–389). New York: The Guilford Press.

Kagan, S. L., Carroll, J., Comer, J. P., & Scott-Little, C. (2006). Alignment: A missing link in early childhood transitions? *Young Children, 61*(5), 26–32.

Katz, L. (1993). *Five perspectives on quality in early childhood programs.* Urbana, IL: ERIC Clearinghouse on Elementary and Early Childhood Education. [ERIC Document Reproduction Service No. ED 351–148].

Kirylo, J. D. (2006). Preferential option for the poor: Making a pedagogical choice. *Childhood Education, 82*(5), 266–270.

Kroeger, J., & Cardy, T. (2006). Documentation: A hard to reach place. *Early Childhood Education Journal, 33*(6), 389–398.

MacDonald, S. (1997). *The portfolio and its use: A road map for assessment.* Little Rock, AR: Southern Early Childhood Association.

Madaus, G. F., & Tan, A. D. A. (1993). The growth of assessment. In G. Cawelti (Ed.), *Challenges and achievements of American education* (pp. 53–79). Alexandria, VA: Association for Supervision and Curriculum Development.

McAfee, O., & Leong, D. J. (2007). *Assessing and guiding young children's development and learning* (4th ed.). Boston: Allyn & Bacon.

McConnell, S. R. (2000). Assessment in early intervention and special education: Building on the past to project into our future. *Topics in Early Childhood Special Education, 20*(1), 43–48.

McLean, M. (2000). *Conducting child assessments.* CLAS Technical Report No. 2. Champaign: University of Illinois at Urbana-Champaign, Early Childhood Research Institute on Culturally and Linguistically Appropriate Services.

McTighe, J. (1997). What happens between assessment? *Educational Leadership, 54*(4), 6–12.

Meisels, S., & Atkins-Burnett, S. (2004). The Head Start National Reporting System. A Critique. *Young Children Beyond the Journal,* January 2004. [Online]. Available at *http:// journal.naeyc.org/btj/200401/meisels.pdf*

Meisels, S. J. (1995). *Performance assessment in early childhood education: The work sampling system.* Urbana, IL: ERIC Clearinghouse [ERIC Digest No. EDO-PS-95–6].

Mindes, G. (2007). *Assessing young children* (3rd ed.). Upper Saddle River, NJ: Merrill/Prentice Hall.

National Association for the Education of Young Children. (2003). *Early childhood curriculum, assessment, and program evaluation: Building an effective, accountable system in programs for children birth through age 8* [Online]. Position statement. Washington, DC: Author. Available at *www.naeyc.org/about/positions/cape.asp.*

National Association for the Education of Young Children. (2005). *NAEYC program standards and accreditation criteria: The mark of quality in childhood education* [Online]. Washington, DC: Author. Available at *www.naeyc.or/accreditation/standards.*

National Association for the Education of Young Children & National Association of Early Childhood Specialists in State Departments of Education. (2003). *Joint position statement. Early childhood curriculum, assessment, and program evaluation: Building an effective, accountable system in programs for children birth through age 8.* [Online]. Available at *www.naeyc.org/resources/position_statements/pscape.asp.*

Neill, M. (2001). Leaving many children behind. *Dissent, 36*(4), 12–18.

New, R. (2003). Reggio Emilia: New ways to think about schooling. *Educational Leadership, 60*(7), 34–38.

Nieto, S. (2005). *Why we tech.* New York: Teachers College Press.

Nilsen, B. A. (1999). *Week by week: Plans for observing and recording young children.* Albany, NY: Delmar.

Perrone, V. (1991). On standardized testing. *Childhood Education, 67,* 131–142.

Perrone, V. (1997). Toward an education of consequence: Connecting assessment, teaching, and learning. In A. L. Goodman (Ed.), *Assessment for equity and inclusion* (pp. 305–315). New York: Routledge.

Popham, W. J. (2000). *Testing! Testing! What every parent should know about school tests.* Boston: Allyn & Bacon.

Popham, W. J. (2004). *Classroom assessment: What teachers need to know* (4th ed.). Boston: Allyn & Bacon.

Power, B. M. (1996). *Taking note: Improving your observational notetaking.* York, ME: Stenhouse.

Project Zero. (2003). *Making teaching visible: Documenting individual and group learning as professional development.* Cambridge, MA: Project Zero. Available from the NAEYC.

Puckett, M. B., & Black, J. K. (2000). *Authentic assessment of the young child: Celebrating development and learning* (2nd ed.). Upper Saddle River, NJ: Merrill/Prentice Hall.

Rinaldi, C. (1998). Project curriculum constructed through documentation—*progettazione*: An interview with Lella Gandini. In C. Edwards, L. Gandini, & G. Forman (Eds.), *The hundred languages of children: The Reggio Emilia approach—Advanced reflections* (2nd ed., pp. 113–125). Greenwich, CT: Ablex.

Rinaldi, C. (2001). Documentation and assessment: What is the relationship? In Project Zero (Ed.), *Making learning visible: Children as individual and group learners* (pp. 78–93). Reggio Emilia, Italy: Reggio Children.

Rinaldi, C. (2004). The relationship between documentation and assessment. *Innovations in Early Education: The International Reggio Exchange, 11*(1), 1–4.

Rose, L. C., & Gallup, A. M. (2007). 38th Annual Phi Delta Kappa/Gallup Poll of the Public's Attitudes Toward the Public Schools. Retrieved February 15, 2007. [Online]. Available at from http://www.pdkintl.org/kappan/ k0609pol.htm#teachers.

Rotbert, I. C. (2001). A self-fulfilling prophecy. *Phi Delta Kappan, 83*(2), 170–171.

Salvia, J., & Yesseldyke, J. E. (1995). *Assessment* (6th ed.). Boston: Houghton Mifflin.

Seidel, S. (2003). Appendix D: Collaborative assessment conference protocol. In Project Zero, Cambridgeport School, Cambridgeport Children's Center, Ezra H. Baker School, & John Simpkins School (Eds.), *Making teaching visible: Documenting individual and group learning as professional development* (p. 85). Cambridge, MA: Project Zero.

Smith, Y., & Goodwin, A. L. (1997). The democratic, child-centered classroom: Provisioning for a vision. In A. L. Goodwin (Ed.), *Assessment for equity and inclusion* (pp. 101–120). New York: Routledge.

Strickland, D. S. (2006). Language and literacy in kindergarten. In D. F. Gullo (Ed.), *K today: Teaching and learning in the kindergarten year* (pp. 73–84). Washington, DC: National Association for the Education of Young Children.

Tolbert, L., & Theobald, P. (2006). Finding their place in the community: Urban education outside the classroom. *Childhood Education, 82*(5), 271–274.

Turner, T., & Krechevsky, M. (2003). Who are the teachers? Who are the learners? *Educational Leadership, 60*(7), 40–43.

U.S. Department of Education. (2004). *No Child Left Behind: A toolkit for teachers* (Rev. ed.). Jessup, MD: Education Publications Center.

U.S. Government Accountability Office (GAO). (2005). Head Start: Further development could allow results of new test to be used for decision making [Online]. Available at *www.gao.gov/new.items/d05343.pdf.*

Vecchi, V. (2001). The curiosity to understand. In C. Guidici, C. Rinaldi, & M. Krechevsky (Eds.), *Making learning visible: Children as individual and group learners in Italy*. Rome, Italy: Reggio Children.

Wiggins, G. (1998). *Educative assessment: Designing assessments to inform and improve student performance.* San Francisco, CA: Jossey-Bass.

Wortham, S. (2005). *Assessment in early childhood education* (4th ed.). Upper Saddle River, NJ: Merrill/Prentice Hall.

Recommended Websites

AlternativeAssessment
www.ncrel.org/sdrs/areas/issues/content/cntareas/science/sc5alter.htm

Authentic Assessment
http://mailer.fsu.edu/jflake/assess.html

Measurement and Evaluation
Criterion Versus Norm-Referenced Testing www.valdosta.edu/~whuitt/psy702/measeval/crnmref.html

Modern Thinking on Assessment
www.ed.psu.edu/dept/~ae-insys-wfed/insys/esd/assessment/menu.html

Chapter 10

Adams, S. K., & Baronberg, J. (2005). *Promoting positive behavior: Guidance strategies for early childhood settings.* Upper Saddle River, NJ: Merrill/Prentice Hall.

Beaty, J. (1995). *Converting conflicts in preschool.* Fort Worth, TX: Harcourt Brace.

Beaty, J. J. (2006). *50 early childhood guidance strategies.* Upper Saddle River, NJ: Merrill/Prentice Hall.

Berk, L. E. (2006). Looking at kindergarten children. In D. F. Gullo (Ed.), *K today: Teaching and learning in the kindergarten year* (pp. 11–25). Washington, DC: National Association for the Education of Young Children.

Boyer, E. (1995). *The basic school: A community for learning.* Carnegie Foundation for the Advancement of Teaching.

Bronson, M. B. (2006). Developing social and emotional competence. In D. F. Gullo (Ed.), *K today: Teaching and learning in the kindergarten year* (pp. 47–56). Washington, DC: National Association for the Education of Young Children.

Carter, M. (1992). Disciplinarians or transformers? Training teachers for conflict resolution. *Child Care Information Exchange, 84,* 46–51.

Children's Defense Fund. (2002). [Online]. Available at *www.childrensdefense.org.*

Comstock, G., & Strasburger, V. C. (1990). Deceptive appearances: Television violence and aggressive behavior. *Journal of Adolescent Health Care, 11,* 31–34.

Conrad, N. K. (1997). Unpublished manuscript. Johnstown, PA: University of Pittsburgh, Johnstown.

Daros, D., & Kovach, B. A. (1998). Assisting toddlers and caregivers during conflict resolutions: Interactions that promote socialization. *Childhood Education, 75*(1), 25–30.

Deci, E. L., & Ryan, R. M. (1985). *Intrinsic motivation and self-determination in human behavior.* New York: Plenum.

Dietz, W. H., & Strasburger, V. C. (1991). Children, adolescents, and television. *Current Problems in Pediatrics, 21,* 8–31.

Dinkmeyer, D., & McKay, G. (1989). *Systematic training for effective parenting* (3rd ed.). Minneapolis, MN: American Guidance Service.

Edelman, M. W. (1992). *The measure of our success: A letter to my children and yours.* Boston: Beacon Press.

Eisenberg, N. (1992). *The caring child.* Cambridge, MA: Harvard University Press.

Elementary Educators. (2006). *Creating a safe and friendly school.* Turners Falls, MA: Northeast Foundation for Children.

Fields, M. V., & Boesser, C. (1998). *Constructive guidance and discipline* (2nd ed.). Upper Saddle River, NJ: Merrill/Prentice Hall.

Flicker, E. S., & Hoffman, J. A. (2002). Developmental discipline in the early childhood classroom. *Young Children, 57*(5), 82–89.

Gannon, B., & Mncayi, P. (1996). You *can* get there from here. *Reaching Today's Youth, 1*(1), 55–57.

Gartrell, D. (2001). Replacing time-out: Part one. Using guidance to build an encouraging classroom. *Young Children, 56*(6), 8–16.

Gartrell, D. (2006). Guidance matters: Boys and men teachers. *Young Children, 61*(3), 92–93.

Glasser, W. (1992). *The quality school: Managing students without coercion.* New York: Harper & Row.

Gordon, A. M., & Browne, K. W. (2006). *Beginning essentials in early childhood education.* Clifton Park, NY: Delmar Learning.

Groves, B. M. (1996). Growing up in a violent world: The impact of family and community violence on young children and their families. In E. J. Erwin (Ed.), *Putting children first: Visions for a brighter future for young children and their families* (pp. 31–52). Baltimore: Paul H. Brookes.

Gurian, M., & Stevens, K. (2005). *The mind of boys: Saving our sons from falling behind in school and life.* San Francisco: Jossey-Bass.

Henley, M. (1996). Teaching self-control to young children. *Reaching Today's Youth, 1*(1), 13–16.

Heroman, C., & Copple, C. (2006). Teaching in the kindergarten year. In D. F. Gullo (Ed.), *K today: Teaching and learning in the kindergarten year* (pp. 59–72). Washington, DC: National Association for the Education of Young Children.

Hewitt, D. (1995). So this is normal too? Teachers and parents working out developmental issues in young children. St. Paul, MN: Redleaf Press. [Online]. Available at http://education-world.com/aadmin/admin022.shtml.

Isenberg, J. P., & Jalongo, M. R. (2005). *Creative thinking and arts-based learning: Preschool through fourth grade.* (4th ed.). Upper Saddle River, NJ: Merrill/Prentice Hall.

Jalongo, M. R. (1987). Do "security" blankets belong in preschool? *Young Children, 42,* 3–8.

Jalongo, M. R. (1992). *Creating communities: The role of the teacher in the 21st century.* Bloomington, IN: National Educational Service.

Jalongo, M. R. (1996). Looking beyond the labels. *Early Childhood Education Journal, 23*(3), 127–129.

Johnson, D. W., & Johnson, R. T. (1996). Conflict resolution and peer mediation programs in elementary and secondary schools: A review of the research. *Review of Educational Research, 66*(4), 459–506.

Kaiser, B., & Rasminsky, J. S. (2006). *Challenging behavior in young children: Understanding, preventing, and responding effectively* (2nd ed.). Boston: Allyn & Bacon.

Kohn, A. (1996). *Beyond discipline: From compliance to community.* Alexandria, VA: Association for Supervision and Curriculum Development.

Kostelnik, M. J., Stein, L. C., & Whiren, A. P. (1988). Children's self-esteem: The verbal environment. *Childhood Education, 65*(1), 29–32.

Krahl, C., & Jalongo, M. R. (1998). Creating caring classroom communities: Advice from an intervention specialist. *Childhood Education, 75*(2), 83–89.

Lerman, S. (1984). *Responsive parenting.* Circle Pines, MN: American Guidance Service.

Levin, D. E. (2002). *Teaching young children in violent times: Building a peaceable classroom* (2nd ed.). New York: Educators for Social Responsibility.

Lewis, R. (2001). Classroom discipline and student responsibility: The students' view. *Teaching and Teacher Education, 17*(3), 307–319.

Luke, J. L., & Myers, C. M. (1994). Toward peace: Using literature to aid conflict resolution. *Childhood Education, 71*(2), 66–67.

Maag, J. W. (2001). Rewarded by punishment: Reflections on the disuse of positive reinforcement in schools. *Teaching Exceptional Children, 67*(2), 173–186.

Marion, M. (2007). *Guidance of young children* (7th ed.). Upper Saddle River, NJ: Merrill/Prentice Hall.

Martin, L. A., Chiodo, J. J., & Chang, L. (2001). First year teachers: Looking back after three years. *Action in Teacher Education, 23*(1), 55–63.

Maslow, A. (1968). *Toward a psychology of being* (2nd ed.). Princeton, NJ: Van Nostrand.

May, R. (1972). *Power and influence.* New York: W. W. Norton.

May, R. (1998). Power and innocence: A search for the sources of violence. (reissue edition). New York: W. W. Norton.

McAfee, O., Leong, D. J., & Bodrova, E. (2004). *Basics of assessment: A primer for early childhood educators.* Washington, DC: National Association for the Education of Young Children.

McClurg, L. G. (1998). Building an ethical community in the classroom: Community meeting. *Young Children, 53*(2), 30–35.

McDevitt, T. M., & Ormrod, J. E. (2007). *Child development: Educating and working with children and adolescents* (3rd ed.). Upper Saddle River, NJ: Merrill/Prentice Hall.

Mindes, G. (2006). Social studies in kindergarten. In D. F. Gullo (Ed.), *K today: Teaching and learning in the kindergarten year* (pp. 107–115). Washington, DC: National Association for the Education of Young Children.

Moore, T. (1992). *Care of the soul.* New York: Harper Perennial.

National Association for the Education of Young Children & National Association of Early Childhood Specialists in State Departments of Education. (2003). *Early childhood curriculum, assessment, and program evaluation: Building an effective, accountable system in programs for children birth through age 8* [Online]. Joint position statement. Washington, DC: NAEYC. Available at *www.naeyc.org/about/positions/ pdf/pscape.pdf.*

National Association for the Education of Young Children. (1996). *Early years are learning years: Teaching children not to be—Or be victims of—Bullies.* Washington, DC: Author.

National Educational Service. (1996). Boys' Town. *Reaching Today's Youth, 1*(1), 50–51.

Nelsen, J., Erwin, C., & Duffy, R. (1995). *Positive discipline for preschoolers: For their early years—Raising children who are responsible and resourceful.* Rocklin, CA: Prima Publishing.

Ostrosky, M. M., & Jung, E. Y. (2006). Building positive teacher–child relationships. *Early Childhood Education Journal, 28,* 144–146.

Paley, V. (1992). *You can't say you can't play.* Cambridge, MA: Harvard University Press.

Perry, D. G., Kussel, S. J., & Perry, L. C. (1988). Victims of peer aggression. *Developmental Psychology, 24,* 807–814.

Porter, L. (1999). Discipline in early childhood. In L. E. Berk (Ed.), *Landscapes of development: An anthology of readings* (pp. 295–308). Belmont, CA: Wadsworth.

Preusse, K. (2006). Fostering prosocial behavior in young children. In K. Paciorek (Ed.), *Annual Editions: Early Childhood Education 06/07* (27th ed., pp. 181–184). Dubuque, IA: McGraw-Hill.

Ramsey, P. G. (1991). *Making friends in school: Promoting peer relationships in early childhood.* New York: Teachers College Press.

Richardson, V., & Fallona, C. (2001). Classroom management as method and manner. *Journal of Curriculum Studies, 33*(6), 705–728.

Rief, S. F. (1993). *How to reach and teach ADD/ADHD children: Practical techniques, strategies, and interventions for helping children with attention problems and hyperactivity.* West Nyack, NJ: The Center for Applied Research in Education.

Rodd, J. (1996). *Understanding young children's behavior.* New York: Teachers College Press.

Rodgers, D. B. (1998). Research in review: Supporting autonomy in young children. *Young Children, 53*(3), 75–80.

Severson, H., & Walker, H. (2002). Proactive approaches for identifying children at risk for sociobehavioral problems. In K. Lane, F. M. Gresham, & T. O'Shaughnessy (Eds.), *Interventions for children with or at-risk for emotional and behavioral disorders* (pp. 33–53). Boston: Allyn & Bacon.

Sherman, J., Rasmussen, C. & Baydala, L. (2006). Think positively: How some characteristics of ADHD can be adaptive and accepted in the classroom. *Childhood Education, 82*(4), 196.

Shore, C. (2003). *The many faces of childhood: Diversity in development.* Boston: Allyn & Bacon.

Silvestri, L. (2001). Pre-service teachers' self-reported knowledge of classroom management. *Education, 121*(3), 575–580.

Simmons, B. J., Stallsworth, K., & Wentzel, H. (1999). Television violence and its effects on young children. *Early Childhood Education Journal, 26*(3), 149–154.

Snyder, J. (2002). Reinforcement and coercion mechanisms in the development of antisocial behavior: Peer relationships. In J. Reid, G. Patterson, & L. Snyder (Eds.), *Antisocial behavior in children and adolescents: A developmental analysis and model for intervention* (pp. 101–122). Washington, DC: American Psychological Association.

Stone, J. (1993). Caregiver and teacher language—Responsive or restrictive? *Young Children, 48*(4), 12–18.

Strachota, B. (1996). *On their side: Helping children take charge of learning.* Greenfield, MA: Northeast Foundation for Children.

Sylwester, R. (1994). How emotions affect learning. *Educational Leadership, 52*(2), 60–65.

Tobin, L. (1991). *What do you do with a child like this?* Duluth, MN: Whole Person Associates.

Walker, H. M., Ramsey, E., & Gresham, F. M. (2003/2004). Heading off disruptive behavior: How early intervention can reduce defiant behavior—And win back teaching time. *American Educator, 29*, pp. 6, 8–21, 46.

Washington, V. (1996). Creating an ideal world for children. In E. J. Erwin (Ed.), *Putting children first: Visions for a brighter future for young children and their families* (pp. 135–136). Baltimore: Paul H. Brookes.

Wein, C. A. (2006). From policing to participation: Overturning the rules and creating amiable classrooms. In K. Paciorek (Ed.), *Annual Editions 2006/7* (pp. 133–139). Dubuque, IA: McGraw-Hill.

Children's Books

Henkes, K. (1985). *Bailey goes camping.* New York: Greenwillow.

Hutchinson, P. (1983). *You'll soon grow into them, Titch.* New York: Penguin/Puffin.

Kellogg, S. (1976). *Much bigger than Martin.* New York: Dial.

Chapter 11

Allen, M., Brown, P., & Finlay, B. (1992). *Helping children by strengthening families.* Washington, DC: Children's Defense Fund.

Baum, A. C., & McMurray-Schwarz, P. (2004). Preservice teachers' beliefs about family involvement: Implications for teacher education. *Early Childhood Education Journal, 32*(1), 57–61.

Berger, E. (2004). *Parents as partners in education: Families and schools working together* (6th ed.). Upper Saddle River, NJ: Merrill/Prentice Hall.

Berry, C. F., & Mindes, G. (1993). *Theme-based curriculum: Goals, themes, activities and planning guides for 4's and 5's.* Glenview, IL: Good Year.

Better Homes Fund. (1999). *America's homeless children: New outcasts. A public policy report from the Better Homes Fund.* Newton, MA: Author.

Boyer, E. L. (1995). *The basic school: A community for learning.* Princeton, NJ: Carnegie Foundation for the Advancement of Teaching.

Bredekamp, S., & Copple, C. (Eds.). (1997). *Developmentally appropriate practice in early childhood programs* (Rev. ed.). Washington, DC: National Association for the Education of Young Children.

Briggs, N. L., Jalongo, M. R., & Brown, L. (1997). In J. P. Isenberg & M. R. Jalongo (Eds.), *Major trends and issues in early childhood: Challenges, controversies, and insights.* New York: Teachers College Press.

Bullough, R. V., & Gitlin, A. D. (2001). *Becoming a student of teaching: Linking knowledge production and practice* (2nd ed.). New York: Routledge Falmer.

Ceglowski, D., & Bacigalupa, C. (2002). Four perspectives on child care quality. *Early Childhood Education Journal, 30*(2), 87–92.

Chavkin, N. (1990). Joining forces: Education for a changing population. *Educational Horizons, 68*(4), 190–196.

Children's Defense Fund. (2006). *State of America's children,* 2005. Washington, DC: Author.

Christenson, S. L., & Sheridan, S. M. (2001). *Schools and families: Creating essential connections for learning.* New York: The Guilford Press.

Christenson, S. L. (2004). The family–school partnership: An opportunity to promote the learning competence of all students. *School Psychology Review, 33*(1), 83–104.

Davies, D. (1991). Schools reaching out: Family, school, and community partnerships for student success. *Phi Delta Kappan, 72*(5), 376–382.

Diaz, C. F. (2001). *Multicultural education for the 21st century.* Boston: Longman.

Elkind, D. (1994). *Ties that stress: The new family imbalance.* Cambridge, MA: Harvard University Press.

Elkind, D. (1995). School and family in the postmodern world. *Phi Delta Kappan, 77*(1), 8–14.

Epstein, J. L., Sanders, M. G., Simon, B. S., Salinas, K. C., Jansorn, N. R., & VanVoorhis, F. L. (2002). *School, family, and community partnerships: Your handbook for action* (2nd ed.). Thousand Oaks, CA: Corwin Press.

Fantuzzo, J., McWayne, C., Perry, M. A., & Childs, S. (2004). Multiple dimensions of family involvement and their relations to behavioral and learning competencies for urban, low-income children. *School Psychology Review, 33*(4), 467–480.

Friedman, B., & Berkeley, T. R. (2002). Encouraging fathers to participate in the school experiences of young children: The teacher's role. *Early Childhood Education Journal, 29*(3), p. 209.

Galinsky, E., Shubilla, L., Willer, B., Levine, J., & Daniel, J. (1994). State and community planning for early childhood systems. *Young Children, 49*(2), 54–57.

Garmston, R. J. (2005). *The presenter's fieldbook: A practical guide.* Norwood, MA: Christopher-Gordon.

Gennarelli, C. (2004). Family ties: Communicating with families: Children lead the way. *Young Children, 59*(1), p. 98.

Gonzalez-Mena, J. (2006). *The young child in the family and the community* (4th ed.). Upper Saddle River, NJ: Merrill/Prentice Hall.

Grumet, M. (1988). *Bitter milk: Women and teaching.* Amherst, MA: University of Massachusetts.

Hanson, M. F., & Gilkerson, D. (1996). Children born from artificial reproductive technology: Implications for children, parents, and caregivers. *Early Childhood Education Journal, 23*(3), 131–134.

Hayes, R. L. (1987). The reconstruction of educational experience: The parent conference. *Education, 107*(3), 305–309.

Henderson, A. T., Marburger, C. L., & Ooms, T. (1992). *Beyond the bake sale: An education guide to working with parents.* Washington, DC: National Committee for Citizens in Education.

Jehlen, A. (2006). Second time around. *NEA Today, 24*(7), p. 21.

Kagan, S. (1990). Readiness 2000: Rethinking rhetoric and responsibility. *Phi Delta Kappan, 72*(4), 272–279.

Kagan, S., Powell, D., Weissbourd, B., & Zigler, E. (1987). *America's family support programs: Perspectives and prospects.* New Haven, CT: Yale University Press.

Kantor, D., & Lehr, W. (1975). *Inside the family.* San Francisco: Jossey-Bass.

Kendall, F. E. (1996). *Diversity in the classroom: New approaches to the education of young children* (2nd ed.). New York: Teachers College Press.

Knopf, H. T., & Swick, K. J. (2007). How parents feel about their child's teacher/school: Implifications for early childhood professionals. *Early Childhood Education Journal, 34*(4). 291–296.

Lawrence-Lightfoot, S. (2003). *The essential conversation: What parents and teachers can learn from each other.* New York: Random House.

Lawson, M. (2003). School–family relations in context: Parent and teacher perceptions of parent involvement. *Urban Education, 38*(1), 77–133.

Lewis, A. (1991). Coordinating services: Do we have the will? *Phi Delta Kappan, 72*(5), 340–341.

Liess, E. (1995). Eat-in, share-in, read-in: An integrated, cooperative, end-of-year program for parents of first graders. *Day Care and Early Education, 22*(4).

Lundgren, D., & Morrison, J. W. (2002). Involving Spanish-speaking families in early education programs. *Young Children, 58*(3), 88–95.

McBride, B. A., & Rane, T. R. (1997). Father/male involvement in early childhood programs: Issues and challenges. *Early Childhood Education Journal, 25*(1), 11–15.

McDevitt, T. M., & Ormrod, J. E. (2007). *Child development: Educating and working with children and adolescents* (3rd ed.). Upper Saddle River, NJ: Merrill/Prentice Hall.

Mensing, J. F., French, D., Fuller, B., & Kagan, S. L. (2000). Child care selection under welfare reform: How mothers balance work requirements and parenting. *Early Education & Development, 11,* 573–595.

National Low Income Housing Coalition. (2004). *Out of reach 2004: America's housing wage climbs.*

National Research Council. (2004). *Eager to learn: Educating our preschoolers.* Committee on Early Childhood Pedagogy. B. Bowman, M. Donovan, & M. Burns (Eds.). Commission on Behavioral and Social Sciences and Education. Washington, DC: National Academy Press.

Pena, D. (2000). Parent involvement: Influencing factors and implications. *Journal of Educational Research, 94,* 42–54.

Pena, D. (2000). Sharing power? An experience of Mexican American parents serving on a campus advisory council. *The School Community Journal, 10*(1), 61–84.

Powell, D. (1991). How schools support families: Critical policy tensions. *The Elementary School Journal, 91*(3), 307–319.

Richmond, J., & Kotelchuck, M. (1984). Commentary on changed lives. In J. Berrueta-Clement, L. Schweinhart, S. Barnett, A. Epstein, & D. Weikart (Eds.), *Changed lives: The effect of the Perry Preschool Program on youths through age 19.* Ypsilanti, MI: High Scope Press.

Rinaldi, C. (2000). Values in education. Speech presented at Mills College, Oakland California, March.

Roberts, R., Wasik, B., Casto, G., & Ramey, C. (1991). Family support in the home: Programs, policy, and social change. *American Psychologist, 46*(2), 131–137.

Rosenthal, D. M., & Sawyers, J. Y. (1996). Building successful home/school partnerships. *Childhood Education* 72(4) 194–200.

Sachs, J. (2005). *The end of poverty: Possibilities for our time.* New York: Penguin Press.

Seplocha, H. (2004). Partnerships for learning: Conferencing with families. *Young Children, 59*(5), 96–99.

Swick, K. (2004a). Communicating effectively with parents and families who are homeless. *Early Childhood Education Journal, 32*(3), 211–216.

Swick, K. (2004b). *Empowering parents, families, schools, and communities during the early childhood years.* Champaign, IL: Stipes.

Swick, K. (2004c). What parents seek in relations with early childhood family helpers. *Early Childhood Education Journal, 32*(3), 217–220.

Swick, K., & Hooks, L. (2005). Parental experiences and beliefs regarding inclusive placements of their special needs children. *Early Childhood Education Journal, 32*(6), 1–6.

Swick, K. J., Boutte, G., & van Scoy, I. (1995). *Family involvement in multicultural learning.* Urbana, IL: ERIC Clearinghouse on Elementary and Early Childhood Education. [ERIC Digest EDO-PS-95-2].

U.S. Department of Health and Human Services. (1990). *Project Head Start.* Washington, DC: Department of Health and Human Services.

Chapter 12

Baptiste, N., & Sheerer, M. (1997). Negotiating the challenges of the "survival" stage of professional development. *Early Childhood Education Journal, 24*(4), 265–268.

Berliner, D. C. (1994a). Developmental stages in the lives of early childhood educators. In S. G. Goffin & D. E. Day (Eds.), *New perspectives in early childhood education: Bringing practitioners into the debate* (pp. 120–128). New York: Teachers College Press.

Berliner, D. C. (1994b). Expertise: The wonder of exemplary performances. In C. C. Block & J. Mangieri (Eds.), *Creating powerful thinking in teachers and students: Diverse perspectives.* Fort Worth, TX: Harcourt Brace.

Balck, A., & Davern, L. (1998, February). When a preservice teacher meets the classroom team. *Educational Leadership*, pp. 52–54.

Bluestein, J. (Comp.). (1995). *Mentors, master teachers, and Mrs. MacGregor: Stories of teachers making a difference.* Deerfield Beach, FL: Health Communications.

Bullough, R. V., & Gitlin, A. D. (2001). *Becoming a student of teaching: Linking knowledge production and practice* (2nd ed.). New York: RoutledgeFalmer.

Carbo, M. (1997). *What every principal should know about teaching reading*. Syosset, NY: National Reading Styles Institute.

Caulfield, R. (1997). Professionalism in early care and education. *Early Childhood Education Journal, 24*(4), 261–264.

Clandinin, J. D., Davies, A., Hogan, P., & Kennard, B. (1993). *Learning to teach, teaching to learn*. New York: Teachers College Press.

Clark, C. M. (1996). *Thoughtful teaching*. New York: Teachers College Press.

Clark, C. M., & Yinger, R. J. (1977). Research on teacher thinking. *Curriculum Inquiry, 7*(4), 270–304.

Connelly, M. F., & Clandinin, J. D. (1988). *Teachers as curriculum planners: Narratives of experience.* New York: Teachers College Press.

Conroy, P. (1987). *The water is wide.* New York: Bantam.

Cryer, D., & Phillipsen, L. (1997). Quality details: A close-up look at child care program strengths and weaknesses. *Young Children, 52*(2), 51–61.

Darling-Hammond, L., & Bransford, J. (2005). *Preparing teachers for a changing world: What teachers should learn and be able to do.* San Francisco: Jossey-Bass.

Darling-Hammond, L., & Sykes, G. (Eds.). (1999). *Teaching as the learning profession: Handbook of policy and practice.* San Francisco, CA: Jossey-Bass.

Darling-Hammond, L., Wise, A. E., & Klein, S. P. (1999). *A license to teach: Raising standards for teaching.* San Francisco, CA: Jossey-Bass.

Dollas, R. H. (1992). *Voices of beginning teachers: Visions and realities.* New York: Teachers College Press.

Editors of *Education Week.* (2002, January 10). *Quality counts 2002: Building blocks for success* [Special issue].

Essa, E. (2002). *Introduction to early childhood* (4th ed.). Albany, NY: Delmar.

Farris, P. J. (1996). *Teaching: Bearing the torch.* Madison, WI: Brown & Benchmark.

Feeney, S., Christensen, D., & Moravcik, E. (2005). *Who am I in the lives of children?* (7th ed.). Upper Saddle River, NJ: Prentice Hall.

Fox, M. (1993). *Radical reflections: Passionate opinions on teaching, learning, and living.* San Diego, CA: Harcourt Brace Jovanovich.

Gallas, K. (1994). *The languages of learning: How children talk, write, dance, draw, and sing their understanding of the world.* New York: Teachers College Press.

Gharavi, G. J. (1993). Music skills for preschool teachers: Needs and solutions. *Arts Education Policy Review, 94*(3), 27–30.

Grant, C., & Zeichner, K. (1984). *Preparing for reflective teaching.* Boston: Allyn & Bacon.

Graves, D. (2001). Build energy with colleagues. *Language Arts, 79*(1), 12–19.

Hayden, T. L. (1980). *One child.* Boston: Little, Brown.

Herndon, J. (1985). *Notes from a schoolteacher*. New York: Simon & Schuster.

Hillman, C. B. (1988). *Teaching four-year-olds: A personal journey*. Bloomington, IN: Phi Delta Kappa.

Ingersoll, R., & Smith, T. (2003). The wrong solution to the teacher shortage. *Educational Leadership, 60*(8), 30–33.

Jalongo, M. R., & Isenberg, J. P. (1995). *Teachers stories: From personal narrative to professional insight.* San Francisco, CA: Jossey-Bass.

Johnson, S. M. (2006). *Finders and keepers: Helping new teachers survive and thrive in our schools.* San Francisco: Jossey-Bass.

Kane, P. R. (Ed.). (1991). *The first year of teaching: Real world stories from America's teachers.* New York: Teachers College Press.

Katz, L. (1977). *Talks with teachers.* Washington, DC: National Association for the Education of Young Children.

Katz, L. (1995). *Talks with teachers of young children: A collection.* Norwood, NJ: Ablex.

Keizer, G. (1988). *No place but here: A teacher's vocation in a rural community.* New York: Penguin.

Kidder, T. (1989). *Among schoolchildren.* Boston: Houghton Mifflin.

Knowles, M. (1975). *Self-directed learning: A guide for learners and teachers.* Boston: Cambridge.

Kohl, H. (1967). *36 children.* New York: American Library.

LaBoskey, V. K. (1994). *Development of reflective practice: A study of preservice teachers.* New York: Teachers College Press.

Lampert, M. (2001). *Teaching problems and the problems of teaching.* New Haven, CT: Yale University Press.

Lieberman, A. (1995). Practices that support teacher development. *Phi Delta Kappan, 76*(8), 591–596.

Little, J. W. (2001). Professional development in pursuit of school reform. In A. Lieberman & L. Miller (Eds.), *Teachers caught in the action: Professional development that matters* (pp. 23–44). New York: Teachers College Press.

MacDonald, R. E. (1991). *A handbook of basic skills and strategies for beginning teachers: Facing the challenge of teaching in today's schools*. White Plains, NY: Longman.

Meier, D. (1997). *Life in small moments: Learning in an urban classroom*. New York: Teachers College Press.

National Center for Early Development and Learning. (2000a, May). *Spotlight #22: Director of teacher-prep institutions*. Chapel Hill, NC: Author.

National Center for Early Development and Learning. (2000b, November). *Spotlight #28: Teacher prep and diversity*. Chapel Hill, NC: Author.

National Education Association. (2003). *Status of the American public school teacher, 2000–2001.* Washington, DC: Author.

Newman, J. (Ed.). (1990). *Finding our own way*. Portsmouth, NH: Heinemann.

Nieto, S. (2003). *What keeps teachers going?* New York: Teachers College Press.

Nieto, S. (2005). *Why we teach.* New York: Teachers College Press.

Nobscot Corporation. (2004). Retention management and metrics [Online]. Available at *www.nobscot.com/survey/index.cfm.*

Paley, V. G. (1981). *Wally's stories.* Cambridge, MA: Cambridge University Press.

Paley, V. G. (1997). *The girl with the brown crayon.* Cambridge, MA: Cambridge University Press.

Power, B. M., & Hubbard, R. S. (1996). *Oops! What we learn when our teaching fails.* York, ME: Stenhouse.

Putnam, R., & Borko, H. (2000). What do new views of knowledge and thinking have to say about research on teacher learning? *Educational Researcher, 29*(1), 4–16.

Reynolds, A. (1992). What is competent beginning teaching? A review of the literature. *Review of Educational Research, 62*(1), 1–35.

Rubin, L. (1996). *The transcendent child: Tales of triumph over the past.* New York: Basic Books.

Ryan, K. (1986). *The induction of new teachers.* Bloomington, IN: Phi Delta Kappa (Fastback #237).

Saracho O. N., & Spodek, B. (1993). Professionalism and the preparation of early childhood education practitioners. *Early Child Development and Care, 89,* 1–17.

Sparks, D., & Hirsh, S. (1997). *A new vision for staff development.* Alexandria, VA: Association for Supervision and Curriculum Development.

Strachota, B. (1996). *On their side: Helping children take charge of learning.* Greenfield, MA: Northeast Foundation for Children.

Stronge, J. H. (2002). *Qualities of effective teachers.* Alexandria, VA: Association for Supervision and Curriculum Development.

Swick, K. J., & Hanes, M. L. (1987). *The developing teacher.* Champaign, IL: Stipes.

Thompson, J. G. (2002). *First year teachers' survival kit.* San Francisco: Jossey-Bass.

Tye, B., & O'Brien, L. (2002). Why are experienced teachers leaving the profession? *Phi Delta Kappan, 84*(1), 24–32.

UNESCO. (1997). *Portraits in courage: Teachers in difficult circumstances.* Paris, France: Author.

VanderVen, K. (1991). The relationship between notions of caregiving held by early childhood practitioners and stages of career development. In B. Poking Chan (Ed.), *Early childhood towards the 21st century: A worldwide perspective.* Hong Kong: Yew Chung Publishing.

Wasley, P. (1994). *Stirring the chalkdust: Case studies of teachers in the midst of change.* New York: Teachers College Press.

Wong, H. K., & Wong, R. T. (2004). *The first days of school: How to be an effective teacher.* Alexandria, VA: Association for Supervision and Curriculum Development.

Wood, F. H., Thompson, S. R., & Russell, F. (1981). Designing effective staff development programs. In B. Dillon-Peterson (Ed.), *Effective staff development/organization development.* Alexandria, VA: Association for Supervision and Curriculum Development.

Name Index

Abelson, R.P., 68
Abraham, M., 214
Adams, S. K., 360
Adler, S. M., 35
Aldridge, D. P., 8, 324
Alexander, K. L., 313
Allen, K. E., 160, 198, 211
Allen, M., 401
Allington, R., 221
Allison, J., 304–305
American Alliance for Health, Physical Education, Recreation, and Dance (AAHPERD), 206
American Montessori Society (AMS), 57
American Psychological Association, 150, 153, 158
Anderson, L., 68
Ardley, N., 242
Arends, R., 261, 263, 279, 284, 287, 289, 305
Aries, P., 43
ASCD Advisory Panel on Improving Student Achievement, 228
Association for Childhood Education International (ACEI), 47
Association for Childhood Education International (ACEI) National Council for the Accreditation for Teacher Education, 397
Association for Supervision and Curriculum Development, 193
Association of Teacher Educators, 211
Atkins-Burnett, S., 224
Ayers, W., 11, 24, 228

Bacigalupa, C., 381
Bainbridge, W., 221
Baldwin, S. C., 14
Ball, D. L., 13
Bandura, A., 149, 168, 175, 228
Bandyk, J. E., 313
Banks, C. A., 149, 154, 242
Banks, J., 80, 242
Banks, J. A., 73, 80, 81, 100, 134, 149, 154
Baptiste, N., 425
Barbour, C., 86
Barbour, D., 243, 244
Barbour, N. H., 86
Barnett, S. W., 35, 183, 415
Barnett, W., 35
Barnett, W. S., 228
Baronberg, J., 360
Baum, A. C., 396
Baydala, L., 345
Beal, K., 276
Beaty, J. J., 362, 364
Beaumont, K., 135
Bellamy, M. L., 287
Benham, A., 242
Benson, T. R., 340
Bergen, D., 133
Berger, E., 392, 395–396
Berk, D., 282
Berk, L. E., 110, 111, 119, 122, 125, 129, 135, 165, 169, 171, 173, 345
Berkeley, T. R., 392
Berliner, D. C., 287, 425
Berns, R., 134, 152
Berns, R. M., 174
Berry, C. F., 384
Best, S., 213
Better Homes Fund, 385
Bidner, J., 68
Bigge, J., 213
Birmingham, C., 12, 13, 68
Bizar, M., 150
Black, A., 424
Black, J., 119, 122, 133
Black, J. K., 317
Black, P., 195
Bloch, M. N., 43
Bluestein, J., 428
Blythe, T., 282
Bodrova, E., 152, 158
Boesser, C., 354
Bolton, G., 15
Borgia, E., 339
Borko, H., 287, 415
Boschee, F., 223, 251, 252
Boutte, G., 390
Bowman, B., 305
Bown, O. H., 11, 26
Boyer, E. L., 6, 22, 23, 362, 391
Bozzi, L., 26
Brainard, M. B., 314
Bransford, J., 427
Bransford, J. D., 149, 151, 156
Brazelton, T. B., 74, 87, 113
Bredekamp. S., 18, 111, 134, 135, 140, 156, 157, 160, 183, 184, 185, 190, 193, 195, 199, 203, 220, 224, 225, 226, 227, 230, 231, 232, 236, 239, 243, 247, 251, 255, 279, 284, 289, 313, 397
Breitborde, M., 190, 193
Brickman, J., 203
Briggs, N. L., 379, 392
Britain, L., 228
Bronfenbrenner, U., 58, 85, 141–42
Bronson, M. B., 53, 343
Brooks-Gunn, J., 75
Brown, A. I., 149, 151, 156
Brown, D. F., 68
Brown, L., 392
Brown, M., 35
Brown, P., 401
Brown, P. S., 208, 210
Browne, K. B., 22
Bruner, J., 171, 172, 176, 252
Buchanan, A. M., 14
Buchanan, T. K., 68
Bucker, K. T., 239
Bullough, R. V., 68, 397, 413
Burg, S. S., 323
Burns, D., 240
Burns, M. S., 305, 419
Burts, D. C., 68
Bush, George W., 313

Capone, A., 198, 244
Capps, R., 221
Carbo, M., 61, 413
Cardy, T., 333
Cargiulo, R. M., 132
Carle, E., 194, 281
Carnegie Corporation of New York, 226, 228
Carnegie Task Force on Meeting the Needs of Young Children, 186
Carothers, S. A., 11
Carpenter-LaGattuta, A., 13

Carroll, J., 335
Carroll, T., 6
Carter, M., 188, 195, 200, 332, 355
Cassidy, D. J., 68
Casto, G., 408
Caulfield, R., 424
Ceglowski, D., 381
Center for the Child Care Workforce and Human Services Policy Center, 35
Chaille, C., 228
Chang, L., 345
Chapman, J., 8
Chard, S. C., 221, 242, 247, 251, 281, 290, 293, 326, 333
Charlesworth, R., 68, 127, 236, 238
Chavkin, N., 401
Children's Defense Fund, 6, 73, 77, 84, 111, 186, 346, 381, 384
Childs, S., 393
Chilvers, D., 15
Chinn, P. C., 74, 81
Chomsky, N., 166, 175
Chrisenson, S. L., 390, 393, 396
Christensen, D., 39, 262, 263, 279, 290, 421
Christie, J., 196
Cizek, C. J., 323
Clandinin, J. D., 426
Clark, C., 286
Clark, C. M., 287, 419, 430
Clarke-Stewart, A., 197
Clayton, M. K., 188, 197, 200
Clements, D., 163, 165
Cleverley, J., 43, 48
Clifford, R. M., 50, 65, 185, 198, 200, 207, 211
Cochran-Smith, M., 81
Cocking, R. R., 149, 151, 156
Colker, L. J., 206, 247
Colton, A. B., 20
Comenius, J., 40, 47
Comer, J. P., 311, 335
Commission on Behavioral and Social Sciences and Education, 156, 226
Committee for Economic Development, 261
Comstock, G., 355
Connelly, M. F., 426
Conrad, N. K., 377
Conroy, P., 425
Cook, T., 183
Cooney, M. H., 190
Cooper, J. M., 244, 286, 287, 289
Copple, C., 18, 111, 134, 135, 140, 160, 183, 184, 185, 190, 193, 195, 199, 203, 224, 225, 226, 230, 245, 247, 279, 284, 289, 347, 397
Corson, D., 199
Cowdery, G. E., 160, 198, 211
Cruickshank, D., 8
Crumpacker, S., 195
Cryer, D., 185, 195, 198, 200, 207, 211, 413
Csikszentmihalyi, M., 11, 26, 28
Cunningham-Eidson, C., 290
Curtis, D., 188, 195, 200, 276, 332
Cyer, D., 65

Dale-Easley, S., 332
Daniel, J., 393
Daniels, D. H., 153
Daniels, H., 150
Darling-Hammond, L., 6, 16, 313, 336, 416, 418, 419, 426, 427, 433
Darlington, R., 228
Daros, D., 359
Darwin, C., 48
Davern, L., 424
Davidson, A., 426
Davidson, F., 100
Davies, D., 392
Day, C. B., 155
Day Care Workers of America, 55
Deci, E. L., 347
DeLong, A., 203
DeMause, L., 39
Denton, P., 158
Derman-Sparks, L., 75, 82
DeVries, R., 140
Dewdney, A., 137
Dewey, J., 8, 15, 41, 158, 228, 240, 247, 252
Diamond, K. E., 313
Diaz, C. F., 398
Diener, P. L., 213, 214
Dietz, W. H., 355
Dinkmeyer, D., 347
Division for Early Childhood of the Council for Exceptional Children, 133
Division of Early Childhood (DEC), National Association for the Education of Young Children (NAEYC), 211
Dixon, S., 15
Dodge, D., 240, 241, 247
Dollas, R. H., 425
Donovan, M. S., 149
Donovan, S., 305
Driscoll, A., 51, 53, 259, 263, 279, 286
Duch, H., 58
Duffy, R., 359
Duhon, G., 13
Duncan, G., 75, 183
Dunn, S., 286

Eby, J. W., 15
Edelman, M. W., 71, 373
Edelman, P., 77, 85
Editors of Education Week, 313, 415
Edmonds, R., 73, 90, 101
Educational Testing Service (ETS), 321
Education Week, 35
Edwards, C., 59, 60, 184, 190, 195, 247
Edwards, V. B., 221
Eggen, P. D., 149, 150, 242, 263, 277, 286, 287, 305
Eisenberg, N., 355
Elementary Educators, 349
Eliot, A. A., 47
Elkind, D., 382
Emilia, R., 59, 60
English, K., 141
Entwisle, D. R., 313
Epinosa, L. M., 78
Epstein, A. S., 57, 58, 59
Epstein, J. L., 397
Erikson, E. H., 111, 135–38
Erwin, C., 359
Erwin, E. J., 61, 66
Espinosa, L. M., 78
Essa, E., 425
Exelby, B., 188, 197, 198

Falk, B., 219, 326
Fallona, C., 345
Fang, Z., 68
Fantuzzo, J., 393
Farris, P. J., 418
Federal Interagency Forum on Health and Family Statistics, 111
Feeney, S., 39, 89, 94, 262, 263, 279, 290, 421
Fennimore, B. S., 20, 80, 83, 90, 91, 93, 96, 97, 98
Fewell, R. R., 336
Fields, M. V., 353, 354

Finlay, B., 401
Firlik, R., 197
Flack, M., 159
Fleegle, P. O., 68
Fleener, C. O., 239
Fleet, A., 332
Flynn, L., 211
Forman, G., 59, 60, 184, 189, 195, 247
Fox, M., 428
Fraser, M. W., 94
Fraser, S., 185
Freeman, E. B., 68
Freeman, N. K., 94
Freeman, R., 60
Freiberg, H. J., 259, 263, 279, 286
French, D., 356, 381
Friedman, B., 392
Froebel, F., 41, 56
Fromberg, D. P., 159, 160, 161
Frost, J. L., 159, 160, 162, 208, 210, 212
Frye, M. A., 181, 197, 200
Fuller, B., 26, 381
Fuller. F. F., 11
Fulton, K., 6

Galinsky, E., 393, 416
Gallagher, K. C., 128, 129, 156
Gallas, K., 427
Gallup, A. M., 313
Galper, A., 276
Gandini, L., 59, 60, 184, 189, 195, 247, 333
Gannon, B., 348
Garcia, E., 323
Gardner, H., 149, 151, 153, 173, 176, 177, 281
Gargiulo, R. M., 132, 144
Garmston, R. J., 406
Garreau, M., 190, 203
Gartrell, D., 345, 351
Gay, G., 76, 102, 198, 228
Genishi, C., 326, 339
Gennarelli, C., 399
Gerzog, G., 165
Gesell, A., 48, 166, 175
Gestwicki, C., 185
Gharavi, G. J., 418
Gilkerson, D., 381
Gitlin, A. D., 68, 397, 413
Glasgow, K., 21, 36
Glasser, W., 348
Glatthorn, A., 223, 251, 252
Glickman, C. D., 8, 324
Goffin, S. G., 86
Goldhaber, J., 198, 244
Goleman, D., 125, 153, 157
Gollnick, D. M., 74, 81
Gonzalez-Mena, J., 81, 381
Goodhart, R. L., 74, 316
Goodwin, A. L., 75, 316
Gordon, A., 22, 279, 284
Gorrill, L., 349
Greenberg, M. T., 320
Greenspan, S. I., 52, 113
Greenspan, S. J., 74, 87
Gregory, K., 158
Greshman, F. M., 349
Grifalconi, A., 243
Griffin, P., 419
Groark, C. J., 320
Gronlund, G., 206, 210, 231, 284
Groves, B. M., 355
Grudlund, G., 52
Grumet, M., 408
Grunwald, L., 52
Gullo, D. F., 314, 316, 324, 325, 339
Guralnick, M. J., 133
Gurian, M., 345

Hale-Jinks, C., 415
Hallahan, D. P., 128, 133
Hamre, B. K., 207
Han, E., 10
Hanes, M. L., 418, 425
Hansen, D. T., 262
Hanson, M. F., 381
Hargreaves, A., 53
Harle, A., 24
Harms, T., 50, 65, 185, 198, 200, 207, 209, 211
Hart, C. H., 68
Hartle, L., 101
Hatch, J. A., 68
Haughland, S. W., 163, 165
Hayden, T. L., 426
Hayes, R. L., 393
Hedges, L., 183
Heider, K., 6
Heller, K., 213
Helm, A., 332
Helm, J. H., 332
Helterbran, V., 24
Henderson, A. T., 392
Hendrick, J., 18, 184, 229
Hendron, J., 426
Henkes, K., 141, 366
Henley, M., 356
Henniger, M. L., 152
Henson, K., 221, 223
Hernandez, H., 154
Heroman, C., 245, 247, 347
Herrell, A. L., 15
Hesse, K., 141
Hewett, V. M., 60
Hiebert, J., 282
Hill, P. S., 47
Hillman, C. B., 428
Hillman, E., 137
Hirsch, E. D., 252
Hirsh, S., 418
Hoban, T., 238
Hoberman, M. A., 243
Hodgkinson, H., 261
Hoffman, C., 73
Hogan, P., 426
Hoge, P., 14, 68
Hohman, M., 216
Hohmann, C. F., 59
Holloway, S. D., 26
Holzer, H. J., 77, 85
Hooks, L., 390, 391
Hooks, W., 137
Hoot, J. L., 64
Hout, M., 73
Howard, F., 14, 68
Howe, H., 55
Howes, C., 100
Hubbard, R. S., 427
Hull, K., 198, 244
Hustedt, J. T., 35, 183, 415
Hutchins, P., 238
Hutchinson, P., 366
Hyson, M., 225, 422
Hyun, E., 224

Ingersoll, R., 6, 415
International Reading Association/ National Council of Teachers of English, 322
Irvine, J. J., 76, 90, 94, 102
Isbell, R. T., 188, 197, 198
Isenberg, J. P., 3, 68, 69, 113, 160, 162, 186, 190, 197, 198, 205, 311, 346, 428

Jackman, H., 289
Jackman, H. L., 152, 183, 221, 229, 230, 245
Jackson, P., 222
Jalongo, M. R., 6, 24, 68, 69, 160, 162, 186, 190, 197, 198, 205, 311, 322, 339, 346, 362, 364, 365, 379, 392, 428

Jansen, A., 282
Jansorn, N. R., 397
Jehlen, A., 388
Jenkins, J., 293
Jensen, A. R., 79
Jensen, E., 52, 321
Jensen, J. M., 94
Jensen, R., 289
Johnson, J., 196
Johnson, J. E., 56, 57, 59, 79
Johnson, L., 68
Johnson, S. M., 6, 53, 73, 415
Johnston, J., 228, 253
Johnston, P. H., 320
Jones, C., 287
Jones, E., 195, 242, 290
Jones, J., 225
Jones, M., 26
Jordan, M. L., 15
Jung, E. Y., 358
Jung, K., 35

Kagan, S. L., 335, 381, 392, 408, 429
Kahn, A. J., 56
Kaiser, B., 345
Kalkman, D. L., 153
Kamerman, S. B., 56
Kamii, C., 140
Kaminsky, J. A., 333
Kane, P. R., 425
Kantor, D., 382
Kantrowtiz, B., 215
Kardos, S. M., 6
Katz, L. G., 25, 221, 242, 247, 251, 281, 290, 293, 326, 333, 425
Kauchak, D., 149, 150, 242
Kauchak, D. P., 263, 277, 286, 287, 305
Kauffman, D., 6
Kauffman, J. M., 128, 133
Keefe, J., 293
Keizer, G., 425
Kellogg, S., 366
Kelly, E., 81
Kemple, K., 415
Kendall, F. E., 396, 406
Kennard, B., 426
Kennedy, C., 190, 203
Kidder, T., 426
Kieff, J., 211
Kiley, T., 289
Kilpatrick, W. H., 240, 247
Kirylo, J. D., 323
Klein, S. P., 416
Knopf, H., 391, 415
Knowles, M., 424
Kochendorfer, L., 28
Kohl, H., 425
Kohn, A., 147, 183, 349, 351
Kontos, S., 199
Koppelman, K. L., 74
Korthagen, F., 13, 14
Kostelnik, M., 158, 220, 236, 239, 285, 293, 298, 365
Kotelchuck, M., 408
Kovach, B. A., 359
Kowalski, K., 68
Kozol, J., 55, 90
Krahl, C., 346
Kritchevsky, S., 188
Kroeger, J., 333
Kumashiro, K., 86
Kussel, S. J., 359

LaBoskey, V. K., 426
Lackney, J. A., 195, 196
Ladson-Billings, G., 100
Lampert, M., 419
Landry, S. H., 226
Lanny, C., 35
LaParo, K. M., 207
Lascarides, V. C., 47
Law, N., 17
Lawler-Prince, D., 287
Lawrence, J. M., 68
Lawrence-Lightfoot, S., 391, 399
Lawson, M., 399
Lazar, L., 228
Lee, H., 12
LeFrancois, G., 43
Lehr, W., 382
Leong, D. J., 152, 158, 316, 331, 332
Lerman, S., 355
Levin, D. E., 355
Levine, J., 393
Levine, M., 226
Lewin, T., 221
Lewis, A., 408
Lewis, R., 345
Lieberman, A., 416
Liebovich, B. J., 35
Liess, E., 401
Lillard, P. P., 57
Lind, K., 236, 238
Little, J. W., 415
Liu, E., 6
Locke, J., 40, 167, 175
Lombardi, J., 86
Lowman, L., 186
Lucas, T., 198
Luke, J. L., 367
Lundgren, D., 391
Luther, M., 40, 47
Lynch, R. G., 149

Maag, J. W., 345
MacDonald, R. E., 426, 431
MacDonalid, S., 339
Madaus, G. F., 321
Magliaro, S., 261
Mann, H., 41
Many, J., 14, 68
Marburger, C. L., 392
Marion, M., 360
Martin, L. A., 345
Martinez-Beck, I., 6, 35, 58, 59, 183, 345, 355, 356, 373, 415, 417, 421
Maslow, A. H., 113, 142–43, 346
Matas, C., 138
May, R., 364
Mayer, M., 276
McAdoo, L., 57, 58
McAfee, O., 316, 332
McAuliffe, C., 47
McBride, B. A., 392
McCall, R., 320
McClurg, L. G., 362
McCombs, B. L., 152, 153, 154, 158
McConnell, S. R., 336
McDevitt, T. M., 347, 381
McDonald, J. P., 5
McDonald, R. E., 431
McDonough, S. C., 44
McGinn, D., 215
McIntyre, J., 13
McKay, G., 347
McLean, M., 313
McLean, S. V., 187, 205
McMullen, M. B., 15
McMurray-Schwarz, P., 396
McTighe, J., 245, 332
McWayne, C., 393
McWilliams, R., 211
Meacham, A. N, 73
Mehaffie, K. E., 320
Meier, D., 425
Meisels, S. J., 224, 321, 325
Mensing, J. F., 381
Meyer, R. J., 33
Miller, L., 158
Mindes, G., 316, 358, 384
Mitchell, K., 332

Mncayi, P., 348
Moffit, M., 17
Mondale, W., 91
Montessori, M., 41, 57
Montgomery, W., 198, 199, 244
Moore, E., 17
Moore, G. T., 196
Moore, T., 373
Moran, J., 203
Moravcik, E., 39, 262, 263, 279, 290, 421
Morris, A., 282
Morris, L., 214
Morrison, J. W., 391
Morrow, L. M., 221, 236, 239
Mosley, J., 68
Moyer, J., 10
Mueller, A., 68
Mumpower, J. O., 181, 197, 200
Murphy, J., 193
Myers, C. M., 367

National Academy of Early Childhood Programs, 195, 197
National Association for the Education of Young Children (NAEYC), 47, 55, 133, 134, 144, 145, 165, 183, 184, 189, 195, 198, 199, 206, 226, 228, 229, 231, 232, 233, 243, 244, 285, 313, 322, 367, 410
National Association of Early Childhood Teacher Educators, 55
National Association of Elementary School Principals, 305
National Board for Professional Teaching Standards (NBPTS), 232, 233, 236, 415
National Center for Early Development and Learning (NECDL), 261, 415
National Center for Education Statistics, 73
National Center for Health Statistics, 111
National Commission on Excellence in Education, 223
National Education Association, 415
National Education Service, 359
National Institute of Child Health and Development Early Child Care Research Network (NICHD), 207
National Low Income Housing Coalition, 384
National Study Group for the Affirmative Development of Academic Ability, 228
NBPTS. *See* National Board for Professional Teaching Standards (NBPTS)
NECDL. *See* National Center for Early Development and Learning (NECDL)
Neill, M., 313
Nelsen, J., 359
Nelson, K. L., 281, 284
Neugebauer, R., 46
New, R., 334
New, R. S., 60
Newman, J., 427
Nieto, S., 6, 11, 73, 80, 100, 101, 337, 420
Nilsen, B. A., 332, 339
Nimmo, J., 242, 290
Noddings, N., 11, 24, 75, 94, 193

O'Brien, L., 415
O'Dell, S., 138
Odom, S., 211
Offner, P., 77, 85
Olson, L. S., 313
Ooms, T., 392
Ormrod, J. E., 347, 381
Osborn, D. K., 35, 43, 46
Ostrosky, M. M., 358
Overfield, R., 17
Owen, R., 41

Paasche, C. L., 349
Pajares, M. F., 68
Paley, V. G., 100, 366, 428
Palmer, P., 231
Parten, M., 163
Patterson, C., 332
Pelo, A., 100
Pena, D., 391
Perham, M., 242
Perini, M. J., 281, 285
Perkins, D., 282
Perrone, V., 322, 333
Perry, D. G., 359
Perry, L. C., 359
Perry, M. A., 393
Peske, H. G., 6
Pestalozzi, J. H., 40
Peters, W., 30
Peterson, P. L., 287
Phillips, D., 149, 151
Phillips, D. A., 128
Phillips, D. C., 43, 48
Phillipsen, L., 65, 195, 413
Piaget, J., 48, 111, 115, 138–141, 153, 160, 163, 170–171, 175, 240, 244, 252, 371
Pianta, R. C., 207
Picar, R., 206
Plato, 40
Popham, W. J., 320, 326
Poppe, J., 6
Porter, L., 352, 358
Posner, G., 251
Postman, N., 43, 66
Powell, D., 389, 392
Power, B. M., 328, 332, 427
Pratt, C., 47
Pre-K Education in the States, 261
Prescott, E., 188, 195
Pretti-Fontczak, K., 68
Preusse, K., 356
Preyer, W., 48
Price, G. G., 43
Prince, K. M., 281, 284
Project Zero, 326, 332
Puckett, M. B., 119, 122, 133, 317
Putnam, R., 415

Quisenberry, N., 13

Raines, S. R., 228, 253
Rambusch/McCormick,N., 57
Ramey, C., 408
Ramsey, E., 349
Ramsey, P. G., 75, 76, 82, 99, 101, 371
Ramsisini, K., 203
Rand, M., 13
Rane, T. R., 392
Rasminsky, J. S., 345
Rasmussen, C., 345
Raver, C., 224
Rawls, J., 86
Readdick, C. A., 195
Reagan, A. J., 313
Ream, R., 261
Reifel, S., 159, 160, 162
Reynolds, A., 426
Rice, G. G., 43
Richardson, V., 345
Richmond, J., 408
Rief, S. F., 359
Rieg, S., 24
Rinaldi, C., 333, 400
Ritchie, S., 100
Rivkin, M., 208
Robert, I. C., 313
Roberts, R., 408
Robertson, J., 332

Robin, K., 183, 415
Robin, K. B., 35
Robinson, A., 34, 98
Rodd, J., 355
Rodgers, D. B., 347
Rogers, R., 320
Rogoff, B., 44
Roopnarine, J. L., 56, 57, 59, 79
Rose, L. C., 313
Rose, T. D., 68
Rosegrant, T., 156, 157, 220, 226, 231, 232, 233, 239, 243, 245, 251, 279, 313
Rosenthal, D. M., 390
Rousseau, J.-J., 40, 166, 175
Rowe, J., 242
Rubin, L., 427
Rudisill, M. E., 14
Ruhmann, L., 186
Russell, F., 420
Ryan, K., 21, 244, 418, 425
Ryan, R. M., 347

Saarni, C., 158
Sachs, J., 381
Salinas, K. C., 397
Salvia, J., 326
Sameroff, A., 44
Sanders, L., 287
Sanders, M. G., 397
Sanoff, H., 198
Santrock, J. W., 66, 109, 111, 113, 117, 122, 125, 139, 141, 151, 166, 168
Sapon-Shevin, M., 22
Saracho, O. N., 416
Sarama, J., 163, 165
Saunders, R., 140
Sawyers, J. Y., 390
Schickendanz, J., 65
Schon, D. A., 11, 15
Schorr, L., 94
Schulman, K. L., 35, 415
Schurz, C., 47
Schweinhart, L. J., 57, 58, 59, 228
Scott-Little, C., 335
Scully, P., 243, 244
Scully, P. A., 86
Seefeldt, C., 224, 231, 239, 243, 244, 276, 279
Seidel, S., 333
Seitz, H., 242
Sendak, M., 137
Senn, M., 91
Seplocha, H., 402, 404
Severson, H., 349
Shambaugh, N., 261
Sheehan, J. J., 84
Sheerer, M., 425
Shefatya, L., 163
Shelton, M., 26
Sheridan, S. M., 390, 393, 396
Sherman, J., 345
Shonkoff, J. P., 128, 149, 151
Shore, C., 350
Shorr, L., 94
Shubilla, L., 393
Shulman, K., 183
Sigel, I. E., 68, 140
Silver, H. F., 281, 285
Silverstri, L., 345
Simmons, B. J., 355
Simon, B. S., 397
Skinner, B. F., 167, 175, 252
Skyes, G., 416
Smilansky, S., 163
Smith, A. B., 46
Smith, L. J., 340
Smith, T., 415
Smith, Y., 316
Snow, C., 419
Snyder, A., 47
Snyder, J., 359
Snyder, T., 73
Socrates, 47
Soderman, A., 158, 220, 236, 239, 285
Sparks, D., 418
Sparks-Langer, G. M., 20
Spier, P., 243
Spodek, B., 416
Spring, J., 77
Springer, M., 123
Squires, D., 232
Stallsworth, K., 355
Stamp, L. N., 322, 339
Stark, D. R., 34, 98
Starks, E., 17
Stegelin, D. A., 101
Stein, L. C., 365
Stevens, E., 84
Stevens, K., 345
Stipek, D., 221
Stone, J., 355
Stone, J. G., 99
Strachota, B., 361, 428
Strasburger, V. C., 355
Strickland, D. S., 328
Strom, B., 349
Strom, S. M., 24
Strong, R. W., 281, 285
Stronge, J. H., 15, 427
Styfco, S. J., 58
Surbeck, E., 10
Sutterby, J. A., 208, 210
Swadener, B. B., 103
Swaminathan, S., 163, 165
Swick, K. J., 35, 387, 390, 391, 399, 418, 425
Swim, T. J., 60
Swiniarski, L., 189, 193
Sylwester, R., 52, 362, 363

Taggart, G. L., 8, 11, 13
Tan, A. D. A., 321
Tegano, D., 203
Tennyson, W. W., 24
Theobald, P., 313
Thomas, M. D., 221
Thompson, J. G., 426
Thompson, R. A., 129
Thompson, S. R., 420
Thorndike, E., 167, 175
Thornton, C. P., 208
Tiedt, I., 198, 228, 242, 281
Tiedt, P., 198, 228, 242, 281
Tobin, L., 360, 377
Tolbert, L., 313
Tomlinson, C., 245, 290
Trawick-Smith, J., 196, 197
Trealese, J., 259
Trudeau, K., 24
Tuchman, B., 43
Tye, B., 415

U.S. Bureau of the Census, 73
U.S. Department of Agriculture, 381
U.S. Department of Education, 206, 313
U.S. Department of Health and Human Services, 382
UNESCO, 428

Vakil, S., 60
VanderVen, K., 426
Van Scoy, I., 390
VanVoorhis, F. L., 397
Vartulli, S., 68
Vasalos, A., 13, 14
Vecchi, V., 333
Villegas, A. M., 198
Vygotsky, L., 111, 150, 151, 152, 153, 160, 172, 176, 244

Wald, P., 214
Walker, H., 349

Walker, H. M., 349
Walling, C., 188
Walsh, B., 56
Wardle, F., 196
Warren, E., 72
Washington, V., 346
Wasik, B., 408
Wasley, P., 87, 427
Wassermann, S., 160, 188
Watson, J., 167, 175
Weikart, D. P., 59, 216, 228
Wein, C. A., 345, 351
Weissbourd, B., 392
Weissman, P., 18, 184, 229
Wellhousen, K., 208
Wentzel, H., 355
Wheeler, E., 369–370
Whiren, A., 158, 220, 236, 239, 285
Whiren, A. P., 365
Whisler, J. S., 152, 154
Whitbeck, D. A., 12, 68
White, C. S., 113
White, R., 196
White, V. F., 68
Whitehead, B., 223, 251, 252
Wieder, S., 52
Wien, C. A., 99
Wiggins, G., 324
Wilcox-Herzog, A., 199
Willer, B., 393
Williams, K. C., 190
Williams, L. R., 76
Williams-Browne, K., 279, 284
Wilson, A. P., 8, 11, 13
Wise, A. E., 416
Wolery, M., 211
Wong, H. K., 426
Wong, R. T., 426
Wood, C., 122
Wood, G. H., 84
Wood, H., 420
Woolfolk, A., 138, 139, 148, 150, 166, 168, 169, 170, 261, 279, 284, 285
Wortham, S. G., 47, 159, 160, 162, 198, 199, 224, 229, 232, 239, 243, 315–316, 321, 325
Wright, J., 163, 165
Wright, K., 101
Wyman, A., 47, 54

Yesseldyke, J. E., 326
Yinger, R. J., 430

Zak, M., 151
Zaslow, M., 6, 58, 59, 183, 345, 355, 356, 373, 415, 417, 421
Zigler, E., 58, 224, 392

Subject Index

Abused children, 381
Academic needs, 214
Acceptance, 113, 377
Access
  for children with special needs, 213
  to classroom materials, 201–2
Accountability, planning for, 284
ACEI. *See* Association for Childhood Education International (ACEI)
Achievement tests, 325
Action plan development, in advocacy, 38
Active Experiences for Active Children: Social Studies (Seefeldt & Galper), 276
Active learning, 244
Activism, advocacy as, 98
Activity(ies)
  communicating with families about, 283
  culturally responsive environment and, 199
  planning for, 289, 295–97, 302–3
  to promote self-regulation, 356
  special, 256
  theme and, 298
ADA. *See* Americans with Disabilities Education Act (ADA)
Adaptability, 21–22, 382
Adaptation, in cognitive theory, 170
ADD. *See* Attention deficit disorder (ADD)
ADHD, 345
Adult-designed playgrounds, 212
Adults' interests, children's needs *vs.*, 90–92
Advocacy. *See also* Child advocacy
  in action, 92–93
  as activism, 98
  as caring, 93–94
  definition of, 34
  as ethical decision making, 94–95
  personal, 98
  private-sector, 98
  public policy, 98
  as talk about children, 95–99
Aesthetics, of environment, 184
After-school care, 66–67
Aggression, 355–60
Aggressive behavior, 347, 359, 369, 377
Aggressive play, 367
A House Is a House for Me (Hoberman), 243
Alternative assessment, 324, 489
Amazing Magnets (Rowe & Perham), 242
Ambiance, 195
American Association of Retired Persons Grandparent Information Center, 388
Americans with Disabilities Education Act (ADA), 130
Among School Children (Kidder), 426
Analyzed knowledge, 419
A Nation At Risk: the Imperative for Educational Reform (National Commission on Excellence in Education), 223, 313
Anecdotal assessment, 328
Anecdotal records, 327
Ani's Rocket Ride, 165
Animals, 256
Ani's Playground, 165
Annual yearly progress (AYP), 223
Anti-bias education, 82–83, 155
Anti-bias environment, 198
Appropriate and effective curricula, 226–28
Appropriate assessment methods, 317
Appropriate planning, 295
Art instruction, 213, 256, 257
ASCD. *See* Association for Supervision and Curriculum Development (ASCD)
Ask Mr. Bear (Flack), 159
Assessment. *See also* Assessment methods; Assessment program; Evaluation
  anecdotal, 328
  approaches to, 320–24
  authentic, 324, 489
  categories and levels of, 325
  communicating results of, 318–19
  comprehensive, 318
  curriculum, 333
  defined, 312–16
  early childhood, 313–16, 331
  early childhood practitioner and, 316–20, 331
  individual, 325
  instruction and, 315–16
  performance, 315, 324–26
  planning and, 281–82
  portfolios in, 339–40
  purposes of, 314
  readiness, 325
  technology and, 331
  testing and, 320–24
  unethical, recognizing, 316–17
  websites on, 489
Assessment methods
  administering, scoring, and interpreting, 318
  choosing and developing, 317
  inappropriate, 317
Assessment program
  balanced, indicators of, 334–36
  perspectives on, 333
Association for Childhood Education International (ACEI), 47, 410
Association for Childhood Education International/National Council for the Accreditation for Teacher Education, 397
Association for Supervision and Curriculum Development (ASCD), 460
Association(s). *See also* specific associations
  learning through, 167
  professional, 445–46, 456–62
Associative play, 163, 164
Attention, 364–65, 376
Attention deficit disorder (ADD), 97
Attention getting behavior, 364–65
Attitudes, of early childhood educators, 76
Authentic assessment, 324, 489
Authentic learning experiences, 149–51
Autism, 130

Autobiography, influence of, 67
Autonomy, 136, 346
Awareness, 156, 157
A Way to Integrate Curriculum for Four- and Five-Year Olds (Gryphon House), 276
AYP. *See* Annual yearly progress (AYP)

Baby Danced the Polka (Beaumont), 135
Bailey's Book House, 165
Balanced assessment program, 334–36
Bank Street/Developmental Interaction Approach, 56, 57–58
Bank Street School, 47
Basic needs, in Maslow's theory, 142
Bear Wants More (Wilson & Chapman), 8
Beginning teachers
  classroom management and, 345
  concerns of, 430–33
  planning characteristics of, 288
Behavior. *See also* conflict
  aggressive, 347, 359, 369, 377
  appropriate, and child guidance, 358–59, 368, 371
  attention getting, 364–65
  children's, 348–49
  disruptive, 374–75
  encouraging caring, 157
  inappropriate, 362
  problems, preventing, 358–59
  of reflective practitioners, 17
  violent, 355–60
Behavioral theory of learning, 167–68
Belief/philosophy connection, 67
Beliefs
  curriculum developer and, 230–31
  of teacher about learning, 152
Belonging, need for, 142
Biological influences, 112
Blame shifting, 367
Bodily/kinesthetic intelligence, 174
Books, 213
Brain
  child development and, 126, 128, 129
  research, 155–56
  traumatic injury of, 131
Brain-based learning, principles of, 156
Brainstorming, 255–56, 363
Bribes, 351
Brown decision of 1954, 72
Brown et al. vs. *Board of Education of Topeka,* 72
Bullies, 367

Canadian Association for Young Children, 457
Canadian Child Care Federation, 457
Careful behavior, reflective practitioner and, 15
Caregivers
  distrusting, 381
  education and training of, 422
  facts about, 415
  separating from, 376
  of young children, 16
Caring
  advocacy as, 93–94
  learning environment and, 189, 193
  out-of-school, 398–99
Case knowledge, 417
The Cats in Krasinki Square (Hesse), 141
CDA. *See* Child Development Associate (CDA)
CEC. *See* The Council for Exceptional Children (CEC)
Center-based early childhood care, 381
Center-based learning environments, learning outcomes in, 197–98
Cephalocaudal development, 112
Challenges, 20–21, 75, 184
Change, adapting to, 20–21
Checklists, 327
Child advocacy
  early childhood practitioner's role in, 34–37, 92–98
  guiding principles of, 46–49
  history of early childhood programs, 56–65
  influences on early childhood programs, 37–46, 49–56
  organizations for, 459–60
  perspectives of teachers on, 33–34
  strategies of, 38–39
Child care
  categories of programs, 7–8
  centers during World War II, 49
  full-day, daily plan for, 271
  full-time, cost of, 381
  planning for, 271
  resources for, 464
  strengths and weaknesses of programs, 50
Child development. *See also* Child development theories
  about, 111
  brain and, 126, 128, 129
  characteristics of young children, 111
  definition of development, 110–11
  essential needs in, 113–14
  families and, 126
  of gifted and talented children, 133
  importance of, 126, 127–28
  of infants, 114–16
  key facts about, 111
  knowledge of, 52, 125
  knowledge of learners and, 52
  of learners with exceptionalities, 128, 133
  patterns of development, 111–12
  perspective of teachers on, 109–10
  of preschoolers and kindergartners, 119–21
  promoting, 123–26, 128–34
  reflective practitioners and, 18–19
  of school-age children, 122–23, 124
  of toddlers, 116–19
  understanding, 18–19
Child Development Associate (CDA), 7, 55
Child development theories
  cognitive-developmental theory, 138–41
  ecological theory, 141–42
  hierarchy of needs theory, 142–43
  psychosocial theory, 135–38
Child guidance
  appropriate behavior and, 368, 371, 375–76
  development and need for, 114
  discipline and, 351–55
  effective, 353
  positive strategies for, 360–62
  teachers' role in, 349–51
Child initiated/child directed learning, 158
Child learning evaluator, 17
Children. *See also* Children from diverse backgrounds; Kindergartners; Preschool children/preschoolers; School-age children; Toddlers
  assessment and, 315, 319, 334
  becoming advocate for, 92–98
  building fair chance for, 83–88, 90
  building relationships with, 353, 354

characteristics of, 111, 123
cultural influence on, 155
curriculum developer and knowledge of, 229
with disabilities, 129, 133
disadvantaged, 79
drug-exposed, 338
early childhood practitioners' influence on, 16–24, 88
with exceptional needs, 132, 133
as the future of society, 47
gifted and talented, 133
grouping patterns for, 285
immigrated, 408–10
importance of studying, 48–49
material resources for, 189, 205
needs of, 90–92, 344–49
nurturing, 46–47
nutritious food for, 207
optimizing potential of, 49
planning for, 279, 286
in public preschool program, 221
standardized testing and, 315, 321–22
support services for, 471–72
theoretical perspectives on learning of, 175–76

Children from diverse backgrounds
curriculum and, 230
developmentally appropriate practice and, 227
early child educators and, 78
learner-centered experiences and, 154
learning environment and, 189
planning for, 281, 303, 305, 307
play and, 162
promoting development of, 133–34
strategies for meeting needs of, 287

Children's work, evaluating, 320
Children Today, 410
Children with disabilities, 129–31
Childstats.gov, 381
Circle time, 213
City and Country School, 47
Civil Rights movement, 76–77, 79
Classroom arrangements
for infants and toddlers, 191
meeting learner's needs, 188–89, 193, 196–97
for preschool and kindergartners, 192
for school-age children, 190
ways of, 200–202

Classroom managements. *See* Child guidance
Classroom materials. *See* Materials
Clear roles, in well functioning family, 382
Climate
learning environment and, 189, 199
positive, creating, 356

Coaching, 349, 358
Code of Ethics, 89, 447–55
Cognitive development
of infants, 115, 116
Piaget's theory of, 138–41
play and, 162
of preschoolers/kindergartners, 120, 121
of school-age children, 122–23, 124
of toddlers, 117, 118

Cognitive developmental constructivist theory, 170–72
Cognitive-developmental theory of Piaget, 138–41
Cognitive needs, 113
Cognitive play, 163, 164
Cohesiveness, in well functioning family, 382
Co-learning, creating opportunities for, 152
Collaborating with families
about activities at home, 283
about good learning experience, 153–54
building connection about curriculum, 246
child development insights, 126
common conflict scenarios, 372–73
conducting home visits, 406–7
maintaining positive relationships, 432–33
selecting early childhood program checklist, 26–27
session with parents on portfolio, 336–37
urban public school kindergarten teacher, 104
using learning centers, 194
writing program philosophy statement, 62

Collaboration
early childhood educators and, 22–24
with families, 26–27, 62, 104

Colleague, definition of, 12
Color, in learning environment, 195
Color Me, 165
Commitment
to child care and education, 16–18
to children during Hurricane Katrina, 88
to diversity, 102

Communication
effective, 354–55, 401
with families, 394, 403
in group decisions, 363
informal, 391, 399
inviting, 402–4
in well functioning family, 382

Communication site, 165
Community
building sense of, 22–24
conflict resolution and, 362–63
creating community of learners, 347–48
creating plan of communication with, 101
expectations of, 53
learning environment and, 184–85
local, in indoor environment, 207
planning and, 279
resources, 466
violence in, 355

Community-building strategies, 470
Compensatory education, 53
Competence/competency
child development and need for, 114
definition of, 261, 347
social and emotional, 125

Comprehensive assessment data, 318
Computer(s)
drawing programs, 165
learning and, 163, 165
literacy, 257
materials, 165
and technology, 213

Concept development, 61–62
Concept(s)
of home, 385
planning and, 279, 281

Concept web, National Social Studies standards and, 277
Concrete operational child, 141
Concrete operations stage, 139, 141, 170
Conferences, 399, 404–5
Confidentiality, 96
Configurations, family, 384

Conflict, 355–60. *See also* Conflict resolution
coping with, 364–68
definition of, 362
Conflict resolution
classroom communities and, 362–63
questions and concerns about, 369–70
Constructive play, 163, 164
Constructive theory of learning, 169–74, 177
Constructivism, 48
Constructivist perspective, of curriculum, 253
Content. *See also* Content areas
in appropriate and effective curricula, 226, 228
connecting to the real world, 171–72
curriculum and, 220, 232–36
curriculum developer and, 229
planning and, 279, 281
reflective practitioner and, 21–22
standards, 232, 233
validity of, 322
Content areas
age-appropriate experiences and, 237–38
of early childhood curriculum, 232–33, 234
written curriculum and, 236, 238–39
Context(s)
cultural, 50
curriculum and, 220–21
of school community, 38
task of teaching in, 12–14
Cooperation, in group decisions, 363
Cooperative play, 163, 164
Corporal punishment, 351
Cost, of full-time child care, 381
The Council for Exceptional Children (CEC), 460
Council for Professional recognition, 457
Create Your Own Adventure with Zeke, 165
Credentials, in professional development, 421
Criterion-referenced tests, 322–24
Critical incident, examining, 13–14
Cultural deprivation, 79
Cultural differences, 397–98
Cultural influences, 112, 138, 155
Culturally diverse learners, planning for, 287
Culturally relevant curricula, 228
Culturally responsive curriculum, 242–43
meaningful curriculum as, 243–44
Culturally responsive environment, 198, 199
Cultural setting, 133–34
Culture. *See also* Children from diverse backgrounds
learning and, 155
Curiosity, 53
Curricular environment, 184
Curriculum. *See also* Influences on curriculum; Meaningful curriculum; Taught curriculum; Written curriculum
appropriate and effective, 226–28
assessment of, 333
behavioral perspective of, 253
children's misbehavior and, 348
children's needs and, 21–22
content areas of, 232–36
culturally responsive, 242–43
definition of, 220–21
developmentally appropriate practice and, 224–26
in early childhood education, 100–102, 241
emergent, 242
high-quality, 62–63
importance of, 221–23
integrated, 239–40
measurement and, 335–36
NAEYC guidelines for content, 233
perspectives of teachers on, 219–20
play and, 161
resources for, 442–46, 464
role of developer, 228–31
standards, 52–53
theories about, 251–53
webs, 255
Curriculum organizer, developmental domains as, 238

Daily plans, 263, 270–73
Daniel's Story (Matas), 138
DAP. *See* Developmentally appropriate practices (DAP)
Deaf-blindness, 131
Deafness, 131
Decision-making practitioner, 30
Decisions, group, 363
Declarative knowledge, 419
Deficit terminology, 96–97
Delta Draw, 165
Demographics, 74
Density, 196–97
Despair, ego integrity *vs.,* 137
Destination: Neighborhood, 165
Destination: Time Trip USA, 165
Developmental domains, 236, 238
Developmentally Appropriate Practice in Early Childhood Programs (Bredekamp & Copple), 224
Developmentally appropriate practices (DAP)
curriculum and, 224–26
early childhood education and, 279
good programs and, 51
Developmental screening assessment, 325
Diagnostic assessment, 325
Differentiation, in effective planning, 290
Disability
children with, 129–31
definition of, 128
Disadvantaged child, 79
Disagreement, expressing, 92
Discipline
about, 341
child guidance and, 351–55
definition of, 372
old-fashioned, 351
Displays, 200–201
Disposition(s)
definition of, 14
of early childhood educator, 76
for reflection, 15
reflective practitioner and, 16–25
Disputes
group-entry, 366–67
possession, 364
Disruptive behavior, 374–75
District-, school-, and program-wide assessments, 325
Diverse academic needs, adapting environments for children with, 214
Diverse backgrounds. *See* Children from diverse backgrounds
Diverse group of parents, skills necessary for, 313

Diversity. *See also* Children from diverse backgrounds
challenges and, 75
Civil Rights movement and, 76–77, 79
commitment to, 102
definition of, 73–74
early childhood setting and, 74–75
future outlook of, 102–3
perspectives of teachers on, 71–72
resources on, 464–65
social issues of, 77
Documentation
features of, 333–34
process of, 332–33
The Dollmaker (Film), 45
Domestic violence, 355
Drawings, children's, 327
Drill-and-practice exercises, 168
Drop-in child care program, 7–8
Drug-exposed child, 338–39

Early childhood education
child development and, 127–28
cognitive-developmental theory and, 140
contemporary leaders in, 46
curriculum in, 241
diagnostic/developmental tests, 313
early leaders in, 40–41
lifelong learning skills, 152–53
precepts of, 46–49
psychosocial theory and, 135–38
social learning theory and, 168–69
standards for, 54
time-honored precepts of, 46–49
Early Childhood Environment Rating Scales (ECERS), 209
Early childhood materials, origins of, 42
Early childhood practice
behavioral theory and, 168
Bronfenbrenner's ecological theory and, 141–42
cognitive developmental constructivist theory and, 171–72
Erikson's psychosocial theory and, 135
Maslow's hierarchy of needs theory and, 142–43
maturation theory and, 166–67
multiple intelligences theory and, 173–74
Piaget's cognitive developmental theory and, 140–41
social learning theory and, 168–69
sociocultural constructivist theory and, 172–73
Early childhood practitioners. *See also* Beginning teachers; Professional development; Reflective practitioners; Teaching
about, 8, 17, 64–65, 76
appropriate child talk examples, 97
assessment and, 317
on becoming, 25
characteristics of, 4, 20, 288
child guidance and, 349–51
creating opportunities for co-learning, 152
culturally responsive environment and, 199
curriculum and, 221, 228
ethical responsibility of, 89
families and, 379, 389–91
free and inexpensive materials for, 444–45
improving educational outcomes of children, 78
learning process for, 20
lifelong learning and, 428–30
men as, 420
multicultural education and, 83–90
professional resources for, 447–56
promoting child development and, 123–34
role as, 418–23
self-questioning framework, 12
Early childhood professional. *See* Early childhood practitioners
Early childhood programs
categories of, 7–8
checklist to guide parents in selecting, 26–27
community expectations and, 53
concept development in, 61–62
curriculum standards and, 52–53
educational theories and, 49, 52
essentials for excellence in, 50
ethnic groups in, 63
evaluation criteria and, 53, 55
exemplary, 51–52
financial and material resources for, 55
historical influences on, 37, 38, 43–46
historical overview of, 57–60
human resources and, 55
interdisciplinary approaches in, 63, 65
knowledge of child development and, 52
outside the United States, 64–65
past and present of, 56–65
pedagogy, 56
perspective on quality of, 333
philosophy and goals of, 61
programmatic precepts, 50
respect for individual differences in, 63
social interaction in, 63
social trends and, 49
Eating problems, 377
ECERS. *See* Early Childhood Environment Rating Scales (ECERS)
Ecological developmental theory, 85–86
Ecological Theory of Urie Bronfenbrenner, 141–42
Economic standards, 234
Education
antibias, 82–83, 223
of children, 395–96
multicultural, 76–77, 79–82, 155
in professional development, 420
of young children, 16–18
Educational influences on curriculum, 224
Educational planning, designing, 29
Educational theories, 49, 52
Education for All Handicapped Children (EHA) (P.L. 94-142), 1130
Education of the Handicapped Act (P.L. 99-457), 130
Education Resources Information Center (ERIC) Clearinghouses, 25, 462
Educators' Guides to free materials, 444
Effective communication, 354–55, 401
Effective planning, 288–305
Ego integrity *vs.* despair, 137
EHA. *See* Education for All Handicapped Children (EHA) (P.L. 94-142)
Elementary children, fostering industry in, 137–38
Elementary school programs, 8
Emergent curriculum, 242
Emotional competence, 125
Emotional development
as content areas, 238
early childhood practitioner and, 125
of infants, 115
of kindergartners, 119–20

Emotional development, (*cont.*)
of preschoolers, 119–20
of school-age children, 122
of toddlers, 117
Emotional disorders, 131
Emotional intelligence, 417
Emotional needs, 113
Emotions, human, 362–63
Empowerment, of parents and families, 38
English-as-a-second-language (ESL), 177–78
English language learners
strategies for, 287
struggling to read as, 177–78
Environmental influences, 112
Environment(s). *See also* Space
ambiance in, 195
caring, creating, 125, 369–70
child development and, 113–14
communities, conflict resolution and, 362–63
creating community of learners in, 347–48
culturally responsive, 198, 199
definition of, 183
density in, 196–97
developmentally appropriate practice and, 227
early childhood practitioners' role in, 187–90, 193
evaluating, 320
high-quality, 184–87, 198–211, 217
importance of, 193, 195–98, 204
inclusive, 211, 213–14
indoor, 198–200, 207
labels in, 198–203
for multiple intelligences, 178–79
outdoor, 207–8, 209–10, 212
perspectives of teachers on, 181–82
preventing behavior problems in, 358
sensory-rich, creating, 215–17
Episodic knowledge, 417
Equipment. *See also* Materials
in child care programs, 27
environment and, 186
indoor learning environment and, 203–5
for infants, 27, 205
for kindergartners, 205
for preschoolers, 205
for school-age children, 205
selecting, 205
for toddlers, 27, 205
Equity
in classroom, 99–102
definition of, 73–74
social issues of, 77
ERIC Clearinghouses. *See* Education Resources Information Center (ERIC) Clearinghouses
Erikson psychosocial theory, 135–38
Errors
in observation, 329
recognition, in balanced assessment, 334
ESL. *See* English-as-a-second-language (ESL)
Esteem needs, 142
Ethics
codes of, 89, 447–55
early childhood educators and, 89
making ethical decisions, 24, 94–95
problem-solving strategies and, 24
social justice and, 87–88
Ethnically diverse learners, planning for, 287
Ethnic groups, 63
children from diverse backgrounds and
recognizing contributions of, 63
Evaluation. *See also* Evaluation criteria
early childhood programs and, 53, 55
evaluator role in, 316–19
of families, 26
of high-quality early childhood environments, 209–10
of individual children's progress, 326–32
of indoor environment, 207, 208
observation and, 326–32
of outdoor environment, 210–11, 212
of program effectiveness, 332–34
Evaluation criteria
for brochures, 411
for programs, 53, 55
software, 465–66
Event sampling, 327
Exceptional learner, 128
Exceptional needs children, 132, 133
adapting environments for, 213–15
developmentally appropriate practice and, 227
play and, 160
strategies for meeting needs of, 287
Exercises, drill-and-practice, 168
Exosystem, 141
Expectations
influence of family on, 382
from teachers, parents/ families, 390–91
Experienced teachers, planning characteristics of, 288
Experience(s)
child development and, 112
in early children education, 6
sharing, in advocacy, 38
Experiential or learned curriculum, 252
Expert, adaptive knowledge, 419
Exploration
fostering, 171
in learning cycle, 156, 157
work, play, and, 161
Exploring practitioner, 30

Facts, planning, 261
Failure, fear of, 361
Fairness, in classroom, 99–102
Families. *See also* Collaborating with families; Parent(s); Parents/families
assessment process and, 319
building connection about curriculum, 246
child advocacy and, 38
child development and, 126
collaboration with, 26–27, 62, 104
communication with, 101, 403
configuration of, 384
connecting with, 193
contemporary, 382–91
empowerment of, 38
homeless, 387
involvement of, 393, 395–96
in larger social context, 384–86
learning and, 153–54
learning environment and, 193
participation in balanced assessment, 334
percentage of children in, 381
planning and, 279
positive outlook on, 19–20
respecting diversity in, 386, 388
as social system, 382–84
standards-based kindergarten unit on, 277–79
support services for, 471–72
support system, 27
weekly plan for kindergarten on, 280

Family Child Care Environment Rating Scale (FCCERS), 209
Family child care programs, 7
Family child-care setting, 27
Family Circle, 410
Family resource programs, 392
Family support programs, 392
Family support system, 27
Family violence, 355
FCCERS. *See* Family Child Care Environment Rating Scale (FCCERS)
Federal- and state-mandated assessment, 325
Feeling significant, 368
Financial resources, 55
Finding Our Own Way (Newman), 427
Fine motor, 119
First grade
  daily plan for, 272–73
  long-range plans for, 268–69
  planning for, 268–69, 272–73
The First Year of Teaching: Real World Stories from American's Teachers (Kane), 425
Fit Source (National Child Care Information Center), 206
Five Oaks, 62
Flexibility, 21
Focus on outcomes for students, in reflection, 14
Food insecure household, 381
Formal operational stage, 171
Formal schooling, transition to, 261
Full inclusion, 133

Games with rules, 164
Gardening, outline for project on, 299–301
General written curriculum, 231
Generations United, 388
Generativity, stagnation *vs.*, 137
Geography standards, 234
Gesell, Arnold, 166–67
Gifted children, 133
The Girl with the Brown Crayon (Paley), 428
Goals
  Bank Street/Development Interaction Approach, 58
  early childhood environment and, 185
  of early childhood programs, 61
  in effective planning, 289
  Head Start, 58
  High/Scope, 59
  Montessori method, 57
  Reggio Emilia, 60
Goals 2000: Educate America Act (U.S. Department of Education, 1994), 206
Grandparent-headed households, 388
Grands Place, 388
Greece, brainstorming web about, 257
Gross motor, 119
Group-administered tests, 320
Group child care programs, 7
Group decisions, 363
Group-entry disputes, 366–67
Group learning, planning characteristics for, 285
Guidance. *See* Child guidance
Guidelines
  for collaborating with parents/families, 397
  for curriculum content (NAEYC), 233
Guilt, initiative *vs.*, 136

Head Start, 79, 331
  about, 56, 58–59
  Child Outcomes Framework, 231
  learning outcomes for children, 284
  parents involvement in, 433–34
  reauthorization bill, 221
Health
  environment quality and, 185–86
  goals and age-appropriate experiences, 235, 237
  resources for, 445–46
Health impairment, 131
Hearing, 214
Hearing impairment, 131
Hierarchy of Needs Theory of Abraham Maslow, 142–43
High/Scope, 59
History standards, 234
Home, concept of, 385
Homeless Assistance Act of 2002, 386
Homeless children
  about, 387
  educational rights of, 386
Homelessness, 385
Home visits, conducting, 406–7
Hot Dog with Abbot Avenue (English), 141
Household and found materials, 444–45
Housing insecurity, 385
Human emotions, 362–63
Human environment, 184, 205. *See also* Environment(s)
Human Resources, 55, 466–71
The Hunchback of Notre Dame (Novel), 44
Hurricane Katrina, 88

IDEA. *See* Individuals with Disabilities Education Act (IDEA) (P. L. 101-476); Individuals with Disabilities Education Act of 1990 (IDEA)
Ideas
  in learning environment, 187
  multicultural education as, 81–82
Identifying with children, 361
Identity *vs.* role confusion, 136
IEP. *See* Individualized educational plan (IEP)
IEPs. *See* Individualized education programs (IEPs)
IFSP. Individualized family service plan (IFSP)
If You Give A Mouse A Cookie (Bond), 289
Illegal assessment, recognizing, 316–17
I Love My Family (Beal), 276
IMAC. *See* International Montessori Accreditation Council (IMAC)
Imagination, 363
Imitation, learning through, 167
Immigrated children, 408–10
Inappropriate assessment, recognizing, 316–17
Inappropriate behavior, 362
In-class workshop
  becoming culturally competent teacher, 106
  becoming valued colleague, 434–35
  brainstorming with curriculum Webs, 255–56
  creating high-quality environment, 217
  creating informational brochure, 410–11
  designing children's work portfolios, 339–40
  drafting teaching philosophy, 67–69
  learning environments for multiple intelligences, 178–79
  planning for diverse learners, 307

In-class workshop, (*cont.*)
role-playing ways of talking with children, 375–77
understanding inclusion, 144–45
working with teacher reflection, 30
Inclusion, 63, 132–33, 144–45
Inclusive curriculum, 244
Inclusive environment, 211, 213–14
Independence, child development and need for, 114
Individual assessment, 325
Individual children's progress, evaluating, 325–32
Individual differences, respect for, 63
Individualized educational plan (IEP), 319
Individualized education programs (IEPs), 79, 97
Individualized family service plan (IFSP), 319
Individual learning, 285
Individuals with Disabilities Education Act (IDEA) (P. L. 101-476), 130
Individuals with Disabilities Education Act of 1990 (IDEA), 130
Indoor environment, 198–207, 208
Industry *vs.* inferiority, 136, 137
Infants
classroom arrangement for, 191
criteria for environment, 186
curriculum and, 241
daily planning form for, 270
development of, 114–16
early childhood education programs, 27
materials for, 189, 205, 438–39
nutritious foods for, 207
planning for, 270
psychosocial theory and, 135, 136
Infant/Toddler Environment Rating Scale (ITERS), 209
Inferiority, 136
Influences. *See also* Influences on curriculum
biological and environmental, 112, 138
cultural, 112, 155
standards and, 54
Influences on curriculum
educational, 224
political, 223
social, 223
Informal communication, 391, 399
Informational brochure, creating, 410–11
Information assessment, use of, 316–17
Information site, 165
Initiative *vs.* guilt, 136
Inquiring practitioner, 30
Inquiry, in learning cycle, 157
Inservice educators, 423
Instruction
assessment and, 315–16
measurement and, 335–36
Instructional support team (IST), 29
Integrated curriculum, 239–40
Integrated units, planning for, 290–93, 294–95
Intelligence. *See also* multiple intelligences (MI) theory of learning
bodily/kinesthetic, 174
emotional, 417
interpersonal, 174
intrapersonal, 174, 266
logical/mathematical, 174, 264
musical, 174
naturalist, 174
visual/spatial, 174, 266
Interactions
with families, 393–405
positive, building, 358
Interdisciplinary approaches, subject-matter teaching and, 63, 65
Interdisciplinary teaching. *See* Integrated curriculum
International Montessori Accreditation Council (IMAC), 457
International Reading Association (IRA), 410, 460
International Reading Association/National Council of Teachers of English, 322
Interpersonal intelligence, 174
Interstate New Teacher Assessment and Support Consortium (INTASC) Standards, 456
Interviews, 327
Intimacy *vs.* isolation, 136
Intrapersonal intelligence, 174, 266
Involvement
of families and children in assessment, 319, 334, 368
of family in children's education, 395
IRA. *See* International Reading Association (IRA)
Island of the Blue Dolphins (O'Dell), 138
Isolation, intimacy *vs.*, 136
IST. *See* Instructional support team (IST)
ITERS. *See* Infant/Toddler Environment Rating Scale (ITERS)

Journals
professional, 456–63, 461–62
teachers, 10
Just Grandma and Me (Mayer), 276

KidPix, 165
Kidspiration, 165
Kindergarten. *See also* Kindergartners
full-day schedule, 204
going to, 306–7
integrated subject-area web for, 291
movement, history of, 47
parents' skills necessary for success of, 313
preschool curriculum for, 241
teacher of, 104
weekly plan for, 280
yearly plan for, 264–67
Kindergartners
development of, 119–21
material resources for, 205
planning for, 264–67, 279, 291
room arrangement for, 192
KINship Information Network, 388
Kitten's First Full Moon (Henkes), 141
Knowledge
case, 417
of child development, 52, 125
curriculum developer and, 229
declarative, 419
episodic, 417
expert, adaptive, 419
learning and, 150, 151
pedagogical, 230
propositional, 417
reflective, organized, and analyzed, 419
sharing, 38
situated, can-do procedural, 419
of teaching strategies, 230
Knowledge-base challenges, teaching and, 419
Knowledge-centered perspective of curriculum, 251
Knowledge stable procedural, 419
KWL strategy, 282, 291

Labeling
child guidance and, 361
as observation error, 329
of work areas, 201–2
Language and literacy, 234, 237
Language and Thought of the Child (Piaget), 48
Language arts, 240, 247, 256, 257
Language development
of infants, 115, 116
of preschoolers/kindergartners, 120, 121
of school-age children, 123, 124
of toddlers, 117, 118
The Languages of Learning: How Children Talk, Write, Dance, Draw, and Sing Their Understanding of the World (Gallas), 427
Lanham Act of 1942, 49
Large-scale assessment, 325
The Last Emperor (Film), 44
LD. *See* Learning disability (LD)
Leaders
contemporary, of early childhood education, 46
early, of early childhood education, 40–41
views of childhood, 43
Leadership
in advocacy, 38
imagination and, 363
real, 429
Learner-centered experiences
about, 153–54
brain research and, 155–56
as child initiated and directed, 158
lifelong learning focus, 156–58
meeting diverse learners' needs, 154
Learners. *See also* Learner-centered experiences
diverse, meeting needs of, 287
diverse, planning for, 307
English Language, 177–78
with exceptionalities, 128
Learning. *See also* Learning centers; Learning experiences; Learning theories; Lifelong learning
about, 149
active, 244
authentic, 149–51
brain-based, 156
child initiated and child directed, 158
colearning, 152
cultural influences on, 155
cycle of, 157
definition of, 148–49
early childhood practitioner as facilitator of, 152
facts about, 149
families and, 153–54
group, planning characteristics for, 285
learner-centered experiences, 153–58
perspectives of teachers on, 312–13
play and, 158, 162
as strategy for professional development, 431
teachers' beliefs about, 152
technology and, 163, 165
Learning centers
choosing, 202
early childhood classrooms and, 197–98
resources for, 442–44
using, 194
Learning disability (LD), 97, 131
Learning experiences
authentic, 149–51
good, 153–54
Learning facilitators, 152, 171
Learning process, for early childhood educators, 20
Learning standards, early, 53
Learning theories
about, 174
behavioral, 167–68, 175
cognitive developmental constructive theory, 170–72, 175–76
comparison of, 175–76
constructive, 169–74, 176
definition of theory, 165
maturation, 166–67
multiple intelligences, 173–74, 176
social, 168–69, 175
sociocultural constructivist theory, 172–73
Legislation, for children with disabilities, 129–30. *See also* specific laws
Less developmentally appropriate practice, 225
Lessons, planning for, 289, 295, 302–3
Library-linked resources, 469
Licensing, 416
Life in Small Moments: Learning in an Urban Classroom (Meier), 425
Lifelong learning
learner-centered experiences and, 156–58
teaching skills of, 152–53
Light, 195
Listening standards, 234
Literacy, 248
computer, 257
content areas, 236
difficulties with, 177
language and, 234, 237
play and, 162
as subject area in curriculum
Little Man Tate (Film), 45
Llama, Llama Red Pajama (Dewdney), 135
Logical/mathematical intelligence, 174, 264
Long-term planning, 262–63, 264–69, 290–95
Love, child development and need for, 113
Love, need for, 142

Macrosystem, 141
Make Early Learning Standards Come Alive (Gronlund), 206
Maslow's Hierarchy of Needs theory, 142–43
Materials
access to, 201–2
early childhood programs and, 55
free and inexpensive, 444–45
historical view of, 42
importance of, 203
indoor learning environments, 203–5
for infants, 189, 205, 438–39
for learning centers, 195, 442–44
learning environment and, 186, 189, 199
possession disputes and, 364
for preschoolers, 205, 439–40
for recording observation, 330
for school-age children, 205, 441–42
selecting, 205
for teachers, 444–45
for toddlers, 205, 438–39
Mathematics
age-appropriate experiences and goals of, 237
brainstorming about study of animals, 256
brainstorming about study of Greece, 257
in curriculum, 234, 240, 247
planning for, 264, 272, 292

Mathematics, (*cont.*)
in primary-grade gardening project, 300
themes and units for early childhood, 248
Maturation theory of learning, 166–67
McREL. *See* Mid-Continent Regional Education Laboratories (McREL)
Meaningful curriculum
building, 245–51
characteristics of, 243–44
Measurement
curriculum and, 335–36
limitations of, 335
Media violence, 355
Mentors, Master Teachers, and Mrs. MacGregor: Stories of Teachers Making a Difference (Bluestein), 428
Meritocracy, 84
Mesosystem, 141
Metaphors, 425–428
Microsystem, 141
Mid-Continent Regional Education Laboratories (McREL), 233
Millie's Math House, 265
The Mind of the Child (Preyer), 48
Min-Yo and the Moon Dragon (Hillman), 137
Misbehavior, 345, 348, 353
Misinformation, school learning and, 149
Mistakes, learning from, 20
Mistrust, trust *vs.*, 136
Montessori education method, 57
"Morning Meeting begins at 7:15 PM," 62
Moss Gown (Hooks), 137
Motor abilities, adapting environment for children with, 213
Multicultural education, 76–77, 79–82, 155
to antibias, 82–83
Multicultural environment, 198
Multiculturalism, 221
Multiple disabilities, 131
Multiple intelligences (MI) theory of learning
about, 173
applying eight intelligences, 174
early childhood practice and, 173–74, 177
learning environments for, 178–79
Music, 235, 256, 257
Musical intelligence, 174
My Left Foot (Film), 44

NABE, National Association for Bilingual Education (NABE)
NACCRRA. *See* National Association of Child Care Resource and Referral (NACCRRA)
NAEA. *See* National Art Education Associations (Arts) (NAEA)
NAEYC. *See* National Association for the Education of Young Children (NAEYC)
NAFCC. *See* National Association for Family Child Care (NAFCC)
NAGC. *See* National Association for Gifted Children (NAGC)
National Aging Information Center, 388
National Art Education Associations (Arts) (NAEA), 460
National Association for Bilingual Education (NABE), 460
National Association for Family Child Care (NAFCC), 459
National Association for Gifted Children (NAGC), 461
National Association for the Education of Young Children (NAEYC), 47, 410, 458–59
Code of Ethics, 89, 447–55
guidelines for curriculum content, 233
social studies Web site, 276
National Association of Child Care Resource and Referral (NACCRRA), 457
National Board for Professional Teaching Standards (NBPTS), 415
National Center for Early Development and Learning (NCEDL), 261
National Center for Homeless Education, 386
National Child Care Information Center, 464
National Coalition of the Homeless, 386
National Committee of Grandparents for Children's Rights, 388
National Council for the Social Studies (NCSS), 461
National Council of Teachers of Mathematics (NCTM), 461
National Laboratory of Early Childhood Education, 25
National Law Center on Homelessness & Poverty, 386
National Network for Youth, 386
National Reporting System test, 224
National Science Teachers Association (NSTA), 461
Nativist theory, 175
Naturalist intelligence, 174
NBPTS. *See* National Board for Professional Teaching Standards (NBPTS)
NCLB. *See* No Child Left Behind (NCLB)
NCSS. *See* National Council for the Social Studies (NCSS)
NCTM. *See* National Council of Teachers of Mathematics (NCTM)
NECDL. *See* National Center for Early Development and Learning (NCEDL)
Needs
academic, 214
of children, 90–92, 213, 344–49, 357
curriculum and children's, 21–22
essential, 113–14
of exceptional children, 132
hierarchy of, 142–43
of learners, 287
planning, 259, 284–86
strategies for meeting, 287
The New England Primer, 45
Noah's Ark (Spier), 243
No Child Left Behind (NCLB), 53, 224, 313, 397, 415
Noise, in learning environment, 195
Non-referenced (standardized) tests, 313, 315, 320–22
Notes from a Schoolteacher (Herndon), 426
NSTA. *See* National Science Teachers Association (NSTA)
Nursery school programs, 7
Nursery schools, 47
Nurturing, 46–47
Nutrition, resources for, 445–46
Nutrition and fitness, 206–7

Objectives, in effective planning, 289
Observation
errors in, 329

learning through, 167, 169
materials for recording, 330
processes and methods, 327
as strategy for professional development, 431
in understanding children, 125
Of Children (LeFrancois), 43
"Old-fashioned" discipline, 351
Oliver Twist (Dickens), 44
OMEP. *See* U. S. National Committee of the World Organization for Early Childhood Education (OMEP)
One Child (Hayden), 426
Onlooker play, 163, 164
On Their Side: Helping Children Take Charge of Learning (Strachota), 428
Oops! What We Learn When Our Teaching Fails (Power and Hubbard), 427
Open-ended software, 165
Open-mindedness, 14, 15
Opportunity(ies)
to develop skills, 103
in early childhood education programs, 27
for self-regulation, 169
for social interaction, 63
Orbis Pictus "World of Pictures" (Comenius), 47
Oregon Trail, 165
Organizational resources, 463
Organizations(s), professional, 445–46, 456–62. *See also* specific organizations
Organized knowledge, 419
Orthopedic impairment, 131
Outdoor environment, 207–11, 212
The Out of Sync Child: Recognizing and Coping with Sensory Integration Dysfunction (Kantrowitz and McGinn), 215

Pancakes, Pancakes (Carle), 281
Paper-and-pencil tests, 321, 322, 324
Parallel play, 163, 164
Parent-child relationship, 383–84
Parenting the Second Time Around (PASTA), 388
Parent(s). *See also* Parents/families
checklist for evaluating early childhood programs, 26–27
children play and, 161
curriculum and, 223
discussing portfolios with, 336–37
empowering, 38
interest in children's education, 395
separating from, 376
Parents/families
building rapport with, 400–401
concerns about working with, 389–90
expectations from teachers, 390–91
guidelines for effective interactions with, 393–405
national standards for collaborating, 397
promoting engagement in education, 391–93
Parent's Magazine, 410
Partial inclusion, 133
PASTA. *See Parenting the Second Time Around* (PASTA)
Patience, in group decisions, 363
Pedagogical content knowledge, 230
Pedagogy, 21–22, 56
Peers
to guide learning, 173
support of, 22–24
People, in learning environment, 187
Perceptions of education, children and, 6
Performance assessment
defined, 315
principles of, 324–26
Performance standards, 232
Persistence
children skills and, 53
reflective practitioners and, 15
Personal advocacy, 98
Personal experiences, curriculum developer and, 230–31
Personal history, about, 48
Personality clashes, 366
Personal positions, children's problems and, 88, 90
Pet store project, 249
Philosophy
of early childhood programs, 61
teaching, drafting, 67–69
Physical aggression, reducing, 359–60
Physical characteristics, in indoor environment, 207
Physical education, 235, 237, 257
Physical environment, 184, 205. *See also* Environment(s)
Physical/motor development
of infants, 115, 116
learning environment and, 213
of preschoolers/kindergartners, 119–121
of school-age children, 122, 124
of toddlers, 117
Physical needs, 113
Piaget's Cognitive-Developmental theory, 138–41
"Plan, Do, Review" method (Hohman & Weikart), 216
Planning
about knowledge of children, 279
of accountability, 284
for activities, 295–97, 302–3
of assessing children's learning, 281–82
definition of, 260–62
differences of novice *vs.* expert teachers, 287–88
for diverse learners, 287, 303, 305, 307
for each child's success, 286
early childhood practitioners' role in, 273–283
educational, designing, 29
effective, 288–305
for first grade, 268–69, 272–73
for infants, 270
for instruction about families, 279
for lessons, 289, 295–97, 302–3
long-term, 262–63, 290–95
matrix, 308
need for, 259
for preschoolers, 274–75, 291
for primary-grade children, 292
for projects, 293–95
research on teachers', 286–87
for school age children, 268–69, 292
short-term, 203, 263, 271, 295
successful teaching and, 284–87
teachers' perspectives about, 259–60
thematic units, 298–99
for toddlers, 270
types of, 262–71
unit on famous Americans, 294–95
Play
about, 163
aggressive, 367
associative, 163, 164
children from diverse backgrounds and, 162

Play, *(cont.)*
children's, role of adults in, 212
children's learning and, 158
children with exceptionalities and, 160
cognitive, 162
constructive, 163, 164
cooperative, 163, 164
definition of, 158–60
importance of, 160
for kindergartners, 254–55
learning and, 162
onlooker, 163, 164
parallel, 163, 164
solitary, 163, 164
stages and types of, 163, 164
symbolic, 163, 164
value of, 161
work, exploration, and, 161
Playgrounds, 212
Policy, in preventing disputes, 364
Political influences on curriculum, 223
Portfolios
designing, 339–40
discussing with parents on, 336–37
Portraits in Courage: Teachers in Difficult Circumstances (UNESCO), 426–28
Positive schoolwide approach, 349
Possession disputes, 364
Postmodern family, 382
Power struggles, 365
Pre-K programs, diagnostic/developmental tests for, 313
Preoperational children, 140–41
Preoperational thinking stage, 139, 140, 170
Preschool
curriculum, 241
half-day, weekly plan for, 274–75
half-day schedule, 204
integrated subject-area web for, 291
programs, 7
room arrangement for, 192
Preschool children/preschoolers
childcare programs for, 27
development of, 119–21
material resources for, 205, 439–40
nutritious foods for, 207
planning for, 274–75, 291
psychosocial theory and, 135, 136
themes for, 248
Preservice educators, 345, 423–24
Primary-grade students
integrated subject-area web for, 292
outline for project on gardening, 299–301
Privacy, 195
Private-sector advocacy, 98
Proactive attitude, reflective practitioner and, 16
Problem solving
addressing, 24
inquiry oriented software and, 165
Problem-solving practitioner, 30
Procedural knowledge, 417
Procedures, in effective planning, 289
Process areas, in mathematics, 234
Process(es)
curriculum and, 220
in effective planning, 289
multicultural education as, 81, 82
observation, 327
Professional development
components of, 420–21
definition of, 416
dimensions of, 416
of early childhood educators, 25, 26
facts about, 415
fostering, 423–24
importance of, 422
influences on, 423
public policy and, 429
specialized knowledge and, 416, 417
stages in, 424–28
teachers' perspective on, 413–14
Professional growth. *See* Professional development
Professionalism, in early childhood, 421
Professional knowledge, 417
Professional performance, evaluating, 320
Program effectiveness, evaluating, 320, 332–34
Project Approach in the "Curriculum Planning and Program–Early Childhood Education," 249
Project Healthy Grandparents (Georgia State University), 388
Project(s)
curriculum and, 247–51
gardening, 299–301
planning for, 293–95
plans, 293, 304–5
structure of, 304–5
vs. units, 304
Propositional knowledge, 417
Proximodistal development, 112
Psychosocial theory of Erik Erikson, 135–38
Publication site, 165
Public Law 94-142, 52
Public library, services for children and families, 468
Public policy
advocacy, 98
professional development and, 429
Public preschool program, children in, 221
Public schools
evening art class, 105
kindergarten programs, 8
kindergarten teacher, 104
specialists, 468
Public spaces, fairness in, 102
Punishment, 353
Punitive methods, 345

Qualities of Effective Teachers (Stronge), 427

Radical Reflections: Passionate Opinions on Teaching, Learning, and Living (Fox), 428
Rating scales, 327
Rational behavior, reflective practitioners and, 15–16
The Read Aloud Handbook (Trelease), 259
Readiness assessment, 325
Reading standards, 234
Real leadership, 429
Redbook, 410
Reflection, teacher planning and, 282
Reflective knowledge, 419
Reflective practice. *See also* Reflective practitioners
definition of, 6, 8
effects of, 67–68
getting started with, 11
levels of, 11–14
process of, 8–9, 11
teachers, 3–5
Reflective practitioners. *See also* Early childhood practitioners
characteristics of, 14–16
disposition to become, 16–27
journal keeping by, 10
perspectives of, 3–4
self-questioning framework, 12

Reflective thinking, 8
Reform, multicultural education as, 81, 82
Reggio Emilia, 56, 59–60
Reinforcement, learning through, 167
Relatedness, 346–47
Relationships
  building, 353, 354
  in classroom, 99
Research
  on advocacy, 39
  appropriate early childhood curricula and, 226
  brain, 155–56
  curriculum, 226–28
  as influence on education programs, 49, 52
  on planning, 286–87
Resource(s). *See also* Materials
  community, 466–69
  curriculum, 442–46
  financial, 55
  health, nutrition, and safety, 445–46
  human, 466–70
  learning, 442–44
  in learning environment, 187
  material, 438–42
  professional, 447–56
  storage and organizational, 463
  technology, 463–65
  for unit teaching, 248
Respect
  in group decisions, 363
  for individual differences, 63
  need for, 114
Responsibility
  child development and need for, 114
  in classroom, 100
  for disposition, 14, 15
  in positive learning climate, 189
  of teaching young children, 6
Rewards, 353
Rights, children's, 344–49
Risks
  in advocacy, 38
  taking, reflective practitioners and, 20
Role confusion, identity *vs.*, 136
Role-playing, 375–77
Roots (Television series), 45
Rosie's Walk (Hutchins), 238
Routines, 203
Rubric, 323
Ruggles Street Nursery School, 47
Rules
  games with, 164
  in preventing behavior problems, 358
Running records, 327

SACERS. *See* School Age Care Environment Rating Scale (SACERS)
Safety
  child development and need for, 113
  in classroom, 100
  environment quality and, 185–86
  resources for, 445–46
Savage Inequalities (Kozol), 55
Save My Rain Forest (Zak), 151
Scaffolding, 172
Schedules, 203, 204
School Age Care Environment Rating Scale (SACERS), 209
School-age children
  development of, 122–23, 124
  material resources for, 205, 441–42
  planning for, 268–69, 292
  room arrangement for, 190
School of Infancy (Comenius), 47
School play, 254–55
Schools, 27
  funding of, 221
Science
  brainstorming about study of Greece, 257
  brainstorming for studying animals, 256
  in curriculum, 238, 240, 247
  in first-grade gardening project, 300
  units and themes for early childhood, 234, 248
The Science Book of Magnets (Ardley), 242
Science center, 194
Seclusion, 186
Second grade schedule, 204
Security, child development and need for, 113
Self as teacher, in reflection, 11–12
Self-concept as a learners, children and, 6
Self-control, 53
Self-direction, 53
Self-efficacy, promoting, 169
Self-regulation, 355–66
Self-regulatory behaviors, 345
Senorimotor stage, 139, 170
Sense, 186
Sensorimotor play, 163, 164
Sensorimotor stage, 139
Sensory impairment, adapting environment for children with, 214
Sensory processing disorder (SPD), 215
Sensory-rich environment, creating, 215–17
SES. *See* Socioeconomic status (SES)
Shame and doubt, 136
Shapes, Shapes, Shapes (Hoban), 238
Shifting blame, 367–68
Short-term planning, 263, 271, 295
Simplicity, 186
Situated, can-do procedural knowledge, 419
Size, in learning group, 196
Skeptical behavior, reflective practitioner and, 15
Skills development, 103
Smell, 214
Social and emotional competence, 125
Social characteristics, in indoor environment, 207
Social competence, 125
Social context
  aggressive behavior and, 359
  larger, family in, 384–86
Social density, 196–97
Social development
  of infants, 115, 116
  of kindergartners, 119–20, 121
  of preschoolers, 119–20, 121
  school-age children, 122, 124
  toddlers, 117
Social influences on curriculum, 223
Social interaction, 63, 152
"Socialization", 343
Social justice
  concept of, 86–88
  ethics and, 87–88
Social learning theory 168–69
Social needs, 113
Social play, 164
Social play (Smilansky & Shefatya), 163, 164
Social relations/civics standards, 235
Social settings, 133

Social studies
- brainstorming about study of animals, 256
- brainstorming about study of Greece, 257
- in curriculum, 234, 238, 239, 247
- for primary grades, 296–97
- themes and units for early childhood, 248

Social Studies: A Way to Integrate Curriculum for Four- and Five-Year Olds, 276
Social Studies for the Preschool/Primary Child (Seefeldt), 276
Social support, in well functioning family, 382
Social system, family as, 382–84
Societal trends, 49
Sociocultural constructivist theory, 172–73
Socioeconomic status (SES), 313
Softness, 186
Software evaluation criteria, 465–66
Solitary play, 163, 164
Space
- arrangement of, 188–89, 190–92, 197–98, 200–201
- for children with diverse academic needs, 214
- for children with limited motor abilities, 213
- in learning environment, 187

Spatial density, 197
SPD. *See* Sensory processing disorder (SPD)
Speaking standards, 234
Special gifts and talents, children with, 133
Special needs children
- children with exceptionalities, 238, 287
- gifted, 133
- legislation on, 129–31
- strategies for, 286, 287
- talented, 133

Specific written curriculum, 231
Specimen records, 327
Speech or language impairment, 131
Stability, 186
Stable procedural knowledge, 419
Stagnation, generativity *vs.*, 137
Standardized tests, 313, 315, 320–22
Standardized test scores, 320
Standards
- accountability to, 284
- content, 232
- content area, 234–35
- for early childhood education, 54
- performance, 232
- reading, 234

Standards-based curriculum, 231
Standards-based education, movement for, 311
Stimulation, 186
Stirring the Chalkdust: Case Studies of Teachers in the Midst of Change (Wasley), 427
Storage, 202–3, 463–66
Strategic interactions, 150–51
Strategic thinking, 150
Strategy(ies)
- of Bank Street/Development Interaction Approach, 58
- community-building, 470
- of Head Start, 59
- of High/Scope, 59
- of Montessori method, 57
- positive guidance, 360–62'
- for professional development, 431
- to promote self-regulation, 356
- of Reggio Emilia, 60

Stress management, 356
Structure, of early childhood education programs, 61
Student-led conferences, 318
Student motivation to learn, in balanced assessment, 334
Students
- focus on outcomes for, 14
- preventing behavior problems in, 358

Subject-matter teaching, interdisciplinary approaches to, 63, 65
Success, child development and need for, 114
"Summer loss," 313
Support
- peer, for early childhood educators, 22–24

Support system, family
Swearing, 377
Symbolic play, 163, 164

Taking action, reflective practitioners and, 15–16
Talented children, 133
Tale telling, 377
Talk about children, advocacy as, 95–98
Tantrums, 377
Task of teaching in context, in reflection, 12–13
Tattling, 376
Taught curriculum, 222, 231, 243–44
T.E.A.C.H. program, 422
Teacher/researcher, roles and behaviors of, 17
Teachers. *See* Early childhood practitioners
Teachers' Stories: From Personal Narrative to Professional Insight (Jalongo & Isenberg), 428
Teaching
- definition of, 5–6
- drafting philosophy of, 67–69
- planning and, 282
- positive outlook on, 19–20
- subject-matter, interdisciplinary approaches to, 63, 64
- successful, planning and, 284–86
- unique characteristics of, 418

Teaching Four-Year-Olds: A Personal Journey (Hillman), 428
Teaching strategies, curriculum developer and, 230
Teaching vignette, 68
Teasing and name calling, 367
Technology
- assessment and, 331
- resources, 464–65

Television violence, 355
Tell Me Again About the Night I Was Born (Curtis), 276
Tell Me Tree: All About Trees for Kids (Gibbons), 239
Tested curriculum, 222
Testing. *See also* Tests
- and name calling, 367
- standardized, 313
- *vs.* assessment, 331

Tests
- achievement, 325
- criterion-referenced, 322–24
- paper-and-pencil, 321, 322, 324
- preparation and anxiety, 323
- standardized, 320–21

Textbooks, curriculum and, 241
Texture, in learning environment, 195
Thematic units
- in meaningful curriculum, 245–47
- planning, 298–99
- projects *vs.*, 304

Theories. *See* Learning theories

Thinking
flexibility in, 21
reflective, 8
strategic, 150
Thinkin' Things Collection, 3, 165
Third grade, brainstorming web for, 257
36 Children (Kohl), 425
The Three Little Pigs, 147
Time
for children with diverse academic needs, 214
in early childhood education programs, 27
in learning environment, 187, 209
learning environment and use of, 189
planning and, 282–83
shared, in well functioning family, 382
Time sampling, 327
Timing, in group decisions, 363
Toddlers
curriculum and, 241
daily planning form for, 270
development of, 116–19
in early childhood education programs, 27
environment, 186
material resources for, 189, 205, 438–39
nutritious foods for, 207
planning for, 270
psychosocial theory and, 135, 136
room arrangement for, 191
themes for, 248
Toileting problems, 377
Tolerance, in group decisions, 363
Topics, choosing, 298–99, 304
Touch, 214
Toys, 27
Traditional perspective of curriculum, 251
Training, in professional development, 420–21
The Transcendent Child: Tales of Triumph over the Past (Rubin), 427
Transition objects, 364
Transitions, for children with diverse academic needs, 214
Trees, Leaves, and Bark (Burns), 240
Trees, using literature to integrate curriculum about, 239–40
Trends, societal, 49
Trust *vs.* mistrust, 136
Turn taking, 377
U.S. National Committee of the World Organization for Early Childhood Education (OMEP), 459
Understanding, child development and need for, 113
Unethical assessment, recognizing, 316–17
Uninsured children, number of, 381
Unit approach, in meaningful curriculum, 245–47, 248
United States
kindergarten in, 47
nursery schools in, 47
percentage of children of color in, 221
standardized testing, 313
Units *vs.* projects, 304
Unit teaching, resources for, 248
Urban public schools. *See* Public schools
Utilization, in learning cycle, 157

Value of play, 161
Values, curriculum developer and, 230–31
Verbal expression, 359–60
The Very Hungry Caterpillar (Carle), 338
Viewing and representing standards, 234
Vignette, teaching, 68
The Village of Round and Square Houses (Grifalconi), 243
Violence, 355–60
Vision, 214
Visual arts, 235, 237
Visual impairment, 131
Visual reminders, 356
Visual/spatial intelligence, 174, 266
Voices of Beginning Teachers: Visions and Realities (Dollas), 425

Wally's Stories (Paley), 428
The Water is Wide (Conroy), 425
Websites, 165
American Association of Retired Persons Grandparent Information Center, 388
Association for Childhood Education International/National Council for the Accreditation for Teacher Education, 397
early learning standards, 53
fitness planning and assessment resources, 206
Generations United, 388
Grands Place, 388
Head Start, 59
High/Scope, 59
KINship Information Network, 388
Mid-Continent Regional Education Laboratories, 233
of Montessori method, 57
NAEYC social studies, 276
National Aging Information Center, 388
National Association for the Education of Homeless Children and Youth, 386
National Center for Homeless Education, 386
National Coalition of the Homeless, 386
National Committee of Grandparents for Children's Rights, 388
National Law Center on Homelessness & Poverty, 386
National Network for Youth, 386
No Child Left Behind Act, 397
Reggio Emilia, 60
Weekly plans, 263, 274–75
What I Know, What I Want to Know, What I Learned. *See* KWL Strategy
Where the Wild Things Are (Sendak), 137
Wholeheartedness, 14, 15
Work, exploration, and play, 161
Work board, 201, 202
Working Mother Magazine, 410
Workshops. *See* In-class workshop
Works Progress Administration (WPA), 49
WPA. *See* Works Progress Administration (WPA)
Writing
teaching philosophy, 67–69
teaching vignette, 68–69
Writing standards, 234
Written curriculum, 222
content standards, 232
definition of, 231
organizing, 236–39
performance standards, 232
standards-based curriculum, 231

Zone of proximal development (ZPD), 172, 331
ZPD. *See* Zone of proximal development (ZPD)